To dear Am...

Enjoy the Read

love

Tricia Bennett

Polly Brown

Polly Brown

Tricia Bennett

CREATION
HOUSE
A STRANG COMPANY

POLLY BROWN by Tricia Bennett
Published by Creation House
A Strang Company
600 Rinehart Road
Lake Mary, Florida 32746
www.creationhouse.com

Unless otherwise noted, all Scripture quotations are from the King James Version of the Bible.

Cover design by Terry Clifton

Library of Congress Control Number: 2007926958
International Standard Book Number: 978-1-59979-214-9
First Edition
07 08 09 10 11 — 9 8 7 6 5 4 3 2 1
Printed in the United States of America

This book is dedicated to the orphan inside each one of us.

****

"I will not leave you as orphans; I will come to you!"

ACKNOWLEDGMENTS

WE WANT TO thank our three children, Antonia, Reuben, and James, for supporting our dream, as well as two of our many foster girls, Emma and Anna, who consider us to be their second Mum and Dad, and whom we hold close to our heart.

Also we would like to thank some of the many precious people we have met since leaving the UK a year ago to arrive on American soil, including Dr. Troy Miller and the Potters House and their Turn Around Project (TAP) which helps young people and others to get their lives back on track, including dear Mr. Young who, despite getting old, still packs a powerful hug! And also to all at Youth Challenge of Florida, whom we love so very much. Thank you to Linda Hall and her caring team who do so much to reach into the lives of many at their homeless shelter. A big thanks also goes to Grace Tab for all their support and encouragement towards us. And to Al and Vickie Sikes for their help in setting up our English Tearoom called "Polly's Pantry" (themed on this book), here in Wildwood, near The Villages, in Central Florida.

We came to this country not knowing a single soul, so thank you Liz and Charlie Parrot for inviting us, complete strangers from the UK, to share your special Thanksgiving Day meal within days of our arrival. And thank you to Lorraine Harris (a fellow author), and her husband, Lamont, for their support and friendship and for helping us launch our first book signing in The Villages. Thanks also to my lovely Spanish sister Kenilia and her family, as well as Vivienne and Al Levine for their wonderful friendship and constant encouragement.

Also to our friend Watchman, who visits prisons and schools, and whose music inspires the youth of Great Britain to believe and hope for better things. Thanks also to Roberta Cousins who has abandoned her life in England to rescue children from off the streets in Uganda.

We would like to send our love to Dave and Tisha Knowles, Carlos and Valerie Macuix, Dr. Vija and Margaret Sodera, Jacquie Long, Steve and Georgie Bailey, Chris and Lottie Seaton, Peter and Felicity Wilkes, Kim and Emma Connor, Simon and Catherine Mouatt, as well as dear friends Mike and Suzie Collins who are heading for Canada, and Steve and Carol Bourne in Vero Beach. And to all our other good friends whom sadly we have had to leave behind in England, to embark on this exciting journey with Polly!

And thank you to Tanya Courtenage and all the staff at Betel International for all the work you do rescuing teenagers from drug and other addictions in the UK, for you have saved so many precious lives with your work.

We would also like to thank all the staff of Families For Children, who work so hard to make foster children's lives both safe and happy. Also we would like to make mention of a wonderful school called Michael Ayres Junior in Bognor Regis. Also we would like to thank Rose Green Infant and Junior School, Nyewood Junior, and Bishop Luffa School in Chichester, for working so hard on behalf of my own children as well as for our foster children.

We would also like to thank Allen Quain and all the staff at Creation House who have worked so hard to produce this book.

Our thanks also to The Carpenters House in Eustis, Florida, a privately run Children's Home run by Pat and Linda Manfredi, for letting us have the privilege of becoming aunt and uncle to their sixteen or more, beautiful children. And also we would like to thank Mukkala and his family who pour out their lives daily for the children in our orphanage in India. Also Pastor Solomon and his family in Hyderabad for all they do in their hometown and beyond.

Ooh and I mustn't forget to thank my extremely patient husband, John, who has been a tower of strength in every time of trouble, and has never doubted me, even when I doubted myself! Such men are a rare, rare breed!

CONTENTS

Chapter 1
POLLY'S SAD, HUMDRUM LIFE

"*ONCE UPON A time...*" *began the storyteller. His young, captive audience had his full attention, for all those gathered around truly loved to hear magical tales. The storyteller secretly smiled to himself, opened the book, and began reading.*

A huge medieval castle stood perched high on a steep hill overlooking a sleepy little town in the heart of the English countryside. It had been built centuries before to fight off all the wicked enemies determined to conquer the town and take its inhabitants captive. Many bloody battles had been fought and won there. As news of these most ferocious encounters spread across the kingdom, enemy after enemy was forced to admit that this castle, and therefore this town, was indeed unconquerable. As a result they were given no choice but to turn their attentions to other lands with less fortified castles to take siege and conquer, leaving this little English town to finally enjoy great peace. Therefore the valiant knights of the castle found themselves unexpectedly redundant, with little more to do than twiddle their thumbs and paint their toenails bright red.

Finally there came a time when they grew so bored that, after much debate, they reached the unanimous decision to put their swords back into their scabbards forever. Once they did that, they felt most relieved as they removed their disgracefully heavy armor and hung it up on the personalized pegs provided in the huge, baronial hall. Then, after giving the plants one final watering, they gave each other a kiss and a hug before swapping addresses, each promising to keep in touch (though any knight worth his salt would indeed never break such a vow).

With their good-byes over, they sadly departed the castle forever, stopping only to pick up some postcards as a reminder of all the mischievous fun they'd had together. They then headed home to their families, who had sorely missed them over the years. After their departure, the castle lay idle for hundreds of years. Thick dust gathered in every corner, and their wonderfully shiny suits of armor slowly corroded into little heaps of iron filings on the cold floor.

Eventually this most impressive castle became little more than a tourist attraction that people visited from faraway lands, anxious to walk through the magnificent rooms. Their cameras clicked away furiously as they took numerous pictures, which were eventually stored away and forgotten in an attic somewhere, untouched and gathering dust. That is, of course, until many years later when they returned to the town, this time with friends, to once again tour the magnificent castle and update their photo albums.

However, quite a large part of the castle was out of bounds to the visiting tourists. A big sign that read KEEP OUT OR ELSE! hung on the imposing black gates, making quite certain that any who chose to ignore this notice did so at his or her own peril. Those who did not heed this warning came face-to-face with the vicious dog that patrolled this private section of the castle, with many leaving with the odd chunk or two missing from a leg or an ankle. This savage beast, who answered to the name of Pitstop, was kept ravenously hungry so that he did his job more diligently. He guarded this wing of the castle and was more than delighted to defend it from nosey tourists hoping for a sneaky snapshot.

The out-of-bounds wing, along with the rest of the castle, belonged to an extremely wealthy duke. Many years earlier, he decided to allow it to be used as an orphanage. It was home to nearly thirty or more children who had no mothers or fathers, and therefore, nowhere else to live and to be cared for. This is where our heroine Polly lived, along with her two brothers. They all lived under the watchful eye of Mr. and Mrs. Scumberry, their guardians, whom all the children, Polly included, were required to call Aunt Mildred and Uncle Boritz.

Uncle Boritz was a short, extremely rotund man. But what he lacked in height, he made up for in other ways. He was so well-versed in wielding his power that all who lived under his roof trembled at the very sight of him. His shiny, bald head was shaped like an egg, and his long nose was peppered with warts. He had a large mustache, and he wore a thick pair of black spectacles.

Aunt Mildred, on the other hand, was as tall as a skyscraper and hideously thin, with the exception of her posterior, which was extraordinarily large. Her scrawny neck was bare, as every wisp of her graying hair was scraped off her prim face. Sadly, her thin lips seemed permanently pursed, for very little in life appeared to amuse her. Polly had never witnessed Aunt Mildred's stony face break out into the tiniest of smiles, as with great purpose she strode around the castle in her flat, old-fashioned shoes.

"Now, I think at this stage it would be fair to point out," said the storyteller, "that most young ladies living in castles are princesses, but this was not the case for Polly. Indeed, Polly longed to feel special and wanted, just like other princesses who lived in fine castles. Instead, she had to live with the sad truth that she was an orphan for which no one truly cared. This made Polly very unhappy and, at times, fearful of what her future might hold," said the storyteller, lowering his voice to little more than a whisper. His young and now-captivated audience turned and looked at one another, their eyes visibly widening. For to those present, to have no mother or father seemed awful and quite impossible to imagine. The storyteller paused and smiled at his troubled young audience, for he hoped that by the end of his tale they would be much wiser!

Polly's full name was Polly Esther Brown, and despite being almost eleven years old, she stood 3 feet 10¾ inches tall when she took off her shoes and measured her height against the wall. This made her despair, for she longed to be taller like many of her foster sisters. She was also decidedly thin, and this made her shabby clothes hang rather badly on her waiflike frame. She was not particularly pretty either, for her eyes were not only slightly crossed, but also muddy brown in color, matching her brown, unkempt hair, which fell somewhere between her chin and her shoulders. To make things worse, she had what she considered to be fairly enormous gaps in her slightly crooked teeth. Polly did not make a habit of smiling, because she believed herself to be positively ugly, and this fact alone made her feel most melancholic.

Polly had often secretly thought to herself that maybe, just maybe, if she had been born with blonde, curly hair and blue eyes and with a name such as Pandora, Antonia, Ruby, or Harriet, her mother would have kept her instead of putting her and with her brothers James and Thomas into an orphanage. This thought had been with Polly ever since she discovered thinking as a pastime, and Polly had plenty of time to think, for she was a very lonely young girl.

It was not uncommon for Uncle Boritz to find Polly weeping in a corner. He would observe her over his thick-rimmed glasses as though she were some insect that needed to be crushed underfoot like a cockroach. Indeed, he had little time or sympathy for such sensitive, troubled mites as Polly. He offered no words of comfort to ease her increasing and most apparent distress; in fact, her plight seemed to amuse him. Eventually, having tired of observing her, he would break into a wide grin and cheerfully declare, "Polly, laugh, and the world laughs with you; cry, and you cry alone." Sadly, this would make her weep even more.

For some unfathomable reason, Uncle Boritz never failed to give words of "comfort" whenever he saw her huddled in a corner in this pitiful state. After this he would then break into raucous laughter before turning on his heels to continue down the long corridor. He would give no further thought to her plight as he jangled his big bunch of jailer's keys with Pitstop, his faithful rottweiler, following devotedly in his shadow. The two of them were inseparable and bore an uncanny resemblance to each other; they both had large, yellow teeth and sagging potbellies. As master and beast wound their way down the many long corridors of the castle, Polly could always trace their movements by following the trail of slimy slobber left by Pitstop on the highly polished oak floors.

Today was Polly's eleventh birthday, and she saw no reason to be happy at all, for she had no birthday cards, no presents, no birthday cake, and no party to celebrate the occasion. Why she had ever expected any form of celebration is unclear, for year after year she had hoped in vain that this would be the special year when she would receive a nice present and have a party. On her eleventh birthday she found herself wistfully dreaming and hoping for a pink pair of ballet shoes. But sadly, all the wishing in the world had done her no good, for the day was almost over, and, as usual, she had received nothing but extra cleaning jobs around the vast castle she knew as home. Polly had lived at the castle for six long years, and with each day that passed she found herself getting sadder and sadder. She was beginning to despair that her little life held no hope. She prayed continuously for a miracle, but it never seemed to come.

She had spent these past years feeling utterly desperate for somebody—anybody—to help her and her brothers and come to their rescue. She always faithfully attended church and listened very seriously to the sermons. They made it quite plain that God was standing by, ready to lend a helping hand and perform miracles if people only cared to ask for them. Take, for instance, sweet Mrs. Greta Hornchurch, who had disgracefully skived off church for many weeks as she battled with a serious chest infection. On her return, Father Benedict warmly welcomed her back into the fold and gave thanks from the pulpit for the wonderful miracle of her recovery.

Polly could not help but observe that Greta was still accompanied by a large oxygen tank on wheels, complete with a tent to help her remain conscious throughout the lengthy service. Polly watched intently as the mask covering her nose and mouth clouded with every breath she exhaled. All this led Polly to wonder whether Greta had any hope of making it to the end of the service without collapsing. But not only had she made it, she was also still happily seated in the pew long after the rest of the congregation had left the church to go home and the good father had returned to the vestry. This left Polly to conclude that if miracles did happen, then both Greta and she needed a far larger miracle if either of them were to have any real and lasting hope.

POLLY'S SAD, HUMDRUM LIFE

As she reflected on Father Benedict's rather lengthy talk on the Sermon on the Mount, she recalled the Scripture verse he read from the pulpit: "Blessed are the poor in spirit: for theirs is the kingdom of heaven" (Matt. 5:3). She had thought at the time that this must surely include her, for she felt very poor in every sense of the word. Likewise, when the Father read, "Blessed are they that mourn: for they shall be comforted" (v. 4), again she found herself wondering how she was meant to feel blessed and comforted when she had never before felt any such feeling in her life. By the time Father Benedict said, "Blessed are they which do hunger and thirst after righteousness: for they shall be filled" (v. 6), Polly could hardly contain herself a moment longer, for surely this one really applied to her. After all, she was always hungry as well as thirsty. So Father Benedict's poignant sermon left Polly feeling more anxious than ever for an answer to the overwhelming sadness and loneliness, which were her only companions in life.

She stood in the red phone booth for hours at a time going through numerous possible combinations in an attempt to contact the "Man in the sky," but all had failed. Once, in total desperation, she dialed 9-9-9, because the sign in the phone booth stated "In Case of Emergency, Dial 9-9-9." As Polly considered her ongoing crisis to definitely fall into the category of an emergency, she had finally come to believe that she had hit on God's correct number. She was most disappointed when the only help she was offered was that of the police, ambulance, or fire brigade, for she was more than certain that she required none of these.

She had also taken to writing many urgent letters directly to Him, which she then placed in the various red pillar-boxes in the town. So far He had not replied to any of them, yet she felt certain she had the correct address: Mr. God, Cloud Nine. She knew this to be the correct cloud, because many times she had heard various people say that they were on it. She thought it might be the cloud where people dropped by to join Him for a cup of tea and a bit of sympathy. He poured the tea, and they poured out their problems. On the next line she always wrote "Seventh Heaven." Again, this was because she had often heard people say they were there and had again duly noted that they always smiled when they said it. With this observation, she presumed that God not only gave them a nice cup of tea, accompanied by biscuits or cake, but that He also handed out the very useful advice they needed. She then always finished the envelope with, "Somewhere up in the sky," as the final clue, which she hoped would help the postman deliver it to the right address. Still she received no reply, so on more recent letters, Polly resorted to putting a little note to the postman:

P.S. Dear Mr. Postman, if the address is not entirely correct, would you please be kind enough, at your earliest convenience, to forward it to the next universe?

Yours ever so truly, Polly

As the evening of her eleventh birthday drew to a close, she felt she could no longer control the deep sadness welling up inside, which made her chest feel so tight that her heart felt on the verge of exploding. With the last task of sweeping and scrubbing the front doorsteps finally finished, she flung the wooden brush back into the pail of soapy suds before collapsing in a heap onto the hard, cold steps. Then, with her head cradled between her knees, she burst into uncontrollable sobbing.

She sat there only a matter of minutes when suddenly she heard a warm, comforting voice behind her say, "Hello, Polly."

Polly raised her head and, through a mist of tears, strained to see who it was that had just greeted her.

"I believe this is yours," he said, handing her a faded blue elephant, which had seen better days. "I also believe his name is Langdon. Am I right?"

"Yes, sir. You are correct," simpered Polly, rubbing her eyes so she could get a better look at him.

It did not take her very long to realize that this stranger, dressed in a long, threadbare, brown trench coat, was in fact one of the many gentlemen of the road who knocked at the door of the home asking for something to eat and drink. The man looked tired and strained, and his clothes, including his boots, were peppered with large holes. His hair, though long and straggly, was silvery in appearance, and he had an equally long matching beard. His eyes were a piercing deep blue, and they twinkled when he smiled. Polly was not the least bit frightened because she was so used to talking to these unusual visitors who would ring the doorbell in search of refreshments.

Polly leapt up, holding Langdon tightly to her chest. "Do you want the usual?" she inquired with a little sniff.

"Yes, the usual will do nicely. Thank you," said the man, breaking into a warm smile.

"You must be familiar with what the usual is then?" Polly continued, forcing her face into a grimace, as if to imply that he could change his mind if he wished and would be well advised to do so.

"Indeed, I most certainly am," replied the gentleman of the road as he mimicked Polly by also distorting his face into a grimace. "But as I am hungry enough to eat a horse, the usual will be fine."

"Then the usual it is," announced Polly with a grin. "And I'm so sorry to have kept you waiting." She made a mocking bow, laughing out loud before turning on her heels to push the heavy door open.

As she disappeared inside, the stranger called out to her, "Polly, would you like me to take care of Langdon while you make my mug of tea and sandwich?"

"Thank you, but no thank you," Polly swiftly replied. "I never leave Langdon alone, for he is so special to me. He is my closest friend in the whole universe—oh, as well as Eton, my teddy bear. But Eton is not with me at present, for he's not feeling so good. Too many late nights! I'm sure you understand."

"I know," replied the man.

"Know what?" interjected Polly, feeling a growing irritation towards him.

The man paused before continuing. "You love Eton, but in truth, if you had to choose between the two, it is Langdon you would keep."

"How do you know that?" quizzed Polly.

8   POLLY BROWN

"The reason Langdon is so special," continued the ragged man in an all-knowing manner, "is that he holds inside him all the tears you have ever cried."

Polly was stunned! How could this complete stranger—a homeless man—know anything about her or her secret about Langdon? Could it be possible that he knew other very private things about her? She hoped not.

Before she had time to open her mouth and challenge him further, he carried on.

"Polly, I know a lot about you and your brothers."

Polly took a deep gulp as he continued.

"I know all the terrible things that have happened in your life and the dark and evil things that take place here behind closed doors."

Polly just stared at him in stupefied silence.

"Now, how is my tea coming on?" he asked in the most gentle of voices in his effort to steer the conversation in a different direction. "If you don't go and put that kettle on, I will almost certainly die of thirst."

Polly flashed him a little smile, forgetting that smiling was not something she usually did. As she started to close the door, the man called out to her again.

"Oh, and Polly, before I forget, I have not told you who I am, have I? Allow me to introduce myself."

Polly stopped in her tracks and poked her head back around the door to show some interest.

"My name is Hodgekiss. Jeremiah Hodgekiss at your service," he said, making a low bow at the same time.

"Nice to meet you, Mr. Hodgekiss," said Polly, holding out a hand toward his. "And I have to say that I just love your name, for it sounds like a savory pie!"

Hodgekiss looked slightly amused, and Polly giggled before going on to explain exactly what she meant. "Oh, do please have a slice of Hodgekiss Pie, Mrs. Tattersbury." Polly said slightly mockingly as she pretended to pass a plate. "Oh, thank you so much. I will have just a smidgen, if you don't mind, Mrs. Smythe-Bourne. Your Hodgekiss Pie is after all simply quite delicious."

Polly giggled. "There, see what I mean?" she said, still holding out her hand to shake his.

They shook hands. The likable vagrant smiled back.

"Well, it would be nice to be famous for something, Polly, even if it is Hodgekiss Pie!" He then chuckled, "I have a very good friend called Ralph, another gentleman of the road who drops by here frequently. I am sure you must know him! It was he that told me about you."

Polly nodded. She did know Ralph and his most distinctive smell. (Mind you, most of these well-worn travelers seemed to have a most uninviting odor.) But Polly was much too polite to make mention of this. Instead, she just served them steaming cups of strong, sickly sweet tea, accompanied by thick, moldy cheese sandwiches. On numerous occasions she had sat on the doorstep and listened intently as Ralph or one of the other fellow travelers told lengthy tales of all that happened to them, as well as all the different places their lives on the road had taken them.

Polly ordered Hodgekiss to hang on, and after going back indoors she raced down the long, highly polished corridors until she reached the door of the kitchen. She hoped she would not bump into Aunt Mildred, as this might mean more chores. Luckily for Polly, the kitchen was empty, so she quickly went about cutting two extraordinarily large and disgracefully uneven wedges from a stale loaf that sat on a shelf in the pantry cupboard. She then filled the kettle and placed it on the stove, willing it to boil extra quickly so she could get back to her guest to continue their conversation. Once the tea brewed, she reached up to a high shelf and took one of the large, white china mugs reserved for serving tea to such gentlemen. The mug was terribly chipped, and the inside was stained a very deep brown. She placed it back on the shelf and picked up another. On close inspection, this one turned out to be just as bad and equally disgusting as the other one. "Oh well. It will have to do," she thought to herself. Polly filled the mug up to the brim and beyond, leaving no room for the milk. This situation was soon rectified as, while pouring in the milk, she gave the tea an all-too-vigorous stir, splashing the hot liquid all over the table. The tea was further reduced by the very generous amount of sugar she piled into the mug. Grabbing a tablespoon from the cutlery drawer, she started to count.

"One... two... three... four... five... There, that will do," she said with a distinct air of satisfaction.

She then went to the large, old-fashioned fridge and, upon opening it, took out the only item on the shelf, a large block of questionable cheese. Polly hummed to herself as she busily went about the gruesome task of slicing off the mold that covered every inch of the cheese. She then cut a large piece into long strips and placed them diagonally between the thick pieces of bread.

"There. All finished," she declared with a note of triumph as she gave the sandwich an almighty thump with the palm of her hand in a vain attempt to weld the sandwich together and thereby decrease its mountainous height.

Polly placed the sandwich in an old brown paper bag, picked up the mug of tea, and headed back down the long corridors. Halfway down the second corridor she had a thought. Had she forgotten the sugar? She suddenly could not remember if she had put any in or not. She turned on her heels and raced back to the kitchen, on the way slopping the tea once more over the same highly polished oak floor. She counted out another five spoons of sugar, gave it a quick stir, and took a tiny sip of the tea just to taste it. "Yuk," she thought to herself. "How on earth do people drink this stuff?" With that thought thoroughly sorted, Polly raced back down the hallway, again slopping the tea as she went.

Hodgekiss smiled and thanked Polly as he took the sandwich from her. Polly then handed him the mug of tea before settling back down on the steps. As he peered into the large mug, he could not help but notice that it was less than half full, but it did not matter at all—he liked syrup very much. While Hodgekiss attempted to eat the seriously stale sandwich, Polly talked on incessantly. Usually it was Polly who listened to tired travelers slurping their tea and telling stories, but on this occasion it was Polly's turn to pour out all her woes, including the fact that today was her eleventh birthday and there had been no surprise to look forward to. Hodgekiss listened but remained silent. Polly began to think that maybe, just like everyone else, he was simply not interested.

"That was a most delicious sandwich, Polly," he announced as he poked a lone finger into his mouth to excavate the leftovers stuck between his teeth. He then brushed out the remaining crumbs from his tangled beard.

Polly giggled and said, "You liar. It was awful; admit it!"

Hodgekiss burst out laughing before confessing that he had tasted better food, even from the waste bins at the various train stations he frequented!

"I'm so sorry, Hodgekiss," said Polly. "But there was nothing else to give you. There never is much food in the cupboards. I often go hungry myself." She paused, giving her stomach a little rub, and then added that the other children often went hungry as well. "If we complain, Uncle Boritz always tells us the same thing," she added with a note of resignation in her voice. "'If you are hungry, you will eat stale bread, and if you are thirsty, you will drink water.'" Her voice trailed off.

"Go on, Polly," Hodgekiss urged. "Is there more?"

"Well, yes and no," said Polly. "That is all he ever says, but he must find it very funny, because he always walks off laughing." Polly felt she could trust Hodgekiss, so she carried on. "What is so hard to bear is they have four children of their own who also live at the castle. But they are separated from us by iron bars, and on their side they get to eat really nice food." Polly sighed deeply, making a wry face. "Many a time they walk past us munching on chocolate bars and candies. It makes me feel really bad and my tummy rumbles even more."

Hodgekiss raised his bushy eyebrows to show his concern, but still said nothing, for once Polly was in the flow of things, it was indeed very hard to stop or slow her down.

"Let me tell you now, Hodgekiss, that once a year on New Year's Eve they hold an amazing party and invite all their posh friends, as well as the more favored children, to join them. They spend the whole evening stuffing themselves, and I would have you know that there are twenty-one courses, starting with soup and ending many hours later with coffee and chocolates. The banquet comes to an end in the early hours of the next morning, and then only after many glasses of vintage brandy have been consumed. The cooking preparations take days, and there is probably more food eaten in that one night than I get to eat in a whole year! Can you believe that, Hodgekiss?"

If Hodgekiss had wanted to reply or make any sort of comment, he would have found it very difficult to get a word in edgewise. Polly took a deep breath before continuing.

"Every New Year's Eve, those children who are not allowed to attend, myself included, are shooed off to bed much earlier than usual." Her voice began to crack as she went on with her story. "I lie in bed unable to sleep as I try to ignore my hunger pangs. Even if I cover my ears, I can still hear all the laughter and smell the smells of the fine food that I could only dream of eating wafting up the stairs." Polly felt tears come to her eyes. "When the guests finally leave in the early hours of the morning, the noise of their departure also travels up the stairs, and I hear all the guest's say good-bye." Polly put on a poker face, changing her voice to the similar affected tones of the gushing guests as they prepare to leave the banquet and go home.

"Oh, this has been a most wonderful evening, Mrs. Scumberry."

"Hasn't it just!" agrees another.

"The food was simply superb!" joins in another voice with a rather bloated chortle.

"Yes, positively divine," adds another. "No better still. Absolutely exquisite! Did you try the roast pheasant, Mrs. Oaksbury? Oh right, you had a little smidgen. So tell me now, didn't it taste utterly scrumptious? Mildred dearest, you must stop inviting us to these exceptionally lavish parties, for our waistlines can hardly take any more of your delectable dishes. But it was so awfully kind of you to send us an invitation."

"Hear! Hear!" the other equally boisterous guests chant in unison. Then I hear their keys turning in the ignition followed by the shrieking, high-pitched voice of some lady shouting her grand finale through the open window of the car. "Mildred, both you and Boritz are such wonderful, caring people, and those little orphans are so lucky to have the two of you to look after them. Well, until next time!"

Polly drew breath and lowered her voice as she spoke on, her words tinged with great sadness. The truth is, Hodgekiss would have been there for at least a week if she were to tell all of what went on behind the high, flint walls of this castle.

"I might add, Hodgekiss," said Polly rather sullenly as she continued to unload her woes, "that the next time is never far off. A couple of weeks after the New Year's Eve party is the old peoples' party, where we, the children, get to entertain a load of merry old grannies. Aunt Mildred and Uncle Boritz always busy themselves, refilling cups with more milky tea while making polite conversation, presumably in the hope that when the old dears finally pass on, they will remember to leave a handsome donation to the orphanage," Polly miserably confided. "After all the old people have been shuffled out of the front door, Aunt Mildred and Uncle Boritz congratulate themselves on a most successful event. The next day, just like after their New Year's Eve gathering, we, meaning us foster children, are left to clear away the incredible mountain of leftovers. Only then do we see what we have missed out on. I find it all so unbearable." Polly fell silent as she anxiously wondered whether she had said far too much.

Hodgekiss sat with his head slightly bowed and muttered, "Better is a morsel in the house of a friend than a banquet in the house of your enemy."

"What did you say, Hodgekiss?" Polly asked, sticking a finger in her ear to see if it was blocked.

"Oh, nothing, dear Polly. Nothing at all," Hodgekiss replied. "Though one day you will understand everything, this I promise you."

Polly thought it might be a good idea to change the subject, so, putting on a bright smile, she went on to discuss the weather. She did this purely because she knew that the weather was the favorite subject of every grown-up she had ever met. She knew that just like drinking endless cups of tea, it was a particularly English thing to do, for it showed just how polite and educated one is. Personally, she could not understand this desperate need to discuss it at every gathering. She thought that if someone informed you that their beloved grandmother had suddenly departed, it would be inappropriate to respond with, "Oh dear, I'm so sorry to hear that, but isn't the weather utterly glorious today. Let's hope it stays that way. Would you care to join me for a cup of tea?"

Polly had a sneaky feeling that most people were afraid to talk about real things that truly mattered, and their apparent obsession with the weather was just a way of avoiding baring their heart and souls to each other.

Anyway, with the weather out of the way, she turned her mind back to the more serious matters affecting her young and sadly traumatized life. "Now if you had visited on Saturday," continued Polly, most informatively, "I could have given you a cake as well as a sandwich, Hodgekiss. For Saturday is pocket money day, and with the few pennies I receive, I ask the baker at the shop down the street for threepence worth of stale cakes. Since I go at the end of the day, he gives me a large bag filled with cakes that have been on display in the window and remained unsold. If they have no cakes left over, I try my luck at the fish and chip shop. They also are very kind and happily scoop out all the batter from the large fish fryer and sprinkle it with salt and vinegar for my threepence. Therefore, Saturday is for me the best day of the week. Promise me you will remember this for future visits."

Hodgekiss simply nodded. "That's settled then, isn't it?" Polly declared with a note of triumph.

Suddenly, they were interrupted by the screech of Aunt Mildred's high-pitched voice.

"Polly, Polly, where are you? Come here right now, you little wretch!"

"What on earth is that noise?" Hodgekiss curiously inquired.

"Oh, nothing to concern yourself about," said Polly. "It's probably the cats having a squabble, or some of the children pushing the piano over the polished floors."

"There are no pianos or cats in this castle," he winked.

"Well, we have had pets in the past," Polly replied rather defensively, for she was quite annoyed at being challenged. "But they have all died one way or another. You should see our back garden, Hodgekiss, for it is full of crosses made from twigs, and each spot marks the place where a bird, chicken, or mouse died and is now buried. So maybe there are no cats in the castle, but how would you know what we have indoors?" she rather rudely snapped.

Hodgekiss remained silent, and Polly instantly felt very guilty at taking her frustration out on him by confronting him in such a harsh manner.

"Look, I had better go back inside, Hodgekiss, or I will be in big trouble!"

Hodgekiss nodded his agreement; for he knew that for Polly to ignore Aunt Mildred's demands would indeed spell trouble.

As Polly jumped up from the steps, Hodgekiss asked her to wait just a minute longer.

"I have a little something for you," he said, dipping a hand into his large, shabby coat pocket. He then pulled out a paper bag. "This is a birthday present, specially chosen by me for you, Polly," he said with a smile.

Polly seemed a little reluctant to take the gift from a man who obviously had so little in life, so she started to protest.

"Please take it. It's important to me that you have it," he said with a hint of urgency in his voice.

Polly, running out of time, finally put out her hand to accept the gift, for she did not wish to hurt his feelings. Slipping the wrapped gift into her pocket, she broke into a smile.

"Thank you, Hodgekiss," she said, gently touching his arm at the same time to show her gratitude. "Oh, and by the way, I love the purple and orange striped socks. Where on earth did you find them?"

Hodgekiss looked down at his feet and saw that the socks were plain for all to see as they poked out of the end of his boots. He smiled again before answering her question.

"I found two pairs of them in a dumpster last January, and what's more, they were still in their Christmas wrapping. I guess they were some young lady's unwanted Christmas present, but I love them since they keep each individual toe nicely warmed. I gave the other pair to my friend Ralph, and he's equally delighted with his."

Polly laughed and then commented, "They look great, but I happen to know those particular style of socks are quite a struggle to put on. In fact, they're far worse than gloves."

"Too true, Polly, and that's probably the reason I haven't taken them off once in the past six, or is it nine, months," he admitted sheepishly, breaking into a big grin.

"Well, remind me not to be around the day you decide to give your feet a little air." She laughed as she pinched her nose firmly to make her point.

Hodgekiss nodded and gave her tiny hand a squeeze as he said good-bye. Polly stood for a few moments watching as Hodgekiss limped slowly down the path and out of sight.

Later that evening as Polly got herself ready for bed, she remembered the little parcel. She sat on the bed, and, after removing the brown string, eagerly tore off the brown wrapping paper. The gift revealed itself to be a book. Suddenly Polly heard footsteps approaching, so before she had time to read the title, she quickly switched off the light and hid well down in the bed, for she did not wish to be in any trouble. The knob of the door slowly turned, and a tall, shadowy figure stood in the doorway. Polly peeped from under the covers and could just about see the silhouette of Aunt Mildred standing in the doorway. With every child in the dormitory supposedly fast asleep, the shadow disappeared, and Polly, with ears pricked, listened intently as she heard Aunt Mildred's footsteps heading down the corridor towards the creaky oak stairs. Polly waited a few more seconds before coming out from under the covers. Then she plumped up her thin pillow as best as she could and lay with her arms behind her head, staring into the darkness.

Polly was very pleased that she had a new book to read, for she really loved books but rarely managed to read any. There were plenty of books in the castle, but most of them were locked up in the huge library, and the key to the library door hung on a large set of keys that swung to and fro from the oversized waist of Uncle Boritz!

Eventually, Polly rolled over in the bed and cuddled up to her little companion, Langdon, in an effort to keep warm. Still, she found she could not sleep. Perhaps I am too cold, she reasoned. So she got out of bed and picked up Eton, her teddy bear, and placed him in the bed next to Langdon.

"There. Now with three in the bed, I must surely get warm," she announced loudly in a desperate bid to comfort herself. "Castles are, after all, such cold, drafty places," she muttered before pulling her one thin blanket right up to her chin.

Despite the cold, and as well as having endured a pretty miserable day, Polly felt a little glow inside that felt quite comforting.

After much tossing and turning, sleep refused to come, so Polly found herself reflecting back on the day's events. It was not long before she became aware that something was really troubling her. It was something about Hodgekiss. "How could he have picked a gift especially for her when they had only just met?" she wondered.

After much worrying, Polly reluctantly switched on the bedside light and picked up the book. She read the title out loud, "*The Ugly Duckling.* Oh, that's really great!" she cried. "So he too thinks I'm ugly!" Polly wiped away a tear and unceremoniously dumped the book onto the floor. "This only goes to show that Hodgekiss is just like the rest," she whispered to herself as she cuddled up to Langdon and Eton. "Both of you are really the only friends I have in the whole wide world."

With that thought still in her head, Polly finally fell sound asleep.

Chapter 2
OLIVER THE CATERPILLAR

MANY MONTHS ROLLED by, and numerous odd-looking, and always very smelly, gentlemen of the road knocked at the door to ask for food. Polly would find herself constantly disappointed that Hodgekiss had not bothered to call back. She had served up mountains of stale cheese and volumes of syrupy tea in his absence, and still there had been no sign of him. She hated to admit it, but although she had only met him briefly she really missed him, and soon she began to believe that there was a distinct possibility that he had died. The thought that he would have been alone, lying in some rubbish, only served to make her feel more anxious and sad than ever.

Polly gave up all hope of ever seeing him again, but one day out of the blue the doorbell rang. Polly raced to the front door as usual, and upon opening it discovered Hodgekiss's good friend Ralph sitting most comfortably at the bottom of the steps. Polly could hardly contain her excitement.

"Ralph, it's so good to see you," she exclaimed rather breathlessly, for the run to the door was quite a marathon for her little legs.

"Good to see you too, Polly," responded Ralph with equal enthusiasm as he scratched his unshaven chin.

Just like Hodgekiss, Ralph wore a long, severely stained trench coat, but his coat was green and far more frayed at the cuffs. His eyes matched his coat, although Polly was fairly certain that this was not a deliberate fashion statement on Ralph's behalf; rather, he had picked it up when rummaging through a high mountain of clothes at a rummage sale. Just like his friend Hodgekiss, he too sported the most vulgar shoes, revealing bright orange- and lemon-colored striped socks through the large holes where all the leather stitching had come undone. His brown hair was wildly out of control, as though a comb had never been run through it. Polly also observed that his nails were in desperate need of a manicure, for they were long and dirty. *Unsightly* was the word that immediately sprang to her mind.

Ralph stood up and smiled rather sheepishly. "I'm in a bit of a hurry, Polly, but is there any chance of a nice cup of Rosie Lee and a sandwich?" he politely asked, giving her a little wink.

"Coming right up!" Polly responded most enthusiastically as she then turned on her heels and raced back down the long corridor to the kitchen.

She returned several minutes later with half a cup of piping hot, syrupy tea (the rest was slopped on the floor all down the highly-polished corridor, as usual) and a thick stale cheese sandwich. As she handed the large, chipped mug of tea to Ralph, she decided not to make small talk and came straight to the point with her long list of questions that needed an immediate answer. She drew a deep breath before launching headlong into her interrogation.

"Ralph, have you seen Hodgekiss? I am really worried about him." She did not wait for a reply before carrying on. "I mean, where on earth is he? What has he been doing these past few months? Has he been reported missing? What if he's in need of help? What if he's been run over by a double-decker bus? Worse still, what if a crane has accidentally been dropped on his head? What if..."

Ralph smiled before rudely interrupting her. "Polly, please do me a favor and stop right there," he ordered. "Hodgekiss is very definitely alive and most well."

Polly breathed a deep sigh of relief.

"In fact, I am on my way to see him right now, and this is the reason I am in such a hurry. We have an appointment to meet at the cake shop. Apparently, four o'clock is the deadline if you wish to purchase a rather large bag of their stale cakes. Personally, I can't wait to fill up on stale cakes, for it will certainly be a most splendid dessert after a moldy cheese sandwich!"

Polly did not know whether to laugh or cry. She wanted to do both at the same time. She was relieved to hear that Hodgekiss was fine but upset that she had missed her pocket money, because she had forgotten it was Saturday. What troubled her most was that Hodgekiss had not only failed to pay her a visit but had the nerve to invite another person instead of her to join him at the baker's shop. It had, after all, been her little secret that she had shared with him out of generosity of heart. The cheek of it! She had definitely lost all faith in him. She had spent these past weeks worrying about his health and safety, while he repaid her kindness by going behind her back to scoff cakes that she believed rightfully belonged to her.

Ralph could clearly see her disappointment, but for some reason chose to ignore it. Polly felt pretty miffed and decided it was probably time to leave Ralph and go indoors.

"Well, good-bye, Ralph. I really must go now, for I'm certain that I will be missed, and that will spell trouble," she said, sounding quite disheartened. "But please remember to give Hodgekiss my best wishes, and I hope you both enjoy the cakes," she muttered. What she really wanted to say was that she hoped they both choked on them!

"Don't leave just yet." Ralph begged as he witnessed the look of disappointment on her face. "Hodgekiss hasn't forgotten you, Polly. I promise you. In fact, he instructed me to ask how you are getting on with reading the book that he gave you as a gift on your eleventh birthday."

"Oh, that," said Polly ruefully. "Well, I'm glad you asked, for if I'm allowed to be honest, I did not like it at all."

"Oh! And why is that?" Ralph asked with a deep frown on his face.

Polly paused to collect her thoughts. "Well, the truth is, the ugly duckling turned into a beautiful, gracious swan, and it made me realize that I have absolutely no hope of anything so wonderful happening to me!" Polly felt like crying. "I feel so angry and sad at the same time, Ralph," she admitted, sniffing as she spoke. "Hodgekiss was in very bad taste by giving me that book, which was my only birthday present. For it has only served to make me feel much worse. How could he do such a cruel thing to me?"

Ralph broke out into a smile. "Hodgekiss told me you would say that."

"Well, he was right then, wasn't he?" Polly declared angrily, at the same time feeling somewhat sorry for herself. "Stay right here while I go and fetch the book, and you can give it straight back to him," she ordered.

Ralph obliged, for he had no intention of going anywhere, at least not until he had finished his tea.

"Oh, Polly," he sighed. "You cannot see it now, but the truth is that you are fearfully and wonderfully made." Ralph paused, waiting for Polly to respond. She preferred not to, choosing instead to hang her head in shame and remain silent. Ralph put his fingertips under her chin and tilted it upwards until their eyes met. "Polly, I don't know whether this is the best time, but as I won't be coming back for quite a while, I had better give it to you now." He spoke quietly and almost apologetically.

"Give me what, Ralph?" Polly asked, filled with curiosity.

"Well, Hodgekiss asked me to give you something to look after for him." Ralph reached into his hideously oversized shabby green coat.

"Well, don't keep me in suspense!" Polly demanded. "What precisely does he want me to look after for him?"

Ralph hesitated slightly, for he was more than certain that this small request would be just as misunderstood as the last gift. He was not entirely convinced he could handle an outburst from such a young lady, who at times did little to endear herself to him.

"Polly, it's something Hodgekiss truly treasures, and there are few people he would entrust this most special thing to."

"Well, what does he want me to look after for safe keeping?" she asked, growing more curious by the minute.

"It's a special friend of his who needs to be babysat and constantly monitored," said Ralph. "He knew you were the perfect one to be trusted with it, and that's why I'm here today. So you won't say no, will you?"

Before Polly could give her answer, Ralph quickly grabbed her by the hand, forcing a small jam jar into her open palm.

Polly's eyes widened to the size of large saucers as she peeped into the jar and momentarily examined its contents. For, apart from some green leaves, there was something moving. A look of sheer horror crept over her face. It was a disgusting, black insect!

"Yuck! It's a maggot!" Polly shrieked in such high decibels that Ralph almost jumped out of his coat. "Here, take it back. Please take it back!" she pleaded, frantically turning her head away to one side so she would not have to look at the hideous little thing again. She then thrust the jar up to Ralph's face. "I demand you take it back immediately!" she cried, suddenly feeling very faint.

Ralph started to chuckle. "Oh Polly, what are you so afraid of? Why, it's only a poor little caterpillar. It will do you no harm."

"I hate insects," Polly angrily declared. "Is this his idea of a joke?"

"No, not at all, Polly," Ralph answered. "I am only following my good friend's instructions. He wants you to take care of it for him. It is one of his favorite little creatures."

"Well, then he has rather poor taste in insects," said Polly before somewhat officiously adding, "Tell him to look after it himself if he likes it that much!"

Ralph sighed, and then with a hint of impatience said, "Look, Polly. Hodgekiss would do nothing to hurt or harm you. He just wants you to observe this little fellow and watch him grow."

After much debate, mainly on Polly's side, she finally agreed to keep the caterpillar as long as her terms and conditions were adhered to.

"First of all, I am only prepared to keep it for a matter of weeks, for I'm terribly squeamish when it comes to insects. Secondly, if Pitstop discovers its existence and devours it, then I will not be held responsible. And lastly, Hodgekiss must return and collect him from me as soon as possible," she demanded rather petulantly, "or I will release this *thing* into a field," she said pointing directly at the innocent and defenseless insect that she found so offensive.

"Just like you, Polly, that *thing* has a name," said Ralph. "He's called Oliver, and I am fairly certain he would rather be called by his name than by 'that thing.' Don't you think so?"

"OK, I will try hard to remember that in the future," Polly airily replied.

Ralph breathed a deep sigh of relief, for he was not at all used to dealing with such stubborn and difficult little girls. He would much prefer to be taken off this assignment!

Polly went indoors with the jar, leaving Ralph to finish his tea. She returned later to pick up the mug and take it to the kitchen to be washed. As she picked it up, she noticed a stray white feather lying beside the abandoned mug. "How strange," she thought to herself as she closed the heavy door behind her.

Chapter 3
THE COPPER KETTLE TEAROOM

*T*HE NEXT DAY was Sunday, and after the usual Sunday lunch—two thin slices of pork luncheon meat, a small boiled potato, and a spoonful of peas and carrots—Polly found herself still feeling very hungry. During lunchtime the children would all play games with the luncheon meat, waving it in front of each other's faces since the slices were so thin that they could see through them. This was then followed by two canned peach slices, served with a dollop of custard. Polly could expect nothing more until a tea of bread and jam arrived on the table at six o'clock.

After tea Polly stood in the growing line and waited to get into the bathroom to brush her teeth. Polly did not like brushing her teeth because by the time it came to her turn there was very little pink toothpaste left in the tin, and everyone before her had spat in it to loosen it up to a lather. Polly longed for her own tube of toothpaste. Then it was time for bed, much too early for Polly's liking or for that matter, any of the other children's liking. The routine was precisely the same every day.

Earlier that day after the dishes from Sunday lunch were washed, dried, and put away, Polly found she had very little to do. She knew if she hung around the castle she would be given extra chores, so she decided to go for a walk down through the town and then along the river bank. She felt she knew every tuft of grass along the bank, for she had walked it so often. She used these times to make up little songs and poems to ease her sense of loneliness in this big and cruel world.

As she strolled down the street, she passed by a delightful English tearoom called The Copper Kettle. In a town that had considerably more tearooms than most, she deemed it to be her favorite. It had a wonderful fireplace with a lovely picture over the mantelpiece. Hanging on either side were copper bed warmers and horse brasses along with all sorts of copper and brass effects that added to the tearoom's warmth and charm, making it look so homely and inviting. Delightful English teapots of every size and shape were displayed on a high ledge that spanned the whole length of the tearoom. Once these teapots were sold to customers, more unusual teapots replaced them.

As Polly pressed her nose up against the large, steamy window-pane to peer around the tearoom, it only served to intensify her deep despair.

She longingly looked on as she closely observed families huddled cozily around the tables, talking and laughing together as they delighted in each others' company. Bustling waitresses in black skirts and frilly white aprons attended to their customers' every need as little brass bells on each table constantly rang to inform the waitresses that their assistance was required. Polly watched envi-ously as children munched and crunched their way through hot scones piled with sweet strawberry jam and topped with lashings of thick cream. The ordeal was not over then, for as soon as these were devoured a huge plate of cakes would be placed on the table. The children would choose from chocolate éclairs, raspberry gâteau, and fresh cream meringues topped with a cherry while through candy-striped straws they slurped and burped on large glasses of Coke and lemonade. Waitresses filed past each other to other tables with mind-boggling knickerbocker glories that seemed to reach to the sky, peach sundaes, endless banana splits, and pineapple upside-down cakes. The list of mouth-watering food appeared endless.

Not only did Polly long to just have a little taste of the delights being served up at the tables, but she also had an even deeper longing to just belong. She stared at all the families in the tearoom and chose the one who looked to be the kindest. Then she imagined just what it might be like to be a part of their family. She often had to restrain herself from just sneaking in undetected and quietly pulling up a chair to join them. She would then hope that the family she had picked for that specific day would not notice they had gained an extra child!

Near the fireplace stood an old, worn out spinning wheel that had not been in use for many years. A pile of children's books, as well as the classics by Shakespeare, Dickens, and the Brontës, were neatly stacked on the mantelpiece, with many small stools surrounding the hearth. Polly knew that over many years hundreds of little children sat on these stools as they gathered excitedly around the hearth to listen to stories, poems, and fairy tales read by a storyteller. This tradition no longer existed, for the new owners viewed the book-reading sessions as a complete waste of time. It didn't take much counting on their fat little fingers to conclude that such treats made them no extra money and therefore needed to be dispensed with as quickly as possible!

Polly constantly wished she could own a tearoom such as this. If ever this impossible dream became a reality, her first priority would be to reinstate the book-reading sessions that had given such joy to so many children. The previous owners had even searched the streets to find children who would listen to the stories. They would have been so sad to know this wonderful treat no longer existed. Polly knew they had been such kind and gracious people. The same could not be said for the new owners who now ran the tearoom. Their names were Hilda and Ernest Greedol.

Polly often witnessed Mrs. Greedol flying into a most irrational frenzy, reducing some poor waitress to floods of tears. Many times she had stopped and handed a handkerchief along with words of comfort to one of them as they sat on the steps, much too afraid to go back in and face more of the same. Today was no exception. Polly crouched down next to the young girl and pulled out her hanky.

"You might need this, Emily," she said softly, placing it in between Emily's cupped hands, which where covering her face.

"Oh, hi there, Polly," sniffed Emily. "I didn't realize it was you."

"What have you done to upset the old dragon today?" Polly sympathetically asked.

"Not a lot," replied Emily before going on to explain the latest upset. "A family asked if they could have a jug of water with their meal, as they did not wish their children to have fizzy soda. Mrs. Greedol saw me filling the jug and wanted to know why I agreed to give them water. I simply told her that the family on table nine requested it. She suddenly started fuming and said we were not here to serve them free water, so I should have politely refused and offered to show them our long list of beverages. 'Water does not bring in the money,' she yelled at me. 'Tea, coffee, and fizzy drinks do. Understand that, my girl?' she kept shouting. Honestly, Polly, I have had enough. Not a day goes by without her going on a fault-finding mission, and all of us girls spend our time at work terrified as we wait for her next outburst."

Polly put her arms around Emily and gave her a big hug. "Let me tell you now, Emily, you did the right thing. It costs us nothing to show kindness, and that is something Old Moneybags knows nothing about. You should feel sorry for her."

Polly had only just finished her sentence when she heard a commotion coming from inside the tearoom. She leapt up and peered through the glass window. Needless to say it was Mrs. Greedol. But this time she was shouting at a customer.

"Lumpy? You say my custard is too lumpy?" she roared over the head of the terrified customer, a very slight gentleman with thin, round spectacles. "Well, I'll give you lumpy, you ungrateful little toad," she hollered at the top of her lungs. "Mark my words, you'll be covered with lumps by the time I'm finished with you!" Then, without any warning, she picked up the pudding bowl and emptied it over his head. "Now get out of my tearoom, you oversized ape!" she screamed.

Polly looked on in utter amazement, as did all the customers who had witnessed this most unseemly outburst firsthand. Polly could not help but observe that Mrs. Greedol's insult was a better description of herself than the man she had just assaulted. For she was as fat as a large Jam roly-poly and had the most outrageous shot of bright orange hair, which she attempted to control by scraping to one side. Polly corrected herself: she did not resemble an ape, but an orangutan!

As she stood outside on the pavement in relative safety, Polly continued to watch through the large window. Mr. Greedol had now

POLLY BROWN

rushed from behind the serving counter to where his wife stood with her hand on her hips, eyes blazing, and bosom heaving up and down most rapidly. He tried to restrain her, but he was a very thin, quiet man and certainly no match for her. As he whipped off his green striped apron and attempted to grab her thick, fleshy arm, she dismissively pushed him aside, bent over the table, and physically picked up the offending customer by his jacket lapels. Then, with his legs dangling off the ground, she marched him towards the entrance, pinched his chin between her fingers, and twisted his face to meet hers, eyeball to eyeball.

"I said get out, and that's what I meant!" she thundered, giving him a hard, swift boot that propelled him straight out the door. The poor man landed beside Emily. He looked shaken and dazed as he stood up, and after removing the napkin that was still tucked into his trouser belt, he began wiping away the custard that still dripped from his head. This done, he straightened his crumpled jacket, adjusted his glasses, and hurried down the road as fast as his legs would carry him.

Polly turned to Emily, "I think you may be needed inside," she said with a wry grin, for she felt certain that many of the customers would need some assurance that they were not in for similar "hands-on" service.

Polly decided that she had seen enough action for one day, so, having said good-bye to Emily, she proceeded to walk up the long hill towards home. She had only gone a few feet when a stunning royal blue car drove past, pulling up alongside the curb directly outside the Copper Kettle tearoom. It was a gleaming Rolls-Royce, and therefore it had to be carrying a passenger of immeasurable wealth or, at the very least, someone of immense importance—a dignitary perhaps. Or maybe even royalty! The driver stepped out of the car. He was dressed in a smart navy blue uniform adorned with large, shiny gold buttons. He wore white gloves and a black cap. His black shoes were also highly polished. He made his way to the side of the car and, with much dignity, opened the passenger door.

Out tumbled one young girl after another. After six, Polly stopped counting. The girls alighted from the back of the plush car and stood on the pavement as they waited with great anticipation to enter the tearoom. Polly noticed that all the girls were dressed in beautiful cotton frocks with big bows tied at the back. They had frilly white ankle socks, shiny shoes, and colored ribbons in their flowing, brushed-to-a-shine, long hair. They all looked happy and so beautiful. Polly felt certain they must be real princesses; all that was missing were their diamond tiaras. Polly reasoned that they had probably accidentally left them indoors because they had left their houses in such a hurry. As she stood staring in their direction, she felt strong pangs of jealousy come over her. She thought to herself that life was indeed very unfair.

Minutes later, Mrs. Greedol rushed out and, with all the charm in the world, greeted the girls like they were long, lost friends before directing them through the open door and into the tearoom to the long table reserved especially for them. As they all took their seats, they handed the birthday princess present after present. Polly was transfixed by what she saw. Her nose pressed hard against the large windowpane as every present the birthday girl opened brought squeals of delight. In truth, it was all too much for poor Polly, but agonizing as it was to behold, she could not tear herself away and just go home.

Mrs. Greedol had covered the table with a pristine white linen tablecloth and put out her best china. A huge, beautiful birthday cake covered in pink candles stood elevated on a delicate glass cake stand in the center of the table. Within minutes of being seated, the little young ladies were served delicate, triangular sandwiches followed by teas and cakes, all washed down with cocktails of fizzy fruit juice served from tall-stemmed sparkling wine glasses. The air was filled with great merriment as the girls ate and laughed amongst themselves, totally oblivious to Polly's presence outside the window. Finally, once all the delicious food had been devoured and the table cleared of gift wrapping, paper bows, and empty plates, there remained only the stunningly beautiful birthday cake left to consume.

Polly could see that Mrs. Greedol was waiting in the wings, most anxious to bring the party to a close. She loathed displays of fun and affection with a passion, but she reasoned that she had little choice other than to tolerate them for they brought in a lot money. Having borne the merriment for as long as she was able, Mrs. Greedol grabbed a waitress by her apron strings and ordered her to hurry up and light the candles. The waitress obliged, taking a small box of matches and heading towards the girls' table. Mr. and Mrs. Greedol disappeared from sight, for they had no intention of joining in any of the fun.

The cake's smooth, iced surface had "Princess Charlotte" written on the top in beautiful pink scroll writing, and this special cake held the place of honor in the center of the table. Once the waitress lit all the candles with utmost efficiency, all that remained was to encourage the girls to start singing. The atmosphere in the room was one of celebration. So much so that all the customers present in the tearoom, waitresses included, happily obliged and joined in to sing "Happy Birthday." As the young princess stood up and bent over the cake, her face lit up with pure radiance. She took a deep breath, and with one almighty blow, she blew out every one of the candles.

"We hope you remembered to make a wish, Lottie," cried one of the girls, giving her a friendly nudge.

"Oh yes, I certainly did," replied Charlotte, laughing out loud as she answered her friend.

"Go on, tell us what you wished," urged another friend.

"Yes, go on. Tell us, Lottie!"

"Oh, please do!" the others in complete unison cried.

"Oh, all right then. If you insist," Charlotte replied with a giggle. "I wished that when I grow up, I would meet a wonderfully handsome man who is both rich and famous and that we would live in a huge mansion with our ten children."

"Ten!" interrupted one of the girls loudly, expressing pure disbelief.

"Oh, all right—three," admitted Charlotte. "And then we will live happily ever after." She paused before bursting into uncontrollable laughter that was so infectious it sent the rest of the girls into more fits of giggles.

Polly wished with all her heart that she could be at the table with the girls, joining in the fun and friendship they all seemed to share. She knew that if she were allowed to make a wish, it would be a very different wish than that of young, carefree Charlotte. She would just wish for a loving mother and father to take care of her brothers and herself. She longed for kind people who would not ever harm them, no matter how much they tried their patience. On the contrary, they would do all in their power to encourage them to do well and make the best of their lives. Mummy would smell of sweet rose-scented perfume and have a soft, gentle voice. She would calm all their fears and wipe away all their tears. Daddy would take the boys out for bike rides and show them how to sail a boat and how to catch the sort of fish that normally got away. Polly knew it was a huge wish, but all the same, she longed to be allowed to make such a wish that might just come true! She took a deep breath, for dreaming such a dangerously wild dream was as hopeless as catching a twinkling star.

Suddenly, Mrs. Greedol appeared from behind the food counter and noticed Polly's face glued to the window–her window! She raced to the door, muttering all the way. She flung open the door, leapt out onto the pavement, and then, like a rhinoceros with nostrils flaring, raced towards unsuspecting Polly. Luckily, Polly caught her reflection in the window and turned around just in time to duck. Mrs. Greedol charged at her with her head down, determined to butt her into the next universe. Mrs. Greedol screeched to a halt, but it was too late. She hit the window with a thump. Any harder and the glass window would have shattered. Frustrated at missing her intended target and with her pride as bruised as her bloodied face, Mrs. Greedol had to content herself with shouting and waving her fists in the air. Polly ran away as fast as her little legs could carry her. "Stay away from here, you filthy, dirty girl! We don't want your type here leaving your germs and dirty paw marks on my window pane and scaring off the customers!" she raged.

Polly ran and ran until she could run no more. Mrs. Greedol staggered very shakily back into the tearoom, heading straight for the cupboard that contained the bright red first aid box. She then moved on to the freezer to make up an ice pack.

Chapter 4
BORITZ ON THE WARPATH

*T*HE NEXT MORNING Polly woke up early from her bed and, after getting dressed, made her way down the oak stairs and headed for the kitchen. She was hungry, and it was breakfast time. Polly took a bowl from the cupboard and scooped out a cup of cornflakes from one of the two very large boxes that stood on the pantry floor. They were so large that they nearly came up to Polly's waist. One box contained puffed wheat, the other cornflakes. The simple truth was that she fancied neither, for both cereals tasted like cardboard. They were always very stale, just like the bread. But she knew that nothing else was available to her.

She took the bowl to the counter and poured milk from a large jug onto the cornflakes. The lukewarm liquid was full of thick lumps, not because the milk was old, but because it was powdered milk that had not been stirred properly. The milk substitute was normally made up by one of the foster children with better things to do, so it was always full of thick, powdery lumps that broke up in her mouth and so tasted truly disgusting. The real milk was strictly for the adults' consumption, and she only got to drink cold milk on the few times she managed to sneak into the kitchen and, when no one was looking, take a quick swig from one of the many bottles lined up inside the tall refrigerator. She felt guilty at being so deceitful, but then again, she privately reasoned, this was how things were. For with all the best food under lock and key in Uncle Boritz's private pantry and fresh milk forbidden, she felt God Himself might well understand her small indiscretion.

Polly then made her way to one of the long tables, and, taking her bowl with her, she pulled out a chair and sat down. She knew that before she could take the first mouthful it would be very necessary to catch all the little insects called silverfish that floated to the top of the milk. She observed as she peered into the bowl that they were quite literally swimming for their lives. Using her spoon, she encouraged the drowning insects to the side of the bowl. Once there, she squashed them flat before removing them with a finger, which she then wiped on her dress. Some days this little task seemed to take forever as the little rogues fought hard and long not to be captured. They knew that once caught, their time was up! With seven of the little mites expired, Polly felt confident enough to finally start eating her breakfast. Just then she spotted another silverfish. Polly showed him no mercy as she sent him the way of the others. With her mission accomplished, she now believed she could eat the cereal with no further crisis.

She was only a few mouthfuls into her breakfast when a commotion broke out. Abigail Crumble raced up to the table and anxiously declared, "Polly, come quickly! Uncle Boritz wants us all in his study right now."

"What? This minute?" questioned Polly, for she was very taken by surprise. "But I have not finished my breakfast."

"There's no time for that. He wants us in his study immediately. Come on, Polly," urged Abigail Crumble, tugging hard at Polly's sleeve.

"Why the hurry, Abigail? Let me at least take a few mouthfuls first, for I've only just managed to remove all the silverfish out of my cornflakes," Polly replied, showing her annoyance.

Abigail was quick to answer. "Look, Polly, I don't know the details. I just know that some very heinous crime has been committed, and Uncle is on the warpath."

Polly knew exactly what *heinous* meant, for the Scumberrys used the word constantly. It meant some terrible and usually unforgiveable act.

"Oh, dear!" said Polly despairingly as she reluctantly threw down her spoon and got up from the table. "Well, I had better come quickly then, hadn't I?"

As Polly made her way to Uncle Boritz's study, she could not help but think that there was always some terrible and wicked act to pay for that would find one of them fighting for their lives. Why, it had only been a matter of weeks since the last dreadful deed had been committed by, she was informed, none other than herself! That particular incident began in the usual manner, with all children assembled and sitting cross-legged on the floor of the study feeling puzzled and perplexed as to what was going to happen. They all hoped they would not be kept in the dark for too long. Uncle Boritz waited until they had all quietly settled down before standing up from behind his large desk. With Aunt Mildred sitting sedately by his side, the meeting was officially declared open. Uncle Boritz then went on to announce that he would read the offending article aloud so that everyone could listen and consider the facts before judgment was then passed on this most terrible of poems that Polly had so audaciously written. Before barely a word or utterance had escaped Uncle Boritz's mouth, Aunt Mildred had burst into floods of tears. Uncle Boritz was forced to stop midstream to remind her to hold back the tears until later when they would have a more dramatic impact.

"You're wasting valuable tears, dearest. So please do wait until I've informed the children precisely what wicked act has taken place to require this most urgent meeting," he whispered urgently into her ear.

With that said, the two of them started to look for her hanky. "I thought I put it in my overall pocket," she sniffed apologetically.

"Don't worry, dear, we will find you another," said Uncle Boritz comfortingly. He pulled open one of the side drawers in the desk, and there, perfectly stacked, were a very large number of neatly pressed, clean hankies. "Here, dearest. I keep these handy just for you," he said, almost affectionately.

"Dead right," thought Polly. Handkerchiefs were, after all, a most essential item when it came to Aunt Mildred and any kind of family meeting. Uncle Boritz handed her a bright red one from the large pile and gave her hand a little supportive squeeze.

"Right, let the proceedings begin," he roared. "I think we will start at the beginning."

"That's where most things normally start," Polly thought to herself.

"Could I just interrupt a minute, dearest?" said sniffly Aunt Mildred. Uncle Boritz turned full circle to give her his full attention. "What now, dearest?" he asked, looking rather agitated.

"Well, is there the slightest possibility that I could change the red hanky for a green one? For I do so prefer green," she simpered.

Uncle Boritz attempted to hide his annoyance as he pulled a green one from halfway down the multicolored pile of handkerchiefs and handed it to her, this time refusing to look in her direction. "Right, let's begin."

"Thank you, dearest," Aunt Mildred subserviently said as she proceeded to loudly blow her nose.

"Thank you for what?" snorted a now-incensed Uncle Boritz. For his dear wife was really interrupting his thought pattern.

"Why, dearest, for changing my hanky from a red one to a green one," she answered sweetly.

"That's perfectly all right, pumpkin. Now can I begin?"

"Oh yes, dear, please do," replied Aunt Mildred eagerly. "I'm so sorry if I'm the reason for the delay."

By now, Uncle Boritz could no longer hide his irritation. Had Aunt Mildred said anything further to upset him, the chances were very high that she would have found herself in trouble.

He cleared his throat and started. "Right, everybody, are we settled? We have a most serious situation to deal with. This is Polly's extremely derogatory poem, which was found hidden away in her bedside locker. I feel..."

Before he could get the next word out, Aunt Mildred blew her nose decidedly loud for a second time before reaching out her hand to obtain another hanky from the pile. As she did so, she managed to accidentally knock over her husband's large glass of water. The next few minutes were chaotic. Uncle Boritz tried to stop the water from soaking into the large piles of very important letters that he had not responded to. In the end, all the hankies were used to mop up the mess and prevent the mail from any further water damage! With the task done, Uncle Boritz cleared his throat, yet again, and attempted to address the issues that brought about this most important meeting.

"Children, you need to know..."

"Thank you, dear," said Aunt Mildred. "And I must say how sorry I am for spilling the water all over…"

"Silence in court!" thundered Uncle Boritz, who had clearly quite forgotten that this was meant to be a family meeting taking place in his rather cramped study.

A stunned Aunt Mildred recoiled back into her seat, gently placing the hanky over her nose and mouth in an attempt to remind herself to stay quiet. Now more than ever she knew her beloved husband was, in Abigail Crumble's words, most definitely on the "warpath."

"I will seriously punish anyone else who disrupts this meeting," snarled Uncle Boritz.

Pitstop followed suit, baring his teeth to show total support towards his powerful master. One could have heard a pin drop, as every child held in his or her breath for as long as possible, lest this should be interpreted as an act of defiance, and therefore deserving of the severest of punishments. Finally, Uncle Boritz felt happy to read out Polly's rather disturbing poem.

> Early in the morning before it is dawn,
> I hear the cows go down the town and trample on my
> lawn.

"Right, let's stop there," Uncle Boritz said in a most disgruntled tone of voice.

But before he could proceed, Aunt Mildred started sobbing again. It started quietly, but soon it transformed to loud bawling.

"Hush, hush, dearest sweet pea," urged Uncle Boritz before turning to face Polly.

Aunt Mildred instantly obeyed, for the truth was there was not a real tear in sight!

"So, Polly. Quite whom are you referring to when you mention cows? Is it Aunt Mildred? Is it myself? Or is it, as I suspect, both of us?"

Polly tried to speak up, but was prevented from doing so.

"Quiet, girl," Uncle Boritz fiercely growled. "So now you are referring to us, your devoted caretakers, as cows, are you?"

"No!" cried Polly. "You've got it all wrong. It is just a silly little poem that I made up in the playground, and it has nothing to do with any of you!"

"Nothing to do with us?" roared Uncle Boritz, his face going an even deeper shade of purple. "I most certainly think it does! And Aunt Mildred thinks likewise. Don't you, dear?"

Aunt Mildred was unavailable for comment, for she was far too busy bawling loudly into her soggy handkerchief. The children sat obediently on the floor, not daring to move a muscle. One of the little ones, Percy Pillsbury, started to cry, for he was very frightened. In a matter of moments, all the children were crying out loud, for in truth, they hated to see Aunt Mildred so distressed.

"There, you've upset everybody," Uncle Boritz sneered. "Just as you usually do, you little wretch," he said coldly.

Polly continued in vain to protest her innocence. It fell on deaf ears.

"Silence in court," ordered Uncle Boritz, quite forgetting that he was not in her majesty's courts of law. "It is no use denying it, because you wrote, 'I hear the cows go down the town.' Well, we all live at the top of the hill, don't we, children?" They all nodded in agreement. "And everything that comes up must go down. So, it is perfectly clear to me, as well as to all present at this meeting, that this particularly nasty little poem *is* therefore about *us*! Therefore, no further questioning is necessary, for this is indeed a prima facie case if ever I saw one," he thundered.

"Sorry to interrupt, dear," Aunt Mildred said softly as she was rather reluctant to spoil her husband's magnificent flow. "But quite what does *prima facie* mean? For I fear that none of the children, nor my good self for that matter, have the slightest idea what on earth you are talking about!"

"For heaven's sake, dearest. Loosely translated, it means, 'on the surface,'" he said proudly, feeling totally overcome by his supreme knowledge.

"Yes, but which of the many surfaces are we concerning our good selves with here, dearest? Is it one of the many kitchen surfaces? Or the dining table surface? Better still, is it the..."

"Enough, woman! Yes, enough of this ridiculous and very time-consuming nonsense," he rather loudly roared, for he was no longer able to hide his complete exasperation. "I am not referring to any domestic appliance or apparatus. I am merely saying, in legal terms, that it is very clear, without having to dig any deeper, what Polly means by *cows*. She is clearly and specifically referring to us!"

"Oh, dear. Then that is most wicked and unkind of her," Aunt Mildred agreed.

Before he could be rudely interrupted again, and after taking a deep breath, he announced in a loud, formal manner, "I therefore have little or no choice but to pronounce you guilty and sentence you to three weeks on R.O.P.E."

Polly gasped and gulped at the same time, unable to believe what she was hearing. For she believed she was entirely innocent of any offense, and these were therefore nothing more than trumped-up charges. For this, she was now on R.O.P.E., which was better known to the children as "Relinquishment of All Privileges and Enjoyments."

R.O.P.E. was a sentence worse than death, with every conceivable self-indulgent privilege being removed and replaced by grim and unpleasant chores that needed doing in and around the castle. In Polly's eyes it was little more than slave labor, and three weeks seemed like a lifetime to spend every day from dawn to dusk washing, ironing, cooking, and scrubbing floors and toilets. With no television, no pocket money, no going out to catch a breath of fresh air, and no communication allowed with the other children, Polly often feared she would indeed go mad. With none of the other children allowed to speak to her, she was forced to eat at a separate table along with any other miscreant on R.O.P.E. She even had to put her hand up in the air, just like at school, if she wanted to go anywhere such as the bathroom. To Polly, the whole matter was simply ludicrous. One thing was for certain: if she wasn't "loop the loop" already, then it would only be a matter of time before she was!

Being punished with endless cleaning chores was not the worst of it. If it had been, Polly might well have been able to bear it. But for Polly and some of the other children there was much more to endure. Each Sunday after lunch was over and as soon as the dishes were cleared from the tables, Uncle Boritz would go to his secret cupboard and after a few minutes reappear carrying a large cardboard box in one hand and a big black book in the other. He would then sit at the head of one of the tables and, after placing the box on the table next to him, he would open his big black book. This book caused Polly to shudder from head to foot every time it appeared. Those children who were on R.O.P.E. were then ordered by Uncle Boritz to leave their seats and stand in the center of the dining room.

Polly never failed to note that it was always the same bunch of criminals standing shamefaced in the center of the room with all eyes upon them. Uncle Boritz would not begin until all the offenders were gathered together, their heads hung low in shame. He would empty the contents of his cardboard box onto the table and then spread the contents out for all to view. Every eye fixed a firm gaze on the table as each child longingly coveted each and every item. The gifts comprised of small coloring books, trinkets, little packs of colored pencils, sweet bars, hair slides, and more. There were just a couple of larger, more expensive items such as a hairbrush set and a large bar of chocolate. Most of the items were cheap but colorful. To all the foster children who owned so little, every sweet or trinket was regarded as highly desirable. After allowing the impatient children the opportunity to drool over the gifts, he would then turn his attention to his large black book.

Having opened the book, his cold, steely eyes would scan the open pages, causing every child present to tremble and take deep breaths. They stared intently into his face, hoping for a clue as to whether this week would bring good or bad news for them. Thankfully they would not have to wait too long to find out! Those with the most stars were called up first, so one-by-one they waited to be called to go forward and stand in front of him. Every child sat on the edge of his or her seat, ready to race forward and be given the chance to choose from the spread. The decision-making process could last an eternity, as each lucky child sweat over what gift to pick up, only to change their mind and put back their chosen item and agonize further over what other gift they might prefer. For Polly and all the other children standing in the docks awaiting sentence it was an intolerable wait.

As the goods on the table were of varying value, it was obvious to all present in the room that the more popular the child, the quicker their name was called to go up and make their choice. Their own children, who never normally ate with them, were always in attendance on Sunday, and so it came as no surprise when their names were the first to be picked. In a matter of minutes, all the more expensive gifts were long gone, leaving only the cheap and cheerful gifts to be chosen by the remaining children hoping for a reward. No child ever dared comment on this. However, their favorite foster children did not do too badly either. To be given anything at all made the good children very happy. It also meant that as they sat stroking their new and most precious gift, they cared little as to what fate befell those unfortunate enough to be in the center awaiting severe admonition.

This whole torturous procedure could go on for an eternity before all the little toys were finally gone. He could now turn his attention to the troublemakers, who, having stood in the center for a considerable length of time, were feeling more anxious than ever, as well as afraid of what was in store for them. For their sins, they would be subjected to the most soul-destroying ordeal. Every misdemeanor was read out to all present, and the audience was reminded of every past offense the children in the dock had ever been found guilty of. No naughty child was to be exempt from this character-stripping process. They were to learn if their punishment was to be brought to an end or extended for a further few weeks. And hardly a week went by without a large puddle of tears being left on the floor, the only evidence of their total demise that needed to be hurriedly mopped up at the end of these terrible sessions.

Polly longed with all her heart to move from being labeled wicked to the good side, but if the truth were to be told, she had given up all hope of ever attaining this level of goodness and perfection. She had come to accept that she was thoroughly rotten to the core, and therefore no good thing could or would ever come out of her life.

For Polly to have any hope of choosing a small gift, she had to eliminate all the crosses and gain additional stars. As it took three stars to eliminate just one cross, it had not taken her very long to work out that she had to earn a massive nine stars if Sunday lunchtimes were going to become something to look forward to. She believed there was more chance of flying around the world on Concorde Airlines than getting enough stars to end her misery. As miracles had no place in this castle, her melancholy grew deeper and deeper. Polly and her partners in crime braced themselves each and every Sunday for more pain and further degradation.

Needless to say, Polly hated Sunday lunchtimes with all her being As the children with gifts happily continued to sit, totally absorbed in what they had just won, there was little thought or sympathy for those who remained in the center, waiting to be given the list of grueling chores. But as if all that were not bad enough, on many occasions there was one more punishment yet to be served to Polly!

As she stood before Uncle Boritz, completely stunned at receiving any sentence at all for her innocent poem, she was ordered to raise her head and stand up straight. She had little choice but to obey. He then pulled out his long cane and proceeded to mete out his own special brand of discipline. You can imagine what happened next. It is enough to say that Polly's cries could be heard throughout much of the building, as the noise of her screams traveled down the long, sparsely-furnished corridors. Many a time, her younger brother James tried to intervene and stop Uncle Boritz from his wickedness, but sadly, he was no match, and he was always punished for his unwelcome intervention. So there came a time when James gave up trying to rescue Polly, and he too sat in a comatose trance, just the same as all the other foster children.

When Polly's ordeal finally came to an end and justice had been served, Uncle Boritz dragged her back into the center of the room, still hurling insults at her. He would then turn his attention back to the children sitting at the tables and start pontificating. (Well, what does *pontificate* mean? It means to go on and on and on some more!) He droned on and on about the necessity for utter loyalty to Aunt Mildred and himself. He told them that whatever went on in this castle stayed in the castle and should never be discussed outside its walls. The children all nodded their agreement. They were in no position to do otherwise, or woe betide them! The children knew from previous experience that he would, as usual, go on reminding them that just as their mums and dads had abandoned them, likewise, nobody else would ever want them. It was therefore essential that they all stick together, unless of course they wished to find themselves homeless—something that terrified them all!

Today, as Polly entered the study, she fervently prayed that it would be someone else's turn to be in the hot seat, though she really hoped with all her heart that it would be neither James's nor Thomas's turn to be severely admonished. They too had received more than their fair share of similar punishments, particularly Thomas, who appeared to be struggling to survive in the home and was falling sicker by the day.

Chapter 5
THE MOLE CRISIS

*O*NCE ALL THE children were settled down and sitting cross-legged on the floor, the room fell silent, and nobody dared to even twitch. Uncle Boritz sat behind his vast office desk, which was still piled high with very important letters stacked up against the old typewriter. He appeared to be in no hurry to get the meeting underway and continued to read his newspaper, something Polly found quite unnerving. Eventually Aunt Mildred entered the room, and after closing the study door, she marched like a colonel in chief across the floor before going behind the desk and pulling up a chair beside him. Out came the handkerchief in anticipation that it would be needed. It always was!

Finally, Uncle Boritz looked down and patted Pitstop on the head before folding away his newspaper and standing up to address all present.

"I believe we are all here," he said, scanning his audience of wide-eyed children through the thick lenses of his spectacles, which were perched very precariously on the tip of his nose. "Good, then we will begin." He took the opportunity to take a deep breath.

"Once again, I find myself in the most unpleasant situation of having to break some very bad news to you all: we have a mole in the house!"

The children all gasped in sheer horror. "Ugh, a mole!" shrieked one of the children.

"Yes, that's precisely what I said," Uncle Boritz sternly remarked over his thick-rimmed glasses.

"Can't we just call in the exterminator?" Oliver Beswick, one of the children, dared to ask, feeling very pleased to have had a thought, let alone the courage to express it!

"Yes, I think Oliver's suggestion is a good one," Tommy Pulleyblank piped up.

"Can we keep it as a pet?" pleaded Maisie Madgewick, one of the youngest girls present. "It would be so nice to have a pet. Please don't kill it. Tell me you won't." She then started to cry at the thought of the dear little defenseless mole with its little wet nose mercilessly being killed.

"Silence!" ordered Uncle Boritz, at the same time furrowing his brow as he peered down at them over his thick black spectacles. "You all know by now I will not tolerate being interrupted!"

He paused as if deep in thought, then continued, hands firmly clasped behind his back as he paced up and down the line of children seated on the floor.

"I am not talking about a mole as in an animal, but rather other vermin," he said in a tone that portrayed nothing short of utter contempt. "Yes, we are dealing with a traitor, or should I say fifth columnist?"

"What's a fifth columnist?" Eleanor Apecot asked, pulling a rather perplexed face. None of the other children were in any position to help her out, for they were all equally confused.

"Don't you idiots know anything?" Tommy Pullyblank sneered rather smugly. "Why, it has something to do with the White House in America. They have loads of columns outside their posh buildings," he stated, very delighted at his supreme knowledgeable ability.

"I said silence!" roared Uncle Boritz angrily. "This particular mole is an informant! Yes, someone in our midst has been talking about the very private things that go on in our family life. This viperous little vixen does not care what she tells people. And what's more, if these lies were to be believed, my little whippersnappers, then it might mean that the wicked, terrible people from the child-care agency would come and drag you from your beds in the middle of the night and you would never be seen again."

THE MOLE CRISIS

The air was thick with tension, and one of the little ones started to cry at the thought of these evil, soulless ghouls coming to drag them from their beds in the middle of the night. In seconds, the room was filled with tearful children, terrified for their lives. Uncle Boritz welcomed their tears, for it meant things were truly going as planned. He seized the moment to quickly add, "And yes, both Aunt Mildred as well as my good self would remain deeply broken-hearted for the rest of our lives if, heaven forbid, this were ever to happen. Isn't that so, Mildred?" he said, giving her a sly kick in order to get the urgently-required, tear-jerking response.

"Oh yes, yes children, that would be so terrible. And Uncle and I would miss you all so much," she replied, almost choking on her words.

Uncle Boritz gave her a little pat on her shoulder. "There, there, my dear. Try hard not to get too upset. So you do understand what I am trying to say here, children, don't you? This is why it is of the utmost importance to reveal this traitor and punish her for her treachery!"

"Who is it?" asked Billy Osgood, quite forgetting they were not allowed to interrupt.

"I think on this occasion, we all know who the culprit is," Uncle Boritz slyly replied as he moved away from the desk, placing himself only inches away from Polly, who was innocently sitting down on the floor along with all the other children. The children then turned to each other, rather foolishly attempting to try and guess just who the culprit might be!

Uncle Boritz used this opportunity to move even closer to Polly, placing his right foot down very hard on one of her hands, which were placed on either side of her on the floor. Polly let out a loud squeal.

"Ah ha! The guilty one has finally owned up," he announced gleefully. "Yes, once again we find that it is none other than Polly who has shown disloyalty to our close-knit family."

It was at this point in the procedure that Aunt Mildred, right on cue, begun to sob uncontrollably into her hanky. Seeing Aunt Mildred so very sad and distressed forced the children to cry even louder. Uncle Boritz was now feeling very pleased with himself. His speech had paid off much, as he had predicted it would. He was now free to use whatever physical force he chose, and no one would think any the worse of him. After all was said and done, Polly had committed the most unforgivable crime, and there was no punishment on this earth that the children would now see as too severe a sentence.

"Polly, do you have anything to say before sentencing begins?" Uncle Boritz said, staring rather intensely into her eyes. Not only was Polly completely flabbergasted to find herself yet again in the docks, but she also wondered whether there was any point in protesting, for she knew that her protestations would fall on deaf ears. However, she still decided to try.

"Yes, I do," Polly replied, much too defiantly for Uncle Boritz's liking. "I am not entirely certain what I am guilty of."

"Ah, the offendant, I mean, the defendant, is a liar too," he sneered. "*You*, my girl, were heard talking to one of the homeless men very disparagingly about our yearly entertainment programs, so don't even try to deny it."

"That's very true," Polly quite openly and innocently admitted. "But I only told him about a couple of the many events that take place each year. So you've no need to worry, for I did leave the worst ones out! Like your famous Halloween parties and..." Before Polly could go into any further detail, she was stopped.

"Enough!" roared a very crimson-faced Uncle Boritz. "Your own mouth has condemned you. Stand to attention!"

Before Polly could uncross her legs, he grabbed her by the scruff of the neck and hauled her to her feet.

"Now, will the plaintiff please step forward," Uncle Boritz ordered in a suitably stern tone of voice.

Of course, no one stepped forward, for all in the room were more than a little uncertain as to quite who the plaintiff was! Uncle Boritz stood drumming his fingers on the desktop as he waited for his command to be obeyed. Nobody moved. At that precise moment, the phone rang. As business matters were of the utmost importance to him, he wasted no time in reaching for the phone, and, upon picking up the receiver, he said in a loud and stern voice, "Hello, this is Boritz of Boritz and Boritz International. How may I help you?"

Cecil Bogswater took this breathing space as an opportunity to turn to Bertha Banoffee, who just happened to be sitting next to him, and loudly asked, "Hey, isn't 'Plaintiff' that new board game that's being advertised on the TV?"

"I don't think so," Bertha Banoffee replied before rather thoughtfully adding, "I think I saw an ad that said it had something to do with relieving headaches. Or was it tummy upsets?"

On hearing their debate, Tommy Pullyblank once again came quickly to the rescue. "Wrong again, both of you! A plaintiff is, in fact, someone who has been upset by someone else and needs help to sort things out, so he goes to the police station to make an official complaint. The policeman, upon realizing the seriousness of the problem, then quickly hurries to the train station and gets on a train bound for London. Once he has arrived at Victoria Station, he then takes a red double-decker bus right up to the gates of Buckingham Palace, for by now he has an urgent appointment with the queen."

"Is the bus an open-topped bus?" enquired Bertha Banoffee, "because he might well get a cold if he has no overcoat on."

"How would I know?" Tommy Pullyblank answered, most annoyed at being interrupted by thick-as-a-door-plank Bertha with what he considered to be such a ridiculously stupid question.

"Well, I only asked," Bertha Banoffee rather sulkily sniffed, "because you never mentioned the policeman putting on his coat, and open-topped buses are only nice to travel on when it's sunny. So there, fish face," she said, rather rudely sticking out her tongue to make her point.

Tommy chose to ignore her insult and continued with his most informative talk. "If the queen believes the crisis is, after all, worthy of her consideration, she would then put on her coat and scarf and walk around to 10 Downing Street to see the prime minister. She would take all her corgis with her, for they need the exercise. Then, having pressed the doorbell, she is left with little choice but to stand in the cold while the prime minister rolls out of bed."

"Poor Queen. I wouldn't like her job," Bertha thought privately to herself.

Tommy continued, "After he has put on his underpants and his pin-striped suit, they both stroll back to Buckingham Palace. Once home, the queen goes to the kitchen to put on the kettle before rustling up some cakes in the oven. She's a very good cook, I'll have you know. Only when the teapot is empty and the crisis has been thoroughly chewed over does our prime minister order his security men to take him to the airport, where he then boards a plane bound for America."

"Does he take the corgis with him?" Bertha Banoffee then dared to ask. "I mean, I've always been terribly concerned that those cute pups don't get out enough. It must be quite awful for them being cooped up in that stuffy palace all day." Secretly Bertha was more concerned at the thought of little dogs being taken up in a plane and having to wear seat belts.

"Of course not, stupid," Tommy Pullyblank retorted, for he was most annoyed at being interrupted by Bertha for a second time.

"The corgis remain at the palace with the queen. It is only the prime minister who gets on the plane. Over another cup of tea, normally served with muffins on the lawn of the White House, the president and prime minister have to make the decision as to whether to put both our countries on high alert. The whole procedure is very simple. Really, it is!" he said, most persuasively.

"Ooh!" said Toby Trotter, who just happened to be listening in.

Both pleased and encouraged by his attentive audience, Tommy finished up by saying with considerable authority, "Yes, this is done so that we can all sleep safe and sound in our beds."

"Oh," said Cecil Bogswater.

"Gosh," said Bertha Banoffee. For they were both very impressed indeed.

Uncle Boritz was still on the phone listening intently to the person speaking on the other end of the line. "Well, Mr. Ribald, I think this calls for you to stand firm and claim *caveat emptor*."

The children looked at each other and shrugged, for none of them understood his fancy talk and assumed it therefore must be Japanese or Swahili! They never studied foreign languages in school, and more to the point none of them wanted to! Ears pricked, they continued to listen in on his most important conversation.

"Don't insult me. Of course I know what *caveat emptor* means, Mr. Ribald," Uncle Boritz said, raising his voice to express his annoyance at being asked such an absurd question. He was, however, at the same time, quickly opening a legal reference book similar to a dictionary. He flicked through the pages furiously in an attempt to find the correct translation. He then breathed a sigh of relief, for by now, little beads of sweat were trickling down his forehead. "Yes. I can state with exceeding confidence that it means 'let the buyer beware.' So as far as I am concerned, this should bring to an end your distasteful dispute with the awful Mrs. Crudite, who, I might add, has never shown as much as a modicum of decency with regard to this whole ghastly affair."

He paused to pull a hanky from his trouser pocket before proceeding to wipe away the perspiration that was now pouring profusely down his face. He then stuffed it back into his pocket, deciding at the same time to bring this rather tedious conversation to a swift halt, for his time was very costly. "That's excellent news, Mr. Ribald. I will pop my bill for services rendered in the post today. I really must go now, as I am in a most important business meeting. So thank you and good day to you, sir."

With the conversation brought to a rather abrupt halt, he placed the receiver down heavily and again breathed a sigh of relief. He then bent over the desk to where Aunt Mildred was still seated and proudly said, "I am awfully sorry to have kept you waiting, dearest, but that phone call has just made us a nice packet of money. It is wonderful to make so much of the stuff as a legal adviser, and for doing so little!"

With that said, he licked his lips like a cat that had just got the cream and turned his focus back to the urgent matter at hand. With the delay over, the children stopped all nonsensical talk and bottom-shuffling and focused their attention back on Uncle Boritz and the current mole crisis.

"Now, back to business," he said brightly. For making money always gladdened his otherwise cold, unfeeling heart. Turning towards the children again, he paused for a second and asked. "Well, has the plaintiff come forward?"

POLLY BROWN

Again there was total silence, something that served to confuse Uncle Boritz even further, for he was not used to being disobeyed. He turned to his desk and picked up his glass of water and took a sip, something he always did when he was trying to contain his anger.

Bertha Banoffee used this opportunity to further her last conversation with Tommy Pullyblank by asking him whether he believed the queen's corgis should be allowed to fly first class or business class. Uncle Boritz, having made it to the other side of his desk, was now standing over Aunt Mildred. Bending down, he quietly whispered in her ear, "You, my dear, as well as my good self, are the plaintiff! So it would be very helpful if you would do as I asked and step forward."

"Of course, my dear," she said sweetly, standing up and pushing aside her chair before taking hold of his hand. For she did so want to show herself as an utterly supportive wife, dedicated to all his causes, of which there were so many. She momentarily stood gazing down adoringly at him before making the deepest of sighs. For in truth, she was finding this to be the most trying case.

"I'm so sorry, dearest. I had no idea that you were referring to me," she said apologetically before adding that she'd never been one for big words.

With Aunt Mildred finally at his side, he gave her a little nudge. Aunt Mildred obliged. Out came the hankie again, and with it came loud sobbing. Uncle Boritz now felt satisfied that everything was back on track. Yes, things had looked a bit dodgy for a moment, but he was now finally back in control! Thank goodness! Then suddenly without warning he loudly roared at the top of his lungs, "Habeas corpus!" with his mouth opened so wide so that all present could very clearly see his shuddering tonsils. Pitstop, never given to fear, growled and snarled, for he was equally frightened and intimidated.

"Habeas corpus?" questioned Aunt Mildred, by now most concerned that he had, yet again, clearly forgotten that he was not in the queen's law courts, but merely in his own rather untidy and very dingy study with the little children acting as jurors. Alas, she felt she had little choice but to intervene once again.

"My dearest darling," she said very graciously. "I am so sorry to have to tell you this, but none of us here have the same wonderful intellect as your good self. We are therefore truly struggling to understand one word of what you are saying. And this is making it very difficult to follow any of your orders!" She paused before quickly returning to her seat, very unsure of what would happen next.

Poor Uncle Boritz was more than a little perplexed by his dear wife's most ignorant and unexpected outburst. Nevertheless, he decided that he must forgive her lack of intellect on this occasion.

"I must apologize for my total lack of consideration, sweet pea," he muttered with mock humility.

With his apology graciously accepted by a very relieved Aunt Mildred, he then turned again to his captive, if not slightly confused, jurors. At the top of his voice he roared, "'Let the body be brought before me,' for that's what it means. We are here to decide if this girl is of sound mind or, as I suspect, truly insane before I, or rather we, pass judgment on her."

All the girls in the group turned to each other quite terrified, for they were most concerned as to whether it was one of their bodies he required, and more to the point, why? They all knew the story of Abraham and his son Isaac from their religious education studies. Did he seriously want to sacrifice one of them? And if so, which one? In unison, they all shuffled further back from where Uncle Boritz stood.

"Bring forth the offendant!" he angrily shouted.

"Don't you mean the defendant, dear?" Aunt Mildred mumbled, tugging on his trouser leg before retreating further back into her seat.

"Yes, and before anyone has the impudence to ask who the defendant is, let me make it perfectly clear. I am referring to Polly Brown," he snapped, at the same time pointing a finger in Polly's direction. "So bring her here right now!" he thundered.

Two of the elder boys leapt up from the floor and in an instant, swept Polly clean off her feet, dropping her down on the floor right in front of Uncle Boritz. Pitstop then slowly circled her and sniffed her body. Polly cautiously picked herself up from the floor and stood before her accusers. She hung her head low, biting her trembling bottom lip.

"Mildred dearest, please come here and take over. There's a good woman," Uncle Boritz ordered.

Mildred once again arose from her chair and walked over to where her husband stood. On this occasion, she did not need to ask her husband what to do, for if she was given the honor of being called to her husband's side, it could only mean one thing. She therefore leaned over to remove one of her hard blue leather shoes. As usual, Polly's cries of pain could be heard throughout the long corridors of the castle. When her ordeal finally ended, with all punishment satisfactorily administered, Polly stood. She held her head down as she shook and cried. Both guardians continued to hurl every imaginable insult in her direction. It worked.

Polly slumped to the floor and placed her hands over her ears. For she knew the physical scars would fade in time, but the cruel words and insinuations always entered deep into her heart and mind and would stay as a very unwelcome guest to torment her every single day and night of her young life.

Uncle Boritz stood towering over Polly's limp, profusely shaking body. He was, thank goodness, extremely satisfied. Seeing Polly lying on the ground in a little ball and whimpering pathetically assured him that he had produced the desired effect of crushing her tender spirit to fine dust. Having achieved his goal, he licked his thick lips with great relish, announcing with great pleasure that she was to be placed on R.O.P.E. for a further two months.

"Children, stay well away from her, unless of course you want to catch her most unpleasant condition," he stated. "She is a real mental case, and I have it on the greatest authority that this malady has blighted many of her ancestors, and therefore it runs in her family. Should any of you choose to ignore this warning, then you do so at your own peril. For it is likely that, within a short period of time, you too will become infected. This will almost certainly mean being removed from here to be taken to a special hospital where screams similar to those you have just heard coming from Polly will constantly be heard throughout the building day and night. For all who live there are, without exception, quite mad!" he cautioned, lowering his voice to little more than a whisper as a fiendish smile played on his lips.

All the children sat frozen with horror as, with great relish, he continued to scare the living daylights out of them. Uncle Boritz was feeling most satisfied that his mission was almost accomplished.

"Once inside, you are almost certain to remain incarcerated in a padded cell. And for those of you not clever enough to understand what the term *incarceration* means, let me inform you right now. It means to be locked away *forever.*"

The sound of loud gasps could clearly be heard as the jaw of each child present visibly dropped, as they now grappled with feelings of absolute terror and determined to heed his extremely serious warning. Despite the eerie silence, they all unanimously agreed with Uncle Boritz to keep well away from the beastly, lice-ridden, maggoty Polly Brown.

Polly was finally ordered to get up from the floor and get out of their sight. She hurriedly obeyed. As she limped out of the room, out of the corner of her eye she spied Uncle Boritz walking over to where Gailey Gobbstopper sat on the floor. Pulling out a bag of sweets from his pocket, he placed them in her outstretched hand.

"Good work, Gailey," he said with a smile as he gave her an encouraging pat on the head. "Thank you for letting me know all that you heard them talking about, and let me use this opportunity to remind you, and all present, that careless talk costs lives."

Gailey blushed slightly before tilting her face upwards to smile back at him, most delighted to have been of assistance. He then turned his full attention to all the children who had endured many hours in the study.

"Now children, if you will all come with me," he said cheerily, beckoning them with his outstretched hand to follow him out of his study. "We will go to my private store cupboard and find some goodies as a special treat," said Uncle Boritz, suddenly feeling in a very generous mood. The children broke out into rapturous shrieks of laughter and merriment as they all huddled together and excitedly agreed that sweets would ease the discomfort they endured sitting for many bottom-numbing hours as jurors. They had, after all, been forced to listen to a case in which they had very little interest.

With chocolate bars in their hot little hands and bottles of fizz to suck through straws, it would be only a matter of minutes before the more than grateful children would fail to even remember any of the events they had just witnessed! Uncle Boritz left the room like the Pied Piper with the children dancing behind him as they made their way down the long corridor, heading towards his permanently locked and very private store cupboard. Pitstop slunk along the corridor at the heels of his master, convinced that he too was in for a big treat—a big juicy bone that he could enjoy sinking his long, sharp teeth into. He much preferred mauling and crunching bones to a chocolate bar.

Alone and fighting back the tears, Polly falteringly climbed the long, wooden staircase and headed for the dormitory. She wanted to be left alone, so she silently prayed that none of the other girls would come in, for privacy was something of a luxury that she rarely had. Polly picked up Langdon and, cuddling him in one arm, flung herself onto her bed and pressed her face tightly into the elephant as well as the pillow. She wanted to scream and scream, but nothing would come. She felt furious and angry with Gailey, for she knew only too well that it was always her who spied on everyone and then ran quickly to her master to tell tales. She had done it so often, and for what? A miserable bag of sweets! When she didn't have a spicy tale to tell, she made one up. Polly had little doubt that if anyone would enter the room, it would be Gailey. Gailey took great pleasure in tormenting Polly.

Hardly a day passed without her cruel taunts, and Polly found it so difficult to understand what made Gailey act like this. She would have found it much easier to understand if she had been one of their guardians' own children, but this was not the case. Gailey was in care as a foster child, just the same as Polly. She would tell Polly that she was a loony, just like her brothers; or that she would grow up to be a bag lady, just like her mother; or worse still, that she was so ugly, no one could possibly ever love her. Just like Aunt Mildred and Uncle Boritz, she found the greatest pleasure in inflicting pain on others, particularly Polly and her older brother Thomas.

An hour or so passed before Polly reappeared from under her blanket and sat up on her bed. She peered into the jar that stood on the bedside cabinet. Oliver the caterpillar was still in the jar, weaving and winding his way over the leaves and therefore completely unaware of the drama that had unfolded downstairs in the study. He just continued on as usual, munching and crunching his way through the lettuce leaves that had now sprung large holes. At that moment Polly wished to be a caterpillar, for she patiently observed that all Oliver had to do was pig out on lettuce leaves and sleep. Nothing more and nothing less! No one bothered him. No one called him names and hurt him. He just lived to eat and rest.

Suddenly, the door of the dormitory opened, and she looked up. Polly let out a deep groan, for her unwelcome visitor was none other than Gailey Gobbstopper, the tormentor.

Chapter 6
OLIVER'S RATHER CLEVER
DISAPPEARING ACT

*T*HE NEXT FEW weeks saw Polly hard at work scrubbing floors, peeling endless potatoes, cooking, and feverishly working her way through mountains of ironing. By the time evening arrived she felt utterly exhausted, but she had one final task—to polish thirty or more pairs of shoes for school the next day. The shoes were all lined up on a long table in a freezing cold, dimly-lit basement. Polly found the only way to get through the job was to brush the shoes as hard and furiously as she could, for this helped to keep her warm. Luckily for Polly, she did get help with this chore. It came from a lady who frequently visited the castle and did little errands and tasks for a few hours a week. When she wasn't at the orphanage she was an inmate at the local mental hospital. Polly knew her as Cecilia Crabtree. She was a very troubled woman in her late forties, and she informed Polly on many occasions that her illness had much to do with a nervous disorder. Not that they talked much, for Cecilia was, in Polly's eyes, far too gone for such things. They usually stood side-by-side in absolute silence, brushing the shoes until they shone.

However, Cecilia was prone to sudden outbursts, which would make Polly almost jump out of her shoes. These episodes always came without warning. One minute she was quietly polishing shoes, the next minute she would throw her head back, cursing and shouting insults. Polly often looked up to see if someone was dangling from the ceiling or swinging from the light shade, but there was never anyone there. If there was, Polly was definitely unable to see them. The lighting in this particular room was poor, and she knew her eyesight was bad, but not that bad.

Polly eventually came to believe that Cecilia was actually talking to God, and furthermore she was very angry with Him. Polly understood this completely, for she had real issues with Him as well. However, she chose to deal with her problems quite differently. She would sneak out of the house and go to the nearby graveyard before she started to yell at Him! She preferred to do such things in private. As with Cecilia's outbursts, Polly's conversations with God seemed very one-sided. She would tell Him she couldn't take any more pain and she wished she'd never been born. What's more, she never failed to draw His attention to the starving children in Africa, demanding to know what He was doing about it! Polly had so much to get off her chest that she could be there in the graveyard for hours at a time giving Him a real dressing down. Although venting her frustration helped to make her feel a little better, she still always ended up crying and begging for His help, especially at night times when she hid under the bed cold and frightened. So when all was said and done, none of Cecilia's very odd behavior bothered Polly in the slightest, for she felt the deepest sympathy for her.

However she did have one objection, and a large one at that: she was constantly having to duck to avoid being sprayed by the fountain of spittle that shot up in the air from Cecilia's mouth as she yelled. For as the droplets flew through the air, much of it landed on Polly! Many a shoe-cleaning session ended with Polly rushing to the bathroom to wipe her face with a cloth. She had to admit that she found this to be most objectionable!

As the weeks on R.O.P.E. dragged on, Polly was very tired by the time she climbed the oak stairs for bed, so much so that she forgot about her jar with the caterpillar. Then came a day when, upon peering into the jar, she discovered that little Oliver was no longer there. Polly felt panic welling up inside. She picked up the jar and emptied the contents onto the bedside locker. There was nothing except dried up lettuce leaves. She sifted through these and discovered a long, seriously shriveled piece of what looked like a dried up carcass. She carefully picked it up between her fingers to take a closer look, and it immediately started to crumble. Were these the remains of her caterpillar? Had she unintentionally killed Oliver? Did she starve him to death by failing to provide him the nutrition he required from fresh green leaves? "Oh dear! Poor Oliver," she thought most sadly to herself. Polly felt very guilty that she had neglected this poor defenseless creature, and now it was dead. How on earth could she face Hodgekiss, and, even worse, would he ever forgive her for such a terribly wicked act of cruelty?

Suddenly she heard a little flutter past her ears. She looked up, and there flitting through the air was the most beautiful orange and gold butterfly. Polly looked at the carcass and then at the butterfly before suddenly remembering what she had once learned in a biology lesson at school. In an instant she realized that Oliver was not dead at all, but had been transformed into this new, most beautiful creature. She sat for a few moments transfixed as she watched it flutter from one wall to another. She found it hard to believe that this maggoty insect was now a graceful, delicate thing of immense beauty. Within seconds of that thought she realized she needed to catch it so that Hodgekiss wouldn't be angry with her and they could still be friends.

Polly watched as it fluttered through the air before coming to land on the light shade, drawn by the light. She knew she had to act quickly if she was to have any hope of catching it. The problem was that she was so small and the light shade was so high up, and therefore well beyond her reach. Being a quick thinker, she grabbed the only chair in the room and placed it on her bed. After climbing onto the bed she attempted to climb up onto the chair. It was difficult, for not only did she feel a little shaky, but the chair also appeared fragile as she stood wobbling to and fro. She was disappointed to discover that she was still unable to reach the light shade. So she climbed down from the chair, jumped off the bed, and left the room.

When Polly finally returned, she was carrying yet another chair. This she dutifully placed on top of the other chair before attempting to climb both chairs to reach the light. Polly had obviously never been to the circus, otherwise she would have learned from the clowns that stacking wobbly chairs on top of each other was not a bright idea and she would certainly be doomed to failure.

She proceeded to mount the chairs, eventually reaching the top chair, and then wobbling to and fro with her arms outstretched, she took an almighty swipe at the light shade. She missed. The chairs, with herself still hanging on, tumbled off the bed and crashed to the floor. Polly was momentarily dazed but remained undefeated as she again mounted the chairs to give it another go. Sadly the results were the same, with Polly and the chairs coming to rest on the floor. It took several attempts before she finally gave up, momentarily admitting defeat.

Polly sat on the floor for several minutes, wondering how on earth she could possibly reach up to the ceiling light. She would have given up right then, but the thought of upsetting Hodgekiss with bad news concerning the whereabouts of Oliver gave her renewed determination to find a solution to the problem.

Suddenly, she had what she believed to be a very bright idea that was almost certain to work. She left the room and came back a few minutes later holding a rather large pair of Aunt Mildred's bloomers, which she had retrieved from the washbin! As Polly held them high into the air and swished them to and fro, the bloomers successfully filled up with air like a hot balloon. She was so delighted with the results that she wasted no time in putting the chairs back on the bed, and once she had found her balance, she began frantically waving the bloomers through the air until she successfully gave the light shade an almighty wack, sending the shade into a spin. Seconds later found Polly crashing to the floor with the chairs once again coming to rest on top of her. Nursing a very sore head, she looked to see if she had succeeded in trapping the butterfly in Aunt Mildred's bloomers. There was no sign of Oliver. She looked up at the light shade and didn't see him there either. She peered once more through the legs of Aunt Mildred's baggy bloomers just in case she had accidentally missed him. He definitely wasn't hiding in either leg. She was very dismayed and disappointed not to have caught him.

If he wasn't on the shade or in Aunt Mildred's oversized bloomers, where precisely was he hiding? As she pondered this question, she thought she heard a little flutter. Looking up across the room, she saw that the mischievous little thing had come to rest on the dormitory wardrobe. She stood up and crept quietly over to where it hovered, feeling a sense of impending victory. She crept cautiously towards the wardrobe, hardly daring to breathe, her eyes firmly pinned on the playful little mite that would soon be safe in her grasp. Polly inched closer and closer, but when she found herself just a hair's breadth away from containing it between her cupped hands the butterfly had the audacity to take off, fluttering straight towards the open bedroom window. She raced to shut the window, but it was too late! The mischievous rascal flew out into the dazzling sunlight and to freedom. He was indeed gone forever! Polly stood open-mouthed and mortified before letting out a loud groan that insufficiently expressed the depth of her disappointment and despair.

Slumping onto the floor, she told herself she was now in big trouble with Hodgekiss. He would never forgive her for letting his pet escape. Even worse, she felt certain he would now happily join the growing list of people who hated her. She therefore wished with all her heart she had never accepted the jar, complete with Oliver, from Ralph! Feeling extremely despondent, she picked up Langdon and Eton from the floor, and, with a friend under each arm, she crawled under the bed covers to lament Ollie's sad and very sudden departure.

Months passed by without any sightings of Hodgekiss or Ralph, and Polly continued to feel her usual lonely self. Every time the doorbell rang, she raced with high hopes to open the front door to see if the visitor was either one of them. Her hopes were always dashed. Plenty of rag-tag men turned up during the time of their absence, and Polly always dutifully made them the usual, but she was unable to hide her growing disappointment and no longer enjoyed her conversations with these sad and lonely strangers. There even came a time when she no longer bothered to race to the door, preferring to leave it to one of the other children.

The winter came and went, and with it dark soulless nights and bitterly icy winds. Soon after came the sweet distinctive smell of spring, that permeated the air with its youthful freshness and vibrancy. As nothing much had changed in Polly's young life, it made no difference what time of the year it was, for spring might represent the season of hope and rebirth for others, but for her, it meant nothing but more drudgery.

Then came a day when, after the doorbell rang twice, no one else answered it, so Polly was forced into action. At first she chose to ignore it, thinking to herself that she was tired of always being the one to make the tea and sandwiches for the gentlemen of the road. She decided it was somebody else's turn to make a snack for a hungry, wearied traveler, for she was in no mood to talk to anyone. The doorbell rang again, followed by several more rings, each ring getting longer and more urgent in length. Still, nobody bothered to answer it. Then the noise from the bell rang continuously, for the visitor now had his finger permanently on the button. It was not too long before Polly felt really furious that no one else had gone to the door, and it was now left to her to go, unless she wanted to get even more wound up by the bell's incessant ring. "What a lazy bunch," she thought as she angrily stormed towards the front door. She was determined to give this extremely rude person on the other side a piece of her mind. She flung the door wide open, shouting, "Get your finger off the button, you horrible..." Polly stopped in her tracks. "Hodgekiss!" she yelled with great delight, abandoning all ceremony to fling her arms around his neck and give him one of her special hugs. Hodgekiss nearly fell backwards off the steps.

"Oh, Hodgekiss, am I glad to see you!" she exclaimed, brushing away the tears that were now unashamedly escaping down her cheeks. "I have missed you so much," she confessed.

"I have missed you too, Polly," he said with a smile. "And I would have come a lot sooner if I had known I would get such a wonderfully warm welcome."

"Wait here," Polly commanded as she quickly composed herself. "And I will make the usual for you, and then we can talk. So don't move a muscle, Hodgekiss. Do you hear me? For I will be back in one tick."

She raced down the corridors as if she were competing in a marathon and her very life depended on winning it. The usual was done, setting a new record time not only in making the tea but also in the amount she managed to slop all over the floor as she rushed back to be with her long-lost friend.

POLLY BROWN

Polly settled down on the steps as Hodgekiss slurped his tea from the large, white, disgracefully cracked mug.

"I've missed your special recipe for tea, Polly," he said with a friendly smile. "Although I'm wondering if you've put enough sugar in it!"

"So sorry," replied Polly. "Shall I run back and get you some more?"

"No need," Hodgekiss replied. "I was only joking. I get a year's supply of energy in one go when you make me a cup of tea!" They both laughed out loud.

With all silly talk out of the way, Hodgekiss's tone of voice turned more serious. "How are things going, Polly?" he inquired with a look of deep concern.

"Not too good," Polly rather glumly admitted, her voice tinged with great sadness. "I seem to be in a lot of trouble most of the time. Although I try my very best, nothing seems to work," she said resignedly before adding that she had come to the firm conclusion that she must be a really bad girl. "They constantly tell me that I'm quite beyond redemption, and I think that means I'm beyond all hope."

Hodgekiss went silent, looking deep in thought. Eventually he spoke. "And how is my little friend, the caterpillar?" he asked.

Polly's face turned a deep shade of pink. "Oh...hmm...the caterpillar," she said very quietly. "Well, I'm not too sure how to tell you this, Hodgekiss, but your caterpillar has gone."

"Gone!" said Hodgekiss, pretending to be a little shocked at the news.

"Yes, didn't you hear me the first time when I said he's gone?" mumbled Polly, feeling very embarrassed.

"Gone where?" queried Hodgekiss, playfully expressing the deepest concern as to the real whereabouts of his little friend.

"Ollie's gone on 'oliday," Polly replied, very tongue in cheek.

"On holiday?" queried Hodgekiss.

"Yes, on a long trip to the Bahamas!" she said warily. Polly momentarily paused, waiting to see if Hodgekiss would finally click on to the fact that Oliver would never be coming home again.

However, Hodgekiss's face still appeared blank, and this seemed to irritate her further.

"Look, Hodgekiss. How would I know where he is?" she said, showing her annoyance. "He's just gone! That's all I can tell you at this point."

In truth, Polly felt really guilty. She had hoped the subject of the caterpillar would remain forgotten, never to be brought up, for she believed he would be most upset with her.

"I'm so sorry, Hodgekiss. Really I am. I know he meant a lot to you, and if I could, I would replace him. Let me go and get the jar," she said, feeling most anxious to leave his presence, for discussing this whole unfortunate episode was making her feel distinctly uncomfortable. She got up from where she was sitting with the intention of going indoors to find his empty jar and return it to him. That way he could see for himself that she was not lying, and he would hopefully find it much easier to come to terms with the loss of little Oliver.

"Polly, please don't go," said Hodgekiss. "I think we both know that you didn't lose my caterpillar," he said gently. "No, the little fellow turned into a butterfly, didn't he?" Hodgekiss studied her face in search of the real truth.

"Yes, he did. That is what really happened," Polly reluctantly admitted. "But I felt certain that if I told you what really happened, you would not believe me. Nobody around here ever believes anything I say, even though I always do my best to tell the truth." A lone tear slid slowly down Polly's cheek.

"Polly, I asked you to observe my little friend, didn't I?"

"Yes, you did, and I promise you, I couldn't feel any worse than I do about what happened to him. So please can we drop the subject?" she pleaded. "I know I failed you, but with all the tasks I am expected to complete each day, I barely had the time to look after little Oliver."

More tears tumbled down Polly's hot cheeks as she attempted to explain herself. Hodgekiss lifted up his hand to gently wipe them away.

"I would give you my hanky, but it's never very clean," he said with a grin.

Polly's face broke into a smile at the thought of being given one of Hodgekiss's rather disgusting handkerchiefs. He was right—she wouldn't want to use it under any circumstances!

Hodgekiss continued on in a softly spoken manner. "Polly, when Ollie, or rather Oliver, was in the jar, he had somewhat limited vision. All he saw was the glass around him and the lettuce leaves in front of him. That was the entirety of his world. He was unable to look up at the big world, and he was also incapable of looking down from a height to see the bigger picture. All he knew was what took place within the jar, so he assumed that was all there was. Now if you are honest with yourself, you looked upon him and thought he had a cushy little number, just sleeping and growing fat on lettuce leaves."

"Fat on lettuce leaves! I think not Hodgekiss, for everyone knows that you only eat lettuce leaves if you're on a very strict diet."

"Oh, Polly, stop being so pedantic. It was only a manner of speech, and all I was attempting to get across was that you thought little Ollie had it easy. But this was not so. He went through an almighty struggle to release himself from his cocoon that acted as a restraint, holding him down. Once he became unfettered, and after his near-death experience, he was able to fly away. Now, that is what I call freedom! Yes, Oliver discovered the freedom to choose, something you have never really known inside these walls."

Polly nodded her agreement.

"From the moment he flew out of your window he discovered that the world was not just the space inside a small jam jar, but was in fact bigger and brighter than he could ever have possibly dreamed."

Polly quickly agreed. For she was beginning to see that Hodgekiss had such a wonderful and uncomplicated way of explaining things that gave a sense of reason to her crazy world.

"Polly, just like Ollie the caterpillar, you too will one day turn into a butterfly, and then you will fly away from all this wickedness that has become your only experience of life. There are a lot of wonderful people out there—people willing to help you find freedom—and they will do it without thought of any personal gain," said Hodgekiss in a very matter-of-fact tone of voice.

"Oh, right! Just like my social worker," Polly retorted rather churlishly. "Well, I'll have you know that I have not seen her for well over a year, yet she is supposed to be there to help me when I'm in great need," Polly's voice was raised, betraying her deep sense of anger and frustration.

"Wrong, Polly. You are not listening to me," said Hodgekiss gently but firmly. "Firstly, I was not referring to your social worker. And like it or not, she does pay visits to the castle in the hope of seeing your brothers as well as yourself. You just don't get to see her! Uncle Boritz and Aunt Mildred always give some lame excuse, such as you are too ill or you are out playing. Your guardians have the longest list of excuses I have ever known for you not being available!" Polly lowered her head as she tried to take it all in. "Polly, your biggest enemy is not the social services or your social worker for that matter. No, Polly, your biggest enemy is within!"

"What on earth do you mean by that?" Polly cried. For now she was very confused.

"Oh, my little crushed one, your real enemies are the walls you have built up inside to protect yourself from more pain. They are the real prison bars, and it is these that you will have to defeat before you can find true freedom."

"I don't know what you're talking about Hodgekiss," Polly defensively replied. "The only bars I know are those inside this castle, and if I'm ever lucky enough to leave this awful place, there is no way I'm taking those bars with me—and that's a promise!"

"Oh, Polly. I wish that were true. For even if by some good fortune you manage to leave the castle, sooner or later you will discover that you are still a prisoner. The iron bars will not be those of this castle, but they are just as real. Sadly, for your own protection you have created these invisible bars, and, believe me, Polly, not only will you discover they exist but there will come a time when you realize that they will only work against you."

"So tell me, wise one," she said. "What exactly are these bars that you say I have inside?"

"Well, Polly. Let me explain it more clearly," he replied, choosing to completely ignore her sarcastic tone. "You, my dear, have become trapped and enslaved by fear and torment, as well as by the chains of suspicion and mistrust and a lot more besides."

As their eyes momentarily met and then locked, Polly perceived that he was not intentionally being cruel, for his eyes were indeed filled with deep compassion towards her. She took a deep breath, for she determined to hold herself together at all costs. Hodgekiss moved nearer and leaned over to gently take hold of her hand as he continued to speak to her.

"Polly, these chains are like bindweed that take you captive as they stealthily twist and bind themselves around your heart, threatening to squeeze the very life out of you."

Polly's face visibly dropped as she, feeling sadder than ever, allowed him to continue to expose intimate truths about her, truths that she thought were safely kept hidden. She had tried so hard not to allow such things as fear and jealousy to play any part in her life, but lately her circumstances had truly overwhelmed her. As she gave much thought to his frank words, she found herself admitting that at times she was indeed spiraling uncontrollably down into a deep abyss of horribly dark and depressing thoughts and feelings. This made her feel that life was not worth living. Hot tears began to well up in her eyes, for she was finding it far too painful to listen to Hodgekiss a minute longer.

"Oh, storm-tossed and afflicted one, you did not ask for any of this to happen. But it is important that you do all within your power to get rid of these obstacles one way or another. And what's more, I am inclined to believe that you will," he said, giving her hand a reassuring squeeze.

Polly felt choked up inside, for she had no idea how to react to any of what Hodgekiss had challenged her with. No one had ever talked to her in such a clear, outspoken manner, tinged with gentle affection. However, she still felt stung by his words.

"Polly, better are the wounds of a friend than the kisses of an enemy," he said softly as he attempted to mollify her, for he knew his words were very painful and therefore hard to swallow.

There was a long, awkward silence as Polly pondered what to do or say next. Normally she would have tried to change the subject and discuss the weather or anything else that came to mind. But for once she deliberately held her tongue, choosing not to fill the airspace as she continued to consider his wise words. But his insights had come as a bit of a bombshell to Polly, so she suddenly found herself feeling most unwell. Hodgekiss knew he had plunged her soul into tremendous turmoil and conflict, so he decided it was time to change the conversation. "But enough of this for now, for I wish to ask after your brothers."

Polly closed her eyes and took another deep breath, for although he had changed the subject, in doing so, he had unintentionally managed to introduce the other most painful subject close to her heart. This impromptu meeting was indeed turning into a most tortuous affair for Polly. Hodgekiss waited a moment before coming to her rescue.

"Your youngest brother, James, is coping quite well at the moment. But the same cannot be said for young Thomas. He is, I believe, very sick. I also know that you cry for him every night, for you are so afraid for him. Polly, I need you to believe and fully place your trust in me when I tell you that things around here are going to change for the better."

"How am I supposed to believe in change? Are you blind?" she lamented, almost choking with the pain. "You tell me things that I have no idea how you have come to know. And then you expect me to believe that you, a poor man who only visits here every few months, can help me. Get real, Hodgekiss!" she added rather sharply.

"Polly, you of all people should know that appearances are deceptive. You know firsthand that your guardians deceive all those around them. And you surely need little reminding that you have many times in the past experienced the harshest judgments from others who have written you off as worthless, or to use your own words, 'a complete waste of space.' So why are you judging and doubting me as well as my words of comfort and hope? Just because I look like a dirty, smelly vagrant with nowhere to lay my head doesn't mean that I am one! Yes, dear Polly, never judge a book by its cover, and then you will not go wrong."

"Hodgekiss, I'm really sorry. Please forgive me. I feel like a bear with a sore head at the moment."

"I know, Polly, and believe it or not, I truly understand," Hodgekiss gently replied, for he understood Polly better than she understood herself.

Even with her apology accepted, Polly still felt really guilty at being so unkind and judgmental. Could she ever get anything right? She felt terrible at having implied that Hodgekiss was a nothing and therefore incapable of helping her just because he looked like a ragamuffin. He was absolutely right, and she was absolutely wrong. For this she was deeply sorry and ashamed of herself. She secretly vowed to do her best, never again to judge him or anyone else for that matter.

With his tea and sandwiches finished, and having picked out the bits lodged between his teeth, he stood up to go.

"Oh, don't go just yet!" Polly insisted.

"I'm sorry, Polly, but I do have to go, for there is much I need to do. I want you to carry on taking special care of your brother Thomas, and for my part I am going to travel to a far and distant land in the kingdom of Piadora to collect some sap from the roots of the Hubber Blubber tree to prepare some special medicine for him."

"Piadora? Hubber Blubber tree?" Polly questioned. "Oh, Hodgekiss! I have never heard of such a place or tree."

"Oh yes, my young one. They really do exist." Hodgekiss replied, stroking his silvery beard as he continued, deep in thought. "The Hubber Blubber tree is well known in my kingdom for its most excellent medicinal qualities. Hmm," he said pondering, "I think we might also need some extract from the Hoolie Koolie tree as well if we are to successfully treat Thomas's most grave condition. Yes, I think we will need to concoct a mixture of both."

Piadora? Hubber Blubber? Hoolie Koolie? Was Hodgekiss off his trolley or finally losing all his marbles? She knew for sure that these most extraordinarily named trees had definitely never been mentioned in her biology lessons. And as for the kingdom of Piadora, she was very positive that it was not a real country. She had never seen it mentioned in any of her geography books. Nor for that matter had she sighted it on the huge revolving globe that stood in the corner of the geography classroom. However, she made a mental note to have a really good search of the globe at the next available opportunity. Until then, she felt she had little choice but to give Hodgekiss the benefit of the doubt and try hard to trust him, even though most people she had known had let her down very badly. Polly found herself having to fight off unwelcome and bad thoughts that were now furiously attacking and bombarding her mind. Was this all for real, or had she met a madman?

He brushed the crumbs from off his long, threadbare coat before plunging his hand deep into his pocket and producing a brown paper package, which he placed in Polly's hand.

"Another present?" asked Polly.

"Yes, sort of," Hodgekiss replied.

"Please, not another book," Polly begged. Before Hodgekiss could answer, she decided to confess that she hadn't liked the last one very much.

"I know," said Hodgekiss. "Ralph told me."

"Is there anything Ralph doesn't tell you, Hodgekiss?" Polly asked, somewhat annoyed that nothing in her young life stayed a secret. Hodgekiss smiled before taking hold of her hand to say good-bye.

"Enjoy the book, Polly," he firmly ordered. He then turned and started to limp back down the path.

"Don't be too long before you return, Hodgekiss!" she shouted after him. "Thomas really is sick, so I am relying on you and your Hubber Blubber tree."

Hodgekiss turned and smiled. As he did so, he could see both Aunt Mildred and Uncle Boritz at the door, shouting at Polly to get back to her chores. He watched as Aunt Mildred roughly grabbed Polly by the arm, pulling her through the front door before slamming it shut.

"It is better to have a millstone tied around your neck than harm just one, yes, just one of My little ones," he thought to himself, shaking his head sadly as he disappeared off into the sunset.

Later that night, when only the sound of snoring echoed down the corridors of the castle, Polly took out her flashlight and, with her head tucked under the bedclothes, she opened the little brown package. Yes, it was another book. She read the title. It was called *The Princess and the Pea.*

"Oh, not another ridiculous fairy tale," she groaned.

With that thought sadly expressed, she switched off the torch, flung the book on the floor, and turned over to cuddle her two friends Eton and Langdon. She held them very tightly in her arms to find comfort and much-needed warmth. Finally, in the early hours of the next morning, her heavy eyelids closed and deep sleep as well as inexplicable peace descended upon her.

Chapter 7
SCHOOL, GLORIOUS SCHOOL

*A*s THE DAYS rolled into weeks, nothing much changed in Polly's sad and difficult life. When she was not at school, she spent most of her leisure time on R.O.P.E. doing mountains of chores. "At least it's not the school holidays," Polly thought in her desperate attempt to cheer up and look on the bright side. For attending school meant a break from the hard work, to which she was expected to fully apply herself every waking hour of the day. Not that she liked school very much, for being a child in care—one of the kids from the orphanage—meant she was considered to be a nothing. Even the school's headmaster, Mr. Edwood Batty, said Polly was not worth investing in.

Polly had only one friend in the school, and her name was Letticia Pizani. She had lived in Italy before coming to the school, and at every break she would meet up with Polly and let her have a go on her recorder. Before Letticia came to the school, Polly had felt quite alone and wandered the playground every break, desperately wishing to join in the fun with the other children. The truth was she was too scared to ask, for she feared they would tell her to go away just like everyone else did.

Polly struggled with most of her subjects. She had to admit to loving music, and she had the deepest desire to be able to play a musical instrument, such as the violin or saxophone. But she had never been given the opportunity to borrow one of the violins that the school lent out to pupils because the waiting list was so long. When instruments became available, they were given to those who showed the most potential. So Polly had to settle for playtimes with Letticia and her recorder.

POLLY BROWN

As for most of the subjects on the school curriculum, she was at the bottom of her class, for she simply found it hard to concentrate. The teachers read this to be a distinct lack of cooperation on Polly's part, but the real truth went much deeper. Polly was always worried about what lay in store for her every evening when she arrived back home. She had every reason to be anxious, for hardly a day went by without some form of trouble on her return. She was also desperately concerned for her older brother Thomas, who suffered worse treatment at the castle than she did. For as well as the cruelty meted out to him by their guardians, the other children would also never leave him alone, and he appeared to be getting very ill, something nobody other than Polly seemed the slightest bit concerned about. She felt so powerless to help him. He was never far from her thoughts as she struggled through each day at school.

However, there were two teachers she loved. Their names were Mrs. Bailey, who taught needlework and art and often covered for another teacher for English lessons; and Mr. Beloski, who taught history and science. Both of these teachers saw Polly for who she was rather than for who she wasn't.

Mrs. Bailey was small with short, dark hair and freckles on her rosy cheeks. Her brown eyes appeared to dance when she engaged in any form of conversation, and she had an unusual accent when she spoke. Polly was not certain where she had originally come from, not that it mattered to Polly, for it was enough to just hear her kind voice. Sometimes she broke out into a giggle over something a child had said that tickled her pink. Speaking of pink, Polly knew for certain it was her teacher's favorite color. She wore pink every day—a pink blouse or a pink cardigan or smart pink trousers with matching pink shoes. All this went to match her rosy cheeks. So Polly absolutely adored her, especially as her favorite color was also pink. Polly decided that Mrs. Bailey's house was almost certain to be painted pink with pink carpets and curtains and a pink bathroom suite with shelves filled with bottles of pink bubble bath. She would have loved to visit her house, just to see if she was right.

Mrs. Bailey could often be seen kneeling or squatting when she spoke to a child. Polly would watch, feeling touched by how much this teacher seemed to care. She never hesitated to wipe away a tumbling tear or give a word of encouragement to even the most difficult child, and that included Polly at times.

At the start of every week Mrs. Bailey would make all the children stand up and, after giving each and every child some word of praise, she would then produce her tape measure from out of her pink bag and proceed to measure each of them in turn. As she noted their varying heights, she would smile before declaring, "I do believe you have grown another inch this week, Lavender Bloomingdale."

Nobody, however naughty the child was reputed to be, was ever left out from either the praise or the measuring tape! And it was well known around the school that the children in Mrs. Bailey's class were indeed taller for their age and happier than in any of the other classes! They were also better behaved, for Mrs. Bailey had learned a deep truth, and she applied it with such generosity of heart. No troublesome child ever wanted to make her feel sad and upset. So all the children did their very best and worked hard with all they had within them to please dear, sweet Mrs. Bailey. Therefore, Polly loved her with all her heart, and she secretly wished Mrs. Bailey would adopt her. Then she could come and live in her pink house, and they would live happily ever after, just like they did in fairy tales.

Polly found it hard when other children turned up in the classroom bearing small gifts such as sweets or a crunchy golden apple for Mrs. Bailey, for she had nothing to give to show just how special Polly thought she was. This saddened her, although it served to make her even more determined to produce excellent stories for her dear teacher to read. Her hard work did not go unrewarded, for she always got top marks, and this only served to make her love Mrs. Bailey even more. Often she would arrive home, happily clutching her work, and go in search of her guardians to proudly show the latest piece to them. It often had the words "Excellent piece, Polly. Keep up the good work" scrawled in red ink at the bottom. Not once did she ever hear one tiny word of praise from the mouths of Uncle Boritz or Aunt Mildred. All she ever received were sour words like, "You really think you're something, girl, when the truth is you are a nothing who will never be anything or go anywhere in this life. You probably cheated anyway to get such a high mark. Look how badly you are doing in nearly all your other subjects."

Still Polly kept on trying, hoping that someday they might actually say something nice or encouraging. But sadly it was never to be.

In her art classes Polly did not fare as well. She got very frustrated when what she produced on paper did not match the picture in her head. On these occasions she would ball her work up into a tiny ball and head for the wastebasket. Mrs. Bailey never once got angry with her, for it was as though she secretly understood Polly's deep frustration. So instead of shouting at her, she would take the time to come alongside Polly with some kind word of encouragement.

"Oh Polly, Polly," she would say with her big beautiful smile. "I really like your painting, and it seems to me that all it needs is a little bit more red here or a splash of blue there."

And then she would guide the paintbrush in Polly's hand, muttering, "Excellent, I knew you could do it," as she helped by splashing on some extra color.

She would also look Polly straight in the eye and openly declare, "That talent is in there somewhere, Polly Brown, and all we've got to do is find it! So arise from within this girl and come forth."

All this was said in deep somber tones of voice, which were not really stern at all! She would then catch Polly's eye and break into a smile. It was never too long before Polly was smiling too, and sure enough, it always did the trick. Polly found it so much easier to create whatever she wanted. For as pure contentment filled Polly's heart and mind, it appeared to transform her artwork as well. Mrs. Bailey was a most wonderful teacher.

The same could be said of Mr. Beloski, for he was young, tall, and extremely good-looking; and this was without question the unanimous verdict of all the girls at school. "He is really a Grecian god," they would whisper to each other as they huddled together outside his classroom. They also passed notes on scrappy bits of paper around the classroom, asking each other what they thought of a particular shirt he might be wearing and whether they thought his tie matched the rest of his outfit. Polly would have none of it. She did not care what he wore on the outside, she just knew with a certainty that inside he had a heart of pure gold.

This tall man had sandy brown hair swept to one side and blue eyes. His teeth were quite large, and they seemed to permanently be on show, because he always appeared to be smiling. Polly observed he had only one teeny imperfection—a small brown mole on his cheek, which moved further up his face when he broke out into a smile. Polly could easily forgive him this tiny flaw, for she had to secretly admit to herself that he would, just as the other girls constantly said, make an excellent movie star. She therefore agreed wholeheartedly with the other girls that they could never allow him to leave the school for the sake of becoming a mere film star. He was too much needed as a history and science teacher. They would kidnap him before they allowed anyone to steal him away from their school and their hearts.

As he strode past them in the corridor, all the girls who huddled in groups gossiping would stop all silly conversation and shout down the corridor, "Good morning, Mr. Beloski," before breaking into fits of giggles, something they always did when he walked by. And much to their delight, he never failed to stop and smile before saying good morning back to them in his very polite manner. He seemed quite unaware that his very presence created such a stir or that he was the heartthrob of each and every one of the young, lovesick girls! As Polly was not part of the crowd, she would walk quickly down the corridor with her head down so as not to draw attention to herself. She was therefore very touched whenever Mr. Beloski stopped her in her tracks to say with a bright smile, "Well, good morning to you, Polly Brown. Isn't the weather simply glorious? I'd rather be mowing my lawn than sitting in a hot, stuffy classroom. Never mind, eh. I hope I see you in my class today."

Polly always blushed as she stuttered a greeting back to him. She would happily mow Mr. Beloski's overgrown lawn for him all day and every day and from dawn to dusk if necessary! The truth was, she was very touched that he even noticed her, and even more touched that he considered her worthy of any greeting at all. Such kindness never went unnoticed by Polly, for she never took anything for granted.

Often Mr. Beloski would bring the class to a halt early and finish the lesson by reading a book to them as a small treat. He would read stories such as *The Adventures of Tom Sawyer*. By the end of the story sessions, which Polly wished would go on forever, her spirits were lifted. In fact, they were positively soaring, and for the length of that most special moment in time, life really did seem worth living.

She would never forget the day when, after a history lesson, he called her to one side.

"Polly," he said with a puzzled look on his face. "You are so different from the other children in the orphanage. Why do you think that is?"

Polly felt too tongue-tied to reply, for in truth, she did not know what to say. He then went on to say that she didn't swear or behave badly and she was not rude. "No, you are indeed very different from the other children in the orphanage," he said slowly, as though deep in thought.

Mr. Beloski would never have known that Polly sang and skipped all the way home on that most special day. Her spirit had just taken a giant leap into the realm of hope and happiness, albeit temporarily. Someone had at last recognized that there was something good—something worthwhile—about Polly. She was not just another kid in care.

On her school reports many teachers had unwittingly penned, "Polly seems at odds with the world." At odds! Yes, of course she was at odds. So would they have been if they had to endure the home life Polly was daily subjected to and felt so utterly powerless to change. Apart from the kindness shown by Mrs. Bailey and Mr. Beloski, there was no other teacher who had ever taken the time to sit her down and find out one personal thing about Polly and her life in the orphanage. It was as though she did not exist, and if she did, she was nothing more than a number in a long list of numbers. All this served to deepen Polly's wounds. No teacher had even observed that at dinnertime she ate everybody's leftovers and had gained herself the nickname "the garbage truck" among her fellow pupils. So her school life just went to further convince her that there truly was nobody out there who could really help her. She was a hopeless case to be shunned by a school that cared more about results than helping troubled children who had overwhelming mountains to climb in their everyday life. Most classes found Polly standing at the back of the class facing the wall. Oh! How familiar she was with every brick in every wall at that school, for she had spent endless hours counting each and every one. All this made Mr. Beloski's little chat something of a miracle, and she was in very short supply of much-needed miracles. Oh, how she loved Mr. Beloski and, of course, dear Mrs. Bailey.

Polly often dreamed of going to a finishing school for young ladies, for she had many books on the subject that she had borrowed and failed to return to the school library. She devoured these books with such relish and was convinced that she could be really happy if only she attended one of these very special schools. They had the power to turn her into a real young lady. Having read endless books on the subject, she discerned that all teachers and students alike were always so polite and gracious, and all swearing was strictly forbidden. But she knew only too well that the girls who got to go to these schools were very rich. The incredibly expensive tuition fees are sky high, so the chances of her ever fulfilling that dream were less than zilch. But even this stark reality never stopped her dreaming.

Many times when she was on a bus journey she would find herself staring at a group of girls from Snobitts Public School as they boarded the bus.

The school was a preparatory boarding school for girls, and Mrs. O'Brien was the deputy headmistress in charge of all school outings. Polly would watch fascinated as the very smart young ladies laughed and chattered as they headed towards vacant seats on the bus. She admired their smart uniform, which consisted of a navy pleated pinafore dress and a pristine white blouse underneath. The school tie was red and white stripes, and the whole uniform was finished off with a delightful round navy hat that sported a band of red ribbon. They all wore black shiny shoes and white knee-length socks, and a brown leather satchel hung from the shoulder of every girl.

Polly thought they all looked so well-turned-out compared to her in her stained, frayed uniform that should have been thrown out a long time ago. Polly heard other children making fun of the girls, as well as the name of the school, but Polly never joined in. She decided that the letters stood for School for the Noble and Outstandingly Bright.

She found it hard to understand why this private school, like many other private schools, was referred to as a *public school* when it was anything but open to the public. The local library was a public library, and its doors were open to everyone. The same could be said for the local public swimming pools. Yet these very exclusive schools that cost an absolute fortune to attend called themselves *public schools*. "Surely someone needs to put them right by pointing out this rather glaring contradiction," Polly often thought to herself.

Polly found herself fascinated by Mrs. O'Brien, believing her to be a very posh woman of high intelligence and moral values. She was slim and always immaculately turned out. She had porcelain white skin, thin red smiling lips, and wispy brown hair that was always neatly brushed up in a little bun with absolutely no strays. Her eyes appeared to dance when she spoke, and there was a hint of an accent that betrayed her true Irish heritage.

Polly thought Mrs. O'Brien was not only very attractive, but she also knew in her heart that she would flourish under the tuition of such an inspiring teacher, who also had the keenest wit she had ever known a teacher to possess. She would find herself having a giggle when she heard Mrs. O'Brien addressing one of the girls. "Rowena dearest, kindly remove that chewing gum from out of your mouth, for young ladies should not look or sound like washing machines. What would your mother have to say if she saw you eating in such a disgraceful manner? And Lucinda dear, kindly refrain from dropping your *h*'s, for I do believe you mean to say, 'Antonia, come and sit down here,' not 'ere.' Do you agree? If the good Lord had intended for the letter *h* to be dropped from the alphabet, then I do believe He would have left it out altogether!" She would say this loudly as she pursed her lips and shook her head, pretending to be filled with utter dismay. The girls never failed to giggle as they automatically chorused a "Yes, miss," before following through with her order.

As Polly listened in on their conversations, she found herself at times feeling very jealous. For as they chattered away, she would overhear them discussing their fencing and pony riding lessons, their Cordon Bleu cookery, and their deportment classes. Oh, how Polly longed to be able to walk with great poise, balancing a book on her head while repeating French verse fluently and at the same time cooking confit de canard, carre d'agneau, or crepes suzette with Grand Marnier. Of course, she had absolutely no clue as to what these French dishes were or what they looked like, but they did sound so romantic as she listened in on the girls' idle chitchat about which dish they had just created in their cookery class.

Polly did have the pleasure of cookery lessons at school, but her teacher, Mrs. Greaseball, never gave her the opportunity to try her hand at making any of the delightfully exotic dishes that all the other girls got to prepare and take home at the end of the school day. The reason behind this was that Polly simply could never afford the expensive ingredients. She sadly grew tired of Mrs. Greaseball drawing attention to this unpleasant fact whenever she addressed the class. "Right, girls, pay attention, for tomorrow we will be cooking chicken chasseur. However, Polly, as usual, you will be making bread, as we simply cannot allow you to sit around twiddling your thumbs, can we?"

There had also been numerous occasions when Mrs. Greaseball, upon discovering they were clean out of flour, had most happily resorted to handing Polly a bucket of soapy water and instructing her to spend the lesson cleaning out the shower room instead. Polly wished with all her heart that she could go to a finishing school and learn to become a real lady. Instead, she had to settle for being a low-life kid from an orphanage, written off at school as someone with no academic ability whatsoever and forced to make bread until even the word *bread* made her want to scream. When she finally left school she could look forward to an exciting career as a public convenience cleaner or a shelf stacker at a grocery store or perhaps, if she was really lucky, a baker's assistant! So Polly hated school as much as she hated most of her lessons.

The blustering winds and showers of spring came and went. Then the hazy and warm days of summer passed by, and all too soon it was time for school to begin again. Polly was very relieved, for she had spent most of the summer holidays on R.O.P.E. Now it was the start of a new school year and, hopefully, new beginnings. At least that was what Polly wished.

As she stood in the morning assembly, Polly could not help but note that her two most beloved teachers were absent from the line of tutors that were sitting on stage alongside the headmaster, Mr. Edwood Batty. Polly began to panic and could only hope there was a simple explanation for their absence.

"Maybe they've just missed the bus; or maybe both of them are sick; or maybe they even just simply forgot that today was the start of a new term. Yes, it will be something like that," she thought in her desperate bid to feel reassured and calm her racing heart. At the end of the assembly, everyone sang the hymn *On England's Green and Pleasant Land.* The pupils were ordered to sit down, for it was now time for Mr. Batty to make his usual new-term address. Polly sat down along with all the other children in her row.

The headmaster cleared the nervous tickle in his throat before welcoming all the pupils to a new year, hoping they all had a pleasant, if not wonderful, summer holiday and were ready and fuelled up to give this term their best efforts. He then spoke for quite some time about all the school's achievements in the past year before expressing his hopes for the year to come. Finally, after much paper shuffling, he turned to all his staff that were comfortably seated on the stage and introduced each of them to the pupils. This was done for the benefit of all the new children, and it gave all the older pupils the perfect opportunity to hand around the chewing gum or begin the much-needed whispering concerning any news-worthy gossip.

After all the introductions were over, he called the school to attention, and then, lowering his voice, he announced. "Finally, it is with the deepest regret that I must inform everyone that Mrs. Bailey and Mr. Beloski are no longer with us. I am unable at present to give you any further information as to their sudden departure from this school. But I can say without any fear of contradiction that both of these wonderful teachers will be sorely missed by staff and pupils alike."

On hearing this terrible piece of information, Polly's face instantaneously went ashen as her blood seemed to drain down toward her toes. Mr. Batty paused briefly to reshuffle his papers before going on to tell his attentive audience of pupils which teachers would be standing in for them until suitable replacements could be found. Polly had no interest in any of this. Her head was spinning, and her heart pounded loudly. All she wanted to do was escape.

Sorely missed! Those trite words rang like cathedral bells through her head. Polly wanted to scream and keep screaming until the walls of the assembly hall collapsed on top of her head and finished her off for good. Her two most wonderful teachers in the world were gone forever! And one tiny sentence from the headmaster was all it had taken to bring her whole world crashing down. The only lights shining in her dark, dreary prison of a life had, like a candle, been snuffed out, leaving her absolutely distraught and with little idea as to where to go from here.

She jumped up from where she was sitting and almost passed out. Her rib cage felt as though it was caving in, threatening to crush her lungs to a pulp. She gasped for air as she stumbled blindly towards the teacher who was sitting by and guarding the main exit. Polly blurted out her urgent need for some fresh air, for she felt very faint and nauseous. The teacher noticed how pale she looked and without any further hesitation opened the hall door to allow her to leave the assembly. Polly then raced along the highly polished corridors, not stopping until she found an empty classroom in which to hide.

Having found a secret sanctuary, she closed the classroom door and headed for one of the corners of the room, whereupon she sank down onto her knees in complete despair. There she stayed and just sobbed and sobbed, feeling utterly desolate and inconsolable. She had no idea how to face another minute of school life. In her mind both Mrs. Bailey and Mr. Beloski had really been angels parading as teachers, and now they might just as well be dead, for they were gone forever and she was now utterly alone.

"They did not even say good-bye," she moaned out loud. "How could they leave without telling me?"

She repeated this over and over to herself, shaking her head from side to side as if willing herself to wake up from this hideous nightmare. Did they not know that she would miss them more than any of the other pupils or staff? She wanted the world to stop there and then so that she could jump off. Eventually, she heaved herself up from the floor and, after washing her face in the girls' room, she headed down the corridor and into her first lesson of the day.

That most terrible school day was, for all other pupils, filled with the buzz that a new term brings. All the girls and boys caught up on the summer holiday gossip. For Polly, though, the rest of the day passed in a haze of deep misery. As the last bell rang, she picked up her schoolbag and, dragging it on the ground behind her, she headed for the school gates. As she passed through the gates with her head hung low she failed to notice that she was on a collision course with Mrs. Trouillet, the part-time French teacher. Polly bumped into her, knocking a large stack of papers out of her hands. As the papers flew everywhere, Polly tried to catch them, shouting out an apology as she continued to race after them.

"Why, eef eet eesn't Polly Brown!" she said somewhat surprised as Polly handed back all the papers she had collected.

"Hello, Mrs. Trouillet," said Polly rather breathlessly. "I'm terribly sorry. I was not looking where I was going, but I think I've caught all your papers," she said, forcing a faint smile. The French teacher smiled back.

"Polly, I am so glad to 'ave boomped into you today," she said in delightfully broken English, "for I was geeven this letter to geeve to you by Mr. Beloski when I 'elped him clear out hees classroom during thee school 'oleedays."

Polly stopped in her tracks. "A letter for me?" she spluttered, turning the deepest shade of crimson. "Yes, for you, my dear," Mrs. Trouillet handed Polly the envelope. Polly grabbed it out of her hand and stuffed it in her blazer pocket.

"Thank you so much, Mrs. Trouillet," she said, feeling the deepest sense of gratitude as she fought back fresh tears. "You have no idea how much this means to me."

She then excused herself, mumbling something along the lines that she had forgotten her homework. She turned in her tracks and raced back toward the main school building to find somewhere private to open the sealed letter.

Finding an empty classroom, she then made her way over to a corner so that she could hide away and be well out of sight of any snooping pupils or staff. As soon as she was sure that nobody else was around, she tore open Mr. Beloski's personal letter to her and started to read.

Dear Polly,

By now you will have discovered that I have left the school. I have since heard that Mrs. Bailey has likewise moved on. This must seem like a terrible blow to you. I can only say I am so sorry that I did not have the opportunity to personally see you to say good-bye. Of all the pupils I have taught over the years, I have to say you are the most promising. I know you will find this hard to believe, but I assure you this is the truth. At this moment in time as you read my letter, I feel certain you will be angry with me, but I also know you have an immense capacity to forgive. How do I know this? Well, it is because over the years that I have come to know you, I have on more than one occasion observed you choose to make the difficult, and often seemingly impossible, choice to forgive other pupils when they treat you badly. I want you to promise me that you will never give up on yourself. You have an amazing ability to touch people's lives. You certainly touched mine. I cannot finish this letter without one final thought. It is a quote given by a famous American lady, Eleanor Roosevelt, and I cannot think of anyone who needs to hear it more than you do. "The future belongs to those who believe in the beauty of their dreams." You are a bright young girl with a big heart and big dreams. I pray you will see each and every one of them fulfilled. Trust your heart, Polly, and believe that God above will help you bring them to pass. Until we meet again, sweet dreams.

Yours Truly,

M Beloski

POLLY BROWN

Polly read and reread the precious letter before slowly folding it up and returning it to its envelope. Then, with the greatest of care, she placed it in the inside pocket of her school blazer before cupping her face between her hands to weep. She wept for Mrs. Bailey and Mr. Beloski, and she also wept because no one had ever reached into her heart with such touching words of hope.

Polly must have been there for some time, for eventually she was disturbed. The handle of the classroom door turned and Stanley Horlicks, the school cleaner, poked his head around the door. He was an old man in his late sixties whose hair had said good-bye to his scalp many years previous, but he had a gentle face and kind, crinkly eyes. Polly knew that Stanley suffered from some crippling back condition that meant he moved very slowly as he went about his cleaning tasks, and this made Polly feel very sorry that Stanley had to work at all. She could see his face was often etched with great pain as he shuffled about, but still he always managed a little smile.

Stanley observed Polly sitting on the floor in a crumpled heap, so he was as quiet as a mouse as he tiptoed across the room. He slowly crouched down beside her, and his bones made cracking noises that caused him to wince from the excruciating pain.

"Excuse me, miss," Stanley said most softly and sensitively. "I'm so sorry to disturb you. Are you all right?"

Polly nodded, feeling more than a little embarrassed. She knew she looked a mess because of her red eyes that were sore from crying.

Stanley, being a most gracious and humble man, pretended not to notice.

"I will have to ask you to leave and finish your homework somewhere else, miss, for I have to clean this room before the school caretaker comes in ten minutes to lock up," he said apologetically, giving her a deep look of sympathy as he spoke.

He hovered over her for a minute before getting up and stretching to ease the aches and pains that come with old age and arthritis. He then made the decision to leave the room just for a minute to allow Polly the breathing space necessary to compose herself. For he knew without a shadow of doubt that homework was the last thing that this rather sad young lady had been doing.

"God bless her little cotton socks," Stanley Horlicks quietly muttered under his breath. "School wasn't much better in my days!"

Polly went back to the girls' room to wash her face and compose herself before leaving the building to head for the train station and go home. The platform was almost deserted, for all the children were long gone, presumably all safely home and now enjoying a delicious, hot meal as they chatted to their families about the first day of the new term and other interesting school events.

The last place Polly wanted to go was home to a castle filled with hatred and pain; home to congealed beans on cold, burned toast— that's if she was lucky and there was any left for her. The guard blew his whistle, and the train chugged slowly out of the station. As it gathered speed, Polly leaned back on the headrest and closed her eyes, allowing herself the luxury of thinking back to past times and her already sorely-missed teachers as she wondered where to go from here.

For Polly, the next few weeks at school were little more than a blur. She sat in all the lessons and did nothing more than what was required of her. The new art and English teacher was quite nice, and the substitute history and science teacher could not be faulted. But nobody could or would ever fill the shoes of her much-loved teachers who had abandoned her. The pain of their absence was almost physical, and that pain would not go away.

Chapter 8
THE PEA PROBLEM

*T*HE WEEKS TURNED into months, and with them came the season to be jolly, although Polly could find no earthly reason whatsoever to be jolly. For others, December meant Christmas trees with shimmering baubles, soft white snow, Christmas carols, mince pies, and steaming hot cocoa by a roaring fire. Instead of being able to enjoy these things, Polly had extra chores daily piled upon her, many of which were outside in the freezing cold. And, as a result of the extra chores, Polly forgot that she even had Hodgekiss's latest book in her possession.

One night, upon finding that she had finished her chores earlier than usual, she took herself off to bed to have an early night and hopefully catch up on some much-needed sleep. However, after many hours of tossing and turning from feeling chilled to the bones, she finally acknowledged that sleep was the last thing that was going to come to her.

She rummaged around under the bed until she found her flashlight. After switching it on, she reluctantly got out of her bed to search through her locker for something to read. She shone the light up and down in her seemingly futile search for something new and inspirational to read among the pile of frayed novels that belonged to the school library, many of which were long overdue.

"Now, let me see. I've read that one several times, and no, I didn't particularly get on with that one," she whispered as she discarded each book onto the bedroom floor and continued her search through the mountainous pile of books squeezed into the small locker space.

She was about to give up when her eyes hit on the latest book that Hodgekiss had given her.

"I suppose as a last resort I could give Hodgekiss's latest book offering a try," she mumbled to herself. She then climbed back into bed, taking the book under her covers to read under the glow of her flashlight.

"Once upon a time, high up on a hill, stood a castle," she read.

"So far so good," thought Polly. As she read on, she quickly learned that this book was all about a young prince who yearned to get married. This particular prince lived alone with his mother.

"No wonder he wants to tie the knot," Polly sympathized. "For this poor man is indeed very lonely. He has only his golden oldie mother to talk to." She felt certain that he must have been pretty fed up, as most men were not the least bit interested in talking about the price of vegetables or the latest knitting pattern. The poor prince was probably screaming inside for new and socially acceptable companions. Anyway, he scoured the kingdom in search of a suitable bride.

Many women of noble birth came and presented themselves before the prince, hoping to be the lucky one to become the royal bride. They were all drop-dead gorgeous with beautifully clear skin and pearly white teeth. The prince, however, was not entirely satisfied that he had found the perfect one.

"Men are always so fussy," Polly quietly moaned to herself.

Then one day a poor, bedraggled young urchin turned up at the castle soaking wet. There had been the most dreadful downpour. The prince handed her a royal towel to dry herself off before making her a nice cup of tea. He was, after all, a very thoughtful prince. Within minutes of chatting with her he knew, without a shadow of doubt, that she was the perfect one for him. Wedding bells began to ring loudly in his royal ears. He was thoroughly smitten. "Hmm. How nice, love at first sight," thought Polly.

However, the prince's mother was not entirely convinced that this young girl was a princess, and it was, after all, most essential to have a girl who knew how to behave in such a manner as princesses do. They must have perfect table manners, be able to sing as shrilly as a bird, and have the ability to curtsy correctly. She there-

POLLY BROWN

fore decided to do what all good mothers put in her situation would have done; she interfered! So the prince's mother thought up a plan, which Polly desperately hoped would fail. "What a grouchy old misery-guts. Are they ever satisfied?" thought Polly ruefully, feeling more than a little disgruntled.

The mother put a pea under the poor girl's mattress. If she had a rough night, it meant she really was a princess. If she slept well, unaware of the pea's presence, then good old mother would know for sure that she was indeed a ruthless young impostor. The young maiden indeed had a terrible night and was quite unable to sleep, for she felt something very hard under the mattress.

Now this should have satisfied the prince's mother, but on this occasion it didn't. "Does it ever?" thought Polly, feeling decidedly disgusted. As a result, his mother decided that she needed more proof before she could give her blessing to this potential marriage. So she decided to try the pea trick again, only this time she placed it under ninety-nine mattresses! Polly believed this was a heartless and mean thing to do. She knew only too well that sleep is a very important part of a young girl's beauty routine, and lack of it produces spots! The poor young girl not only had to endure another night of torment, but was also forced to clamber up one hundred mattresses before she could even lie down and close her eyelids.

By this stage in the story, Polly felt so sorry for the young girl and very angry with the mother, whom she felt deserved a good slapping! For being royalty did not excuse her disgraceful behavior. That night, just like the last, the poor and now-exhausted young urchin complained bitterly that she had once again suffered a very bad and sleepless night. On hearing this latest piece of news, the prince's mother finally threw in the towel. She agreed that, having passed this most dreadful test, the young girl really was a princess, and therefore her son could go ahead with the wedding plans.

Polly felt greatly relieved by the good news, for she felt truly convinced that, should the poor girl be required to undergo any further sleepless nights, she would more than likely require cosmetic surgery to remove the dark bags from under her eyes! The happy couple went on to have a very large and extremely expensive wedding due to the thousands of people who lived in the land and were invited to attend. Afterwards they went on a luxurious honeymoon before going on to live happily ever after. "The end," sighed a very sad and freshly tormented Polly.

Having finished the book, she slammed it shut before flinging it violently across the floor of the dormitory, feeling quite discouraged that, yet again, she had been given a book that had a happy ending. Luckily for Polly, all the other girls were sound asleep and were therefore not rudely awakened by her noise. "Oh, how pathetic! I really hate fairy tales," she thought angrily to herself as she switched off her torch and cuddled up to Eton and Langdon. She could not imagine what had possessed her friend Hodgekiss to yet again give her another book that provoked such deep torment to well up from within. Did he have a mean streak like her roommate Gailey Gobbstopper, who took great pleasure in tormenting her day-in and day-out? If so, fine friend he'd turned out to be. Polly turned over in the bed and tried very hard to sleep, but no amount of sheep counting did the trick, for the story she had just read would not go away!

She could have done with the help of matchsticks to keep her drooping eyelids from entirely closing as she sat slumped in her chair through a double math lesson the next morning. She was so tired that she was really struggling to pay any attention at all to the teacher as he droned on and on. Finally the bell rang. She had never been so grateful to hear that bell, for it signified that morning lessons were finally over and it was now lunchtime. As she sat at the table with her dinner tray in front of her, she found herself staring at all the food on her plate. She was pleased to see it was one of her favorite dishes—liver and bacon casserole with a small portion of mashed potatoes, cabbage, and peas. Polly was delighted.

She glanced over at her fellow diners and was very relieved to see they were all deep in idle conversation. She seized the moment to scoop up the peas from her plate and quickly plunge them into the waist pocket of her blazer, pleased that nobody had noticed. Then picking up her fork, and with a smile on her face, she proceeded to demolish every morsel that remained on her plate. She would have picked the plate up and licked it clean if there had been no one else around. But Polly had manners and knew this would not be considered a polite thing to do. She therefore hoped that she would be offered the leftovers from other pupils who did not eat every scrap of their meal. She wasn't to be disappointed.

Later that same day, Polly found herself in the geography room. She waited until the end of class and, once all the pupils had left along with the teacher, quickly sprinted across the classroom towards the globe. She twirled the globe round and round inspecting every inch of it. She pored over America and Australia, followed by Russia and then China. Her in-depth search took her from the Adriatic all the way to the Pacific, then from the Baltic to the Bahamas. Polly scrutinized every inch of the globe as she continued on with her thorough search. Try as she may, she could not find Piadora.

Polly was beginning to feel very discouraged and bitterly disappointed, but then she had the bright idea of fetching the teacher's magnifying glass from her desk drawer. With all the names on the globe now magnified, her searching was made considerably easier. But still, even with the help of the magnifying glass, she was unable to locate Piadora. Just as she was about to give up, her eye caught sight of what she believed she was looking for. She moved in to take a closer look.

"Yes!" she cried out loudly, punching the air with her fist. "Piadora does exist, and I have finally found it. Oh, this is such good news," she cried as she began dancing around the classroom in a state of pure elation.

She could not help but sing and skip all the way to the train station. She was so blissfully happy. Now, for the first time in her young, troubled life, she had real hope. For if Piadora existed, then so did the Hubber Blubber and Hoolie Koolie trees. She could hardly contain her newfound joy. These feelings were totally new to her, and although they were strange, Polly felt grateful to be feeling something other than the usual deep sorrow, or worse still, numbness. She wanted to give Hodgekiss a great big, sloppy kiss on his whiskery cheek.

That evening after tea she made her way to the dormitory and upon placing her hand in her jacket pocket, pulled out a few peas. As she positioned one lone pea under her rather thin mattress, she prayed with all her heart that she would feel it. She then headed for the bathroom to wash her face and brush her teeth before bed. This done, she gathered up her two friends, Eton and Langdon, and with great expectancy, crawled under the covers to wait.

Polly, waited and then waited some more. It was not too long before she felt panic rising inside. Although she was wide awake, she definitely could not feel the pea. "Maybe the pea is more to the left?" she thought to herself as she then quickly moved over towards the wall. Nothing! "Maybe I need to be more over to the right?" she reasoned, turning over and almost falling out of the bed and onto the floor. Still nothing! "Maybe having both Langdon and Eton in bed with me is at the root of my problem," she considered before throwing both of them out of the bed and onto the cold, hard floor. Still, try as she may, she felt nothing. She wiggled backwards and forwards, huffing and puffing, hoping that by repositioning herself she might get to the precise point in the mattress where the pea lay directly under her body. It was useless, for wherever she lay in the bed, the result was just the same. She could not feel the jolly pea!

Such was her desperation that she even resorted to standing on her head in the bed in the vain hope that this might do the trick, but all her futile efforts were useless. There was not one trick in the book that Polly did not attempt that night. She bounced and flounced on her bed as though it were a trampoline in her ridiculous and sorry attempt to feel the pea.

Eventually, her noise woke up all the other girls in the dormitory, who then threatened to throw her out of the window if she did not shut up and let them get back to sleep. Polly obeyed, for she took most threats very seriously. Pulling up the blanket to cover her head, she gave up considering any new ideas and closed her eyes. A lone tear slid down her cheek as she tried to face the bleak truth that her experiment had not only failed dismally but had also proved, beyond all reasonable doubt, that she was not after all the princess she secretly hoped she might be. The next morning she crawled miserably out of bed and, upon lifting the thin mattress, all she discovered was one lone and now-hideously unrecognizable squashed green pea!

The next day as she traveled home from school, she resolved to give it another try. After all, she reasoned, it was fairly common knowledge that most scientists often had to make numerous attempts before their experiments succeeded. She must be equally resilient and work just as hard to find a scientific solution to her pea problem. With a new pea securely positioned under the mattress, she went through the same procedure as she had the day before. Still she could not feel the pea, and another extremely squashed green pea lay as evidence of her failed experiment.

Despite being extremely disheartened, Polly still refused to give up. Being the determined young lady that she was, she went deeper into scientific mode, reasoning with herself that if she were to leave the peas a few days longer, they would go from soft to very hard, and a hard pea would be so much easier to feel. So a few nights later she placed a new but hard, shriveled-up pea under her thin mattress. The next morning found Polly's tender spirit as squashed as the pea as she headed for school, feeling utterly inconsolable. Despite another bad night with a pretty solid pea under her mattress, she had still been unable to feel a jolly thing! It was all very troubling.

Over the next few days, Polly found it hard to concentrate on anything, for the pea problem sought to dominate her every waking moment and therefore overshadowed everything else. Her need to feel like a princess simply overwhelmed her, and soon she began to hate Hodgekiss for ever having given her the book. She was now convinced that he had been rather wickedly stringing her along with false hope. However, even this didn't stop her. For some days later, in what could be considered as a final act of desperation, she scooped, not only her own peas from off her plate, but also every pea that lay abandoned on all other pupils' plates, delicately placing them in her blazer pocket. She made every attempt to keep them safe from being squashed as she went through the afternoon lessons and finally journeyed home.

Once she was back at the castle, she emptied her pocket of peas into an empty plastic bag before giving it a sharp twist. On this triumphant note, she then headed for the freezer section of the fridge, constantly checking the bag on the way to ensure there was no hole for rebel peas to escape. She then proceeded to place the bag deep into the freezer section of the refrigerator. Many days later she returned to the freezer, and with a new and light spring in her step, she took the bag of recently frozen peas and emptied the whole lot under the thin mattress. The frozen peas rolled everywhere. "This has surely got to work," she happily and very optimistically thought to herself.

That night she got into bed, leaving her faithful friends Eton and Langdon on the floor. She apologized to both of them and assured them that they still meant the world to her, but cruel as it may seem, she considered what she was doing to be very necessary. Again Polly suffered a sleepless night, tossing and turning and jumping and bumping around all over the bed before reluctantly surrendering to tiredness and falling asleep. She awoke the next morning and crawled out of bed with a most heavy heart. For despite putting a whole bag of peas under her mattress, and frozen ones at that, she had not felt one of the now-very mushy miserable things! Polly felt very, very angry and disappointed!

That morning she was left to clear up what could only be considered an awful mess of disgustingly mashed up peas from under her mattress, which now rather insultingly bore the most dreadful bright green stain. Polly then headed off to school, feeling the same deep despair that had become her daily experience. For a moment, in the short history of her young and troubled life, she had actually been crazy enough to believe that she might be a princess after all. Now she knew for certain that she was not. She also knew that if she saw Hodgekiss, she would tell him he was a rotten fraud. When she thought of Hodgekiss, she felt so explosive that she made the choice to forget he ever existed. She would never think of him or speak of him ever again! She believed this to be the best solution to the problem. However, this resolution only served to make her feel sadder than ever.

At precisely 11:00 a.m. the next morning, Polly found herself sitting in the geography room, and, once her lesson had come to an end, she chose to linger and wait until all the other pupils had left the classroom, heading for the canteen. Polly found that she couldn't help but take one more peep at the revolving globe, even though it was against her better judgment. She waited until all was quiet on the western front before creeping over to where the globe stood and picking up the magnifying glass from her teacher's desk.

Polly then rolled the globe round and round, her search becoming more frantic by the minute.

"Piadora, come on, Piadora, where are you?" she muttered to herself as the globe whizzed around over and over again. "Arctic…Atlantic…Pacific…come on, Piadora. I know you are hiding, and I'm not leaving here until I find you."

Polly missed lunch altogether as she rolled and searched the globe in her seemingly fruitless endeavor to find Piadora for a second time. It was like looking for a needle in a haystack. Finally she fell to the floor clutching her head.

"I must be going out of my mind," she said out loud. "I definitely saw Piadora the last time I looked, and now it is nowhere to be found!" she wailed bitterly.

Polly could hardly face the afternoon classes, for she was not only decidedly depressed, but also tired and hungry. As she lay in bed that cold, damp night, unable to sleep, her mind and heart in great torment, she felt a thick, suffocating blanket of darkness shroud her. She had no idea what was happening to her, and this really frightened her. Was she on the brink of going mad? After all, she had been warned many times by her guardians that madness ran in her family, and now it seemed as though they had been right all along. The real truth was that she, Polly Brown, was experiencing the dark night of the soul.

Weeks passed without any strangers visiting the castle, and Polly gave up all hope of Hodgekiss returning. She began to believe the reason he had not made any further visits was because he secretly knew he could no longer string her along with his little fantasies about mysterious places and trees that did not exist. He had not returned because he did not want to face the music. However, deep inside she desperately wanted to be proved wrong.

As time went by Polly grew more and more anxious for her brother Thomas, for she had not seen him for a long time but heard many rumors and whisperings that his health was rapidly deteriorating. Her need to see him therefore was growing by the day. As the boys' dormitories were on a different wing and her brother was confined to his bed, she had no idea what to do. She just had this awful sense of urgency that would not leave her.

Finally, there came a day when she decided to throw all caution to the wind and take the big risk of sneaking onto the boys' wing to pay him a visit. She was well aware of the serious consequences that would befall her if she were caught. However, she was missing him so badly that she believed the risk was well worth taking. She waited until nobody was around, and then, despite shaking and trembling all over, she braced herself and, after taking a deep breath, stealthily crept up the hallway and through a door into the dormitory where Thomas slept. Polly was visibly shaken when she reached his bedside, for he was barely recognizable! He was so terribly gaunt. His hair had grown long and was badly matted. His eyes were bloodshot and seriously swollen, and his face was a sickly ashen grey. Polly knelt down by the bed and took hold of his hand. Thomas slowly opened his eyes and then in barely a whisper said, "Polly, is that you?" Polly squeezed his hand before whispering back that it was.

"I am not feeling well," he softly wheezed, his voice crackling as he struggled to take a breath.

"I know, Thomas. I know," she said, fighting back the tears as she spoke.

It was no use. Seeing her brother in so much suffering really was much too painful for her to bear. Polly began to weep unashamedly.

"Polly, please don't cry," begged Thomas. "For you know full well that I hate to see you cry."

"I'm so sorry, Thomas," she whimpered. "But I can't help myself. I cannot stand to see you in this terrible state. I have begged them to take you to the hospital or at least to a doctor, but they simply refuse, saying you're not sick at all and that it's all in your head. Oh, how I hate them!" she cried most piteously.

"Polly, dry your eyes," Thomas begged. "I know that I won't be here much longer and then all my pain will be gone forever." Thomas paused and attempted to squeeze her hand. "It's you that I truly worry about since I'm your older brother and I am supposed to protect you." Tears slid down Thomas's face. "I'm so sorry I have failed you, Polly, for it is you that has tried to look after me when it should have been the other way around."

Polly gently placed her finger on his lips to prevent him from carrying on.

"Enough, Thomas," she gently ordered him. "Brothers and sisters are meant to look out for each other," she said in little more than a whisper and in an attempt to reassure him that she really did not mind. "What really matters is that we have each other. Besides, you have had to put up with so much more than I have. So don't you dare start believing that you have failed me, for that's a downright lie," she sniffed, giving his hand a tight squeeze. "I can say with my hand on my heart that it has been my privilege to have you in my life. It really has."

Thomas gave her a faint smile before asking her to get him a drink of water. She returned, and after puffing up his thin pillows as best as she was able, she tried to help him sit up a little to enable him to take a few sips. It was no use, for Thomas was far too weak and she was not strong enough to help him; she therefore chose to dip her finger into the glass and wet his crusty lips.

"Thank you, dear sister," he wheezed, his large brown eyes glazing over with deep sadness. "But now I need you to go, for I fear that if you are caught, we will both be in big trouble."

Polly hesitated, feeling very reluctant to leave his bedside, for everything inside her wanted to stay and nurse him back to health. She would have stayed by his bedside forever because of her love for Thomas, but deep in her heart she knew he was right. As she stood up, she bent over his weak and limp body, gently wrapping her arms around his neck as she gave him a long, lingering hug in her attempt to transmit some of the deep love she had inside her heart for him.

"I love you so much, Thomas Brown," she said, her heart breaking with the pain of parting. "And I will always love you."

"I love you too, Polly," he replied in a barely audible whisper. "Please look after James, for I know he is worried about me as well. Tell him his big brother has ordered you to, for you know what he's like."

"Yes, I certainly do know." Polly answered, smiling through her tears. "He thinks he's much older than he really is, and he therefore never needs anyone's help. Don't worry, Thomas. I will never stop being there for James, and that's a promise."

"I know, Polly," Thomas faintly whispered as his heavy eyelids began to close. "I know. You never make promises that you don't intend to keep, and that's one of the many things I love about you. Now please go or we will both be in big trouble."

Polly moved forward to kiss his cheek, and with their tears mingling, she gently stroked his clammy forehead with her hand. She then clasped hold of his hand one final time, weaving her fingers into his as the final symbolic gesture of their togetherness. Finally she forced herself to break free and head for the door.

"I will try to sneak in again sometime soon, Thomas," she said falteringly. "But please know that you are never far away from my thoughts, and you always remain in my heart."

As she closed the door behind her, she wiped the tears that were now furiously spilling down her face. With the door firmly shut behind her, she started to softly tiptoe her way down the corridor. She was nearly at the end of the hallway when she was forced to stop, for standing in her path blocking her way was none other than Gailey Gobbstopper.

"Oh, just you wait until I tell Uncle Boritz," she said with an amused smile that betrayed her utter delight. "You are in so much trouble now!"

Chapter 9
GOOD-BYE, THOMAS

*I*T WOULD BE less than a fortnight later when Polly and the other children were ordered to go quickly to Uncle Boritz's study. A family meeting was about to take place. Polly wrongly presumed that this time she knew what dastardly crime had been committed—being caught in the boys' dormitory visiting Thomas. She had known then that Gailey Gobbstopper's threat to tell on her would never remain as just a threat. The thought of being rewarded with sweets was too great an opportunity for Gailey. At least this time Polly would not step through the door totally unaware of what might take place. She therefore took in a deep breath and braced herself for the coming ordeal.

With all the children accounted for, the meeting for once took place on schedule. Polly had only been in the study a short while when she found herself feeling quite disturbed inside, for the atmosphere seemed different—a little too eerie for her liking. Why she felt as she did was something of a mystery, for nothing was out of place. The typewriter still stood central on Uncle Boritz's desk, and mail was stacked up beside it. Pitstop was, as usual, hauntingly close to his master's side with buckets of slimy drool hanging from his large jaw. Aunt Mildred was, as usual, sitting close by, very prepared with her hanky out and ready for use when duty called. So what was different? All she knew was she felt very uneasy.

After what seemed an eternity, Uncle Boritz moved away from behind the desk and slowly came to stand in front of the children. He seemed strangely nervous. "Yes, very edgy," thought Polly to herself.

"Kiddiwinks," he said in a very different and quite subdued tone. "I have some very bad news to tell you all. That's if *bad* is the right word to use concerning the matter that I need to bring to your attention." He then fell silent.

Polly felt puzzled. He never ran out of words, and if he did, he usually had no problem making them up! Uncle Boritz coughed before proceeding. "There is no easy way to tell you this, and I am seriously struggling to put the news in such a way as to make it palatable enough for you to digest."

"Are you about to ration our food?" Cecil Bogswater anxiously asked. For he was most eager to get the meeting over with and get back to watching football on the television, especially as Manchester United was playing Liverpool, and nothing should come in the way of this.

"Surely it can't be that, can it?" interrupted Tommy Pulleyblank, "for we are already on half rations! Uncle Boritz, you told us that the last cuts would be enough to save the orphanage from being closed down. So please tell us now that this is not going to happen," he wailed, looking very glum.

Uncle Boritz still remained silent and deep in thought as he paced up and then down the line of very edgy and anxious children sitting cross-legged on the floor beneath him. Pitstop followed his movements, softly padding behind him, feeling quite dizzy due to his master's somewhat erratic pacing! Aunt Mildred, hanky in waiting, decided to help her husband since he appeared to be struggling to express himself.

"Pay attention, children!" she ordered. "The bad news is simply that Thomas has passed away. There, I've said it. It's now out in the open."

There was a stunned silence. No one had any idea what to say next, and strangely enough, this included Polly, for she had fainted. With that terrible piece of news she had simply slumped into a heap on the floor.

The children remained seated with their eyes directed on Polly. None of them had ever seen someone faint, so they wrongly presumed that she also had dropped dead! No one moved a muscle to help her, with the exception of Pitstop, who cautiously left his master's side. Like a vulture swooping on its defenseless victim, he went to investigate this rather unusual and untidy piece of meat that lay prostrate and motionless on the floor. He had hoped it was a very generous gift of a juicy sheep's head for him to gnaw, so he was most disappointed as he sniffed and slobbered over the heap on the floor, only to discover it was none other than smelly old Polly Brown.

Uncle Boritz remained seated and most quiet, merely observing the situation. Minutes passed before he stood up and reached for his glass. He took a large gulp before throwing the rest of the water directly towards Polly. His aim was most successful. The cold water hit her face, and in just a matter of seconds she came round, moaning and rocking her head from side to side.

"Sit up, girl!" he growled. "I am in no mood for any of your amateur dramatics today."

Polly tried to obey his order, struggling to remain upright, for her whole body felt completely numb and her heart felt as though it had just crashed like an elevator straight down into the pit of her stomach. She wanted to scream, but nothing would come.

Uncle Boritz, having found his tongue, decided to take over all talk from Aunt Mildred. He deemed himself to be much more capable at presenting the determining factors than his dear wife, whom he believed was best suited to staying at home and cleaning the kitchen. After all was said and done, he had years of experience in and out of court at persuading people that black was white and white was black. He therefore considered himself to be quite the expert in this field.

"Yes, sadly, I'm afraid to say he did indeed die some days ago," he informed his shocked audience.

Polly could no longer hear what he was saying, for his voice seemed muffled. "Days ago?" a voice screamed inside her head. "Thomas had died days ago, and nothing had been said earlier?" She could not believe her ears. Neither she nor her little brother had been told. It was as though their feelings were not important. She believed it was a very heartless and cruel act to be told so bluntly, so matter-of-factly, without an ounce of human compassion toward her or her younger brother. She believed that out of decency alone they should have been told in private before the other children.

Words could not express the depth of pain she instantly felt as her helter-skelter emotions went into free fall, leaving her sick in the pit of her stomach. She wanted to remove herself from the room and run until she could run no more. She wanted to run away forever from this hellish place called home! Instead, all she could do was make tiny whimpering noises that arose from a volcanic crater deep inside before escaping through her trembling lips. Her young body felt like a lump of lead, for she was so weighed down with the most unimaginable sorrow.

Ignoring Polly's continuing and very annoying little moans, Uncle Boritz went on to inform all the children that the funeral was arranged and would be taking place during school time, so there was no need for any of them to attend.

"I know he was not the most popular child in the home, but I think we will still all miss him," he said, almost choking on his words as he then paused to wipe the beads of sweat that were now dropping from his lined forehead. "I also think the best thing we can do now is try to put this sad event as far out of our minds as possible, and then it will make it much easier to move on and rebuild our lives. We will then become a much stronger and closer family than we already are."

Uncle Boritz scanned his young audience for any sign of rebellion to his little speech, and much to his relief, there was none. As for Polly, her thoughts and feelings were entirely irrelevant, for he could deal with her later and at his convenience.

Polly looked over in James's direction to see how he was taking the terrible news only to sadly note that he was staring into space, completely expressionless. Polly was quick to realize that this apparent lack of response was simply that he was too young and therefore incapable of taking it all in. She also thought it very cruel for her guardians to arrange for Thomas' funeral to take place during school hours so none of them could attend. This was, after all, her beloved brother they were talking about! And yes, she realized that, like herself, he was unpopular, but why? Polly felt she knew the answer to that one.

Though thoroughly shaken and dizzy, Polly managed to haul her limp body up from the floor. Then with a boldness that up to this minute she had no idea she possessed, she announced, "I'm sorry, Uncle Boritz and Aunt Mildred. I have no intention of ever upsetting you, but I beg you to reconsider and allow me to attend my brother's funeral," she cried, bursting into floods of tears.

"Stop all this nonsense!" roared Uncle Boritz, extremely outraged by her impudence. "I have made it quite plain that none of you will be attending his funeral, for school and an education are of the utmost importance. Do you understand?"

"No, I don't understand. I want to go to the funeral! He was my brother, and I loved him. Please don't do this to me. Let me go," she begged.

Uncle Boritz marched over to where Polly still stood, shaking from head to toe, and pushed her back down onto the floor.

"How dare you defy me! And in such an outrageous manner! You ungrateful, miserable wretch! Do you think you can get away with challenging me in such an abominable way? Well, you'd better think again. Children, you can all see why Polly here will end up in prison one day. For not only does she constantly flout and challenge our authority, but she continually shows us all that she is indeed a defiant upstart, incapable of obeying a single order."

All the children sat motionlessly watching, so very upset with Polly for making trouble and upsetting Uncle Boritz and Aunt Mildred. It made them hate her even more than they already did.

Polly, who now lay sprawled out on the floor, attempted to get back up on her feet. She felt like a boxer in the ring who, having suffered a severe blow to the head, determines to get back on their feet before the count of ten. After many attempts, she was successful, although she was now swaying to and fro as she struggled to remain upright. As she stood before her opponent, she mustered up the courage for one final act of defiance.

"I'm not going to school, but I *am* going to his funeral!" she screamed, closing her eyes tightly as she did so.

Before she could say another word, she felt a piercing pain on the side of her face before slumping for a second time back on to the floor.

Uncle Boritz moved over to where a sobbing Aunt Mildred sat and placed his arms around her shaking torso, for she was so distraught at Polly's disgraceful outburst that she needed to lie down and take her medication. The children that were seated on the floor remained motionless, for they too were equally shocked by Polly's crazy outburst. And it only served to further convince them that Uncle Boritz was absolutely correct in his assessment. Madness really did run in Polly's family! How much longer could poor Aunt Mildred and Uncle Boritz struggle on in their foolish attempt to control and help out this loony who seemed determined to make all their lives a misery. If it weren't for her and her brothers, none of these family sessions would surely ever have to take place, and Aunt Mildred would not need to keep taking medication to control her bad nerves. It must be time for Polly to be removed and at the very least be taken to the local mental institution, if not prison, as their poor uncle had often and quite rightly suggested.

Aunt Mildred sat in the seat sobbing and shaking with no amount of comfort from Uncle Boritz able to calm her down. How dare Polly behave in such a defiant manner when all they had been trying to do was pass on information to the children regarding Thomas's sudden departure. It was bad enough that they would be expected to cough up the money and pay all funeral expenses, and then there was the inconvenience of organizing and attending the funeral themselves, for this would severely interrupt their busy schedules in the process.

However, they could still see the bright side to all of this, for it conveniently served to give them the winning ticket. Aunt Mildred confidently knew, just as her husband also knew, there would not be a single child left who would choose to remain sitting on the fence after Polly's disgraceful outburst. They would indeed all be rooting for Aunt Mildred, and this gave her a great sense of comfort and purpose. She knew it was now time to start bawling again, and the louder the better. Uncle Boritz joined in the pretense by throwing his arms up into the air to convey his total despair.

"Children, I'm at my wit's end. How can we all put up with this for a moment longer? Just look at poor Aunt Mildred. She is in the most terrible state of distress, and this has, as usual, all been bought about by Polly," he said, furrowing his brow to show his deep concern as he patted his wife's shoulder in his bid to comfort her. "Children, as you continually bear witness, this girl lives, day in, day out, to create utter chaos."

He then carefully removed his glasses and wiped both eyes with a hanky, shaking his head. He then systematically cleaned both glass lenses. This little action served to point out that Polly's temper tantrum had even reduced him to tears, and he was a man not usually given to displays of emotion.

"How can Polly do this to us all?" he asked, his deep voice cracking as he continued on with the pretense of struggling to contain his deep distress. One-by-one the children began to cry, for it was all too much for them to bear. They were now frightened that Polly had, on this occasion, pushed things too far. It might even mean that they would all have to leave the orphanage, for it appeared that Aunt Mildred was clearly tinkering on the verge of a nervous breakdown, thanks to sniveling, smelly Polly Brown.

Uncle Boritz turned and glared in Polly's direction.

"*You*, young lady, are going nowhere!" he seethed. "How dare you even think that you can defy us in such an outrageous manner!" Uncle Boritz knew he needed more ammunition if he was going to win this one, and thankfully he had it! "Furthermore, I have yet to bring up the subject of quite what you were doing sneaking into the boys' dormitory, which you most definitely know is strictly out of bounds and therefore forbidden."

Polly, who was still lying incapacitated and sprawled out on the floor with her head spinning, felt unable to answer his question, for it had taken her off guard that Uncle Boritz should change the subject so completely. Surely he must realize that there was nothing sinister in her going to the boys' dormitory, even if she had been wrong in breaking the strict code of the castle on this one occasion.

Uncle Boritz, never one to miss an opportunity, seized this moment to twist the truth in his favor.

"Well, well, you horrid little misfit. I would like to suggest that you were rummaging through the boys' most precious possessions looking for something to steal," he sneered.

Polly still remained lost for words, shocked that he could suggest such an act of wickedness on her part. As she lay on the floor, she made several attempts at sitting up, but found that she couldn't. Her whole body felt like a set of dumbbells. Not only was she completely paralyzed with fear, but also her emotions were now on a very high roller coaster. "How could they make such wicked and utterly false accusations, and at such an awful time as this?" she thought as she attempted to stop herself from shaking. However, she knew, as history had always told her, that she had no hope whatsoever of proving herself innocent.

They had spent years branding her a liar and a thief, to the point where she almost believed it herself. So no amount of protestation on her part would make the slightest bit of difference. There would, as usual, be no one on her side. There would be no supporters or mediator to stand in the gap and get the true facts. She was out on a limb and fighting for her life with the term *innocent until proved guilty* totally reversed!

Polly found it hard to believe how passive and brainwashed the other children were. They never seemed to question anything that was said to them. Uncle Boritz constantly told them that no one else would ever want them. With great relish he made up awful stories concerning their terrible parents. The other children seemed to lap it up, unbelievably encouraging him to tell them more! And the worse the stories got, the more cheerful they became. They all seemed to truly believe their guardians when they were regularly told that God had sent them to run the orphanage to protect them all from this most evil world. What would they do, and where would they all be now had it not been for these wonderful, saintly crusaders of homeless children?

Polly's thoughts were rudely interrupted by a loud bang as Boritz thumped his clenched fist down hard on the desk to get her undivided attention.

"Yes, Polly Brown, you entered the forbidden zone with only one intention in mind, and that was to steal the highly treasured possessions of other poor children," he said snidely. "And as I wish to discuss this no further, you are therefore sentenced to another three weeks on R.O.P.E. So when you are not at school, you will work until you realize that disobedience and attempted theft are not to be tolerated in my castle!"

The children still sat cross-legged on the floor, much too terrified to move. They all secretly wondered why Polly was still making such a stupid, unnecessary fuss! After all, it was only Thomas the loony that had departed from their midst. It was true that they would certainly miss teasing him and tying him to a tree in a potato sack, for he had made such an excellent punch bag! Now they would be forced to search for a replacement victim to torment. This might prove a trifle inconvenient, but they were certain that in the fullness of time another victim could, and would, be found. However, their biggest fear was which of them, besides Polly, would become their guardians' next scapegoat now that Thomas was gone? The thought that they could possibly be next on their guardians' hot list for special attention made each of them shudder. For deep, deep down, never to be expressed, they knew only too well that their guardians were people who took sport and pleasure from the pain of others. Therefore, if they were true to character, with Thomas now out of the way, a suitable replacement would become an urgent priority. Suddenly the idea of Thomas's death did not seem quite so fine.

The children were dismissed, and as they filed out of the room Uncle Boritz shouted at them to stop, for he had forgotten something very important—something he had never failed to state and remind them all of in the past. He began to fear that he really was losing his God-given gift of controlling everything under his power. Heaven forbid that such a thing should ever happen!

"My little whippersnappers," he said, lowering his voice. "I feel I must caution you that if news of Thomas's sudden departure were to somehow leak out of here accidentally through careless talk..." He momentarily faltered as he moved closer towards the children, his eyes widening as big as saucers. "Then you must realize that the child care agency would come and take you all away without any warning whatsoever! You would all find yourselves locked up in the back of their big black van," he whispered in a barely audible voice. "And let me assure you now that none of you would ever be seen again! Of this I am most certain, for having removed you all from our safe castle in the dead of the night, they would then take you to a most secret hideout where men in white jackets would pull out a drawer filled with special, very frightening instruments used only when they wish to interrogate someone."

"What does *interrogate* mean, Uncle Boritz?" whimpered Bertha Banoffee, her large blue eyes widening as they filled up with tears. "It means, Bertha, that they would use all kinds of force to get you to tell them what happened to Thomas," Uncle Boritz replied, his eyes bulging out from their sockets as he endeavored to put great fear into them. "And may I remind you all that there is nothing, no nothing, they would not resort to in order to find out what happened. Why, they might even tie your bodies to chairs and, I hate to say it, but they might...well...er..." he paused, for timing was of the essence.

"Go on. Say it. Get it over with," urged Aunt Mildred, showing great irritation as she spoke. For she had looked up at the clock in the study only to realize that she was now missing *Coronation Street*, her favorite television program.

Uncle Boritz could barely hide his annoyance at being interrupted, but he took a very deep breath and then, softening his voice to that of little more than a whisper, he said. "Well, I hate to say it, girls and boys, but they might even torture you!"

On hearing this, little Sacha Shoesmith drew a deep breath and began to cry. For she was utterly horrified at the thought of the hateful child care agency showing no mercy whatsoever as they slowly pulled out her fingernails, followed by her toenails! And, if they still had not got the information they were after, they would then proceed to gouge out her eyes! She knew, just as the other children knew and believed, from watching old war movies that torture could at times be a most unpleasant experience.

Therefore, as little Sacha and the other children filled their vivid imaginations with the ten most terrifying ways of being tortured, each of them privately resolved that they would never say a word. The decision they all made that most wretched day was, in their little minds, set in concrete. They would never spill the beans and become the castle traitor or the disloyal one responsible for breaking up the family.

POLLY BROWN

Uncle Boritz had not quite finished.

"Of course, children, I am not saying that this would definitely happen, just that it is a real possibility."

He added this as he realized it was always essential to cover his tracks. For heaven forbid that one of the children would accidentally get to meet someone from the child care agency and finally discover they were not the cruel and utterly contemptible people that he had spent much of his lifetime making them out to be. There was a real possibility, if this were ever to happen, that they might well crumble and tell all! This could never be allowed to happen! So, with sweat now pouring profusely from his brow, he finished up by saying, "Children, may I remind all of you that if any of this were to happen, neither Aunt Mildred nor myself would be in any position to help you. Yes, sadly our hands would be completely tied, and we would be unable to come to your rescue. So please, please, remember our little, and very private motto, and repeat it after me. 'What happens in the castle stays in the castle.'"

They all dutifully repeated every word of the motto, nodding continually to show their total allegiance to the family. Uncle Boritz and Aunt Mildred breathed a deep sigh of relief.

Polly stood up to join the end of the growing queue lining up to leave the room, but when it came to her turn, Uncle Boritz moved over and blocked the doorway.

"And where do you think you're going?" he asked coldly. "I haven't finished with you yet. So get back over there," he angrily snapped before turning to shoo the other children away from the open door of the study. "Children, please go and stand patiently by my goodies cupboard, and I will be along shortly to give you all a treat. So hurry up my dears."

With the room now empty of children, that is, with the exception of Polly, he was finally free to do or say whatever he wished. He continued to stand with his arms folded across the doorway, preventing her from escaping. "Stay right where you are, girl!" he barked.

Polly obeyed, for she had no choice. He was, after all, so much bigger than her, and besides, she was in no mood to argue, for she was experiencing such immense pain deep down that she cared very little about anything else her guardians might want to do to her.

"You really take the biscuit, girl, defying me at every corner and undermining my authority," he snarled. "You will not be attending the funeral, for you will be going to school—unless, of course, you want further punishment. Are we clear about that?"

Polly stood with her head hung low and remained silent. She had no idea how best to answer, for she had made up her mind and nothing was going to change it. She instinctively knew that if she were to openly repeat her decision, it would only serve to make things worse than they already were, and she had no desire to escalate things any further.

"Answer me, girl. Do you understand my order?" he bellowed, giving her arm a hard prod as he continued to sneer at her. "I have had quite enough of you and your family. Now at least, there is one less annoying little nuisance to deal with! Get out of my sight before I lose my temper and give you something to really cry about."

Polly wasted no time in obeying, moving at great speed to duck under his outstretched arm in order to get as far away from him as she possibly could.

She staggered and stumbled down the lengthy corridor, struggling to remain upright, for her arms and legs felt like wobbly jelly. She felt she was in a nightmare, only this was for real. She did not want to talk to anyone. She just wanted to be alone to grieve, come to terms with her terrible loss, and work out how she might get to his funeral.

She did not care about any of the threats made that day concerning further possible punishments. She was going to Thomas's funeral no matter what! She reasoned that she had more right to be there than anyone else, and she knew Thomas would have wanted her there. It was settled. She would find a way, although at this moment in time she had very little idea as to how to make it happen. She sadly came to the conclusion that it would be wise to leave James behind and go on her own, for she did not wish to bring any more unnecessary suffering into his life.

Polly decided to go to the only place she knew she would not be disturbed. The place she ran to whenever she needed to sort out her head and find some measure of peace was a little church that was only a short distance away from the castle. As she sang in the choir and regularly attended choir practice, she knew that the small side entrance would still be open, so hopefully she could slip undetected into the church. After lighting a candle for Thomas, she made her way down a passageway before opening a little door that led up some long, winding, narrow steps. She stopped halfway and, taking a left turn, slipped under the thick rope that blocked off a further flight of steps. She then headed up the long and winding steps and made her way towards the belfry, her only place of sanctuary from everything in her crazy, mixed-up little life.

The room that held the bell was very small. It was also very, very dangerous! So Polly took great care as she walked over the rotting wooden planks, some of which were very loose. She often thought that if she accidentally fell, her body would never be found, for the bell tower was out of bounds, and no one except herself ventured up there. This was her secret place, a place she could be alone without any fear of being discovered. She had once seen a black and white movie called *The Hunchback of Notre Dame*. It was about a monster named Quasimodo who was forced to live and hide away in a bell tower. She remembered crying throughout most of the film, for she felt just like him. Deep down inside, she too felt like a monster. She therefore thought it eerily strange that, just like the hunchback, she had a bell tower to live in, even though hers, she believed, was considerably smaller.

Polly had not been to choir practice for a number of weeks, and for this she felt guilty. She even thought that her failure to attend choir had in some strange way been the reason for Thomas's death. Perhaps it was her fault, and God was very angry with her; and perhaps Thomas's dying was meant to teach her a lesson. First her two most wonderful teachers disappear without a trace from school, and then her beloved brother just happens to die. It was all too much of a coincidence for Polly, and the thought that she could have caused all this made her feel even worse.

The truth of why she failed to attend choir was twofold. Firstly, one afternoon after school they had been asked to go to the church for practice much earlier than usual—three thirty to be precise.

Their practice that day was unusually short, and afterwards two sisters named Constance and Beatrice Bickertree happily showed all the young choir members their brand new bikes. Polly had always dreamed of having a bike, and despite never having ridden one before, she used every persuasive method in the book in her desperate bid to get Constance to part with her bike and let her have a little ride. Eventually, and against her better judgment, Constance reluctantly gave Polly the permission to mount the bike and take it for a short spin.

Off she went at great speed, very delighted to have this wonderful opportunity to ride this highly desired machine for the first time ever. The trouble was that the hill was very steep, and Polly had no idea whatsoever as to how to stop the bike. She didn't realize that the bike had special brake handles that, when clutched, would bring the bike to a grinding halt, for up until this moment in time no one had ever even given permission for her to as much as sit on their bike seat. The bike picked up speed as it hurtled down the hill. Polly anxiously held on for her life, her trembling hands clammy with sweat as she struggled to remain in control. She quickly realized that she was in deep trouble and had to do something fast if she was not to have a terrible accident. She knew that there was more than a fifty-fifty chance that she would have a collision with a car or, worse, a truck, if she did not stop this stupid bike before it reached a major road and disaster struck.

Feeling decidedly panicked and afraid, as she and the bike went further out of control, she decided to take a chance and swing the bike very hard to the right, heading straight towards the little hairdressing shop. The front wheel mounted the pavement and then continued to hurtle towards the shop before crashing into the pane glass window. Polly was then hurled through the window, still mounted on the bike, which came to land with an almighty crash, just missing a line of women sitting under hairdryers.

When Polly finally got back on her feet, she, as well as all present, were amazed to discover that she was unharmed, although covered from head to toe in shattered glass. Polly noted that the bike had not fared as well. As it lay on its side on the vinyl floor, its back wheel spun as furiously as Polly's little head. Polly could not fail to notice that it now looked like an entirely different contraption from the one she had originally mounted! The ladies under the dryers had also not fared too well. A large number of the old dears were scared witless by the brief and very sudden catastrophe. Many of them, because of the magnitude of distress suffered on that eventful day, chose to leave the premises with curlers still firmly attached to their heads.

Constance Bickertree's bike was beyond repair. Both wheels were severely buckled, and the handlebars now faced entirely the wrong way. Neither sister ever spoke to Polly again. She was also given a lifetime ban from entering the hairdresser's shop, for the owner was forced to offer free hair styling for a month as a conciliatory gesture to the large amount of deeply distressed women seeking compensation. Polly too paid dearly for her unfortunate episode, for there was a new bike and a new front window to pay for, and as she only received a miserly pittance in pocket money, she sincerely wondered if she would ever receive another penny. She was also placed on R.O.P.E. for many more months to punish her further for her disgracefully wicked misdemeanor.

Polly deeply regretted ruining Constance Bickertree's new bicycle, torturing herself daily with the wish that if she could somehow turn back the clock, then none of this would have happened and Constance would still be friendly. Now she had to face the cold treatment, which meant being completely ostracized by all who attended choir practice. In no time at all, it appeared that the whole jolly town knew every grim detail of her little escapade, and the townsfolk could also be very unforgiving. From the time of the mishap, she had endured hostile glances and people moving to the other side of the pavement and shunning her whenever she passed them on the street corner. Polly was at a complete loss as to how she could ever put things right, although she longed to with her whole heart.

Eventually, Polly did the only thing left open to her. She put on a brave face and still attended choir for several weeks after the incident, even though it meant enduring secretive whispering behind her back. Things finally came to a head when, by pure chance, she discovered that all the other children who attended choir practice were discreetly being paid by the church to sing in the choir. This disclosure had come as a complete shock to Polly.

She had joined the choir at the same time as the other children, for the church had approached the school in search of volunteers. Polly had said yes to the opportunity without any thought of payment for her services. She was just happy to be part of a group that loved to sing. When she discovered that all the other young-sters were secretly being financially rewarded for their attendance, it was too much to bear and left Polly feeling very hurt. She knew that none of the other children suffered lack on the scale that she experienced. Every other child in the choir had warm houses to go home to, loving parents, nice clothes, shiny polished bikes, holidays by the beach, and every other imaginable delight that Polly could only ever dream of having. "Will life ever serve me a better deal?" she bitterly wondered as she struggled to come to terms with yet another cruel blow.

She remained hidden away in the tower, weeping and completely ignoring the stomach pangs that reminded her that she had not eaten all day. Finally, very tired as well as cold, Polly slipped out of the church and hurried home. Her heart raced within her breast as she ran down the road towards the castle, hoping her unexplained absence would go unchecked.

Once inside, she crept quietly up the creaky oak stairs and headed for the dormitory, slipping quietly under the bedclothes so as not to disturb the other girls deep in their slumber. She nestled her head into Langdon's soft body and quietly sobbed until she fell asleep.

Chapter 10
DOCTOR CHIPATTI TO THE RESCUE

HEN POLLY FINALLY woke up the next morning the room was thankfully silent and empty. All the other girls had long left the dormitory for breakfast. Polly felt glad to be left alone, for she was unprepared to face the other children and suffer hurtful jibes, which she found impossible to ignore no matter how hard she tried. Polly therefore remained in the room, sitting on her bed, trying to come to terms with all that had happened the day before. She picked up Eton, who had tumbled onto the floor during the night, and whispered in his ear, "Eton, I need you to be very brave and do something very difficult for both of us. I love you very much, but I am going to have to let you go." A lone tear slid down Polly's face as she clutched Eton very tightly to her chest, remembering back to the day she had found him.

She had gone to the attic for a reason she could not remember. As she moved around the attic, her eyes eventually hit on a large, leather-bound trunk. Being a curious little girl, she wasted no time in opening it. The trunk was laden with old, moth-eaten clothes, and Polly set about emptying the trunk, although she had no idea what she was searching for. Out came one crumpled straw hat after another followed by faded leather bags and old, scuffed shoes. When she was on the verge of abandoning her mission, she suddenly found herself picking up the dismembered arm of a teddy. She momentarily paused, staring at the sad, worn-out limb before deciding that she must continue the search just in case his torso was hidden deeper down in the trunk. If it was, she urgently needed to retrieve it. Finally, her hand came to rest on something soft. Plunging her hand deeper into the trunk, she pulled out the remainder of the teddy.

"You are, I fear, in a very bad way, little man," she solemnly declared as a statement of fact. She observed that, sadly, most of the stuffing was missing from his belly. His eye was damaged and delicately hanging on his cheek by a thread. Polly had felt extremely sorry for him, and, after considerable thought, her conscience dictated that she could not ignore his sad plight by abandoning him back to the trunk for the remainder of his days. He was, after all, in a very sorry state, and she felt it was no coincidence that it had been left to her and not one of the other children to unearth him. He was now her responsibility, and caring for others was what she did best.

Many times she had been called upon to use her caring skills to save animals that had been injured, and this teddy deserved the same respect. So she made the decision to try and save him just as she did whenever she found wounded birds or rabbits lying in the woods writhing in pain. As she stroked the battered teddy, she remembered the terrible day during the summer holidays when she had been out walking through woodland with some of the other children. As they made their way back to the castle in readiness for suppertime, they had discovered a wounded and very frightened hare trapped in some thick bracken. Somehow they managed to catch it before carefully bringing it back to the castle with the full intention of lovingly attending to its injuries. Polly had bandaged its broken leg and placed it in an empty cage filled with fresh straw. She then put in a little saucer of milk and some cabbage leaves, hoping it would eat and build up its strength.

The next morning Polly went to check on him, for she was very concerned to know how the little chap was doing and, more to the point, whether he required further medical attention. She placed her hand in the cage, only to discover that her new friend was missing. She remembered feeling thoroughly sick as she rummaged through the straw, desperate to find the little fellow. There was no sign of him. Polly was both puzzled and panicked. How could he escape when the door of the hutch had been securely locked? She summoned up the help of other children, and in no time at all the search and rescue party was frantically searching the whole garden, desperate to find the injured little hare. But their search proved fruitless, for, despite combing every inch of the garden, their hare was nowhere to be found.

That day the children refused to give up hope that eventually he would be found. They carried on patrolling the garden, inspecting every nook and cranny until they were finally called in to wash their hands before lunch, but not before collectively agreeing to meet up and continue their search as soon as lunch was over. They raced toward the kitchen to wash their hands, gobble down their lunch, and then regroup in the garden to continue their search for Thumper.

As Polly entered the kitchen she felt a bit uneasy, for the smell did not seem familiar. Lunch on Saturdays was always soup made from a miniscule amount of minced beef that had been poured over a boiled potato, a few peas, and a couple of carrots. And as she joined the long queue of hungry children, her eyes fell on the plates of children filing past her as they went in search of a seat. Polly was very surprised to see that instead of the norm, there were thick brown chunks of meat in a rich brown sauce. Now as meat was a luxury rarely served to them, Polly fleetingly had the most terrible thought, but dismissed it as quickly as she had entertained it, for it was indeed a most unbelievably gruesome thought. There was no way on earth that those square lumps on the other children's plates could actually be her wounded hare, could they? As Polly's plate was handed to her from over the counter, she began to tremble as she headed for a vacant seat to join the other children.

Having found a spare seat, she sat down at the table and, after tentatively picking up her knife and fork, simply stared down at her plate, wondering what on earth to do next. Meanwhile, Uncle Boritz entered the room, and upon observing a large group of the children sitting motionless, many just staring into their plates, he decided to jolly them along with encouraging words.

"Children, eat up," he ordered, breaking out into a wide grin, "for you are very lucky today to be eating jugged hare!"

Knives and forks came crashing to the floor as all the younger children, Polly included, started crying.

"Children, children, stop this nonsense immediately and eat up," Uncle Boritz furiously demanded. "For jugged hare is known to be a real delicacy, and therefore you children should all be truly grateful. Besides, the hare was in so much pain that I believe I did the right thing," he smugly added with a grin.

Polly, along with many of the other children, would not and could not obey his order to stop crying. And as far as Polly was concerned there was no way she was ever going to satisfy her hunger by eating what hours earlier had been her wounded pet, no matter how desperately hungry she was. Before long, many more of the children chose to join the mounting army of young protesters, refusing to eat up what only yesterday had been their new friend. Uncle Boritz quickly began to lose his patience, for they were pitting their wills against his. So he quickly determined that they would pay dearly for their act of disgraceful defiance.

The children were forced to sit at the table for the remainder of the day. Finally bedtime arrived and the rebels were all ordered off their numb bottoms and frog-marched upstairs to their respective dormitories. Morning arrived, and Polly was shocked to discover that the matter was not yet over. As they sat down for breakfast, they were served the same plates of jugged hare stew that they had abandoned the night before. Every child involved in the plot sat at the table and continued to stare down at their plate, refusing to open their mouths and eat one jolly morsel.

For their defiance, the children remained seated with the same plates of dried-up stew in front of them, while those that had given in gracefully began eating their normal plate of Sunday lunch. For Polly it had to be the first time ever that Sunday lunch seemed inviting, for wafer-thin luncheon meat served up with a miniscule amount of bland vegetables had always been pretty boring, and therefore unappetizing. But today of all days her greatest wish would have been for the plate of hare stew to miraculously disappear and be replaced by a plate of luncheon meat! With the dinner plates and other crockery washed and put away, the children still remained at the table, steadfast in their determination not to take one bite of the seriously shriveled stew.

Their rebellion lasted well into Sunday afternoon as their stomachs grew hungrier and hungrier and began to gurgle. Uncle Boritz, filled to the brim with rage and frustration, finally dismissed them from out of his sight, sending them, along with their plates, to sit on their own in another room.

Polly's younger brother James was amongst the small band of rebels and was clearly distressed to see Polly so upset, so he decided to be both brave and courageous and offer to eat Polly's for her. Polly willingly agreed and gave James her plate. Her sense of gratitude and relief were to be very short-lived. In no time at all the stew was back on her plate. For to Polly's absolute horror, not only did James fail to digest the stew, but worse still, he vomited it back onto the plate—Polly's plate! Her situation was now worse than ever! For now, she had a plate of thoroughly regurgitated jugged hare to polish off.

Their ordeal only came to an end when Polly decided that firm action was needed to stop this awful crisis from continuing any longer. She marched over to the window and flung it open before turning to each child and removing their plate to throw the contents out of the window and into the garden. Each tear-stained face showed great relief and gratitude as their plate was removed from under their nose, for it meant that their ordeal was over. If this dastardly deed was ever found out, it would be Polly and not any of them who would bear the brunt of any future punishment.

The stew was quickly and gratefully gobbled up by the remaining few scrawny chickens, whose lives had up until now been spared the stewpot. With all remains of the stew finally dispensed with, the children could hopefully put the ordeal behind them. Polly had not felt the slightest bit remorseful concerning the deception, but she did feel a twinge of sadness that there was nothing left of their pet hare to bury in the garden. She also hoped it would not lead to further punishment. Luckily for Polly and the other inmates, no one, not even Uncle Boritz, had the temerity to question their sudden licked-to-a-shine plates. For although her guardians may have suspected foul play, all incriminating evidence was long gone, leaving them unable to prove a thing!

As she looked back on that terrible ordeal, she hoped her newfound friend the teddy bear would indeed be spared the stew pot. Sitting comfortably on her bed, she pulled out her handkerchief and made a temporary tourniquet to hold teddy's arm in place, for she was quite the little expert on bandaging wounds and applying tender loving care. Then, with the freshly-bandaged teddy under one arm and humming a tune under her breath, she left the room to do whatever was necessary to help the poor little fellow, for she deemed him to be a most suitable case for treatment.

That same afternoon she marched to a good friend's house, believing she needed his help and expertise to care for the teddy's injuries. She rang the front doorbell and waited, but no one answered.

Polly turned on her heels, very disappointed that the good doctor was nowhere to be found. As she walked across the gravel on his driveway, she suddenly had the revelation that it was Saturday, and that meant she knew exactly where to find him. He and his wife would without fail be sharing an intimate moment as they dined at the Copper Kettle.

Polly wasted no time and ran as fast as the wind down Main Street until she came to the door of the tearoom. Then, as discreetly as she was able, she pressed her nose up to the window to check if they were inside seated at their usual table. Much to her delight and relief, they were. Polly thought the Chipattis were such a nice couple. He was very swarthy with thick, unruly black eyebrows and a most mischievous grin. Mrs. Chipatti, well, she was as white as a sheet with rosy cheeks. Polly had observed that, unlike the good doctor, she was not Indian at all, as she had light brown curly hair and wore no ring in her nose. Polly had also never seen her in a sari, and neither did she have a red diamond in the center of her forehead.

They shared their house with their two beautiful daughters, as well as every animal imaginable. Every spare room was occupied by hamsters, rabbits, snakes, and even a live giraffe that the doctor had raised from a baby. It made Polly wish at times that she had been born a koala bear or perhaps an exotic reptile, because then they might have welcomed her into the bosom of their unusual and very warm family.

Polly quickly dismissed her ridiculous imaginations before discreetly peering through the window again to check on their progress. She observed that they were still waiting for their main course to be served, so she looked around for a suitable place to sit down to prepare for the long wait as they ate their lunch. Every now and then she jumped up and peered through the window just to check how far through their meal they were. Every time she found herself smiling, for their heads were almost joined together as they met across the small, round table, deep in the art of conversation.

The Chipattis always ordered the same dish for lunch every Saturday, for although it was an English tearoom, the Greedols still made a most delicious chicken curry for them. The Greedols were always happy to oblige and equally happy to charge accordingly.

Polly often watched as two plates of rice topped with yellow stuff arrived piping hot at their table. Next to arrive at the table was a plate that had four small bowls on it. One of the bowls contained coconut, another chopped banana, in the third was brown pickle, and the fourth held chopped up tomatoes. They sprinkled the contents of these little bowls on the top of the bright yellow stuff before they started eating. As they ate their meal with great relish, they crunched on big cream-colored plates called popadoms, which Polly had taken some time to discover weren't plates at all! Polly would watch on quite fascinated, wondering if she would like the taste of curry and popadoms.

The couple were always delighted with their curry meal, which they happily ate, chatting constantly between each mouthful. And Polly observed that they both drank vast volumes of water from the jug that had been brought to their table. They nearly always requested that the water jug be refilled. The reason for their incredible thirst, Polly did not know. All she knew was they were easy to please, and they never ordered anything different from the menu.

It was the same with the Pistachios, an Italian family that came in at the same time every Sunday for their specially made lasagna. Then there was the Corcellut family, who reserved a table every Thursday to sit down to share a quiche cooked in traditional French style. Polly thought that this pie looked very colorful, as well as mouth watering, so she quite fancied trying a slice. Then there was also a Russian family, whose name she could not pronounce, and whom Polly observed were late as usual for their big bowl of steaming Siberian dumplings! Polly never fancied trying these at all, mainly because she had heard along the grapevine that these dumplings were made from horse meat, and she loved horses and ponies far too much to want to eat them!

Polly found it strange that this English tearoom was more than happy to make these unusual dishes for their regulars. But she felt pleased for them, thinking it made people who had come from faraway lands feel at home in England and not quite so homesick. These regulars were obviously delighted with the service they received, and Polly observed that they never failed to leave a generous tip. So, she longed to become a waitress (as well as a nun and a part-time firefighter) when she grew up. This was another good reason why the Copper Kettle was her favorite tearoom in the whole wide world.

Polly continued sitting on the step outside the tearoom, hoping that Mrs. Greedol would not notice and chase her away. She constantly fidgeted, for she found it impossible to remain calm and composed as she waited as patiently as she could ever wait! Would they ever finish lunch and leave? Finally, they emerged out of the tearoom and on to the pavement.

"Why! If it isn't young Polly Brown," Dr. Chipatti said rather cheerily. Polly's face went crimson, as it always did when someone greeted her warmly. "Good morning to you, Polly, and isn't it a beautiful and most fine day," said the good doctor, sporting a huge grin on his face.

"And a good morning to you too, Dr. Chipatti, although I do need to point out that it is one thirty in the afternoon, so you might need to adjust your watch!"

Dr. Chipatti looked down at his watch and laughed before asking, "Well, my dear, what can I do for you this very pleasant afternoon? Have you perhaps come to ask if you can take my pet chinchilla out for a walk?"

"No," replied Polly. "I have something much more important on my mind, and only you can be of assistance. So I really do need your help."

They strolled back to the good doctor's house deep in conversation. Polly filled the doctor in on all the necessary details. The doctor appeared deep in thought, and Polly was forced to hold her breath as she hoped that he would agree to help her.

Finally they arrived at his front door, and the doctor took out a brass key to open the door before looking down into Polly's anxious face. Then, with a big broad smile and eyes filled with compassion, he said, "Well, Polly dear, after hearing this most sad and tragic story of yours, I feel I have little choice but to offer you all the assistance you need."

Polly visibly relaxed before breaking out into a smile.

"Thank you so much, Dr. Chipatti. I don't know what I would have done if you had said *no* to my request."

"Then come this way, young lady," he said, beckoning her through the front door and into the hallway. "But first I must look in on my pet giraffe, for I clean forgot to give him his breakfast this morning!"

Dr. Chipatti then suggested that Polly follow him to his small private study. The room was lined with tall oak bookcases filled to capacity with books that Polly thought only the cleverest of doctors could possibly understand.

"Pop yourself down over there, Polly," said the loveable doctor, directing her towards an empty chair. "I will be back in five minutes, after reassuring dear Cyril that his belated breakfast will be with him shortly."

Polly moved towards the chair.

"Thank you, thank you," she muttered, as she sat down on the seat and made herself comfortable.

As she waited, she gazed up at the many paintings lining the walls, all of which had been painted by the good doctor himself. Polly sighed to herself, for she thought it most unfair that God should bestow such a wealth of talents on one man. If painting and being a doctor and author were not enough, she also knew that he was a brilliant musician. She thought it most unfair that he should sail through life so gifted when others like herself struggled to produce any talent whatsoever! Polly quickly rebuked herself for allowing jealous thoughts to enter her head, for she knew that if she entertained them long enough they would certainly take root in her heart, and that would not be right. He was, after all, a kind-hearted and extraordinary man who used his talents to help others, so she had no right to feel anything other than the deepest gratitude and admiration towards him and his equally delightful family.

Dr. Chipatti kept his word and reappeared less than five minutes later.

"Right, Polly. Let's get down to business. You say you need to borrow one of my books in order to perform an operation?"

"Yes, doctor. That's right. Otherwise I will not have the slightest idea what I'm doing," said Polly, putting on her serious face.

Dr. Chipatti stood by his vast collection of medical and surgical books, stroking his chin with one hand as he began to ponder.

"Right then, young Polly. Are we looking for a book on heart surgery?" he quizzed. "Although I do have a very nice one on liver and kidney transplants!" he rather thoughtfully added. "Or how about this one?" he asked, pulling out an unbelievably thick red book from amongst his collection. "It's called *How to Do a Most Successful Amputation.*"

"What's an amputation?" Polly asked, slightly embarrassed that she had so very little medical knowledge.

The good and kindly doctor smiled before replying. "Well, this informative book will show you how to remove a damaged or diseased limb," he stated as he tentatively flipped through the pages with the clear intention of finding a diagram to show her. "Here, Polly, take a good look."

Polly looked positively horrified. "He's already lost his right arm," she wailed, at the same time giving a small shudder. "So I don't think I want to remove his other one!" she stated most emphatically.

"Hmm, I think not," said Dr. Chipatti, placing the book back on the shelf. There was silence as he paused deep in thought. "I do believe that what we need here, Polly, is a book on reconstructive surgery, don't you?"

Polly readily agreed, for she did not wish to appear too stupid.

"Thank you, doctor," she said visibly showing her relief. Then she lowered her voice to little more than a whisper. "I think you are correct. But tell me, does it also give instructions on how to deal with teddies that have such big splits in their tummies that their guts are now spilling out all over the place?"

"Oh, dearie me," whispered back the doctor. "I don't believe it does. But tell me, Polly, why exactly are we whispering?"

"Oh, sorry, doctor, but I am a little unsure as to whether I should be giving away confidential medical information concerning my patient."

"Polly, do not concern your good self about such things; for this crisis most certainly falls into the category of privileged information. It is therefore vital that you share the gory details with me, especially as his condition appears to be life threatening."

Polly nodded her agreement.

"Yes, it does sound as though the poor chap is in a most terrible state," he muttered, again rubbing his clean-shaven chin to show the depth of his concern. "Here, I think you will need this one as well," he said, pulling out a huge and very dusty green book the size of an encyclopedia that was titled *Extremely Complicated Surgery for Absolute Beginners.*

"This wonderful book deals in great depth with all the practical issues surrounding surgical procedures. It's one I wrote earlier in my career, and to date I've never had an angry letter back informing me that a patient failed to survive as a result of following the useful advice that my book gives," he confided, giving Polly a little wink.

Polly was delighted and thanked him profusely, although she was left secretly wondering if she had the necessary strength required to carry the book all the way home.

"Dr. Chipatti, you have been most kind, but I wonder, could you please do me one more tiny favor?"

"And what might that favor be?" he asked as he concentrated on making sure the line of books in front of him was still perfectly ordered.

"Well, I need to borrow one more book," said Polly rather sheepishly, for she knew these books were extremely expensive and he was showing her such kindness in lending any of them to her. "I also need to ask for a book on eye surgery," she said, biting down hard on her bottom lip and feeling somewhat embarrassed.

"Delicate or general?" quizzed the doctor.

"Oh, definitely delicate," Polly swiftly replied. "For Eton's eyeball is in a dreadful state and is no longer sitting where God intended, but is hanging by a thin thread almost halfway down his chest!"

"Well, goodness gracious me!" exclaimed the kind doctor, shaking his head wearily to convey his utter disbelief. "Then delicate surgery it is," he said airily as he placed the second, equally heavy book in her outstretched hands.

Polly smiled and thanked him for all his help, at the same time assuring him that she would take great care of his precious books and return them as soon as possible. Dr. Chipatti knew she would keep her word and determined to remember to ask after teddy when he next saw her. After all, teddies were very important and precious to most children, his daughters included.

As she staggered towards the door, seriously weighed down by her heavy load, the dear doctor hardly seemed to notice as he placed another two books on top of her already burdensome pile.

"You will also require these two books if teddy is to have any hope of making a successful and speedy recovery," he went on to advise her.

Polly was now seriously struggling to remain upright as she violently swayed backwards then forwards, completely hidden by the mounting pile of books.

"What are their titles?" she called out, her voice very muffled, for her face was now completely obscured. "Can you read them out to me?"

Dr. Chipatti happily obliged and recited the titles of both books out loud. "Well, one is called *How to Keep Your Patient Alive Much Longer Than Hoped For by Using Correct Procedures During Operations.*"

"Oh," said Polly. "Well, I definitely need to take that one then."

Believing Polly to be slightly confused, Dr. Chipatti went on to explain that it was of the utmost importance to give the correct dose of anesthesia to ensure that the patient did not wake up halfway through surgery, but remained calm and perfectly still in a deep sleep.

"Oh," said Polly for a second time. For she was indeed most ignorant when it came to medical matters.

"Yes, but it is of equal importance to make sure that the patient's wound is kept clean of all germs. Otherwise, they will suffer from the most terrible infections, and these can be life-threatening, trust me," said the delightful doctor all-knowingly.

Polly looked visibly shocked at this new piece of information.

"Polly, many a patient who was on the way to a full recovery has faced terrible setbacks due to post-operative infections, for they can cause immense trauma and suffering."

"Oh, my word," muttered Polly despondently. For she was suddenly feeling quite overwhelmed and anxious by the responsibility she was taking on. And she began to secretly question if she was really up to the task ahead. "I had absolutely no idea!"

"I thought as much," said Dr. Chipatti, scratching his head. For he too was now most concerned for the teddy's welfare. "This is why it is of the utmost importance to tell you that failure to observe these procedures may well lead to post-traumatic stress, and I know you would not wish for your patient to go through such an ordeal," he stated, solemnly raising an eyebrow.

Polly acknowledged the seriousness of his lecture by catching his eye and giving a slow nod. For of all the concerns he had expressed, she felt she was most familiar with post-traumatic stress and indeed believed that she suffered from this particular ailment most of the time.

Polly stood quietly as she gave great thought to all the advice the good doctor shared with her, and she gave her word that she would take the greatest of care and diligently follow through his instructions to the letter.

Satisfied that she was taking things seriously, he then went on to read the other title. Its title was *Post-Operative Care in Order to Ensure a Most Pleasing and Happy Recovery.* The lovely doctor was most proud to be the author of this book as well.

Polly was extremely grateful to the doctor for all his time and help and offered to come by later to take his chinchilla out for a very long walk.

"That would be most kind of you, Polly," said the doctor as he opened the front door to allow her to leave. "But you may well find that you will be in surgery for a number of hours if all is to go well. So perhaps tomorrow would be a better day to call by."

Polly readily agreed. She then left the good doctor's house, staggering forwards then backwards like a merry sailor as she cautiously walked down the driveway, attempting to balance her very shaky pile of books.

"And remember to wash your hands thoroughly!" the doctor shouted more as an afterthought. "Good luck."

He closed the front door, smiling to himself as he then went about the task of making Cyril, his now ravenously hungry giraffe, his extremely late breakfast. Cyril was, of course, most delighted and licked his plate clean, for it was without a doubt his favorite meal—very hot and spicy Indian curry!

How Polly made it back to the castle that day we will never know. But being the very determined girl that she was, she not only made it back, but also managed the marathon task of climbing the stairs with her heavy load. She then went straight to the dormitory, where she proceeded to lay out all of the books on her bed. Freed from her heavy load, she then made herself comfortable on the bed, systematically flipping through each book, although not as thoroughly as she possibly should have. She reasoned that time was of the essence, and emergency surgery needed to happen sooner rather than later.

Having scrutinized each individual diagram from the many books that were laid out on the bed, she soon satisfied herself that she now had the general idea and more or less knew where to start and, more importantly, what to do. So with fresh, unwavering confidence, she hastily set about preparing a space on her bedroom locker, knowing that she would have to improvise and use this space as the makeshift operating table.

She placed a clean pillowcase over the surface of the locker before placing a long length of string as well as scissors, a sewing kit, a large roll of sticky tape, a silver-colored emery board, and a plastic bag all on the operating table.

"Perfect," she loudly declared.

POLLY BROWN

Then after rummaging through her bottom drawer, she found a small plastic heart-shaped pendant. Removing the chain from the pendant she placed the small heart on the table alongside the other surgical items. She now felt very optimistic, as she believed that she had all she required. With everything in place she gently put the teddy on the locker, taping him down with sticky tape so he would not move and ruin her delicate workmanship.

She then disappeared into the bathroom to scrub up, using her old toothbrush to get under her nails. Many times she had seen this procedure in her favorite hospital drama, *Emergency Ward 10*, so she felt most confident that she knew exactly what she was doing. Finally, with her sleeves rolled up to her elbows, she picked up a fresh toilet roll as well as a pair of bright yellow rubber gloves normally used for cleaning purposes and headed back to the dormitory.

Standing over her makeshift operating table, she perused the objects she had gathered up just in case she had forgotten any important item that might throw the whole delicate procedure into jeopardy. Thoroughly satisfied that everything was in place, she reached for the large yellow rubber gloves and put them on. The gloves were far too big, but Polly didn't care, for she believed they were very necessary to safeguard against serious infection. The pendant would act as a new heart, the string would replace the teddy's intestinal tract, and balled up toilet tissue would have to make do for his general lack of other organs. She then thoughtfully tied a scarf around the teddy's eyes so he would not have to watch the operation being done on himself. "I'm sorry, but I will have to remove this scarf later on when the time comes for your eye surgery," she dutifully informed him. Then, taking another scarf from her drawer, she bound it around the lower portion of her face to cover her mouth before raising her huge yellow rubber hands in the air for a final stretch. It was time to begin.

The whole procedure seemed to take hours, just as dear Dr. Chipatti had suggested it might. Finally, with the last stitch sewn to hold his eye back in place, she visibly relaxed, wiping her forehead just as they did in hospital dramas when the doctors, after many hours, finally came out of surgery. Polly then bandaged teddy up before placing him in a large polythene bag, thereby creating a germ-free protective barrier for him. She then tucked him up safely in her bed. Polly felt elated! For despite having been involved in a very lengthy and most delicate piece of surgery, she was now supremely optimistic that, as everything had gone according to plan with no unforeseen complications, the operation could be considered a complete success. Being a doctor was so rewarding and such fun. No wonder dear Dr. Chipatti was such a jolly, cheerful chap!

While the teddy went through the rather lengthy recovery process, Polly set about knitting him a bright green waistcoat, complete with a little breast pocket. "He might need that for a pocket watch," she thought to herself. She made the waistcoat, as she had enough foresight to realize that his scars would be visible to all if she did not cover him up. She reasoned he would not be too happy for this to be the case, for scars were indeed very private things not to be on full view to the general public. She knew from personal experience that people could be most unkind to anyone who looked different or had any disability. Polly herself continuously endured this treatment as a result of her wobbly eyes. She would not allow this bear who had already suffered so much to be put through any more needless pain. Of this she was certain. Taking a needle and some gold-colored thread, she set about sewing his name onto the little waistcoat.

A few days later, when she was satisfied that he was well enough to sit up in the bed, she removed the plastic bag, and after giving him a hug gently forced his arms into his green waistcoat, doing up the coat with the two gold buttons that she had borrowed from Aunt Mildred's large button jar. She then stood back to admire him. She was more than satisfied. In fact, she felt very proud of her workmanship. She then attached an old broken pocket watch to his waistcoat, slipping the watch face into the tiny pocket before reading his name out loud to see if she had spelled it correctly. Sewing his name on the front of the waistcoat had been of the utmost importance. It was just as important as the surgery itself, for quite rightly she did not wish for anybody to take him, mistakenly believing he was theirs.

As she stood back admiring her teddy, so handsome and regal in his new outfit, she decided he should be given a title to honor his bravery. Putting his life in her hands had been a very coura-geous thing to do! She also felt the title should reflect the generous assistance given to her by the wonderful Dr. Chipatti. She there-fore decided to privately knight him, Sir Eton Popadom de Chipatti. However, she preferred to keep things simple on a day-to-day basis and just call him Eton, keeping his full official title private and their little secret.

All this had taken place a long time ago, and because they had been through so much together, Polly had a special love for Eton as well as Langdon, her faded blue elephant. The three were insepa-rable. And now on this terribly sad day, she was about to part with him forever! She removed the stopwatch from his pocket, replacing it with a little folded-up note before giving him a quick kiss. She snugly placed him in her schoolbag and crept most stealthily out of the castle grounds, heading for the town on her secret mission to find the funeral parlor.

Chapter 11
FLUSTERED BY FEATHERS

*P*OLLY STOOD OUTSIDE the old building looking up. In the window there was a beautiful floral display, and in very large gold and black letters painted on the window were the words *Pinecoffin and Sons Funeral Directors*. Polly believed she must be at the right place, for it was the only place in town that dealt with such delicate matters. She also vaguely knew the proprietor's son, Jeremy Pinecoffin, from school since he was in the year above her. She summoned up courage and walked in.

Behind the desk sat a desperately thin woman with the brightest shot of frizzy red hair Polly had ever seen. Not only was she on the phone, but she was also rather cleverly filing her long nails at the same time, ensuring that the front desk was covered in a thin veil of dust from the nail filings. The receptionist continued talking, totally ignoring Polly's presence. Polly stood and patiently waited. She watched as the lady rested the receiver between her chin and shoulder and then unscrewed the top from a small glass bottle before applying cherry red paint to each individual nail on her long, bony hands.

Polly, who was standing on the other side of the desk, began to think that either Lady Rednails had not seen her or otherwise was deliberately ignoring her, and as she was now finding the lengthy wait rather tedious, she decided to loudly cough in the sincere hope of gaining her attention. It didn't work. So Polly coughed again, only this time with more enthusiasm, but still the talkative lady continued to chatter down the phone line about the film she had seen the night before, oblivious to the fact that she was being extremely rude. Polly eventually got so fed up with being ignored that she decided there was only one thing left to do. She went into a deliberate choking fit, coughing and spluttering to the point where it looked as though she was about to have a seizure. It worked. The lady stopped her incessant chatter and turned her head full circle to look over in Polly's direction before rather reluctantly muttering, something about having to go and quickly placing the receiver down.

"Well, hello there," she said somberly. "And what can I do to help you?" Polly stood up straight and returned the greeting before taking a deep breath. "My name is Polly Brown, and I am looking for my brother Thomas Brown."

"Well you won't find him in here, dear!" replied the receptionist.

"Oh dear," responded Polly rather glumly, feeling very defeated by the news.

"I'm sorry, my dear, but this place is for those who have departed to go on to higher things," she said, her eyes looking upwards as she spoke.

Polly joined her in looking up at the ceiling before shaking her head.

"Look, I don't think you quite understand. My brother has departed, and I need your help to give him something."

"Well, if he has, as you say, departed," she said lowering her voice to little more than a whisper, "then he certainly won't be wanting anything, dear," she responded in an all-knowing manner. "Well, nothing except your prayers to ask that he makes it to the right place," she said rather sanctimoniously, again turning her eyes upwards then downward towards the floor.

Feeling slightly puzzled and confused, Polly followed her eyes, wondering quite what she meant.

"Oh, I don't think he will be going down there," she winced, momentarily feeling quite insulted, "for he was a wonderful and very kind brother."

"That's what they all say once a relative has departed this earth," said the woman airily.

Polly refused to listen any further, preferring to delve into her schoolbag in search of Eton. "Please, please help me, for I have no one else I can turn to," she pleaded.

The lady with the red nails could see how upset Polly was and felt quite sorry for her. She shook her hands in front of her face before blowing on each individual nail to dry them further. She then picked up a large black book from the desk and, after blowing the filing dust from its hard-backed cover, she opened it up and finally began to address Polly's pressing situation.

"Right. Let me see," she said tartly as she proceeded to thumb through the black book. "Ah, yes. We do have a Thomas Brown booked in after all," she brightly announced as she thumbed down the pages. "Yes, he is due for burial on Tuesday at two o'clock at St. Winifreds Church. And I have to say it is a beautiful church as far as churches go. It's sixteenth century, I'll have you know, so it has quite a history." She then did another quick blow on her nails to encourage the red paint to dry as she moved away from her desk and came to stand in front of Polly. "Come to think of it, I do remember Thomas being brought here, and I also remember his guardians," she said, pulling a long face before moving closer and stooping down until she was eye to eye with Polly. "Oh yes, his guardians," she said, lowering her tone to almost a whisper and pursing her bright red lips. "Yes, I remember them all right! Not only did they decline to have any flowers for the funeral, the mean things, but they also ordered the cheapest coffin possible. Then they had the cheek to complain that this was more than they wished to pay! I won't tell you what I thought about that, for it is much too naughty for tender little ears as yours to hear."

Polly smiled, for as young as she was, she had some idea of what the receptionist might well have thought. The lady graciously held out her hand for Polly to take hold of and allow herself to be led down a long, narrow passageway and then down some steep steps into a basement room.

"Wait here a minute!" commanded the lady with the red nail polish that still had not finished drying.

Polly obeyed and stayed put. The lady then opened the door that was in front of them and shouted, "Here, Bert. I hope you haven't sealed up the coffin of that little boy. What's his name?" she said, quickly turning back to face Polly.

"Thomas," Polly interjected.

"Yes, his name's Thomas, Thomas Brown, and there's a young girl here who wishes to see him."

"Nope. The good news is that the coffin is still open, me darlin', as I haven't got round to closing it up yet," came the cheery but muffled reply from inside the room.

"That's great news," said the receptionist. "For this young lady wants you to put her teddy bear into his coffin. Something to do with helping him not to feel lonely anymore! So can you come and take the teddy from her? Understand it's more than my job's worth to allow her to enter the room?" she called out loudly.

Suddenly Bert appeared through the door, most anxious to be of assistance.

"Thank you so much," whispered Polly, her eyes moist with fresh tears. "And please, can you make sure that the little note in his waistcoat does not fall out," she pleaded.

"I will see to it that it doesn't, miss," said Bert, flashing Polly a compassionate smile that revealed more than a few missing teeth. Polly smiled back before trustingly handing Eton over to Bert. He then closed the door firmly behind him as he needed to get back to his busy work schedule.

She was just about to turn and leave when she heard a sudden commotion from behind the now firmly shut door. They were noises that suggested all was not well. Suddenly, and without warning, the door sprang open and out jumped Bert, covered from head to toe in white feathers. He struggled to speak. The lady with the long nails reeled back in horror.

"Bert, look at you! You look a right mess. What on earth is going on?" she demanded to know.

"I have no idea!" spluttered Bert as he attempted to spit out the feathers that had flown into his mouth. "All I did was remove the lid from the young lad's coffin, and without warning, thousands of feathers flew out of the box!"

Polly stood in stunned silence. Lady Lacquernails could only let out a small gasp, then cry, "What did you say, Bert?" for she believed she had not heard correctly.

Bert repeated himself, saying he had done absolutely nothing except open the box, and the feathers had sprung from nowhere, catching him completely unaware.

"Stay here, my dear," the lady with varnished nails crisply ordered as she placed a firm hand on Polly's shoulder and steered her to one side so that she would not be able to see into the room filled with coffins. Then slowly and tentatively, the lady walked through the open door to where Bert and his coffins resided, for she needed to see for herself just exactly what was going on.

As she stood peering into the open box, the air surrounding her was thick with white feathers still swirling and fluttering around. Without warning a feather came to rest on one of her fingernails, sticking to a freshly painted bright red nail. Then another one did the same, followed by another. She frantically attempted to pull the feathers off, but they refused to be removed.

"Some doves or pigeons must have flown in while we weren't looking," she anxiously suggested to Bert, her ruby lips quivering as she spoke. For she was beginning to feel quite disconcerted as well claustrophobic and wished to get back to the front desk as quickly as possible.

"I don't think so," answered Bert. "There are no windows down here, and I am very careful to close all the coffins very tightly when they are brought down. Besides, the pigeons around here aren't normally this white, and these feathers are white as white can be!"

As they stood for some time feeling exceedingly troubled and perplexed, they were unable to come up with one plausible explanation. For instance, could the pillow have accidentally burst open, spilling its contents? Or perhaps a bird had laid its eggs and now their chicks had hatched inside an open coffin? No, nothing they came up with seemed the slightest bit logical or worthy of another moment's consideration.

Suddenly they heard the sound of a car pulling up in the backyard. It was the owner of the funeral home, Mr. Pinecoffin.

"Quick, Bert, I will help you clear up this awful mess," said the receptionist. "If Mr. Pinecoffin sees the state of this room, both of us will be out of a job!"

Between the two of them they hurriedly scooped up handful after handful of the feathers that had come to settle on the floor, quickly throwing them back in the box. Luckily, Bert suddenly remembered the teddy and quickly placed him into the box, checking first that the little note was still in his waistcoat pocket. It was. After placing the lid firmly back down, he then used the full weight of his body to lean on the box, ensuring that it remained firmly shut. Satisfied, he then pulled out his hammer and some long nails from his deep overall pocket. After a few extremely loud and very hearty bangs, the box was, in his estimation, now thoroughly secured.

Bert breathed a deep sigh of relief, for now nobody would know anything of what had taken place and therefore his job was no longer on the line. The lady was also very grateful that everything was once again in order. She grabbed Polly's hand and rushed her back up the steps and towards the front door just as Mr. Pinecoffin was coming in through the back entrance. Giving Polly a quick peck on the cheek, she ushered her quickly out onto the street pavement before racing back into the reception area, for she needed to get back behind the desk as quickly as possible. She straightened her dress and attempted to brush off the last remaining feathers before hastily taking her seat and then pretending to be fully occupied with filing important letters.

"Good morning, Miss Lushblush," said Mr. Pinecoffin rather briskly as he popped his head through the doorway to acknowledge her.

Lady Rednails chose not to look up. Not because she was a rude employee, but because she was desperately trying hard to look busy, and was hiding both hands underneath a pile of old files. However, she did manage a smile in the direction of her boss before putting her head back down as she continued on with the pretense of being hard at work.

"It's been a very quiet day so far," commented Mr. Pinecoffin.

"Yes, sir, it most certainly has," replied Miss Lushblush.

With all perfunctory conversation out of the way, Mr. Pinecoffin hastily turned and went directly to his office to get on with business, for he was most behind with the bills.

"Whew! We made it," were the only words that came forth from the ruby red lips of the extremely anxious lady, for *quiet* was not the word she would have used to describe her unusual morning.

With her boss well out of sight she dropped the files down onto the desk and then raised both hands into the air to observe her fingernails. The feathers were still firmly attached! After rummaging around in her black bag, she finally produced a bottle of nail polish remover.

"This had better do the job," she whispered as she attempted to remove the remaining white feathers that were still fiercely glued to her very long red nails.

Polly felt happy as she walked up the hill towards home. She knew she would miss Eton so much, but she also felt that the sacrifice was worth it. She had given him to Thomas to save him from being lonely, and that felt good. Her thoughts turned to her little note. She hadn't really known what to write, but in the end, she felt that what she had written perfectly expressed her heart.

Dear Thomas,

I never got to say good-bye to you, and now you are gone. Oh, how I already miss you. I hope that you will be happier in heaven, for it is supposed to be a very nice place. If you find yourself getting bored, don't hesitate to ask God for some paper, paint, and brushes, because I am quite certain He will be as impressed with your pictures as I have always been, and I have heard He can be quite generous. While we're on the subject of generosity, could you give Him a little nudge and remind Him that He needs to pay a lot more attention to the starving children in Africa and India. Oh, and I mustn't forget Brazil, for they could really do with His help at the moment! And please could you emphasize that many will die of hunger and awful diseases if He does not act fast. Also speaking of food or, in this case, lack of it, please could you very casually slip into the conversation that

POLLY BROWN

all the children in the castle are struggling with hunger issues as well. You really must stress the urgency of this fact, Thomas, for He really does need to take His hands out of His pockets and tackle these serious problems A.S.A.P. By the way, Thomas, if God gets upset by you telling Him all this, please feel totally free to point the blame in my direction. I think that's only fair.

I promise to keep a beady eye on James, but also to never ever forget you. We will meet again, only next time we will be free from all the pain and heartache we have become so used to. When this happens I will sing songs and you can inspire me to write a lot of crazy poems. Of course, that's when we're not doing loads of cartwheels in fields filled with wild poppies. Remember the poppy field, Thomas? James will be with us, and we will then be reunited as a family. I wonder what James would like to do to pass the time away in heaven? I know! He can make loads of model airplanes and ships while you paint me even more of your lovely pictures of mountains and rivers. Until that day, remember that I will always love you. God bless, my most wonderful brother. P. S. I have left Eton with you so that you will not be lonely or cold. He has promised me that he will do all he can to keep you warm and snug at night, just the same as he did for me.

Oodles of Love,

Polly felt much lighter inside as she headed for home, feeling very pleased with her letter. She believed that for the first time in her life she had actually managed to write a letter that went straight to the heart of the matter. Hopefully it would make Thomas laugh when he read it, and maybe, just maybe, God also might smile as He took time out to read it! Polly hoped that might happen, especially as this letter was nowhere near as long as most of her writings.

Polly knew she had very little problem articulating herself. But she also knew that she had always struggled to keep specifically to a point. She always somehow managed to go around the houses, and it was always quite by accident. At school, when she was asked to write an essay, she was ready with her pen long before all the other children had even unzipped their pencil cases, and once she put pen to paper she was unstoppable. She would feel the flow and write till either her hand ached or she was ordered to stop. Even then, she was very reluctant to obey the command and put her pen down.

Polly cared little for grammar or correct punctuation. Her main ambition was to just get the story down on paper. Besides, she had always struggled with the whole concept of grammar and punctuation and felt truly incapable of understanding why it was necessary. She despaired of ever being able to master it. Mrs. O'Bleak, one of the part-time English teachers, likewise despaired of Polly's lack of grammar and at times became very cross with her, ordering her to take back the piece of work and sort it.

On one occasion she thought she had come up with the perfect solution to her little problem. No such luck! Mrs. O'Bleak had completely rejected her plan, declaring it to be most unacceptable. Her solution was to place a full stop after every ten words and systematically do the same thing over and over until she came to the end of her piece of work. Polly was as pleased as punch with her new method, and she was therefore very surprised that Mrs. O'Bleak did not feel likewise. Polly was forced to do it all again. According to Mrs. O'Bleak, her writing now made little or no sense at all. Polly had felt most disappointed, for she really had done her very best. She would have to try harder, for she hated upsetting anyone, including straight-laced Mrs. O'Bleak. If she was given a poem or story and asked to give a short summary to show she understood the piece, she found this just as impossible. She always ended up with her summary being at least ten times longer than the original story or poem, for she found she had so much to say.

However, there was one English lesson where she would look as blank as her white sheet of paper and spend the whole lesson unable to write a thing. This happened every first day of a new term when Mrs. O'Bleak would stand at her desk and say, "Now, children, I would like you all to write me an essay describing all the exciting things you have done during your school holidays. The child who writes the best story will, of course, collect another gold star."

Polly knew for certain that she could attain no gold star, for her story was simply that she never did much in the holidays. All she seemed to do was cook, clean, and scrub floors. When she wasn't doing these chores, she would walk for miles around the town through hills and fields. Apart from all the times she pressed her nose up to the window of the Copper Kettle, enviously watching on as families sat and ate together discussing their plans to tour the castle, there was little else to write about.

Polly knew it was quite out of the question to write the truth, because she had always been drilled to do otherwise by Uncle Boritz. "What happens in the castle stays in the castle." Therefore she was at a complete loss as to what precisely she was allowed to write. Polly would stare at the blank sheet of paper, feeling equally blank, for with no inspiration coursing through her mind and no poetic words flowing forth from her pen, she felt well-and-truly stuck. If telling the truth spelled trouble, as it had done so many times in the past, then lying made her feel equally uncomfortable.

Polly would look over in Gailey Gobbstopper's direction only to find Gailey having no such difficulty. She would be sitting, head down, writing away most furiously. When Gailey's essay was finally read to the class, it was a tale of pure fantasy. Its lengthy pages were filled with nonstop adventures that left most of the class feeling extremely envious, for they had only been to Spain for their holidays! Gailey Gobbstopper, however, had managed to sail the oceans, stopping off to visit the seven wonders of the world before heading home. All this miraculously in just five short weeks! During her vacation, she'd eaten endless mind-boggling breakfasts and sat at the captain's dining table devouring sumptuous gourmet cuisine every jolly evening. And when her feet finally touched dry land, she still found the time to go horse riding on one of her many ponies that she kept at the castle! Sadly, Gailey even believed that she was one of the Scumberry's own children, although the rest of the world knew different.

Mrs. O'Bleak never seemed to question Polly's unusual lack of written work on these occasions or, for that matter, Gailey's extensive, fast-paced, over-the-top summer holiday program of events. Something obviously did not add up as they both lived under the same roof, yet she chose to ignore this glaring difference. Polly hated the first day back at school more than any other day.

Bringing her thoughts back to the present, Polly continued her walk home from the funeral home, smiling to herself, for she deemed that her little expedition had been more successful than she could ever have hoped for. She had come away knowing everything she needed to know regarding her brother's funeral, and she had not even had to ask or beg for them. The nice lady had volunteered all the necessary details, such as time and date and where the service was to be held. This all served to make Polly feel very delighted, as well as thoroughly satisfied with her outing.

She sang to herself as she wandered home, openly declaring, "Thomas will have flowers on Tuesday. Where from? I have no idea, but he will have flowers and lots of them!"

She continued singing right up to the front door of the castle. Her only problem now was how to make it to the funeral without Uncle Boritz and Aunt Mildred ever finding out!

She walked inside and was halfway up the stairs when she was greeted by Bertha Banoffee and Tommy Pulleyblank.

"You're in trouble again!" stated Bertha, pulling an extremely childish face. "They want you in their study immediately."

Polly said nothing. She just shrugged her shoulders with seeming indifference, dropped her schoolbag by the bottom of the stairs, and turned on her heels to make her way toward the study. Having arrived outside the study door, she timidly knocked, expecting to hear a voice from the other side call out for her to enter. But when no such command came, she knocked on the door again, only this time harder. Still she heard nothing. She then slowly pushed open the door and, with great fear and trepidation, cautiously entered the study. She was very surprised to discover that the room was empty. There was no sign of either guardian.

Polly stood with hands behind her back, staring at the ceiling for a few minutes before giving herself permission to look around the room. She scanned the rows of thick, dusty books lining the many shelves of the large oak bookcases. Before long, her eyes hit Uncle Boritz's untidy desk and then his old fashioned typewriter that still had a sheet of white paper stuck in the machine. At first she ignored it, choosing to turn her attention to the grandfather clock with its large ornate face. Still neither of her guardians appeared. Her eyes went back to the typewriter, and it seemed to be inviting her to move closer. Polly inwardly rebuked herself for even giving thought to reading someone else's private and most personal mail, for it was not something she had ever done before. Yet, as she stood there alone waiting for her guardians, the piece of paper stuck in the typewriter became more and more irresistible with every minute that ticked by.

Eventually, curiosity got the better of her, and she wandered around the desk and stood before the old typewriter, her eyes glancing down at the letter. It was addressed for the attention of Miss Dogsbody, care of the social services. It was also incorrectly dated. It should have read the seventeenth of May; instead it read the seventeenth of October. The letter was five months ahead of itself! What on earth was going on? Perplexed by the incorrect dating on the letter, Polly allowed her curiosity to run away with her, and she proceeded to read the letter.

Dear Miss Dogsbody,

We regret to inform you that Thomas Brown has disappeared, and with him some £20 of our hard-earned money. After much investigation into his whereabouts, it appears that for a long time Thomas had the somewhat daft idea of going to America in search of his real father. All the children were thoroughly interviewed by us, and of those children that Thomas had confided in all told us the exact same story. It appears that Thomas was very determined to go ahead with his plan in spite of their efforts to dissuade him. As the children had no desire to get Thomas into trouble, none of them thought to report their concerns to us, for they just saw this as another of Thomas's pie-in-the-sky dreams that would, like the rest of his little fantasies, amount to nothing, particularly as he had no way of financing this little adventure. That is, until he stole our money, for which the children are most upset as it will mean serious temporary cutbacks in all their wonderful activities.

There is therefore no need for you to come and pay us a visit as there is very little more that we can tell you at present, although we assure you that we will not rest until we have exhausted all avenues in our desperate bid to find Thomas and bring him back safely into the bosom of our big and most wonderful family.

I think you will wish to agree with me that it is the responsibility of your department to reimburse us with £20 to cover our loss. I am certain this is not the sort of scandal the social services would want the general public to get wind of, as it would do much to damage your department's otherwise faultless record. I am therefore sure you would wish us to stay well away from being investigated about a missing boy and our missing money. I have to point out that this would in fact be quite difficult, as Mellbury Clifftop of the Daily Times is not only a close friend of ours, but has an extraordinary knack of sniffing out newsworthy stories. Therefore I cannot guarantee that one or more of the children will not accidentally let slip that Thomas is to date still missing. Of course we will do all in our power to prevent such a thing from happening.

We think that until Thomas is found alive and well (probably living it up in America or Canada at our expense), your department should continue with the payments for his board and lodging as he still has a bed here, ready for when he finally returns safely to the nest. Assuring you of our continued care of all the delightful children we are so fortunate to take care of.

Yours sincerely,

Mr. Scumberry

Mr. Scumberry, Dop. Dop. Dip. Hon. B.C.S.M.E.C.C. (British and Colonial Standards of Most Excellent Child Care)

Having reached the end of the letter, Polly started to shake from head to toe, feeling instantly very nauseated to the very pit of her stomach. How could Uncle Boritz write such terrible lies?

As usual, she was completely powerless to do anything. Her heart filled with despair as she tried to comprehend the enormity of the deceit that had just been revealed as a direct result of reading the letter. How on earth could Thomas ever be found, when he had passed from this life and was about to be buried? She was also very distressed that they were ruining her beloved brother's character by suggesting he had stolen this incredible sum of money. She felt certain that Miss Dogsbody and all her department would fail to make any sort of investigation in an effort to find out the truth. After all was said and done, they too, like everyone else, were completely besotted with both her guardian angels. The letter surely would be read, stamped with an official rubber stamp, then filed away forever in some large, dingy warehouse, never to see the light of day again.

Polly felt very angry with this group of people who were meant to care for them. She wondered where it would all end. In the case of her guardians, she thought she knew. Their ability to deceive all those around them—the school, the church, even the social services—might not even end when they finally departed this earth. She believed there was the distinct possibility that some bright spark would have the idea of building a memorial in their honor. Or worse, they would be declared by the church to be saints. Then they would officially become known as Saint Mildred and Saint Boritz. Just the thought of such an event ever happening made her squirm.

Suddenly Polly thought she heard footsteps. She wasted no time and raced from behind the desk and sat down on a chair as far away from Uncle Boritz's desk as possible. The last thing she wanted was for her guardians to discover that she had taken a sneaky peek at their letter. Aunt Mildred came in first and Uncle Boritz followed close behind. Following in their footsteps and the last to enter was Pitstop, his teeth exposed as he glanced Polly's way. They gave no explanation for their absence from the office, preferring to launch into their usual tirade of accusations.

"And where have you been, young lady?" Aunt Mildred demanded to know. "We have been searching all over the castle and its grounds in our endeavor to find you."

Polly remained silent, for she had no intention of telling either of them about her little secret outing.

"You know full well that you are confined to the castle when you are on R.O.P.E.," stated Uncle Boritz very angrily. "You are really pushing my patience to the limit, you little wretch. And for all your impudence, rest assured we will be doubling your workload."

"Oh, good," said Aunt Mildred, giving a small but sinister smile before adding her twopence worth. "I have to say, Polly, we have been most fortunate in being able to dispense with both Mrs. Saddlebag and Mrs. Grimespot, the part-time cleaners. For with you to take their place and do all the chores, we simply have no further need of them!"

Polly did not need to be told any of this, for she had already worked things out for herself a long time ago, and that fact was that her guardians loved saving their money for the finer things of life. For just as making money sent their hearts of stone into a positive spin, so did hoarding it and spending it on little lavish treats. So if Polly could save them money, all was well. She believed this was the main reason behind her continually being placed on R.O.P.E., as they conjured up reason after reason to keep her hard at work.

Polly was not afraid of all the hard work, for she did every task conscientiously, but she was more than afraid of losing her mind, as week after week she was kept a virtual prisoner within the castle walls. She often wondered how much more she could endure before she really did become mentally unbalanced, intensifying her very real fear of going insane.

Chapter 12
IT IS GOOD TO BE A CRACKED POT

*A*s HER GUARDIANS appeared to have much on their minds, Polly was spared the usual lengthy sermon and was quickly dismissed from their sight. They ordered her to get back to work, for the kitchen floor needed her attention. As she got down on her hands and knees with her pail and hard brush to begin the task of scrubbing she could hear the wind picking up outside. It was not long before it was positively howling. Soon it began to thunder, and this was closely followed by violent lightning that tore down from the heavens, lighting up the whole sky with its brilliance.

Polly was grateful to be safely indoors, for she had always been afraid of thunder and lightning. She knew she still had the shoes to clean before she could go and hide under the covers, and this meant going down into the dark and freezing basement. Later that same evening, as she set about doing the final chore of the day, she found it impossible to stay warm. She frantically set about polishing the long rows of shoes on her own. Cecilia had long gone home.

The light in the dimly lit room kept dimming and then flashing brightly, causing her to shudder with fear as she stood alone before the long rows of shoes. Polly was convinced that the reason she was colder than usual was because the room temperature had dropped to well below zero, so she worked faster than ever in the hope of preventing her chapped hands from becoming number than they already were.

She had not been tackling the chore very long when there was a knock on the back door of the basement. Polly was mystified as to who could be behind the door, for all visitors normally came to the front door of the castle. Therefore, it was with much caution that she dropped what she was doing and slowly made her way towards the door.

"Who's there?" she called out, her shaky voice betraying her underlying fear and apprehension.

The knock got louder, and Polly's hands began to shake as she reached for the bolt and cried out for a second time, urgently wishing to know who was on the other side.

"Polly, it's me, Ralph. Please let me in," came the muffled voice from the other side of the heavily bolted door. Polly quickly unbolted the creaky door to allow him to come in from the cold.

"Ralph," she delightfully cried, "It's really lovely to see you, but what on earth are you doing here at this very late hour?"

"I've come to see you, Polly," he said with a grin.

"Well, you're quite out of luck if you're hungry, Ralph, for I can't make you the usual," she responded apologetically. "The kitchen is now locked up and is therefore out of bounds."

"That's perfectly fine with me, Polly," Ralph replied, giving his belly a quick pat. "I've already eaten. Hodgekiss told me about this great little fish and chip shop where they scoop out all the batter into a bag before showering it with salt and vinegar. And all this for just threepence," he said with a big grin lighting up his face. "I don't have to tell you, but it's a most wonderful find. Hodgekiss and I have been eating there regularly! In fact I do believe it has become our local!"

"You lily-livered weasels!" cried Polly, instantly feeling upset and exasperated with the two of them.

All thoughts of being frozen and fearful were instantly banished as poor Polly stood there fuming! First they sneakily sabotage her cake shop, and now her local fish and chip shop. "They certainly have a lot of cheek," thought a now-furious Polly. She took in a deep breath and picked up another shoe from the row, which she then began to frantically brush in an effort to dispel her sense of outrage towards both men. She clenched her teeth lest anything too hasty or unkind should slip out.

"Cat got your tongue, Polly?" Ralph asked good-humoredly.

It Is Good to Be a Cracked Pot

Polly ignored him, feverishly continuing to brush the shoe she was holding in her hand.

"Come on, Polly. Don't hold out on me. Looking so mad and angry doesn't suit you. Really, it doesn't," he said playfully.

Polly still continued brushing away at the same shoe, ignoring Ralph completely.

"If you brush that shoe any harder, before long there will be a nice hole in the toe, and then you can give them to Hodgekiss," Ralph suggested with another grin.

"Speaking of Hodgekiss, how is he doing?" Polly asked, her voice strained as she continued to stare down at the shoe, still waiting for her anger to dissolve. "He promised to come and visit me and yet I have neither seen nor heard from him for quite some time! Now I get to hear that he has been visiting my fish and chip shop regularly. How could he be so inconsiderate?" she snapped.

"Hodgekiss is doing just fine, Polly. At present he's back in Piadora," Ralph cheerily replied.

"I bet he is," Polly angrily thought to herself. "Fine and fat on my stale cakes and chip batter! What rotten little scoundrels they have turned out to be!" Polly thought, grimacing as she considered how taken in by them both she had been.

"Well, I hope the weather is nice for him in Piadora," she commented, slightly tongue in cheek.

"From what he has told me, the weather is absolutely perfect. But then it always is," Ralph chirpily replied. "I really must take some time off and go to Piadora, for I'm certain that I must be due a break," he sighed.

"Oh, come on," said Polly, no longer able to conceal her irritation. "Surely you don't really expect me to believe your far-fetched tales about the kingdom of Piadora, along with your delusions about the Hubber Blubber and the Hoolie Koolie tree. Please tell me that it really is all just make-believe."

Ralph stopped grinning.

"I assure you, Polly, Piadora most certainly does exist. And as for the Hubber Blubber and the Hoolie Koolie tree, they are most real too," he said sternly, pretending to be offended.

Polly did not know whether to laugh or cry, so she settled for the latter. "Ralph," she cried through a mist of tears. "Ralph, are you as mad as Hodgekiss?"

Ralph looked offended. "I assure you that I am neither mad nor crazy, for I have spent much of my time in the kingdom of Piadora, and I find it quite offensive that you should think I would lie about such things."

Polly quickly apologized, for she reminded herself that Hodgekiss had swiftly pulled her up for making judgments on others based on how they appeared.

Ralph accepted Polly's apology and went on to ask how Thomas was doing.

"I have some medicine for him," he said brightly, taking a small vial out from his overcoat pocket.

"Don't bother!" responded Polly rather abruptly, for, in truth, she had suddenly become most sad at being reminded of her beloved brother Thomas and how much he had suffered.

"Don't be silly, Polly," said Ralph. "This medicine has come all the way from Piadora especially for Thomas. Here, take it," he said offering her a small vial full of purplish liquid.

"No, thank you, Ralph. I really have no need of it and neither does Thomas. He died last week." Polly's voice trailed off as she struggled to find the right words to continue. "So please thank Hodgekiss for going to so much effort on Thomas's behalf, but his help has come far too late to save him."

Her eyes brimmed with fresh tears, and she felt absolutely wretched. Ralph remained conspicuously silent as he allowed Polly the breathing space to continue pouring out all her frustration, for he could see she was nearing breaking point.

"I have to be honest when I say I really trusted Hodgekiss to help us, Ralph. I feel terribly let down by him, for he promised me he would do all he could for us," she sniffed. Her voice was also beginning to crack, but she needed to talk to get it all of her chest. "And as you might well be aware, we have nobody in the world who cares a jot or tittle about us, and that's no word of a lie. So I was really counting on him, and now it is too late, for Thomas has well-and-truly gone." Polly began to tremble as she talked on. "His funeral is on Tuesday, and I have been told by my guardians that I am not even allowed to attend it! Oh, how I hate them!"

Ralph put his arm around Polly in an attempt to comfort her. Polly was touched by his gesture, but thought that no amount of comfort would remove this huge mountain of pain that was growing daily inside her, for she was so angry and hurt by just about everything in life. Ralph clearly observed that she was indeed suffering from a broken and crushed spirit and that she could hardly take any more.

"Polly, hate is a most terrible thing. It is a disease that most deceitfully and very stealthily gnaws away the marrow from our bones. It works silently and effectively. One moment you feel good about being angry and the hate feels well-deserved. However, it will eventually turn and ravage you, for that is its nature. It will bring you nothing but misery and unhappiness, and when it has finally done its work, it strikes yet another deadly blow."

"Oh, and what might that be?" Polly angrily asked through her vale of tears.

"Disease and death, to be precise," Ralph replied. "Oh yes, hate is such an ugly thing, Polly. It shrouds the mind and soul and ultimately takes over the body, and I have to strongly suggest that I feel you do not wear it well," he added in a soft voice, brimming over with deep compassion. "For you were made for higher things."

"Well, I really don't care about so-called higher things. I just want to go and be with Thomas," she cried defensively. "For life has brought me nothing but pain and sorrow, and no matter how hard I try, I feel powerless to change anything. I am a mess, a mistake, a monster, and a freak!" she cried.

"Polly, stop right there! Not only is all this untrue, but you are rushing headlong into a real pity party, and this will do you no good at all."

"Don't tell me what to do, Ralph, for I'm so sick of obeying everyone else's orders. If I want a pity party, then I'll have one. I am, after all, a useless mess, or to use my uncle's words, a blithering idiot, doomed to failure in just about everything I do."

"Polly, I will leave this instant if you continue to judge yourself so harshly. For you are none of these things. Yes, it is true to say there is a lot of mess in your life, but it's a mess that you did not create. I can also tell you with much authority that whatsoever a man thinks in his heart, then that he will be. So you urgently need to pay some attention to how you see yourself and how you speak. Only you have the power to change that."

Polly remained dumbstruck as the anger continued to rise within her. Ralph welcomed her silence, because it meant he could still continue to give her advice that, if listened to, might eventually help her.

"Look, Polly, I know you feel very battered and bruised at this moment in time, but just hear me out. There is an old adage that you need to hear, like it or not. 'He that hath no rule over his own spirit and emotions is like a city that is broken down and without walls.'"

"Precisely what are you getting at?" Polly seethed.

"Well, the sad truth is that you need to work on yourself, for you are like a wounded animal in a corner, fighting for your life. You feel both afraid and vulnerable, and this allows others to plunder then trample all over you, leaving you crushed and feeling pretty hopeless."

Listening to all this information was just too much for Polly's ears, and she soon felt very charged up. How dare this rather presumptuous, scraggy vagrant—a loser who hardly knew her—presume he could lecture her on how to change her life!

"Ralph, you should try writing a self-help book, for it would probably be a bestseller," she said tongue in cheek. "Not that I would read it, for I already have enough of your great wisdom to contend with," she chided. "Then perhaps you could afford to take baths and buy some deodorant, you stupid, pompous scallywag." She was now feeling very rattled.

Ralph chose to remain silent, allowing her derisory insults to wash off his back. Even his silence seemed to upset her further, as she mistakenly saw even this as an act of such great piousness. So she continued to pour out her wrath.

"Yes, Ralph, you're obviously a man of great wisdom. So perhaps you should consider a new career helping others with your amazing insights into life and the universe. And then maybe, just maybe, you could then buy yourself a smart suit," she contemptuously spat in his direction. "Then not only will we be able to see how refined you truly are, but also that you too were born for higher things in life. Until then, you certainly have no right to lecture me on anything!"

With Polly clean out of words, the room fell into a deathly hush. Polly instantly felt ashamed and embarrassed by her very hurtful outburst. Ralph remained standing in complete silence as he searched his mind for the right words to give this traumatized young maiden some comfort and hope in her tragically difficult situation. In truth, he wanted to weep for her and found it difficult not to break down, for he was feeling the full impact of her pain.

Polly pretty soon found herself feeling very awkward and uncomfortable with the long drawn-out silence. So she decided to pick up from where she had left off, only this time in a more humble and gracious manner.

"Let's face it, Ralph," Polly wept, "I am nothing but a crackpot!"

"Crackpot is good, Polly," replied Ralph with a relaxed, gentle smile.

"Good!" exclaimed Polly. "How on earth can a crackpot be good?"

Ralph paused for a moment before telling her a most ancient story: "Listen to me, Polly," he softly ordered.

Polly responded by making a face, but she obeyed, showing some interest, albeit resignedly.

"There once was a man who had to travel many miles to get down to the river and fetch water. On each shoulder he carried a pot. One pot was perfect, with no visible defects."

"You mean no cracks?" interrupted Polly.

"Yes, that's precisely what I mean," Ralph replied.

"The other pot was full of cracks. Each day the man walked miles to the river and, upon arriving at the waters edge, he filled both pots full to the brim with water. As he traveled home, the cracked pot leaked continuously. The master therefore had to make many more trips than he should have, due to the cracked pot. One day the cracked pot turned to its master saying, 'Oh master, I am so sorry that I am such a burden on you. For if it wasn't for me and all my awful cracks, you would have no need to travel so many times to the river to collect extra water.'

"The master turned to the cracked pot and smiled. 'I know you are cracked, but to me you are just perfect.'

"The cracked pot was now very confused. The master then turned to the cracked pot and said. 'Look down at the dusty path that we travel each day and you will see that on your side are the most beautiful flowers, and it is you that waters them each day. Nothing delights me more than to see those beautiful flowers, for it makes my journey into something so magically wonderful and special.'"

Polly made another face, this time to convey that she was not entirely convinced. "Nice story, Ralph, but it won't work. For at the end of a day a cracked pot is a useless vessel that should be thrown away and then replaced by something better."

"Oh, Polly, don't throw the baby out with the bathwater. Yes, it is true that you have many cracks in your pot—I mean life! But as a result, you have a wonderful ability to give yourself to others. You see things that others are unable to see, and you think nothing of going the extra mile to help out wherever you can. This is truly a great gift, Polly, but you seem unable or unprepared to acknowledge this truth." He momentarily paused, for he knew by the look on her face she was still not convinced.

"Polly, do you remember the evening of the Girl Guides awards presentation?"

"Oh, great. You had to bring that up now!" thought Polly, feeling quite furious. For the last thing she wished to do was remember something she had spent a considerable length of time trying hard to forget!

"If I am right, and I nearly always am," said Ralph slightly tongue in cheek, "you, Polly, my dear, received the award for the best Girl Guide of the year!"

Ralph was correct. Polly, who had never received an award for anything, was innocently sitting alongside all the other girl guides. As far as she was aware the ceremony was over and all the awards had been given out. They had gone to people like Cynthia Molespot for her most brilliant cello performance, and to Angela Kettledrum for having collected all three cookery badges. Cassandra duPlantis never failed to get the most prestigious award for her most excellent contributions on just about every camping expedition that had ever taken place in the universe. The girls who received the awards exceeded everybody's expectations in just about everything they did. Polly had not even hoped for an award, for she knew that such honor was well beyond her reach.

Suddenly, the organizer announced that they had created a special award, and with it, a new badge. And this was to be given to the girl who had shown herself to be worthy of the title "best Girl Guide of the year." Polly was only half listening, as the lady standing at the microphone told one story after another of some unknown young girl who had continuously put herself out to help others. The girls all sat in nail-biting trepidation, anxiously waiting to know who the winner of this new badge was. Finally it was announced.

"This award goes to Polly Brown." Polly heard her name but did not respond. "Will Polly Brown please come forward?" said the lady with the microphone, standing behind the high podium.

Still Polly refused to come forward. This was not because Polly was being stubborn—quite the contrary. It was because no one had ever given her any type of award before. All her seemingly heroic deeds that they saw as so wonderful were, to Polly, her usual way of life. She had no choice but to respond if she thought she could do anything to help anybody. It was part of her nature. She certainly did not think that this deserved being given any sort of high praise or accolade!

Polly had to be pushed forward that evening by the other Girl Guides, who were standing by her side.

"Polly, it's *you* they are talking about," they insisted.

She still stood glued to the spot.

"Polly, please go up and receive the jolly award or we'll be here all night," they pleaded.

Polly was still most reluctant to move. It took the girls on either side of her to give her an almighty shove that forced her out of the line. Only then did she move forward towards the podium. Even as she walked towards the lady with the microphone she hesitated, for she truly expected that they would burst out laughing and then cry out: "Only joking, ha ha." Or worse still, for the lady at the front to look embarrassed and say "So sorry, dear!" as she ever so slowly thumbed down her list, suddenly stopping to say, "I can't find it, dear! No, I've checked and your name is not on here. So see here, it wasn't your name I called out; it was actually Polly Brownslow. So, if you'd be kind enough to return to your seat, dear, I think that would be best, don't you?"

Polly would then have turned scarlet, and wished for the end of the world to take place instantly, for she loathed the awful feelings humiliation brought to her soul. As she stepped out to receive the award, unlike the other girls she did not wallow or glory in her twenty seconds of fame. Polly knew only great fear as she shook the lady's hand and accepted the award. For all these reasons Polly would have much preferred that particular night to stay well out of their conversation!

Polly was getting really behind with the shoe polishing and decided that she should ask Ralph to go.

"Pitstop will be coming here to sleep for the night, Ralph," she said, fearful for his safety. "And if Uncle Boritz finds I have not finished the shoes, or worse still, discovers I am talking to someone, I will be in real trouble. So please go now."

"Look, Polly," replied Ralph. "Your so-called uncle is fast asleep, and so, for that matter, is Pitstop." Polly looked slightly puzzled. "How on earth do you know that, Ralph?" she asked. Ralph smiled. "Let's just say it was with a little help from a tranquilizer."

"What? Both of them?" questioned Polly, feeling shocked as well as amused.

"Yes, both of them," Ralph sheepishly replied. Polly laughed and turned to Ralph, looking suitably concerned.

"Oh, Ralph, how could you? Pills are not good for you. You must surely know that," she giggled.

"Ah yes, dear Polly," he said. "But these were no ordinary pills. Oh, no! These were made from the sap of the Hoolie Koolie tree, and they are guaranteed to keep them fast asleep for the whole night and probably much of tomorrow as well!"

Polly laughed. "Is there any condition the sap of the Hoolie Koolie and Hubber Blubber trees won't fix?" she asked, attempting to be serious.

"Not as far as I know!" Ralph replied with a straight face.

Polly accepted Ralph's help, and they carried on talking as they finished polishing the rows of lined-up shoes. Polly thought it was a much more pleasant task with Ralph than with dear Cecilia Crabtree. Ralph's undesirable smell seemed on this occasion more bearable, and Polly deemed it to be far more preferable than having to constantly duck the fountains of spittle Cecilia showered upon her.

"How did you like the last book?" Ralph asked.

"Well, I don't think it will come as any surprise to you, Ralph, but just like the previous one I have to admit that I didn't like it very much. Oh, don't get me wrong, the story's great, but, yet again, it made my sadness feel worse than ever," she sniffed. "Yes, it was just as painful to read as the one about the ugly duckling. Let's face it, Ralph; they are wonderful fairy tales. But that's the point. At the end of the day they are tales made up by fairies for fairies."

Ralph raised an eyebrow. "Oh, Polly. We all have to deal with secret heartache and disappointment, and you could say that fairy tales give us all hope."

"OK, but the point I'm really trying to make is they all end happily ever after, and I know that life just isn't like that."

Ralph agreed. "Hodgekiss told me you'd say that," he mused. "You're right, Polly. They are at the end of the day just fairy tales. But let me tell you, there is an ancient book filled with stories of ordinary people just like you and me. They were nobodies with no hope and no future, but they had dreams and they followed after them until they took hold of them.

"Oh, right," said Polly sullenly. "And who precisely are these people? And more importantly, where can I find this so-called ancient book?"

"First things first, Polly," said Ralph. "One of the many stories is about a young shepherd boy who is the least in his family. He gets to kill a giant and eventually becomes a king."

"Well, then that counts me out as usual, for I have no strength at all," she mournfully stated, flexing her arm at the same time. "Go on, Ralph. Have a good feel, and you will see for yourself that there's not a hint of a measly muscle anywhere. Truth is, I'm really very puny."

"Oh, Polly! The shepherd boy was not strong," laughed Ralph. "No, quite the contrary. He was puny too! They put the heavy armor on him, and he pretty soon discovered that he could not move a muscle, for he was so weighed down. Eventually he declined all offers of protective clothing, preferring to go into battle in the clothes he stood up in. Polly, I have to tell you that there was not one soldier on the battlefield that believed this young boy could kill the giant, but none of them wanted to volunteer for the job either, so they were left with no choice but to let him have a go. If the young boy had listened to their opinions, there is little doubt that he would have changed his mind. But he refused to listen to anything but what his heart told him, and that was that he had been chosen to defeat this most terrible giant, who, I might add, had never known defeat. When the giant saw his opponent was nothing more than a little whippersnapper, he could not help but burst into fits of laughter, shouting out; 'Ooh stop, you're really scaring me,' whilst clutching hold of his belly to roar, 'You'll soon be nothing but mincemeat in my burger bun.'

"While the whole army of Israel watched on, shaking and scared witless by the giant Goliath and his threats, the young David, without any of the usual weapons at his disposal, marched out onto the battlefield. Reaching into his pouch of smooth pebbles, he placed one in his sling. He then bravely stood before his terrifying opponent, sized him up, sent up a prayer, and took aim. The pebble flew through the air at ninety miles an hour before smashing through Goliath's forehead like a bullet. Goliath collapsed onto his knees before crashing nose-first into the dust."

"Fantastic," remarked Polly.

"A miracle," commented Ralph. "David then used the giant's own sword to cut off his head, just for good measure."

"I bet that was to make sure he was really dead," added Polly with a shudder, getting very carried away with the grim and gory details of the story as she pictured the giant's messy brain matter scattered across the battlefield.

"Yes, I'm sure it wasn't a pretty sight," admitted Ralph.

"Pretty gruesome, I would imagine," Polly replied with a small smile, lighting up her face.

"Precisely. And Polly, I would imagine there was not one Israelite whose jaw did not drop down to his knees with sheer disbelief at what they had witnessed before their very eyes. Also try and imagine the panic of Goliath's army. They decided to make a very hasty retreat."

Polly grinned and thanked Ralph for sharing this story of hope with her. Ralph gave a deep sigh as he admitted, "I just love that story. It is indeed one of my favorites."

"All right. You've mentioned one. Now give me another example," ordered Polly. Ralph kindly obliged.

"Well, another accurately-recorded tale is of an equally young man named Joseph. This young boy was a dreamer, and just like you, Polly, he dreamed big. As a result, all his brothers hated him."

"That's just like me with the other children in this castle," cried Polly excitedly.

"Yes," said Ralph. "And in Joseph's case the brothers plotted to kill him."

"They'd kill me too if they could get away with it!" Polly insisted.

"I'm sure they would," Ralph thought to himself. "Anyway, after many terrible trials, Joseph became the second most important person in the land. And, Polly, the icing on the cake was that he got to control the food storehouse for the whole land of Egypt. Now tell me, how amazing is that!"

Ralph now had Polly's undivided attention. "Yes! Joseph was able to eat like a king and distribute whatever food he fancied, seven days a week, three hundred sixty-five days of the year!" Ralph informed her, licking his lips with great relish. "He could also be as generous as he wished to whomever he wanted to help. Now that's powerful stuff, don't you think?"

Polly stood in stunned silence, her mind working overtime. Was Ralph trying to hint that maybe something as truly amazing might possibly happen to her one day? Did it mean that there was a real possibility that one day she could find herself becoming England's prime minister, and thereby control the country's wealth? That would surely mean she had control over all the food being transported in and out of the country.

"Oh, wow!" Polly gasped, hardly able to contain her excitement as her irrepressible imagination ran riot.

She knew she'd have no problem accepting the job when it was offered to her. And if not prime minister of England, then how about minister for agriculture, for she figured that post surely had to involve food. Finally she decided that if none of those positions were available, she would very happily settle for becoming the new owner of the Copper Kettle tearoom. She would change the name to Polly's Pantry Royal Tearoom, and then she would do the most wonderful prince and princess birthday parties. She would also serve the finest Hodgekiss pies, Piadora puddings, pizzani lasagnas, and so on. Oh, not forgetting wonderful sandwiches, only this time with freshly baked bread. Polly's mouth began to water just thinking about the endless possibilities that owning the tearoom would bring.

"Yes," she thought rather excitedly, "all the food would be made and served up with ladles of love." Polly shook her head as if to tell herself to wake up and stop daydreaming, for none of this would or could possibly ever happen to a pathetic little wretch such as Polly Brown.

Ralph smiled, for he knew her thoughts. "Polly, the story of Joseph is real. It is a true account of historical events that happened to a real man in a real place, and it is recorded in this most ancient of books. And although I cannot predict what your future holds, I can say that if you dare to have faith, then anything is possible. Yes, Polly, anything!"

Polly still remained absolutely silent. She was not convinced by his stories, although she had little choice but to conclude that if they were true then they were pretty amazing.

"Polly, people who insist on playing it safe rarely fulfill their dreams. For it takes great persistence and courage to follow after them."

She was impressed with Ralph's thought-provoking insights, but certainly not ready to back down. As she could talk the hind legs off the back of a donkey, she determined that she wasn't finished yet!

"Well, that's all well and good, Ralph, but if, like me, you lived in an orphanage that feels more like a prison, what then?"

"Well, believe it or not, Polly, even that is covered in this most ancient of books. For there was a whole nation of people called the Israelites, and these dear people lived in bondage and slavery in a place called Egypt under a tyrant king who went by the name of Pharaoh. Every day brought them more pain and affliction."

"Oh, I know what that's like," interrupted Polly.

"Then one day they were released from their years of slavery," continued Ralph, most determined to finish his story.

"At first they were delighted with their newfound freedom. But after spending years in the desert going around and around in circles, they became very fed up. The reason they were stuck in the desert so long was simply because they were afraid to go and take the land they had been promised. Oh, they had seen miracles all right. Even getting out from under Pharaoh's feet had been against all the odds. But in truth they carried all their old bondages, or rather baggage, with them," he said, slowly shaking his head.

"Ralph, what was their baggage?" Polly asked, for she was most curious to know all. "I mean, if I had a long journey ahead of me, I would never take my bed or my bedside locker with me. And I would certainly leave the curtains for the next people. And there would be no point whatsoever in taking the fridge, for without electricity it would never work properly, would it Ralph?"

Ralph smiled a smile of light despair. "Well, Polly, I'm not actually referring to physical items such as household furniture. No, I am referring to the affairs of the heart and mind. It was undoubtedly all the fear and failure of the past that troubled and gripped them like a vise, refusing to let go. They were unable to abandon these chains of the mind that tied them down and zapped their courage. So, having heard that giants were occupying the land they were heading for, they sat down and accepted defeat as their lot in life. Polly, can you believe it? Fear actually prevented them from fulfilling their dream of living in a new land flowing with milk and honey!"

When Polly heard the word *milk*, she couldn't help interrupting Ralph again. After all, milk was a really big issue to Polly. She loved the stuff but hated the lumpy, powdery liquid that she and the other foster children were forced to pour over their stale cereal every day. Now he was really talking her language.

"Ralph," said Polly thoughtfully. "I really love milk, so I can't believe that the promise of as much as they could drink was not enough to persuade them to get off their backsides and have a jolly good try at giving those giants a good beating. I would at least have considered throwing a brick or two their way if I thought I might just be able to get hold of a bottle of the real stuff. As much as I adore honey, I love cold, fresh milk even more."

Ralph forgave Polly for yet again interrupting him. For he was beginning to get quite used to this talkative young lady who could not only divert conversations, but who could also easily turn every comment into a lengthy debate. However, he hoped this assignment would not turn into a lifetime commission as she grappled and argued every detail in their rather extensive conversations. He scratched his head as he pondered over this troublesome thought before continuing on with his story.

"Now, Polly, you might be interested to know that there were two men who had been young lads when they left Egypt. Once they saw what they were going to miss if they hung around in the desert, they were having none of it. They determined to go after their dream and take the land, regardless of the personal cost. The two lads tried their hardest to persuade all the tribes to find the courage and join them. They even sneaked into the land and brought back grapes so large and juicy they could hardly carry them. But sadly, even this failed to persuade all the others to get off their rumps and at the very least have a good try to take the land. Not only were the tribes not prepared to listen but also they even considered going back to the land in which they had once been slaves. Can you believe that, Polly?"

It was now Polly's turn to smile, for she could well believe it. The chances were very high that she would have been among those who chose to stay and take their chances in the desert, for her problem with fear was no different from theirs. She would have been positively terrified! So perhaps after all, the promise of as much milk as she could drink might not have been enough to persuade her.

However, she chose to keep this tiny thought from Ralph as he soldiered on with the story.

"The two brave and very courageous men were Joshua and Caleb. I believe the name Joshua means 'wholehearted,'" said Ralph, showing great excitement as he continued on. "So while all the people in the desert stood around whining about their lot in life, Joshua and Caleb refused to be fainthearted. Oh, they almost certainly had to deal with their fears, but they decided to go anyway! So there you have it, Polly. Of all the people who left Egypt and the land of slavery, these two were the only ones who got to live in the new land that they had been promised many years beforehand. I believe this to be an amazingly true story, for it shows you what faith mixed with determination can do for any person who will run with their dreams."

"Oh, they are wonderful stories, Ralph. Truly they are, but all my dreams are dead. I don't feel like I have any future at all," she said, feeling instantly discouraged and defeated. "Besides, all your stories are about men of valor and courage. You have failed to even mention a woman who went on to greatness. And if you hadn't noticed, I just happen to be a girl of little strength—and a pretty useless one at that!"

"Polly, what's your middle name?" quizzed Ralph, deliberately choosing to ignore her personal character assassination.

"I don't have one," said Polly sadly. "I'm just plain old Polly Brown."

"I don't believe that to be true," said Ralph, gently challenging her.

"No, really Ralph. I don't have a middle name," she insisted.

"All right," said Ralph. "But I happen to know that when you were confirmed, you were given another name, were you not?"

"Yes," said Polly rather hesitantly, "but I did not choose it. No, all the other children were allowed to choose a name they liked, but my guardians chose mine for me, and I hate it."

"Go on, Polly," urged Ralph. "Spill the beans and tell me what name you were given."

Polly felt put in a corner. She was beginning to feel most uncomfortable. So it was with the greatest reluctance that she confided her middle name. "Please don't laugh at me, will you, Ralph?" she begged.

She took a deep breath. Then, after much hesitation and in little more than a whisper, she muttered, "It's Esther."

"Esther!" exclaimed Ralph very loudly. "Why, that's a wonderful name."

"Oh, sure, it's really great. Polly Esther Brown." She waited for Ralph to click on. He didn't. "Polyester. Don't you see the problem?"

Ralph looked confused, for he appeared not to see what she was driving at.

"Oh, come on, Ralph," said Polly, feeling rather agitated. "Do I have to spell it out for you? I mean, are you really that thick? *Polyester!*"

Ralph still did not appear to understand what Polly was getting at, forcing her to become even more exasperated with him.

"Ralph, do you live on this planet or are you from another universe?"

Ralph refused to be drawn into such a line of questioning.

"Look, Ralph. Polyester is a cheap, clingy material," she cried. "So even my name is a byword, something to laugh at. Not only am I Polly Brown, a sad and sorry excuse for a human being, but even my name is a joke as well. It was just one more thing to humiliate me. And the other children often use it to mock and ridicule me much of the time." Polly looked at Ralph despairingly, at the same time thinking, "He's as thick as the cheese sandwiches I make for him if he is unable to clearly see what I'm going on about."

"You will have to forgive my ignorance, Polly, but I can only see what I wish to see, and I would sincerely advise you to do likewise. People can only hurt you if you choose to let them. As for me, I prefer to think on things that are wonderful and of good report."

"Oh! So what you are really saying, Ralph, is that sticks and stones will break my bones, but words will never hurt me. Well, you're quite wrong," Polly rather glumly insisted. "Whoever made up that saying obviously had no idea what they were talking about, Ralph. For when I'm beaten, it hurts, but that pain is, in time, little more than a memory. However, the terrible things that have been said to me, particularly by Aunt Mildred and Uncle Boritz, are then constantly repeated by the children. Well, those words not only hurt like crazy, but they live on to torment me day and night. Those scars are here to stay!" she yelled.

"Oh, Polly," said Ralph very softly. "These scars that have wounded you so deeply are caused by the despicable words of cowards and bullies, and you have suffered much by allowing yourself to take them on board. It is you who has given those words permission to take root in your heart and soul. Yes, Polly, and these have become the seemingly insurmountable giants in your land. It is these that you will need to conquer."

"I can't. At least not while I remain imprisoned in this horrible orphanage," she lamented. "Gailey Gobbstopper is the worst of all. She sleeps in the next bed, and she taunts me every night with her unkind words until I feel I am screaming inside. She only stops when she finally falls asleep. She was also really cruel and horrid to Thomas. He found it equally unbearable."

As Ralph listened to Polly, he felt nothing but the deepest compassion for her, for he witnessed that her heart was indeed near to breaking. He also knew that deep down she felt responsible for what happened to Thomas, and no amount of words on his part would dissuade her of this lie. However, he wholeheartedly agreed with Polly's diagnosis that she had no hope while she remained in the orphanage. All necessary healing could only take place once Polly was finally away from this home. He knew from much experience that this type of scarring could take many years and as many tears to heal. He therefore resigned himself to making the deepest of sighs.

Ralph waited until Polly had run out of steam, and then, giving her a gentle pat on the back, said, "Polly, I want to go back to your middle name. As I mentioned earlier, it is a lovely name. Now, I know it was chosen with the intention of hurting you further, but you asked me for a true tale that had a woman as the heroine. Well, there are many women in this ancient book who, despite hideous trials and tribulations, went on to do amazing exploits. The one I wish to tell you about is the story of a young girl who, funnily enough, was named Esther. Let me assure you, Polly, this story is no fairy tale. Just like the other tales I have shared with you this night, this too is a historical fact."

Polly dried her eyes, and for once she listened intently.

"Just like you, Polly, Esther was an orphan. And what happened to her parents is sadly not recorded. She was alone in life and was raised by her uncle, and they were poor. Also Esther was a Jew, and just like you, Polly, she and her people were despised. So she had to keep her true identity a secret. I am not going to tell you the whole story, for I want you to go in search and find the ancient book. When you do find it, you must promise to read her story. It is a wonderful story where she not only gets to become queen, but, against all the odds, she also saves all her people. She went through great persecution and trials, but she was a woman of courage who stood by her convictions. I think you are very like her, Polly!"

Polly felt touched that Ralph could liken her to anyone who had courage, for she saw herself as little more than a useless blob.

She chose not to share this little detail with him, for she was in too much despair.

"So are you saying that you want me to go and search high and low in order to find this so-called ancient book, Ralph?" Polly asked, her voice tinged with annoyance. "If the book is hidden, then it will probably take me years of hunting around until I find it. Oh, that's just perfect, isn't it? Well, I can't do it, for I am tired and fed up with looking for answers."

"You will become more tired running away from finding answers than going in search of them, Polly," Ralph said meaningfully. "Look, Polly, nothing in life just happens by chance. What I mean is that all that has happened in your young life is for a purpose, just like Esther was born to save her people."

"And just who are my people?" Polly asked despairingly.

"I think you already know the answer to that one," responded Ralph.

"Oh, why do you speak in riddles, Ralph?" cried Polly, quite exasperated as she wondered where this conversation was going. "You know I am an orphan, and therefore I have no people, unlike this so-called Esther. I'm 'Polly Nobody.' Nobody cares and nobody listens. I'm a real nobody's child."

"Look, Polly, when you eventually free yourself from all this self-hatred and self-loathing that is clouding your heart and mind, then there will come a day when you will recognize who your people truly are. And then you will thank God. He made you Polly Brown with Esther as your middle name. Trust me, for I never lie."

Polly was well-and-truly stumped. And as she stood, momentarily silenced by the thought that maybe, just maybe, she had been born for some useful purpose, she was left with no choice but to give in. Yes, surrender. And for the first time ever she found herself ignoring, even denying, the tormenting voices that were constantly invading her heart and mind. For they whispered to her that Hodgekiss, Ralph, Piadora, and Hoolie Koolie trees were little more than ridiculous fantasies that beckoned her to follow after them to the brink of a cliff and then far beyond into a world of complete madness!

The time was getting very late, and with the shoes all polished and shining, Polly asked Ralph if he would pass on something that she wanted Hodgekiss to have. He said he would be seeing him very shortly and would be happy to pass on whatever Polly wished to give him. Polly thanked him and plunged her hand into the bottom of her pocket at the side of her frock. She pulled the small item out and handed it to Ralph. It was a packet of toothpicks.

"I think he needs these," said Polly with a smile.

Ralph smiled back and replied, "I do believe you could be right, Polly."

With their conversation over, he buttoned up his coat with the one remaining button that was still attached, and, giving Polly a light peck on the cheek, he turned on his heels and left, closing the back door behind him.

Polly turned off the light and left the room, heading for the staircase and bed. She felt very tired and frail, and she still had to think up a way of getting to Thomas's funeral. The last thing she remembered as she got into bed was giving a big yawn. For Polly to fall asleep so suddenly with no huffing and puffing as she wrestled with the pillow and the bedclothes was something of a miracle. What she did not know was that this would be the first of many miracles as she got closer to going on the adventure of a lifetime!

Chapter 13
THE POPPY FIELD

*T*HE NEXT DAY there was a most disconcerting rumor circulating amongst the children at the orphanage. At first Polly wondered what on earth was going on and feared another family meeting might well be the reason for all the secretive whisperings. After much persuasion and pleading from Polly, Cecil Bogswater broke ranks and told her the latest piece of salacious gossip that was causing sensational ripples within the walls of the castle. Polly found herself smiling as she listened, hoping and praying that there was some truth to Cecil's wild story. She knew from past experience that most events in the castle tended to get more colorful and spiced up as the news passed between informants. On this occasion Cecil's story proved to be true, as it was confirmed by Tommy Pulleyblank and Bertha Banoffee later that morning.

Apparently Aunt Mildred had been unable to rouse either Uncle Boritz or Pitstop, whom she found stretched out on top of her husband. Poor Aunt Mildred had been scared witless at the thought that her dear husband, whom she relied on for everything, may suddenly have departed from this earth. Sadly, she also secretly believed there was every possibility that he had been murdered by a foster child out for revenge, and therefore she could be next! This possibility had frightened her so much that she believed she was in urgent need of protection.

She therefore was somewhat hysterical as she raced to the phone and demanded that Dr. Glumchops abandon his early morning surgery and get up to the castle immediately. When the doctor arrived on the scene, he was unable to help until he had calmed Aunt Mildred down with the help of an injection into her overtly large rear end. Only after the medication had sufficiently done its work was he able to reassure her that Boritz was not dead, just mysteriously and temporarily incapacitated. Although he did have to admit that until Pitstop was physically removed from on top of his master, he would be unable to give Uncle Boritz a more thorough medical examination. As Pitstop weighed a ton, Dr. Glumchops was left with little choice but to call in the local haulage firm—Bodgit, Dodgit, and Hoppitt—who, with the help of a large and very strong hoist, were happily able to lift the limp body of the beast down from the bed. Then and only then was the doctor able to make a clear medical diagnosis and administer the correct dosage of drugs that were deemed vital to bring her poor, comatose husband back to his senses.

Many hours later he was still feeling too weak and exhausted to leave his bed, and he was now complaining of a thumping headache that resisted all medication. The condition of Pitstop was equally poor, and as a result neither party were to be seen strolling around the castle for the next few days, giving Polly a much-needed and very welcome break.

Tuesday arrived in no time at all, and by the time the sun had graced the sky with its appearance Polly was already up and ahead of schedule. This was after all a very important day, and she had much to get on with. After the usual small and very unsatisfying bowl of stale cornflakes, she set off to school as usual, but with one addition to her schoolbag. This was the jar that had been home to Hodgekiss's caterpillar until it transformed to a butterfly.

Polly feared the morning lessons would never come to an end. Every time she looked up at the clock face the hands seemed to barely move.

But finally the various smells of boiled cabbage and chips wafted down the corridors and into the classrooms, alerting the studious pupils' rumbling tummies to the excellent news that lunch break had almost arrived. The dinner gong eventually boomed, informing all pupils that the morning lessons were over, much to Polly's great relief.

She hung back to avoid the inevitable stampede for the cafeteria before picking up her schoolbag and leaving the classroom. After heading down the steps that led to the hallway, she then turned in the opposite direction to avoid the noisy lunchtime queue of hungry pupils anxious to get into the canteen for today's special. She then quietly slipped out of school to avoid detection, keeping her head down low as she left the premises and headed for home. She had allowed herself plenty of time, in fact, way too much time. But this did not matter to Polly, for it meant she could go on her mission to pick some fresh flowers for Thomas.

What she was totally unaware of at that moment in time was that Gailey Gobbstopper had followed her, watching her disappear through the school gates, and then headed back into school to report Polly's truancy to Edwood Batty, the headmaster.

Gailey was very proud of herself as he opened the absenteeism book to write Polly's name down, for she knew that after lunch there would be a certain phone call made to the castle, and Uncle Boritz would be fuming. So as she went to join the remainder of the lunch queue, great joy filled her heart and did not leave, even when she discovered that all the specials had been finished, leaving only braised liver with boiled cabbage. Normally this would have deeply upset her, but not today, for today she had witnessed Polly's deceit and wickedness in disobeying Uncle Boritz. She was extremely excited knowing that she would undoubtedly receive a reward of goodies and sweets, as well as witness Polly's punishment. After almost falling asleep in the many boring morning lessons, this had unexpectedly turned into a wonderful day for Gailey.

The sun was shining brightly; the sky was a perfect azure blue; and the birds of the air were singing praises as they flitted from one treetop to another. All this caused Polly's tender spirit to feel lifted as she got off the train. She started to walk in the opposite direction from her normal route, for she had a special job to do before attending her brother's funeral. Polly walked for what felt like miles. After leaving the main road she headed down a long, winding lane and then through a lush, green meadow filled with beautiful flowers that she was unable to name.

Eventually she stopped by a gate and, looking over the cornfields, she saw what she was after—a field full of wild poppies that she and Thomas had many times walked through together. It was their field, where they shared their highs and lows as well as all their dreams as they lay sucking on long grasses and basking in the warm sun. Today it looked stunningly beautiful, as usual, to Polly. The sun bent down to kiss the golden corn, and the red poppies intertwined and added such rich color as they swayed to and fro in the gentle breeze.

She climbed over the gate and made her way through the golden cornfields, taking great care not to trample down the corn as she did so, for she knew that if she damaged the corn the farmer would be most unhappy with her. Soon she arrived at her poppy field. As she had plenty of time on her hands, she lay down in the long grass and allowed her thoughts to fill with memories of Thomas.

Polly smiled as she remembered how Thomas had tried so hard to protect her when they first arrived at the castle. Both of her brothers, as well as she, had been so frightened, and nobody had done anything to allay their fears. There had been no social worker to sit and talk to them about why they had been brought there or how long they would be staying. Nobody in the castle introduced himself or made them feel even the tiniest bit welcome. In fact, Polly got the distinct impression that they were not wanted. Over the years much had happened to both Thomas and herself to prove this to be the case.

There was one occasion that he had always brought up in their conversations. This event had taken place only days after their arrival at the castle. Polly had been instructed to sit on a chair that had been placed at the top of the staircase. Within seconds, her light golden hair had been mercilessly and forcibly chopped off. Polly had struggled, and Thomas, who happened to walk by, stopped in his tracks, shouting, "Leave my sister alone. Get off her right now!" He had then rushed over to Polly and attempted to remove the scissors from the lady cutting her hair. The result had been a most irregular cut that more resembled a pudding bowl and left poor Polly very upset. She believed she now looked more hideous than ever.

She had always loved her hair, and it had up until now always been brushed and then braided with ribbons tied on both ends. But now there was no longer the time or a willing pair of hands available to do this seemingly meaningless task. Therefore the decision to chop off her long hair had been deemed most necessary by Aunt

Mildred. Polly had burst into tears and hugged Thomas, crying, "Thomas, please help me! Get me out of this place."

On witnessing Polly's distress, Thomas had also begun to cry, at the same time promising he would do all that he could to help her. But he also admitted to Polly that things did look pretty hopeless. She would never forget that day and how touched she had been at Thomas's efforts to protect her. Polly wished every day for her hair to grow long again, but her guardians refused point blank to allow such frivolous indulgence. She was given no choice but to have short hair with no style whatsoever. This went a long way in making her feel like a hideously ugly monster. Oh, how she missed her braids!

Thomas had never spoken truer words than he did that day when he told Polly things looked pretty hopeless. It would only be a matter of time before he fell sick and could no longer be of any help to Polly and her younger brother.

They had only been in the home a matter of weeks before they came to realize that all was not well. The awful truth that they were not wanted began to dawn on them. Unbeknownst to Polly and her brothers at the time, Aunt Mildred had made it perfectly clear to Uncle Boritz that she was finding it hard enough to cope with the ones she already had.

Uncle Boritz had obviously ignored her pleas and had gone behind her back in agreeing to take them in. Therefore, from the moment of their arrival they were forced to face the awful fact that they were uninvited guests! Aunt Mildred made it quite plain that she could not bear the sight of any of them, or apparently their smell either. When they were in her presence, she distinctly raised her nose in the air and looked away, choosing to ignore them. The other children were also quick to realize that this was indeed their opportunity to gain the favor of their guardians, so they acted likewise. Polly and her brothers were therefore treated like outcasts, and this left them feeling ostracized and, at times, very confused.

On the rare occasions when treats such as sweets were handed out, they were often excluded. Birthdays and Christmas were the worst times of all. The other children would whisper to her, "We can see they don't like you at all," as they more than happily sneered at the cheap gift that had been Polly's only present. In both

Thomas's and Polly's case there had been birthdays when nothing arrived at all!

On every child's birthday, Uncle Boritz would always promise a goodie box. This box comprised of small goodie bags, packets of crisps, and a can of coke. Many times Polly witnessed an anxious foster brother or sister spending much time looking for Uncle and their unclaimed and highly desired box. Polly found herself in the same boat when it came to her birthday, playing hide and sneak with the elusive box and sneaking around the castle desperately seeking out Uncle Boritz. Sadly, if he had not been tracked down by the next day, it was considered too late, and there was no longer any entitlement to the box. So the hunt for Uncle Boritz caused great anxiety not only to Polly, but also to the other children as well.

It was quite different however when it was one of their own children's birthday celebrations, for then all the stops were pulled out. Nothing was too much trouble. A big cake arrived from the baker, and all the children were expected to produce presents.

Despite Aunt Mildred's growing hatred of Polly and her brothers, Polly had the deepest desire to please Aunt Mildred. The sad truth was Polly really did love her and desperately wanted that love returned. Then there came a day when she found the opportunity she had been waiting for—Aunt Mildred's birthday. Polly knew that to find something special would prove to be extremely difficult, for she had received no pocket money for some weeks as part of her long list of punishments. But she did have in her possession a necklace that she treasured. The diamonds were of course plastic, but to Polly they were the real things. As Polly caressed the necklace between her fingers, she made the very tough decision to give it to Aunt Mildred as her gift.

Polly had so little in the way of personal possessions, but she felt the sacrifice would be worth it. She made a small tag and wrote £1,000,000 on it, and then tied it securely onto the necklace before wrapping it in brown paper. She could hardly wait to give Aunt Mildred her special gift, for she believed that upon opening and seeing it was Polly's special diamond necklace, Aunt Mildred would at last realize that Polly cared for her and all their problems would be in the past. Aunt Mildred would then kiss her and tell her how much she really loved her. "The possibilities are indeed endless," Polly thought most excitedly.

The children had to wait until after lunch before presenting their gifts, for this was always how it was done for her guardians. No such ceremony took place for any of the other children, Polly always noticed. It was as if none of their celebrations counted. With the tables cleared of all plates and cutlery, Aunt Mildred eventually sat down and all the children fought to be first in the line up to present her with their gift. At last it was Polly's turn, and with great excitement she rushed forward, thrusting the package into Aunt Mildred's open hand. The room fell silent. Every eye was on Aunt Mildred as she tore open the little package, causing the plastic diamond necklace to drop on to the table.

"What on earth is this?" cried Aunt Mildred in disgust as she dangled the necklace for all to see.

"It's my special gift to show you that I love you," stammered Polly.

Aunt Mildred continued to finger the necklace, and then her eyes met with the small price tag. She burst into hysterical laughter. The children joined in, laughing almost as loudly as Aunt Mildred. Polly began to feel panicky, for she could not understand why Aunt Mildred was laughing so hysterically.

"One million pounds?" she sneered. "Boritz, come here quickly and take a look at Polly's hideously ridiculous present to me. This sniveling child thinks I was born yesterday."

Uncle Boritz rushed forward to peer through his thick glasses at the price tag before laughing out loud. The necklace was then passed from child to child so that all present could be witness to Polly's more than pathetic attempt at fraud. They all continued laughing uncontrollably as Aunt Mildred turned on Polly and shouted, "Get out of my sight, you miserable little blighter. You don't love me. In fact *you*, my girl, could never love anybody. For you are nothing but a liar and a cheat," she hissed.

Within just a matter of seconds, all the children joined in the fun, hissing and booing in Polly's direction.

But Aunt Mildred wasn't finished yet. "Here take back your cheap, miserable present," she yelled, "for I want nothing from you or your pathetic brothers."

Venom continued to pour from her mouth as she tossed the precious piece of jewelry into the air. The necklace dropped to the floor and broke, scattering the artificial diamonds everywhere.

Polly fell to her knees, hot tears burning her cheeks, as she attempted to pick up all the diamonds from the floor. Her futile attempt to gather them up was somewhat hampered as the children standing around started a game of football by kicking the diamonds across the room to each other. As Polly continued to grovel around on the floor, desperately attempting to retrieve them, she was kicked numerous times in the head and on her body. Eventually she was forced to give up and make a hasty retreat from the room.

Nobody spoke to Polly for days after that incident, and Polly kept well clear of Aunt Mildred and Uncle Boritz. She felt so humiliated. Much of the time she stayed under the bedclothes with only Langdon and Eton as her companions. She played events of that terrible day over and over in her head as she tried hard to understand and come to terms with what had taken place.

Thomas had, on too numerous occasions to mention, been subjected to similar treatment. Polly remembered back to one specific time when it was Mother's Day, and the children were again queuing up to present their gifts. Thomas was rarely given his pocket money, for they found every reason under the sun to withhold it from him. Polly had tried to help out by giving him all she had, and that was a bright, shiny penny. Thomas was very grateful and spent the penny buying something for Aunt Mildred. He bought her a penny chew, and then, because the gift was so small, he had the bright idea of wrapping it up a number of times. This made his gift look far more substantial. He waited at the end of the long line of children, eager to be called forward to present his gift. Again silence fell as all eyes were on Aunt Mildred as she unraveled layer after layer of paper. When the final wrapping had been discarded, she held the penny chew high in the air and screeched, "And what do you call this?" before throwing the penny chew to the floor in disgust. She then pulled out her hanky and started to cry. Uncle Boritz was fuming. He ordered Thomas to go back to his seat immediately.

All the children present on that most special of occasions started to cry, for Aunt Mildred's special day had been totally hijacked and destroyed by the loony. And if her day was wrecked, then their day was ruined as well. They believed that Thomas was therefore a wicked and very cruel person who deserved the beating he was about to get. Thomas curled up in a ball to stave off the blows and punches from the children who, like a pack of wolves, surrounded him, baying for blood. It was right for them to be granted permission to mete out their own brand of justice. So it was many blows later before Thomas was finally able to flee from the room and find a place to hide away. Such was the venom of those who sought his blood.

These events were typical in Thomas's short life. Needless to say, when his birthday came around, Uncle Boritz had the perfect opportunity for revenge. And as he was never a man to miss an opportunity, he called the children to gather around the table before placing one tiny little present by Thomas's dinner plate. As Thomas had no other relatives, this was all he received. All the children suspected they were in for some kind of amusement, for it was unheard of to gather all the children around the table on the birthday of a foster child, and the lowliest of them all at that! Something worth watching was surely about to happen! Polly watched their glee-filled faces as they waited with eager anticipation to witness the hurt this gift was more than likely to bring. Thomas dutifully tore open the package, unwrapping layer after layer of paper, until the gift tumbled out. It was a small plastic pencil sharpener.

All the children roared with laughter, with the exception of Polly, who instantly felt beside herself on Thomas's behalf. She stood for a few moments feeling his intense pain. The children began to jeer and mock Thomas as they got immense satisfaction from witnessing his disappointment at the paltry gift. Uncle Boritz and Aunt Mildred joined in the party, for it was turning into a most successful and fun event. They laughed until Uncle Boritz could hardly keep upright, clutching his belly as he continued to crease up. This encouraged the children to laugh even louder. If Polly could have done something, anything, to prevent her brother's terrible ordeal, she would have. But sadly she felt as powerless as ever. Polly just watched in horror, her heart pounding in almost as frenzied a fashion as their laughter.

When Uncle Boritz was done, he ordered Aunt Mildred to come with him to their sitting room. This was a clear signal to the children present to finish the job. Within seconds Thomas was curled up in a little ball on the floor, covering his face with his hands to protect himself from the repeated blows raining down on him from so many.

It was not too long before Polly felt that she was unable to take any more, but she was unable to save him. Neither could she just stand by and watch. She raced to her bedroom locker in search of something to give him, for she was desperate to let him know that he was worth so much more than a pencil sharpener. He was worth more than the whole wide world to her, and she needed him to know this.

Polly would have given him any and every possession she owned, but all she had were a number of broken, secondhand toys, and most of these were old dolls. Sadly, she had nothing of any value at all. But she still decided that she wanted to give him all that she had, for she loved him so much and felt this was the only way she could show it. Scooping up some of her broken dolls, she went in search of Thomas. She found him in a dark corner, bruised and hiding from everyone. Polly crept up beside him and knelt down.

"Here, Thomas. You can have all of my toys," she said in little more than a whisper, large tears streaming down her face.

Thomas remained motionless in a ball. Polly could do nothing except curl up beside him, putting one outstretched arm over his shoulder to say she loved him. She felt so helpless and powerless to do anything to take away his pain that day. As she lay curled up beside him, she wept not only for Thomas, but also for the children who had attacked him. For even though she was so young, she knew they were just puppets controlled by their master and willing to do anything he ordered. They too wanted desperately to be loved.

In the end, the only difference between them and Polly was that they were prepared to do anything to get it!

This scene would find itself being repeated many times over the years. Polly felt the treatment dished out to her brother far exceeded anything that she had to endure. Thomas, as a result, became a recluse. He preferred his own company to that of others, and as he was rarely invited to join in with the other children, he appeared to accept isolation as his little lot in life. He could often be found sitting down with odd sheets of plain paper drawing the most amazing pictures. Polly would gaze at them for ages, for they seemed utterly magical to her. She realized that her brother was wonderfully gifted.

However, the other children did not see things in the same light, and they wanted it both ways. They excluded him from all activities, complaining bitterly if for some unforeseen reason he had to be involved in an outing or event. However, they also seemed equally annoyed if he was minding his own business and quietly drawing. They saw it as their business to put a stop to it. Sadly, the main offender was Gailey Gobbstopper, who took pure delight in tormenting him just as she did Polly. She would race over and grab hold of his pen, or worse still, rip the piece of paper away from him and tear it into little pieces as she ran as fast as she could from the room. Thomas, now utterly distraught, would leap up from his chair and race after her, desperate to salvage what was left of his drawing and, at the same time, give her or the offender a hard thump.

In Gailey's case, she would then run to the safety of older children, begging their protection. They would happily oblige, forming a circle around her. Thomas would then be harshly stopped if he dared to come near. All he wanted was his pen and what was left of his picture. He would accept the picture torn or screwed up as long as he could have it back. If the children refused, he would come nearer, determined not to leave without taking back what belonged to him. By this point in their little game, Thomas was usually worked up into an extreme state of agitation. Even seeing Thomas worked up into a terrible frenzy seemed to provoke them into going further still with their spiteful games. As there were far more of them, Thomas always came out worse, as they hounded him like a fox, throwing endless punches with their clenched fists or giving brutally hard kicks. Normally Gailey Gobbstopper held back, watching Thomas receive his beating. Her facial expression conveyed nothing short of pure elation as she watched blow after blow rain down on his bloodied face and body. The severity of these blows was increased if perchance he had managed to catch up with her and hit her before she made it to the safety of older children.

It was not too long before other children copied Gailey in her fun and frivolous antics. Thomas had found there was nowhere he was safe where he could just be left alone to draw to his heart's content. It became normal for Thomas to receive not only a hard beating from the older children, but also further punishment from Uncle Boritz and Aunt Mildred for fighting. Out came the rod, and Thomas would be on the receiving end of a publicly administered almighty thrashing. All this had over the years become quite routine, leaving Polly in the most agonizing state of distress.

She no longer frantically rocked her head from side to side as she lay on the pillow every night crying out "Mummy, Mummy. I want my Mummy," for she no longer wished to waste her tears on someone who would never come. Instead, she now hid under the covers crying for her brother Thomas.

The local doctor, Ebeneezer Glumchops, visited once a week, and being a family friend, he always stayed for tea. Just like Uncle Boritz, this man was also very rotund, and his suit, which he always wore on every visit, was at the very least three sizes too small. His jacket, when done up, saw the buttons straining to remain fastened. One big heave and Polly figured they would definitely fly off in all directions. They also shared the same style in glasses and wit. They would sit in Uncle Boritz's plush sitting room and, over a delicious tea of salmon and cucumber sandwiches, scones and jam, followed by many huge slices of Queen Victoria's sponge cake, they cheerfully discussed all the things they had in common, which gave them a most united friendship.

Polly was often required to push the tea trolley down the hall and into the room where Dr. Glumchops was entertained. More than once, Polly had the wicked thought of stealing a sandwich or scone while no one was looking. She would stop the trolley outside the sitting room door and, before knocking and waiting to hear if she had permission to enter, her fingers would find themselves lingering most wantonly over the sandwiches and cakes. Luckily, common sense always prevailed, for she knew the punishment would not match the crime if it were to be discovered that she had stolen any delightful morsel from the tea trolley that was clearly intended for their mouths alone. There were never any leftovers from that trolley, and Polly decided that either they had the appetites of elephants or whatever remained untouched made its way up to their private quarters to be polished off by their own family. What was absolutely certain was that none of it ever went back to the general kitchen to find its way into the mouths of the hungry foster children.

As Polly entered the room, Uncle Boritz and Dr. Glumchops were as always sitting like fat cats having just got the cream, their large bellies stuffed full of food and giving each other one compliment after another. If there were a sick child that needed the doctor's attention, they would then be sent for, but never before the doctor had been fed and watered. If, as happened on a number of occasions, the doctor was unable to pay his weekly visit and a child had the temerity to be unwell, then the child in question had little choice but to wait until Dr. Glumchops was once again available.

Luckily, the doctor was not given to taking long holidays, otherwise a sick child's condition might become critical, and then what would happen? They either saw Ebeneezer Glumchops or continued to suffer in silence. For dear Ebeneezer was considered by Uncle Boritz, along with many other dignitaries such as Edwood Batty, the headmaster, to be part of his closely knit family. Thomas was regularly called in, but the many pills that were prescribed by Dr. Glumchops did nothing to help his rapidly deteriorating condition. They only made things worse. Therefore Polly believed that the panacea he truly required was not on offer. And what exactly was this? Well, Polly thought they should give up plying him with brightly colored pills and instead try plying him with some mercy and tender loving care. For crazy as it may seem, she truly believed that this might work.

Before long, Polly was under a similar medical program as her brother Thomas. She was forced to take all sorts of pills to help her sleep as well as others to help her stay awake and many more besides. All this was to alleviate her sickness that manifested itself with long bouts of the deepest sadness. But no amount of red, green, and yellow medication did anything to combat her worsening malady, and this only served to mystify Aunt Mildred and Uncle Boritz further. They had, after all, done all in their power to find the root cause of her mysterious and deep melancholy. As he often stood over her pondering the enormity of her most peculiar condition, Uncle Boritz believed Polly had totally failed to heed his helpful and very sound words of advice: "Laugh and the world laughs with you. Cry and you cry alone." If she wouldn't help herself, then he was at a complete loss as to how to help her any further. She obviously liked having this black cloud hanging over her.

She remembered one occasion when, having been checked over thoroughly by the doctor with the aid of his cold stethoscope, Ebeneezer Glumchops had then sat back on the comfy chair reserved for important visitors and informed Uncle Boritz that Polly had a most irregular heartbeat. He then turned his attention to Polly, casually informing her that if she did not calm down, there was every possibility that she would indeed suffer a fatal heart attack. He then began to chortle loudly, his fat face bloating even further as his laughter gained momentum. Uncle Boritz found it equally funny and could not help but join in the merriment. Polly stood in silence as the two chuckled on, stopping only to continue their discussion as to what other further pills should be administered to prevent such a thing from happening.

Polly wanted no further pills and considered a heart attack might just be the answer she was looking for to get her out of the castle forever. She therefore couldn't wait for it to happen. Especially as it turned out that not one jolly pill prescribed by Dr. Glumchops had done a thing to save the life of her now-departed brother.

Just like Thomas, Polly was eventually taken to other doctors that specialized in the area of broken hearts. Polly felt like a flea under the microscope as they huddled together, frantically shaking their heads as they pondered and reflected on the possible root cause of her problem. Their language was littered with long words that sounded as though they came from another planet. They offered endless theories concerning her most sad and quickly deteriorating condition.

There came a day when it dawned on Polly that she alone held the solution to her malady. Therefore she could, if allowed, save them time and many hours of hypothesizing, which must cost someone loads of money. She felt strongly that all that was truly required was for her to be allowed to talk with them in private without the presence of her guardians. Polly knew this thought was indeed as outrageous as many of her other ideas, for her guardians always insisted on being involved, believing that their presence was very much needed at every session, because they were so concerned for her welfare.

Also, if she could be allowed to talk, she would need firm guarantees that all she said would remain confidential. On one of the rare occasions Miss Dogsbody visited the castle to see the children, Polly had unwittingly begun to share just how unhappy she really was. The social worker had then gone behind her back and discussed this with her guardians. It resulted in a most terrible family session for Polly, where she had been convicted of gross misconduct and disloyalty to the family. She had vowed there and then never to trust another social worker ever again.

In fact she had no reason to worry, for after that episode she never did see another social worker. They had only ever visited once or twice in the five or six years that she had lived at the castle. In truth their complete absence had no worse impact on her sad life.

However, one social worker did come to the castle regularly, albeit once a year, and her name was Mrs. Oddbodd. Polly often watched Uncle Boritz stand at the window taking pictures of her sitting on the wooden bench in the garden. She presumed that this was because this very ancient lady just loved to get out into the fresh air. She would then peer out of another window to see what it was about this lady that Uncle Boritz thought was so fascinating that he needed to take so many pictures. She was nothing to look at. In fact not only was she old with thinning white hair, but also her face was very shriveled, making her seem very haggard. Polly felt certain that this lady was no glamour queen! So if Uncle Boritz's pictures were not intended to grace some fashion magazine, it made Polly all the more curious as to what it was that Uncle Boritz saw in her that made her so worthy of all this personal attention.

As Polly gazed down on her from a window, Mrs. Oddbodd would quietly slip her hand into the side pocket of her coat and bring out a small bottle. After a few swigs, she would then return it back into her pocket just as discreetly, but not before Uncle Boritz had got his secret snapshot. Because Polly was so young, she had no idea what any of this truly meant. For he always seemed to be taking pictures of everybody, and most of the time, the object of his photo had no idea whatsoever that they were having their picture taken. All she knew was that photography had become something of a passion for Uncle Boritz, who became so consumed with his new hobby that he had turned one small room into a dark room so he could content himself developing all his rolls of film.

Uncle Boritz continued to remain more than happy for Mrs. Oddbodd to pay her annual visit, welcoming her with open arms whilst others barely got past the front door. And if perchance a social worker were invited into the castle, they would find themselves being led towards his luxurious private sitting room to be privately entertained by this charismatic man, well away from the itching ears of the children.

No social worker had ever ventured into the foster children's section of the house, and none of them were invited to. Had they done so, Polly wondered what they would make of everything, particularly the large iron bars that segregated Uncle Boritz's children and their living quarters from that of the foster children's abysmally bleak section of the house. They only got to see the plush side, with thick pile carpets and enough antiques to keep an auction room in plentiful supply for a very long time. So they left most impressed with the standard of living these wonderful carers were providing for the little outcasts. They therefore need only pay the odd and most brief of visits with Uncle Boritz ushering them out of the door as fast as possible. For without wanting to appear rude, he had so much to do for his little dears.

Polly had long made up her mind that if she ever again became brave enough to disclose how unhappy she truly felt, this could only happen if she could be guaranteed a new identity. She would only feel safe if her face was changed, along with her name and where she lived. She had come to believe that if she were ever given the permission to talk with an honest, open heart, then she would no doubt need protection for the rest of her days.

None of the so-called experts ever ventured to ask Polly, or Thomas for that matter, why they felt so sad and broken-hearted. As the doctors failed to delve into this most obvious and crucial connection between being so unloved and their melancholy, Polly could only leave them to continue serving up multiple prescriptions of colored pills that would supposedly cure the symptoms of heartache. Meanwhile, they also sent letters to one another, suggesting other suitable remedies, such as the possibility of long-term institutionalization.

It seemed that Polly was much wiser than her so-called professional counselors. For she knew more than anyone that broken hearts are rarely diagnosed in one or two sessions and can never be put back together by brightly colored pills. Despite this personal revelation, she was more than happy to leave the orphanage and her guardians for the sanctuary of another institution if it meant nice nurses and a future free of Gailey Gobbstopper's taunts. For Thomas and Polly, all the observation in the world, as well as the endless medication, was in her eyes a complete waste of time.

As Polly lay stretched out on the grass in the large field, she watched the poppies swaying in the gentle breeze, and she felt close to Thomas. They had both loved this special field. She felt safe talking Thomas, even though he was not there. As she lay in the sunshine and talked nonstop of her love for him and all her dreams, she felt it was right to share her most private desires and reassure him that he had a permanently special place in her heart. Tears slid down both her cheeks as she thought about their few special times together and how she had longed with all her heart to put things right for him. But now it was too late. That day in the field she told him that she felt she needed his forgiveness for all her failure to get help.

As she continued to lie in the field of long grass with the warmth of the sun caressing and comforting her body, her thoughts went back to the many occasions when all the children were ordered to put on their coats and Wellington boots, for they were going to be taken out for the day on a walk.

The first few times this happened, Polly had been delighted. But eventually, along with many of the other children, she grew sick of these walks. The reason was that they were not allowed to return until evening, and by then their bodies were weak with exhaustion and their little legs wracked with pain. They were also expected to do these walks every day of the holidays, and there was a limit to how many different trails they could wander down. It was a wonder there was no excitement left as their coats were forcibly put on them. They were always hungry, as the carer was only ever given a pack of sausages to cook on his stove and a loaf of bread with which to feed them all.

This carer, Mr. Peawee, was a most hearty gentleman who always dressed like a hiker. He wore a thick tweed jacket and a strange hat, and a long, thick walking stick accompanied him on every trip. He wore huge leather boots, and on his back he carried a knapsack, necessary for carrying essential items such as food, drinking water, a little stove, and a frying pan. With all these items securely in his bag, Mr. Peawee would then frogmarch the reluctant little troopers out of the front door to go on the next wild expedition. Any that dared to straggle in the forlorn hope of getting left behind felt the sharp boot of Aunt Mildred as she accompanied them to the front door and out into the fresh air. Rain or shine, every holiday was the same.

Polly remembered many times when her younger brother James got lost in the fields, for he was so small for his age, and the corn and wheat towered high above him. James getting lost became such a concern that an answer to the problem needed to be found. Luckily the solution was not too long in coming. Mr. Peawee got the inspired idea of tying a strong rope around James's tiny waist, and an older child was given the other end of the rope. He was then ordered to hold on tightly and under no circumstances let go of the rope as they walked through fields with long grass. If James went missing, then everybody grouped together and lent a hand in tugging hard on the rope. They would carry on pulling as hard as they could until he emerged safely out of the field usually plastered from head to toe in fresh mud and still lying on his belly. He would then jump up, attempt to brush off the dirt, and continue walking on with the rope still tied around him just in case they ventured into any other fields with tall grass.

Thomas had often commented to Polly that he found it strange that James didn't seem to mind any of this treatment; at least that's how it appeared to be. It would be a long time before Polly realized that James never complained or seemed to cry even when he was really hurt. He preferred to visit his imaginary planets that were filled with rockets and spacecrafts and anything that had nothing to do with living in this world with all its heartache and pain.

On these long treks Polly was often ordered to carry Mr. Peawee's knapsack for him, and the weight of his bag at times put quite a strain on her back and legs. At night the pain in her legs felt unbearable, and as a result sleep refused to come. If she was not crying for Thomas or for some awful event that had taken place, she would be crying due to the pain in her joints. She was often harshly rebuked by Aunt Mildred if she made any complaint about pain anywhere in her body. So she had little choice but to suffer in silence.

On hearing her anguished cries, Mr. Peawee started caring for Polly in a way that caused Polly to feel even more distressed, and it was not too long before she lost all trust in mankind. After many years, there came a day when this terrible truth came to light. Polly was punished for her participation in this most unmentionable saga. For despite only being five years old when the offenses concerned first began, she was deemed to be the irresponsible party because of her "wayward manner." Therefore they determined that she was without question the thoroughly guilty one in this whole sad affair, and Uncle Boritz was left to see to it that she was suitably punished for her unmentionable and most disgraceful misconduct that had been going on for many years right under their very noses.

As for Mr. Peawee, Uncle Boritz had, at the time of the deeply disturbing revelation, determined that the best thing was for Mr. Peawee to disappear immediately without trace and thus prevent any scandal that might well involve his home coming under the scrutinous eye of the social services. Also, as any inquiry of a serious nature might involve the police, he became very anxious to bring the whole unpleasant saga to an end with the least amount of fuss and attention.

Happily and very luckily for him, the police also loved visiting and came regularly to the castle. They enjoyed the entertainment Uncle Boritz provided along with a nice hot cup of steaming tea, which was always served up with a nice slice of cake. However, he could not entirely rely on his friendship with them if the seriousness of this terrible problem were discovered. His influence might take him a long way, but the risk involved was much too great.

And so this most loving and hardworking carer had his services dispensed with overnight. That same evening, Mr. Peawee's very smelly room was hastily emptied of all his belongings. Once darkness fell, Uncle Boritz led him most quietly to a small side entrance and bade him farewell, at the same time ordering him to never speak a word about any of it no matter what the circumstances. In fact, it would be best to deny ever working at the castle. Mr. Peawee readily agreed, for he was not an entirely stupid man. He knew full well that when Uncle Boritz wielded all his power and influence, it would, without a shadow of doubt, ruin the rest of his life. In his many years of service, he had witnessed others who, having intentionally or unintentionally crossed Uncle Boritz, rarely lived on to tell the tale. If by some miracle they did, their lives and reputations were normally left in tatters.

As Uncle Boritz closed the door behind him, he prayed most fervently that this would be swept under the carpet and become the end of this very trying little matter. All the same, he decided to fully cover his tracks just in case this was not to be the end. He was not a man readily given to trusting others, because he had been betrayed by business acquaintances many times in the past. He headed hastily towards his study and put a large sheet of paper into the ancient typewriter. He feverishly began composing a letter to Miss Dogsbody, Polly's elusive social worker. He began by complaining that Polly's imagination was now well-and-truly out of control, so further visits to expert doctors would indeed be required.

He hoped and believed this letter would do the trick and that Miss Dogsbody would, upon receipt of the letter, be fully persuaded that all appropriate action was being put into place by her extremely concerned guardians. His very thoughtful letter did much to suggest that not only would a visit by her be very time consuming, but also he feared that it would be fairly unproductive. Polly really needed further examination by specialists who deal with problems in the head as opposed to the heart.

He rightly reminded her that this was an area in which she had no experience, so she should not even begin to meddle. Although he was much too polite and gracious to express it in such undermining terms, Uncle Boritz rightly concluded that if things went to plan, she would stamp the letter and then store it with all other correspondence concerning Polly and her brothers. Eventually the letter, along with all other correspondence, would be boxed up ready for shipment to a vast warehouse. Once there, it would be placed with millions of other officially stamped documents, never to see the light of day again. They would be lost forever like some archeological document. He felt more than hopeful that the elusive Miss Dogsbody would stay true to form and busy herself with more important tasks that were closer to home and required her urgent attention.

Nobody ever came along to replace this committed carer except for a number of most peculiar and inexperienced people that were willing to work for a pittance. Most of these new arrivals had such deep-rooted problems that their stay in the castle was always short and filled with trouble. Polly observed that they always looked so sad when the inevitable happened and they were finally instructed to leave the castle. For the castle had not only provided them with a roof over their heads, but it had also been a welcome sanctuary in protecting them from the cruel world, which just like the children, they too found very hard to cope with.

As a direct result of Mr. Peawee's dismissal, all other holidays found the children left to their own devices. It was therefore not too long before some of the children, so bored with no money in their pockets and no one available to pay them any attention, turned to other more questionable ways to spend their days during the weekends and holidays.

Although this made Uncle Boritz and Aunt Mildred very upset, the positive side of the children's exploits meant that the terribly friendly police officers were at the castle far more regularly than they otherwise might have been, and it served to help prove what wonderful people her guardians were. Who else would be crazy enough to take on the burden of such troublesome children and cope with all their very trying misdemeanors? Therefore, local policemen could often be found tucking into large slices of Queen Victoria's cake and drinking endless cups of tea as Uncle Boritz filled their ears with the latest mischievous and often overdramatized antics of the foster children. As Uncle Boritz so loved their company, it went a long way to make him feel most happy and content.

As well as her legs, Polly's teeth really hurt as well, for her mouth was overcrowded and her teeth were crumbling. Why this was she had no idea. It certainly had nothing to do with eating too many sweets. She therefore concluded that the root of the problem lay with her rarely getting enough fruit to eat. Many times she heard others say, "An apple a day keeps the dentist away."

Polly had often thought to herself that there was less than a fine chance of getting an apple a month, let alone a day, so she apportioned all blame for this pain on apples. She had to admit that if she were given an apple each day, she would not eat it but keep it safe to give to her wonderful teacher, Mrs. Bailey, who had disappeared from her life so suddenly.

The other alternative to her condition was that the toothpaste they used to clean their teeth was not only cheap, but was solid as a rock. The bright pink paste came packaged in red cellophane in a small, circular tin. One child after another would open the tin, and if there was no sink at their disposal, they would happily spit on the hard, round lump of toothpaste before applying the bristles of their brush to grind the paste until frothy bubbles were produced. As child after child resorted to this unhygienic and rather gross method, Polly would find that she preferred not to clean her teeth at all. Besides, by the time it came to her turn, there was rarely anything left in the tin except pink frothy spittle with which to brush her teeth.

Whenever Polly went with Thomas and James and a small party of the other children on a visit to the local dentist, she was always terrified. Like most children she was frightened of going to the dentist, but as far as Polly was concerned, she had more reason than most to be afraid. Egor Treblinka was their dentist. He was a thin, wiry man with equally thin, wiry grey hair and matching thin, wiry, circular glasses that were permanently perched on the end of his nose.

Polly also had reason to believe that Egor was as blind as a bat. His drill never stayed on the tooth in question but would slip and slide from tooth to tooth, making huge holes in them all. He simply had the greatest of difficulty keeping to the designated area requiring immediate treatment. Since Polly hated the drill, he would give her numerous injections to numb the specific area he intended to work on. The needle looked like an instrument of torture to Polly, and she wasn't that wrong! For he was forced to make several attempts at hitting the correct section of gum, and he never seemed satisfied until Polly's whole face was thoroughly numb!

As he then bent over her to inspect her teeth more thoroughly, Polly often felt more than overwhelmed by his terribly stale breath and was therefore very anxious for him to get the task over with as quickly as possible. But sadly, every session went on for what seemed an eternity, for Egor loved drilling and filling cavities more than anything else in the world. With Polly's whole face now thoroughly paralyzed and at least five holes ready and waiting to be filled, he would patiently wait for his dental nurse to hand him a bowl of thick gunk that she had made up with the help of a small pestle and mortar. As with everything else he did, the thick, off-white paste seemed to go everywhere once it was applied.

Polly would go home with the now-hardened filling paste stuck in her hair, caked on her face, and as far up into her nose as anything could possibly venture, momentarily making simple breathing a very arduous task. When the last in the little group finally left the dentist chair, they would all head for the door to walk back to the castle together. Most of the time they would find themselves spitting out the fresh fillings on the way home, and another appointment would then have to be made for an emergency visit. None of the children deliberately did this as some form of rebellious defiance, for it wasn't as though any of them wished for regular visits to Mr. Treblinka's dingy dental practice. It was just that their fresh fillings never seemed to stay in place long enough for them to make it up the hill and back home to the castle.

So Polly had little faith in either doctor or dentist, or in any adult for that matter. For she felt very betrayed and let down by every authorative figure who came into her sad little life. When she thought of dear Thomas, she felt really upset and angry, for she was convinced that Thomas would still be alive and well if Dr. Chipatti, instead of Dr. Glumchops, had been the one making weekly visits to the castle for tea!

Chapter 14
THE FUNERAL

*P*OLLY AWOKE FROM her daydreaming and rubbed her sleepy eyes as she gave a big yawn. She noticed that the sun had gone down at least two feet since she last looked up. She knew she would miss the funeral if she stayed daydreaming any longer, so after hurriedly jumping up and brushing herself down, she decided to hurry up and pick some of the beautiful, rich red, velvety poppies that she knew Thomas so loved. Clutching a large bunch in her hand, she then went to the church graveyard as quickly as her little legs would allow.

She had not been walking long when she came across a wooded grove, and as she ventured on she stumbled into an area bursting with millions of bluebells. With great delight she picked as many as she had time for, adding these to her bunch of flowers and moving on. It was not too long before she saw an open field filled with stationary caravans and camper vans.

On seeing the vehicles in the field, memories instantly flooded back into Polly's mind of one very fateful day. She remembered that some delightful nuns had offered to take them on a short holiday to this campsite. Polly had never been to a campsite before, and as a group of them set off, she had no idea that this time would also be their last.

She remembered that the nuns were very kind to them and loved telling stories, especially one particular nun who happily informed them all that before becoming a nun, she had once been a royal taster. This delightful lady, dressed from head to toe in her penguin outfit, had many more eventful stories to tell than the rest of the nuns put together. Polly decided they were all really lovely, for they made nice cups of tea and seemed to want to spend time with them, something she was not used to. And so it came as no great personal revelation when she decided to add becoming a nun to her constantly growing list of potential careers.

They had been at the site for only a few days when the incident happened. It all took place so quickly. One minute Polly was with the other children having a story read to them before tea, and the next minute panic and mayhem broke out. The nuns rushed all the children from inside the caravan into the field as they tried to make sense of what was happening. Polly looked up and could clearly see that fire was raining down from heaven, or so she thought. She wondered if she or the nuns had done something to upset God, as great lumps of burning wood were falling from the air directly onto the roof of their stationary caravan. But then she realized that all the other caravaners were experiencing the same terrifying plight, and they hadn't, after all, been personally singled out.

While Polly and the other children continued to enjoy this unplanned fireworks display, the nuns had lost their inner joy and appeared to be more in a state of shock. In a matter of seconds other frightened vacationers ran up to the nuns shouting that help was urgently needed if the whole field of caravans was not to go up in smoke, but nobody seemed to know quite what to do. It wasn't long before two large, bright red fire engines pulled up to the gate entrance of the field and firefighters began to pull out their long hoses. There was a problem; their hoses were not long enough to reach up into the trees of the thickly dense wood, which by now was well-and-truly ablaze and lighting up the sky.

With nightfall having arrived, it was like the biggest bonfire and fireworks party Polly had ever seen. The furnace crackled and continued to spit its most fearsome load of fireballs down on all the caravans and tents in the field below. The fire crew became as desperate as the campers and knew that something had to be done quickly. Everyone present was asked to form a human chain, and then buckets of water were handed from person to person until it reached the firefighters standing at the end of the long line. Polly felt a truly tangible sense of excitement as she stood in the line taking and then passing bucket after bucket of sloshing water, which soaked her clothes and feet. As her heartbeat quickened within her breast, she felt gloriously exhilarated by the whole experience, for it left her wondering if there was any possibility of her becoming a part-time firefighter as well as a nun when she grew up! She was, after all, having so much fun, and for once in her life she was finally feeling a real sense of achievement and purpose.

Despite everyone working hard to pass the buckets down the line, the fire appeared to be gaining momentum and was spreading further out of their control. The nuns huddled together and agreed amongst themselves that the children should be removed for their own safety and returned to the castle.

The chief nun ordered the children to gather around for a head count. A younger nun then started the counting, touching the top of each head as she did so.

"One...two...three...Cecil Bogswater, go and stand over by Bertha so I get my figures right. There's a dear," she ordered in a most stern fashion. "Now, where was I? Ah, yes...four...five...six ...seven. Yes, I do believe that everyone is all present and correct, Sister," she delightedly announced.

"Wait a minute," one of the other nuns anxiously cried out. "I feel certain that we brought eight children with us on this trip."

"I don't think so," replied another nun with just as much certainty.

"I am absolutely sure we are all here," insisted the nun who had been responsible for the head count.

"No. Someone is definitely missing!" piped up another nun, making a quick sign of the cross as she stood shivering from the cold.

"Oh, dear, this is all so dreadfully confusing, admitted the head nun. "I had better mention this to the fire chief, for it would be simply awful if one of ours was to be discovered missing in such terrible circumstances. We will do one further head count just to make absolutely certain. Sister Anastasia, please count the children again, and Sister Gertrude, go and get the register from the caravan."

Sister Gertrude instantly obeyed the order, risking life and limb to reenter the caravan in search of the register, the only real evidence of how many children they had brought with them on this trip.

She was gone for several minutes but came back very distressed, for the elusive register was nowhere to be found. She could only stutter as she sought to inform her superiors of the problem. After much thought the head nun decided there was no other choice open to them other than to bring the possibility of a missing child to the fire chief's attention. She did this immediately.

All the children were completely kept in the dark as to the identity of the potentially missing person! "It is all most disconcerting," thought one of the nuns, for with the second headcount done, no one seemed any the wiser. So if anyone was actually missing, then Polly presumed it must be one of the nuns who had gone up into the woods for a quick tinkle!

In seconds, two burly firemen armed with huge axes and bearing thick ropes headed up into the wooded area. Polly watched, quite taken with their courage and bravery. They were not gone long. As they headed back down and onto the open field from the woods, the two had become three.

Everyone present watched with a mixture of horror and delight as the child held by his rescuers was finally whisked out of the woods and away from danger. The child was unrecognizable to any of the growing audience of anxious onlookers, for he looked like a chimney sweep. He was black from head to toe and his frizzled hair was smoking and standing on end. Everyone wondered whose party this child was from. Polly was fairly certain that this most poor, sad creature could not possibly be one of their little group. Both courageous firefighters had a firm grip on the child's shoulders as they frogmarched him back to base camp for an extensive interview. Then the mystery child stood in the limelight and was hosed down by ice-cold water that cascaded over his blackened torso. The black grime and soot soon washed away until finally the true identity of the missing person was revealed, for the perpetrator of the crime turned out to be none other than Thomas.

One of the firefighters, while handing him back to the most grateful nuns, remarked, "I think we can say with great confidence that we have found our culprit! Once we have this fire under control, someone from our department will be in touch with Mr. Scumberry! The nuns thanked all the firefighters before quickly loading the children into the back of their station wagon. This done they then hastily abandoned the site before news could spread that the nuns were in possession of the culprit and that he was hidden under a blanket in their camper for reasons of personal safety! The poor and serenely gentle nuns had never in their lives seen a riot, let alone been involved in one! Therefore they were not prepared to take any further risks by staying!

Back at the castle the children were all ordered to go to the bathroom and get washed before bed. Thomas, on the other hand, was frogmarched down the corridor to Uncle Boritz's study for further interrogation. It later emerged that Thomas had taken some matches as well as a wad of paper from the caravan and then ventured into the woods to experiment and make a small fire, just like they did on the all-day hikes. It turned out that the clipped-together wad of paper that was used to help get his little fire started had in fact been the property of the chief nun. It contained the names of all the children in their party! Polly knew the punishment Thomas received had been most severe, for she did not see him again for many days!

Polly could not help but smile as she thought back to that most serious affair. Poor Thomas. He was always such an inquisitive child! When he wasn't drawing, he was always in the middle of some scientific project. Polly was amazed by his desire to create new inventions. He really was a nutty professor trapped in a child's body. She knew he was a real genius, and this fact, for some unknown reason, seemed to threaten his guardians immensely. They made it their personal mission to destroy all his creativity. In doing so, they destroyed Thomas.

As Polly made her way to the church, the sun was beating down on her back and there was little more than a light breeze in the air. It was, in Polly's eyes, a most perfect day to be going to church.

She made it to the cemetery just in time to watch the procession of pallbearers walk with the coffin balanced on their shoulders to where a large, oblong hole had been dug in the ground. The vicar, dressed most formally in a black robe covered by his white frilly smock, stood most solemnly beside the burial site. Aunt Mildred in her large ostentatious hat walked equally solemnly behind the coffin, looking, terribly delicate and fragile as Uncle Boritz held her arm most supportively to prevent her from fainting from grief. Polly hid behind a tombstone some distance away so as not to be seen, but near enough to hear all that was to be said.

There were to be no other mourners at the graveside that day. There had been no mourners to weep while he was alive and suffering, so why should there be any now that Thomas, her beloved brother, was dead? No one had cared for him and protected him in life. It was therefore up to God to take on the role of caring for him, and she hoped that He would do a much better job. For that's what Polly had always been told that God promised to do. However, it seemed to Polly that few people she had ever met in her young life kept their promises, so why should God be any different?

Polly crouched behind the tombstone, peering out from time to time.

"Dearly beloved, we are gathered here..." started the vicar as he read from his little book with the deepest tones of solemnity, causing Aunt Mildred to burst into most grievous sobbing. Uncle Boritz as usual was on hand with the famous hanky. The vicar graciously paused to allow her the time to express her deep sense of grief.

It all started innocently enough with just a few spots of rain on her cheek, which then turned to a drizzle. The sun used this as the perfect excuse to make a very hasty retreat behind the grey clouds. Pretty soon the gentle breeze changed its mood completely and quickly became quite blustery. Polly looked up at the sky, and she could clearly see that the most dark, thundery clouds were now rolling in and threatening what had been, up until this moment in time, a most perfect day. Seconds later, the heavens burst opened to empty great bowls of water onto the earth below. Pretty soon Polly found herself soaked through to the skin. She really didn't seem to mind at all, for she felt that the sudden downpour was really quite poetic. She believed that there was every possibility that each and every rain droplet was a genuine tear from heaven. The very angels themselves were very considerately standing in as mourners at Thomas's funeral. Polly smiled to herself at having had such a silly thought. She was, however, very grateful for this downpour, for it seemed the perfect, heaven-sent opportunity to fill her jar with water, something that she had given no thought to until this moment.

Polly rummaged through her schoolbag, and, after producing the little jam jar, she carefully balanced it on the top of the tombstone to catch the rainwater. She then crouched back down to watch. Unbeknownst to Polly, the graveyard had another visitor that day. He too was crouched behind a similar tombstone also watching.

The rain became heavier and heavier as dark clouds rolled and crashed angrily through the sky. Then came thunder and with it very loud bangs that caused Polly to shudder as great bolts of lightning shot through the clouds, many of which came very near to where the vicar and her guardians were standing. The wind blew up further and began to ferociously howl, forcing poor Aunt Mildred to hold on very tightly to her most expensive hat.

Polly, though thoroughly soaked to the skin, continued to crouch behind the tombstone, peering continuously to see how things were going. Ralph, equally soaked, did likewise. The vicar was now racing through the order of service, skipping many of the hymns that were originally on his service sheet because he wished to be back at home out of the wind and rain, which was now threatening to become a most serious storm. His task was made much worse, for his frock kept blowing up, smothering his face and making it quite impossible to perform this service with any sense of dignity.

He hastily beckoned the coffin bearers to come forward and lower the coffin into the freshly dug hole, which they proceeded to do at quite a fast pace. Everyone wished to go home and get dry in front of a roaring fire. Aunt Mildred inched closer to watch the coffin as it descended into the hole until it finally came to rest on the ground, allowing the coffin bearers to pull up the ropes before moving away to stand nearby. Aunt Mildred should have been satisfied that she had seen enough, but instead moved even closer to peer into the hole one final time and thereby satisfy her morbid curiosity.

Suddenly, and without warning, she slipped. There was simply nothing anyone could have done to prevent the mishap. One minute she was on the surface of the hole peering down; the next, she was falling headfirst into the freshly dug grave! On impact, her body struck the coffin with such force that its lid not only flew off, but shot like a bat out of hell out of the hole and up into the air before eventually coming to rest at the feet of the vicar. This poor man of the cloth stood like a statue in stupefied amazement.

Aunt Mildred was now lying on top of the open coffin at the bottom of this most deep hole. She let out an almighty scream as the coffin bearers, along with Uncle Boritz, moved with the greatest of speed to rescue her. Uncle Boritz was nearer than anyone else, so he flung himself down on the muddy ground before attempting to reach in and take hold of Aunt Mildred's outstretched arms to pull her out. He heaved and heaved, going quite purple in the face, as he tried with all his might to pull his beloved wife out of the deep hole. It was useless, for the earth around the hole was soft and now very muddy, and the poor man had nothing solid to hold on to. Moments later, Uncle Boritz was battling against being slowly sucked headfirst into the hole to join his wife. He let out a loud yelp before doing his final disappearing act into the deep abyss, landing directly on top of his wife's larger-than-life posterior. Now both of them were stuck in the hole and in most urgent need of assistance!

The coffin bearers all gathered round, anxious to give all the help they possibly could. They felt it best to use their ropes and form a human chain, thus preventing any of them from falling into the grave and joining the Scumberrys. It worked! Minutes later both victims arose from the grave and staggered like zombies as far away from the hole as possible. As they stood some distance away, Polly found herself releasing a small giggle. For both her guardians looked absolutely unrecognizable due to the brown sludge that now covered them from head to foot. Polly observed their frantic efforts to clean themselves off, but as they only had several of Aunt Mildred's hankies at their disposal, their attempts were largely in vain. Polly could not help but let out a further giggle, for they looked such a ridiculous sight.

Uncle Boritz removed his thick glasses and gave them a wipe with one of the hankies before abandoning Aunt Mildred to walk over to the vicar with the intention of encouraging him to continue on with the service. As he walked towards the vicar, there was a sudden strong gust of wind. Uncle Boritz turned around just in time to see hundreds of feathers fly up from the hole and begin to swirl and flutter in the air above the grave. The coffin bearers were aghast and just stood looking up heaven's way, mouths wide open in awe of what they were witnessing. The vicar, too, stood motionless and unable to decide whether or not he was witnessing his first miracle or the opening scenes of a horror movie. If the latter was true, he promised God he would never watch one again!

Polly was eventually forced to cover her mouth to stifle the giggles that were now threatening to expose her presence in the cemetery. Ralph did likewise, for like Polly, he certainly did not wish to be discovered. Polly remembered back to the strange happenings at the funeral home and how the feathers had been stuffed back in the coffin before the director returned. Now they were out of the box for a second time, she wondered what on earth would happen next! She did not have to wait too long to find out. The feathers that had been circling in the air began to fall like raindrops, many landing on all those participating in the funeral service.

"Atchoo! Atchoo," sneezed Aunt Mildred as a stray feather landed on her nose and then appeared to make its way up her right nostril.

She let out a scream for assistance as she alerted her husband to her crisis. He in turn abandoned the vicar and immediately raced back to her side. He then struggled to remove the offending feather that was now protruding from her right nostril. It refused to budge.

"Get my tweezers from my bag," yelled a very distraught Aunt Mildred as she pointed towards her handbag, which still lay abandoned on the ground near the grave.

Uncle Boritz obliged, moving most cautiously. He did not wish to fall into the hole again. He therefore very wisely got down on all fours as he scrambled in the mud attempting to retrieve her bag. Finally he had it firmly in his possession. He then began to rummage through it in search of his dear wife's tweezers. Try as he may, he could not find them.

"The tweezers are definitely in there, you incompetent buffoon!" she hollered at the top of her lungs.

Uncle Boritz chose to ignore her histrionics as he continued his frustrating search of her large handbag, still looking for the elusive tweezers, but to no avail.

Meanwhile, the vicar still stood on the other side of the grave, silent and disturbed. Never in all his years in the ministry had he performed a funeral service that had been reduced to such a fiasco! The white feathers continued to circle above them until one-by-one they came to settle on Aunt Mildred and Uncle Boritz, forcing him to remove his glasses, for he could no longer see out of them. It was no use; the feathers still kept coming. Before long, both of them were engulfed by hundreds of them.

Aunt Mildred was by now very irate and began hurling insult after insult at poor, flustered Uncle Boritz. For now every inch of her disproportionate anatomy was covered in the wretched, itching feathers. Finally, out of sheer desperation he picked up her handbag and shook out all the contents. As everything but the kitchen sink fell onto the muddied ground, he blindly groped around in his seemingly futile effort to put his hands on her stupid tweezers!

Uncle Boritz was in such a panic that he did not notice that a neatly folded piece of paper from among her personal belongings had flown away, landing nearby on a vase of flowers that was perched on an adjacent grave.

"Get that piece of paper, for it is an important piece of evidence!" screamed Aunt Mildred.

Uncle Boritz rose from his knees and hurriedly raced after it. He was within inches of retrieving this important piece of paper when a gust of wind blew it higher up into the air. Uncle Boritz, still covered in feathers, raced after it with his arms outstretched in the hope of finally catching it. The paper seemed to be playing with him. For each time he almost had it in his grasp, another rush of wind blew it further away. Eventually he gave up the chase and lamely staggered back in Aunt Mildred's direction. He struggled to see where he was going, for by now he was so covered in feathers that he could not see a jolly thing.

As he walked with arms outstretched back towards Aunt Mildred he suddenly slipped again, and in trying to prevent another fall he grabbed hold of her, pulling her down on top of him. On witnessing

POLLY BROWN

this, the coffin bearers rushed to give their assistance. They were, after all, trained to be helpful in such extremely sensitive jobs as theirs was normally meant to be. As Aunt Mildred and Uncle Boritz finally got to their feet, they began to experience a new and very uncomfortable emotion called humiliation, and they did not like it at all. They felt so embarrassed by all that had happened to them, and they were extremely upset that the vicar as well as others had borne witness to their total demise. Therefore instead of showing gratitude, they turned on the coffin bearers and proceeded to curse and shout at them.

Unable to face any more, the poor and most baffled coffin bearers turned on their heels and made a run for the church and its sanctuary. Not only did they seek to get under cover from the dreadful weather conditions, but they also sought to get as far away as possible from the Scumberrys.

Meanwhile, the vicar still stood frozen to the spot. He was thoroughly soaked to the skin, and his sermon book was as wide open as his mouth. Polly could not help but feel sorry for this man of the cloth, but not quite so sorry for her guardians, who were not only hideously tarred and feathered, but still screaming obscenities in each other's direction.

By this point in the whole affair, the vicar, having noticed that the coffin bearers had made a run for it, decided to do likewise! He therefore hastily left the scene, preferring to opt for the solitude and sanctity of his chapel to finish his prayers for Thomas. He thought about how much Thomas must have needed them when he was alive, and he felt a sense of overwhelming sadness as he prayed for Thomas's safe passage into the arms of Jesus. Unbeknownst to him, his prayers on this most difficult day had in fact already been answered long before he dropped to his knees.

Within minutes of the vicar and coffin bearers' hasty departure, the rain ceased and the sun came out from its hiding place to beat down on the soaked-to-the-skin young lady. Polly hardly noticed that she was drenched, for she had been so absorbed by the farcical events that she had witnessed from her hiding place. She smiled to herself as she observed that Uncle Boritz had come off much worse than Aunt Mildred. For Mildred was the owner of the large handbag, which she had seemed very happy to turn into an offensive weapon as she struck her husband blow after blow as they left the graveyard to go back home to the castle.

Although the graveyard was now empty, Polly deemed it wise to stay hidden just a little longer. She stretched out on the sodden grass to allow the sun's warmth to dry her off. The other secret visitor who had been hiding behind a tomb decided to do likewise.

Ralph took off his old leather boots to wiggle his toes and then hung his trench coat on a tombstone before likewise stretching out on the grass to dry out under the warmth of the sun. He smiled to himself as he thought this had been the most eventful and fun funeral he had ever attended. As both of them lay on the grass in the graveyard, Polly still totally unaware of Ralph's presence, the grave digger, Ernie Shwartskoff, came along with Bert from the funeral home. Bert had been ordered to join Ernie at the cemetery, having been urgently contacted by Mr. Pinecoffin, and ordered to make his way to the graveyard to reseal the coffin. This time they used extra long nails!

Ernie stood leaning heavily on his spade while Bert jumped down into the hole where the coffin still sat. As he hammered in the extra long nails, Ernie commented that this whole funeral had seemed quite spooky from the start.

"Where on earth did all those white feathers come from, Bert?" he asked, looking down the hole as Bert hammered away.

Bert looked up and shrugged his shoulders. "Beats me, Ernie," he said with a grin. "Not only have these little feathers been the cause of much mischief, but their very existence is still something of a mystery."

With the coffin lid safely secured, Bert called out to Ernie to give him a hand out of the hole. Ernie happily obliged, holding out his hand and pulling hard until Bert came up to the surface.

"There, that should do it. Nothing should open that coffin again," he triumphantly declared, "for I've used the longest nails I could find."

Both men stood for a moment as they had a good chuckle. Ernie then took the large spade he had been leaning on and began filling in the hole with the earth that stood piled high beside the burial site. He whistled merrily as he got on with the job. In no time at all the large mound had disappeared and the ground was then leveled off. He paused along with his friend to admire his workmanship. He then placed a friendly arm on Bert's shoulder as they walked out of the cemetery together, deep in conversation about the length, depth, and breadth of the next grave that Ernie was required to dig in time for tomorrow's funeral.

Chapter 15
IN DOMINUM SPIRITUM SANCTUM

*P*OLLY THOUGHT IT was now safe to come out from where she had been resting. As she stood up from the ground she checked to see that all was clear. It was. She placed the wild poppies and bluebells into the jar that was now filled with rainwater and headed over to where Thomas lay at rest. She placed the jar on the freshly-filled grave before gently falling down on her knees to say a prayer for Thomas. She still had absolutely no idea that she was being observed from a distance.

Polly found herself at a complete loss as she wondered precisely what prayers she should say, for her emptiness consumed her. She had no "order of service" or little prayer book to help her. Without these aids, she was very unsure where to put the *thees* and *thous* that were put into most prayers. She believed that these were obviously the keys to getting God's full attention. She thought she would have a good try anyway. She cleared her throat and began. She chose her sternest and most holier-than-thou voice, which was pretty similar to that of the dear vicar.

> *O Lord, Thou knowest all my ways, and I therefore beseech Thee to hearken unto my voice and inclineth Thine ear unto me and pitieth me in all my troubles. For mine eye is consumed with much grief, and my bones are therefore consumed even unto my bowels. For only Thou, O Lord, knoweth the way that I should take, and Thou must surely in Thine good judgments cometh to mine aid and giveth me Thy deepest consolation that only cometh from Thy right hand, or is it Your left?*

Polly paused to consider whether it was God's right hand or whether it was His left. She could not remember which one of God's hands was the one that was so often referred to when praying. It was very important, after all, to get it right if there was to be even the slimmest chance of persuading Him to act on her behalf and give her a helping hand.

"Oh, dear," she cried forlornly. "I will be here all day if I don't get it right. So I think I will have to settle for the left hand and just hope for the best."

Ralph, who was within earshot, could not help but make a deep groan as he remained very curious as to what on earth was going to come forth next from this unusual young lady. He therefore continued to listen in on Polly.

For I waiteth upon Thee, O Lord, and putteth all my trust in Thee. For I hopeth that when Thou hast tried me, You will bringeth me forth from the pit and setteth my feet upon Thy rocks and establish me in Thy great kindness.

Polly stopped and made a similar groan to that of Ralph's before finally admitting defeat and giving up. She was most impressed with her words, and there was no denying she would, if she were a man, make a most credible minister, but the sad truth was that she hadn't the slightest idea what she was going on about. "No," she admitted to herself, "it was all pure gobbledygook!" She usually spoke from her heart and said whatever she needed to say in her words. Therefore she felt most frustrated and dissatisfied with her failure to express herself and thereby discharge her burden.

Ralph was nodding in perfect agreement with Polly's assessment of her very unsatisfactory communication with God. He hoped and prayed that she would have the courage and conviction to be herself and start speaking from her heart.

For many years Polly had sung in the choir, and again, she had to confess that she understood very little of what she was saying and wondered if God might well be in the same position. After all, what does *In Dominum Spiritum Sanctum* and *Qui tollis peccata mundi* and other such utterances really mean?

Polly admitted to herself that she really had very little idea as to what was the best method to get God to pay her some attention. She felt that most of what she said or repeated after the priest bore little resemblance to how she felt inside. It all served to make Him seem very far away and quite unreachable. Polly mistakenly suspected that God used this secret code only with bishops, cardinals, and priests, but cared little when it came to communicating with commoners such as herself, who could only understand plain English. This crisis appeared to come to a head as she knelt there alone and heartbroken at Thomas's grave. Her beloved brother was gone, and she could no longer keep up the pretense of feeling fine and doing what she felt was expected of her. Inside she was screaming and in need of real answers to the hideousness of her life on this earth.

She slumped down by his graveside and pondered what she should do. Luckily it was not too long before she had a bright idea. She would sing her favorite church hymn that she always sang when she was alone with only her private thoughts for companionship. As she knew all the words of this hymn by heart, she decided that singing it might be the best option after all. She would at least give it a go. With this settled in her mind, she opened her mouth and began.

The LORD is my shepherd; I shall not want. He maketh me to lie down...

Within minutes of starting, her voice began to crack causing her to falter, so she stopped her singing, even though she had only just begun. Her heart felt like a lead weight, and therefore every attempt to pray seemed utterly futile. She believed she might as well give up and go home, for what she truly needed was a real heart-to-heart with God, as she was so weighed down with her cares and woes. She therefore made the snap decision to go for it! Yes, really launch right in!

I'm so sorry, God. But I really don't feel like singing today, for I have much in my heart that I need to say, and I'm beginning

*to feel that this may be the perfect time and place to get it all off
my chest if that's OK with You.*

She paused for a second, straining to hear an answer. Whether
she was hoping for a thundering voice from the heavens to bellow
down, "I'm here, and I'm listening," or "Oh, no! Not you again,
Polly Brown!" will remain a mystery. What is known is that she
only waited a matter of seconds before advancing most forthrightly
into her speech in a way that only Polly knew how! For she was very
experienced in expressing such matters of the heart with no holds
barred! There was to be no holding back by this young lady as she
spilled out all her deepest concerns that day by the graveside.

*I thought not, for as usual You are probably far too busy to
talk to me. Well, I'm going to say it anyway, and I would like
to start with the words of this hymn that I've been told is really
a psalm. Now, I know You didn't write it with Your own fair
hands, but as far as I am aware, You supposedly inspired the
person who did. To me that is the same thing. Therefore, as far
as I am concerned, You must take on some, if not all, responsibility for its interpretation.*

Polly paused to draw breath before continuing on.

*Well, this all leads up to me saying that I think we need an
open discussion concerning the content of this hymn, don't
You think? For starters, Your psalm begins, "The Lord is my
shepherd; I shall not want." Well, I am going to stop there, for
I need to inform You that I am most definitely wanting! Yes,
I am wanting so badly that it hurts like crazy. I want a mother
to take care of me and tell me that she loves me. I want You
to take real care of Thomas, and I also want You to help me
get out of this horrid orphanage, because I really can't take
any more. I'm sorry, God, to have to talk to You in such an
outspoken manner, but I cannot hold all this in much longer.
I know You may think I am utterly selfish for complaining
when there are so many children in the world who have no food*

or a bed to sleep in. But I am screaming inside, and I have no other person to share all this pain with.

As Polly paused to wipe away the tears that were streaming down her face, Ralph felt the depths of her distress and desperately wanted to come out from behind his hiding place to give her a reassuring hug. Nonetheless, he chose to restrain himself from intervening, for he felt that it was best for her to remain ignorant of his presence in the graveyard. He chose instead to privately shed a few tears on her behalf.

You go on to say, and I quote, "He maketh me to lie down in green pastures." Well, that's all very nice, but if You hadn't noticed, I am not a cow! So a field full of green grass to chew on is therefore of no use to me whatsoever! All I want is a real home and a real family with nice food to fill my tummy once in a while. So I do think it would be wise of You to get those words changed for starters!

Polly paused to take another deep breath as she continued to confront Him on this very personal matter.

Leaving aside the still waters bit, You then go on to say that You restore my soul. Well, I may be a bit of an idiot at times, but nowhere in my biology books is there any reference to the soul as an organ. I've seen plenty of hearts, livers, lungs, and kidneys. They are all in the books along with illustrations of what they look like, but there is definitely no picture of a soul! So how can You possibly claim to restore something that clearly does not exist? Need I go on?

Ralph smiled at her rhetorical question, for he knew with much certainty that there was no way Polly Brown would finish until she had exhausted every avenue available to her. He had, after all, come to know Polly and her little ways only too well. He therefore gave a deep sigh.

Polly looked down towards the earth that covered Thomas's coffin and apologized to Thomas, saying she promised she would get down to talking about his needs just as soon as she had got everything off her chest. She knew he would understand.

You further claim, "Yea, though I walk through the valley of the shadow of death, I will fear no evil." Well, I feel this one really needs further explaining! For my whole life is spent in fear, and I assure You it is no shadow; it truly is the real thing. The evil that encompasses me is so dark that I feel like I am dying all day long. I therefore feel I have little choice but to ask what on earth are You going on about? I do hope that at some time in the near future, after You've given some thought to my question, You will be able give me a satisfactory answer.

Polly took a hanky from her pocket and wiped her eyes.

And I have to say that I am particularly concerned about the next bit, for You say, "Thy rod and thy staff they comfort me." Well, speaking of rods, I have had so many beatings, and I can assure you, hand on heart, that they have given me absolutely no comfort at all. Have You ever had a beating? I'm pretty certain that if You had You would have no trouble agreeing that You gained no comfort from them whatsoever!

Polly paused as she instantly realized that she had gone too far. She had made a real blunder. She felt pretty stupid as she considered past Easter Sunday services, which never failed to remind all the parishioners about what happened to his only Son. For not only was He beaten beyond recognition, but He was also nailed to a cross and left to die. This time she had really blown it! She continued, very apologetically.

I'm sorry God. Please ignore the last bit. In fact, pretend I never said it. It must have been absolutely awful for You to watch on and feel powerless to stop it, so please understand my outburst. It's just that I have had to watch Thomas take many beatings for things that he, too, was innocent of. So I'm really so sorry. I really didn't mean to be so heartless.

Polly wiped away the tears that were now streaming down her face quite out of control. Ralph also looked around for something to wipe away his tears, for he really needed to get a grip on himself. In sheer desperation he pulled off one of his dirty and very pungent striped socks and proceeded to wipe his face before blowing his nose into his sock as quietly as he was able. Finally, after many blows, Ralph took his crumpled sock and, using both hands, he stretched it back into shape before struggling to put it back on his bare foot. Polly, having blown her nose, also put her hanky back in her pocket before carrying on her seemingly one-sided conversation with her Maker.

> *But come to think of it, she sadly said, I also think canes, or rods if you prefer, should be banned from use in orphanages and all schools. My brothers have all been given the cane for the most stupid little things, so to think that all Your staff in heaven are going around giving the rod willy nilly makes me wonder if I would really like heaven at all!*

Ralph, who was still listening in on Polly's conversation, felt nothing short of the deepest sadness for her. He felt sadder still that all her experiences in life had led her to believe that God above was something of a cruel tyrant or a hard taskmaster. It made him want to start weeping all over again. He declined, purely because he felt much too exhausted to pull off his other sock. Separating each toe and then placing each of them into their own individual cubby hole was more than a bit of a challenge, at least as far as he was concerned.

"You'd have to be an angel to stay around and listen to Polly when she got into the full flow," he muttered rather resignedly.

He could only hope there would come a time when she would realize that God's arms of love were already around her. Until that day he could do little but watch on, feeling nothing but the deepest compassion for this extremely hurt and damaged young lady.

> *You go on later to say, "Thou anointest my head with oil." Again I find myself having to stop You there to point out that if You hadn't already noticed, I have extremely dry hair with*

awful split ends. It may well have a lot to do with the cheap shampoo I'm forced to use, but no way does this excuse get You off the hook! I can say with absolute certainty that I am missing out on this special offer. None of this free "anointment oil" has ever touched one measly wisp of my hair! So I wonder if You could turn a blind eye to my little outburst and still do me the kindness of popping by one night when you have a free moment to apply a little of this conditioner to my very dull and lifeless hair!

Oh, and while You're at it, please could You give me a generous dollop of this oil. I would really appreciate hair like Cassandra Catchpole's. Her hair is so shimmeringly shiny and glossy that it gives her the perfect excuse to flaunt herself, swinging her head from side to side as she swans around the school like some trumped-up glamour queen. I have to admit that I find this more than a trifle upsetting, for I've come to believe You're accidentally giving her my portion of anointment oil. I promise You that she really doesn't need it. The truth is she already has lots of lovely clothes and beautifully straight teeth. It all makes me feel quite sick because it's not fair! I really need Your assurance that You will look into this little matter on my behalf.

Polly pulled out her hanky again, this time to have a good blow. She then began laughing out loud.

You tell me that my cup runneth over. Well, God, You're quite right about that! I obviously don't need to tell You that I'm constantly in trouble for filling my mug to the brim and slopping water or tea all over the place. But I bet You do the same! Be honest, You know You do!

Polly paused and listened intently. She took the silence to mean a firm yes. Encouraged by this, she went on.

Well, it's good to know I'm not the only one with this terrible habit. We must make more effort not to do this, don't You think? In Your case it would be advisable to clear up all spills

as soon as they happen, otherwise the angels could well find
themselves sliding all over the place, quite possibly slipping off a
cloud, then falling to the earth with a hard thump.

Ralph also chuckled to himself as he thought this extraordinary and most outspoken child has an unusually keen sense of imagination. He drew closer to listen further.

Now on to the next bit. You say, "Goodness and mercy shall
follow me all the days of my life." Well, God, I would really
love this to be the case, but to date I have found nothing but
unhappiness and trouble, and therefore mercy is a word that
I have the greatest difficulty understanding. Have I got it all
wrong? I have heard of Mercedes! This sounds almost the same
as mercies, and they are very expensive cars, I believe. Is that
what You're trying to tell me? Is there some undercover opera-
tion going on and I am being constantly watched and monitored
by secret agents from inside their Mercedes? Surely Gailey
Gobbstopper couldn't be involved, could she? Hmm…maybe
not, for she could never afford such an expensive car on three-
pence a week. So who else could it be? If this is the case, then
I can only thank You for being so kind as to warn me. I will
certainly be on my guard, for it goes a long way in explaining
why I can do nothing in secret without being found out.

At this point, Ralph had to cover his mouth, for he was afraid if he laughed too loudly his cover would be well-and-truly blown. He came to the conclusion that Polly would make a most excellent politician, for he had never met so young a lady who could keep going for so long. She would indeed make an excellent candidate for the House of Lords.

Polly, on the other hand, felt so much better for having had this little talk with God. She felt the anger was beginning to leave her, taking with it the dark, ugly cloud that had hung over her head. So she was now feeling a whole heap lighter. She believed she was almost there in terms of letting off steam, and she resolved to hurry things up, for she did not want to be late home and be in more trouble, as well as miss tea.

Finally, God, You tell me that "I will dwell in the house of the Lord for ever." Well, again, this is a real problem to me. If You had invited me to stay forever a few months ago, I would have been very happy to oblige. But now I have these two friends. Yes, they are gentlemen of the road, but I tell you, God, they are really very nice ragamuffins with extraordinarily good hearts. One of them, a man called Ralph, has told me there may be some purpose to all the things I am going through. He has encouraged me to follow my dreams, of which I am most proud to say I have many. So I need to make it perfectly clear that while I am very happy to pop in for a cup of tea and a chat, I do need to stress that I can only stay a while, for I have important things that I need to achieve. So, what I am trying to say in the politest way that I know how is that I'm not entirely sure about the "for ever" bit, at least not at the moment! Now please don't get mad at me about that! My decision is not set in concrete, and in time I might well change my mind. We'll just have to wait and see!

Ralph secretly nodded in agreement.

Oh, and one more thing that I nearly forgot to mention, but it is of extreme importance. You have never given me the exact details on how to find You. How can I possibly pay a visit if I have absolutely no idea where You reside? Surely anyone with an ounce of courtesy would think to give a map of some kind if they were giving out a lot of invites? I even took the liberty of popping into our local estate agents, Sting and Chargemore, to ask them if Your house had ever been on the market. Because, crazy as it might sound, I thought that maybe if it had, they would be able to look it up and print off some useful directions. They went to great lengths to assure me that although they had sold thousands of houses over the years, Yours wasn't one of them. So sadly they were unable to be of any assistance whatsoever to me.

With this in mind, I feel somebody has got to risk all and be honest with You and spell out that in future You really do need to send very clear directions to all persons that You've kindly invited. This will go a long way towards preventing any further disappointment. So I look forward to receiving written confirmation of Your address and whereabouts at Your earliest convenience. Also, if You don't mind, a little map or sketch would also be really appreciated.

Ralph looked on despairingly, for he was most concerned that Polly would be there all night if she kept thinking of new things to discuss and debate. Still, Polly continued to chatter on, rearranging the poppies and bluebells that were in the glass jar as she spoke.

Now, about Thomas, for he's the real reason I am here today. I really need You to take great care of him for me. Please tell Your staff to spare him the rod, for he has had a lifetime of being given the cane—sometimes for no reason at all! So he really does not deserve to be punished anymore. I hope You agree with me on that one. Also, if You find him crying in a corner, I do think it would be really nice if You could see Your way to putting an arm around his shoulder, or better still, could You give him a little hug and wipe away his tears. I used to do that when he was badly hurting, she gulped, wiping away her own tears as she spoke. Please ask him if he liked my little note, and finally, I am quite certain he will forget to ask You for drawing paper and pencils. So please, please, God, can You make sure he gets some? He will be so happy painting and drawing. You never know, You might even get to like some of his pictures! So promise me You won't forget.

After she finished saying all that needed to be said, Polly stood up from the ground and remained motionless with her eyes firmly shut. She had seen this minute of silence done many times in church on special occasions, so she thought she was following correct procedure by doing it. Ralph felt extremely grateful, for it was the first time he had ever witnessed Polly wide awake and not talking!

Polly moved away from the graveside, blowing Thomas a final kiss. Then with a single tear sliding slowly down her cheek, she said, "Good-bye for now, my precious one," before hastily turning on her heels to leave the cemetery.

As she opened the church gate to leave, she looked back at the grave and her jar of flowers one more time. She could not help but observe that the wild poppies that earlier in the day had stood so tall and majestic were now wilted. She smiled to herself, for she truly believed that they too had bowed their heads in prayer and now appeared to be bleeding all over Thomas's little grave. She winced as she thought that it must be the sunlight doing funny tricks.

Ralph, who had watched the whole funeral from beginning to end from behind a tombstone, breathed a deep sigh of relief as he thought to himself, "She is, I believe, most definitely ready to leave the orphanage and go on her journey." He then made an even deeper sigh as he thought to himself, "Thank goodness she only knows the twenty-third psalm from the church hymnal. What would have happened had she known there were a further one hundred forty-nine psalms that she could take issue with!"

Ralph was fairly certain that if Polly discovered their existence, he would certainly be in for a long night. God help everyone if this should ever happen. He would in such a case be well advised to book into a local hotel for a fortnight at the very least! He shook his head as he pondered such an event ever taking place. He hoped that by the time Polly discovered the other psalms in that most ancient of books, she would be wiser and much more trusting towards her Maker! He shook his head again as he got up to leave, for he knew with much certainty that for Polly the road ahead would be strewn with many trials and tribulations. It would at times be most treacherous, and she would indeed go through many dark nights of the soul before she found that dreams do finally come true and with them, much joy and freedom. He therefore hoped and prayed that Polly would have the very necessary courage to take a leap into the unknown and follow her destiny.

Chapter 16
TRUTH COMES IN A DAY

*A*s POLLY WALKED out of the graveyard she noticed a piece of folded paper. She stooped down to pick it up with the clear intention of disposing of it in the nearest wastebasket. But as she held it in her hand she found herself unfolding it. She instantly felt very guilty as she discovered it was a letter and therefore may be of a personal nature to its owner. However, curiosity prevailed and she started to read it. She was very surprised to discover that the letter was addressed to the Scumberrys and more surprised, if not shocked, when she read it contents.

Dear Mr. and Mrs. Scumberry,

My name is Camilla Ascot, and I am a very distant relative of Polly Brown and her brothers Thomas and James. I have been working for many years with the poor and needy in darkest Bolivia. Therefore I had no idea that these children had been taken into the care of the social services.

As soon as this most sad news became known to me, I got on a plane and came back to England in search of them. Once home on English soil, I arranged for an interview with the social services in the hope of getting the necessary information. To my surprise, that information was not forthcoming. I was told the reason for this secrecy is that all their information is regarded as highly confidential and that, as I was not an immediate relative, they were in no position to help me with my search. I have therefore taken it upon myself to approach every orphanage and private home for children in care in the hope that eventually I would find them or at least get a positive lead as to where they might be.

To date, I have had no response whatsoever. So with all possible leads exhausted, I am turning to you as a last resort. I am feeling most forlorn and frustrated in my efforts, for I cannot bear to think of these children alone and without any real hope. Their mother wrote many times telling me how wonderful and beautiful they were as babies, and I am therefore quite certain that she was very distressed at having to give them away. From what little I have found out, she fell on hard times, losing her job and then her home, and she was finally forced to live on the streets in London, taking refuge in shelters and going from soup kitchen to soup kitchen in search of the food and comfort that The Salvation Army give to so many lost and weary homeless souls. (God bless them for their wonderful work.) Had I known any of this I would certainly have done all I could to help her. But I think she allowed her pride to prevent her from writing and asking for my help. Sadly, she caught pneumonia, and with no shelter to take refuge, she died alone in an alley. She was found by some of her friends, clutching a photograph of the children in her frozen hand.

At this point Polly started to uncontrollably tremble, before breaking down in tears as she wept for this unknown woman who went by the name of Mother. She found it unbearable to think that her mummy had died alone and in such a terrible manner. Her guardians had always led her to believe that her mother was a woman of ill repute, and this belief had been expressed in many of the so-called private family sessions. Her guardians told all present that Polly would end up exactly the same as her mother. For at the end of the day it was in her genes, just as madness was! Polly had therefore determined that she would never wear a pair of jeans if this was going to be the end result!

The children had used this terrible and most false piece of information to cruelly taunt Polly—especially dear Gailey Gobbstopper, who slept in the next bed. She made it her mission to gather up every piece of salacious information she could in order to make Polly's nights terrible! Sadly, Gailey and many of the other children were more than willing to call Polly the most terrible names associated with this usually-never-talked-about and most undesirable trade. Only now did Polly know that like most other things, it was an absolute lie! This made her weep even more. She finally took control of herself and read on.

Luckily, the friend who discovered her body had many friends in The Salvation Army, and as they specialize in tracing family members the organization attempted to contact any other living relatives, to no avail. With only the possessions found by her side in a carrier bag, they were eventually forced to give up looking, and her belongings were disposed of, with the exception of a pile of photographs. Many of these are of the children as babies. These I now have in my possession, ready to give to the children if ever I'm lucky enough to find them. I want to help these children in any way that I can. Although they must be between six and twelve years of age by now, I enclose a photo of them as babies in the hope that you might recognize them.

If you can be of any assistance in my pursuit to find these children, I would be eternally grateful and indebted to you. For my time in England is fast running out, and it is only a matter of time before I head back to Bolivia to oversee my next project. I am sure that you are aware that only one in seven people in the world have a tap with running water. This is most shocking, don't you think? I am therefore heading up a project that will provide many poor villages with clean running water so that the villagers will be able to drink from it, as well as give water to their animals and sustain their crops.

It is indeed most wonderful to know that we are all on the same side, working to give love and hope to those in great need—suffering souls that are dying daily without any help. God bless you for the personal sacrifice you are making to ensure that deprived, unfortunate children are given a warm and loving home, thereby ensuring they have futures filled with great promise. It is good to know that there are others in this sometimes-selfish world in which we live who wish to make it a better place to live. I therefore enclose a small donation of £100 to be spent on the children in your good care.

Yours sincerely,

Camilla Ascot

P. S. I leave for Bolivia in just under six months, so I would appreciate an early reply. Thank you so kindly for taking the time to read my letter. If you are unable to be of any assistance, I would be most grateful if you would return the most precious photos of the children back to me at your earliest convenience.

To say that Polly was shocked is to underestimate the depth of pain she experienced as the contents of the letter were slowly and painfully revealed to her. Her heart was pounding so fast that she felt it might well explode as she struggled to understand what was going on. Polly noted that the letter was dated and was therefore some nine months old. Sadly the address had been obliterated by large lines of blue ink. Why had Uncle Boritz and Aunt Mildred never mentioned the letter? Polly felt as though she was going crazy. If her relative had been informed that they were all living at the castle, surely she would have come for them? Worse still, Thomas would still be alive. She felt sick to the pit of her stomach. She had consistently prayed to God to be rescued, and He had, after all, heard her prayers. But all hope was now gone, for her cruel and very deceitful guardians had as usual sabotaged her only hope and chance of freedom. Polly wept bitterly.

Instead of going straight home as she had originally planned, she now decided to make one small detour. She knew she was running late, and this in itself would cause much suspicion at home. What difference would a few more minutes make? She therefore turned on her heels and headed back to the church.

Once inside, she headed up to the altar and lit a candle for Thomas, as well as for her mother. She then knelt down and prayed in silence until the candle had fully melted and the flame finally died. Then she got up from her knees and, with a still-heavy heart and tears tumbling down her cheeks, she walked out of the church, shutting the door quietly as she left before heading home to the castle. She had been coping so well until she found that stupid little folded piece of paper. She now wished that she had never opened it up to read its contents, for then she would have been none the wiser. Her heart felt so heavy and her life so beyond all hope as she opened the door and crept back inside the castle, wanting to find a small dark corner to sort out her confused thoughts and weep alone.

On her walk home that evening she found herself going back in time to a specific day in a history lesson. After the lesson was over and all the other students had left the classroom, she had gone up to his desk to challenge dear Mr. Beloski over certain events they had discussed in that lesson which had greatly disturbed her. Polly had always enjoyed learning about the historical events that had shaped the world over thousands of years. But she was also often very distressed when she learned for the first time about rulers and their wars, where so many people lost their lives due to the arrogance of some terrible and wicked tyrant. She could understand the need to fight, for it was very important to defend your country, but she had nothing but anger towards those who purely wished to extend their boundaries and killed innocent people as a result of their power and greed.

She hated evil and injustice with a passion. She had just finished a book on King Arthur, and in the book she had read, "War is the trade of kings." Polly felt it was high time all these so-called kings became satisfied and content with what they already had instead of being greedy and wanting what did not belong to them. She felt strongly that these kings had a duty to do all within their power to make their subjects' lives as safe and happy as possible, specifically looking out for those citizens that needed more help, such as the poor and downtrodden. That's why kings were born, wasn't it? Besides which, they got to live in beautiful castles and eat wonderful, scrumptious food, and that privilege alone should make them more merciful and generous, or so she thought. So Polly rightly believed that true kings ruled over their people with honor and integrity, and any that didn't do this were imposters who should feel very ashamed of themselves!

"Why is there so much hate in the world?" she had asked him, desperately seeking some suitably acceptable and consoling explanation. Mr. Beloski had stopped marking the papers in front of him and paused, toying with his pen as he gave thoughtful consideration to her question.

"Come on, Mr. Beloski, I need a truthful answer," she urged, completely misunderstanding the reason behind his reticence to give a quick answer off the top of his head.

"Sometimes there is no right answer to a question, Polly," he gently replied.

"Well, that's crazy," said Polly rather abrasively. "For if all those in power around the world know and see terrible wickedness going on under their noses, then why do they often appear to stand by, doing little or nothing whatsoever to help? I find it all makes me feel not only very sad, but also very angry."

Mr. Beloski had agreed that history often had a way of troubling the heart and conscience.

"Polly, not everyone is as concerned as you about getting to the bottom of everything. In fact, most of us prefer to hide our heads in the sand and just hope a problem will go away," he said, looking directly into her eyes. For he hoped she would just accept that this was the way things were and always had been throughout the history of mankind. She wouldn't!

"Mr. Beloski," she cried very despairingly. "How will we ever learn to change this world for the better if we do not face the mistakes of the past, even choosing at times to deny that certain events even took place?"

"Oh, Polly," Mr. Beloski rather drily replied. "For the bright young student that you are, you ask too many questions. But listen to me, one thing I can assure you is that lies may last a lifetime, but truth comes in a day."

Polly had never forgotten dear Mr. Beloski or those powerful and unforgettable words of hope, for they had entered deep into her being and seemed permanently engraved on her heart. Those few words regarding the uncovering of lies had given her such comfort many times when she witnessed grave injustices.

But now, as she thought back to those powerful words of consolation, she found it hard—if not impossible—to believe that they held any truth. If they did, how was it that her guardians had managed to get away with deception all these years without ever being discovered, and were still deceiving all around them? She did not think that any history book would ever record the tragic events that had taken place in children's homes up and down the country, hers included. And if that was the case, how would the social services ever recognize that mistakes had been made? And more to the point, would they, like kings, ever seek to put their mistakes right? For if the social services were supposed to protect them from further pain in their damaged and seriously troubled lives, she felt they had much explaining to do.

Uncle Boritz had always made it perfectly clear that no one would ever listen to a child, especially if the story in question came from the mouths of children in care. They were all deemed to be not only the lowest of the low but also compulsive liars who made up fanciful stories for no particular reason other than to get attention. He had been proven absolutely correct in his assessment that to spill the beans was a complete waste of time, and this infuriated her further. She was very angry with a body of people whom she had never met, as they held her life and many other children's fragile lives in their hands. They seemingly used little more than a nod of their head, and their official rubber stamp when making life-changing decisions that so often bore very serious consequences.

Unless they fully acknowledged their guilt, changed their ways, and took their heads out of the sand, history would feel free to repeat itself time and time again. To Polly's way of thinking, nothing made any sense at all. She was extremely wearied and tired of living in a world that made no sense…a world that seemed upside down…a world filled with injustice and prejudice…a world that appeared to say that right was wrong and wrong was right. What sort of world was that? Polly felt certain that mankind was heading for the deep abyss unless it woke up and turned from all that was threatening to destroy it. She seriously wondered if this could possibly ever happen. She truly hoped so.

When Polly walked through the front door she was greeted by her extremely upset guardians. Their very posture immediately told Polly that both of them were very angry indeed!

"And what time do you call this, girl?" hissed Aunt Mildred, her thin lips twitching and both hands hugging her hips.

Polly looked up and immediately noticed that a few remaining small feathers were still caught up in her tight locks, and this made her want to break into a smile. However, she forced herself to remain not only straight-faced but also equally tight-lipped about where and what she had been doing that day. She was far too sad to care and much too tired to reply.

"Well, you sniveling little wretch, you're really in for the high jump now," sneered Uncle Boritz. "In fact you will be severely punished for your downright impudence. Take my word for it, young lady! Your troubles are only just about to begin, for a little birdie told me you left the school early today," he said with an air of all-knowing pomposity.

Polly felt certain she knew exactly who the little birdie was. Still she kept silent, and this only served to make her guardians more furious than ever.

"Get upstairs now, and that's an order!" yelled a red-faced Aunt Mildred. "You're far too late for any food; tea-time finished hours ago. So for part of your punishment you can go to bed hungry, and we will see you in the office tomorrow morning without fail. Do you clearly understand? Our office first thing!"

Although Polly had not eaten a thing since breakfast, she had become so used to being hungry that to go without tea was no big deal to her. She was just very relieved and happy to be dismissed and sent straight to her room. Her day had, in many ways, been most grueling, and she needed the space to be alone with her thoughts. Polly went to the bathroom, and after cleaning her teeth she got into her pajamas and wearily made her way back to the dormitory. She tiptoed past all the other beds that were occupied by young ladies deep in their slumber and picked up Langdon from the floor where he lay before pulling down the bedclothes to get into bed. As she turned on the small lamp on her bedside locker, her eye caught something sitting on the top of the locker. It was a plain brown package tied up with string. She sat on her bed and proceeded to open it. As she tore open the packaging, a small white feather fluttered onto the bed. Polly picked it up and smiled, for she assumed it must have got itself trapped in her clothes earlier in the day at the graveyard. She placed it on her locker before continuing on somewhat cautiously to unravel the brown string that was tied tightly around the package. As she pulled away layer after layer of brown paper packaging, a bright, shiny object fell to the floor. Polly picked it up and immediately realized it was a signet ring that on closer inspection bore a strange, regal coat of arms. Polly placed it to one side as she continued to unravel the parcel. The gift revealed itself to be yet another book.

"Oh, no. Not another book to make me feel worse than I already do," she moaned.

Polly sat and stared at the book cover for quite a lengthy period of time, for this book seemed different from the others she had previously been given. One difference was there was no title on the cover to tell her what the story might be about. This book was a lavish gold in color, and its cover was embellished with tiny delicate gold sequins. Polly thought it looked most expensive. *Precious* was the word that sprung to mind. Finally, she took a deep breath and opened it up only to discover, much to her surprise, that all the pages were blank. There were many pages, but none had any print whatsoever. Polly leafed through the pages from beginning to end many times just to make sure that she was not imagining it all. But still she came to the same conclusion that this strange little book contained no story. Perhaps it was a mistake, and the defective book had slipped through the printer's net without being discovered! Polly felt very puzzled. What was the point in a book if there was nothing inside to read?

As she flipped through blank page after blank page for one final time, a little note slipped to the floor and came to settle by her feet. She picked it up and read it. It was from Ralph.

Dear Polly,

I know that today has been most trying for you, and you must be feeling pretty terrible. But I want you to know that you are not on your own, even though you may feel like you are at this most difficult time. Hodgekiss asked me to pop in and invite you to come to tea at his house. As I was flying by—oops, sorry—came by the castle, I was informed by a young girl who brought me tea and my regular sandwich that you were not in. (I have to tell you that neither the tea nor the sandwich were anything as nice as when you make them.) I was most disappointed not to have our regular chat. I have come to look forward to them. Anyhow, I took the liberty of asking the young lady if she would kindly leave my little package on your bedside locker.

Polly, by the time you get to read my note, you will have discovered that this special book holds no words. This is meant to be. You no longer need other people's fairy tales to give you hope (or discouragement in your case), for it is time for you to embark on your own personal journey of self-discovery.

So this book is your book. Yes, you, dear sweet Polly Brown, are being given the wonderful opportunity to rewrite your life. That is, if you are willing and courageous enough to take the risk and make the journey to Hodgekiss's house for tea. If you decide to come, I would be no true friend if I did not warn you from the start that there will be dangers involved, some of which might even be considered perilous. For the pathway is at times very narrow and hazardous, and most give up long before they have Piadora in their sights or within their grasp. Yes, I need to be honest and up front with you when I say that without a shadow of a doubt, you will face giants—many of them from within. But in the time I have come to know you, Miss Polly Brown, I have seen that there is great courage and determination within your spirit. Therefore, I feel certain and confident in my conviction that if anyone can make it, it will be you.

I've enclosed a small map with details of how to get there, along with a gold signet ring that you will need to be wearing. It will ensure your entry into Piadora. But be warned! It is vital that you do not lose this ring, for it is a most essential item. Without it, the gates of Piadora will remain firmly shut, refusing to allow you in.

There is only one thing left to say. Because the terrain is at times treacherous, with many mountains that will be necessary to climb, you cannot bring any baggage—oops, I mean luggage—with you. It will hinder your progress and might even prevent you from reaching your destination. However, you are allowed to pack your schoolbag with small, essential items such as a toothbrush and flannel, hairbrush, a couple of changes of underclothes, and any other necessary items.

I must also inform you that you have permission to bring one nonessential item that you consider very special. However, I cannot stress enough the importance that you make sure that you choose one item and no more. We both look forward to seeing you for tea, and I promise you that this will be the best banquet you will ever attend. I know you will find this extremely hard to believe, but just think of it, Polly: all the pizzas, pastas, and knickerbocker glories you can eat! In fact every imaginable delight that your heart has ever wished for will be available to you! I might take this opportunity to add that even more wonderful than the food is the atmosphere of pure joy and contentment that fills the hearts of all who get to attend. I promise you, hand on heart, that the difficulties you may face getting here will be well worth it. It will be the experience of a lifetime that you will not wish to miss. I leave it with you to make the choice of whether to stay at the castle and continue to suffer a very painful and slow death with the very life force being sucked out of you, or risk all and come in search of Piadora.

Love,

Ralph

Polly's stomach began to rumble at the mention of all this most wonderful food. She thought back to Uncle Boritz's New Year's Eve banquets and how she had always longed to be invited. Now finally she was going to taste scrumptious food beyond her wildest imaginings, and she could hardly wait.

Polly read the note over and over to herself. But as she considered what the journey might mean, such as leaving all her toys behind, and worse still, leaving her little brother James to the mercy of her guardians, the shadowy doubts began to rise within her. She really wanted to go, but she admitted that she was very afraid. What if Gailey Gobbstopper or, worse still, her guardians followed her and caught up with her? Polly could not imagine what fate would befall her in this instance. She felt certain that, were she to be caught, they would think up the worst punishment imaginable. Fear gripped her heart at that possibility. What if Piadora turned out to be a load of nonsense? Yes, that was possible too! And what if she died on the way from influenza due to extreme cold or, worse still, from terrible hunger? She found herself smiling at that one, for what was she thinking? She was always cold, as well as hungry!

Polly sat for a long time, one minute deciding to go, the next minute changing her mind. She felt she was going crazy. Where was her daisy when she needed it so badly? It would make her decision-making process a whole heap easier if she could just keep picking off tiny petals while chanting, "Shall I? Shan't I?" allowing the last petal to determine the outcome, whether favorable or not.

She was about to turn off the light and continue her decision-making in the morning when her eye caught hold of the book still sitting on top of the locker. She paused and thought, "What have I got to lose? There is nothing for me here except more pain and heartache. I will never know for certain what I will have missed if I do not make this journey. And more to the point, I would love to rewrite my life and change my life forever; especially since my dear brother Thomas is no longer here and in need of my support. And James, well, unless I get the help I need, I am in no position to help him either. Polly knew she would just have to hope that he would survive until she returned. After weighing up all the pros and cons, Polly came to the firm conclusion that it was now or never.

She once more picked up the book and opened it up at the first page. She blinked and looked again. Surely she was not imagining it. Her eyes were not playing tricks! There was definitely some writing on the first page. She flicked the page over, then the next, until she reached the last page. She discovered that all other pages were still blank. She went back to the first page and read.

The princess, whose name was Polly, sat on her bed, most anxious to make the right decision: should she leave on her journey of discovery or not? Eventually she chose not to listen to the many murky whisperings that came from within and were getting louder and louder by the minute. They challenged her decision to break free from the castle and embrace the journey, for these cruel and ugly fears had gripped her by her heart and were now screaming their orders as they forbade her to leave. They also warned her of the terrible consequences that would befall her if she disobeyed their strict orders. These demons had indeed plagued her over the years and were not willing to leave and abandon ship without a fight. They had, after all, lived with her and become her only friends when no one else was prepared to befriend such a pitiful loser. They alone had rightful ownership of the princess.

Eventually, after much deliberation, the princess stood up from her bed and declared, "I have had enough of all the pain living in this castle brings, and as I am a girl of much strength and great determination, I must make plans to leave. I cannot stay here forever. If I do, I will surely die. This may be dreaming the impossible dream, but I must follow after it with all my heart and soul. And if the worst happens and I die on the way, then at least I will have tried." With the right decision made, she got up from the bed to get dressed before taking her book from on top of the bedside locker. She then slipped the signet ring on her finger, and with her schoolbag slung over her shoulder, she picked up her chosen and most prized possession before heading toward the door of the castle and freedom. The start of her journey had just begun.

———◆———

Polly turned over the page. Nothing! This page and all the rest of the pages still remained blank. She closed the book and got up from the bed to get dressed and make the necessary final preparations for her journey.

Polly had no problem deciding which of all her possessions she deemed to be the most prized. It was, of course, Langdon, her blue elephant. He held all the tears that she had ever cried. Besides which, she reminded herself, an elephant never forgets, which was very important as Polly believed herself to be an extremely forgetful person. She therefore considered Langdon to be a most dependable elephant and one on whom she could truly rely to see her through any storm in life that she had to face.

That night Polly had the most difficult, if not unpleasant, task of saying good-bye to all her friends. She had never found good-byes easy, and this time was to be no exception. For her toys were the only friends she had ever known in her disappointingly cruel world. Therefore, Polly felt an immense and overwhelming sense of grief at the prospect of parting with any of them. There was Suishi, the one-eyed crocodile. He was really a doorstopper. And there was also Cecil, her giraffe, who always sat alone, decidedly aloof, as he perched on her pillow, his main job being to guard her pajamas, lest they be taken by another child! He would need at least two hugs, as well as a kiss good-bye.

Oh, and she nearly forgot Percy and Petunia, her stuffed penguins who had just got officially engaged. They stood entwined in each other's flippers on the windowsill. Rather than separate the loving couple, Polly embraced them both, and before placing a lace hanky on top of Petunia's head she carefully explained to both of them that it was necessary to bring forward their wedding ceremony, as she had to go away and it might be for quite a while. She went on to assure them that one day soon they would have a real celebration, complete with confetti. But for the time being all wedding plans had to remain on hold. So she quietly whispered, "I pronounce you man and wife," before turning to Percy to suggest, "You may now kiss the bride." She turned both their heads to face one another and brought their beaks together. "Oh, how I love weddings!" she declared, breaking into a hushed little giggle.

Polly left the dormitory and headed for the bathroom to grab her flannel and toothbrush. She then made her way back into the dormitory and gathered up her friends one more time for a final session of hugs and wet kisses. She then placed the little gold book and the envelope containing the map and note into her schoolbag along with her flannel and toothbrush and some spare red ribbons before reaching into her pencil case to choose a pen. This item was necessary so that she could write down her many thoughts and feelings on the blank pages of the little gold book that Ralph had given her. She put the pen in the pocket of her white smock overdress before finally placing the signet ring on her middle finger as a final act. It fit perfectly. As she twisted the ring on her finger, she looked down at the unusual royal crest and wondered what the coat of arms stood for. With everything she required now securely stowed away in her schoolbag, she picked up Langdon and crept on tiptoe out of the dormitory and then stealthily along the landing before creeping as quietly as she was able down the creaky oak staircase, heading for the front door. She had quite a struggle on her hands as she attempted to unbolt the stiff lock on the front door. Thankfully it finally gave, and as quietly as she could she slipped out of the castle, not forgetting to close the door behind her.

To tell you the truth, she did not shut the door properly. For reason had taken hold of her and reminded her that it might be wise, if not cautionary, to leave the door on the latch, just in case there was some unforeseeable reason to return. This way she could sneak back into the castle with no problem. So she left it just a bit open with the bolt resting on the latch. "Anybody with an atom of sense would probably do the same thing," she told herself.

Polly groaned inwardly as she instantly felt the cold, bitter wind biting into her thin body, causing her to shudder. She hugged Langdon tighter to her chest in an effort to keep warm as she groped her way in the dark across the quadrangle towards the big, black gates. Her heart was pounding so loudly in her ears that she became convinced that Pitstop would be woken from his slumber and come after her for his dinner! As the wind continued to whip up all around her, she soon began to have a change of mind. Oh, how much she needed a daisy to help in the decision-making process and help conquer her double-minded thoughts. So, after much deliberation, she decided in her wisdom that she had not chosen the best of nights to leave the orphanage. Perhaps it would be better for her to go back inside and give more thought and attention to the final preparations before leaving the castle. In fact, what on earth had possessed her to choose this most unsuitable night to go on such a quest in the first place?

With her mind now settled, she turned on her heels, and with feelings of great relief, walked back across the quadrangle heading towards the front door. As she reached for the door handle, which was only inches from her grasp, a sudden strong gust of wind came from nowhere. Before she could reach out her hand to push open the door, it slammed shut. And with it went her one and only opportunity to creep back upstairs and get back into her bed without anyone knowing she had ever been missing.

"Oh, no!" gasped Polly as she frantically pushed against the door in a vain attempt to open it. It was to no avail, for, try as she may, there was no way this heavy, baronial door was going to allow her to pass through it. Her heart sank as she realized that she was well-and-truly stuck outside in the cold and dark. With the front door now firmly shut, Polly knew that she had only one of two choices. The first was to ring the bell and face the might and fury of Uncle Boritz and Aunt Mildred. The second was to turn around and head for the open road and Hodgekiss's house in Piadora. She knew deep inside that there was only one choice she could possibly make, and that was to move forward and stick to her original decision to leave.

She had not gone very far when the heavens burst open, releasing large droplets of rain that made loud splitter splatter noises as they made contact with her coat. "Oh, that's just what I need now," she moaned out loud. "First I have the wind to endure, and now I have the rain as well. Some adventure this is turning out to be, and I've only just started!"

She hugged Langdon more tightly, feeling hopelessly insecure about what she was doing. It was not too long before she began to feel quite panicky. It was pitch black outside in the cold and dark, and she had quite forgotten to pack her torch or take a quick look at her map to check which way she was meant to be going. She pulled out the letter from her pocket and unfolded the map, but it was hopeless, she couldn't see a thing, and the map was very quickly going limp and soggy due to the rain. Polly looked up to the sky in search of the moon, hoping it might help her to see the map more clearly. However, even the moon was obscured by the many bad-tempered clouds that were patrolling the sky. Already she felt as though the odds were heavily stacked against her, and she felt a trifle angry with herself for not having studied the map while she was still indoors in the warm. What a prize idiot she was already turning out to be, and she hadn't even left the grounds of the castle!

Chapter 17
CLOSE EVERY DOOR TO ME

*P*OLLY WALKED RESIGNEDLY out of the big, black gates and slowly headed down the road. She had no idea where she was going, and if she did not know where she was meant to be going, the chances were very high indeed that she'd end up somewhere else. Sooner or later she would discover that she was going in completely the wrong direction. As she had no idea what to do next, she sat down on the curb in the rain and shot up a quick prayer.

> *Dear God, I don't know if You remember me, but my name is Polly Brown. If ever there was a time when I needed Your help, that time has got to be now. I have to admit that I have never felt so afraid, alone, and stupid to think that I had the courage or ability to leave all I have ever known and go on a trip to a place I have never seen and only heard of. I know You have every reason to ignore me, especially after the way I spoke to You at the graveyard, but I can only say I am very sorry for my outburst. Please feel free to discuss this with me, but not at the moment, as I'm feeling rather delicate and sensitive—well, touchy to be precise. I hope you can forgive me, as well as understand that I cannot make this journey on my own. So please, please comfort me when I'm feeling scared and watch over me from above, I beg you.*

Polly started to sob as despair filled her heart. The wind gathered momentum as it joined forces to mercilessly mock her for choosing to leave on such a night as this. Suddenly she thought she heard a noise. Her heart almost leapt into her mouth, and she began trembling from head to toe. She strained her ears to see if her imagination was beginning to run riot, or had she really heard something? As she craned her neck in the direction she believed the strange noise was coming from, she felt certain she could hear someone singing, albeit very quietly. She looked around, but all she could see was thick, foggy darkness. Then she thought she could see the outline of a figure. Her heart started pounding faster. She jumped up from the curb and gingerly shouted out into the darkness, her voice betraying great fear. "Who's there?" No one answered. Trembling and now very afraid, she walked a more few paces towards the shadowy figure, stretching out an arm towards what she perceived was the outline of a ghost. Nothing! No, she was truly alone. The strange sound was barely audible as she strained her ears further in an attempt to recognize who or what it might be. Perhaps it was just the wind making these unusual but gentle noises. She listened harder still. Yes, she could definitely hear the small, faint voice of someone singing.

> Come my Princess, come with me
> I'm calling you this day
> To live carefree, is to trust in me
> There is no other way.
> To ignore this call, would be a shame
> For I've seen the tears you've cried
> A crown for your head, is why I bled
> I cannot be denied.

Polly sat back down on the curb of the pavement and broke into a smile as she thought that things couldn't get much worse, for now on top of everything else she was hallucinating! She decided this must be the result of extreme cold and hunger, coupled with tiredness. She had read that mountaineers experienced this sort of thing when nearing the summit of a mountain, and apparently this was due to the air becoming thinner and the brain becoming starved of oxygen. When this happened they started to see and imagine all sorts of things—at least that's what the book had said. She took consolation from knowing that at the very least it was a recognized medical condition and not just complete insanity taking hold of her.

Suddenly she heard footsteps approaching from the distance. They were getting nearer and nearer, and their pace was getting faster and faster. Who on earth could it be coming her way at this late hour of the night? Her heart raced as the footsteps came closer, not stopping until they were right up beside her. Polly instantly froze with fear and plunged her head into her lap, too terrified to look up and face whatever, or whoever, it was now standing right beside her. She heard the sound of heavy breathing and her heart began skipping beats as blood-curdling fear took its loathsome grip on her.

"Hello, Polly," whispered a gentle voice as a hand came to rest gently on her shoulder. Polly breathed a deep sigh of relief, and all fear vanished in an instant.

"Ralph, thank goodness it's only you," said Polly nervously. "You really had me scared for a moment. What on earth are you doing out here in the cold in the middle of the night?"

"I could ask you the same thing," replied Ralph.

"It's a long story, Ralph," said Polly wearily. "To tell you the truth, I think I've made another of my rather stupid mistakes. Not only am I cold, tired, and hungry, but if I do head back to the orphanage I will be in so much trouble that I can hardly face it." Polly buried her face in her hands. "Oh, Ralph, I have no idea what to do next—really I haven't."

Ralph stepped down from the curb before settling down on the pavement next to her. He placed an arm around her shoulder in an effort to comfort her.

"Oh, Polly," he said in a slightly mischievous tone of voice as he shook his head from side to side. "You really have got yourself into quite a pickle this time!"

"Yes, I have," Polly tearfully admitted. "I wasn't running away this time—honest." She momentarily hesitated, thinking how on earth she could explain to Ralph precisely what she was doing sitting on a curb with Langdon in tow and in the middle of the night! But she decided to have a go anyway. "I know this might sound pretty stupid, Ralph, but I read the note you left me inside a book, and I took it to mean that I was meant to immediately leave the castle and start on the journey. But I'm beginning to think that as usual I have completely misread the situation. Don't you think so?"

Ralph thought long and hard before answering. "Look, Polly, don't take offense when I say that no journey is taken without weighing up the personal cost, and I think I am right in saying that on most adventures things happen good and bad. Yes, many things catch us unaware, making it difficult to anticipate everything that could possibly happen. We just have to deal with it. We either gird up our loins, so to speak, taking hold of the challenge, or we turn back to our safe, comfortable lives."

"Comfortable?" exclaimed Polly, feeling very insulted. "I would not describe my life as comfortable, Ralph. In fact, it's anything but!"

"Sorry, Polly," Ralph replied. "That was probably the wrong choice of words. Perhaps safe or predictable would be more appropriate?"

"Oh, give me a break, Ralph," cried Polly, now feeling very exasperated. "My life is neither safe nor predictable. In fact most of the time I wish it was," she groaned loudly. "I never know what to expect when I get through the door each day, and I've never had the feeling I'm safe—never!"

"I guess what I'm trying to say," said Ralph again rather apologetically, "is that sometimes we would rather stick with what we know and are used to than face any sort of change. You want change, don't you, Polly?"

"How can you ask me such a question, Ralph?" Polly furiously demanded to know. "You know only too well that I do."

"Oh, I most certainly know you do, but do you? For it is one thing to know you want change, but quite another to do something about it!"

Polly admitted to herself that even as desperate as she was to get out of the orphanage, she had gone through quite a battle of the mind. She felt her name should be changed from Polly to Yo-yo, as she went up and down so much, constantly procrastinating whenever it came to making any firm commitment or decision.

"Oh, Ralph," she tearfully cried. "I really do want to believe in Piadora and have tea with Hodgekiss. But deep down I am so afraid that I haven't got what it takes to make the journey. I have so little confidence and even less ability to survive outside the orphanage.

So what hope do I really have?" she asked, her heart welling up with great sadness.

"Well, that makes you a most excellent candidate then," stated Ralph rather delightedly.

"What on earth do you mean by that?" challenged Polly.

"I mean that if you don't think you can do it, then the greater the joy when you actually surprise yourself by achieving it," he replied. Polly turned to look at him, her eyes conveying that she was indeed feeling most puzzled and perplexed. "Look, Polly, there are many people who have great confidence in their own abilities, and they determine that they will conquer all challenges that cross their path. They visualize their goalpost and decide that nothing will get in the way. They have every confidence in their own ability, and therefore they go through life with all around cheering them on and congratulating them with each success. They rightfully experience immense pride in their ability to succeed. But how much deeper will your joy be when, with very little going for you and with no one to cheer you on, you make it to the goalpost?"

Ralph waited for Polly to speak up, but no answer came forth from her lips so he answered the question for her. "I can tell you for certain that you will experience nothing short of pure elation as well as deep gratitude that you, Polly Brown, have achieved the impossible. Now, young lady, isn't that the best ending you could ever wish for? A dream come true?"

"Yes, it is a pretty amazing thought," said Polly, finally finding her tongue and speaking up. "But if I'm honest, Ralph, I don't know if I believe in happy endings."

"Well then, that is where the root of your problem lies," said Ralph, a tinge of sadness in his voice. "For if you don't believe in happy endings, why make this journey in the first place?" Ralph paused and looked her straight between the eyes. "Polly, if you want to reach for your dreams, then you must follow them with all your heart. I think I am correct when I say that every world-class athlete trains every day, rain or shine. They face each day knowing that exercise is crucial, that is, if they want success. A true athlete will be consumed with the desire to win, and as a result all they can see ahead of them is obtaining the prize. So that cup or medal will have them out there training, even when they have an injury. That is how great their determination is to succeed. If they gave up at the first hurdle, collapsing at the first sign of pain and discomfort, then they would have no right to their moment of glory, would they?"

Polly nodded her head, her eyes moist with fresh tears.

"Yes, dear Polly, if you want your dreams to come true, then you must not only become more resilient to life's many obstacles, but you must also be more resolute in your thinking as you follow after your goals with your whole heart and all your strength."

Polly fell silent, for she knew Ralph was right. She knew she wanted to believe that her dreams would come true, but inside everything screamed that they never would and that she was indeed a prize idiot if she believed that she, of all people, was capable of achieving anything!

Ralph believed it was time to bring the conversation to a close, for he felt he had given her plenty to chew over. He also knew that the next few days would prove fairly tough for Polly, for her head was as full of contradictions as her heart was full of turmoil. She had a lifetime of deep fear and mistrust to fight and conquer, and these inner demons would not disappear overnight! However, he decided to give Polly one final thought-provoking insight.

"Polly, I have a good and very dear friend whose name is Nippy Mango. He once said something that I believe to be true for many of us who struggle with all kinds of deep issues in our lives. His observations and insights have touched me very deeply over the years."

Polly perked up and listened intently. "Go on, Ralph. Tell me, what did this Mungo chap—or whatever his name is—tell you?"

"Hold on, Polly, for I'm just about to get around to that. He said, 'There is no easy way to walk to freedom, and most of us will have to pass through the valley of the shadow of death a number of times before we reach the mountaintop of our dreams.' I believe Nippy Mango was a very wise man, for he had indeed walked the same trail of hardship and despair as you have. But once he had come through his difficulties, he was clearly able to see that all things are possible to those who believe."

Polly felt very comforted to hear that someone other than herself had found the struggle for freedom a most difficult and frustrating quest. And it made her more determined than ever to continue on and climb whatever mountains were necessary in order to get to her destination, and this was the kingdom of Piadora. Oh, and not forgetting that the prize for completing this journey would be tea and cakes with Hodgekiss. Ralph smiled and put his hand into his rather deep pocket before pulling out a brown paper bag.

"Here, Polly. You might like to have these?" he said thoughtfully.

"What are they?" questioned Polly.

"If you look inside then you will be able to see for yourself," replied Ralph, most good-humoredly.

Polly opened the bag and plunged her small hand inside to pull out the contents.

"Why, it's a pair of blinders!" she exclaimed, feeling rather shocked as well as highly insulted. "What on earth would I want these for, Ralph? For surely they are what horses wear on their heads."

"Yes, Polly, I know that, but people who are following after their dreams need to wear them as well. For if you put them on, you will then notice that you can only see ahead, and therefore you will not be distracted from achieving your goal by all that is going on around you."

Polly laughed, for she could see Ralph had a good point.

"Carry on looking, for there is still something else in the bag," Ralph informed her.

"Oh! I thought the bag was now empty," she exclaimed before turning the bag upside-down to give it a hard shake.

Out fell a small, see-through polythene bag. Polly picked it up and could see that the bag contained earplugs. She laughed out loud and then turned to Ralph. "Are these so I don't have to listen to your words of wisdom anymore, Ralph?"

Ralph joined in the laughter. "If that's what you want to think, Polly, that's fine with me. But no, the real reason for my giving them to you is that, as you make your journey, many will try to discourage you, happily telling you it's much too dangerous, or worse still, that it will never happen. They will seek to persuade you to abandon your dream entirely, pouring plenty of cold water on your enthusiasm by their words of failure and discouragement. And what you need to understand is such people have no dream they wish to see fulfilled, otherwise very little courage or conviction to follow after it. So, Polly Brown, if they can't have what they want, they will not be too happy to see you reach the finish line. You need to take what I'm saying fully on board, Polly, for this need to discourage others seems to be inbred into the very nature of many. Therefore, when you meet such people, it is considered best that you put your earplugs in and your blinders on. And having done so, you must politely decline from engaging in all dangerous and idle conversation with such folks. For I believe the whisperings going on inside your head will be enough for you to contend with, without the extra pressure of unwelcome and off-putting advice from other travelers."

Polly willingly agreed to do what Ralph had helpfully suggested. So she placed the blinders and earplugs into her schoolbag along with all her other possessions.

Having fastened the buckles on her schoolbag, she began to shudder, for the cold was really beginning to get to her. Ralph was quick to notice, and decided it was time to get up and leave.

"Polly, I am on my way to meet up with some good friends of mine and wondered if you might like to come and join us?"

She readily agreed, feeling extremely grateful for the invite, for she felt in desperate need of some companionship. Ralph was the first one up from the ground, and he held out his large hand to pull her up from the pavement. They then journeyed together, talking and laughing as they continued on towards their destination. It was not too long before Ralph caught sight of his friends in the distance standing around an open fire, their arms outstretched towards its fiercesome flames as they attempted to keep warm. Ralph felt Polly's hesitation and her reluctance to advance any further forward to meet them. So he turned to directly face her and told her she had nothing to fear, for after all these were his friends.

"They are real ragamuffins with hearts of pure gold," he said reassuringly.

As Ralph walked towards his friends, Polly clung on tightly to his arm, still feeling very unsure about whether she should have come with him. But all this uncertainty evaporated when a large number of them rushed over to greet them.

"It's good to see you, Ralph," shouted one of the travelers rather hoarsely as he came up to give Ralph a warm hug.

"Yes, we've all really missed you," shouted another.

"Come and stand by the fire, for it will keep you warm," interrupted a haggard but kindly woman in a tattered shawl. "And I will roast some delicious chestnuts on the fire. So quick, come closer and introduce us to your little friend."

Ralph took Polly by her free hand, for her other was tightly holding on to Langdon. He led her towards the warmth of the fire.

He then introduced Polly. "Friends, this young lady is called Polly Brown, and she is a good friend of mine."

"Well, if she's a good friend of yours, then she's a friend of ours too," piped up one of the travelers.

They all nodded in agreement before moving forward to introduce themselves to Polly. Every greeting was so warm and friendly that Polly's arm began to ache from the amount of handshakes she received.

"Pleased to meet you, Miss Polly," said one friendly voice after another. There were so many of them that Polly was afraid she would never remember all their names. But on a more positive note, all fear vanished as young Polly started to relax.

"Give the girl a warm mug of Rosie Lea, Dot," shouted one of the women.

Polly had no idea what sort of drink Rosie Lea was, but it didn't take her long to find out. A large mug of hot sweet tea was placed in her hands. This was soon followed by a very questionable-looking sandwich, its filling completely unrecognizable to Polly, even after she had taken a large bite! But as she was so hungry, she just gratefully accepted it, wolfing it down in a matter of seconds.

Later that same night she was given a small paper bag filled with some rather nice roasted chestnuts, which again she polished off in no time at all. Polly noticed that all those gathered around the fire seemed to really love Ralph, and he in turn seemed to love and accept them just as much. Polly found being there a strange but liberating experience.

All her life, and on too numerous an occasion to mention, she had been warned not to speak to strangers. She had done her very best to strictly adhere to this. For Uncle Boritz had gone to great lengths to make sure all the children were made fully aware of the many dangers that were lurking outside the castle. There were also the possible consequences of not following his strong and very sound advice. But here in this magical moment in time, she felt safe to leave all such advice to one side. For this strange night, meeting up with these scruffy outcasts of society, was indeed turning into a most unusual experience. With Ralph constantly at her side, she felt safe and secure as well as happy.

As she huddled around the fire with Ralph and his friends, she listened to all their personal stories—stories of such hardship and sadness that made her want to weep.

There was an ancient-looking man named Mordecai Monkfish, and Polly listened most intently as he told the saddest stories. His young son, who had been the apple of his eye, had drowned while on a fishing trip. Mordecai had always warned his son of the many dangers when going down to the river. And he had spent the time ever since that fateful day apportioning all blame to himself for not having been there to rescue his son. With the loss of his son too painful to bear, he had turned to alcohol to stifle his anguish and torment. He had then lost his job and his wife, for she ordered him to leave the family house when she could no longer cope with the loss of her son and seeing her husband fall apart at the seams. Mordecai was full of deep regrets and shame, and he told Polly he wished he could turn the clock back, for he would have sought to solve his problems in other ways—any way but the bottle! He had been on the road for some twenty years, and the bottle was now his closest companion.

Then it was the turn of his fellow traveler, Ichabod Grimshaw, to tell his tale. He also had suffered much. He had been young in years when he had been called up to go and serve in his country's war, and sadly he had never fully recovered from all he saw and experienced. He had finally come home after helping to bury many of his fellow soldiers who had become close friends. There had been no hero's welcome for him or for his fellow soldiers who, having survived the madness of war, made it home only to discover that their towns-folk were angry at them for going to war in the first place. It had made no difference that they had obeyed the call to go to war. They wished to serve and defend their fine country. Many of his friends were still missing, never having returned. And of those who did come back, many since had chosen to end their lives, unable to live with the nightmares that were to constantly haunt them.

"Polly, you need to understand something," Ichabod explained, his voice cracking under the weight of his words. "Wars will only cease when clear-thinking, decent men refuse to fight. For having seen the real horror of war, I can honestly say there really are no winners. Yes, war is a most terrible thing to behold! And I think that those of us who have witnessed the hideous darkness and terror that war brings, never stop seeing its horror."

Polly knew exactly what he was talking about, for she too felt she had been through a war. Her war had, of course, been very different from the one Ichabod had experienced. Nonetheless, she had been bloodied on the battlefield of life and had sustained real injuries as a result. She therefore considered herself to be just as much a casualty and therefore in need of a healer. Her memories were like open wounds, bleeding constantly and refusing to be healed. And just like Ichabod, they served as a constant reminder of the terror she had experienced at the hands of others. She therefore reached out her hand to touch his to reassure him that she not only understood but also felt the depth of his pain. Yes, his pain had become her pain. As she listened most intently to this man, whose very soul appeared to have been destroyed, she felt nothing but the deepest sorrow on his behalf.

Ichabod felt touched by young Polly's gesture, and pondered how a girl of such a tender age could understand and empathize with what he'd been through in life, as well as accept him in his current state: a raggedy, smelly old ragamuffin, who most of society steered well clear of. He could only speculate as to the horrors she had endured in her young life that went to make her the deeply caring and understanding young lady that she was.

Poor Ichabod had struggled in his effort to return to normal life, but had found it impossible to do so, preferring to take to the highways and byways and walk—then walk some more—in his futile attempt to ease his pain.

Polly wept openly as she listened, privately thinking, "Where do you go when there's nowhere to go, and you don't want to be where you are?" Eventually she could no longer restrain herself, and she reached over and flung her arms around his scraggy neck.

"Oh, dear sweet Ichabod, I am so sorry that all this has happened to you. Please believe me when I say that I truly wish there was something I could do to take your pain away."

Ichabod fought as hard as he had on the battlefield to hold back the tears, but to no avail. In no time at all he lost his fight to remain in control, and with it went all reasoning. To be hugged, and so warmly, by a young, caring girl was more than a man of his years could withstand, especially since he had completely forgotten for years too numerous to mention the long lost emotion that the touch of a hand or the warmth of a gentle smile could bring. Within just a matter of seconds, he could no longer hold on to the tears that had remained hidden and stored away all these years, refusing to come forth and bring healing to his broken heart.

"Thank you, young lady. You giving me this hug is making me feel all cracked up inside. Yes, quite wobbly!" he sniffed as he struggled to control the depth of emotions that now had been unleashed. For he did not want to break down completely and frighten Polly, or himself for that matter!

What he did not know that night as he embraced her was that Polly would not have been the slightest bit afraid, for she was so used to tears, her own as well as others. She felt really comfortable and at home around open and honest people who showed their vulnerability, for such people touched her to the very core of her soul. What really frightened her were people who were decidedly superior and delighted in making her feel small or insignificant, people who made her feel worthless. It was this kind of people who made Polly most afraid.

Ralph watched on and said nothing. He just sat and observed young Polly, hoping with all his heart that she would make it to Piadora for her sake, as well as for the sake of others who needed the love and openness that this young girl radiated from deep within.

For the first time since they met, he felt glad that it was he who had volunteered for the special assignment of directing Polly towards her destination. He therefore smiled secretly before noticing a feather flutter past him. He watched its flight path until it landed on the ground before coming to the full realization that there was a large pile of feathers growing in number gathering around his feet. "Oh, dearie me," he thought to himself. If I stand near this fire much longer, then pretty soon I will be as naked as a plucked chicken! He rather furtively delved into his long trench coat pocket and produced a small dustpan and brush. Then after checking that no one was watching, he discreetly began sweeping up the pile of feathers. When the task was done he put the dustpan and brush, along with all the loose white feathers, back into his pocket.

Ralph breathed a sigh of relief, for he had almost been found out, and now was definitely not the right time for him to have to do any explaining!

Luckily, Polly had not noticed Ralph sweeping up his feathers, for she was too busy listening most intently to a rather plump, red-headed lady who had introduced herself to Polly as Morag McCrutchfield. She told Polly that she too had been living on the streets for many years after being thrown out of her home at the tender age of sixteen by her drunken, abusive father. She had lived on her wits on the streets ever since, going from soup kitchen to soup kitchen with a rusty, broken-down shopping cart that was filled to overflowing with all the seemingly insignificant worldly possessions that she had accrued over her years. She had braved the harshest of English winters by stuffing realms of newspaper down her coat in an effort to keep warm. Despite all her hardship, this well-worn lady was so warm and jolly in character. She made Polly feel so welcome. She even pulled out a jumper from her many plastic bags for Polly to wear. Polly felt both humbled and touched to be in their presence and find real acceptance, something she had never experienced in her young life.

"Here, put this on, love," she said to Polly with a huge grin on her craggy face. "Or you'll catch a death of a cold, that's for sure."

Polly grinned back and thanked her before putting it on. Morag then picked out an old newspaper from the cart and, taking piece after piece, she screwed them up before handing some to Polly.

"Here, my dear. Stuff some of this down your jumper, for it will do much to keep out the bitter cold."

Polly giggled, but obeyed. She instantly felt much warmer. As she continued to listen to many other sadder-than-sad tales, she felt that even if there had been no fire to stand next to, the very warmth that came from these unusual and most bedraggled outcasts would have been enough. She began to experience a melting inside her heart as she talked and communed with them. In the past she had been guilty of shunning such people, for she could only view these raga-muffins with disgust. Now having heard just some of the stories, she felt deeply ashamed. That night around the fire, Polly discovered that judging such people only serves to harden the heart, but compassion does much to melt it away.

They had been talking for hours when Ichabod turned to Ralph and asked about Hodgekiss.

"Yes, where is he?" asked one of the travelers.

"We have not seen him for some time," piped up another.

Ralph smiled and then said, "He is fine and well, but rather busy at present organizing a huge banquet, I believe."

"Well, please tell him that we miss him," interrupted another of the travelers.

"Yes, tell him we really love it when he pays us a visit," said Mordecai, "he somehow manages to give us such hope and strength to carry on. It just isn't the same when he's not here."

They all nodded their agreement.

"Yes, and he really makes us laugh," interjected another traveler. "So be sure to tell him we are in real need of a few belly laughs to keep us warm on these cold winter nights."

Ralph smiled and promised to pass their greetings on to Hodgekiss when he next caught up with him.

With all conversation ended and all available scraps of food consumed, a man with a grey beard, funny brown hat, and matching grey jacket suggested to those present that it was now time for a good sing-along. His idea was met with real enthusiasm by all gathered, so he opened his bag and produced an accordion. His friend standing beside him, who also sported a beard, likewise produced an instrument. Polly was not certain if it was a violin or viola or something she had heard referred to as a fiddle, but all she knew was when the bow made contact with the strings the sound that came forth was so sweet that the strings of her fragile heart were most affected.

"Well, what shall we sing then, folks?" asked the man with a squeeze box.

The next few moments were chaotic as everyone cried out for this or that song; there were so many requests that Polly felt they could spend all the rest of the night if they were to get through singing all the songs.

Finally, the man in the blue jacket with the violin made the choice for them. In seconds they were all singing "Danny Boy."

The travelers sang with great gusto, and although their voices were rough from years of hard drinking and smoking, none of this seemed to matter as the musicians' instruments did much to mellow the sounds that filled the air around the campfire. Polly looked at all the faces of those singing, faces that had seemed so hardened by life's tragedies, and yet, as they glowed in the light of the fire she saw raw pain and beauty in their eyes, and it made her want to weep some more.

They went on to sing "You'll Never Walk Alone." Polly knew and loved this song as much as the travelers, although she did think it strange that they would want to sing this song, as just like herself they had walked through life with only loneliness and despair for companionship. Polly noticed that many an eye was decidedly moist as they sang on, not wishing for the song to end. She laughed as they started the next song called "Show Me the Way to Go Home." She sang along, desperately trying not to burst into fits of laughter, for she knew that once again, just like herself, they would all love to find their way home. Yes, home to the warmth of a real fire and the arms of a real, loving family, as well as delicious hot food and a warm, cozy bed. Instead they had to settle for lamenting and dreaming of such things. Finally, after many more golden oldies had been sung, including "Pack Up Your Troubles in Your Old Kit Bag," the two raggedy musicians decided to call it a day, or rather a night.

"No, can we have just one more?" pleaded a lady in a red shawl as she drank from an open beer bottle.

"Yes, go on. Just one more tune," urged her giggly friend as she too swigged from a bottle. "Yes, can we sing 'Streets of London'? For we haven't sung that one in ages," urged another traveler as he dragged deeply on his pipe.

Both musicians gave in and once again picked up their instruments from the ground, for they were more than happy to oblige such an appreciative audience.

Polly had never heard this song before, but as she listened to the words she began to tremble inside. By the time they got to a line in the song that referred to all her belongings making up just two carrier bags, Polly broke down completely as she thought of her mother and how she had died on the streets, alone, with one carrier bag as the only evidence that she had ever existed on this earth! Oh, how she missed this unknown woman, even though she could not remember a thing about her. She would have loved a photo, yes, just one little picture of her mother to treasure and place under her pillow at night. She could then have talked and felt close to her. Instead, she had spent years rocking her head violently from side to side as she cried out, "Mummy, I want my mummy!" until she finally fell asleep, which more often than not did not happen until the early hours of the next day.

The music and singing tailed off as the travelers became aware of Polly's deep distress. Morag rushed over and swept her up into her arms, saying, "There, there, little lamb. You'll be all right. Yes, everything will be all right."

Morag produced a handkerchief and proceeded to wipe away Polly's tears as she whispered words of great comfort in her ear. Polly apologized for her outburst, for she felt embarrassed and ashamed to have spoiled their wonderful time of singing.

"Now stop that, young lady," ordered Morag gently but firmly. "You must rid yourself of all this guilt and shame, Polly, for this garment was never intended for you. Oh no, it does not belong to you, and it never has."

All who had gathered around Polly agreed, most concerned for her welfare. But Polly was not listening, for shame was such a well-known and comfortable companion to her that she was not ready to give it a good hard kick, thereby booting it out of her life and heart once and for all. But all was not lost, for in that moment it dawned on her that although she had left behind the castle with its huge prison bars, she had still taken with her the iron bars that guarded and protected her tender heart, and she had no way of knowing how to break free of these ugly monsters. They had, after all, crept in most stealthily and taken her completely unaware, and now they acted like a fortress, hell-bent in their desire to keep her imprisoned.

Morag decided that the best thing to do was sing another song to take Polly's mind off this last song that had affected her so deeply. She turned to Polly and asked her if she knew a song about hope that she would like to sing. Polly did not think she did. She knew a song about the sinking of the *Titanic* that they sang in music lessons at school, but she felt that would make her cry more. Morag wholeheartedly agreed that that song was best left alone. Polly thought for quite a while before coming up with a suggestion that might do the trick.

"Morag," she said, sniffing a little as she spoke. "I do have a little song that I made up myself."

"Then let's hear it," cried Morag enthusiastically.

"Yes, let's hear it, Polly," the ragamuffins in unison shouted.

"The musicians will pick up the tune very easily, for they have trained their ears to do so," Morag added.

Everyone around Polly urged her to teach it to them. Polly showed some hesitancy, for she believed they might ridicule her song and consider it pretty pathetic. But in the end, her friends were so persistent that she threw caution to the wind and started to sing. In seconds, just as the musicians had promised, they joined in and the air was filled with such tender sweetness as bow touched string before touching cords in their hearts. It was as if the musicians had known and played the song for many years, but Polly knew that this was impossible, for she really had made this little song up all by herself!

> *Give, give me love, 'cos that's just what I need,*
> *I need real love, yes, the kind that never fails,*
> *You need it too, so we'll go hand in hand*
> *Refusing to give up, as we travel unknown roads*
> *In search of our promised land.*

All those gathered around the fire clapped and encouraged Polly to continue singing, for they loved both the words and the music of her simple gentle song. Polly felt encouraged as all fear of rejection left her, so she sang louder.

> *Give, give me peace, when my world comes tumbling down,*
> *The grace to cope, and find fresh hope*
> *As my troubles reach high ground*

You need it too, so we'll go hand in hand
And collect enough for both, from our promised land.

Give, give me faith, to meet my every need,
I need real faith, if I'm ever to succeed
You need it too, so we'll go hand in hand
And collect enough for both
From our promised land.

By this point everyone was humming along or otherwise bringing out hankies from their pockets to stifle the deep pain that was threatening to engulf them if given permission, and would most certainly manifest itself in the form of plentiful tears.

Give, give me joy, every minute of the day
For without love, the faith, the peace,
It won't come my way.
You need it too, so we'll all join our hands
And collect enough for all

"All together now,"

When we reach the promised land.

Once the rag-tag travelers had picked up all the words and the tune, there appeared to be no stopping them, and they seemed happy to spend the rest of the night singing it over and over again. Polly felt deeply touched by this, but not as touched as all the travelers felt towards this young lady who had come into their midst and brought something with her. Quite what they were unable to put their fingers on, but they all knew without any discussion taking place between them that when she left their company there would be a hole that nobody else could fill.

Polly stayed with the group until dawn broke. Ralph then told her that it was important for her to leave and go on her journey. Polly felt truly sad and was most reluctant to leave them behind.

"Look, Ralph," she said, "why can't all these good people come with me to Piadora? They could all use a good meal. Please let me take them with me on my journey."

Ralph sighed before answering. He knew she would not find his reply easy to swallow.

"I'm so sorry, Polly, for it is really kind of you to make such a nice suggestion. It's just not possible."

"And why not?" retorted Polly, feeling quite rattled that Ralph had shown a complete lack of enthusiasm towards her rather brilliant suggestion. "Surely, you could at least ask them on my behalf, Ralph, for they have the right to make up their own minds as to whether to come or not."

"You're right, Polly. They do have that right to make their own decision, and let me assure you that over the years all of them have more than once been invited by Hodgekiss to come to Piadora. But sadly, for all sorts of reasons, mostly personal and private, none of them have been able to face the journey."

"What? They refused to come? Even after they heard about the banquet?" said Polly showing great surprise, "That's unbelievable!"

"Yes, I know it sounds hard to believe, but it's true to say that over the many years I have known them they have all declined many invitations to join us. And now my job is just to be a good friend and listener to them. I care deeply for each and every one of them, as does Hodgekiss. When we are not able to be here with all our good friends, well then, we do all we can to make sure they are looked after. One of my many tasks is to leave little parcels of food in the trash bins of all the places they frequent, but you must never tell them of this, for they might take offense. You must therefore keep this as our little secret.

"Then, is that why there are never any stale cakes left over these days when I venture down to the cake shop?" Polly asked, looking Ralph directly in the face, for she wanted a straight answer.

"Yes, I'm afraid so," said Ralph rather sheepishly.

"Oh Ralph, why on earth didn't you tell me?" she said, suddenly feeling very guilty about her churlish attitude towards both of them.

"The fish and chip shop, too?"

"Yes, I'm afraid the chip shop, too," he admitted, lowering his head as he went rather red in the face.

"Well, that explains a lot then, doesn't it?" said Polly, pretending to be a bit annoyed.

She then broke out into a smile as she thought how disappointed she had been the last few times she had gone in search of the cakes, only to find there were none left. For she had wrongly assumed that greedy Ralph and Hodgekiss had bought up all the leftover cakes to devour all by themselves.

"Don't worry, Ralph. I don't mind; really I don't. Their need is much greater than mine, but I still wish you'd told me."

"I hoped you would see things that way," Ralph sighed. "Talking of cakes, I saved some for you from my last visit to the shop. You will need something to keep you going; here, please take them."

Polly was grateful to Ralph and took the bag of cakes from him.

"Can I please say good-bye to them all before I leave?"

"Of course you can and must," Ralph cheerily replied.

Polly shook the hand of all who were still standing around the fire that now was little more than a pile of glowing embers. She also pulled off the jumper and tried to give it back to Morag, the bag lady.

"You keep it, love," Morag insisted, "for your need of it is probably much greater than mine. So just think of me whenever you put it on. It will do much to kindle the glow inside of you, me darlin', so take great care. Promise me you will."

Polly nodded and then waved everyone good-bye as she walked away from the group of kind ragamuffins that still huddled around the glowing embers of the once-bright fire. She turned around for one final glance in their direction, and as she did, she felt a surge of love toward them all. Polly paused, and then without warning broke away from all her English reserve (not that she had much of that in the first place)! She raced back, rushing up to Morag and throwing her arms tightly around her to give her an overwhelmingly huge hug.

"You take good care of yourself, too, Morag," Polly whispered, her eyes glistening with tears.

"Go on, poppet. It really is time for you to leave, or you'll have us all in tears," she said softly to Polly, her voice cracking as she spoke.

Morag then hastily put her mitten-covered hand up to her eyes as she brushed away a tear that was flowing unchecked down her craggy, rosy cheek. "God bless you, darlin' little Polly. And may He keep you safe from all harm," she sniffed.

Ralph, who was standing only a short distance from them, came over and took Polly by the hand to gently lead her away. Morag stood still, clutching her shabby shawl tightly around her as she waved Polly off.

As she walked away, Polly experienced a deep sense of loss and sadness, but her loss was not as deep as that of the band of travelers. For despite having only just met her the previous night, there was not one of them who did not immediately feel the impact of her leaving. They would have many interesting conversations in the future as they huddled together around their fires discussing this brave young girl who went by the name of Polly Brown.

Chapter 18
POLLY'S NEAR-DEATH EXPERIENCE

*R*ALPH INSISTED ON taking Polly to the bus stop. "I believe you need to get on the number seven bus, and it will be here very shortly," he said. "It is the bright red double-decker one, so remember that, Polly. This is the bus that you must get on," he insisted as he rummaged deep into his shabby trench coat pocket and pulled out a shiny silver sixpence.

Ralph handed her the brightly colored coin, pressing it urgently into the palm of her hand. "You will need this for the fare," he said, giving her a warm hug. He then looked into her eyes and promised to meet up with her again when she arrived in Piadora.

Polly watched Ralph as he walked back down the dusty road until he disappeared from sight. Minutes later she saw a large red double-decker bus in the distance, with a large black number seven on the front.

In no time at all she was safely on board and climbing the steep stairs of the bus. Upstairs on the bus was empty, so Polly had her pick of seats from which to choose. Soon she was comfortably seated with her schoolbag safely stowed in the overhead locker. She gave Langdon the window seat because she knew he would be bursting with excitement as he viewed the glorious English countryside from out of the large window. As it journeyed on, the bus cheerily wound its way down long winding lanes and over quaint little bridges that it had quite a struggle to squeeze through.

Polly thought she was settled comfortably when she suddenly felt as though she was sitting on something rather lumpy. She wriggled around, and then stood up to look down at the seat to find out what was causing her discomfort. She was very surprised, if not alarmed, to see a large pebble mysteriously lying on the seat. Polly felt puzzled, for she was more than certain that the seat had been empty when she first sat down, and she was convinced that she would have noticed the stone's presence on the seat before now. She picked it up to take a closer look and discovered that it was inscribed with the word *compassion*. Polly thought this was rather strange, but decided to keep it. So she pulled down her schoolbag and popped it safely inside. At the same time she decided that this might be an excellent moment in time to write something in her diary. She wanted to write down the names of all the travelers she had met around the camp fire so that she could always remember them. She also wanted to write something about leaving the orphanage and the feelings of fear she had faced. She delved into her schoolbag for her gold book and pen, and then sat back down to start writing. Polly found herself taken by surprise to discover that, just as before, the book had writing on the formerly clean pages. It had miraculously happened again!

———————

After the young and very inexperienced princess had made the difficult decision to leave the castle, she pretty soon found herself floundering. She had even wished for a daisy to make the decision for her. Now how crazy is that? Luckily, though, for some unfathomable reason, the door to the castle accidentally shut itself, leaving the princess with no other option than to begin her journey. Saying good-bye to all her friends had been quite a sad moment, but now she would discover new and very real friends—as well as enemies—as she made her way to Piadora. The princess was absolutely right, not to mention wise, to pray for guidance from above, for she would need all the help she could get along the way.

Ralph gave the princess the wonderful opportunity of meeting some of his loveable ragamuffin friends, and she had found herself filled to overflowing with the milk of human kindness towards them. For the prin-

cess discovered that, like herself, they had their story to tell. Many of these outcasts had been abandoned as well as misunderstood by a society that saw them as nothing more than misfits to be shunned and despised for their contemptible lifestyle. And yet the princess was given the privilege of hearing firsthand what had caused their total demise and fall from grace, and her heart welled up with unflinching compassion towards them. These vagrants would really miss the princess, such was the impact of her care and concern for them. As she continued on with her journey she would soon find herself bumping into many others who also needed to know the same love and compassion she had shown to Mordecai and all the other battle-wearied travelers.

For now, though, she could relax and just enjoy all the views of the glorious English countryside as she sat upstairs on the double-decker bus. It had also not gone unnoticed that she gave Langdon very preferential treatment by kindly offering him the window seat so that he could get the best view. She was indeed turning out to be a very gracious princess if ever there was one!

Polly smiled and then stood up and put her pen and gold book back into her schoolbag for safekeeping. She only had the time to sit back down on her seat when the ticket inspector climbed the stairs and made his way toward her.

"Please, sir, may I have a ticket to go to the seaside," said Polly, hardly able to contain her excitement.

"Which one do you want?" the bus conductor asked, "for there are many bays on this particular route."

Polly pulled out her map and opened it up, pinpointing the place where she was meant to be going. The conductor adjusted his horn-rimmed glasses so that he could see more clearly. He followed her finger to the precise spot.

"Ah yes, Banana Bay. I've never been there, miss, although I have heard of it, and it is supposed to be quite a nice place," he said as he straightened his peaked conductor's cap.

"I've also heard that," said Polly with a smile.

"That'll be sixpence altogether then, miss. Four and a halfpenny for your ticket and one and a halfpenny for your little blue friend," he said as he wound the small dial on the peculiar machine that he had draped around his neck.

The machine made a funny whirring noise before the tickets popped out. Polly handed over her shiny sixpence as soon as she received the tickets.

"Have a good day then, miss, won't you?" said the friendly conductor with a big smile.

"I certainly intend to," Polly replied.

She then closed her eyes and thought back to her newfound friends that she was already sorely missing.

How long Polly was on the bus is neither here or there. Luckily for her, she suddenly opened her eyes just in time to hear the conductor call out: "Attention everybody, this is the stop for Banana Bay."

Polly jumped up and collected her bag from the overhead storage space, and then with Langdon safely tucked under her arm, she made her way back down the winding stairs before stepping off the bus into the warm hazy sunshine.

Polly took out her map and studied it, for she had every intention of getting to Piadora as quickly as she could. But as the sun shone so gloriously in the sky, she soon thought there would be no harm in going down to the beach and perhaps, if the tide was in, taking a quick swim. She therefore took the folded-up map, put it back inside her small gold book, and popped them both back into her schoolbag for safety. With this done she then headed with Langdon towards the promenade to choose a perfect place for them to sit down on the beach.

The beach at Banana Bay was stunning, with the softest white powdery sand that stretched as far as the eye could see. Yes, there was enough sand for Langdon to make a million sandcastles, complete with turrets if he so wished, thought Polly most excitedly. And as if that was not enough in itself, the sea looked wonderfully inviting,

POLLY BROWN

too. It was the deepest crystal clear blue with small frothy waves mischievously chasing each other to get to the shoreline first.

The beach was rapidly filling up with people, mainly families, who had chosen to have a family day out. Having set up base in a very pleasant spot she sat alone, enviously watching family after family set up camp on the beach, laughing and chatting most happily as they struggled to tiptoe over the very hot sand without burning their feet. As soon as they had chosen the perfect spot they then set about making themselves comfortable, bringing out multiple beach towels before pulling bright buckets and spades out of equally-colorful bags for the children to play with . This was then closely followed by large and small picnic hampers, windbreakers, and brightly colored umbrellas—in fact all the paraphernalia that families insist on taking with them whenever they decide to spend a day at the beach.

Once settled, mums covered their children's writhing bodies with thick white sun cream while the children continued to impatiently wriggle, desperate in their desire to be released and get in the water. Dads were left to have the all-too-familiar fight with stubborn deck-chairs that never play by the rules. They battled against all odds to set them up without getting fingers and hands pinched between the wooden struts. Polly observed that many dads, as usual, lost this battle and could be seen hopping up and down on one leg as they clutched a couple of painfully pinched and sore fingers, which now urgently required a bandage.

As family after family settled down to enjoy this most glorious day, Polly felt decidedly lonely inside. She had such a deep need to belong, and whenever she saw families out and about enjoying their togetherness it served to make her sense of loneliness and isolation feel all the more desperate and unbearable. She knew many families that did not speak to each other due to some disagreement. She had heard of one family where the sisters had not spoken to each other for years. Polly found this unbelievable, for, to her way of thinking, having family was the most precious gift on Earth and nothing should be allowed to destroy that, especially a stupid argument. Polly observed that most families did not appreciate this wonderful gift as much as they ought. But for herself, who had no real family, she knew she would do all within her power to hold on and to treasure such a gift. Polly gave a deep sigh before rebuking herself for allowing such sad feelings to descend upon her on such a beautiful day.

After a while she decided to move elsewhere. So she gathered up her belongings and headed over towards some rocks to find another nice spot to lie down. She placed her schoolbag closely by her side and then folded the jumper Morag had given her, positioning it underneath her head to make her feel just that little bit more comfortable. She allowed Langdon to lie down beside her, for she felt that he too could benefit from a nice bit of sunbathing. Polly had no towel or personal effects, such as a windbreaker or chair, but this did not matter. She just stretched out fully on the sand and sifted the silky grains between her fingers as she allowed the sun to caress her body with its warmth, occasionally twisting the little ring on her finger as she fondly thought back to her meetings with Ralph and Hodgekiss. Funny enough, thinking of those two rogues always made her smile, and she couldn't say precisely why they had this effect on her, other than that at the end of the day they were quite loveable vagabonds!

It was not too long before she began to experience a wonderful sense of well-being. It was not something she usually experienced, and as she basked in the sunshine she also basked in this newfound contentment. She really appreciated the quietness and solitude with no Aunt Mildred or Uncle Boritz breathing down her neck and finding endless chores for her to do, nor Gailey Gobbstopper to chant cruel tormenting words in her ear. No, it was just Polly at peace with herself and the world, and this new experience felt simply great.

As she had been up all night talking to Ralph and his ragamuffin friends, she was happy but also exhausted. It was therefore no surprise that before you could say, "Bob's your uncle," she had fallen into a peaceful slumber.

When much later she woke up, she realized she must have been asleep for some time, for although the sun was still burning brightly, it had fallen a couple of feet from its original position in the sky. Polly felt extremely hot and sticky as she sat up to look around her. She was pleased to see that there were still plenty of people on the beach. One family had buried their two children up to their necks in sand. Polly hoped that this was purely for fun and that they would in time dig them out. Children wandered by the seashore, nibbling on large clouds of pink cotton candy on long wooden sticks, while others licked enormous ice cream cones. She could also hear a variety of different musical sounds that rang through the air before fusing together as people lay in the sun listening to their favorite radio station.

Polly would have loved an ice cream to cool her down, but she had no money for such a luxury and, as she wasn't hungry enough to fancy one of the stale cakes from the bag Ralph had given her for her journey, she therefore decided to go for a swim. She realized she had no swimsuit with her, but she figured that as the sun was still shining and it was still hot, her clothes quickly would dry off in the sun afterward. So she picked herself up and, after kicking off her shoes, instructed Langdon to watch over her possessions and then headed down towards the water's edge. As she did so, she noticed a lot of people waving. Polly waved back, thinking that this was indeed a most friendly beach that she'd found. As she neared the shore people still seemed to be waving. Polly thought this to be a little odd. After all, she had already waved back. So she waved her hands in the air once again as she neared the water's edge. Suddenly she heard various cries and screams coming from the sea. To her horror she quickly realized that they were not waving at her, but were actually waving to get her attention; the cries she heard were actually the pitiful pleas of people drowning.

Polly panicked. What on earth could she do to help them? There were far too many of them for her to attempt saving on her own. She made the snap decision to alert the people on the beach, and then they could all wade in and help these poor people. She turned on her heels and rushed over to the first group of people she could find.

"Help me! Please help me!" she cried. The small group looked up at her feeling most annoyed before an extremely large lady in a polka dot swimsuit and wide-brimmed straw hat piped up, "We came here for a bit of peace and quiet, young lady, so be off with you. Just leave us alone. That's a dear. Now what was I saying before I was so rudely interrupted, Clarissa? Ah yes,..."

"But you don't understand. There are a lot of people drowning in the sea," she stammered as she pointed towards the shoreline.

"Didn't you hear me the first time, girl? Just go away and leave us alone, or I will call the police and have you arrested for being such a nuisance!"

Polly fled and raced up to the next group. The gentleman was putting sun cream on his wife's back while the children that were sitting nearby slurped on bottles of sugar-filled lemonade.

"Please, sir, I am so sorry to bother you, but I really need your help, for there are many people drowning in the sea, and I cannot save them all by myself."

The man looked up at Polly and sighed, before saying, "Sorry, love, my hands are covered in cream, and I have not finished applying it to the wife's back. Give me ten more minutes and then I will see what I can do to help."

Ten more minutes! Polly panicked as she turned towards the shoreline and could still see many heads and arms flailing as they struggled to keep their heads above the water.

"Please, sir. Ten minutes will be far too late. They need our help now!"

"Sorry, love. As I've already said, I have my orders, and that is to put this here cream on the wife's back. My life won't be worth living if I don't get to cover her back thoroughly," he said, giving Polly a wink.

"You're quite right about that," intervened the lady who despite being covered in white cream turned over to take a better look at Polly. "My needs come first, so if you can't wait that long, then you'll have to find your help from somewhere else," she said rather snottily before turning back on her stomach and saying, "Stick a bit more cream on my shoulders, love, will you? For that's where I go most red."

The man squirted half the tube of cream on her shoulders and began to rub it in, ignoring Polly and her plight as he did so.

Polly turned on her heels, for she was feeling absolutely exasperated at their lack of concern for all the desperate people who needed their help. But she was not about to give up. Through the corner of her eye she saw a man and woman who had just left the water's edge and were walking back to their deckchairs. Polly raced over just as they were picking up their towels to dry themselves off.

"Excuse me," said Polly breathlessly. "I really need your help." She then pointed out towards the sea before continuing on. "Look, there are lots of people drowning, and I can't get anyone to help save them," she said with pure desperation.

They looked over towards the sea, and then they turned to each other, shrugging their shoulders. "Look, young lady, can't you see we're wet? We've just come out of the sea and we have no wish to go back in again, for we need to dry off. So you'd better ask someone else. Look, there are some folks over there. Now why don't you go and ask them," said the man pointing over towards some rocks.

Polly followed his pointing finger. Yes, she could see them sitting peacefully on deckchairs, but they were an old and most frail couple who never in a million years would be up to the task, for Polly quite rightly believed that she would probably end up having to save them as well. No, they definitely would not have the strength required to be of any assistance to her.

She therefore moved on, this time to a man helping his two young boys build a huge impressive sandcastle.

"Come and join us," said the man invitingly to Polly, for he wrongly thought that she was coming over to ask if she could join in.

"Oh, sir, I really would love to, but I have a matter of extreme urgency, and I really do need your help."

The man put down his spade. "How can I help?" he asked, showing a measure of concern as he put his hand on his forehead to shield his eyes from the sun.

Polly pointed towards the sea and cried out, "Look, all these people are drowning, and I cannot rescue them all by myself."

The man looked over towards the sea, still shielding his eyes as he did so, but Polly noticed distinct signs of hesitation in his eyes. "Look, love, I would help you, truly I would, but I only get to see my young boys every other weekend since I split with the wife. So my time with them is very precious, therefore I will have to decline your request for my assistance in helping you. You can stay here, though, and help us finish this sandcastle if you like. The boys would really appreciate some help, wouldn't you boys?" The two brothers looked up and smiled before nodding.

"Sorry, but I can't stay, much as I'd love to," said Polly, now very agitated and feeling close to tears.

She rushed from one group to the next and it was the same. Oh, the excuses were different, and some seemed most genuine in their concern and desire to help, but sadly none were available or prepared to abandon the pleasure of the afternoon to assist Polly. With no help at hand, a very desperate Polly threw caution to the wind and just raced into the sea in a last-ditch effort to do what she could. Within seconds the sea went from calm to extremely rough, and the waves grew higher and higher. She struggled to swim as the waves hit and lashed at her with the full might of their fury. Still she swam on, her body aching all over, but she was not prepared to give up. Suddenly she saw a Royal Navy frigate coming toward her. As she looked harder she realized that it was a battleship. Polly winced and shook her head, thinking she was now imagining things, for she had no idea what such a ship would be doing at Banana Bay.

She continued to be battered by the waves as the ship drew nearer. Polly coughed and spluttered as she bobbed up and down like a warning buoy, her mouth and lungs filling up with sea water. As one final gigantic wave grabbed hold and launched her high into the air Polly managed to read the big, bold, black name painted on the side of the ship. It read *H.M.S. Freedom.*

No sooner had she read its name than she realized to her horror that it was heading straight at her. Polly then did what she usually did—she panicked. She summoned up all her strength and began to swim for her life. Yes, a life that up until this point in time she had not believed was worth fighting for. It was all to no avail, for the ship was moving so fast, though how many knots she had no idea. It was enough to say that the vessel was racing toward her at full steam, threatening at the very least to pull her under, or worse, crush her tiny body into a million little pieces.

Polly was now well-and-truly frightened. Her heart was pounding furiously, and all seemed hopeless as she fought against every wave in her desperate bid for air. Seconds later the vessel was almost on top of her, when suddenly a large wave pushed her clear of its path. Polly disappeared from sight as she was forcibly sucked under, the water swirling around her and dragging her with great force toward the ocean bed. She knew in that instant that she was drowning. Her lungs felt near to bursting as they filled with water and her life flashed before her eyes in a most spectacular fashion. With that over, for she had not lived too many years, she gave up her struggle to survive and fell unconscious onto the sea bed.

Polly awoke to find many people standing over her. She was in such a state of shock that she was unable to speak.

"Roll her over onto her side," ordered the man who sounded like the captain, for he had a gruff but authorative voice.

Another man, who had a gold, braided band around his pointed flat cap, quickly acknowledged the order, "Yes, Captain, I'll do that, for I'm sure she has taken in much water."

He gently rolled Polly onto her side, and she immediately began to be sick as the pea green liquid emptied from her lungs and stomach. After this, Polly remembered nothing, for she blanked out.

When she finally awoke she felt as if she were in a dream, for everything appeared very hazy, and although she could hear many voices talking above her head their voices appeared very slurred and muffled. She moaned and shook her head from side to side, and this alerted the captain to the fact that she was coming round. Yes, thankfully alive and well, although he had to admit there had been a few dodgy moments when he, as well as the whole crew, thought that they had lost her.

"Where am I?" Polly asked the captain with the kind eyes and silvery beard.

"You're on a lifeboat, young lady. In fact a Royal National Lifeboat, to be precise," he gently replied. "And I have to say that you're very lucky to be alive. There's been a lot of praying for you on this boat, as your heart stopped numerous times. Now tell me dear, what is your name?"

Despite being weak, Polly smiled and quietly said, "Polly—Polly Brown," before drifting back into a deep sleep.

She awoke many hours later, and this time the whole crew was sitting around her bed, peering intently into her eyes.

"What happened to me?" Polly asked the captain, whose full title was Captain Cuthbert Codswallop. "I mean, one minute I was in the water trying to rescue all these people who were drowning, and then..." Polly cut short her sentence as she immediately felt immense anguish remembering all those poor drowning people.

"Please tell me the truth," she said, her eyes welling up with tears. "Did you manage to save any of them?"

The captain took hold of Polly's hand as he falteringly answered her. "Polly, we did indeed manage to save a few of them, but for many it was too late." He paused to take a deep sigh and Polly started to sob.

"That's why I went into the water in the first place," she cried, "for I could see so many of them, and they were all fighting for their lives as they cried out for help. I asked so many people who were on the beach to help me, but no one would listen." She turned her head away from the captain as tears slid down her cheeks. "I cannot bear to think of how much they suffered," she whimpered.

Captain Codswallop gently squeezed Polly's hand as he looked down at her most concerned. "Polly, you did all you could, and no one could have asked more of you. Why, you are lucky to be alive yourself! The crew and I think you are a most courageous young lady." All the crew who were sitting by her bed wholeheartedly agreed. She was indeed a very brave girl. "I think there might well be a medal for bravery given to you in the not-too-distant future," he added while he gently squeezed her hand for a second time.

"Thank you, sir. Forgive me if I appear ungrateful, but I don't want any medals. I would gladly forgo any award just to have saved one of the lives of all those helpless people. So as far as I'm concerned there is absolutely nothing to honor."

The captain smiled as he thought to himself how rare a breed this young lady was in a world that seemed only to care about themselves, with many receiving accolades for next to nothing. He quickly decided that he would very much like her to join the Royal Navy when she was older.

After eating her way through a large plate of the good captain's fish pie, which was named Codswallop Pie after him, Polly spent the rest of her time on board playing chess with the crew members and drinking quite a few cups of hot and very sweet tea. Polly was having such a good time that she felt very disappointed when the captain told her they would be landing very shortly and therefore her time was almost up.

The boat headed for the shore, and Polly reluctantly disembarked onto the wharf. As she jumped ashore, she suddenly realized that she had no shoes on her feet, and it dawned on her that she was also missing the jumper given to her by Morag as well as her most precious gold-covered book with the map safely tucked inside; in fact she was missing her schoolbag with all her precious belongings. Suddenly her thoughts turned to the worst loss of all. She gulped, as tears instantly sprang to her eyes, for she was shocked to realize that she had also lost her beloved Langdon, for she had left him on the beach to watch over her possessions. Polly felt truly dismayed. The lifeboat was just about to leave the quayside, with the last ropes having been pulled in, thereby releasing the vessel from its mooring, when Captain Codswallop suddenly ordered the crew to stop.

"Wait here," he commanded them as he leapt from the vessel onto the quayside. He then ran towards Polly. "Here, Polly, I almost forgot to give you these back to you," he said as he handed over her schoolbag and her elephant.

Polly felt instantly relieved and on the verge of tears, only this time out of sheer gratitude towards Captain Codswallop and his crew.

"I sent one of my men ashore in our rowing boat to get your things," he said with a twinkle in his eye as he gave her the warmest of smiles. "We also hand-washed your schoolbag as it was stinky and full of sand and seaweed. Oh, and I hope you don't mind that we also gave your elephant a quick hose down, as he was also smelling a bit iffy!" he chortled.

"Dear Captain, How come you knew I had left all my possessions on the beach?" she quizzed, anxious for an immediate answer.

"Well, not many young ladies take to the sea fully clothed, and might I add without any shoes on their feet," he said as both of them automatically looked down at her bare feet.

The captain then produced her shoes, which he had been hiding behind his back. Polly laughed as she took her shoes from him, and after placing them back on her feet, she gave the wonderful, kind captain a bear hug, which was rapidly becoming known as a *Polly hug*. The captain thought he was never going to be released from her grip as she clung to him for so long. Finally Polly's lengthy embrace came to an end, and she let go of him. She then stood on the quayside with Langdon under one arm, waving and blowing kisses to the crew of the lifeboat. The crew returned the gesture, blowing a lot of kisses back in her direction as they set sail on another rescue mission. Polly giggled as she watched some of the crew almost topple overboard as they continued to wave good-bye while climbing up the mast.

With the lifeboat having disappeared into the sunset, Polly went in search of a bench so that she could check the contents of her schoolbag, just to make sure she still had everything. She pulled out the jumper Morag had lent her, for the day was drawing to a close and she did not wish to catch a cold. She was also hungry enough to try one of Ralph's stale cakes. As she pulled out the cake bag, a small, smooth stone dropped to the ground. Polly leaned over and picked it up. It had the word *courage* cut deeply into its otherwise-smooth surface. Polly thought this strange until, upon peering into the bag again, she discovered a little note. It was from Captain Codswallop.

My dear Polly,

I hope by now you have fully recovered from your ordeal, although I need to warn you that you may feel a bit weepy in the days to come. This will be due to the shock of experiencing a near-drowning. Don't worry. Given time, this will pass.

I have to say that my crew were very taken with you, and therefore they wanted to leave you with something to remember us by. We unanimously agreed that, though you were so reluctant to consider a medal for your bravery, we would make it our business to ensure that you got one anyway. So when I sent one of my men to pick up your belongings from the beach he also went in search of a smooth pebble to carve out the word courage. As far as we, the crew of the lifeboat, are concerned, you have your medal. Please keep it *in remembrance of your special time with us. Take care and God bless you.*

Much love,

Captain Goodalhap.

Polly gazed at the pebble and couldn't help but smile. She then proceeded to eat a number of the stale cakes that, for some reason, seemed anything but stale, but as though they had just been freshly baked. Once her hunger was satisfied, she poked around in her carrier bag for her gold book, for she felt compelled to record all the unusual and rather dramatic events that had befallen her. She pulled out a pen from her pocket and then turned to the next fresh page in her personalized diary. However, this time round she wasn't the least bit surprised to discover that her newest adventures had already been added to her diary. And, I might add, not by her fair hand.

The princess, with Langdon safely by her side, took the red number seven bus that travels along the coastal route before getting off at Banana Bay, a most delightful sandy bay if ever there was one! After scrutinizing her map to see where she was next headed, she chose to consult with Langdon on whether to press on or use this opportunity to take a well-earned break. After much thought and great deliberation, she wrongly decided to sidetrack from her most important journey and take time out with Langdon to go down onto the beach to sunbathe and build sandcastles together, a decision that would most certainly cost her dearly. Yes, that most impulsive of decisions almost cost the princess her life and Langdon's as well. For he was such a scruffy little elephant that any conscientious person, upon reading one of the many posters saying Keep Britain

Tidy would certainly not have thought twice about binning him! Alternatively, he might well have suffered severe sunstroke as he sat for many hours on the beach guarding her personal possessions. Worst of all, he could well have been washed out to sea with the tide, only to find himself becoming a lunch snack for a mighty whale with an especially huge appetite for abandoned blue elephants! And all this for half a day's leisure! However, even though this impromptu break was not part of the original plan, it still worked for the good, for it gave Polly the chance to discover the gift of great courage that had been deposited deep within her. It also opened her eyes to how blind and selfish others around her could be at times, thinking only of themselves and preferring to ignore the plight of others in deep need. The princess learned many painful lessons that day, lessons that, if remembered, would save her much future grief. Once she was reunited with Langdon, the princess felt happy and grateful to be alive, thanks to the rather splendid efforts of Captain Codswallop and his delightful crew. She even admitted to herself that she was now feeling very positive about carrying on her journey to Piadora to have tea and cakes with Ralph and Hodgekiss, her ragamuffin friends.

Polly shut her gold-covered book and returned it to the safety of her schoolbag before taking out her folded map, which she then began to study closely. She now felt a real sense of urgency to reach her destination as quickly as possible before any further embarrassing incidents occurred. She therefore determined to set off first thing in the morning, as soon as the sun rose. Curling up on the bench with Langdon close at her side, Polly pretty quickly fell into a deep slumber.

Chapter 19
THE VALLEY OF LOST SOULS

*P*OLLY AWOKE EARLY to the cheery sound of birds singing, and after straightening the crumpled smock that went over her dress, she stood up to have a good stretch before giving Langdon his usual good-morning kiss. Then with her schoolbag on her shoulder she said good-bye to Banana Bay and its quaint little town filled with whitewashed fisherman cottages, and headed out into the open countryside.

She walked for many hours, humming the tunes of her favorite songs as she strolled along with seemingly not a care in the world. This contented state of being was not to last for too long, for soon she found herself well off the beaten track and feeling very lost. She quickly decided that she must have taken a wrong turn, so she stopped and pulled out her map to check that all was well. But rather sadly she discovered that she was unable to confirm her exact position, as she was unable to understand or recognize any of the identification symbols that usually act as a useful aid.

Feeling helpless as well as hopeless, she decided to simply follow her instincts and carry on down the long, meandering, dusty lane and then down further through a valley before trudging up and over a very steep hill. If she had felt lost before, she now felt as thoroughly lost as anyone could ever be. Luckily she spied a signpost not far away in the distance. She raced toward it, feeling totally convinced that this signpost would be her salvation and get her out of this sticky mess by showing her the direction she needed to take. Polly stood directly under the sign, which hung on a tall pole. She looked upwards to read it and became very concerned that she had never seen or heard of any such place before. The sign said Welcome to the Valley of Lost Souls. Underneath in smaller writing it said: "Only careful and considerate drivers welcome in this desert."

"Desert!" shouted Polly, "Goodness gracious me, then I really am as lost as lost can be, for there is absolutely no mention of a desert of any description on my little map," she groaned.

Polly felt most alarmed as to why anyone would want to call a place by such a peculiar and most worrying name. And as she considered its strange name, "Valley of Lost Souls," she shuddered, for she could only hope that it didn't mean that she, too, was destined to become one of those already lost forever! She did admit to herself that most of the time she felt very lost indeed, but she had rather hoped that this extraordinary journey to Piadora would bring to an end all such soul-searching. Then she would find herself becoming free of the inner torment and feelings of hopelessness that took great liberties by making their home in her heart, troubling her constantly as they acted like landlords demanding blood for their money.

The sun was beating down hard on Polly's back, making her feel uncomfortably hot and sticky. So she sat down on a rock with Langdon and wiped away the beads of perspiration that were trickling down her forehead. She felt quite tired and drained of energy. She was also thirsty, for she had been walking for many hours. As her eyes scanned the horizon, she thought she could see a lake. She felt instantly encouraged, for this meant that she and Langdon could have a quick swim and possibly a drink as well. Leaping up from the rock, she raced as fast as her legs would allow toward the lake. Pretty soon she was clean out of breath, but as she looked around, she found herself very shocked to discover that there was no lake and therefore no water to be found. It was purely a mirage! Gasping for breath and feeling very distressed, she slumped down onto her knees and buried her head in her hands.

Polly did not stay on her knees for too long because she realized that her need of water was becoming urgent, so she had little choice but to trudge on. By noon, the sun was at its fiercest as it continued, most provocatively, to stalk her, and yet she still struggled along hoping against all odds to find a shelter. Later that same day her feet broke out into painful blisters and her face also began to peel due to pretty serious sunburn. But there was worse to come since it was only a short while before her need for water went from urgent to critical and her tongue began to cleave to the roof of her mouth. With still no water in sight, she walked on like a haunted man with swollen eyes, cracked lips, and her face and hands like dried out leather.

Polly had no other choice but to continue walking in the forlorn hope that at some point she would either reach a landmark that could help her or people and houses that might be willing to provide her with some food and shelter. But it was not to be.

Eventually, it began to get dark, and with the dark came extreme cold as the desert temperature plummeted to well below freezing. And still Polly stumbled along like a dead man, staring straight ahead as though she were some sort of battery-operated robot who perfunctorily zig-zags around in circles until its energy source finally runs out.

And so it was well into the night before she found herself in the middle of a large canyon with huge mountainous rocks on either side. Groping her way toward a mountain, she happened perchance to discover a small cave where she could take refuge from the harsh cold. She cautiously entered the cave, clutching Langdon very close. It was pitch-black inside, but she thought she could hear the sound of water trickling, or rather, dripping like a tap, though she was much too scared to investigate where it was coming from. Besides which, she could only see as far as the end of her nose.

"Thank goodness it's empty. Let's hope this place is safe," she said to Langdon, jumping slightly as the sound of her voice echoing through the cave gave her more reason than ever to feel anxious and afraid. Polly then collapsed on the ground and, with Langdon at her side, fell fast asleep.

When she finally woke up she rubbed her eyes, for the sun was pouring into the cave almost blinding her with its brightness. Polly yawned and felt instant pain from deep within her parched throat, and she immediately realized that her need to find water was now crucial, so she headed deeper into the cave until she came across a wet rock. Looking up, she noticed droplets of water dripping down onto the rock, so she held out a cupped hand until it became filled and then with the deepest gratitude she had ever experienced, she brought her lips down into her cupped hands and lapped up the water with her tongue. Polly had to do this a number of times as the drips were quite slow in coming, but she did not care. She was prepared to be patient and stand with her hands cupped for as long as it took, just for the privilege of collecting the water to quench her thirst.

Finally her thirst was satisfied, so she headed back to where she had left Langdon and all her other worldly possessions. She pondered as to whether to continue on with her journey or stay in the cave until help finally arrived. But then she panicked as she thought to herself that she was probably being overly optimistic as far as being rescued was concerned. I mean, was there ever going to be a search party, especially when she had never disclosed to anyone her intention to leave? And she certainly could not rely on her guardians to alert the police of her absence, for they went to considerable lengths to cover up all mishaps that happened at the castle. To cap it all, she was lost in the middle of a dusty desert, which could mean weeks, months, or even years before she was finally found.

As Polly pondered such a dreadful fate, she shuddered, the images of her mummified body—complete with hollow eye sockets and a dried-up tongue—flashing before her very eyes. It seemed a most unpleasant, if not thoroughly disagreeable, way in which to end her life. So after much agonizing over what was to become of her, it became crystal clear that she must move on, and the sooner the better.

Polly picked up Langdon and gathered up her possessions, leaving the cool of the cave to stagger back out into the blazing heat of the desert once again. She staggered and stumbled, then staggered some more as she struggled to remain upright due to the intense heat of the sun that was beating down hard on her back. As she climbed over one sand dune after another, she could only further despair, for as far as her eye could see, there was nothing ahead but more desert. She had tried faithfully to follow the route on her map, but with only sand, followed by more jolly sand, she wondered whether she was just going around in circles. The situation was rapidly turning into yet another rather desperate crisis.

On the verge of collapsing through heat stroke and exhaustion, Polly was then to have her worst fears confirmed. Upon looking straight ahead she discovered that she was back at the cave, and had, as she suspected, just been going round and round in circles. She wanted to scream, but her mouth was so dry and her throat so swollen that no noise would come forth from her lips. She headed deep into the cave in search of the dripping water to alleviate her parched throat that felt like sandpaper. This done, she headed back to the cave entrance, and once more sat down to weep. And as she wept, she asked herself a very familiar question: "Why was everything in life such a struggle? Surely she was entitled to have a few things go right for her. I mean, that couldn't be seen as unreasonable, could it?"

Polly sat for many hours with what seemed like a black cloud hanging over her, as tormenting thoughts invaded her mind with just about every unfair event that had ever happened to her. It was not too long before she began to feel angry and very frustrated, so much so that, despite her very swollen throat and tongue, she stood up and attempted to let out a yell as she stamped her feet in the dust. All this achieved was to send clouds of dust into the air above her, which, once breathed in, caused her to immediately start choking.

"I can't get anything right, can I?" she raged in little more than a hoarse whisper. "I am a complete waste of space, a blob that someone ought to stamp on and then scrape from the bottom of their shoe. I hate my life, and I hate Ralph for giving me false hope. I also hate Hodgekiss for inviting me to tea. It's probably just some stupid joke anyway, and as usual the last laugh will be on me."

She was so furious and angry with just about everything in life that she temporarily abandoned all self-control, and without thinking she flung poor innocent Langdon into the air as far as she could. She watched on horrified by her actions as a very dizzy Langdon spun round and round in the air before coming to land with a hard thump on the sand, squashing his long trunk as he did so.

"What have I done?" Polly mumbled as she raced over to where he lay, dazed on the ground. Polly frantically brushed off all the sand that was now in his eyes and sticking to his hot, furry body. "Oh, Langdon, I'm so, so sorry. I don't know what came over me! Honest, I don't. I am just so mad at myself for ever having agreed to go on this ridiculous quest in the first place. If I knew how to get out of this horrid dustbowl and go home, then I would, whatever the consequences," she whispered in his ear. "I would not care what Uncle Boritz and Aunt Mildred did to me, for they have taken away my life anyway. I feel like a helpless, hopeless, dead man walking, hollow and empty, and with no hope for my future. So please forgive me, Langdon, for I now feel really terrible."

Polly planted a kiss on Langdon's trunk, and despite her swollen throat making all utterances jolly painful, she continued to talk to her blue, and very dazed, companion.

She then fell silent as she pondered her current Polly crisis. "Perhaps I should turn back and head for home, for at least if I go back to the castle there will be a bed for me, as well as food and water. Yes, we were better off in the castle. So perhaps going home is the wisest thing to do after all!"

No sooner had she spoken than Polly heard a noise. At first it was very faint, but as she strained hard to listen, she quickly determined that she could definitely hear whimpering.

"Shhh! Langdon," she said, covering his flappy ears with her hand. "Can you hear what I'm hearing?"

The noise appeared to be coming from behind a small group of rocks not far from where Polly was standing. She walked very cautiously over toward the rocks and peered behind them. What she saw next visibly shocked her. For lying on the ground, curled up in a tight ball, lay a young girl with only the threadbare remains of her dress covering up her trembling body. Polly was horrified to see that her hands were bound behind her back, and she had masking tape over her mouth. "Who could have done such a dreadful thing to this poor and very precious little girl?" she pondered, instantly experiencing strong feelings of anger and shock. However, despite feeling very weepy and emotional, Polly took a deep breath to help her regain control of her feelings, and then she knelt down to untie the distraught and terrified little girl. This done, she then very gently attempted to remove the tape that bound the girl's mouth.

Polly noticed that her feet were bare and bloodied, as were her arms, so they would need bandaging. In an instant she forgot her own pressingly urgent problems as she knelt down and caressed the forehead of this girl who resembled one of the frightened animals that

Polly was forever rescuing. The young girl responded by curling up even tighter. Her whole body was shaking and quivering from fear. Polly took her woolly cardigan from out of her schoolbag and placed it gently over her body. She then placed Langdon in the girl's arms before lying down beside her with an arm over her in her attempt to persuade the little girl that she was now completely safe. Polly instinctively knew that it was best to say nothing, choosing instead to continue stroking her head as she cuddled up close to her.

How much time passed before the little girl opened her mouth and found the courage to speak is not known. Polly had no wristwatch and therefore no way of knowing the time of day. But eventually the little girl opened her eyes and began to communicate.

"Thank you," she whispered in a voice barely audible through trembling lips.

Polly smiled down at her and then hugged her again. "You don't have to say anything unless you want to," said Polly very gently to the little girl whose eyes were filled with terror.

The little girl gave a little smile. "My name is Jessica Julestone, and I think I'm seven years old."

"Well, Jessica, seven is a wonderful and most magical age to be, for I was once that age, although it seems like a long time ago. Now, let me introduce myself. I am Polly, and my elephant that's cuddling up to you, well, he is called Langdon. But, whatever you do, don't call him Lang, for he gets most upset if people shorten his name."

The little girl gave a faint-hearted smile and nodded her agreement. Young Jessica felt completely safe with Polly. So much so that in no time at all she uncurled and sat up, still clutching the jumper and Langdon to keep warm. Polly realized that Jessica was still shivering, so she encouraged Jessica to let go of Morag's woolly jumper and put it on. It was much too big for her, but it didn't matter as it could at least help regulate her body temperature and stay warm. She then took off her shoes and put them on Jessica's small feet.

"Look, I know they are probably far too big for your small feet, but they will have to do for the moment, Jessica. Do you want to stand up and try to walk?"

Jessica nodded, so Polly helped her get up from the ground, and, still holding her arm to steady her, they clumsily walked a few paces together before both of them collapsed in a heap on the ground.

"Never mind," said Polly brightly. "We will have another try later."

It was not too long before Jessica decided to tell Polly what had happened to her, and how she had come to end up in the desert.

"Polly," she said quietly with tears welling up in her eyes. "Last night I was fast asleep, safely tucked in my bed, when suddenly these strangers with two savage hounds at their side burst into my room and woke me up. They told me I had to go with them. Oh Polly, I was so frightened." Jessica began to cry.

Polly gently squeezed her arm in an endeavor to give comfort. "Look, Jessica, you don't have to tell me if you don't want to."

"Oh, but I do!" she cried.

Polly squeezed Jessica's arm for a second time, encouraging her to calm down and take it easy.

"Well, I tried to hide under the bedcovers, but it did not work," she cried, faltering badly as the words stuck in her throat. "But they dragged me from the bed, and one of them put his hand over my mouth to keep me from screaming. My mummy and daddy were fast asleep in the next room, and I wanted to let them know that something awful was happening to me, but I could not cry for help since my mouth was covered and I could hardly breathe."

Jessica continued to sob as she spoke. Her words did not come easily, for she was in a bad state of shock. When she did speak, she continuously broke down. Polly understood and let her continue with her story at her own pace. Polly knew only too well that Jessica was so traumatized that she required gentle handling, as well as tons of patience, if she was going to finish pouring out all the terrible details of what had happened to her.

"I want my Mummy," Jessica cried most piteously, shaking from head to foot.

Polly's eyes welled up with tears as the strength of those few words uttered by Jessica hit her heart with a massive thump. For those were the precise heart-wrenching and gut-churning, emotionally loaded words that Polly had continuously screamed out from deep inside her being for as many years as she could remember!

"There were three of them; two men and one lady, and some dogs that growled all the time and had huge, sharp teeth. Oh Polly, they looked as though they were going to gobble me up. I was dragged down the stairs and then bundled out of the front door and into the back of a car that then drove off very fast. Oh Polly, I was so afraid," she sobbed as she looked deep into Polly's eyes in the hope that she might understand the terror she had faced.

She was not disappointed. She could see clearly that Polly really understood the depth of what she had been through, for her eyes held nothing but the deepest compassion for her. Jessica felt deeply relieved that it had been Polly and not someone else who had found her.

"I bet you were absolutely petrified, Jessica," Polly said comfortingly as she continued to stroke Jessica's matted hair.

Jessica nodded and went back to her story. "Well, as I lay curled up and shaking on the backseat, the lady who was in the back of the car with me took out some rope and bound my hands behind my back, and then tied a scarf around my eyes so that I could no longer see." Jessica broke down again at this point, and Polly could do little but hug her tightly. "I could hear them discussing what to do with me. And I remember the lady had a funny name like Sookie, or Spooky, or something like that," she wailed. "I tried not to listen, because they talked about selling me to people who buy children, and they also said something about throwing me in the river to drown, or giving me to their dogs for their lunch. Polly, I was so afraid, so frightened," she whimpered. "I had no idea why they wanted me. Eventually they stopped the car, and I was ordered to get out. I could not see anything, so the lady pushed me out of the car, and then she got out herself and dragged me back up on my feet. Then the three of them got back into the car, and I could hear plenty of shouting, arguing, and barking, for their voices were so angry. The men wanted to keep me alive and get some money for my safe return."

"That's called ransom money, Jessica," Polly interjected.

"And I could hear the lady say she wanted to hand me over to her friend, Van something. I can't remember the name, but luckily for me she must have changed her mind."

Jessica started to tremble and shake so badly that Polly wrapped her arms even tighter around her, just as she used to do to calm Thomas down.

"Suddenly everything went silent," Jessica sniffed as she brushed away the tears that had been flowing steadily down her cheeks. "They stopped arguing, and that moment was the worst, Polly, for I had no idea what they were planning. Jessica coughed and sputtered, still struggling to get the words out. "While I stood there trembling from head to toe, I started to pray for help, for I had no one else to turn to. I said a little prayer that my mummy always says with me at bedtime, and just thinking of Mummy's soft skin and sweet-smelling hair helped me to not feel so afraid. It must have worked because suddenly, without any warning, they just sped off, leaving me standing alone in the middle of the desert."

"Oh, dear sweet Jessica, this must have been most terrible for you. But thank goodness they left you alive, and how amazing that your simple prayer was answered in your real hour of need. I think that is both precious and wonderful. But I think it would be wise to leave the rest of your story until later, for you are very weak and tired. So now it is very important for you to rest."

Jessica closed her eyes and allowed Polly to stroke her forehead until finally she fell asleep still cradled in Polly's lap. Polly felt very worried for her, but there was nothing she could do except hold Jessica tightly and pray a similar prayer to that of Jessica's for help to come, and quickly. For Polly knew that they needed to get out of the desert as soon as possible. Jessica urgently needed to get to a hospital so that her wounds could be cleaned and bandaged up before they attempted to fix her heart. She believed that if Jessica was to survive this most terrible ordeal, then she needed the help of people who knew what to do in such extreme cases. Knowing all this and being able to do nothing but wait and hope made Polly feel very frustrated and thoroughly powerless. All she could hope was for something out of the ordinary—possibly miraculous—to happen; yes, something unforeseen to get them out of this terrible mess.

Polly was really glad that she had been there to help Jessica. What would have happened to this most precious and frightened little girl if she had been left alone in the desert with no one to help her? Polly shuddered at such a thought. She knew that Jessica's ordeal would not end once help came. She could be taken to a hospital and all the wounds on her arms and legs would in time heal, but the restoration of her heart, well, that could take much longer, possibly years!

It was some hours later before Jessica awoke, and Polly noticed that she began to tremble again. "Polly, I miss my mummy and daddy so much," she cried. "The thought that I might never see them again is so awful." Jessica began to bawl loudly, her cries echoing through the cave most disturbingly. Polly felt so helpless that she began to cry as well, for in truth their plight seemed completely overwhelming and hopeless.

Finally they both ran out of tears and just lay exhausted in each other's arms for comfort.

Jessica went on some hours later to tell Polly how she had stumbled through the desert with her hands behind her back. Blindfolded and with sticky tape covering her mouth, she had stumbled over rocks that cut her hands and feet to ribbons. She had ripped her nightdress on the same obstacles, and that's how it had come to be in shreds. Eventually, the scarf had slipped down from her eyes and Jessica had been just as afraid without the blindfold, for she felt very panicky when she realized she had no clue as to where she was. As she walked on, many people had gone past her, some sitting high up on camels, their saddlebags bulging with spices and beans as well as pots and pans that clunked and clanged with every step the camels took. Strange-looking men followed behind the camels with brightly colored turbans on their heads as they walked through the sand. Others remained in front as they led their heavily-laden camels over the sandy dustbowl toward their destination.

Jessica had tried to scream out for help, but was prevented from doing so as her mouth was still taped. She still tried hard to get their attention by kicking up as much sand as she could in her futile attempt to make them aware of her existence, but all her attempts were in vain, for they had sadly failed to notice her because they were so caught up in their own concerns of getting to the marketplace. Other strangers had also passed by her, chatting incessantly as they walked in groups, but none had stopped to give her assistance. As Jessica still had tape around her mouth and her hands were bound with rope behind her back, she had at one point fallen to her knees in desperation in front of a large crowd of tourists, who had just disembarked from a coach to stretch their legs. Yet still no one came to her rescue, for they were all caught up with taking group photos and snapshots of lone palm trees and clusters of camels. Unbelievably, many of the tourists had simply walked over her limp body as they strived to get a better picture. One man even angrily kicked her to one side as he took a snapshot, for he most certainly didn't want this strange-looking object included in the family picture. Indeed, he felt she was most inconsiderate to be lying there at all, obstructing his path.

Jessica therefore had little choice but to pull herself up from the ground and with painful, bleeding legs and feet she staggered on, stumbling continuously and falling into razor-sharp briar bushes that ripped further into her flesh. Her face had become cracked and shriveled as she walked in the blazing heat of the day, and her eyes had become swollen and filled with sand, which she had no way of removing. She had braved the most terrible weather conditions, ranging from ice snowstorms to searing hot sand blizzards, which made her feel as though she were being stung by millions of bees.

Still she continued to stagger and stumble on through the desert, desperate for help. She had collapsed too many times to count from the intense sweltering heat of the scorching sun that beat down upon her. And her only protection had been the remains of her nightdress that still partially clung to her body. At one point she had become so dehydrated and delusional that she imagined she had seen water, so she made one final attempt to walk toward it before falling down to finally pass out behind the rocks, near to where Polly had found her. Yes, the poor darling had amazingly survived the most terrifying ordeal imaginable, but she was not out of the woods yet! For if help didn't arrive soon, Polly knew there was no hope of Jessica making it home, except in a body bag.

Polly continued to silently pray for help to come as she carried on stroking Jessica's tangled and matted blonde hair, lying closer than ever to her so that her heat would help to keep Jessica's body temperature from plummeting. Polly noted that Jessica was becoming worse by the minute, her breathing at times very shallow and her skin cold and clammy.

Polly wrapped her arms around her even tighter as she prayed for a miracle. She also used the time to reflect back on her life, and her thoughts turned to a similar trauma that had happened to her. It was a deeply painful memory, but lying in a cave in the middle of the desert with Jessica hanging onto life by a thread she could not help but turn her thoughts back to the terrible day when she and her siblings had first arrived at the castle.

She remembered so vividly the day they were forced to leave the children's home they had grown up in to be taken without warning to live at the castle. It was a bitterly cold December evening and Polly, who was just five years old at the time, had been ordered to go into the sitting room by one of the two extremely well-proportioned middle-aged sisters named Molly and Maisie Brimstone that ran this no-nonsense children's home with military precision. At the time Polly had no idea as to why they needed to speak to her. She therefore happily obliged. When she opened the door to enter, she found her two brothers were already there standing in the middle of the room, awaiting further instructions. Polly walked over and joined them. They stood in complete silence, most innocent and unsuspecting of the fate that was about to befall them.

It was not too long a wait before both ladies marched in, accompanied by the most portly gentleman they had ever set eyes upon. The man was shown to a comfortable chair, and once seated he was handed a cup of hot tea, followed by a nice thick slice of Victoria sponge, which Polly duly noted he polished off in no time at all. Polly had always wondered why it was called Victoria sponge cake. I mean, did it belong to Victoria, and if so, was that Victoria the very famous queen who had reigned over England so many years ago? If it turned out that this cake was indeed Queen Victoria's, then how come she was still making them all these years later when she was supposed to have died many years ago? And more to the point, how come everyone she knew, without exception, was allowed to eat a piece? She had never met the most hospitable Queen Victoria, but hoped that one day she might actually catch her alive and well in the kitchen, popping some of her sponge cakes into the oven. Then she would tell her how wonderfully delicious and oh-so-light her cakes were. Perhaps she might be able to persuade her majesty to give her a copy of her secret recipe!

Polly's wishful thinking was brought to an abrupt end when she and her two brothers were beckoned by Molly Brimstone to come forward and stand in a straight line in front of the still-seated gentleman. There was to be no introduction whatsoever. As the children stood, heads hung low, he finally pulled himself up from the chair, circling and looking them up and down as he did so. Polly felt very uncomfortable. Having come full circle, he then came to stand facing them directly, staring them up and down as he continued to deliberate whether he wanted these sad- and sorry-looking creatures. Polly felt as though they were slaves being purchased at some market, the only difference being the absence of chains around their hands and feet.

"Well, what do you think, sir?" Molly Brimstone asked, for of the two of them she was nearly always the mouthpiece.

He remained silent as he continued to observe the trembling children. There was no warmth about this man. His eyes seemed totally cold and lifeless.

Finally he spoke. His words were very deliberate as he asked, "Will they be any trouble?"

"Oh no, sir," replied Molly Brimstone. "No, we certainly keep them in order here, don't we, Maisie?" she said over-enthusiastically as she turned to face her sister for verbal agreement.

"We most certainly do," replied Maisie Brimstone as she got out of her chair and moved hastily towards the gentleman, anxious to refill his teacup.

Still he hesitated from giving any sign that he was interested in the children, who stood most pathetically with their heads hung low before him. Molly Brimstone was beginning to experience immense agitation and began to believe that he was on the verge of changing his mind. She therefore turned to Polly and snarled, "Stand up straight, girl, and stop slumping, otherwise I will have to fetch the broom from the kitchen cupboard and slide it down your back to help improve your disgraceful posture!"

She dropped all scowling as she turned to face the silent gentleman and with a smile alighting her hard-nosed face. She then went to great lengths in her endeavor to assure him that not only was her offer good, but also that he would be making a terrible mistake if he turned it down.

"They're in very good health, sir. Truly they are." She reached out and grabbed hold of Polly's chin, prizing her mouth open as wide as she was able to. "Here look, sir, see what I mean? Her teeth might be crooked, but otherwise she's all there."

"That will not be necessary," said the man, his steely eyes remaining firmly fixed on Polly as he spoke. "You say they are orphans with no living relatives, am I correct?"

"Yes sir, they're orphans all right," Molly Brimstone sniggered as she sycophantically fawned all over her potential client, most anxious to please him. "Yes, their father was I think of Italian descent, and he's long gone…and the children's mother, well, she had no interest in them whatsoever! Put them all in care at her earliest convenience. Yes, they've all been in children's homes within months of being born. And I can tell you right now, sir, there has never been as much as one visitor to see them. So nobody has the slightest interest whatsoever in these poor little blighters! Yes, I do believe they could disappear from this earth upon which we live, and nobody would ever know or miss them!" she said with a wide and wicked grin on her face.

"Good, that's settled then. I will take them," he said coldly, as he placed his hand out towards Molly Brimstone to shake on it, and thereby finalize the deal.

"That's good news, sir, and I promise that you won't be sorry." Molly clasped her hands with sheer delight and broke out into a huge smile.

Polly and her brothers were then frogmarched by Maisie to the cloakroom where their little coats hung, while Molly Brimstone stayed behind and took care of the finer details with the gentleman.

"Children, put your coats on at once," instructed Maisie, with an air of pompous officialdom normally reserved for her sister. Polly found it hard to respond, for she felt numb with shock. She glanced over in the direction of her brothers, and they seemed equally bewildered and were struggling just as much to respond to Maisie's latest order.

"I said right now!" Maisie thundered as she began, rather roughly I might add, to force Thomas's arm into the sleeve of his coat.

Polly felt hysterical as Maisie then attempted to force a coat onto her slightly built frame. She understandably put up quite a struggle, preferring to lunge towards Maisie, grabbing fistfuls of fatty flesh that hung in pleats from her ample thighs and arms. And having successfully grabbed hold, she refused to let go, hanging on to Maisie as though her very life depended on it. She looked directly into Maisie's eyes and pleaded, "Please don't do this to us, I beg you."

Maisie's face remained expressionless as Polly searched her face for just a hint of compassion. There was none to be found. "Get off me, girl," she growled.

"No, I'm not going," Polly screamed. "You can't make me! Please, please help me!" Polly cried, her sad and despair-filled eyes brimming with tears. Maisie remained unmoved, calling instead for her sister to come quickly to give her much-needed assistance.

In a matter of seconds her sister had excused herself from the gentleman's presence and raced at full speed to her sister's side to help her. She gave Polly a quick whack around the head. "This'll sort you out, girl," she hollered.

Though thoroughly dazed, Polly was not about to give up her firm grip on Maisie's flesh. She fought hard and long as she bit, scratched, and kicked like a wild animal caught in a hunter's trap. If the fight had been a fair one-on-one, there was every chance she would have come out on the winning side. It would have been a fight to the death, but sadly, she was no match against these sumo wrestlers, and eventually she was forced to admit defeat. Both women eventually had her lying prostrate on the floor, with both of them sitting on top of her as they forcibly stuffed her arms down her coat sleeves. With her coat on, Polly was dragged to her feet and placed in an arm lock by Molly Brimstone, who was more than a potential champion for the boxing ring.

Polly was still not about to give up, for she would rather be killed than taken alive from this place to be sent elsewhere. So she had to be dragged, screaming and kicking, all the way to the waiting black car that was parked in the driveway. She tried with all her might to break free, but to no avail. It was useless, for her wrestlers had weight as well as strength on their side, and they used it to the full to ensure she made it to the car. Her brothers put up no such fight. They just walked in dumb silence toward the car, climbing onto the rear seats and then sitting like stiff boards as they waited for further instructions. Polly was then bundled like a limp rag doll onto the seat beside her brothers.

She felt nothing short of terrified, for she was completely convinced that they were being kidnapped. A lady sat in the front passenger seat and did not even move her head to look in their direction. The gentleman stood by the car with his hands deep in his pockets until he was satisfied that they were all there and the back doors of the car were well-and-truly locked in order to prevent them from escaping. He then walked to the front door of the vehicle and, after climbing in and placing his black leather gloves on the dashboard, rolled down the window and bid Molly and Maisie Brimstone farewell. Both ladies turned towards the light of the open front door, and without so much as a good-bye or soft word of comfort to the terrified children, they shut the front door behind them.

Polly turned her head in one final attempt to catch a glimpse of what had been their home, and therefore all the security they had ever known. It was useless! She was much too small and the seats too low down for her to see out of the window. Besides, it was very dark. The tears tumbled profusely down Polly's cheeks as they drove down the driveway and headed out onto the open road. She was in a state of fear as well as confusion. Polly felt as though she was being physically ripped apart by being taken away from everything she had ever known. No words could express the depth of that feeling. They had not even been allowed to say good-bye to their other companions in misery, and Maisie Brimstone's final words of encouragement had been nothing more than, "Right, girl, do as we say and behave yourself!"

Behave herself? Polly wanted to scream and scream some more, for nothing had prepared her for an ordeal of this enormity! But only uncontrollable sobbing sprang forth from her lips as her teeth rattled and her body quaked with fear.

The journey to wherever they were being taken seemed to last an eternity. The gentleman who had called at the home sat passively in the front seat of the car, and no conversation took place between him and his lady passenger. The tension in the car was therefore unbearable. Polly's cries became louder and louder as fear and panic took its firm hold on her. Still, the man did not as much as flinch. No, he never turned to face Polly and her brothers to offer as much as a hanky, preferring instead to look straight ahead, watching the wipers go backwards and forwards over the windshield as it started to rain rather heavily. Polly believed that they might as well have been a car full of groceries for the lack of concern that was being shown towards them. Were they to be sold as slaves? Or worse still, were they being abducted? Would they be murdered in some dark woods, never to be found? Or finally, were they being sent to prison for, in Molly Brimstone's own words, "unacceptable naughtiness."

There came a point in the long and terrifying journey when Polly's anguished cries really began to irritate the silent gentleman. He chose this moment in time to ask his equally-silent lady companion to search through a bag that he had placed down by her feet. After rummaging around in the bag, she produced three chocolate bars and handed one to each of them. I might add that this was not done through some kind gesture towards them, but to encourage Polly to shut up, for she was giving him quite a headache, and he believed her noise was also preventing him from concentrating fully on the slick road ahead.

The last thing Polly wanted was a chocolate bar. No, all she desperately wanted was a cuddle and a few words of tender reassurance, but sadly, neither of these were on offer that most terrible of nights. Polly tried hard to force the chocolate down, for it felt as though it was stuck in her paralyzed throat, so great was the level of fear she was experiencing. Within minutes, she was sick. Yes, sick all down her black gaberdine raincoat, sick all over her shoes, and sick all over the floor of the moving vehicle. This disgraceful and unexpected happening forced the gentleman to quickly wind down his side window in an effort to dispel the unpleasant acrid aroma as he continued to concentrate as best he could.

The long journey finally came to an end when the car turned off the main road and headed down a gravel pathway, coming to a sudden halt in front of the largest towering black gates. Seconds later, the large black gates slowly opened and then closed behind them as the car drove through into a large open space, coming to a halt under an oak tree. Polly could hear the crunch of the gravel under the tires, then the rear door was flung open and the children were ordered to get out.

Polly stumbled as she alighted from the car, hurting the palms of her hands on the gravel as she attempted to break her fall. Looking up, and despite the darkness, she could see the definitive outline of a castle. Yes, this was most definitely a castle. She had seen plenty of pictures of these buildings in books at her nursery school. However, she had to admit that she'd never seen anything like this before. It was tall, gloomy, and archaic, with huge flint walls that rose high into the clouds and then beyond. Every way she looked her surroundings felt hostile, making her heart race even faster from terrifying fear. She stood by the car shuddering as the ice-cold wind whipped around her, showing no compassion as it mercilessly bit into her young and tender flesh.

Then a hand hit down hard on her shoulder, and before she had time to understand what was going on, she and her brothers were frogmarched across the large quadrangle in single file toward a baronial door. Polly and her brothers walked with heads down in stupefied silence, for pure terror was clutching at their loudly-pounding hearts. The only other noise was the crunch of gravel under their feet as they walked, most afraid, toward the front door. The large wooden door squeaked loudly as it opened and then shut behind them. Polly then heard the sound of the massive black locks as the door was then bolted. Once inside, they were quickly ushered down a bleak, long corridor and into a side room where they were ordered to sit down at a table. Once seated, lukewarm tea accompanied by a plate of brown bread and butter was served to them along with the order to "eat up."

Polly, who was still covered in sick, attempted to obey, but once again found herself trying to force food down her dry throat to no avail. For try as she may, she could not swallow the bread that felt like hard lumps of rock, even when she took a few gulps of cold weak tea to wash the bread down. And, as she dared to look up from the table, she could see the faces of many children staring directly at them from behind different pieces of furniture in the room. Polly instantly discerned that all their eyes held great sadness as well as morbid curiosity. She felt so uncomfortable with her every move being watched. She was very relieved when finally they were dismissed by someone in authority and then accompanied up the large oak stairs before heading towards the dormitories.

Polly and her brothers were together, that is, until they reached the top of the stairs, when without warning they were parted. For the first time that day the boys let out a little whimper as they tried and failed to grad hold of Polly's hand for help and comfort. It was to no avail as hands stronger than theirs physically separated them, the boys down one corridor and Polly down another as they headed toward their sleeping quarters. On the way to the dormitory, she noted a picture of Jesus on the wall. It had Him pointing both hands towards His heart, which was lit up in gold. It gave her no comfort.

Halfway down the long corridor the silent helper stopped and opened a door. Polly was then beckoned to go into the room. Polly reluctantly moved towards the silent lady and the door. She stopped and peered in. Her eyes hastily scanned the bleak room before settling on two rather formidable-looking rows of ancient, creaky beds. The room was otherwise very sparsely furnished with only the minimum perfunctory furniture, such as bedside lockers and a large old-fashioned brown wardrobe.

A firm hand pressed lightly down on her shoulders, suggesting she should move towards an empty, freshly-made-up bed with a bare locker by its side. It was the last bed in the room, and farthest from the door, so it was up against a wall. Strange as it may seem, having the wall on one side made her feel a tiny bit safer, simply because it was something immoveable. She was then ordered to undress and change into pajamas that were neatly folded by her pillow. The room was freezing cold, so she struggled to remove her clothes and put on the pajamas. The carer, who stood by silently watching, stripped back the bed, ordering her to quickly get in. Polly dutifully obeyed, clambering as quickly as she could between the sheets. She desperately wanted a bath, for she was still covered in sick, but she was much too afraid to ask for anything. Her plastic carrier bag, containing all her worldly possessions, was then hastily dropped down beside the bedside locker by the mysterious and silent carer.

Polly covered her head under the thin blanket in her futile and desperate bid to escape the world and blot out all that was happening to her. Her helper stood a moment and then moved back toward the door to switch off the light. Polly listened intently as she heard the pitter-patter of her unknown carer's footsteps heading down the long corridor towards the creaky oak staircase. Then she was gone. Polly would later learn the identity of this mysterious carer. Her name was Miss Scrimp and she was normally in charge of the laundry room.

Polly hid under the thin bed clothing and cried into the pillow as she attempted to stifle the deep sobs that rose up like an active volcano from deep within her breast. As she lay there in the dark, frightened and shivering from cold, she was unable to sleep. She felt so worried for her brothers. Were they all right? James hated the dark, so would he cry and then come and try to find her? Who were all those name-less children she had seen peering at them? Had they been taken to prison after all? And if so, was it because she had borrowed one of the other children's red pencil sharpeners and not given it back? Polly couldn't think of any other incident that could have caused the Brim-stones to have them sent away to be locked up forever in a castle. After all, being only five years old, she hadn't yet been given enough time to build any sort of impressive criminal career.

Polly felt exhausted by the stream of questions swimming around inside her head; questions that would, in the fullness of time, be answered, but at this present time gave her no hope or assurance when she so desperately needed it. All she knew that most terrible of nights was that she had been left with the sneaking suspicion that this was no holiday camp where they could pack their bags and leave after two weeks. Oh no! This place felt more like the very bowels of hell! And if not its bowels, then most certainly its mouth, for she felt as though she were being slowly sucked in to be agonizingly devoured! Nothing could, or would, in the years to come, persuade her otherwise!

With those big black gates firmly shut behind her, she would very soon come to realize that she was locked in and, worse still, there was to be no way of escape! Yes, I think it is fair to say that Polly and her brothers had been well-and-truly "hung, drawn, and quartered" by the social services, a shameless body of people to whom she, as well as her brothers, had been entrusted!

As Polly remembered back on the events of that most terrible of days, she likened it to that of Jessica's kidnapping. The whole episode had been a truly terrifying ordeal, and just like Jessica, there had been nobody to help her. The same had been true ever since! She felt as though her hands were bound behind her back, for she was powerless to do anything. Also, she might as well have had sticky tape around her mouth, for nobody had ever listened to her or asked her to share her feelings regarding any decision that was being made concerning her family members or herself. As a result, Polly felt that, just like Jessica, she had stumbled around in the darkness, torn and bleeding from wounds that never healed as she searched for hope and reason to her crazy roller-coaster life. And just as Jessica had kicked up sand in her attempt to be noticed, the same could be said for Polly. No matter how much fuss she kicked up in her attempt to be heard, it was as though she didn't exist.

She had given up all hope of help ever coming, for she and her siblings were just pawns on a chessboard to be moved from here to there at the whim of the faceless people from the social services. These unknown individuals happily stamped all documents without a flicker of thought as to the impact that their decisions—or their hideous effects—would have on the tender hearts and souls of pain-filled children who were already suffering terribly from having no mummy or daddy to love and care for them. It made Polly want to weep.

Jessica had been found virtually naked by Polly and curled up in a ball, too terrified to move. Polly felt equally naked and vulnerable as she had constantly faced life's most cruel elements that sought to mercilessly cuff and buffet her battered, exposed soul. It left her screaming inside for someone—anyone—to come along and rescue her and her brothers, for they were all suffering from broken spirits that would eventually be considered irreparable! She may not have suffered the visible cuts and bruises that Jessica had all over her arms and legs, but inside she felt equally cut to ribbons. She hoped with all her heart that Jessica would quickly be reunited with her mummy and daddy, for she knew that to go through childhood unprotected and without these precious people was to be left in a constant state of grieving.

Polly felt caught in this permanent state of mourning and had often dreamt that her parents would one day, out of the blue, turn up at the castle door and say there had been some terrible mistake, and they had carelessly mislaid the children while out shopping in the supermarket. They would then take Polly and her brothers away from this horrible place to finally live as a family and be happy ever after. Until that day came, Polly felt like a victim of war, struggling to battle on with large pieces of razor-sharp shrapnel still deeply embedded into her flesh. Yes, a fully paid-up member of the walking wounded, or was it more like the walking dead?

As she remained in the cave, cradling Jessica's limp body, she hoped Jessica's story would, unlike her own, have a happy ending. She knew if it was left up to her, she would do all in her power to make it so. As the hours ticked by and Jessica continued to whimper and pitifully cry, she could only carry on caressing her forehead, whispering soft words of comfort and reassurance in her ear, something no one had ever before done for her.

Chapter 20
HOPE IN YOUR HEART HOSPITAL

SUDDENLY, WHEN ALL hope seemed lost Polly thought she heard a noise coming from outside the cave. She thought she was going crazy, for it sounded like a car. She then told herself that this could not be, for she had never before heard of a car being driven through the desert. She got up from the floor of the cave, telling Jessica to stay where she was, she cautiously made her way to the cave's entrance.

As she climbed out of the cave, shielding her eyes from the scorching sun she could hardly believe what she saw, for she hadn't been imagining things. Parked just a few meters from the cave entrance was a cherry red Mini car with a brightly-colored Union Jack painted on its roof. Leaning against the car were two boys that Polly recognized and knew to be best friends who spent their every waking moment together, for they loved the same recreational activities.

Polly had always found it most amusing that they shared the first name, with only their surnames being different. The sandy, fair-haired boy was called Justin Kase, and the leaner, darker-haired boy was called Justin Thyme. And as far as Polly was concerned they were indeed just in time, for Jessica needed help, and she needed it now! Polly broke into instant laughter, for she was deliriously happy to see the two of them. She wasted no time at all, racing breathlessly over to where they stood deep in conversation as they poured over a map they had just spread out over the hood of their car.

"Justin," she cried out twice over so that both boys were acknowledged. "I cannot imagine what possessed you both to drive out here into the heart of the desert, but I am so glad to see you both!" she squealed as she flung herself into the arms of Justin Kase, who, taken by surprise, lurched backwards in astonishment. She then moved towards Justin Thyme to give him an equally emotional hug. Both boys went a deep shade of purple, feeling very relieved to be in the middle of the desert with no friends around to witness Polly's seemingly over-the-top display of emotion!

"It's good to see you, too, Polly," declared Justin Thyme as he warmly greeted her. "And to answer your question, we have no idea whatsoever as to how we ended up here!"

Justin Kase nodded. "Yes, we were actually on our way to a place called Piadora, because we overheard two rather shabby and decidedly stinky men discussing a banquet they were going to at this strange place. And then we heard them say that all the food would be free of charge to anyone who cared to turn up. That's right, isn't it, Justin?"

His friend continued nodding before rudely butting into the conversation. "Yes, Polly, we heard them discussing the menu, and I can tell you now it sounds like an awesome event. There will be pizzas galore and pasta and ice cream and hamburgers by the dozen."

"With chips. Don't forget to mention the chips," interrupted Justin Kase.

"Yes, you can have chips with everything," said Justin Thyme, his mouth watering as he spoke. "Well, we couldn't turn down such an offer, could we? And although we weren't actually invited," he said rather sheepishly while winking at his friend, "we discovered a rather tatty old map of Piadora that the men accidentally left behind on the bench, so we decided to invite ourselves to the party."

"Yes, crash the event," interrupted his friend. "We were doing really well, time-wise, until we hit upon a car rally and some bloke called Phil Fastrack invited us to take part in it. Well, I don't need to tell you, Polly, both of us love a good race."

His friend grinned and nodded back most heartily. "So we both signed on the dotted line as we believed a little detour would be OK and we would make up for the lost time later. What made it more tempting was that first prize was a hundred pounds, and as I'm still paying my mum back for this car, we figured we could win the race in record time and then get back on track toward Piadora in time for the grub."

Justin Kase continued to stand, arms folded, with a permanent cheeky grin on his face as he nodded his agreement at all his friend had said. "Things were going really well. So much so that we found ourselves well ahead of all the other racing drivers. Then, with the first prize almost in our grasp, we suddenly took a wrong turn. I am still mystified as to how this happened, for Justin here is a first-class map reader."

"It was the signpost in the middle of the road that totally threw me," interrupted Justin Thyme as he tried to justify his actions. "Quite what it was doing in the middle of the road is anyone's guess, but the signpost definitely directed us to turn right off the beaten track. At first I did question it, for there was no mention of this route on my map, but the sign definitely said "Winning Route, this way." So I threw caution to the wind and told Justin to turn off and head for the desert. It didn't take us long to realize that we'd made a terrible mistake, but by then we were well-and-truly lost. So we stopped here at the rocks to take another good look at our map, and hopefully figure out what to do next."

Polly inwardly smiled at their story, for she was becoming very familiar with odd things happening that had no rhyme or reason to them. Indeed no earthly explanation whatsoever!

Polly directed the boys into the cave where Jessica was sitting being watched over by Langdon, and as they walked she told the boys of Jessica's ordeal. Both of them felt disappointed that they would have to abandon the racing rally, but they were in full agreement that the girls' need of help was far more important.

As soon as they both set eyes on Jessica, they appeared very shocked at her bad condition. Justin Kase immediately went back to the car to get his large backpack. He returned a few minutes later and placed it on the ground before squatting down to undo all the zips. Polly watched on in sheer amusement, for there appeared to be nothing that he had not thought to pack for his journey.

"You'd have thought you were going on a long expedition for at least a year, Justin," she declared with a sense of amusement. "I have never seen so many items come out of a bag. It's like watching *Mary Poppins*! Do you have a standard lamp in there?"

Polly was correct in her thinking, for Justin produced, not only a sleeping bag, but pen knives, saucepans, a hammer, screwdrivers, notepads, needle and thread, clothes, including smelly socks, hiking boots, torch, and whistles; the list of all he produced was endless and some items were, to say the least, most surprising! At the end of the day Polly would not have been the least surprised if he had pulled out a full sized forklift truck from his bag, such was the extraordinary amount of things he had forced into it.

"They don't call me Justin Kase for nothing, Polly. Oh no! I never go anywhere without packing all I need and more, just in case of any emergency," he beamed.

Finally he produced the item that he had been looking for: a large, bright-red first-aid kit with a huge white cross on its lid.

"There you go. I knew it would only be a matter of time before I put my hands on it." He pulled the first-aid kit out of his backpack and handed it to Polly. "Now if this doesn't only go to prove that I am right in my way of thinking that we must always consider taking everything that we might possibly need. Yes, my motto from my days in the scouts is 'Be prepared,' and therefore I always am!"

Polly thanked him and set about binding Jessica's wounds from the plentiful bandages that were in his first-aid kit. Justin then produced a large bottle of water for the girls to drink, as well as a bag of stale cakes. Polly thought it best not to ask Justin where he had gotten the cakes from, for she believed she knew the answer to that!

Finally, both boys helped to carry Jessica to the car before placing her down very gently on the backseat. Polly then picked up all her belongings, including Langdon, and squeezed into the back of the Mini alongside Jessica. The boys got into the front of the car and pinpointed the nearest hospital. Justin Thyme then switched on the ignition and started the car up. Polly had no problem believing he was a natural-born racing driver, as she found herself holding on for dear life to a small looped strap that was in the exterior of the car. As they made the journey, there were times when she thought it would not only be Jessica that required urgent medical attention, but all of them if he did not slow down!

Polly needn't have feared, for although Justin Thyme was a fast driver, he was also a very capable and experienced driver as well.

Unbeknown to Polly, his father was a racing driver who took him to the racetrack most weekends, so he had taught Justin well.

Finally they arrived at Hope in Your Heart Hospital, and Jessica was helped out of the car and onto a stretcher by a team of professional nurses and doctors. Polly went with them, for she needed to fill out the many forms that hospitals seem to require. The boys, having done their duty, told Polly that they were most anxious to be on their way, for neither of them liked hospitals. They hoped the girls would fully understand. Polly thanked them for all their help, for she was extremely grateful that they had been so willing to do all they could, but she also felt that they were not being entirely honest and that their keenness to leave had more to do with getting to Piadora and the banquet. It left her feeling slightly anxious as she believed that both boys had such huge appetites that she very much doubted there would be any food left for her by the time she finally got there!

Although Polly could not fill in all the details, she did her best. She also decided to ask the doctor who had presented her with the forms if she could stay until she knew that Jessica was out of danger. The kind doctor, whose name was Dr. Loveheart, sported a small goatee beard and had smiling eyes. He suggested to Polly that she might like to stay in the guest suite that was used for relatives of sick family members. There she could make herself a cup of hot, sweet tea and have a rest, as Jessica would be in hospital for quite some time.

As they walked down the highly-polished corridor towards the guest suite, Polly implored Dr. Loveheart to do all he could to find Jessica's mummy and daddy.

"I cannot stress enough how important it is to find them," Polly informed the kind doctor, "so please do all you can," she pleaded before adding, "I am certain that if she is reunited with them her recovery will be much quicker, so I beg you to ask the receptionist to call the police and get them to help. Promise me you will," she urged.

Dr. Loveheart reassured Polly that the police had already been contacted and would be arriving at the hospital very shortly. He also told her that they would probably like to speak to her first, as it was most important for Polly to help paint a picture of where Jessica had been found and the details of her condition at the time of being discovered. Polly agreed it might be helpful and said she would do all she could if it helped to find the perpetrators of this terrible crime.

As they were talking, Polly noticed a small white feather flutter to the ground and land beside her bare feet. She felt embarrassed, for she had forgotten that she had given Jessica her shoes and therefore was not only barefoot, but barefoot in a hospital where everybody was required to dress properly and for reasons of hygiene, this included shoes.

"I apologize for coming into your nice, clean hospital barefoot," she stuttered, at the same time going red in the face, "but I lent mine to Jessica."

"I know," replied Dr. Loveheart with a huge grin. "Don't worry, Polly, I will bring them with me when I return to report on Jessica's condition."

Polly was grateful, for she knew it would be difficult to continue on her journey without them. Dr. Loveheart led Polly down a number of long corridors and then into the guest suite.

"Polly, put the kettle on and make us both a nice cup of tea," he said, a little tongue-in-cheek as he ushered her through the open door. "The kettle is just over there. I just need to have a word with my colleague Dr. Heartthrob, and then I will come back for that cup. I do hope you know how to make a decent brew?"

Polly flashed him a smile and assured him that she did. "I was always making mugs of tea for men who stopped by at the orphanage, and to date none of them have ever complained," she said, wide-eyed and innocently.

"Well, Polly, that's good to hear. So I will see you shortly, and we can talk further."

The doctor was about to leave the room when Polly suddenly had a thought, "Dr. Loveheart, please can you give this to Jessica," she said as she handed over her most prized possession. The doctor took the little blue elephant from Polly. "And tell her that she can borrow him until her parents are found, for he will do much to comfort her," she added as an afterthought.

Dr. Loveheart bade Polly farewell and left to go in search of Dr. Heartthrob to sound out his professional opinion concerning Jessica and medication, leaving Polly to make herself at home in the guest suite. Polly busied herself making a large pot of tea and decided to have a cup while she waited for Dr. Loveheart to reappear. She then made herself comfortable on the large sofa and, having drained her cup, promptly fell into a fitful sleep.

She awoke some time later to find an officious-looking police constable standing over her. She sat up quickly, for she was instantly filled with dread. Had her past finally caught up with her? Did the police believe that Polly was behind Jessica's kidnapping? If so, were they here to arrest her? Panic spread through her body as she believed her worst fears were about to be realized. All this and more raced through her imagination, causing her heart to beat faster than ever.

She had met a lot of policemen in the past when they visited the castle to have cups of tea with her guardians, and she had always been very worried that they were going to lock her away for the crimes she had committed. Yes, crimes like the poem she had written and other such heinous acts that had caused Aunt Mildred and Uncle Boritz such distress. In truth, they had told her on many occasions that she was so wicked that it was only a matter of time before she would find herself locked away behind prison bars, and her crimes were of such magnitude that the keys to her cell would almost certainly be thrown away for good.

Polly therefore felt most uneasy and, if she were honest, guilty. For as crazy as it might seem, she had always been made to feel guilty concerning things she had done, or had omitted to do, or was otherwise preparing to do! It seemed that even the thought was enough evidence to find her guilty and therefore deserving of a stiff sentence, if not the maximum sentence afforded to such hardened criminals such as the likes of young Polly Brown.

The policeman, whose name was Bob Locke, could see that Polly was not at all comfortable with his presence in the room, and this did much to puzzle him. After all, she was a hero. Yes, a very brave girl, who at the very least deserved an award for bravery. He even thought it would be very nice if Polly joined the British constabulary when she was old enough, as she was just the sort of young lady they would like to have on their force. So as he unfastened the bright gold button on his breast pocket to pull out his thick incident book and record the details, he gave her a warm smile and patted her on the shoulder, saying, "Well done, miss."

Even this seemingly friendly interaction served to confuse Polly even more. Why would an officer of the law be so nice and kind? For it made no sense to her way of thinking, and not only did it make her feel uncomfortable and a trifle embarrassed but it heightened her suspicious leanings as well.

As Polly chatted away to the very nice constable with the bell-shaped hard-topped hat, completed by a silver badge on the front, she felt all her nervousness and mistrust melt away. That is, once she had established in her mind that she was not in any sort of trouble with the law. She quickly decided that Bob Locke was a very nice man after all, and therefore she had nothing to fear.

She was also very surprised to hear from Officer Locke that the police were considering awarding her a medal for her charitable act in saving Jessica. Polly made it perfectly clear that she did not want any sort of award, for she had only done what anyone else would have done. Bob Locke disagreed but chose not to tell her so. He smiled to himself as he thought that Polly would make a most excellent and caring officer on his task force. He had almost finished interviewing Polly when Dr. Loveheart knocked on the door and poked his head around the corner.

"How's that cup of tea going, Polly?" he asked with a wide grin.

"Oh dear," replied Polly, "I made it quite a while ago, so I think it is almost certain to be stewed. I will quickly brew up another pot."

Soon Dr. Loveheart, Officer Locke, and Polly were in possession of a cup of fresh, warm, disgracefully sweet tea made by Polly's fair hands. Neither Dr. Loveheart or Officer Locke thought it appropriate to tell her that she had gone way over the top with the sugar so that it therefore tasted more like syrup than tea, for both men were far too polite and gentlemanly. While sipping his tea, Dr. Loveheart decided that this was as good a time as any to update Polly on Jessica's progress. Polly was delighted to hear that while she had been snoozing, young Jessica's parents had been traced and were at this very moment by her bedside.

"Excellent," cried Polly, "that is such good news!"

"I thought that would make you happy," said Dr. Loveheart with a smile. "And, as promised, here are your shoes, oh, and of course, Langdon as well." He placed the items in her hand.

"Polly, Jessica's parents wish to meet with you to say a big thank you. Would that be all right?" asked the doctor.

Polly declined the offer. "I'm really sorry, Dr. Loveheart," she said apologetically. "I would love to meet them, really I would, but I have stayed far too long and I must quickly leave the hospital, for I have some very private and urgent matters that I must attend too. Can you tell them that I'm so glad Jessica is safe and in good hands, and perhaps we can meet up at a later date once Jessica has made a full recovery?"

Dr. Loveheart smiled at Polly, saying he fully understood. "I will just slip back to Jessica's bedside and let them know that it is not possible. But first, I think I need another cup of tea. Anyone else like a refill?" he asked as he made his way over toward the kettle.

Polly leapt off the sofa and offered to make some more tea. The good doctor declined her kind offer, for his stomach was still feeling a bit queasy from the last cup she made. Officer Locke on the other hand held up his cup to express that he wouldn't mind another cup if it was going. After all, it is well known that British bobbies never turn down the offer of another cup of tea, as it serves to help them concentrate more effectively as they scribble down and then go over the he said-she said facts of the case in question.

Officer Locke asked Polly a few more questions before closing his notepad, at the same time informing her that for the time being, he had all the information he required. Then, leaving only the dregs of his tea in the cup, he stood up and with a huge warm smile that lit up his entire face as he bid her farewell. Polly smiled at the constable, feeling very glad to have met him, for their little timely rendezvous had done much to restore her confidence in the British bobby!

After the constable had left to go back to the police station, Polly picked up her schoolbag containing all her possessions and slung it over her shoulder. Then with Langdon in one hand and her shoes in the other, she quietly left the room and tiptoed down the corridor. Once outside the hospital, she sat on the wide steps to put her shoes back on. As she slipped her shoe onto her right foot, it felt distinctly uncomfortable, so she pulled it off and shook it. She was completely taken by surprise when out tumbled a small smooth stone. Polly cautiously picked it up and quickly noticed that, just like her other pebbles, this too had a word inscribed on its smooth surface.

The engraved letters spelled the word *goodness*.

Polly was thoroughly stumped as to how it got there, but she was far too tired to allow free reign to the multitude of theories that were ready and willing to occupy her mind for the next twenty-four hours. She wisely decided to place it in her pocket along with the other two and forget about it. She then slipped on the other shoe only to find that it also seemed strangely uncomfortable. So once again she removed the shoe and shook it. However, on this occasion nothing revealed itself. So she then resorted to peering inside the shoe before placing her fingers into it. She could see clearly that something was stuck inside and, trapping the mysterious blockage between her fingers, she pulled it out. It turned out to be an envelope that had obviously been folded up a number of times. She carefully opened it up and began to read its content.

Dear Polly,

Nothing can express the depth of gratitude we feel toward you for rescuing our very precious daughter. Please accept this monetary gift as a small gesture on our part to say a big thank you. We knew if we gave it to you in person you would probably refuse to accept it, so we felt it would be better to do it this way. We know you need the money, for a friend of yours named Ralph popped in to see Jessica, and he told us that you had a plane to catch and this is why you are in such a hurry to leave the hospital. Have a safe trip and keep in touch, for Jessica has told us you are now her best friend ever. Take care.

Mr. + Mrs. Julestone

Polly felt deeply moved by the letter. She put the money safely in her pocket before pulling her precious gold book out of her schoolbag. She opened it up to a fresh page, and as she did so, she again noticed the words had been written for her. It read:

The princess was very tired, for she had been through quite an ordeal. Her time in the desert had been such a difficult and painful experience that she had nearly thrown in the towel, even giving in to thoughts that told her she would be far better off if she went back home to the castle. Luckily these thoughts were only temporary, as was her understandable outburst of rage. Thankfully, Langdon was only slightly injured, suffering a small bump, which left him nursing a sore head and trunk for the next couple of hours. However, the princess came up trumps in the end, for when she discovered a young girl who not only had been kidnapped but also left for dead in the desert, the princess immediately dropped all concern for herself and her future, choosing instead to devote herself to helping the extremely distressed and very bewildered child. She put on both goodness and kindness and spent all her energy doing all within her power to ease the young girl's most terrible plight, for Jessica's pain became her pain.

The princess even insisted on staying at the hospital until she knew Jessica had her family safely at her bedside. She did all this in spite of knowing that she was probably jeopardizing everything. It seemed a certainty that this unforeseen hold-up would result in her arriving at Piadora far too late for anything but cold leftovers. But to Polly, it no longer mattered, for such was the goodness that arose from within the spirit of this young maiden. It was a gift that had been there all the time, just waiting for the right moment to be released.

The young princess also dealt with her suspicion and mistrust for officers of the law, for she discovered that many of them truly do serve to protect young and very vulnerable ladies, such as Jessica and the princess. She had therefore learned many lessons through the trials and tribulations of her days in the hot, dusty desert. She now needed to hurry and get herself ready to catch a plane. The black London cab arrived in perfect time to get her to the airport, with the cabbie leaning out of the window to cry, "Taxi. I've come to take you to the airport, miss!" The princess got up from the hospital steps, and with Langdon safely tucked under one arm and her schoolbag over her shoulder, she climbed into the taxi to continue her most exciting adventure.

———

Polly closed the gold book and placed it carefully back in her schoolbag, along with all her other possessions. She then picked up Langdon and held him close. As she did so, a big black London cab pulled up right beside her, and with the engine still running the cabbie poked his head out of the window and shouted; "Your taxi, miss, to take you to the airport."

Polly climbed into the backseat of the car and then closed her eyes as she reflected back on all the strange events that had taken place over the past few days. The taxi then drove carefully out of the grounds of Hope in Your Heart Hospital before making its way in the direction of the airport at high speed.

Chapter 21
MANY MISUNDERSTANDINGS

*I*N NO TIME at all, the taxi pulled up outside the taxi rank that was specially reserved for dropping passengers off. Polly paid her fare and thanked the nice cabbie driver, not forgetting to tip him, before heading toward the doors of the airport terminal.

The inside of the building was not only huge, but bustling with travelers and their bursting-at-the-seams suitcases as they raced to and fro with trolleys stacked precariously high with their luggage. Observing all the busyness left Polly feeling a little bit scared.

Finally she made her way over to where two very glamorous ladies with highly polished nails were sitting behind a long desk tapping on computers. Polly had to stand on tiptoe, and even then she was not too certain whether the ladies would be able to see her there, for with the computers blocking her view and the service desk being so high she felt very insignificant.

"Excuse me," she said in the most grown-up voice she could put on.

Still the ladies chatted excitedly because they had not heard her, nor could they see her. She needed to think of a way of catching their attention. She made a loud coughing noise before waving both arms in the air, and as Langdon was being held in one of her hands, it did much to make him feel terribly dizzy and sick to the pit of his furry little tummy. Her plan worked! Both ladies eventually stopped chatting and peered over their computers to take a better look.

Polly smiled and then said again, "Excuse me, but I really do need your assistance, for I need to catch a plane to Piadora and so I was wondering if you could help me."

The two exquisitely dressed ladies looked at each quizzically before answering.

"Piadora? I have never heard of such a place!" remarked the taller one of the two, who had her long, blonde hair swept up in a bun, most of which was covered by a red-white-and-blue hat.

"No, neither have I," stated her equally smartly-dressed companion with short dark hair and deep green eyes. "Don't you think that you've got yourself a little bit confused young lady, and the place you really want to travel to is Paris?"

"Ooh, I love Paris," interrupted the blonde lady dreamily, "Yes, Paris is definitely the 'in place' to travel to, for it's so romantic, and the food is simply divine. Shall we book you on a plane to Paris then, young lady?"

"No, thank you," replied Polly. "For although I'm sure Paris is, just as you say, a most wonderful place with food to die for, I cannot go there because I am expected in Piadora for tea at a friend's house. He would think I was most rude if he ever got to hear that I had chosen to go elsewhere to eat. In fact, I'm certain he would feel so upset that he would never invite me to his house ever again!"

"Without wishing to appear rude either, miss," interjected the blonde lady, "Do you think there is just the smallest of possibilities that you have the name of the country wrong or the spelling of it incorrect?" she suggested, drumming her highly polished nails on the counter as she spoke.

"I don't think so," replied Polly. "In fact, I am quite certain that I have got it right, and Piadora, not Paris, is where I am meant to be flying to. So please, I really do need your help and advice."

Polly, who was now feeling most frustrated, pulled out her map and then placed it on the counter for the ladies to unfold and then look at. Both peered most anxiously at Polly's map, agreeing and then disagreeing as to where this country might possibly be.

Polly began to feel a little unnerved. For if the ladies had no idea where it was, then what hope had she of ever finding it? After all, she considered herself to be a most inexperienced traveler. Yes, her travels had been extremely limited, with Polly never having ventured farther afield than the town in which she lived. She stood waiting as patiently as she was ever able to wait, anxiously biting her nails as she did so, in the forlorn hope that the ladies might finally shed some light on her growing travel crisis. She was on the verge of giving up all hope when one of them finally spoke.

"I think I know the answer to your travel problem," she said with a smile. Polly immediately perked up. "Yes, what you need to do is travel to Rio de Janeiro in Brazil, and once there, you will then need to take an internal flight to the Iguaçu Falls. Finally, you will need to take a boat downstream before heading up into the mountains. Yes, I'm quite certain that is where you will find Piadora."

Polly thanked them, for she was most grateful for their help. She then politely asked, "Where do I need to go to buy a ticket to Brazil then?"

"You can get one here," said the kind hostess with the blonde hair tied up on a bun. "But I will need to see your passport."

"What's a passport?" Polly asked with a troubled look etched on her face, for she had never seen one before.

"It's a little book with a gold British emblem embossed on its cover, and inside it has a nice little picture of you, dear," replied the nice lady.

"Oh dear," said Polly, feeling instantly disappointed, "I don't think I have one of those, and I certainly have no picture of myself, for I am so terribly ugly. Please tell me the truth...Are very ugly people allowed on planes? For if not, I have no idea as to what I am going to do," she wailed.

The ladies looked at each other before breaking into a smile. "Yes, even if you were Quasimodo you would still be allowed on the plane," said the blonde lady before breaking out into fits of giggles, her friend then following suit.

"Well, that's all right then," said Polly, her voice betraying sheer relief, although she had absolutely no idea as to why they found her very reasonable question so funny. However, she decided not to pursue the matter any further.

"I may not have a photograph or a passport, but I do have a royal emblem on my signet ring," she said, placing her hand on the desk. "Will this do instead?"

Both ladies peered at the ring before the blonde lady replied to Polly's question. "Well, that's all right then, for I do believe that wearing that ring will get you anywhere you wish to go."

"Is Langdon allowed to travel on the plane with me?" Polly asked. "Or does he require a passport or ring as well?" She lifted Langdon above her head and once again waved him in the air so they could take a good look at him.

"No, I think as long as he stays close to you at all times and doesn't charge off anywhere, then I do believe there should be no problem," replied the blonde lady with a smile as she issued Polly a ticket.

"Do you wish to have any baggage checked in?" asked her equally delightful companion.

"No, I don't think so," Polly wistfully replied. "For I have very few possessions and I take them with me wherever I go, but thank you for asking."

Polly breathed a deep sigh of relief as she thought to herself that she was finding her time at the airport a very pleasant and trouble-free experience. She beamed back at both ladies as she produced the envelope that contained the money. In minutes, she had been checked in and was clutching her ticket tightly in her hand.

Polly made her way to gate seven, where the ladies had instructed her to head. They also informed her that she would be traveling with BOAC. Polly asked them what that meant. The nice ladies informed her that it stood for British Oversees Air Carrier.

She was glad they had been so helpful in giving her directions. The airport was so large, and Polly had absolutely no idea which gate she needed among the many corridors and glass tunnels that all served to make Polly feel thoroughly confused.

Once she made it through one set of gates, she was directed by a very serious uniformed gentleman with a peaked cap to join a long line. Polly hadn't the slightest idea what they were all lining up for. She wondered if it was to get free sweets and ice cream. She certainly hoped so. As the line got shorter and she reached the beginning of the queue, she was most disappointed to discover that she had not been standing in the line for free goodies, but they wanted her to remove her schoolbag from her back and place it on a long black surface that was moving. Polly did as she was told and then watched as her bag of most precious items went down what looked like the production line in a factory, only to be finally gobbled up by a large metal, oblong machine.

This made her most anxious until the man standing behind her in the queue told her that it would come out the other side, and once checked over by security, it would be handed back to her. She was delighted to hear this good news, as the bag held all her worldly possessions and she did not want to lose them to the hungry X-ray machine that was happily devouring everything that came its way!

Polly was then ordered by a man in a uniform to place Langdon on the moving security line. She was quite reluctant to part with Langdon and therefore hesitated. Having given her the order, he then momentarily turned his head to deal with a customer who appeared to require his immediate assistance. The very demanding lady then commandeered him toward her rather large mound of luggage. In doing so, he abandoned the security checkout and left the line momentarily unsupervised. A bad decision if ever there was one, and one that he would have many years to reflect back on!

For Polly, having followed through his last order, which was to place Langdon on the conveyer belt, took it upon herself to jump up onto the moving line as well. For she naturally assumed that if Langdon was required to go down the moving line, then she too was expected to do likewise! She also could not bear the thought of being separated from Langdon, even if it was only for a few minutes. She had, after all, experienced the deepest sense of loss when she accidentally left him on the beach in the near-drowning crisis, so she was not prepared for anything like that to happen again!

"Langdon," she rather furtively whispered in his ear. "Where you go, I go."

With her intentions now clearly out in the open, Polly then climbed up on the conveyor belt and lay out flat, giving a quick stretch as she did so. For she did not wish to bump her head or get her hair tangled in the man-eating machine. The machine had a strange rubber fringe that looked something like tentacles as it flapped to and fro, covering each item that moved slowly toward it before utterly consuming it all. She smiled to herself as she thought how much fun all this was, lying back with not a care in the world.

Seconds later she was looking up and waving good-bye to Langdon as he disappeared from sight into the man-eating machine. Polly was also just about to disappear from sight when she was suddenly spotted by a security man who was halfway through searching a lady's purse. The man's jaw fell open in sheer disbelief, and he immediately abandoned his investigative search to race as quickly as his legs would allow him over to where Polly happily lay outstretched, about to be swallowed up into the machine. By the time he reached the conveyor belt only Polly's lower limbs were still visible, much to the horror of all the onlookers, for the upper portion of her body had long gone out of sight. Although it was very dark and dismal inside the man-eating machine, the young girl's smiling face, complete with detailed bone structure, could be viewed quite nicely on the televised scanner!

The uniformed man lunged at Polly, grabbing her by the feet. But to his utter despair, only her shoes came off in his hands. And with each passing second, there was becoming less of Polly to grab hold of. A woman who was watching screamed before fainting. Nobody went to the poor woman's aid because all eyes were firmly fixed on the Polly crisis. In fact, the lady fainting had been good news to some of the eager spectators, for with her now lying flat on the floor conveniently out of the way, they now had a much better view of the drama that was unfolding before their very eyes. Some even hurriedly reached into their bags to get out their cameras, for this was one picture they certainly wanted in their photo albums!

The uniformed man tried again, and this time he was more successful, for he managed to get a firm grip on both of Polly's ankles. He wasted no time in giving an almighty tug. Thankfully it worked, and Polly found herself moving from great darkness into light as her torso was dragged free from the conveyor belt with its man-eating manacle!

As Polly was pulled back down the moving line, she smiled up at the faces of all the curious spectators who had gathered around to watch the rescue and took the time to wave in the direction of the flashing cameras. The onlookers unanimously agreed that she had been a very lucky girl who had been saved just in time, thanks to the quick-thinking uniformed gentleman.

Polly sat up and continued to wave at everybody, thinking how nice and friendly they all were at this airport. That is, with the exception of the uniformed officer, for he had, only scowls for Polly, as he picked her up from the offending and still-moving machine. He took it upon himself to rather harshly plunk her back down on the ground, well out of harm's way. His quick action had certainly saved Polly from serious injury, something Polly seemed quite unaware of. Yes, she had no idea that she had almost brought security at the airport to a complete standstill! All she knew was that she was trying to be helpful and obedient, and this rather rude man had grabbed her by the ankles, giving her an awful fright.

After placing her back on her two feet, the security guard explained to Polly that the machine was only intended for luggage. This confused Polly further, for no way did she view Langdon as "luggage." Oh no! He was, after all, her very special elephant who required the same amount of respect as anyone else!

Polly was then steered to the area where she had been meant to go through, and where she could be searched if necessary. She had no choice but to obey, for the uniformed gentleman had both his hands firmly on her shoulders as he moved her in the right direction. Once she had been searched up and down by a lady with what looked like a gun (although quite what they were looking for, she had no idea!), she was then reunited with her schoolbag and Langdon. She hugged him tightly and promised him that she would never allow him to be separated from her ever again! She thought she might even write a letter to the airport authorities explaining that this should not be allowed to happen to any child ever again, as favorite toys were very afraid when they were separated from their young owners. Yes, she would definitely write a stiff formal letter as soon as she got home from her journey to Piadora.

Polly found a vacant seat and made herself comfortable while she waited to be called to board the plane. The area she sat in was crowded mainly with families who were about to go on holiday. Suddenly there was an announcement over the loud speaker. Polly listened intently as did the other passengers.

"Attention, all passengers! We are sorry to have to inform you that your flight has been delayed, and will not be departing until 1800 hours."

Polly looked up at the clock on the wall and quickly realized that she now had another two hours on her hands. All those sitting nearby began to moan and groan, and she heard many suggesting to their equally fed-up partners that they might as well go back to the duty-free shop. Polly had no idea what this shop had in its store, but she decided she might as well follow the crowd and find out.

Polly stopped short of the entrance and looked up. Yes, it definitely said duty-free. Polly then wrongly assumed that this must mean that everything in the shop was free, and therefore everybody could help themselves to whatever their heart desired. This made perfect sense to her, for she now understood why, after the broadcast, there had been a mass exodus from the waiting area to come to this shop.

"How nice they were to be so considerate and generous," thought Polly as she came to the conclusion that this must be the airline's way of apologizing for the inconvenience the travelers were now suffering due to the delay.

As she walked down the aisles of the shop, she saw many of the travelers filling up shopping baskets with cases of beer, bottles of liquor and fine wines, as well as long boxes of cigarettes. "Is it any wonder that so many people have medical problems when they're giving this stuff away for free?" Polly thought to herself. They should come and see for themselves the terrible effects of years of hard drinking and the toll of misery this had brought to her friends around the campfire. And then they might realize just how much misery and unhappiness this disgusting-tasting stuff could cause.

How did Polly actually know this stuff tasted quite disgusting? Well, although Polly had only ever tried alcohol once, her little faux pas had made her so unwell that she had never quite been able to put this little indiscretion behind her. Her guardians' eldest daughter had held her wedding reception at the castle, and many of the children were called upon to act as waiters and serve both food and drink. Polly had been delighted when she had been handed a whole tray of glasses filled to the brim with Sherry, which was intended for the guests but had in truth been drunk by her good self. Had she been caught, she would have paid dearly for her indiscretion. But on this occasion, as her guardians were more concerned with mingling with the guests, she wasn't missed when she slunk out of the room carrying the tray of refills brimming over with the sickly sweet liquid. She had found a nice quiet spot away from all the merriment, and then she sat down in a corner and decided to try some. The first glass was gone in seconds, and this was shortly followed by the next, which turned out to be one too many.

A short while later Polly attempted to get up from the floor, only to discover to her sheer horror that she couldn't. She panicked, thinking this stuff had, for her sins, paralyzed her for life. A short time later, she passed out and remembered nothing else.

By the time she came round, the wedding feast was well-and-truly over, and thankfully nobody had discovered her. Eventually, she found she could move her legs, and, despite a crashing headache, she was able to pull herself up from the floor. She immediately felt sick as all the furniture and walls began to playfully sway backwards and forwards, making her feel truly dizzy and more nauseated then ever! She decided that the best thing she could do was get out of the castle into the fresh air, so she staggered to the front door of the castle, and, once outside, began to walk down the hill. She had only taken a few faltering steps when she toppled over and, unbelievable as it might seem, began to roll headfirst down the hill.

Polly had been very lucky to escape serious injury, for the hill was very steep indeed. Apart from sustaining a few bruises, she escaped lightly with no broken bones or the loss of any more teeth. She had to admit that her headache, which had already been pretty awful before her leave of absence, had now gone from bad to worse. She was forced to crawl back to the castle on her hands and knees. Not, I might add, a very ladylike thing to do. Once home, she then made it up the creaky oak stairs and crawled slowly along the corridor, barely making it into the dormitory. Feeling now quite ill, she threw herself onto the bed. She heard the crack as she accidentally managed to hit her head on the adjacent wall, taking her headache from a level five to a level ten in a matter of a split second!

Polly had stayed in bed for the rest of the day, feeling terribly sick as the ceiling spun above her. It would be many days later before she felt like her old self, such were the effects of her little indiscretion.

Therefore, as she stood watching the travelers in the shop fill baskets with bottle after bottle of this stuff that makes you feel extremely unwell, she found herself very puzzled as to why all these travelers wished to make themselves sick when they were about to go on holiday! No, it made no sense at all to Polly's way of thinking.

As she cared little for any of the goods that the grown-ups were loading into the baskets, she decided to wander into the toy section of the shop. And after spending a considerable amount of time browsing through the rows of interesting items, fascinated by all that was on offer, she came across a small blue torch that she considered might well come in handy at some point on her travels. Besides which, she had accidentally forgotten to pack her torch. It was still hidden under the pillow at home, ready for nighttime reading sessions. So Polly took her schoolbag from her shoulders and, after opening it, placed the torch inside her bag along with the rest of her possessions. She then walked out of the shop, feeling pleased as punch at having found such a useful item.

She was walking back toward the waiting area when suddenly she felt a strong hand come to rest firmly on her shoulder and heard a very fierce voice speak, "Excuse me, miss, but please will you step this way with me?"

Polly swung round to see the face of a security guard looking angrily down at her. She had no idea why he was so upset, so she sincerely informed him that although she would love to come with him and perhaps have a cup of tea, she was unable to, for she had a plane to catch. The man became even angrier with Polly, his face going a deep red as he told her that he had no intention of giving her a cup of anything. He just needed to search her bag.

Before Polly could utter another word, she was frogmarched back into the shop and then taken into a tiny room to be searched. Polly still could not understand what was troubling the gentleman. Was it that the plane had been delayed? For she understood perfectly, after all, this had upset a lot of the passengers.

"Stand here, miss, and hand me your bag," said the uniformed man rather gruffly.

Polly willingly obliged. She then watched on as this most fearsome man upended her schoolbag, scattering its contents all over the floor.

"Look," said Polly, feeling quite agitated and annoyed, "you are welcome to help yourself to anything that I have, with the exception of Langdon, for he is mine for keeps," she said, preferring to keep the elephant close at hand as she hugged him to her chest. "None of my stuff is worth very much, but if your need is greater than mine, then I will willingly part with any of my other possessions that might take your fancy," she said wide-eyed and very innocently.

Poor Polly still had absolutely no idea whatsoever that she was in big trouble. The frightfully angry man continued to ignore her as he sifted through her personal belongings. Polly soon realized she wasn't getting through to him and decided to try harder.

"Look, I don't know if I should tell you this. Not that it's a secret anymore, for many of the other passengers have already found out. But everything on the shelves in the duty-free shop is going for nothing! Can you believe it?"

The officious man looked up at Polly and frowned, but still not a word passed from his pursed lips as he continued to riffle through her possessions. Polly continued on, undeterred.

"There's a big notice outside the shop. Come and take a good look, and then you can see for yourself if you don't believe me! And the shop is filled to overflowing with all kinds of goodies, all far more valuable and much nicer than anything that's in my schoolbag. That's a promise. So please don't waste any more time on me," she pleaded. "Otherwise, there will be nothing left in the shop for you to take," she wailed with a growing sense of urgency in her voice.

The angry man looked up from where he was crouched on the floor as he searched rather thoroughly through all her possessions, and he shook his head in pure disbelief. Polly didn't seem to notice his expression, choosing to ramble on some more.

"Look, if we quickly go now, there's bound to be something fairly nice left, for all the other passengers are grabbing as much as they can in large wire baskets. If you come with me, I can show you.

POLLY BROWN

I am even happy to carry a basket for you if that will help!" said Polly in a last-ditch effort to soften the heart of this stern-looking man.

"That will not be necessary, miss," said the security officer very officiously, his face deadpan as he held up the offending item. "This torch has not been paid for. I am therefore placing you under arrest, and although you have a right to remain silent, anything you say will be used as evidence against you in a court of law. I have called for the assistance of a police officer, and when he arrives, he will be taking you into custody."

Polly felt her knees buckle, and she then passed out.

With the help of smelling salts, administered directly under her nose, she came round to discover many people gathered round and staring directly down at her. Some passengers even had the audacity to prod and poke her as though she were some gone-off piece of meat. She came to her senses and sat up, still having no idea what had happened to her. The last thing she remembered was having her schoolbag emptied by an officious looking man who, for some reason, seemed really upset with her. Then she remembered nothing else, for everything went blank.

The policeman, who had been called to the scene, dutifully informed her that she was under arrest for having stolen a torch from the duty-free shop. It was left to Polly to tearfully explain that because the notice above the shop had said Duty-free, she had therefore genuinely believed that everything in the shop was free for the taking. She had wrongly presumed that this was why all the passengers had been loading up the wire baskets with gifts.

"I thought that the airline decided to do something really kind and generous because many of the passengers were very miffed by the announcement that the plane had been severely delayed," she sniffed in her miserable attempt to explain herself.

She felt absolutely terrible that as a result of her misdemeanor she would now be branded a thief. She then became even more concerned and upset at the thought that she would probably be sent to prison for many years, or worse still, the Tower of London—and for life! Polly began to cry at the thought of being locked away in that frightfully old and gloomy tower that had in the past been home to many a traitor to England. She was not entirely sure that she would cope very well if she were to spend the rest of her days shackled in irons in the dank, smelly dungeons of the tower with hundreds of deathwatch beetles as her only companions. And the thought that she might well be forced to catch and eat these disgusting creatures, along with the odd sewer rat, made her cry even louder, for Polly sadly realized that if all this were to happen she would never get to go to Piadora. She also hoped that England did not routinely use the hangman's noose or the guillotine as a method of serving out justice to such hardened criminals as herself!

"There, there," said the policeman in the hard bell-shaped custodian helmet as he gently patted her on the back in a bid to comfort her. "I will speak to the management and explain everything. I am certain they will understand."

"Look, I have the money to pay for the torch, and you can have this ring as well, if you like. Please take it," she implored, holding out her very shaky hand so that he could see for himself that she really did have the money to pay for the torch. "Please take it, for I really need to have a torch for my journey; really I do. Especially as I rather stupidly left mine back at the castle," she cried. "And here, take an extra pound note and buy the manager a nice box of chocolates, for I hate to think I have caused him such distress," she tearfully said as she wiped her eyes with her handkerchief.

The British bobby could clearly see that she had made a genuine mistake, and it took a lot of effort on his part not to break out into a smile. As he took the money from Polly's hand, she made a further request.

"I know I don't deserve it, but please while you're sorting out this dreadful misunderstanding on my behalf, is there a tiny chance that you could pick me up a packet of chewing gum for my journey? I would be very grateful if you help me."

The police officer obliged, smiling down at her as he took another pound note from her outstretched hand. He then disappeared off the scene, presumably to go and sort things out with the management and also to purchase a packet of chewing gum for Polly, for he was, like most British bobbies, a very kind and understanding man, indeed!

Meanwhile, Polly still sat on the floor being observed like an insect under the microscope by all the morbidly curious passengers who had joined the crowd of people anxious to know what the disturbance was about. Worse still, their numbers were growing by the minute. Polly felt utterly humiliated as she continued to sit on the ground surrounded by people, all wishing to intently stare at her. And as she sat alone and afraid, she thought to herself that she would never wish to become a pop star, for she would hate to draw such large crowds as they did wherever they went. Was it any wonder they went wild and smashed up their rooms when they finally arrived at their hotel?

She began to feel quite claustrophobic as the crowd pressed further into her for closer inspection. At this point, Polly would have paid any amount of money to have the ground open up beneath her and swallow her up whole, bringing an end to this very unpleasant crisis that had completely ruined an otherwise pleasant day. Unbeknown to Polly, it was about to get much worse.

"Attention, all passengers! Will the remaining passengers for flight 777 kindly make their way to the gate for boarding. The plane is due to take off in precisely ten minutes."

"Oh no," Polly inwardly groaned. "That's me, and I'm about to miss my plane." Minutes later there was a second, more urgent message over the sound system.

"Attention, all passengers. This is the final call for all passengers flying to Brazil with BOAC. We are still missing one passenger. If a Miss Polly Brown values her life at all, will she kindly do us the great pleasure and get off her backside to make her way to the gate immediately. For we now have a number of very irate passengers on board!"

Polly felt desperate, for she realized that it was now more than likely that she would miss her plane. She had so been enjoying her time at the airport, what with everybody being so kind and helpful, but now it had turned into a complete nightmare!

Eventually the police constable returned, and, after making his way through the very large crowd of people still gathered around Polly, he crouched down and informed her that the matter was sorted, and therefore no charges were being pressed.

"You are now free to go on your way, miss," he said, giving her another friendly pat on the back.

Polly breathed a deep sigh of relief as she thanked the friendly bobby for his kindness. He then handed her the packet of chewing gum.

"I hope I chose the right flavor, miss," he said with a large beam on his face. Polly smiled back, informing him that strawberry flavor was indeed her favorite. She wasted no time in getting up from the floor and, putting the flashlight and chewing gum into her schoolbag, she grabbed Langdon and hurriedly waved good-bye to the humungous and ever-growing crowd of people who were still gathered around her as she anxiously pushed past them and raced toward the gate to catch her plane.

Polly arrived at the gate area only to discover there was nobody behind the desk to check her ticket. Earlier, before the unfortunate delay, there had definitely been a very nice couple of ladies standing behind the desk, dressed in pristine navy blue uniforms with red-white-and-blue scarves elegantly draped around their necks. But now the desk stood empty. She turned and looked around the seating area, only to discover to her horror that this too had no signs of life, for all the seats that had previously been occupied by disgruntled travelers were now vacant. All that remained as evidence that this particular area had earlier been filled with many fed-up passengers was the large amount of discarded cans, bottles, plastic cups, and half-eaten sandwiches, as well as other rubbish that lay strewn across the seating area.

Polly thought that she might have a word or two with the passengers once the plane had taken off. For she thought it was extremely important to ask them if they had ever seen one of the many Keep Britain Tidy posters that were pinned up on walls and trees all around the country. After all was said and done, England was such a pretty little country, and it was of the utmost importance to keep it that way. Yes, she thought it was well worth reminding them of this small but really significant fact before they arrived in another country and littered that one as well!

Polly could clearly see through the huge glass-paned window that there was still a plane on the concourse. So she decided that she would make a last-ditch attempt to get on board. She went through a dark and rather breezy tunnel, and at the end of the tunnel she found herself going through a funny accordion bit of tunnel that was attached to the plane door.

As she stepped onto the plane she experienced great relief, but this was to be very short-lived. As she walked down the aisle, heading for her seat, she became very concerned that no other passengers, or even cabin crew, were on board. Polly tried to dismiss this small, bothersome detail, preferring to walk down to the rear of the plane and find her numbered seat. She stopped by her seat and placed her schoolbag in the overhead locker before slumping into her seat to rest her weary legs. She then put Langdon in the window seat and adjusted the safety belt to his size. She then closed her eyes, took a deep breath, and relaxed.

After what seemed an eternity, she began to feel a little anxious and concerned that no passengers or crew had turned up to take their seats. She thought that the airline really needed to get their act together, for she had been sitting alone on this plane for at least an hour, and still no nice hostess had even bothered to come round and offer her as much as a slurp from a can of cola! She had always heard from other vacationers in the past that BOAC was an excellent bunch to travel with and that their service was considered to be the best in the world, so she felt pretty neglected and decidedly miffed at the poor quality of service she was being treated to. She hoped there would be a drink and a hot meal served soon; then perhaps she would begin to feel better.

Time marches on, and still there was no sign of anyone else on board the plane, and yet still she continued to brush aside all disconcerting thoughts that she might well be on the wrong plane. Eventually she decided to stand up and have a good stretch and walkabout. So she made her way to the center aisle and began to walk and skip, bend and stretch, and walk some more. She walked the entire length of the plane, back and forth more times than she cared to count, but still no staff or passengers turned up. She stopped at one of the hostess serving stations, where she could see a large pile of newspapers, as well as an equally large pile of plain white paper and packs of felt-tip coloring crayons. She ignored the newspapers, for they were obviously for the enjoyment of the adult passengers to read while they waited for take off. But she decided to help herself to a large number of sheets of plain white paper and a pack of crayons so she could amuse herself drawing until the plane eventually took off from the airport.

Polly sat contentedly drawing picture after picture for what she considered to be an extremely long time. But after a while, she began to lose all patience and felt very fed up that still no passengers or lovely air hostesses had filed onto the plane and filled up all the unoccupied seats. "What on earth is going on?" she wondered. Polly sat in her seat furiously waiting and waiting before finally her eyelids closed and she fell fast asleep.

She awoke to discover that not only was it nighttime, but the plane was high in the sky, well on the way to its destination. Polly thought it mighty peculiar that both seats in her row were still empty. She decided to peer up the aisle and see just how many passengers had boarded the plane because she could hear no movement or excited chitchat from other travelers as she sat alone in the dark with only the whir of the engines keeping her company.

She hoped the absence of familiar noise was because the passengers were all sleeping, but she felt disappointed as she thought that she must have missed the food trolley due to dozing off. Polly strained her neck, scanning the aisle for any sign of movement. It was no use, for other than the tiny lights that lit up the aisle, she could see nothing! She lay back in her seat wishing that morning would soon come round, and hopefully with it, some breakfast.

Chapter 22
STORMING THE PLANE

*I*T WAS WELL into the early hours of the morning before Polly looked out of the window, to see that the sky was still cloaked in darkness. Suddenly, a voice broke the silence, making an announcement over the intercom.

"This is your captain speaking. Will you please fasten your seatbelts, for we will be landing shortly and if you need to use the bathroom, now is your last chance."

Polly felt gutted that no breakfast was going to be served and decided there and then that any future travel arrangements would be made with a more hospitable airline that considered serving the passengers a hot breakfast of great importance. But leaving that aside, she was still considerably grateful to the captain for his impromptu reminder that it was everyone's last chance to use the restroom. So she removed the seatbelt and climbed into the aisle, heading for the bathroom.

The door to the little cubicle read "Engaged." So Polly waited out of sight for the small room to become free, for she felt that was the polite thing to do. Seconds later she heard the click of the door and peered around the corner as she waited for it to be vacated. What she saw next shocked her to the core of her being! Whatever it was that very merrily bounced down the aisle of the plane bore absolutely no resemblance to a human being. Yes, whatever this thing was—and there appeared to be many of them—it was definitely not the sort of clientele Polly expected to find traveling on a British plane to Brazil!

She gasped and then covered her mouth, for she realized that doing so was definitely in her best interest. As the captain had failed to turn off the sound system, she could clearly hear all that was going on in the cockpit. Polly was immobilized, yes, frozen to the spot, as she listened in.

"Tower, come in tower. We need permission to land."

"Request accepted, and permission granted," came the speedy and most cheery reply. "Oh! And do have a nice day, won't you?"

"I'll give you a nice day if you don't shut up," growled the captain. "Just give me a quick update on the present situation, and then let me land this plane!" he thundered.

Polly decided that this particular captain could not possibly be a British pilot, for they were all meant to be such polite and extremely well-spoken gentlemen who would never in a million years speak to anyone in such a disgraceful tone of voice. Her worst fears were confirmed. There was definitely something very wrong!

She decided that her best bet was to sneak back to her seat, quickly grab Langdon and her other belongings, and then find somewhere safe and well out of view to hide. She had spent many years playing hide-and-seek, so she was a bit of an expert at such covert operations. Having discreetly grabbed her schoolbag from the overhead locker without being seen, she then crouched down by a window seat, her ears pricked as she watched from the crack between the seats and continued to listen in on the mysterious captain's conversation with ground control.

"Well, Sniveling Obedience, have you managed to find a suitable runway that we can land on?" snorted the captain, whose name, she would find out later, was Vanaspi.

"I have indeed, Captain," came the short and very swift reply. "But you must land quickly, before the French authorities become aware of your presence."

"Oh no, not France!" thought Polly, absolutely horrified. For she distinctly remembered telling those two very nice ladies at the airport desk that, although Paris sounded lovely, her rendezvous was in Brazil!

"Understood," replied the captain rather snappily. "I am just going to give my servants—I mean, passengers—a quick update. Then we will be ready to land in ten minutes. So please make sure that our runway is fully lit up, Sniveling Obedience, or you will pay with your life for any mistakes, and that's a promise! Over and out."

The captain left his seat to come out of the cockpit. Seconds later he was standing in the aisle, where normally very beautiful air hostesses show off the safety procedures to all the passengers—procedures such as where the emergency exits are positioned in case of a crisis, as well as how to put on an oxygen mask—to make them more at ease and comfortable.

Polly was at a complete loss for words as she looked down the aisle to where the captain stood. No words in Polly's limited vocabulary could get anywhere near expressing how hideous and frightening this man appeared. She thought it very possible that he and his passengers might be aliens from another planet. And if this were the case then they would do well to go right back to where they had come from, for they were certainly not welcome to touch English soil. She was fairly certain that the prime minister would think likewise, and the president of the United States would probably have very similar feelings if he were to be approached by these monsters asking for a long-term residency permit.

The captain stood still, a presence of pure evil surrounding him as he opened his misshaped mouth to address his passengers.

"I have just spoken to Sniveling Obedience, and he has informed me that some of our colleagues have successfully taken over part of the airport tower. We will be landing shortly. He has also informed me that Polly Brown has gone missing, although our spies are at present doing all in their power to track her down. They will not rest until they have her in their custody."

Polly felt great panic begin to rise, for she was terribly frightened, as well as very confused, as to why these hideous monsters were after her. She had, after all, settled up fully concerning the horrible and most unpleasant matter of the duty-free shop! The kind and understanding bobby had even bought her the strawberry chewing gum she had asked for! Surely he would not have been so happy to oblige in making this kind gesture if she was still on Britain's "Ten Most Wanted" list, would he?

Her thoughts were going as fast and haywire as her heartbeat, for she was struggling to take in all that was now happening to her. All she had wanted was a lovely, comfortable plane ride to Brazil, with a nice hot meal served by delightful, friendly air hostesses. Now she was in France on board a plane with terrorists, and, to cap it all, she had to date received no hot meal. No, not as much as a single salty peanut! Things did not look very hopeful at that moment in time for young Polly Brown.

"Now listen to me, you bunch of moronic day-trippers," the captain snarled. "You will all remember that over the last few months we have done much to wear this poor girl down. Despair here had done a most excellent job in making her truly believe that she had no hope, when suddenly, out of the blue, she decided to go on this very misguided journey to Piadora. It is therefore of the utmost importance to make sure that she never makes it."

All present agreed that this had now become a matter of the highest priority! So they nodded their fat, ugly heads and hissed at the captain to let him know they were ready and willing to follow any order he might care to give them as soon as they disembarked from the plane.

"Now, where is Self-Pity?" the captain sharply asked, his face seriously scrunched up as his eyes scrutinized every row of seats in search of the greasy little toad!

"I'm here, Captain!" answered a most depressed and very subdued voice from the back of the plane.

"Well, get up here right now!" ordered the captain menacingly.

Down from the seat slid the most gruesomely vile, hairy blob that, having left his seat, proceeded to bounce up to the captain, leaving a black, sticky trail the whole length of the aisle as he came to stand before his master.

"Well, well, Self-Pity, I know you have been in continuous negotiations with Polly throughout the last few weeks, and I am therefore anxious to know how well you are progressing. So give me an update. Also, try to keep to the point, and please, not too much weeping and wailing. My nerves can't take it at the moment."

Polly listened, feeling both shocked and puzzled. Who was this revolting thing that not only claimed to know her, but also had the cheek to say he often had conversations with her? She felt angry and insulted, but far too afraid to speak out, for to do so would reveal her presence in the cabin.

"I was doing quite nicely," slobbered Self-Pity, "especially when I had her to myself in the desert, for she had nobody to comfort her or give her the encouragement to go on. Yes, I was having such fun tormenting her, when suddenly she discovered little Jessica and then sadly she no longer had the time to listen to me. I still thought I would have plenty of opportunity because both girls were stranded inside a cave with no way of escape. But then these two rather dumb idiots came along in their car. A Mini, I believe—very popular with the British! And then rather annoyingly, before I even had the time to cough or blink, the lads agreed to assist them by taking them to the nearest hospital. I'm so sorry, Master," he pathetically drooled. "But don't despair, for I feel very certain that plenty more opportunities will present themselves long before she ever gets anywhere near reaching Piadora!"

The captain, trying very hard to contain his rage, reluctantly agreed with Self-Pity and ordered him to get back to his seat. Persecution, who was sitting next to him, could not help but mock and jeer in Self-Pity's direction as he glumly made his way back down the aisle to his seat. Persecution then stood up, making a gross gesture in his bid to make the master aware of his presence. The master caught his eye and beckoned him to come forward. He then slunk out of his chair and casually strolled up to the front, leaving a green trail of slobber and slime all the way.

"Are you meant to be on this plane?" the captain asked Persecution.

Persecution wasted no time in answering his master, spitting small black balls of hair from his mouth as he spoke.

"I know that I wasn't invited to come, but then I thought to myself, 'Why not? For the more the merrier.' Besides, Master, I have been feeling very lonely since Polly left the orphanage. For with Polly and her brother gone, I have had very little to do to make myself useful. Sadly for us, their guardians have not got round to choosing another victim to replace them. Yes, and until they hurry up and make their choice, I do believe that I can be of more use to you, Master, by coming on this mission," he sullenly replied.

The captain stood and said nothing, for he was giving consideration to Persecution's plea to be allowed to stay and become involved in the execution of his master's evil and malicious plan. He was about to boot him out of a plane window when he suddenly smiled to himself, for he quickly realized that Persecution could indeed still play an important role in his plan concerning Polly's downfall. He therefore ordered him to go back to his seat before addressing all present.

"As most of you are aware, we seem to have lost touch with Polly, at least for the time being. It is vital that we catch up with this young lady and once again take her hostage."

Polly gave another gasp before frantically placing a hand over her mouth, for she needed to avoid detection. The word *hostage* screamed in her head and filled every atom of her body with terror. The evil captain continued on with his address.

"By now, Polly will be both weak and hungry, and this, I believe, is a perfect opportunity to catch her unaware." He then paused, scanning each individual blob, anxious to see if they were taking in everything he said. "By the way, where is that little cripple, Addiction?" he angrily demanded to know.

"He's in the hold, Master. He discovered hundreds of bottles of alcohol and large boxes of Belgian chocolate down there. Yes, whether you knew it or not, he's been down in the hold for the whole journey, stuffing his fat, hairy face," hissed Binge as he rather delightedly informed the captain of Addiction's whereabouts.

However, he failed to mention that he too had also been down in the hold, doing likewise for much of the journey. In fact, he had only recently returned to his seat after a very lengthy session in the bathroom, where he had been extremely sick.

"Well, will someone go and drag him back here to face my wrath before he drinks himself unconscious!" seethed the captain, baring his gangrenous, splintered teeth.

In seconds, yet another hideous ball of guck was bouncing to the front of the cabin, only this one had razor-sharp fangs. Moments later, Addiction stood, or rather, sycophantically bowed and groveled at his master's feet, still clutching a half-drunk bottle of wine.

"Yes, Master—hic—what can I do to be of service?—Hic, hic," Addiction asked, squirming as he hung his head low in order to prevent all further eye contact.

"Well, for one, you can wipe all that disgusting chocolate from around your face, you revolting, despicable miscreant! And then you can tell me who gave you permission to leave your seat in the first place, or the permission to stuff your disgustingly ugly, fat face?" he thundered.

"You did, master! That's why I exist—hic—to stuff myself stupid with anything and everything. You know full well that my job is to latch like a leech onto my host, because it was you who gave me the job in the first place," he snickered, hiccupping continuously as he attempted to answer his master. "Yes, myself as well as Craving, who incidentally is still down in the hold, have had ourselves a wonderful feast, and he is still down there, eating your share of the chocolate," he mischievously confided. "You've always allowed us to take this course of action as we begin to take control of our unwitting victim. Yes, you have to agree with me when I say that together we make a superbly successful team, ruining the lives of many an idiot in this sneaky, well-thought-out manner," he answered with a snort.

With the exception of Polly, all present on board the plane began to snicker and squeal as they delighted themselves in just how professionally Addiction did his job and how many thousands of lives he had managed to destroy over the years. The ugly little mug did, after all, deserve much praise, as well as chocolate, for all his hard and surprisingly effortless work behind the scenes. They were also quite overcome with joy as they considered that Craving would really be in for the high jump as soon as their master got hold of him. For they knew with much certainty that, at the very least, Craving would be squashed into a small ball and then thrown as far as the captain could throw him. Knowing their captain's cricketing skills as well as they did, they were all convinced that Craving would more than likely find himself being batted into another orbit! That is, until he begged and screamed and had a major tantrum, making Vanaspi frighteningly consumed with rage. Their master would at this point seemingly relent and allow him to return to his side in readiness of his next assignment. Then he would use the opportunity to get him back some more. Such was the root of vindictiveness inbred into his very nature.

"Be quiet, all of you," the captain sternly ordered. "Now, Polly will hopefully find herself meeting up with Soogara and her hounds, Grovelock and Grubstick," he said, flashing a wicked smile. "And it is very important that you, Addiction," he said pointing directly at him, "are there to meet Polly. In fact, it would be a good idea to take Binge and Craving along with you on this occasion."

Binge started to jump up and down in his seat at being given this most special covert operation. He was so full of glee that thick and very pungent black liquid began to squirt from his pointed ears, landing and covering many of the others as he continued to bounce up and down on the seat.

"Addiction, it's your job to make sure that she falls for Soogara's charms, and Craving will have already seen to it that her sweet tooth is really playing up before Binge goes in to finish the job. Make sure you do not fail me, for if you do, you know the consequences will be harsh!"

The black hairy blobs nodded and shuddered in unison as they considered all that would happen to them if everything did not go according to the plan. Their master was indeed a hard taskmaster and quite impossible to please. They all knew with absolute certainty that failure was not an option!

The master stood for a few minutes in absolute silence as he perused his motley crew and hoped they where up to the task.

"Deceit, stop playing with those headphones and come down here right now!" the loathsome captain commanded. "And drag Malice along with you, for I'm not that stupid. I can see him hiding under the seat next to you."

Deceit slithered off his chair and headed forward to the front of the cabin, bowing and fawning ingratiatingly as he did so, with Malice reluctantly following hard on his heels. He stood before his master slobbering, "Your wish is my command, oh master of the universe— oh jewel-encrusted star of the Orion—oh star-spangled…"

"Zip it before I personally decapitate you!" spat the captain. Deceit instantly obeyed, firmly shutting his mouth to allow no further utterances to spew forth.

Polly, who was still watching, felt utterly mortified and in a state of shock. She slowly shook her head as if, by doing so, she might wake

POLLY BROWN

up and discover that this was just another of her horrible nightmares. She knew she had to take a firm grip of herself and think of some way of escaping from the plane. She also felt it was her responsibility to think up a plan or way of alerting the French authorities to let them know that the plane was in the hands of frightfully evil terrorists and insurgents. The trouble was she had absolutely no idea as to what she could possibly do. To make matters a whole lot worse, her legs felt like jelly and her whole body refused to stop shaking. She therefore closed her eyes momentarily and did the only thing she thought she could do. Yes, this was her last resort. She closed her eyes tight and silently sent up a prayer for help.

The captain continued to bark his instructions to what Polly was now convinced were his servants, for they certainly were on no holiday, and they appeared to have little choice other than to obey every whim and command he thundered in their direction.

Malice now moved from behind Deceit in order to greet the captain. Polly had no idea what was said to him, for the captain bent down and whispered directly into Malice's ear. The captain then stood up straight and with a smile on his face said, "Good, yes, I think this plan of yours is brilliant. Well done, both of you. You may go back to your seats."

Both blobs turned and headed back down the aisle toward their seat, Deceit bouncing and bashing into many of the empty seats as he made his way back. At one point he stopped to scratch his hairy, lice-filled head, and as he did so, his fingers became instantly covered in hundreds of tiny insects, which he simply brushed into the palm of his hand before popping them, one-by-one, into his cavernous mouth. Polly watched on feeling thoroughly sickened.

The captain then gave his final address.

"Right, listen up, all you vomitous cretins," he ordered, a dark scowl engulfing his face. "You should all have an envelope in your possession, giving precise details of your individual roles that are necessary if we are to hasten Polly's downfall. Those of you aboard whom I have not managed to speak with, please do not worry, for I will catch up with you later." He then deliberately fixed his dark, soulless eyes on Jealousy, who now looked very anxious and upset that he had missed out by not being called forward. "And that includes you, Jealousy, for I can see you sulking over there in the corner seat." Jealousy shrugged his wimpy shoulders and closed his dolefully sad eyes as he continued to smolder, for he found it quite unbearable to have been ignored by his master while others around him got the master's personal attention.

"Right, now where was I?" said the captain. "Oh yes, pay attention everyone. Eventually we will be meeting up with Hagora and Egor, who are at present guarding the control tower from any inquisitive persons who might call the French authorities for help. Finally, I have given orders to Carnage to organize just a teeny weenie train accident so that all attention is diverted from our presence here on French soil."

"Can we go with him?" Misery and Despair shouted back at the same time. "For you know we get so much pleasure helping Carnage wreak havoc."

"No, that is not possible," snarled the captain.

"But you promised me I could go with him on the next mission," retorted Misery miserably.

"Yes, I know I did, but I have changed my mind," the captain snapped back.

"Well, that's not fair. You promised me," wailed Misery as he hung his head low in bitter disappointment.

"Silence, you fool!" snapped the very angry, as well as extremely agitated, captain. "You know full well that I am the father of lies, and therefore I never keep my promises. If you had wanted a fair and faithful master you should have stayed on the other side. Now put a sock in it before I do something to you that I will never regret."

The captain paused for a moment, privately thinking how much he truly hated insubordinates. He then cleared his hairy throat and turned to finish his address.

"Remember, everyone, we may not have found Polly yet, but we still have much work to do in the meantime—important work, such as taking the French president hostage and storming the Eiffel Tower," he said with a menacing smile. "Oh, and before I completely forget, I have one final word of warning for Addiction and Craving. If I discover you have abandoned your post, opting to head for the nearest French restaurant, both of you will be dealt with most severely!"

All the slimeballs started to crease up at the thought of these two lovable rogues sitting with red-checked napkins tied haphazardly round their scrawny little necks as they tucked carte blanche into escargot provençal along with mountains of garlic bread while swigging back endless bottles of French wine. These two less-than-adorable numskulls were much admired for being so very out of control and gluttonous.

"Pay attention, all of you!" screamed the captain as he lashed out at the nearest miscreants sitting close by in their seats. He had, understandably, suffered enough of their disruptive and foolish behavior and needed to remind them who was boss. "My instructions are very detailed and precise, so make sure, all of you, that you read them very carefully, for I will not tolerate incompetence of any description. Do I make myself perfectly clear?"

"Yes, perfectly clear, Master," they all whined in unison.

"Yes, my little protégés, let me warn and remind you one final time: failure is not an option."

"Yes, we all understand. Failure is not an option. Failure is not an option, oh master of the universe," they repeated as they fawned and then stood united to toast their master and his wonderfully wicked mission.

"Good, then let's get on with the task at hand," he said with an evil glint in his eye before turning quickly on his heels to head back into the cockpit and prepare to land the plane.

Suddenly, the runway beneath the plane lit up with a million tiny lights, and moments later the plane swiftly descended until the rubber from the wheels hit the tarmac surface of the runway.

Finally the plane came to a halt. All lights inside the plane and on the runway were put out, leaving Polly and all inside the cabin in utter darkness. The smell of evil was tangible. The air inside the cabin was thick with tension.

Polly felt really scared and realized that if she was to have any hope of escaping, now was the time. Any hesitation on her part could spell disaster, so whatever she had planned she needed to do it as fast as she could. Seconds later she heard the click of numerous seatbelts as they were unfastened within a split second of each other.

Polly suddenly had an idea. She reached into her schoolbag as quietly as she was able and pulled out her new torch. She breathed a sigh of relief as she discovered that she had picked up a boxed item that miraculously, for once, had batteries provided. She lifted her eyes to the heavens and whispered, "Thank You," before crouching down near the window seat at the back of the plane to place the batteries inside the torch. Taking off the silver foil from a piece of chewing gum, she quickly popped it in her mouth and then frantically began chewing away. She then began to flash the torch out of the window in the direction of the airport control tower, for she wanted to alert the French authorities to this most terrible and urgent crisis. She knew how to do Morse code, for she remembered seeing it done numerous times before when she had watched *A Night to Remember* on the television. It was, after all, one of her favorite black-and-white movies about the sinking of the *Titanic*.

As she flashed her torch, she struggled to remember if it was "dot...dot...dot," followed by "dash...dash...dash," followed by one more round of "dot...dot...dot." She hoped she had it the right way round for her sake, as well as the whole of France.

She then pulled out a large sheet of drawing paper, and with a black felt-tip pen, began to scrawl in large letters on the paper.

HELP, MY NAME IS POLLY BROWN. NOT ONLY AM I ENGLISH, BUT I'M VERY PROUD OF IT. THIS PLANE HAS BEEN TAKEN OVER BY TERRORISTS WHO ARE ABOUT TO DO SOME OUTRAGEOUS ACTS OF WICKEDNESS ON YOUR SOIL. SO PLEASE CAN YOU CONTACT THE BRITISH EMBASSY AND ASK FOR THE SPECIAL ARMED SERVICES (SAS)? I RATHER URGENTLY NEED THEIR ASSISTANCE!

THANK YOU, Polly

Polly went over all the lettering with a bright yellow fluorescent pen to highlight her most urgent note. She then spat out her chewing gum into the palm of her hand. This rather disgusting act was very necessary, because it acted as an adhesive to help keep the note pinned to the window of the plane. She felt guilty putting the sticky stuff on the clean window. Chewing gum should only be thrown away into bins; otherwise it sticks to the heels of shoes, making a disgusting mess that is virtually impossible to remove. But she hoped the airline would understand the dreadfulness of her plight and readily forgive her seemingly slovenly behavior. She continued to flash the torch toward the tower, at the same time praying under her breath for help to come, and quickly.

All she could do was continue to crouch between the passenger seats and wait. Polly was in complete despair of ever being rescued when, after what seemed an eternity, the Fifth Cavalry finally arrived on the scene.

To use the word *arrived* implies that by some reasonable means, Polly was finally freed from her captors. This certainly was not the case, for as Polly was about to discover, the British government does not take kindly to any acts of violence and it therefore does not negotiate with terrorists! And, I might add, neither does the SAS.

At precisely seven minutes past six, the emergency doors over the airliner's wings at the front and rear of the fuselage were all blown open by special explosive charges. Seconds later, stun grenades were thrown into the fuselage. Then there was a terrifyingly loud bang followed closely by a bright flash, its light so blinding that Polly instantly covered her eyes with her hands.

Seconds later assault teams stormed the plane. Polly remained hidden as a most intense battle took place. Hails of bullets rang through the cabin as the SAS men with their Heckler & Koch MP5 submachine guns emptied magazine after magazine as they fought to take control of the plane.

Polly eventually arose from under the seat, peering most cautiously out of her window only to see soldiers from one of the four squadrons, dressed from head to toe in camouflage with ropes tied around their waists, hoisting themselves up the side of the plane. Seconds later, as she continued to stare out of the window, she came eyeball-to-eyeball with one of the team members who gave her a quick wink as he continued to rappel up onto the roof of the plane. Soon after, they burst into the cabin. After throwing flash bangs, they then rolled smoke grenades down the aisle. Polly felt she could hardly breathe as thick smoke filled the cabin. Then she heard shouting, coupled with yet more bursts of gunfire from fully automatic weapons before all fell eerily silent.

Polly instantly fell back onto the floor and then remained crouched under the seat, her eyes streaming due to the thick haze of smoke. She coughed and spluttered, hardly able to breathe. She wanted to jump up from where she was hiding to let all in the plane know she was there, but she wisely chose to remain hidden just in case there was any further action. Also, being the very sensible girl that she was, she had no wish to be shot dead when she was innocent of all crimes other than the unfortunate misunderstanding back at the airport; she felt she did not deserve to die under a hail of bullets just for that tiny misdemeanor.

Suddenly, she heard very determined footsteps making their way down the aisle of the plane. Polly didn't dare look up, for she was much too afraid. Then she heard voices.

"Colonel Slaughterhouse, I've found her!" said a low but very delighted voice.

"That's excellent news, Corporal Beanpod," came the equally merry reply. "Now go and tell Lieutenant Snodgrass that he may call off his men, for I do believe that, as usual, we have the situation fully under our control."

"Yes, sir," said Corporal Beanpod, giving a salute while standing to attention at the same time. Colonel Slaughterhouse then walked up the aisle before crouching down to address Polly.

"Well, hello there, old boy," he said in his most fierce and stiff upper-lip English accent before putting out his hand for Polly to shake. "That was a close shave, even if I say it myself, old sprout," continued the colonel.

Polly looked up and tentatively placed her hand in his. She felt most cautious and reserved as they shook hands, for she needed reassurance that he was on the "good" side and part of the rescue team. His grasp was distinctly firm as he squeezed her small and

POLLY BROWN

frail hand. She looked him up and down, her eyes momentarily halting as she stared at his white mustache that curled upwards at both ends. As she looked into his blue eyes, she could see a twinkle. Only then did she breathe a deep sigh of relief and begin to shake his hand in a more affirmative manner.

"Thank you for rescuing me," said Polly most sincerely.

"Don't mention it, old boy," replied the strong soldier with the turned-up mustache.

"Well, it's really nice to meet you," said Polly as she waited for him to let go of his overly firm grasp of her hand.

"It's awfully nice to meet you, too, old bean," he said with a smile before sneezing as a white feather fluttered down in front of his nose. Much to Polly's relief, he let go of her blood-drained hand to pull out a handkerchief from his pocket.

Polly had little time to notice the feather, for by now there appeared to be many faces peering down at her, and thankfully they were all smiling. The colonel lifted Polly from the floor and then introduced her to his men, of which there were many. She was introduced to Sergeant Major Ramsbottom, Staff Sergeant Prior Palmer, Major Woodlouse, and many more of the lovely soldiers from the SAS Polly hugged each and every one of them, for she was most grateful that they had rescued her and thereby "delivered her from all evil" as she had prayed she would be earlier on that most terrible of days.

The good colonel smiled before saying, "Come on, old boy, the brigadier is waiting outside to meet you in person, for you are indeed a very brave young lady. Yes, a most courageous little sausage, if ever I met one. I do believe that if girls where allowed to join the SAS, we would love to have you sign up," he said, giving her a hearty slap on the back. "But sadly this is extremely dangerous work that is better left in the capable hands of grownups," he said with a loud chortle.

Polly agreed wholeheartedly with the colonel on his diagnosis, for she had to admit that she had been very frightened and had felt limp like jelly throughout most of her ordeal. As she filed past the seats that previously had been occupied by the horrible "things," she noticed that all that remained as evidence that they ever existed were puddles of thick, black sludge that lay in pools on the seats and trailed all down the aisle. Polly sighed as she thought of the poor cleaning ladies who would certainly have their work cut out for them as they struggled to scrub the seats of the ghastly smelling slime and muck that now stained the vacated seats. She was so concerned at the amount of work those cleaning ladies needed to do in cleaning up that she placed her hand into a pocket and pulled out a few pound notes, for she wanted to leave a tip for the poor ladies as a little encouragement.

The soldiers lined both sides of the steps and politely saluted Polly as she disembarked from the plane. She felt like royalty as she took each step down until her feet reached the tarmac. She thought that Queen Victoria could stick with her sponge-making sessions, for this was indeed much more fun. As she alighted from the plane she looked up into the sky. There above her she could hear the noise of the Red Arrows display team as they very stylishly wrote in every color of the rainbow across the sky. Polly smiled and had a lift in her step as she walked across the tarmac to the tune of "Land of Hope and Glory," which was being played by the Queen's Color Squadron along with a Royal Air Force band. She found herself feeling all cracked up inside as she listened to the music being played. She felt touched as she thought to herself how wonderful and talented the Red Arrows were, as well as the Queen's Color Squadron, along with the RAF contingent. They would never be fully aware of just how much their thoughtful and overwhelming efforts had gone to making her feel very proud to be British!

Polly was taken over to meet the brigadier who stood waiting most patiently to greet her. He was joined also by the French president, Monsieur Legume, who was still tucking his shirt into his trousers, as he had only just got out of bed and had rushed straight to the airport in only a matter of minutes.

"Well done, old chap—I mean, Polly—for that was a close call," said the brigadier warmly and enthusiastically as he stuck out a hand to greet her.

"What was a close call?" Polly asked, a little unsure if they were on the same line of thinking.

"Well, my dear, if you had not alerted the tower when you did, those terrorists would have escaped and gone ahead with their most incomprehensible act, and that's a certainty," said the brigadier, arching his eyebrow to show the seriousness of the matter.

"Oh," replied Polly, feeling a proud sense of achievement.

"Yes, I've witnessed firsthand the reprehensible acts these men do, and it leaves the most terrible trail of carnage," he said with a sniff.

"How did you know that my name is Polly?" she asked, a puzzled look written all over her face. The brigadier chortled out loud and pointed to her large piece of paper, still pinned by chewing gum to the plane window.

"Oh, my goodness," she mumbled, feeling most embarrassed, for she had clearly forgotten that she had written the note. There had been so much high drama going on all around her.

She was also very glad she had left a tip for the cleaning ladies, for as if clearing up the considerable mess the terrorists had left behind was not enough for the poor dear ladies to contend with, they now had *her* chewed up gum to scrape off the plane's window. She sincerely hoped they would forgive her.

Polly then shook hands with Monsieur Legume, the French president.

"Bonsieur, Miss Polly," he said in broken English. "Eet ees so veree good to meet up weeth you, mon petit choux."

Polly smiled back at him, most unsure as to what her proper response should be, especially as her French was so very poor. She wished in that moment that she had paid more attention in her French classes! Mr. Legume did not seem to mind and continued on.

"Polly, I theenk you are a veree brave ladee and I have onlee one thing left to say to you." He then proceeded to speak much too fast and, worst still, in French.

Polly now had absolutely no idea what he was talking about, so she answered as best she could. "Well, thank you for saying how much you like England, I too think it is a very nice place. You should visit it sometime."

The French president shook Polly's hand one more time before saying, "Au-revoir."

He then turned and headed back toward the terminal in search of a cup of strong black coffee and perhaps, if he was very fortunate, an aspirin or two.

Polly turned her attention back to the brigadier, for, being a very English man, she found him much easier to understand. She went on to say how amazed she was to get help, and so quickly, on French soil. The brigadier smiled before answering her question.

"Well, young Polly, the French authorities saw your flashlight SOS and your note. And for once," he said turning his eyes up into his head, "Yes, for once they took quick action and phoned our dear prime minister, who in turn called the queen at Buckingham Palace. Luckily, she had just taken her curlers out, and was just about to get into bed when the call came through. If the call had come just ten minutes later, the chances are very high that she would have been fast asleep, and therefore most grumpy at the thought of having to get out of bed."

Polly laughed, for she knew how grumpy she felt when she was tired and was forced to get up and go to school.

The brigadier continued on. "Well, Polly, once the queen was dressed and her tiara was firmly in place, she put on her white elbow-length gloves and made her way to 10 Downing Street (taking her corgis with her, of course, for they needed the exercise). She had quite a lengthy wait, let me tell you now, for the prime minister had also long gone to bed. Once dressed, he walked back to the palace with the queen, and they sat up discussing the crisis over tea and cakes. Tea, I might add, that was very much needed if they were to stay awake long enough to come to a reasonable resolution concerning your crisis. It was very quickly decided—but not before the prime minister had helped himself to a second serving of cake—that this situation ranked as a category ten on her list of importance. It was therefore decided to call for the help of the SAS. They were, of course, about to ring the president of the United States of America to get his views on the matter, but the prime minister remembered that he was on holiday, so there was a high probability that he would be out in his fishing boat and therefore unobtainable!"

"So Tommy Pulleyblank was right after all!" said Polly as her mind flashed back to the day of the mole crisis.

"Who's Tommy Pulleyblank?" asked the brigadier.

"Oh, never mind," replied Polly as her thoughts continued to go back in time to her very sad life at the castle.

"Well, Polly, as I was saying, we called up the French president, Monsieur Legume, to obtain his permission to land our specialist team on French soil. At first, he was not a happy bunny, for he was very insistent that it should be left to the Foreign Legion to storm the plane. However, when we told him that our dear queen had specifically requested that you, dear Polly, be rescued by our own Special Armed Services, he reluctantly agreed to allow our boys to take over the operation. And, if the truth be known, he was more than likely a little worse for wear, so in no position to put up much of an argument."

Polly raised an eyebrow to express that she didn't understand what "worse for wear" meant.

"Tipsy, Polly, tipsy. For the French love the odd bottle of rich and fruity red wine. It's a very important part of their tradition, the same way that we Brits like our tea," chortled the brigadier. "And if you ask me, I think he definitely is still slightly the worse for wear, for it was only last night that he officiated a state banquet," he snickered, giving her a little nudge at the same time. "Yes, they certainly love their wine almost as much as we British love our nice pot of tea. Speaking of which, I could really use some tea right now. How about you, old bean?"

Polly admitted that she was rather thirsty after her traumatic flight from England with no refreshments.

"That's settled then," said the brigadier as he placed an arm over her shoulder and commandeered her towards the airport terminal.

He then ordered Corporal Beanpod to make up a fresh brew and bring it to them.

"The French can't be trusted to make a good cup of tea, old girl, so we'll make our own, in the good old fashioned way that only us Brits know how," he said with a wink and a smile.

Over their cup of tea, Polly went on rather glumly to tell the brigadier about her trip to Piadora and how it had been ruined by the set of unfortunate events that had taken place ever since she had set foot in the airport terminal. The brigadier listened intently before saying, "Leave it with me, my dear girl."

He then disappeared and went in search of the French president. Meanwhile Polly patiently sat and finished her cup of tea.

"Well, Polly, I have sorted things out for you," he said on his return. "I have just spoken to Monsieur Legume, as I found him in the airport cafeteria downing a cup of rather strong black coffee. You wouldn't happen to have an aspirin on you, would you?"

Polly shook her head. The brigadier acknowledged her answer and then continued on. "Anyway, we have decided to fly you first class to Brazil on none-other than Concorde Airlines!" said the brigadier with a big beam on his face. "In fact, we have agreed that no expense should be spared in giving you the holiday of a lifetime. So we've decided to up the stakes and make it an around-the-world trip, stopping off wherever your little heart desires. Now how's that for service with a smile?"

Polly flung her arms around the slightly embarrassed brigadier, for she was so overwhelmed with gratitude. With the brigadier's face now a deep purple, he informed her that he had organized for her to stay in a top-class hotel for the night, while all the necessary preparations were made. He also told her she could eat whatever she wished from the à la carte menu and have a deep soak in a bath filled with bubbles, as well as a good night's sleep in a huge four-poster bed.

Polly's gratitude was much too deep to express, for not only had she been saved but she had known nothing but kindness and decency since her dramatic rescue by the wonderful SAS She would certainly send them a box of chocolates when she next got the opportunity. And now the icing on the cake was to be told she was getting a free around-the-world trip aboard Concorde. She really was being treated as though she were royalty!

Polly said her good-byes to the brigadier, and as she did so, he said to her, "Oh Polly, I have one more thing to tell you."

"What's that?" she asked.

"It's a message from the French president, for when I told him about all that had happened to you since you arrived at the airport, he told me to give you this message, "Reculer Pour Mieux Sauter."

"Oh thanks," said Polly, a little mystified, for she had absolutely no idea what it meant, but she wasn't prepared to let on this fact to the very wise and capable brigadier.

"Well, brigadier, please tell the president that I will pop by and see him for a cup of tea when I'm next in France, would you?" she said brightly as she turned to leave the cafeteria, flanked by his men.

"I will, Polly, and now you must let my men escort you to your hotel."

Polly waved good-bye to the brigadier as she left the concourse accompanied by some of his men. She was very delighted to discover that the vehicle she would be traveling in was pink, for as you will remember, pink was her favorite color. Yes, she was going to her hotel in the SAS's Pink Panther Land Rover. "Perfect, absolutely perfect," she said to herself as she climbed on board and was driven away from the airport.

As they were driving along, Polly took the opportunity to tell the boys how much she loved pink, and then she asked them why their vehicle was that specific color. They informed her that the reason it was pink was to help the vehicle blend into the pink haze often encountered in desert terrain. Polly marveled at their intelligence and wisdom in choosing pink as the color for their vehicles. Soon she arrived at her destination, and, after giving the whole squadron of elite men a big hug and a kiss, she waved them good-bye and headed inside the hotel lobby.

After a wonderful meal, Polly filled the bath with a whole bottle of champagne bubble bath that she had seen standing and waiting to be used on the bathroom shelf. The whole bathroom soon filled up with bubbles, some even floating up to the ceiling. She then slipped into the bath for a nice, relaxing soak, remembering to take off her ring and balancing it on the side of the bathtub. As she reached out to take one of the small soaps that lay in a gold bowl beside the bath, she found that it was not soap, but indeed a smooth stone she had picked up. As she held it in the palm of her hand she saw that this one had writing on its smooth surface like the other stones, only the inscribed word was, as usual, different. *Endurance.*

"How nice," thought Polly, but in truth she had no idea what it meant. She still thought she would add it to her collection of stones once she had finished in the bathroom. As soon as she was ready for bed, she put the smooth stone with the others she had collected. She then remembered that she had left her ring in the bathroom, so she leapt out of the bed and went in search of it. With the ring safely back on her finger, she jumped back into the bed and pulled out her pen and gold book, opening the book at a fresh page to record the events of the day, only to discover her diary had already been written in for her:

The poor princess had indeed endured a most terrible day filled with frustration and many misunderstandings. She had known nothing but fear as she witnessed the frightening events that had taken place on the plane. Had it not been for her strawberry-flavored chewing gum and torch, there was every possibility that she might not have made it out of the plane alive. In hindsight the terrible misunderstanding at the duty-free shop had worked for the good, and therefore to her advantage.

As the whole of France slept soundly in their beds, they would never know that the princess had saved their country from a terrible fate. However, the princess had not gone unrewarded, for she was now going to be treated like the princess she truly was by being given the opportunity to fly around the world on none other than Concorde.

She would use this trip to her advantage, stopping off in India, South Africa, Brazil, and many other countries. Yes, she would visit every land where her people lived and quietly suffered. Her trip would serve to confirm that she was indeed a princess to the poor and downtrodden, as well as the hungry and the outcast—something she must never forget. The princess would be well advised to heed the warning that if she got too caught up in the trimmings and refinery of being a princess, she would lose sight of

POLLY BROWN

her gift, and that gift was: seeing what many others chose to ignore.

The princess enjoyed a delightful champagne bubble bath before discovering yet another stone, this one having the word endurance written most beautifully on its smooth surface. She had at the time of its discovery no idea what this word meant, but now she knew and understood that it meant to "hang on in times of great trouble." Yes, she had indeed endured and come through many fiery trials on that most terrible of days, and she had come through them a much stronger person.

She had also come to learn another truth in the words given to her by the French president. As the young princess had rarely paid attention in her French classes, she had been quite unable to translate the meaning of reculer pour mieux sauter, and therefore, its hidden truth. But loosely translated, it meant that sometimes you have to take a step backwards to go forward better. The princess now understood that, just as an athlete attempting the long jump takes steps backwards to ensure their jump will take them further, the princess missing her plane and then being taken hostage had resulted in her being propelled further toward her destiny.

Tomorrow would be another day, and she had her around-the-world trip to look forward to. She would at some future stage be invited to come home by boat, or rather ship. Yes, she would also experience the delights of a cruise on the luxurious Queen Mary, but for the moment, all she needed to concentrate on and enjoy was her impending flight aboard Concorde.

The princess yawned out loud before closing her book and settling down for the night, for she knew, as all true princesses knew, that her beauty sleep was of *the utmost importance and lack of it most certainly does produce spots!*

———◦•◦———

Polly smiled and then gave a big yawn as she closed the book and cuddled up to Langdon. She fell sound asleep, dreaming the sweetest of dreams.

Chapter 23
PEDRO AND THE STREET CHILDREN

$\mathcal{P}$OLLY AWOKE THE next morning to the sound of birds singing. As she happily lay in the four-post bed and had a good stretch, she rubbed her eyes to remind herself that she really was not dreaming. Then, twisting the signet ring on her finger, she broke out into a smile. She lay in the bed, her eyes surveying the extremely plush room and most extravagant furnishings before leaping out of bed to go and run herself another refreshing bubble bath. On this occasion she decided to take Langdon into the bathroom with her, for she felt that he was beginning to smell quite disgusting and could benefit from a quick dip. After getting dressed, she was served a wonderfully tasty full English breakfast on silver platters as well as a nice big pot of tea.

No sooner had she finished scraping up the last tasty morsels on her plate when Corporal Beanpod knocked on the bedroom door to inform her that he had come to take her back to the airport, where her plane awaited her. Polly picked up her schoolbag and tucked a now very clean and sweet-smelling Langdon under her arm before following after the corporal.

"Phew, old sprout!" sniffed the corporal. "Where is that pungent smell coming from?" he asked, screwing up his nose to convey his sheer disgust.

Polly politely informed him that it was coming from Langdon, and that the so-called disgusting smell was, she would have him know, expensive French perfume. She thought he smelled simply divine.

"After taking off the top and smelling it, I felt Langdon deserved a little treat, so I poured the whole bottle over him, and I think he now smells utterly gorgeous," she said, sniffing into Langdon's fur.

Some treat, thought Corporal Beanpod to himself, for he much preferred the smell of stun grenades and jungle sweat to that of fancy French perfume.

The drive to the airport did not take too long, and once there, the corporal took her straight up to the steps of the aircraft, dispensing with the need to go through the terminal with its passport control, customs, and X-ray machines, for which Polly was indeed extremely relieved and thankful.

The corporal then said good-bye to her, for he was urgently needed on another specialist mission. Polly would not allow him to leave without giving him a final and rather lengthy hug, planting a kiss on his cheek as she did so.

As the corporal headed back to his vehicle, he sniffed himself.

"Good grief! Now I stink to high heaven of French perfume!" he groaned.

He knew for certain that his fellow SAS colleagues would make fun of him, and he would never live it down if he turned up at his next assignment smelling like a bouquet of flowers! The corporal therefore made a small detour into the airport terminal in search of the bathroom to have a quick shower before changing into his spare camouflage jacket, for so strong was the pungent smell on poor Corporal Beanpod!

Polly boarded the plane and was shown to her seat by two delightful and exquisitely-dressed air hostesses, who Polly thought smelled as equally divine as Langdon. Once in her seat, which she thought more resembled the bathtub she had just been in, she then fastened her seatbelt and placed Langdon close to her in the next seat. Adjusting her seat back almost into the sleeping position, Polly then lay fully stretched out, feeling as though she was in seventh heaven.

As she sat back in her luxurious seat, the two flight attendants, Amanda and Annabel, approached her with a large mountain of comics, coloring books, and a big bag of sweets for her and Langdon to munch their merry way through.

Eventually, Polly heard the captain over the loud speaker.

"Good morning to you, Polly Brown and Langdon," he said in a most stiff and British upper-crust accent. "My name is Captain

Philemon Plimsol, and I will be your captain on your around-the-world trip aboard this magnificent supersonic jet. Isn't she a mighty fine baby?" the captain added, referring very fondly, of course, to his beautiful and sleek plane. "Well, Polly, I hope that both Langdon and your good self had a perfect night's sleep and are ready for this adventure of a lifetime!" Polly giggled before popping a boiled sweet into her mouth. "We will be cruising at an altitude of…" Polly switched off at this point, for she hated anything technical.

Polly then watched as the flight attendant named Amanda performed the ritual safety procedure, taking a careful note as to where the safety cots were situated, for although these were normally used to carry babies and infants to safety she knew she would require one for Langdon, should the need arise.

Captain Plimsol then continued his address.

"Today our wonderful in-flight chef, whose name is Bernie, will be providing us with a lunch of either Hodgekiss Pie or roast rib of beef. The former is a most tasty steak-and-mushroom pie topped with a piecrust that I have to say is as thick as my English accent. New potatoes will be served alongside this dish as well as the freshest vegetables that were picked from my grandmother's garden only this morning. My grandmother's name is Edna, and she asked me to say hi to you, Polly, on her behalf. She will be praying that you and Langdon have a most wonderful trip. Now, back to the menu. Where was I? And if Hodgekiss pie doesn't take your fancy, you may prefer to choose the other option of the finest of English roast beef, accompanied by horserubbish—I mean, *horseradish*—sauce and the lightest, fluffiest Yorkshire puddings, again served up with grandma's finest and freshest vegetables, full of essential vitamins to keep you fit and healthy. And we all know how vitally important being healthy and fit is, don't we, Polly?" said the good captain.

Polly giggled and nodded her head at the same time.

"And, as if that is not enough to make your mouth water and your tummy rumble, the desserts are simply superb as well. Here you have a choice of mouth-watering Piadora pudding—this is a delightful pudding of hot chocolate cake, ice cream, and fluffy meringue topped with whipped cream and finished off with chocolate sauce, or you can opt for Mrs. Bailey's hot apple pie, made with crunchy and very juicy English Bramleys. Again, I have to tell you that these juicy apples come from my Aunt Winnie's apple tree, and she too wants to wish you well on your journey. This rather delicious pudding comes topped with a generous portion of thick, creamy custard as well as ice cream, if you so desire.

Polly felt her tummy begin to rumble and wondered if she would be allowed to sample a bit of everything, for she would be getting to taste food that up until this moment in time she had only ever had the luxury of dreaming of.

The captain went on, "Drinks will be served on a request basis. That means, Polly, should you or Langdon fancy a drink of any description, with the exception of alcohol of course, then please feel free to ask one of the hostesses, and they will be delighted to oblige. Personally, I could do with a nice cup of tea. How about you, Polly? I'm certain Amanda or Annabel, our two lovely hostesses, will make us a nice cup as soon as they are able, won't you girls?"

Polly noticed that both hostesses were blushing furiously, and she decided that both girls liked the good captain very much. Polly's only fancy, though, was to get her hands on some of the scrumptious food that the captain was reading from the menu. She felt on cloud nine just listening to him, but he wasn't finished yet.

"For afternoon tea we will then be serving warm, freshly baked scones with English strawberry or raspberry preserve, topped with whipped cream. And if that does not fill your tummy to overflowing, then we have a large and varied selection of gateaux, including Queen Victoria's homemade sponge. It goes without saying that this will be accompanied by a nice, big teapot of freshly-brewed English tea."

Polly giggled as she thought that Queen Victoria had certainly made sure that she would never be forgotten, for it seemed that her cake was on offer everywhere she went!

"Finally, Polly, please feel free to browse through our extensive video library, for I am certain you will find plenty of your favorite films on offer. My personal favorite is *A Night To Remember*. Oh, and I love *The Sound of Music* just as much. Perhaps you will join me later for a sing-along, so I hope you know the words to "Climb Every Mountain" as well as I do! Then there's *Mary Poppins*. Isn't she such a poppet? If none of these take your fancy, then how about *It's a Wonderful Life*?" The captain's voice began to crack as he went on to admit that he always cried when he watched that one! "Oh dear," he exclaimed. "There are so many wonderful films in the library, I fear that I may well have to put the plane on autopilot and come and sit next to you and Langdon so that I can watch them all," he said, giving the deepest of sighs.

Polly laughed, and thought it would be very nice if all the crew sat and watched the films with her and Langdon. Then they could all partake in the sumptuous food and turn the trip into a most wonderful party!

By the time their plane landed in Rio de Janiero, both Polly and Langdon were most reluctant to disembark from the plane, for they had experienced such a lot of fun on board. However, the real truth lay more with the magnificent food they had demolished en route and which, I might add, had caused them to pile on the pounds!

Polly refused to leave her seat and only did so after the whole crew went to extraordinarily great lengths to persuade her that, apart from refueling, the jet would remain stationary until she safely returned. To encourage Polly and Langdon to disembark, they also filled her schoolbag with cakes, sweets, and every other goody that they had on board, as well as filling a large carrier bag with comics, coloring books, and felt-tip pens. Still Polly would not undo her seatbelt until she had their promise of waiting officially put in writing by the good and most patient captain. Such was her mistrust concerning people keeping their word!

With the captain's written guarantee clutched tightly in one hand, Polly then staggered down the steps of the plane, seriously weighed down by all the gifts she had been given. Once outside the terminal, she then boarded a bus that had just pulled up at the bus stop. She quickly made her way to an empty seat and with great relief placed Langdon and the carrier bag, along with her schoolbag, on the vacant seat that was next to her. She then gave Langdon a cuddle as she waited for the bus to start up and take her on a tour around Rio. As she looked out of the window seat, taking in all the views, her delight soon turned to horror as she saw thin, half-naked children on the streets, crouched under cardboard that was held up by thin sticks. She got up from her seat and after putting her schoolbag on her back, picked up Langdon and the carrier bag and proceeded to head to the front of the bus.

"Please, sir, can you stop the bus, for I need to get off here," she politely asked the driver.

Luckily for Polly, the bus driver, who normally only spoke Portuguese, was able to understand her request, for he had been taking evening classes in English for a lengthy period of time.

"I am so sorry, miss, but this is not our usual stop. Besides, I have my orders to take you to the beautiful shopping malls," he said most cheerfully.

"But I don't want to go to any shopping malls, sir," replied Polly rather forcefully.

"Oh! But wait until you see them," answered the bus driver, most persuasively. "For our shopping malls are filled to overflowing with the most beautiful clothes and most wonderful toys, as well as every unimaginable treat that your heart could ever possibly desire."

"I'm truly sorry, but I've changed my mind," said Polly. "I no longer wish to go shopping. I just want to get off here."

The bus driver acted as though he had not heard Polly's request, as he continued to keep his eyes on the road ahead.

"Please, sir, don't you understand? Please stop and let me off now, for I have no desire to jump off a moving bus and injure myself," she wailed.

"I tell you what," said the bus driver, momentarily taking his eyes off the road ahead to speak to her. "Why don't you go to the shopping malls first? And then you can stop here on the way back. This way, you get the best of both worlds," came his cheery reply to her request.

"No, I don't think so," Polly replied. "Please just stop this bus, before I scream and force you to stop."

"That would be a most unwise thing to do, miss. I would be forced to call the police, for this would constitute a public disturbance," he retorted, at the same time hiding his panic at the thought of hearing one of Polly's ear-bending screams, which he believed would surely amount to pure torture!

"Do your worst, sir. I really don't care, for I have tried to be polite and tell you that my deepest desire at this moment in time is to get off this bus!" she begged. "So please, please help me by stopping it, and allow me to go on my way," she rather petulantly demanded.

The bus driver reluctantly obliged and turned the large wheel of the bus full circle, swerving off the road before coming to a standstill with his engine still running. As he opened the electronically operated door of the bus to let her off, he suddenly sneezed.

"Bless you," shouted Polly in the driver's direction.

The driver smiled before answering back. "Thank you, miss, for I am indeed very blessed."

Polly flashed him a quick smile before turning on her heels and heading back in the direction of the poor street children.

The bus driver was in no hurry to get back into the stream of traffic, preferring to sit with the engine still running as he watched Polly through his side mirror. He saw her walk back to where the children sat under cardboard makeshift houses, and he couldn't help but break into a smile as he thought to himself, "Yes, I am most blessed. For this headstrong and somewhat precocious young lady has indeed all the hallmarks of being a true princess. He then waited for a gap in the stream of traffic, before pulling out of the lane to go on his way. As he waited for the gap in the traffic to materialize, white feathers began to fall at his feet.

"Oh, bless my little cotton socks," he muttered under his breath. "This heat is really getting the better of me, and I'm rapidly losing my feathers. Thank goodness I've got my dustpan and brush with me, or this could have turned into quite an embarrassing situation."

He then drove off, taking all his other passengers to the city center with its wonderful and very exclusive shopping malls.

Polly approached the children with the sad eyes and empty bellies who lived in the gutters, but when she began to try and talk with them she quickly discovered that sadly they did not speak the same language. Within minutes she felt frustrated that she had not tried harder in her French classes. She did not seem to realize that, even if she had been top of her French class, it would have made no difference, for these sad and virtually-naked children only spoke Portuguese. Polly then suddenly had an idea, for she remembered that she had a lot of food in her schoolbag. She quickly removed the bag from her shoulder and emptied the contents onto the ground. Out tumbled fruit buns, packets of chips, chocolate bars, and sweets galore. The children eagerly crowded around her as she crouched down, and then handed each child something from her large pile of goodies that in no time at all had completely disappeared. Polly watched as each face that had formerly looked so sad now lit up and glowed with pleasure as they ripped open the wrapper to savagely devour the contents.

Polly felt her eyes go very moist as she watched, holding back the tears of sadness that she felt for every one of them. She then reached out to every thin-framed, dirty-faced child and hugged them in a way that might well suggest this could possibly be their last hug ever. There was not one child who did not respond to Polly, as they likewise showed no restraint in their response. Polly began to realize that day on the streets of Rio that the language of love needs no interpretation and therefore no interpreter.

Polly sat down on the pavement with the children, supervising them. They colored in the pictures from the wealth of books she had been given, and the number of children wanting to join in the fun began to multiply. Before long there were so many young ones, all hoping for a felt-tip marker and a picture to color, that it was only a matter of time before she had completely run out of supplies. This saddened and frustrated Polly, but it made her determine that as soon as she got back to the airport she would inform the captain of all she had seen and get him to empty the plane of all remaining sweets and coloring books so that she could leave them with the street children.

As Polly was taken on a tour of the favelas, she soon parted with her torch to a couple with ten children that lived in one of the shacks. She knew it wasn't much, but it was all she had. She also knew with certainty that if the man kept switching the torch on and off in the manner he was doing, the batteries would run out pretty quickly and they would once again find themselves sitting in the dark with no money to buy new batteries. Still, as she sat in the dingy room with the man shining his newly-acquired torch backwards and forwards onto the children's faces, she could not help smiling at seeing the children laugh and giggle with joy at the magic light. She knew that experiencing even a few minutes of happiness was better than never having experienced it at all.

After many hours of coloring, and just as many hours of hugging, the children led Polly, along with Langdon, up into other districts packed with favelas so that she could meet other street children and their families. Polly could not hide her shock or tears as she witnessed firsthand the terrible conditions that these people endured. There were mothers dressed in rags with crying, hungry babies in their arms and old men with deeply-lined, leathery-looking faces, all of which betrayed a lifetime of struggle and hopelessness. Old men wobbled by on sticks, scrawny flea-bitten dogs barked and gnashed their teeth, and beautiful but dirty children played football in the narrow streets with empty, rusty cans. To cap it all, the stench from poor hygiene was almost unbearable to Polly, as open sewers ran past her feet.

Polly felt as though her heart was well-and-truly going to break as she allowed the children to guide her through the narrow streets filled with pain and deep misery. Such was her distress at all she was witnessing that day. As she toured the area, the crowd that followed her began to swell in numbers. It was not too long before she found a young boy in the crowd named Ricardo who had a reasonable smattering of English. Polly was delighted at this news, for it made understanding their sad and often painful stories much easier, although as she sat and listened to their harrowing stories, she felt she could hardly bear to hear any more. Just like Polly, these dear and poor people felt helpless, yes, utterly powerless to change their lives. Polly was told that the Brazilian government had partnered with Paraguay to build the largest dam in the world, and that although it provided 25 percent of all Brazil's electricity and had cost them billions, not one of these dear souls stood to benefit from this luxury. They still sat in the dark and dank squalor of their shacks wondering how on earth to feed and clothe themselves.

Ricardo then took Polly to the house of one of his friends. Polly assumed that this hunchbacked, wizened old lady was in her sixties and was therefore very surprised to learn that she was actually only in her late thirties. This dear lady lived in a small pig barn with her two young daughters. Her son, Ricardo informed her, was in prison. Polly was most curious to know why her son, whose name was Pedro, was imprisoned. Had he murdered somebody or robbed a bank? Ricardo forced a faint smile at Polly's line of questioning.

"Oh Polly, he has done neither. Little Pedro is only nine years old, and he was caught stealing food to feed his mother and sisters, as well as himself."

"How long has he been in prison?" Polly asked Ricardo, for she was deeply saddened by all she had heard.

"Well, it must be getting on for nearly a year," Ricardo replied, turning to talk in Portuguese to the wizened old lady just to confirm he had given Polly the correct facts.

"A year!" said Polly, visibly showing how shocked she was.

"Yes, it's almost a year, and today this lady must go to the prison and sit before the prison board to hear if her son has reformed enough to be allowed out."

"Well, I must go with her," announced a most determined Polly.

Later that afternoon Polly arrived at the prison gates with Pedro's mother and Ricardo. They were kept waiting for what felt like an eternity before they were ordered to come through and take a seat at the end of a very large and long table.

Polly felt most uncomfortable, as did her two companions, for although you could hear a pin drop there was a distinct air of officialdom pervading the room. Sitting at the other end of the very long table was a most severe woman with grayish hair scraped up tightly into a bun and thin round spectacles perched precariously on the end of her rather long nose. She acknowledged their presence with little more than a dismissive nod. To both her left and to her right sat four equally officious gentlemen who also appeared not to notice their presence in the room. They were deep in conversation and stopped only to take the odd puff from their thick cigars. The air in the room quickly filled with thick clouds of smoke that caused Polly's eyes to water and made her cough. Even this did little to draw attention to their presence in the room. The spectacled lady continued to shuffle her very important papers, occasionally peering over her glasses in Polly's direction. It all felt so intimidating and somewhat frightening to Polly and her humble companions.

Polly gave the mother's hand a supportive squeeze to reassure her that she was not on her own. She then took a deep breath and reminded herself that fear was a thing of the past. She was here to support the dear, wizened mother of Pedro, and reminded herself that she had much experience of meetings of this nature thanks to the family sessions in the orphanage.

Within minutes a small, frail boy with the deepest sad eyes and shock of black hair was brought into the room, flanked by hefty prison officers on both sides, lest he should stupidly try and escape. He was ordered to hold out both his arms in front of him, and once he had obeyed this order one of the officers then produced a key and began to unlock the handcuffs from around his tiny wrists. Polly caught Pedro's eye and gave him a smile. He made a faint smile back to her as he rubbed his sore wrists. He was then ordered to stand to one side and pay attention as a list of his offenses was read out by a most serious and rather snooty bespectacled lady. Pedro hung his head in the deepest of shame as the long list was solemnly read out to all present. "Oh boy, I've been here before," thought Polly to herself as she sat witnessing poor Pedro's utter demise.

Pedro's mother sat in silence, her head hung uncomfortably low like that of her son. The officious-looking lady directed her attention to the boy and began to talk to him in his native language. As she spoke, his head appeared to hang lower than ever. Polly noticed his lips were trembling and tears were spilling down his cheeks.

"What is she saying?" Polly asked Ricardo.

"Well, Polly, she read out his list of crimes, and now she is telling him that the list of offenses is so very long, she is not entirely certain if he has spent long enough in prison to be truly remorseful. She then said she would have to discuss the issue with her colleagues before coming to any firm decision."

"That's crazy, Ricardo," whispered Polly, "all he has done is steal food so that his family and he can survive. How can they possibly keep him from his family for a minute longer?"

"Well, Polly, they view such crimes as pure wickedness that must be dealt with most severely, and this prison is full of little boys who are guilty of the same offenses."

"Well, it's utterly disgraceful," declared Polly. "In fact, it's outrageous, and they should go on trial themselves for punishing these poor children in such a shameful manner." She folded her arms as if making some statement of her contempt of the whole procedure.

"Shush, Polly, or they will hear you, and then you will be in deep trouble."

Polly huffed and puffed in a most defiant manner as a full-blown discussion was held between the gray-haired lady and her board of governors. The officious gray-haired lady with the delicate wiry spectacles finally turned to the little boy and began to talk to, or rather to address, him. By now there was a small puddle of tears forming on the floor by the young boy's bare feet. Polly wanted nothing more than to rush over and wipe away his tears, but she knew better than to follow her instinct.

"What is she saying now, Ricardo?" asked Polly most urgently.

"She is telling him that he is a very bad boy who has bought great disgrace on his family," Ricardo replied.

"Absolute nonsense!" shouted Polly very angrily.

The officials turned and stared in Polly's direction, for although they did not understand quite what she had just shouted, they had been rather rudely interrupted and were quite rightly most offended. Ricardo, who was just as startled by Polly's untimely outburst, turned to Polly and suggested that she remain quiet, otherwise she might be forcibly removed from the room by little Pedro's rather hefty prison wardens.

"Look, Polly not only could it make things worse for Pedro, but they might throw you in prison as well for contempt," he said, pleading with her to see reason. "Polly, he could end up getting extra months added to his sentence if you offend them any further than you have already," he added anxiously.

"Well, let them be offended! They need to be offended," replied Polly, completely ignoring Ricardo's request to stay out of it and remain calm. "I cannot stand and listen to this utter balderdash another minute longer, for the whole situation is just as farcical as some of the trials I have been put through," she responded loudly and most defiantly.

"Please be quiet for Pedro's sake, Polly," urged Ricardo, getting more agitated by the moment, his voice becoming more anxious than ever. Polly reluctantly agreed and sat back, taking a deep breath in order to help herself remain calm.

Finally, young Pedro was instructed by the officious lady with the spectacles to hold his head up and pay attention so that she could inform him of their unanimous decision. As she peered down at the young boy with the sad eyes, neither her face, which was as set as stone, or her voice betrayed any emotion as she coldly informed him of the decision they had come to. Polly turned to Ricardo and asked him to explain to her quite what was happening and what their final verdict was based on.

"Well, sadly, Polly, they have decided that he needs another six months in prison to remind him of the severity of his crimes."

Polly could contain herself no longer, "HIS CRIMES?" she shouted angrily, before yelling, "This court is an absolute sham, and they are the guilty ones, not poor Pedro. Yes, they are guilty of one of the biggest crimes against humanity by keeping this poor child here and away from the love and care of his family. No, this definitely is not right, there has been no justice served here today," she stated very angrily. "Ricardo, help me. I need to challenge their decision, please interpret for me."

Ricardo was given no choice, as Polly rather roughly pulled him up from his chair by the neck of his T-shirt.

"Excuse me, madam, but I need permission to speak," announced Polly in the direction of all the officials who had just started to get up from their chairs with the clear intention of leaving the room. "Come on, Ricardo. Translate for me," urged Polly, at the same time knowing she would not accept no as an answer if he declined to offer his services as a translator.

Ricardo reluctantly obeyed, feeling he had little choice, for Polly seemed most determined to have her say. The officials stared in their direction before resignedly sitting back down on their seats, one man lighting another fat cigar in his bid to while away the time as well as control himself from showing the full extent of his outrage at this rude and rather rebellious little troublemaker who would pay dearly for her interference at this meeting.

Polly drew a breath, for in truth she had no idea what she was going to say. She had been given no time at all to rehearse any speech, so she did what she always did in such difficult situations; she launched into her Churchill mode and spoke from her heart, Ricardo reluctantly translating her words for the sake of all those present. Polly continued on, oblivious to the tension that was now building up in the room as the angry and understandably offended governors were forced to listen to this little upstart.

Having finally got their full attention, Polly turned and pointed at the frail mother who sat weeping into her hanky. With all hope having been drained away, she grieved that she would not be taking her precious, beloved son home with her to join his little sisters in their humble home.

Polly stood up and prayed for the right words to come forth.

"This poor woman has today lost a son. Yes, for the next six months she will be separated from her little boy, whom she loves with a passion and has not seen for almost a year. For her, his absence has already felt like a life sentence, which she is serving as well as Pedro. She has already suffered the shame of having her young son imprisoned , but she came here today praying for mercy and compassion and in truth she has received none."

Polly paused, but not for too long, for she could see that they were anything but amused by her most rebellious challenge.

"I think the real truth is that no sentence you impose today will make any difference. Adding a further six months is very wrong too and will serve no purpose in making him a good boy as opposed to a bad one. Little Pedro here," she said, pointing towards the frightened little boy with the sad eyes, "was in truth served a life sentence from the moment he arrived in this world to let out a whimper. Yes, his biggest crime was to be born at all. To be born into a family that has no hope or future and that can only survive by living on their wits—including stealing other people's food—cannot and should not be viewed as some heinous crime that deserves such a hefty punishment." Polly gathered her thoughts while Ricardo attempted to loosely interpret her message in as palatable a form as he could, for he knew her challenge would be very hard for the parole governors to swallow.

"Before you leave this room, I want to ask you one final question, and one which I hope you will have the courage and honesty to answer. If you were living in a hovel and your mother and two young sisters were starving, would you not do all in your power to help them? If that meant you had little choice but to steal food from those who have plenty, would you not seize the opportunity to do so? I can tell you that I too have at times been so hungry, but probably never to the level poor Pedro and his family have endured. And yes, I can honestly admit there have been times in the past when I resorted to stealing food," Polly confessed, patting her stomach as she continued to address the stiff-necked and very unimpressed governors.

"I felt guilty, as I'm sure little Pedro here must also have felt, but I might add that the overwhelming desire to survive was placed by God inside all of us. There is surely a high probability that none of us would exist today if that were not the truth. Just as the animal kingdom, according to what my teachers tell me, is based on the survival of the fittest, so is the whole of mankind. I entreat you today, before you drive home to your comfortable, plush houses and sit down to eat a delicious and lovingly prepared meal, to consider just how blessed you really are. And as you prepare to sleep in your warm, comfortable beds, I ask you all: even if your bodies enjoy a restful slumber, can your consciences sleep soundly knowing that this poor lady and her children have no bed to sleep in, and that she and her family will therefore have to ignore the deepest of hunger pangs before the luxury of sleep ever comes to them? Please, please if you have any heart in you at all, I beg you to change your mind and let this poor boy go free to be reunited with his family."

With all said and done, Polly wiped away the tears that were now tumbling down her cheeks before slumping back down in her seat. Ricardo gave her a hug, for, despite being uncomfortable and afraid at being her interpreter, he was glad to have been of service. He felt proud of her moving and impassioned speech, and though he hated to admit it, it had brought tears to his eyes as well.

However, this was not the case as far as the governors of the board were concerned. There was not a moist eye among them as they sat most straight-faced, for they certainly did not share

Ricardo's feelings regarding Polly's emotional appeal. No, they were incapable of that! They instead, felt nothing short of outrage and disgust that she should have the audacity to challenge their humanity. Who on earth did she think she was to think that she had the right to address them in such an unbelievably rude manner? Yes, their pride was sorely wounded, and it would take many weeks, and probably much counseling, before their confidence would be fully restored, enabling them to continue their important jobs as governors of the prison parole board.

The bespectacled lady arose slowly from her chair and ordered the prison officers to come forward before shouting an order to them in Portuguese. With her order given, the hefty wardens moved over towards Polly, and before she knew what was happening they had her firmly in their grip and stood ready to frogmarch her out of the room. Ricardo shouted out in Polly's direction.

"Polly, you have just been sentenced to a week's imprisonment for your insulting outburst. And don't say anymore or they will put you in complete isolation!"

Before Polly could call back to Ricardo, she was forcibly removed from the room, something that gave the governors great comfort as they watched on before turning to stroke each others' bruised and damaged egos with words of deep consolation. Seconds later the hefty guards returned to make sure Ricardo, as well as Pedro's mother, left the prison without further incident. Then Pedro too was taken back to the squalid cells to continue his sentence along with the hundreds of other street children who lived without hope behind bars.

Pedro's mother openly wept and struggled to remain upright as she was forcibly led toward the tall, imposing prison gates, wondering if she would ever see her son again! For sadly, she had heard many horrific stories of what happened to the imprisoned children once the lights went out!

Polly, on the other hand, was dragged kicking and screaming down the long, dimly lit corridors and then down some steep steps before a door was unlocked and she was thrown inside. As she picked herself up from the floor, she found herself surrounded by hundreds of curious faces staring at her. Their eyes expressed both pain and concern. Again, Polly found herself unable to communicate with them, for they all spoke Portuguese. Just as before, it would not be too long before she overcame this difficulty, for not only did she experience the reality of the awful conditions the children were forced to endure, but she also heard their screams in the night. She could do nothing but pray that not only would her ordeal end, but all these little children would find some deliverance as well from their sad, wretched lives.

The week in prison was therefore spent hugging and wiping away the tears of many children who were lonely, very desperate, and also at the mercy of the prison guards. Polly wept much during that long and fear-filled week, and she prayed that one day she would be old enough and empowered enough to bring much-needed change.

Polly was very relieved when Ricardo turned up at the prison and was allowed to see her, even though it was only for a short time. She immediately had him working very hard translating between her and the children as each of them told their heart-rending stories of how they had come to be imprisoned. Many more tears were shed as each individual story was shared, and Polly could do little but console them as she listened on. She did, however, teach them her little song, "Give Me Love," and she shared with them all about Hodgekiss and Ralph and her journey to Piadora.

As the children huddled around her, holding on to her every word that was dutifully interpreted by Ricardo, their sad, pain-filled eyes began to sparkle like diamonds, and Polly felt a real sense of hope and purpose returning to light up the heart of each and every child that was present in the cell. As news travels very fast in such places, it was not too long before there was not a man, woman, or child in the prison who had not heard Polly's story. They too longed to visit Piadora and meet Ralph and Hodgekiss. When crushed lives know nothing but the deepest sense of despair, any glimmer of hope is worth hanging on to.

As the women sentenced to work in the laundry room boiled linen in large metal drums and scrubbed bed sheets with their painful and sorely cracked hands, they huddled together and whispered of Hubber Blubber and Hoolie Koolie trees, as well as all the other amazing things Polly had told the children. Likewise, the shackled and broken-spirited men forced to labor under the intensely fierce heat of the sun breaking up the ground and concrete found themselves humming Polly's song. Even the hardest and vilest of men held prisoner on death row found it quite a catchy little number that rather surprisingly raised their spirits. There was not one prisoner who, having heard her story, did not long with all their heart to visit Piadora and see for themselves what a wonderful place it was.

What troubled Polly most was the realization that virtually all of the children were incarcerated for stealing food, something she considered to be absolutely crazy. She also discovered that all of the children had two big dreams: to be granted an education so they could change their lives forever and to be back with their mothers and fathers. Sadly, most of the children believed that both dreams were well-and-truly beyond their grasp and verged on the impossible.

Polly experienced the depths of their anguish, for she too knew the depth of pain that struggling through life brought, especially when coupled with the absence of love and nurturing that comes from belonging, something so many seemed to take for granted. She therefore determined in her heart that she would never forget these precious little ones, and she would try to work harder at school. Then maybe—just maybe—one day she would find herself in a job that gave her enough clout to be able to change the lives of these poor souls once and for all. In the meantime, if she ever made it to Piadora for tea, she would tell Hodgekiss and Ralph of all she had seen and experienced and maybe they could do something to help. She certainly hoped so.

Chapter 24
I SAY, ANYONE FOR TENNIS?

*B*Y THE TIME Polly's week of imprisonment was finally at its end, she found herself very reluctant to leave the prison and the children. The squalid conditions which she had endured over the past week could only be described as horrendous. But she had also experienced the deepest acceptance she had ever known, and to Polly that was worth any amount of discomfort.

Ricardo was waiting outside the prison the day she was released, ready and willing to take her back to the favelas before she got herself into any more trouble. He felt that there was a high probability of that happening, for he had come to know Polly and her little ways.

Polly kept Ricardo waiting for quite a while as she hugged each tear-stained cheek, her final child being little Pedro. She looked into his eyes and promised to do all she could to help him and all his other companions in misery. As she gave him a final hug and told him that she loved him, she vowed she would never forget any of them—never!

It was therefore with the greatest reluctance that she finally boarded the bus that had pulled up outside the prison. Once on board she sat with her face glued to the window as the big black gates of the institution were firmly shut and locked. She felt deeply sad and knew she would miss her newfound friends, but then she thought of poor Captain Plimsol and his two lovely hostesses, Amanda and Annabel, who had been kept waiting, and she very much hoped they would forgive her for her over-extended stay in Brazil.

On the bus, Ricardo handed Langdon back to Polly, for she had left him with Ricardo for safekeeping. She had to admit that she was extremely glad Langdon had been spared the same atrocious treatment she had received since her arrival at the prison. She hugged Langdon closely to her and, stroking his fur, promised never to be parted from him again. Polly then sat back in her seat and had a little catnap.

When she finally woke up, she found herself back in one of the poorest districts of Rio de Janiero. She then changed buses and boarded one that was heading for the airport.

As she said good-bye to Ricardo and thanked him for all his help, a crowd gathered. It appeared as though the whole town of the poorest people had turned up most impromptu to say good-bye to Polly, the strange young English girl with the blue elephant.

The bus driver grew most impatient as Polly attempted to hug each person and not leave anyone out. The only trouble was the gathering crowd was growing larger by the minute, making it quite impossible to give everyone her little personalized hug good-bye. She was eventually left with no choice other than to give a final wave before going in search of a vacant seat for Langdon and herself. This was much to the relief of the anxious bus driver, who was beginning to sweat profusely, for he had a timetable to keep to and really did not wish to lose his job.

As the bus driver started the engine and then drove off, Polly continued waving until the crowd had become little more than tiny dots on the horizon. She then sat back and once again closed her eyes. As she thought back to all the suffering and hardship she had witnessed, the tears began to silently flow. She vowed that if ever she was in a better position to do anything, she would not hesitate to help these poor and desperate people.

Soon the bus pulled into the airport terminal, and Polly headed toward her plane with Langdon neatly tucked under her arm for safety. She was met on the concourse by Amanda and Annabel, who boarded the plane alongside her, taking her all the way down the aisle until they reached her seat.

"Come on, Polly, have you had a great week?" asked Annabel, who was all ears and wanting to know every detail of how the week had gone.

"Yes, Polly, tell all. Come on, spill the beans, for we're both dying to know," chipped in Amanda.

Polly found herself incapable of answering them, so troubled and burdened was her little soul by all she had seen and witnessed in her short time in Brazil. The lovely hostesses were most surprised to note that she had not returned to the plane laden with packages and shopping bags, as most of their clients usually did.

"Why, Polly, where are all your shopping bags? We were both looking forward to seeing what you bought. So come on, where are all the snazzy new shoes and funky jewelry? Where are you hiding them?" Amanda quizzed.

Polly felt embarrassed at her sad disposition and feared that the lovely ladies would mistake her silence for ingratitude, so she asked to be excused and headed for the restroom. As soon as she had locked the door from the inside, she sat down on the toilet seat and wept mainly through frustration as she wondered what on earth she could do to help all these people, for their pain had now become her pain. Eventually there was a knock on the cubicle door. It was Amanda.

"Polly, are you all right?" she called out with great concern. There was no reply. Amanda knocked on the door for a second time. Still no reply.

Amanda decided to try one more time in the hope of getting a reply, for she could not understand what, if anything, could possibly be wrong. Finally Polly answered, much to Amanda's relief.

"No, I'm not all right, Amanda, and I don't think I will ever be right again," announced Polly through the closed door.

"Are you feeling ill, Polly?" Amanda quizzed, "Do you need an aspirin? I can get some from the cupboard. We have plenty on board."

"Thanks, Amanda, but I feel there is no pill on this earth that will help me at this time," replied Polly most disconsolate.

"Shall I get Captain Plimsol to come and have a word with you?" suggested Amanda.

"No, I don't think he can help either," stated Polly wearily.

"Well, please come out, Polly, for we are all very concerned for you." Amanda pleaded as she placed her ear close to the door in order to hear Polly's reply.

It did not come. Amanda, nervous of the silence, decided she had better call on Captain Plimsol and get him involved, for she believed Polly would listen to him. After all, she and her hostess friend Annabel hung on to every word that came forth from the darling captain's mouth, so he was their best bet.

She therefore left the cabin and headed for the cockpit to inform the utterly gorgeous captain of her troubling predicament. Captain Plimsol, on hearing that Polly had locked herself in the restroom and was refusing to come out, left his seat to sprint quickly down the aisle in the direction of the locked cubicle. He stopped outside and gave the door a loud knock.

"Hi, Polly, this is Captain Plimsol. I hear we have a problem."

"We most certainly do," Polly retorted.

"Well, I can't help you unless you tell me what is going on," said Captain Plimsol, jogging on the spot as he spoke, for keeping the blood flowing nicely around his body was of the utmost importance to him.

"Well, Captain Plimsol, I have just witnessed some of the most terrible suffering I have ever seen, and I can't just leave Brazil pretending that I never saw it," she mournfully replied.

"Oh Polly, trust me when I say that I really do understand," said Captain Plimsol. "It is all very sad, but quite what can be done about it? I don't have the answer to that one, for the problem is seemingly insurmountable," he said with a heavy heart as he attempted to acknowledge Polly's deep concern. "Yes, if we came up with anything to help them, it would be a mere drop in the ocean. As you probably realize, the problem is so widespread."

"Well, I don't wish to appear rude, Captain Plimsol, for as everyone on board this plane knows, you really are a lovely man. But if everybody thought that way, then nobody would do anything, would they!" she said, feeling very disgruntled.

"I agree, Polly, really I do," admitted the good captain, "but what exactly are you thinking of doing?" he asked with a note of resignation in his voice, for he wanted to solve the problem as quickly as possible, then get back to the cockpit to make the necessary preparations for take off.

"I'm glad you asked me that question," Polly replied, "for I do have a few suggestions that I would like you to consider. Firstly, how about arranging for a consignment of food and clothing to be taken into the poor districts every week? Secondly, I would like you to find a compassionate human rights lawyer for Pedro and all his companions in the prison. Thirdly, I would very much like to become a member of the parole board to make sure justice is carried out for all the children who are confined within its walls."

"Is that it?" asked the captain as he anxiously wiped his forehead and repositioned his hat.

"Yes, I think that will do for now, but if I come up with anything else, I will let you know."

"Well, that's very decent of you, Polly," replied the captain, slightly tongue-in-cheek.

"I can probably organize the first request, Polly, but I'm not too sure about the other two," he said in his attempt to appease her.

"Well, that's just not good enough," retorted Polly from behind the closed door, "for I cannot leave Brazil without doing more to help my friends."

"Polly, you need to hear me out when I say that I never negotiate with little terrorists," said Captain Plimsol, by now feeling pretty fed up with Polly's defiance. "In fact, if you persist in remaining locked away inside this cubicle, I will be left with little choice other than to call in the SAS for their assistance."

"Good," retorted Polly sullenly. "I look forward to meeting Colonel Slaughterhouse again, if only to hear what he has to say on the matter."

"Look, Polly, we are all doing our best to help you, so please try to be reasonable," pleaded the patient captain. "I'm sure you realize that Colonel Slaughterhouse has better things to do with his time than to storm this plane to rescue the crew from your unreasonable demands. Come on, Polly, you know that the colonel loves action, and I'm fairly certain that if you continue this standoff, you will sooner or later discover that you have bitten off a lot more than you can chew."

"I don't care," Polly shouted back angrily. "I can't turn my back on those poor little defenseless children, so Colonel Slaughterhouse can do his worst, for I'm not opening the door until my demands have been fully met—*and* within a specified time frame."

"Oh, and what time frame is that, Polly?" the very frustrated captain asked.

"Now, how would I know the answer to that? I mean, what amount of time do terrorists usually give as they wait to have their demands met?" Polly replied, a little too snottily for the captain's liking.

Captain Plimsol gave a deep sigh, for he could see he was getting absolutely nowhere with Polly. It was therefore with the greatest of reluctance that he abandoned his efforts to talk her out of her standoff. So it was with a resigned spirit that he turned and sprinted back to the cockpit in order to make contact with the colonel. He hoped that the SAS would do a better job than he had managed in talking some sense into her. After all, they were highly trained in the art of negotiating, whereas his skills lay more in flying planes and thrashing friends at the odd game of tennis.

Polly was locked away for what seemed an eternity before there was a knock on the cubicle door.

"Polly, this is Colonel Slaughterhouse. I hope you will talk to me, old sport, for I have come a long way. Yes, I was in the middle of a good piece of the action, with smoke grenades going off all around me, when I took Captain Plimsol's emergency call. So you had better be willing to talk to me, old chap." He paused for a moment as he waited for her response. Nothing! "Polly, I've also brought Corporal Beanpod with me, so if you would prefer to speak to him, please just say so." Still there was no response from Polly. "Look here, old girl, you can't stay forever in this rather small and confined space. So why don't you just open the door, and then we can all have a good hearty chat over a nice cup of tea. How about it, old sprout?"

Polly reluctantly caved in, for the thought of a nice cup of tea did seem a rather good idea, as she privately conceded that she was extremely thirsty. Moments later, she slowly unbolted the door and emerged, looking decidedly sheepish from the small cubicle.

Colonel Slaughterhouse was both delighted and disappointed at the same time. Delighted that the siege was well-and-truly over without incident, and disappointed that he had not been given the opportunity of even pulling a pin from a smoke grenade, for he did so enjoy action. Still, at the end of the day he had to admit that he was very relieved Polly had not put up a fight, for privately he had a soft spot for the little whippersnapper, and he did so admire her steely determination.

Amanda and Annabel hurried off to make a pot of tea while the good colonel, along with Corporal Beanpod, sat and listened to Polly's long list of grievances. After much tea and an equal amount of negotiation, it was agreed that Polly's first and second demand could be fulfilled. Her third demand, however, was impossible to fulfill at this present time, and the colonel was happily able to make Polly see reason over this demand. He advised her to wait until she was much older, and therefore much wiser, before becoming involved on the political world, for she would need great wisdom if she was to take on the many unjust social issues that went on not only in Brazil, but sadly all around the world. Polly wisely agreed to heed their advice and settle for her first two demands being met. She then apologized to the colonel for causing so much trouble.

"Apology accepted, old sprout," said Colonel Slaughterhouse with a big grin, as he gave Polly an "old boy's" slap on the back with such unintentional force that it caused some of Polly's tea to spill from her cup.

"Yes, don't mention it, old bean," echoed Corporal Beanpod, "Now that everything's happily sorted, is there any possibility of getting a bungee jump in while we're still here?"

"Bungee jump? Did I hear you right? You want to go bungee jumping?" said Polly, feeling miffed that Corporal Beanpod would ask such a thing after all her intense and seriously sensitive negotiations.

Colonel Slaughterhouse roared with laughter. "Oh Polly, what Corporal Beanpod is really asking for is a banana split dessert. It's our favorite treat in the regiment, well, next to Mrs. Beeton's brandy-soaked Christmas pudding."

"Banana split!" echoed Polly.

"Yes, that really is Beanpod's favorite," the Colonel wickedly confided. "Yes, it's made with a nice ripe banana, sliced in two, with a scoop each of chocolate and strawberry ice cream, topped with lashings of whipped cream and chocolate strands. He really is rather greedy and impertinent to make such a request," said the colonel, furrowing his brow playfully to show his disapproval. "Especially when I have noted that he has already downed two rather large slices of Victoria sponge and polished off the last chocolate éclair," he chortled loudly.

Polly began to laugh, not because Corporal Beanpod had the impudence to ask for a bungee jump banana split, but because she found Colonel Slaughterhouse's raucous and spontaneous fits of laughter so infectious.

Amanda, not wishing to appear rude, offered to bring the colonel a bungee jump as well.

"Thank you, but no thank you, my dear," replied the colonel, stroking his upturned whiskers. "If I eat another thing, I will have no room for tonight's supper of meatloaf. Now that's what I call real food. Yes, real gut-busting, wind-breaking nosh that fills me up a treat, old girl."

Seconds later Corporal Beanpod was tucking into a rather large bungee jump, but not before he was again further reprimanded by the colonel for being so greedy.

"You will put on too much weight, my boy, and then you will have to go back to military school, and you know what will happen to you once there," whispered the colonel most gleefully. Corporal Beanpod nodded, but still continued to cram his mouth with spoonful after spoonful of ice cream. "Yes, you will be forced to go on a diet, but worse, you will spend the next few months back at squadron headquarters square bashing, old boy. So if I were you, I'd make that your last mouthful," said the colonel with a chuckle before turning back to face Polly.

"Now, Polly, where was I? Oh yes, you must now put this whole rather ghastly episode behind you, old sport," said the colonel cheerfully as he brushed off all remaining cake crumbs from his upturned mustache. "As far as we're concerned, it was well worth the time and effort to come all this way just for the nice pot of tea, rather splendid cakes, and in, Beanpod's case, the bungee jump dessert. But now, I really must get back to my men, for heaven only knows what they will have got up to in my absence. Chances are they will have gotten their knickers in a real twist and are now in some tight spot that only I can get them out of."

Polly smiled and then walked with them to the exit of the plane stopping only to give them both a hug. Corporal Beanpod shrunk back as Polly approached him with arms wide open, for he remembered her last hug and did not wish a repeat performance. He wanted to go back to the jungle smelling of sweaty socks, gunpowder smoke, elephant dung, and monkey droppings. Anything but exquisite French perfume! So it was with great hesitation and an equal amount of reluctance that he allowed Polly to give him a lingering hug. He did however decline to be kissed by her on his mud-stained cheek that still bore the traces of chocolate ice cream, for he believed there were limits to how much of a softy he was prepared to be!

Just as he was about to leave the plane, he plunged his hand into the breast pocket of his uniform.

"Here, Polly, have this little gift as something to remember me by."

Polly looked down to see just what he had placed in her hand. It turned out to be a book titled, *SAS Survival Guide.*

"Thanks," mumbled Polly as she continued to stare at the title.

"I think you might need it in the future, for it might help you stay out of trouble," said the corporal with a big grin. "Besides, it has plenty of practical advice from the experts, and if nothing else it will be a constant reminder that not only do we exist, but we also do our best in every situation and crisis we encounter. So you'll take great care of the book, won't you, Polly? Also promise me that you won't ever forget us."

Polly thanked Corporal Beanpod and promised she would never forget them, no never in a million years, for they had been so kind to her. She also felt bad that she had nothing to offer him in exchange for his kind gift.

"I could give you this little ring that I was once given by a kind gentleman of the road," she said to Corporal Beanpod. "I'm not sure if it's worth very much, though," she said as an afterthought, twisting the ring around on her finger as she spoke.

The corporal laughed. "Thanks, Polly, but you keep it, for I am certain the other men would really begin to wonder about me if

I returned to my battalion in camouflage and sporting a dress ring! Somehow I don't think that would go down too well, do you?"

"I guess you have a point," said Polly with a smile, "but if you don't take it, then I don't think it will be too long before you entirely forget me," she said with a tinge of sadness.

"Forget Polly Brown? No, I don't think so," said the corporal with a cheeky grin. "I think you've made certain that you will always be remembered. Trust me on that one."

Polly smiled back at the corporal and promised to take great care of his book. She stood at the top of the steps to watch them disembark from the plane, and then she watched as they drove away in their rather snazzy-looking pink jeep. Then heading back to her seat, Polly pulled down her schoolbag from the overhead locker and safely tucked the book inside along with all her other worldly possessions.

She was about to sit down and make herself comfy when she changed her mind and headed toward the cockpit. She realized that it was imperative for her to apologize to dear Captain Plimsol, for she knew she had tried his patience to the limit, and she hoped a sincere apology and a shaking of hands would suffice. She needn't have worried, for the good captain was just thoroughly relieved that the siege was finally over, and without incident. Yes, just happy that his "baby" remained fully intact. His sleek jet had survived the arrival of Colonel Slaughterhouse and his troopers without sustaining any damage whatsoever, and for this he was most truly grateful.

For Captain Plimsol was not a stupid man, and he knew that the sometimes "gung ho" colonel was like a fish without water if he did not have smoke grenades in one hand and a semiautomatic in the other. So at the end of the day, he and his jet had come off lightly. Now, all that was left for him to do before take off was change his socks and spray some deodorant under his arms, for unlike the lovely Corporal Beanpod, he much preferred the distinctive smell of heady aftershave to that of stale sweat and smelly socks. With this done, he put on his smart, pristine uniform and then sat down in his chair to await orders from the control tower, telling him he could now taxi down the runway and prepare for take off.

Once in the air, the captain asked Polly if she was now hungry enough to eat, for he had the most wonderful menu of Indian curries for her perusal. Polly declined the offer, telling the good captain she was so tired and exhausted that she felt she could easily sleep for a week. The captain smiled and agreed to leave disclosing the menu until the following day. He told her that he too would abstain from the evening meal, as he needed to lose a few pounds if he was to remain fighting fit, although he did think he had more than likely sweated off a few pounds, what with all the worry of the SAS arriving on the scene.

Amanda and Annabel, who were both listening in, turned to each other and smiled, for they did not agree with the captain's assessment of needing to lose a few pounds. They both thought he looked utterly gorgeous just the way he was.

"It's not easy staying trim when you are sitting down all day and night in a plane," he informatively told Polly. "And it's even harder when delicious, mouth-watering food is constantly being served," he said with a smile that showed off his perfect, gleaming white teeth.

"So I will bid you good night, Polly, and let's hope tomorrow will be a more peaceful and uneventful day, eh?"

Polly smiled and agreed to do her best to stay out of trouble. This news did much to gladden the good captain's heart.

"If you're a good girl, we can even watch *It's a Wonderful Life* again, how about that?" he said with his big, impish grin.

Polly felt delighted and said good night, feeling happily reassured that her misdemeanor was now a thing of the past. She found this hard to come to terms with, for in the past her history of crimes had always been repeatedly dragged up at every available opportunity by her guardians. Polly settled down with Langdon in her arms, and with the lights in the cabin dimmed, she fell asleep almost instantly.

Amanda and Annabel left her as soon as they heard the first hint of a snore and went to make themselves, as well as the rather gorgeous Captain Plimsol, another nice cup of hot Earl Grey with a slice of lemon. While they prepared the refreshments, they chattered on excitedly about all the unusual events that had taken place on the plane that day.

By lunchtime the following day they were almost at their next destination. All that needed to be done was for Captain Plimsol to read out the lunchtime menu so that Polly could choose what to eat. Then they could all watch a movie together, although he wasn't too sure if he could face watching *The Sound of Music* for the third time in only twenty-four hours. Polly perked up as the good captain, over the speaker, read from the extensive menu.

"Well, Polly, for lunch today, we thought we would give you a taste of India, especially since that's where we're headed. I hope you like spices and seasonings, for our curries are nothing short of heavenly."

"Yes, simply divine," Annabel interjected as she was at present in the cockpit serving the captain with a late morning cup of tea.

"Firstly, we have a wonderful bhuna gosht. This traditional dish comes from Delhi, and this is one of dear Dr. Chipatti's favorite curries, as well as that of Cyril, his rather greedy pet giraffe. This is a most delicious lamb curry with aromatic stir-fried spices. However, if that doesn't tickle your taste buds, then why don't you try some pista chicken? This delightfully creamy chicken and pistachio korma will be served up with rice and popadoms. Also, we have on offer prawns in a sweet and hot curry accompanied by yellow rice and lentils. And finally we have a fish molee. This is fillets of fish in a delicately flavored curry sauce, served on a bed of dill-flavored rice," said the captain, licking his very kissable lips in anticipation of the first mouthful of one of these very delightful dishes. "So Polly, out of all of these yummy delights, which particular dish tickles your fancy?"

"Well, they all sound very nice, but please may I just have egg and chips, sunny-side up?" Polly asked very politely.

"You mean egg and French fries!" repeated the captain, totally taken by surprise by her simple request. "Oh, but Polly, you must surely give one of these wonderful and utterly scrumptious curries a try?"

"Yes, I know I should, but what if I find I don't like a particular dish. What then?" Polly anxiously asked. "It's not as though there is an open window that I can throw it out of," she said, thinking back to the jugged hare episode at the orphanage.

The good captain saw her point.

"I certainly wouldn't want to upset or offend Bernie the chef, who has spent an awful amount of time making these exotic dishes…" she continued, her voice trailing off.

"Polly," the captain cut in, "why don't you just try a little smidgen of each dish, and then if you still think you would prefer egg and chips, I will ask Bernie to cook some for you," said the captain, trying to be helpful. "Or perhaps you would like to try a few mouthfuls of my favorite dish: shepherds pie with lashings of gravy, eh?"

Polly really enjoyed her egg and chips, or French fries, as the captain preferred to call them. In no time at all she had eaten every morsel on her plate, which washed down very nicely with the large glass of lemonade. This was then followed by a disgracefully huge knickerbocker glory, as well as an exceptionally large portion of pineapple upside-down cake, served with piping hot custard. Polly ate until she had no room for any more. "They can keep their curries to themselves," she thought most contentedly to herself, for she had thoroughly enjoyed her lunch, minus all aromatic spices and herbs.

The plane thankfully landed in Bombay later that afternoon and without further incident. Polly and Langdon happily disembarked from the plane without giving the crew a difficult time, although Polly did ask if there was any possibility of filling her schoolbag with comics and sweets. She was delighted to hear that this had already been done by Amanda. Soon Polly was walking through the artistically brightly-colored, hustling, bustling streets of Bombay, dodging doddery old men on equally dodgy bikes as she meandered through the streets with Langdon tucked securely under her arm.

This time, just as in Brazil, she found herself alarmed and horrified by the sight of poor, painfully thin children living on the streets and dressed in rags. Again she saw prematurely aged women with crying babies and old, blind men, many with only one leg, hobbling along and begging on the street corners. She once again felt saddened to the very core by all the atrocious suffering going on around her.

In no time at all she emptied her schoolbag of all the comics and sweets, which she then shared amongst the children. There was not one child who did not show immense pleasure at being given a sweet or chocolate bar. Polly felt touched as they eagerly shook her hand and beamed the most beautiful smiles from hearts filled with the deepest joy and gratitude. Polly found it touching, as well as difficult to believe, that these street children could be so grateful at her seemingly pitiful gifts. "Anyone would think I had handed each of them a million pounds," she thought privately to herself.

On this occasion Polly did not hang around too long on the streets, for the sweltering heat and stench were unbearable, and besides, she was once again feeling very distressed by all she was seeing. She knew if she stayed longer, her feelings might lead to another explosive outburst back on the plane, and she could not allow this to happen again to dear Captain Plimsol and the lovely Amanda and Annabel. No, this time she needed a more diplomatic solution to the problem.

Later the same day, and after she was safely back on the plane, Polly asked Amanda if there was the possibility of a quick chat with the captain. She was quite disappointed when Amanda informed her that the good captain was not at present on board, for he had gone for a quick game of tennis with Captain Bumble, his copilot. However, she went on to reassure Polly that she did not think it would be too long before they returned. So Polly sat down with Langdon and waited.

Amanda was right. Polly did not have to wait too long for the captain to return. She watched from a window as he bounded up the steps three at a time, dressed from head to toe in white and holding a racket under one arm. Once on board, the captain casually headed towards the bathroom to take a cool shower and then change back into his neat, prestigious uniform with gold braiding. Amanda caught up with him just in time and told him that Polly needed to speak to him rather urgently. Captain Plimsol sighed, feeling very reluctant to abandon his shower, but all the same, he gave in to the request and headed down the cabin aisle to talk to Polly. He asked Amanda to make them a pot of tea, for he had the sinking feeling that he might be with Polly for some time. He smiled as he sat down, propping his tennis racket on one of the vacant seats.

"Hi there, old sport," he said with a cheerful grin. "I say, would you like to play a spot of tennis with me?"

"I'm sorry, Captain Plimsol, but never in my life have I even picked up a tennis racket, let alone swung one," she admitted rather ruefully. "Anyway, I'm not too sure that I would be able to play tennis, for I have extremely poor sight," she said, pointing a finger towards one of her eyes.

"I'm sorry to hear that, Polly," said the captain rather disappointed. "I was hoping you would give me a game, for I do so love the sport."

Amanda and Annabel, who were standing nearby making a pot of tea, started to quietly giggle, for both of them would have loved an invitation to play tennis with the rather gorgeous Captain Plimsol, and neither girl would have ever declined such an offer, even if their hands had never before as much as touched a tennis racket!

"Well, Polly, even if you don't play, surely you must watch Wimbledon on the television?"

"No, I don't think I ever have," Polly replied. "All I ever get to see is wrestling on Saturday afternoons, and I really hate that."

"Well, perhaps one day you will be lucky enough to go to Wimbledon and actually watch a live match. It is the most wonderful experience, believe you me. Oh, and when you do go, be sure to buy a bowl of English strawberries and cream. I must admit this is one occasion where I turn a blind eye and do not count the calories. For I often have two or three bowls of strawberries and cream, all washed down with a couple of glasses of sparkling champagne," he cheerily confessed.

Polly produced a lame smile, for she could not help liking the captain and his enthusiasm for just about everything in life. She just wished that she had even the teeniest bit of his spark and zest for life and all its pleasures instead of horrible sadness that at times seemed to zap the very life out of her. As they sat drinking tea together with Langdon close at her side, Polly unburdened herself of all her latest anxieties, for her heart was once again very heavy indeed.

Luckily for Polly, not only was the captain jolly good looking, but an equally jolly good listener who also liked to drink considerable amounts of tea. So, much as he suspected, he remained seated for a rather lengthy amount of time as Polly sought consolation as well as sound advice from this kindly man who had many years of experience behind him. Before long, he found himself being pressured to do all within his power to get a consignment of food and clothing to them. He told her he would have to go higher up in the chain of command, but promised her that he would try his hardest. Before leaving his seat to go back to the cockpit and make the urgent phone call to the boss of the airline company, he turned to Polly and said, "Look Polly, we still have many other cities to visit, and what concerns me most is that you will see similar scenes wherever we land. We will be going on to Hyderabad and Delhi, as well as many other countries on other continents," he said, a look of great consternation written all over his face. "And my main concern is that if we keep handing out large consignments at every destination, our company will pretty soon go bankrupt."

"Oh dear," muttered Polly.

"Yes, and then before too long, Concorde will be a thing of the past, with future generations having to look at pictures in history books just to see what the world once looked like!"

Polly understood the poor captain's predicament, but she also felt a deeper sense of urgency to help the desperate, suffering children that she kept meeting. Soon she came up with what she considered a very bright idea: perhaps at some time in the future an appeal could be made each time the jet took off with its wealthy passengers, who she believed could easily afford to give a generous contribution without ever feeling the pinch.

The captain was not entirely certain that Polly's idea would go down well with the company chairman, for he knew that rich travelers would more than likely feel most annoyed, if not intimidated, at the prospect of being asked to part with their money every time they came aboard. No, if they had paid thousands of pounds for the luxury and privacy of flying to their destination aboard Concorde, the last thing they would want to concern themselves with was other people's troubles. The captain knew only too well that such harassment might well force their rich clientele to look elsewhere to other competitive airlines for future flights.

He did not tell Polly all of this, for he did not wish to make her any more upset than she already was. But he did promise that as soon as he had drained the dregs of his tea, he would go back to the cockpit and phone the company chairman for a little chat.

Polly felt deeply grateful to Captain Plimsol. After handing his empty cup to Amanda, he picked up his racket and headed back to the cockpit, privately promising himself that he would take that urgently needed shower as soon as he had spoken to the chairman of the board on Polly's behalf.

Captain Plimsol returned to the cabin some time later to inform Polly that he had indeed made the phone call on her behalf and that the chairman's response had not only been sympathetic, but also favorable.

"He's agreed to bring it up at the next board meeting, Polly, but please don't get your hopes up too high, for he is only one of many on the board." Polly nodded. "However the good news is that until then, you are free to help yourself to supplies of sweets and coloring books whenever you venture into a new city."

"Brilliant. I feel better already," responded Polly enthusiastically, for the news had gone a long way in gladdening her otherwise heavy heart.

"I'm glad that's sorted you out, Polly," said Captain Plimsol. "I was beginning to think I was dealing with Mother Teresa and the Pope all rolled into one!" Polly laughed at his keen sense of humor.

"Speaking of the Pope, I was wondering..." Polly stopped short, suddenly feeling that she would be well out of order to continue on and verbalize her unusual request.

"Well, speak up, Polly. What was it you wanted to ask?" said the good captain.

"Oh, nothing," replied Polly. "Really it was nothing."

If Polly had unwisely continued with her request, the good captain might well have found himself filled with dismay, for Polly, suffering from tired legs, had momentarily wondered if just like the Pope's Popemobile she too could be allowed to have a vehicle on wheels. After all, it made perfect sense, for she could take much more with her as well as cover a greater area. And it would do much to relieve the bunions that were now beginning to develop on her toes. After much serious consideration, she decided to hold her tongue and put up with painfully swollen ankles, for even she knew better than to push her luck too far!

That evening after yet another plate of fried egg and chips, Polly settled down with all the cabin crew to watch *It's a Wonderful Life* for the umpteenth time. As she watched the movie, it made her wish that one day she too would understand why she had been born into a life of such sadness and whether there ever would come a day when any of it would finally make sense. With that thought meandering its way through her mind and the film credits going up on the screen, Polly dozed off, still cuddling Langdon tightly in her arms.

Amanda found a blanket to tuck her in, and Annabel dimmed the cabin lights before heading towards the galley area to make the rest of the crew and the lovely Captain Plimsol a fresh cup of Earl Grey tea served with a slice of lemon. While the tea was left standing to brew, she hunted around in an overhead locker for the Scottish shortbread which she knew the darling captain loved. "How does he stay so sleek and handsome," she pondered as she lingered to study the disgracefully high fat content figures printed on the shortbread wrapper.

"Bless him," she whispered with a giggle before placing an extra shortbread finger on the gorgeous captain's plate.

With the tea brewing nicely in the pot, she picked up her tray and headed for the cockpit to join the rest of the crew.

Chapter 25
ANOTHER DARK NIGHT OF THE SOUL

*T*HE NEXT MORNING found Polly and the crew of Concorde well on their way to Durban, followed by Cape Town in South Africa. Again Polly found herself shunning the glamour and opulence of these beautiful cities, preferring to head out into the townships and see with her own two eyes the immense poverty that many people had to endure. Again she found herself meeting sad children like little Pedro. Their names were different, and much more difficult for her to pronounce, but their plight was just the same, and their despair equally recognizable. As usual, Polly found herself desperate but powerless to change anything.

Polly did have to admit that despite all the hardships she had witnessed in her travels, the children had something unusual—a richness, yes, an inner joy—that appeared to exude from their beings. They broke out into the most beautiful smiles at the drop of a hat. How could this be when they had experienced nothing but hunger and hardship? Yet love and laughter came so quickly when they gathered to kick an empty tin can around the streets. They also showed such immense gratitude when handed a small, insignificant bar of chocolate. This made no sense at all, and it served to confuse her further. There could be no denying that there was something profoundly rich about these poor countries, for the hardship seemed to make them more alive and passionate, with more ability to give of themselves to others. Could it be that despite having nothing, they in truth were the rich ones and those with too much wealth or comfort were actually the poorer ones?

She found herself continually perplexed by this nagging thought as she emptied her backpack time and time again to joyous huddles of wide-eyed children that always grew in number wherever she went. Finally, after endless kissing and an equal amount of hugging, she hurriedly made her way back to the airport to board the supersonic jet as it was getting late and she was looking forward to her next hot meal. Amanda and Annabel were standing by the steps ready to greet her.

"Did you have a wonderful day, Polly?" Annabel asked with an air of excitement in her voice. "I mean, isn't Cape Town just about the most beautiful place on Earth? I bet you took the cable car up to the top of the mountain to see for yourself. For the views over the bay are just breathtaking, don't you think?"

Before Polly could give any reply, Amanda jumped in.

"Yes, Annabel, I agree with you. The views over the bay are simply stunning, and often you can see whales and dolphins swimming in the clear blue water below. It's simply wonderful." Amanda smiled as she patted Polly's shoulder. "Polly, I do hope you took Langdon on a safari tour so he could see some of his relatives? For the elephants walking with their babies in tow is such a wonderfully cute sight to behold. So tell me, please do. Did you take Langdon to meet up with them?"

Polly gave no reply, choosing to remain silent. For once again, she was having a serious fit of the blues. So she just shook her head, and proceeded to wearily climb the steps up to the plane. Once on board, she headed for her seat, and after placing Langdon down next to her she sunk back into her seat and closed her eyes.

Amanda and Annabel both looked at each other, shrugging their shoulders as if to say that as usual neither of them had the slightest idea as to what was upsetting Polly. The sad truth was that they were both finding it very hard to understand why, having been given the gift of the trip of a lifetime, Polly wasn't showing more excitement and coming back from each city with camel loads of goodies and presents? If nothing else, they thought, at least lots of beautiful new shoes, for both hostesses had a real weakness for new shoes. Yes, if the truth were to be known, both girls were well on their way to becoming the next Imelda Marcos, with the competition being very close as to which one of them had the fullest wardrobe stuffed with hundreds of pairs of shoes. So to both girls' way of thinking, none of Polly's behavior made any sense at all.

Amanda crouched down by Polly's seat in a final effort to communicate with her while Annabel went to pour Polly a cool glass of lemonade.

"Polly, do you want to talk about whatever is bothering you?" Amanda asked, feeling very concerned.

Polly remained silent, her eyes firmly shut. Annabel joined Amanda in crouching down in the aisle as she then attempted to place the glass of lemonade in Polly's hand. Still Polly would not open her eyes or take hold of the glass. Both girls looked at each other resignedly and decided to leave her alone until she was ready and willing to talk.

What neither girl knew—and Polly felt they would never understand—was that she was feeling desperately homesick. But homesick for where? Polly hated the orphanage so much that to long to be back there was nothing short of crazy. But as she sat in her seat with her eyes firmly shut, she found herself being confronted by the same vision that constantly haunted her, a vision of a little girl aged around five or six, sitting on a chair in a dark empty room, constantly crying "I want my mummy; I want my mummy." Nobody ever entered the room to answer her call, and her cries seemed not only to get louder but also more heart-rending as she sat alone in the dark in a state of deep distress. Often when Polly was finding life difficult, she would find herself picturing this disturbing scene. Only recently, she had begun to realize that the little girl was, in fact, none other than herself.

Polly had spent years rocking her head back and forth, crying over and over for her mother. But no amount of rocking brought her mother to her side, and only after completely exhausting herself did sleep ever come. She had tried hard to imagine a warm, sweet, tender woman with a delicate string of pearls around her neck, bending over her to stroke her hair and whisper kind and touching words as she wiped away her tears. Oh, how she had always longed for the comfort and sense of security that mothers bring. To Polly's way of thinking, parents were the most precious gift any child could be given, and cut the deepest wound imaginable if they were absent from a child's life. She knew for certain that no amount of fancy clothes and classy shoes could ever fill that void. Yes, she'd forgo every imaginable luxury for the gift of having parents, for their absence in her life had done much to cause turbulence in her heart that felt crippling in its impact. This turmoil never seemed to subside in its strength and seemed happy to engulf and overwhelm Polly at the drop of a hat. It sought to invade and highly influence just about every event of her young life as it continued to wreak its trail of total havoc.

Polly thought back to a day at the beach when at the young age of four years old, she had been in the care of Molly and Maisie Brimstone. They had gone to the beach as a treat. Polly had just been given a new turquoise stretchy swimsuit to replace the dark blue, bubbly old costume that, like a sponge, never failed to hold in the water until long after she came out of the sea. It was horrible, for as well as keeping her cold and clammy as it stuck like superglue to her skin, it also made her feel ugly. Therefore, the joy of being presented with a new rather trendy costume had felt indescribable, so great was her joy at the surprise gift. Once she had the costume on, she dispensed with all self-control as she raced down the shoreline and began to skip and dance through the small soap-sud waves that rushed up the beach to meet her.

The water was so chillingly cold that as the suds covered her toes she screamed with delight. However, from her guardians' perspective, she had quite clearly forgotten her place, and therefore needed to be taken down a peg or two. They seemed incapable of appreciating that Polly's delirious state of happiness had nothing to do with her being a show-off, but simply that she felt wonderful and like a little princess for the first time in her otherwise forlorn life. Before she had the opportunity of even getting the costume fully wet, one of the other children was ordered to run and fetch her, for Maisie and Molly required her presence back at base camp.

Polly obeyed the command and immediately raced up the beach as fast as her legs would allow. She hardly noticed the pain of the sharp pebbles under her feet, so great was the rush of adrenaline that came from experiencing such newfound happiness.

Finally, a little out of breath, she reached the area where her two guardians sat. Their overgenerous bodies overlapped on striped deckchairs that appeared to be on the verge of collapsing under the strain of their weight. Polly innocently assumed she had been called because it was now lunchtime, and they wanted everyone present before the large wicker hamper was opened for the sandwiches to be handed out.

As she approached them she saw one of the girls, Carol, sitting beside the ladies crying, and Maisie was patting her on the shoulder in an attempt to comfort her. Polly had no idea what the problem was, and therefore never considered that she could possibly be the root cause of young Carol's plight. She therefore arrived on the scene still excited and very, very happy.

"Come here immediately, Polly Brown," Molly officiously demanded.

Polly, though perplexed by Molly's gruff tone of voice, immediately obeyed.

"We have all had quite enough of your prancing and parading around as you try to make the other children jealous," she sneered.

Polly stood in a stupefied silence as Maisie pulled the face of sobbing Carol further into the cleavage of her heaving bosom. However, Carol did manage to flash a wicked smile in Polly's direction on her way down into Maisie's ample chest. Before Polly could speak out, Molly jumped to her feet, and without prior warning, she lunged towards Polly. In just a matter of seconds Polly's new stretchy turquoise costume was forcibly stripped from her waiflike frame, leaving her cold and exposed, as well as completely shocked.

Despite being only four years old, Polly felt instantly humiliated and quickly grabbed hold of a towel to cover her exposed and shivering body. She then raced over to where her clothes sat nearby in a small pile. Gathering them up rather frantically in her arms, she then rushed up the beach in search of the public facilities so she could put her clothes back on. Hot tears stung her eyes as they mingled with sand. Her cheeks were also burning as she fought back the awful sense of humiliation she was experiencing. Once inside the ladies room, she locked herself in one of the cubicles and slumped down on the seat. With her towel still wrapped around her, she began shaking and crying as she tried to come to terms with what had taken place. Eventually she forced herself to put her clothes back on, for she feared she would be in further trouble if she remained absent too long. Then as she stood up to open the cubicle door, she found it was stuck. She began to panic, trying desperately to push the thick bolt back and free herself from the stall. All her attempts were futile. She finally admitted defeat and slumped to the floor weeping loudly as she cried out for help.

Her cries for help eventually caught the attention of other vacationers, and it was not too long before she was rescued and released from her temporary prison. Polly was shaking so badly from her ordeal that all the ladies were most concerned for her welfare. Suddenly one of the ladies bent down to look in Polly's tear-stained face, and once their eyes met, she took it upon herself to ask what in any other situation would be considered a reasonable question.

"Little girl, please stop crying. Where is your mummy?"

She presumably asked that oh-so-explosive little question in total innocence so that Polly and her mother could be reunited. Instantly, Polly felt a sharp stabbing pain in her heart as she opened her mouth and began to stammer, "I have no mummy," before making a further spectacle of herself by collapsing in a heap down by the group of ladies' feet. Her grief at being publicly humiliated by the removal of her swimwear had been bad enough, and being locked in the stall had been pretty terrifying. However, the awful realization that she had no mummy to help or comfort her suddenly superseded both other painful events, forcing them way down the trauma Richter scale. The concerned lady had asked the same question that tormented Polly every single day of her young life, and it had never been satisfactorily answered. Where *was* her mummy? At that painful moment in time it forced Polly to sob deeper than ever at her loss.

The group of very concerned ladies made it their business to take Polly back to where her guardians sat, and one lady kindly took it upon herself to explain that Polly had accidentally got herself locked in the bathroom stall. Polly was grateful that it was not left up to her to give a satisfactory excuse for her rather lengthy absence, but

POLLY BROWN

rather another adult to whom both guardians would think twice before expressing anything other than gratitude.

With the ladies gone and well out of earshot, Polly was ordered to sit down on the pebbles and remain in their presence for the rest of the afternoon. As she tried to make herself comfortable, Molly handed her one of the last remaining sandwiches, which she gratefully accepted. But as she took her first bite into the bread her eye caught a glimpse of Carol. Suddenly, from deep down inside, she started to feel those old familiar rumbles of distress, similar to that of a volcano, warning that an eruption is imminent, and once again she found herself struggling to contain her emotions. Fresh tears began to spill down her cheeks, splashing onto her half-eaten sandwich, which she was now struggling to eat as she experienced an overwhelming sense of loss, for down on the shoreline Carol was strutting like a peacock adorned in the turquoise swimsuit which Polly had briefly loved.

Polly did not know how to cope with the rest of the day on the beach. She could only pray with all her heart that Maisie and Molly would relent and find it in their hearts to give her back her new swimsuit, even if it was not to be on this bright and hot sunny day. It was never to happen.

So, as Polly sat on the plane with both hostesses quietly pondering and confused as to what the root of Polly's problem really was, Polly felt miserably depressed. Both girls remained hidden in the galley area sipping tea and feeling quite puzzled. After all, Polly was being treated like royalty with her every seemingly indulgent whim being met, and yet not showing an ounce of gratitude. How could she be so spoiled and ungrateful? Both girls were beginning to feel pretty impatient with her, though they were loath to voice their disapproval of what they perceived as ingratitude while in her presence.

Polly remained equally silent and melancholic, for she too felt incapable of expressing what she was really feeling. The truth was simply that there was nothing she wanted to buy; all she wanted was a mother and father, and she knew that there was no shop on this planet that sold them. She also felt that if such valuable items were on sale, they would surely cost millions of pounds and would therefore be well beyond her reach.

So traveling the length and breadth of the globe and witnessing firsthand such heartbreaking scenes in every country her feet touched had served to make her anguish deeper and her feelings of being homesick intolerable, for the sickening truth was that she had no real home to go to and no family to love and be loved by.

Finally, Polly asked Amanda if Captain Plimsol was available, as she needed to have another heart-to-heart with him. Amanda agreed to go and look for him. She came back minutes later and informed Polly that the good captain was out playing tennis but would be back soon. She made Polly agree to eat something while they waited. Polly didn't argue, for she was very hungry from all her traveling on foot.

"What do you fancy, Polly?" quizzed Amanda, "and don't say egg and chips, please."

"I'd like to try some pasta," Polly replied, her face visibly brightening up. "I used to dream of trying some of Mrs. Pizzani's lasagna that they used to make at the Copper Kettle tearoom. So do you think Bernie would be able to make such a dish? And if he is unable to produce that, then is there any possibility of having some creamy chicken and ham carbonara? I always wanted to try some of that."

"Well, funnily enough, both meals are available, for Mrs. Pizzani sent our chef Bernie some of her secret recipes when she heard that you were on board," Amanda cheerfully informed her. "So which will it be? Tell me now, and I will get Bernie to rustle up some nice, comforting food for you."

Polly decided on the lasagna served on a bed of crisp lettuce with a nice potato and a big dollop of mayonnaise. She was not to be disappointed and ate every mouthful of the huge plateful, declaring it to be exceedingly and deliciously scrumptious. With the floral pattern almost licked off her plate, she finally announced to the girls that she was full. However, it is important to note that Polly still managed to polish off a whole bowl of chocolate and banana trifle before calling it a day.

No sooner had she finished when Captain Plimsol leapt up the steps and into the cabin. Amanda quickly took him aside and explained that Polly wished to talk with him.

"This time around, not before I've taken a shower," he said with a smile that made Amanda feel giddy and all gooey inside. Twenty minutes later he emerged looking handsome and bronzed. The air inside the cabin now filled with the smell of expensive aftershave that made both hostesses swoon some more.

Having sat down beside Polly, he then asked Annabel to make a very large pot of tea and bring it to them. So, while Polly poured out her heart, the good captain poured out endless cups of tea and listened sympathetically to the long list of things troubling her. Polly finally ended the conversation by asking him if she could be taken back home to England.

The captain was surprised and told her that they still had many places to visit. Did she not want to go to Australia? And then after Australia he had China in mind as the next possible place to touch down. Polly shook her head. He even suggested Thailand as a strong possibility, as it was definitely becoming a new hot spot for tourists. It had plenty of nightlife, as well as fabulous sandy beaches that went on for miles.

Polly admitted that it all sounded very wonderful, and she was very grateful to all the crew, the chef included, for they had all made it a really wonderful trip, but she really was tired and homesick, so she hoped they would understand her reticence in not wishing to continue on with the journey.

"Dear Captain Plimsol, I just want to go home," she pleaded.

The good captain agreed to Polly's request, but with one condition attached.

"Oh dear," groaned Polly. "I am not certain that I am going to like what I hear. Please, captain, do there have to be any conditions?" she wailed.

"Absolutely, my dear," declared the captain, giving a wide grin that exposed his beautifully straight and gleaming white teeth. "Look, Polly, we have all tried very hard to meet your demands. Now it is my turn."

Polly looked at the captain wistfully. "Oh, go on then. Tell me what the condition is."

The good captain put his hand into his pocket and pulled out an envelope, which he then handed over to Polly. Polly was taken by surprise.

"What's in the envelope?" she anxiously asked.

"If you hang on a minute, I'm just about to tell you," he replied, at the same time making a deep sigh to show his slight annoyance at Polly's impatience. "Polly, we are at present heading for New York in America, because both Amanda and Annabel's families live there, and they have not seen them since the start of this trip. I think you will agree with me that both girls need some time off."

Polly nodded her head in perfect agreement, while the captain took another sip of tea. "Well, Polly, I think it would be a very nice idea for you to travel back home to England on a very special ship. Her name is the *Queen Mary*, and she is setting sail from New York tomorrow at midday. The captain of this luxury vessel is a personal friend of mine, in fact he is one of my tennis partners who I've never quite managed to thrash yet," he said with a sheepish grin. "Anyway, I took it upon myself to contact Hector a week or so ago, and besides discussing this year's Wimbledon tournament I also took it upon myself to tell him all about you."

Polly remained silent, giving her full attention to all the captain was sharing.

"I then went on to ask if there were any unoccupied cabins left, as I felt you were beginning to get homesick. Hector readily agreed to help me out, and so inside the envelope you will find the ticket and everything you need for Langdon and your good self to make it home safely to England's green and pleasant land. So, Polly, what do you think?" the captain asked as he observed her face in search of a positive response.

Polly leapt to her feet and moved over in his direction as fast as any international tennis player he had ever seen. She then flung her arms around his neck, planting a big kiss on his clean-shaven, sweet-smelling chin.

"Thank you, Captain Plimsol. Thank you so kindly," she cried excitedly. "Both Langdon and I cannot thank you enough for all the kindness and patience you have shown us both, and I can tell you now that neither of us will ever forget you." Polly paused to

POLLY BROWN

take a deep breath. "If ever I fail to remember any of these events, Langdon will most certainly remind me, for as you well know an elephant never forgets."

The Captain smiled as he patted Polly's shoulder. "Well, Polly, I think you can now release me from your bear hug before I expire."

"Oops, I didn't realize I was hugging you so tightly," she said, her face going a deep shade of crimson.

Amanda and Annabel enviously watched on, sighing deeply as they found themselves wishing that they were back at Polly's age so they too could get away with giving the lovely captain such a demonstrative hug.

"Come on, Polly. It's time to leave the captain to chart the next course for Concorde," Amanda stated with a grin.

"Yes, Polly, the girls will help you pack and fill your backpack with lots of goodies. And then when we land, I will personally drive you to the dock and make sure you are well settled in your cabin before I leave."

"Oh Captain, you do not have to do all this for me. I am certain I can find my way to the docks," said Polly. "Please, you have already gone more than the extra mile by giving me this ticket."

"Sorry, Polly, I'm taking you, and that's the end of it. My decision is final. Besides, I do have a selfish reason for personally escorting you to the docks to board the *Queen Mary*."

"Oh, and what's that?" Polly asked, displaying a large amount of curiosity.

"Why, to have a good game of tennis with the captain, of course," replied Captain Plimsol. "I would have thought you would have been able to guess that one. Yes, I do believe I have considerably improved my game since he and I last met up, and now I'm hoping to give him a good thrashing," he said with a chuckle. "He's an ex-Wimbledon player, I'll have you know. So I don't think Captain Humdinger will take losing a game to me too lightly."

Polly joined in the laughter, for she was finally beginning to feel considerably happier, thanks to Captain Plimsol and his generous heart.

"Oh Polly, one more thing," said the captain more as an afterthought. "Have you heard of a new pop group called Freddie Fruitless and the Backsliders?"

"Have I heard of them!" said a very excited Polly. "Everybody is talking about them, for they have become really famous," she said, immediately humming their latest release.

"Well, Captain Humdinger informs me that they will be on board, as they are on a world tour, so isn't that just peachy?"

Polly clasped her hands in delight at the good news, and as she did so, all thoughts concerning poor, hungry children such as Pedro completely disappeared, for she was about to fulfill something beyond her wildest dreams: to meet none other than her favorite pop idol, Freddie Fruitless, in the flesh, along with the rest of the band. All the excitement of this happening left Polly feeling thoroughly overwhelmed. She leapt up from her seat and gave the darling captain a big kiss on the cheek, which caused another tremendous surge of jealousy to rush through the hearts of Amanda and Annabel as they both watched on most enviously.

The next day, as promised, Captain Plimsol escorted Polly from the plane, but not before Polly had said her good-byes to all the crew, in particular Amanda and Annabel, as well as Bernie the onboard chef. Bernie was so touched when she complimented him on all his wonderful cooking that he produced a little lunchbox, informing her that he had made her some very special sandwiches and added a couple of large slices of Victoria sponge. Polly was delighted and plunked a kiss on his plump cheek, which immediately turned to bright pink. Amanda, not to be outdone, gave Polly a bottle of expensive perfume, and Annabel generously donated one of her favorite lipsticks, telling Polly the color would definitely suit her and that it might come in handy one day.

With their good-byes said and all hugging out of the way, Polly climbed into the bright yellow taxi along with Captain Plimsol and they headed for the docks and the *Queen Mary*. When the taxi halted and Polly stepped out of the taxi, her jaw dropped ninety degrees as she stared in awe and amazement at the beautiful vessel that she was about to board.

POLLY BROWN

Chapter 26
ALL ABOARD THE *QUEEN MARY*

ONCE ON BOARD, Captain Plimsol took Polly to the officers' quarters to introduce her to all the ship's staff, as well as to pick up the key to her cabin. He also wanted her to meet Hector Humdinger, the proud captain of this fine ship.

Polly had to stifle her giggles as Captain Humdinger held out his hand to introduce himself, for he was already in his white shirt and shorts, revealing two extremely hairy legs. Polly duly observed that he had very large feet. He also had a tidy but very whiskery white beard, which he permanently appeared to be stroking, and piercing deep green eyes which seemed to mischievously sparkle. His attire was topped off by a rather trendy headband around his forehead and a racket under one arm.

"Couldn't waste valuable tennis time, Polly," explained Hector Humdinger, "Yes, time is clearly of the essence. Isn't that right, Plimsol?" he said as he made a facial expression that suggested he was disappointed with Captain Plimsol for not being suitably dressed for tennis, for this would mean certain delay in getting onto the court.

Captain Plimsol smiled back at his impatient and rather impertinent friend before asking permission to escort Polly to her cabin. After she was settled in, he would then come back to the officers' quarters to get changed as quickly as Hector could say "Jack Robinson." Captain Humdinger readily agreed and handed Polly the key to her cabin before informing her that she was invited to sit at his table for dinner that evening. Polly and Captain Plimsol then excused themselves and went in search of Polly's cabin.

Once they had found it and opened the door, Polly went ahead of the captain and placed Langdon and her backpack on the bed. She then turned around to say good-bye and thank him for all he had done for her, only to discover that he had completely disappeared. Polly was puzzled, so she raced over to the cabin door and looked both ways down the corridor. There was no sign of him or anyone else for that matter. This left Polly very perplexed, as she had only turned her back for a matter of seconds. As she closed the door of the cabin and walked towards where Langdon was lying trunk down on the bed, she saw that a couple of feathers had come to land on the polished floor of the cabin. She went over to where they lay and carefully picked them up from the floor, feeling most confused as to why they were there. She felt she needed an answer, so she went over to the bed and checked the pillows to see if they were filled with feathers. They were. She breathed a sigh of relief. Obviously the feathers had escaped while the cabin staff plumped up the pillows as they went about their job of making up the cabin bed.

Polly felt overcome with tiredness and, as it was still some time until dinner, she lay on the bed cuddling Langdon tightly to her chest, feeling very excited. For the thought of dinner at the captain's table, as well as the opportunity of meeting Freddie Fruitless, was causing quite a stir in her heart.

Polly woke up from her catnap to discover time was marching on and she had less than an hour to get ready for her dinner engagement. She decided that she still had plenty of time to run a bath. And as she happily lay soaking in a cloud of jasmine-scented bubbles, her hand reached for the soap dish. As she scooped the dish contents into her hand, she realized that she was not holding soap but another rather large pebble covered in frothy bubbles. She immediately brushed the bubbles away with her fingers and, as she looked at the pebble, she could see a word gouged into the glassy surface. The letters spelled out the word *kindness* in beautifully scripted writing.

Polly did not react at all, for she had become very used to weird and strange things happening, so she just placed it on the side of the bath and determined to put it with the rest of the smooth pebbles in her backpack as soon as she was out of the bath and dry. This new find also served as a little reminder that it was time to write in her gold diary about all the amazing things she had seen on her travels. Oh, and she must not forget to mention that she was now on board the *Queen Mary* and was going to meet her dream hero, the wonderful Freddie Fruitless and the Backsliders.

Polly wasted no time in getting dry, and with a big, white, fluffy towel wrapped around her torso and a smaller, equally fluffy towel wrapped in a turban around her head, she headed for the bed where her schoolbag still lay. She wished to write down her first impressions of the *Queen Mary* and Hector Humdinger. Polly was both surprised and delighted to see that a lovely new dress and matching shoes had been placed on her bed. She read the little note attached to the dress.

Dear Polly,

It's been a real pleasure meeting you. I hope you enjoy your journey home on the Queen Mary, and do please try to stay out of trouble. If and when we meet again, I hope you will have taken up tennis as a hobby, because exercise is good for the soul as well as the body. See you at Wimbledon! I will save you a strawberry...or two!

Best Wishes,

Captain Phinsof

P. S. Hope you like the dress and shoes; Amanda and Annabel picked them out for you, as, rather cheekily, they didn't altogether trust my fashion sense!

Polly smiled and folded up the note to safely tuck amongst her belongings. Then after much rummaging through her bag, she finally produced her pen and the little gold book, which she opened at a fresh page this time. As pen touched paper, words somewhat magically appeared on the fresh white page. Polly dropped her pen and began to read each line as it appeared on the page before her very eyes.

———•••———

The princess had successfully completed her trip of a lifetime, and in doing so, she had experienced the highest level of luxury: flying around the world on Concorde. She had sampled international cuisine with all its delicacies and eaten like a queen. She experienced the delight of being waited on hand and foot by the lovely Amanda and Annabel. She had for the first time tasted what it was like to be a real princess, and she had enjoyed every moment of it. She had also proven that she could be trusted with such privileges, as she ignored her own natural desire to shop until she dropped. The princess had chosen instead to reach into the hearts of all the poor and abandoned that she met in each city, giving them comfort and hope in whatever small way she could.

She had, however, experienced a few hiccups on the way, such as locking herself in the washroom until her outrageous demands were met, thereby giving not only dear Captain Plimsol great grief, but also Colonel Slaughterhouse, who was only appeased by receiving a very nice pot of tea with cakes for all his trouble. However, she had learned through all her mistakes that threats and tantrums are clearly no way to resolve any crisis, and sometimes invaluable lessons can only be learned the hard way.

She had also ignored the blisters on her swollen feet and quite rightly resisted asking for a mobility car similar to that of the Pope's to get herself around the various cities. She was, after all, unlike the Pope: very

POLLY BROWN

young and in need of regular exercise, so such a mode of transport would have been considered a most self-indulgent request, and therefore quite out of the question. She had begun to understand that there is no gain without pain, and for this she had earned an award for great kindness in the form of a pebble.

The princess now found herself sailing back to England on none other than the luxury British liner named the Queen Mary. She would now find herself socializing and dining with the upper echelons of society, and it was up to the princess as to whether she allowed such things to go to her head or not. She would spend the next few days in the lap of luxury, but there would also be challenges. Would the princess heed the warning that not all things are as they seem? Also the princess would have to make the hard choice between continuing her search for Piadora (something she had seemingly abandoned, at least for the present) in preference to joining up and traveling the globe with Freddie Fruitless and his entourage. This would be a difficult choice for her to make, as the pop stars' lives seemed so intoxicatingly exciting, and in truth, she, like many others, had come to utterly idolize this gorgeous hunk of a man. Only time would tell which choice the princess would make.

Polly closed the gold book and carefully placed it back in her schoolbag along with her pen. She then dried her hair and put on her new dress and shoes before picking up Langdon and heading out of the door. On her way out of the cabin she suddenly remembered she had forgotten to take the pebble from the bathroom. She rushed back and picked it up and then placed it in her bag along with the other pebbles for safekeeping. She then closed the cabin door and headed quickly to the dining room. For she did not wish to keep Captain Hector Humdinger waiting.

The doors leading into the dining room where opened by two footmen who bowed as she entered. Polly giggled out of embarrassment as she found the pomp and ceremony a little bit excessive for her liking. Once in the dining room Polly found herself instantly mesmerized by the many breathtakingly magnificent chandeliers, as well as the impeccably-decorated banqueting tables that stretched as far as the eye could see.

"Absolutely exquisite," followed by, "fit for a king," was all she could mutter under her breath as she felt a rush of excitement that this night was going to be a truly special occasion, never to be repeated. As far as the eye could see there were long tables covered in pristine white tableclothes. They were adorned by the most visually stunning floral displays that dominated each table, and each display included just about every flower on the planet, which exuded the most delightful fragrances that filled the air with their sweetness. Each individual table had many tall and elaborately decorated elegant silver candelabras, with lighted candles that significantly added to the sense of grandeur and splendor of the dining room.

As Polly's eyes scanned the long tables, she could see that every place setting had more than the usual amount of silver cutlery, and she guessed this was because the guests would make their way through endless different courses, similar to that of Uncle Boritz's lavish New Year's Eve dinners, only better. Every setting had a number of different sized handcut crystal glasses that gleamed under the lighting, and each setting had a personalized card with the name of each guest written on in beautiful lettering. In one corner of the room a string quartet was preparing to sit down and start entertaining the guests with sweet music. Many of the musicians were tightening their strings. As her eyes continued to feast on all the glitz and glamour of this banqueting hall, Polly found herself being escorted to the head table, where Captain Humdinger was already standing ready to welcome each guest that had been invited to join him at his table.

"Good evening, Polly" said the captain with a warm and most welcoming smile as he beckoned her to take a seat right beside him.

Polly smiled back before sliding as graciously as she was able onto the chair which had been pulled away from the table by one of the waiters.

"Well, Polly, you are in for a treat tonight, for the food on this ship is simply superb," grinned the captain before declaring, "I am so hungry I could eat a whole stuffed pig."

As Polly pictured the captain with bib and tucker under chin, and knife and fork ready to dig into a whole pig on an enormous silver platter, she made a grimace. The captain laughed and then went on to explain that his tennis match with Captain Plimsol had gone on for hours, because both were equally determined to win.

"We pretty much played a whole tournament!" declared the captain enthusiastically. "Right now I could eat a horse."

"Who won?" inquired Polly gingerly.

"Me, of course," said Captain Humdinger with a huge grin. "Captain Plimsol is a fine player, but he is no match for me, and I do have the added advantage of having tennis courts on this ship," he confided. "I therefore have ample opportunity to improve my serve, although at times it has been a close shave. However, the day he does win will be the day I give up being the captain of this ship, although I have no intention of retiring from this beauty for many years to come," he said with a glint in his eye. "Until that day comes, he will have to face losing every game." With that said, Captain Humdinger picked up his glass of sherry and raised it in the air. "A toast to Captain Plimsol and many more games of tennis," he said gleefully before downing the sherry in one triumphant gulp.

Just then more of the captain's guests arrived and stood in line waiting to be greeted by him. Soon the captain's table was filled with the exception of four chairs that remained unoccupied. Polly soon discovered that these vacant seats were for her wonderful pop idol Freddie Fruitless and his backing group of female vocalists.

The captain ordered a member of the waiting staff to go in search of them as it was not good etiquette to keep all his other guests waiting any longer. The waiter nodded his agreement and left the dining hall, noting their cabin numbers on a small slip of paper before leaving. Eventually the waiter returned looking slightly disheveled and harassed and whispered something into the captain's ear. Polly watched as the captain nodded, saying, "I see," repeatedly in response to the information he was being given by the waiter. At one point he seemed to raise an eyebrow as if somewhat concerned. He then thanked the waiter and turned to address his table of guests, stroking his whiskers as he spoke.

"It appears that our guests of honor know little about the code of conduct we enjoy on this ship. They have been quite rude to members of my staff who were sent to advise them that we are all sitting here awaiting their presence at this table." The captain paused to clear his throat and then continued, "But it appears that when you are a rich pop star you no longer need to live by the same courtesies as the rest of us. I therefore suggest that we refill our glasses with some more Chateau Latour and let the banquet commence."

"Hear, hear!" came the unanimous response from the very hungry guests.

The banquet was a most sumptuous feast of every imaginable delicacy, ranging from caviar to fresh lobster. Polly declined the Pâté de Foie Gras, as well as the gleaming black lumpy stuff. She also declined the roast pheasant and stuffed pigeon, but luckily, and much to her relief, she noted that English rib of beef with horseradish sauce was also on the menu. Her decision made, in no time at all Polly was happily tucking into a large serving of roast beef with fresh vegetables, at the same time helping herself not to one or two, but three large Yorkshire puddings to accompany the meat on her plate. Polly was almost through her second helping of sherry trifle topped with ice cream and fresh cream when Freddie and his entourage finally made their very belated entrance into the dining hall.

Polly observed that Freddie seemed in a most foul mood as he made his way across to the table, pushing aside every waiter that attempted to greet him. His female backing group seemed equally out of sorts, their long faces hanging in the deepest of sulks as they followed behind him. The captain stood up from his seat to person-ally greet them, but Freddie dismissed him in a most abrasive manner before rather rudely flinging himself down into the seat the waiter had just pulled out from under the table.

Over the next hour Polly watched as the churlish group constantly complained that this or that was not right, or the homemade soup was too cold and then too hot as overstretched waiters sought to keep them happy. Finally, after the group had drunk exorbitant volumes of Chateau Latour, as well as equal volumes of vintage Krug Champagne, they finally appeared to relax and settle down. Polly took this opportunity to introduce herself.

"Hi, Freddie. I am Polly, and I think I'm your number one fan. I really love you. I think you're wonderful, really I do."

Freddie smirked, for he was a little taken aback and also slightly amused that this young lady should be so innocent and forthright in her manner.

"Wow, that's really great, Polly," he said, smiling as he spoke. "It's good to know that you have such good taste."

Over the next course—which Polly declined, as it was a lot of smelly cheese accompanied by savory biscuits and served with a glass of port—she discovered why Freddie was in such a bad mood.

"One of my female backers has just told me she intends to quit as soon as the ship docks in England," he angrily confided. "Now where am I going to find myself another singer at such short notice?"

Before Polly could come up with a suggestion, Freddie raised an arm high into the air and clicked his fingers as he tried to get one of the waiters' immediate attention. A waiter obliged and rushed to his side.

"Is there anything more I can get you, sir?" he asked very politely.

"Yes, there is. You can fill up my glass with more port," Freddie said, waving his glass under the waiter's nose. "And by the way, what on earth do you call this?" he snapped as he prodded the food on his plate before stabbing his index finger into the middle of a soft creamy cheese.

"It's called cheese, sir, and I believe that's the French brie you have just stuck your finger into," answered the waiter very patiently.

"Yes, you dumb fool, I can see that," sneered Freddie impatiently. "But I can also see that this cheese is not fit for half-starved mice to eat, let alone humans. Besides, it stinks, you half wit."

"I'm sorry, sir, but it is supposed to look and smell like that," responded the waiter with polite firmness.

"Well, I don't care. Go and get me some more, and hurry up," snapped Freddie, who was becoming more irate by the moment.

"Certainly sir," replied the waiter, keeping his dignity as he discreetly whipped the offending plate of cheeses from under Freddie's nose in a most professional manner before heading off in the direction of the kitchen.

"Right, now where was I?" said Freddie as he attempted to compose himself. "I do so hate having to deal with the riffraff, and it seems to me that most waiters and hotel staff fall into that category," he remarked, raising his eyes into his head to show total boredom before tossing his head back and running his fingers through his hair.

Polly chose to ignore his inflammatory remarks, preferring to believe that he was just upset and therefore having an off day. "Everybody is allowed one of those once in a while," she thought to herself in an effort to excuse Freddie's atrocious behavior.

"Yes, Polly, I was in the middle of telling you that I am about to lose one of my female vocalists, wasn't I?"

"Yes, you were." Polly then hesitated for a moment before blurting out, "But, Freddie, I may have the perfect solution to your problem."

"Go on. I'm listening," said Freddie.

"Well, Freddie, I could help out if you like," said Polly very enthusiastically.

"What? You?" retorted Freddie, throwing his head back further and laughing out loud. "I may be desperate, but not that desperate!"

"Don't laugh at me like that," said Polly, choosing to ignore his insult. "I can sing, really I can. I have sung in a choir for the last couple of years. So give me a chance," she pleaded before adding, "Would you like me to sing something now? I am more than happy to sing any one of your songs, for I know all the words by heart," she innocently asked, feeling very excited.

"No thanks, although I'm sure your voice can't be much worse than listening to the strains of Bach coming from over there," he said scornfully, at the same time pointing a finger offensively in the direction of the string quartet. "But spare me the honor, for I have had enough grief today. Besides, I'm very tired and a little worse for wear, for even their wine is pretty disgusting," he groaned as he downed the last dregs of the wine and crashed the crystal glass back down on the table.

He then held onto the table as he levered himself up from his chair, grabbing hold of the tablecloth as he did so. The tablecloth and the unused cutlery started to come off the table and crashed to the floor. All the guests present in the dining room turned to look in their direction, including one gentleman who reached out to prevent the large floral display from toppling over. Finally, Freddie staggered across the dining room, stumbling into a dining hall pillar as he attempted to make his way out of the dining hall, struggling like a blind man to see his way to the exit.

Captain Humdinger watched, stroking his beard while he patiently observed the young, hedonistic star. On this occasion he chose to hold his tongue and say nothing. Oh, he was indeed more than willing to step in and order Freddie and his band out of his dining room. There was no denying that he would have done so if Freddie had uttered one more offensive word to any of his guests or staff, but for the moment he decided to allow wisdom to take its course and wait for an opportune moment, something he knew would not be long in coming.

Despite Freddie's rather sad behavior, Polly really enjoyed the evening. The captain had been very amusing and witty, telling one joke after another. The food also had been delicious, and the wine had flowed all night, although, I hasten to add, none in Polly's direction. She had pineapple and orange juice all evening, and this was much more to her liking.

Finally, great tiredness swept over her, and she could no longer keep her eyes open, at least not without the help of matchsticks. After thanking Captain Humdinger for his wonderful hospitality, she excused herself and Langdon and left the dining hall to make her way to the cabin and bed.

On her way down the long corridor she heard shouting, and she very quickly determined that it was coming from the first-class cabin suite of none other than Freddie Fruitless. Polly crept nearer to find out exactly what was going on. As she neared the door, it was suddenly flung open, and a young female member of staff was forced out of the door and into the corridor. Her bucket with cleaning materials followed after her, the contents spilling all over the floor. Polly went over to the young girl and placed her arm on her shoulder before asking her what the problem was.

"He's been sick everywhere, and I've been instructed to clean it up and change his sheets. But he is completely out of control and keeps shouting offensive words at me," the young girl whimpered. "I am so afraid that if he complains to the management, then I will lose my job," she cried.

Polly gave her a sympathetic hug. "Stay here a minute, and I will see if I can get some sense out of him," Polly gently ordered the maid.

Polly knocked on the cabin door, but Freddie chose to ignore her. Polly would not be beaten and continued to knock.

"Go away, you miscreant. You are giving me a headache!" he shouted, adding a few more obscenities intended to demoralize the girls and get them to stop harassing him.

"I'm going nowhere until you let me in," Polly defiantly retaliated. "This poor girl has a job to do, and you are preventing her from doing it. So please do the right thing and let us in, and I promise we will be out of your cabin in no time at all." Still there was complete silence, so Polly continued knocking only harder.

Eventually, Freddie ran out of steam as well as expletives, and he found himself forced into opening the cabin door and agreeing to let Polly and the maid inside as long as the job of clearing up was done quickly as well as to his liking. Polly wasted no time in grabbing the young girl's hand and hauled her, along with her bucket of cleaning agents, back into the cabin.

"We are going to get through this together," she whispered to the young girl. "For as we all know, many hands make light work. Wait here, for I just need to put Langdon down on the coffee table, and then we can get started."

As Polly and the maid cleared up, Freddie Fruitless continued to be sick. Eventually he crashed down onto the leather sofa and passed out, leaving Polly and the maid thoroughly relieved. They retraced his steps, stooping down low to clean up his pungent mess.

Finally, the cabin was clean and his bed made up with fresh linen. Then with a number of squirts from a can of room freshener

POLLY BROWN

the room was once again as fresh as a daisy. With Freddie still out for the count and sprawled across the sofa, the girls took the opportunity to exit the room as quickly and quietly as possible. Outside his room, the maid hugged Polly.

"Thank you. You are so kind," she said with a sweet smile.

"Nonsense," Polly retorted as she gave the maid's hand a tight squeeze. "I am sure you would have done the same for me. And listen, if you need my help again, don't hesitate to give me a call. I'm in cabin 27 B, on D deck."

The maid squeezed Polly's hand tightly and said good night before quickly heading back to her quarters as fast as her legs would take her. As Polly placed Langdon between the fresh linen sheets and climbed into bed, she found herself hoping that Freddie's behavior was just an out-of-character blip. She certainly hoped so, for everyone's sake.

The next day found Polly and Langdon stretched out on deck chairs on the promenade deck, for the weather was perfect with just a hint of a breeze. Later the same day Polly found herself joined by a lovely Scottish woman who introduced herself as Roberta before drawing up a deckchair to join her. Polly was glad of the company, and before long they were deep in conversation. Polly was amazed to learn that Roberta was on her way back to England from a little-known place in Africa where she had set up a medical center to rescue young girls from the street. She was also amazed by Roberta's bravery and courage, as there had been much opposition from local people who were losing serious money. There were now considerably fewer young girls to sell into slavery.

"What made you give up your life and comforts to go and help them?" Polly asked wide-eyed and full of curiosity.

Roberta did not hesitate in her reply as she explained that she had simply read an article and been so moved with compassion that she had felt the deepest compulsion to sell all she had and get out there to rescue these defenseless children.

"All this was some fifteen years ago," she informed Polly. "But I am now on my way back to England, as my funds have run out. I am not entirely certain at this present time what to do next, but

I am confident that I will find new ways of funding my project; I certainly hope so for the children's sakes as well as mine."

Polly could only admire Roberta for her fortitude and courage to abandon all her comforts and be so selfless, and she hoped that by some unforeseeable means the money would flood in and thereby greatly encourage Roberta to continue her clinic. As they talked on, two odd-looking females that looked more like penguins walked towards them, stopping by their chair to greet them.

"Good afternoon, Roberta," greeted one of the ladies, who was rather unusually dressed from head to toe in a habit. Polly recognized the outfit as being similar to that of the nuns who had taken her on that fateful holiday to the campsite, so she determined that these two ladies were indeed nuns from some different order.

Roberta looked up and placed her hand over her brow to shield her eyes from the sun before acknowledging the greeting.

"Oh, hi, Sister Thomasina and Sister Augustus. Why don't you come and join us? There are plenty of chairs available," she added before jumping up from her seat and pulling up a couple of empty deck chairs.

"We would love to join you, but not before you introduce us to your young friend," said Sister Thomasina with a warm smile.

"Of course, I apologize for being so rude. This is Polly Brown, and her elephant is called Langdon. That's correct, isn't it, Polly?" said Roberta with a slight note of hesitancy. She hoped she had remembered the elephant's name correctly.

Polly nodded and then stuck out a hand to shake both ladies' hands consecutively. Both sisters sat down, and before long they were all deep in conversation. Polly again found herself very taken with these two nuns, for they had traveled the world many times over and, just like Roberta, they had sacrificed everything to help the poor and needy. As she listened to their stories she found herself laughing because both sisters had so many amusing stories to recount. As they spoke of their exploits, Polly noticed that although most of their head was covered their faces shone.

"Sister Augustus, please tell Polly the story of when you almost got eaten by a crocodile," goaded Sister Thomasina, giggling as she gave her companion a little nudge in the ribs.

"Oh, I don't think I had better tell her that one. Surely not," replied Sister Augustus in barely a whisper before breaking out into loud laughter.

"Oh, go on. Please tell the story, for I am certain Polly would love to hear how moments after you had asked our good Lord to provide some food for the hungry villagers you ended up wrestling in the water with the crocodile. Tell her how you punched it in the eye just as it was about to take you under," cried Sister Thomasina as her eyes filled up with water due to too much laughter.

"I don't think it's an appropriate story for Polly to hear," retorted Sister Augustus in a slightly tongue-in-cheek manner. "After all, what will she think of me when she hears that not only did I punch it in the eye but that my powerful punch by some miracle killed the little whippersnapper instantly?" she said snapping her fingers to add dramatic impact to her story.

Sister Augustus began to laugh so much that tears were streaming down her cheeks. "And I have to say we cooked the most wonderful crocodile stew that fed all the African villagers for a whole week!" she informed her captive audience as seriously as she was able, for by now she was scrunched up with laughing and beginning to cough. "Now, doesn't the good Lord work in mysterious ways, His wonders to perform?" she stated before cracking up again, this time holding her belly even tighter.

They were quite a spectacle to behold, the four of them sitting in deckchairs holding their aching stomachs as they laughed and laughed some more at both of the sisters' antics. Up until this moment in time, Polly had no idea that nuns had any sense of humor at all, and better still, could be such fun and so entertaining. She also found it hard to imagine that they could keep their sense of humor and joyful perspective on life when their travels often took them to some of the darkest places on the globe where hope was often in very short supply.

The ladies were interrupted by a steward with a tray that held a large pot of tea and a plate of wickedly fattening cream cakes. Sister Augustus quickly sobered up as she attempted to pour the tea from the pot into the rather delicate bone china cups without making any splashes, as she had not the slightest wish to accidentally scald anyone with hot tea. And as they all sipped their refreshing tea, Sister Augustus took on a more serious tone of voice.

"Polly, did you know that the three richest people in the world now control more wealth than all six hundred million people living in the least-developed countries?"

"Surely not," replied Polly, rather surprised by this revelation.

"Yes, sadly this is a statistical fact, isn't it, Sister Thomasina?" Her friend nodded in Polly's direction. "And all we can do is use the money and talents that we are given to help those who come our way. Yes, some might say that there are those who have already had their reward on Earth while others, like dear Roberta here, will have to wait until heaven to receive theirs," she added with a sigh.

"And until that time, we must joyfully do all we can within our power with the knowledge that we are making a difference, albeit small," interrupted Sister Thomasina with a warm smile. "Now drink up, Polly, for your tea is getting cold, and do me the kindness of eating the last gooey chocolate éclair before I completely lose all willpower and devour it myself," she said laughingly as she pushed the plate toward Polly.

Polly willingly obliged, for she had been eyeing up the last cake for quite some time but had not wished to appear too greedy. Polly quickly polished off the éclair in a matter of seconds and was handed a paper napkin by Roberta to wipe off all traces of chocolate that still lingered around her mouth.

Roberta then turned toward the sisters and suggested a good stroll around the deck might well be in order to burn up some calories. The sisters agreed and invited Polly to join them. As they walked and breathed in the fresh air, they passed Freddie Fruitless's cabin suite, and again, they sadly witnessed a terrible commotion. This time it was the steward falling out of the cabin door backwards, with a plate of cakes following closely behind. Both steward and cakes landed sprawled out over the deck. The sisters helped the poor gentleman to his feet while Roberta and Polly scraped up whatever they could of the squashed cakes from the floor of the deck.

"Not, I presume, to his majesty's liking!" remarked Sister Thomasina to the steward before giving him a friendly little wink.

The steward gave a wry smile back and nodded before thanking them for their help. He then headed back towards the kitchen.

The ladies continued their walk, talking and laughing as they made their way along the decks.

"Have you seen all there is to see on this ship, Polly?" inquired Roberta.

Polly confessed that she had spent most of her time in the cabin with Langdon as they tried to catch up on their sleep, but she said she intended to go to the theater that night because *The Sound of Music* was showing.

"Do you like the musical, Polly?" asked Sister Thomasina.

"Like it? I love it!" said Polly, somewhat overenthusiastically. "I watched it at least five times with Captain Plimsol, for it was also one of his favorite films," she informed them.

"Well, what's your favorite bit in the film?" interrupted Sister Augustus.

Polly did not have to think too long. "It has to be the bit where Mother Superior sings 'Climb every Mountain,'" replied Polly without the tiniest bit of hesitation.

Without any warning Sister Augustus began to sing the song, and Polly could not help smiling, for she sang it with just as much passion as the Mother Superior had done in the film. Polly joined in the finale. They then all broke out into uncontrollable fits of the giggles.

"Oh dear, Polly, you really must take on board all the advice of that wonderful song and follow every highway until your dreams become a reality, and they will," she enthused before taking on a more serious tone of voice. "Yes, they will, Polly, if you follow them with all your heart, never giving up on yourself or your dreams," she said, patting Polly on her head as she spoke.

Roberta then broke into the conversation, offering to take Polly and the sisters on a guided tour of the ship before dinner, and so they all agreed to congregate in one of the lounges later that day.

Soon the time arrived for Polly to meet up with her new friends, so with Langdon tucked under one arm, she headed for the agreed meet-up point. The others were already there and waiting. Roberta made an excellent tour guide, and as they walked together she informed her little group of many fascinating facts concerning the ship.

"Did you know that this beautiful ocean liner was built in my country?" she asked them. The group admitted that they had no idea where it had been built.

"Oh yes, Scotland may be just a wee place, but we know how to build big. Yes, she was built in Clydebank for Cunard, and her maiden voyage took place on May 27, 1936."

The group remained silent just listening to Roberta as she continued to provide them with fact after fact concerning the history of the vessel. "She has over two thousand portholes, and the weight of her anchor is a mere forty-five tons."

"Wow!" exclaimed Polly. "That is some anchor!"

"Yes, Polly, and I'll have you know that she has twelve decks; the one we were sunbathing on this morning was the promenade deck, and its length is an awesome 28.19 meters long. She has 27 boilers, so think how many men are working in unbearably hot conditions as they continuously fuel these boilers."

"It doesn't bear thinking about," replied Polly before adding, "That's one job I would really hate to do."

"Well, thank goodness you're a refined, genteel lady," interrupted Sister Augustus, "and such things are left in the hands of strong, capable men."

Polly smiled, for it was the first time in her life that she had been addressed as a refined young lady, and she liked it.

"Yes, I think we must thank the good Lord that He made us the fairer sex and, therefore, more delicate," declared Sister Thomasina, raising her eyes upwards as she spoke.

"Did you know that Sir Winston Churchill has been a guest on this ship a number of times?" announced Roberta very cheerfully. "And as well as that, during the war she was used to carry the wounded back home to American soil. This majestic and powerful vessel carried home almost thirteen thousand G. I. brides and their children. Now that's a wonderfully romantic fact, isn't it, Polly?"

Polly nodded, preferring to remain quiet, for she was really enjoying soaking up all Roberta's fascinating facts as they wandered around the magnificent vessel. As they toured the first-class galley, they stopped to look at a huge oil painting that depicted a peaceful

English landscape. Roberta stopped in her tracks, her eyes momentarily lingering as she took in the magnificence of the scene.

"Oh, how I love England, for it is truly a beautiful place. I wonder if after all these years it will still look the same," she said before wistfully adding, "although I have to confess to you ladies that I love Scotland more."

"And so you should," Sister Augustus chipped in. "After all, it is your birthplace, and we all tend to have a soft spot for the place we were born, don't we, Polly?" Polly remained silent, and this only encouraged Sister Augustus to probe a little deeper. "Come to think of it, Polly, where in England were you born?" she asked most innocently.

Polly shrugged her shoulders before admitting that she had no idea where she had been born. She then confessed that she had very little information regarding any part of her life and that this made her feel as if she had a huge hole inside her.

Sister Augustus took the opportunity to give Polly's hand a little squeeze before informing her, "It matters not a jot or tittle where you came from, Polly. What truly matters is where you will end up, and I do believe many doors will open up for you in the future, so be sure to keep in touch. Promise me you will."

Polly promised all present to write to them, and the sisters promised to continually remember Polly in their prayers. Polly felt touched by their kindness.

They were nearing the end of their tour when they passed by a large room. Polly peered through the door just as Roberta informed the group that this was a casino. It was a place where gentlemen played card games and where those with more money than sense could, if they so desired, gamble away vast fortunes of their wealth.

On hearing the word *money*, Polly turned to Roberta, asking her to hold onto Langdon. Then quick as a flash, she abandoned the group and raced into the room. Before anyone could stop her, she grabbed a chair and climbed up to stand on it. Once upright, she then shouted at the top of her voice.

"Gentlemen, please can I have your attention."

Roberta and the two sisters could only stand at the door with jaws dropped, watching and wondering to themselves what on earth this sassy young girl was going to do and say next. They did not have to wait too long to find out.

To be honest, as Polly stood on the chair, she too had little idea as to quite what she intended to say. She just knew she had to say something, especially since all eyes were now on her. Everyone was quite puzzled as they waited to hear what this young girl had to say that was of such importance that she had interrupted their enjoyment.

Polly cleared her throat and opened her mouth, and then all that was in her tender heart just began to flow.

"Gentlemen, I apologize for interrupting you in this manner, but I beg you to give me just a few minutes of your time and hear me out. I am on my way home after traveling around the world, and on my travels I have seen firsthand the terrible amount of suffering that exists in so many cities and countries all over the world. Many children have little or no food, and most do not even have the privilege of clean drinking water. I have witnessed such a great level of suffering, and I have felt completely powerless to do anything to help."

Polly felt the tears start to sprout from her eyes, but she did nothing to prevent them from coming, and as they spilled down her cheeks and splashed on her shoes, she still continued to address her stunned audience. Polly addressed her audience with passion and eloquence well beyond her years; so much so that no one could fail to be touched by her words. Even the sisters found themselves lifting up the white bibs of their habits to have a good sniffle.

She spoke with immense clarity and compassion as she relived her jail sentence with Pedro and his Brazilian friends, and she then went on to tell them all about the streets of India and South Africa. Amazingly, her audience remained spellbound as she then spoke of children in orphanages in England and revealed hidden truths about their suffering, much of which remained hidden behind closed doors. By the close of her rather lengthy speech there was hardly a dry eye in the place. Roberta and the sisters remained standing in the doorway, their jaws still gaping and their eyes firmly glued on Polly, for she was nowhere near finished!

"Gentlemen, I have recently been informed that the three richest people in the world now control more wealth than all six hundred million people living in the least developed countries. Now I ask you, is that not a sad and startling piece of information? And today I would implore each of you to search your hearts and ask yourselves this question: can I take all my wealth with me when I die? And hopefully the answer to that one is an overwhelming NO. Then ask yourself this one: after I'm gone, will there be occasion to bitterly regret keeping all that I owned to myself? You see, gentlemen, God above may have blessed you with abundant wealth, and He most certainly is not against us using money to have good fun and frolics, however, I have come to believe that He intended the fortunate among us to use some of our excess wealth to help and relieve those in dire need."

Polly paused to take a breath, and she used the opportunity to ask someone to fetch a wastebasket. Roberta immediately obliged by bending down and picking up the wastebasket that was near the door exit. She then cautiously made her way over to where Polly still stood on the chair and handed it to her.

"Go for it, girl," she whispered encouragingly.

Polly took the basket from Roberta, and with a big broad smile on her face remarked that she fully intended to. Roberta then quietly tiptoed her way back to the exit door to once again join the sisters.

"Now, I know I have probably offended some of you here by challenging you in this unusual manner. But as you lay down your next wad of money in a bid to win or perhaps lose more, think about this. You have no idea how many days you have left on this earth, for all our days are, I believe, numbered. And this money may or may not make you considerably richer than you already are, but the greatest reward that provokes our Father in heaven to shine on you is for you to give generously out of the abundance of your hearts.

"So, gentlemen, with that in mind, I implore you this day to exercise those heart muscles and urge you to open up your fat wallets out of concern and deep compassion for others to give to such a cause as I have spoken of."

Polly paused and cleared her throat, using this brief interlude to scan the room for pockets of resistance to her heartfelt speech. It appeared there was none. "I would also like to leave you with one final thought that Sister Thomasina mentioned to me earlier in the day, and that thought is, 'God is no man's debtor.'"

Polly quietly got down from the chair, and then with the basket in her hand, she boldly walked up to every gentleman in the room, brazenly placing the basket right in front of their noses. Some gave rather reluctantly, not wishing their friends to consider them stingy, and others wiped tears from their faces as they generously emptied out the entire contents of their wallets. Some preferred to write checks, and as Polly stood over them waiting, they found themselves changing the amount to higher, then even higher amounts before scrawling their signatures on the bottom. As Polly strolled around the room one could hear a pin drop, for with the exception of scribbling on open checkbooks, the room remained utterly silent.

Suddenly two croupiers, along with a number of stewards, arrived in the room, and upon seeing their potential profits going into a wastebasket instead of the usual company coffers, they furiously marched toward Polly, harshly ordering her to stop. Of course Polly had not given her speech for nothing, so she was not about to hand over her wastebasket stuffed with money and checks. With this in mind she ran around the room as fast as she could in her effort to avoid being captured. Neither the stewards nor the croupiers were a match for her, and they soon found themselves quite out of breath.

Polly used their lack of stamina to her advantage and made a dash for the exit door where the sisters still stood alongside Roberta. As she passed through the door, she breathlessly whispered to Sister Augustus, "Here, take this."

The good sister quickly and happily obliged by hastily tucking the wastebasket under her habit for safety. She knew with unmistakable certainty that no steward or croupier would wish to personally search her, a sister of mercy, in pursuit of the missing basket. Yes, that would be unthinkable! The sisters and Roberta remained standing wide-eyed and innocent by the exit door as they waited to see what would happen next.

The croupiers and stewards quickly congregated to devise a strategy before leaving by the exit door to split up and go in search of the girl and the basket of money. Happily, after many hours of searching, they were still unable to discover her hiding place, perhaps because the ship was so big and therefore plentiful in secret places to hide away without being discovered. Anyway, they were sadly forced to abandon the hunt for Polly and go back to their normal duties.

"We are certain to meet up with her at dinner," one of the stewards reassured the forlorn croupiers. "And then she will have a lot of explaining to do."

All the staff involved in the treasure hunt were greatly comforted by the belief that Polly could not hide away forever. She would be caught and then they would get the money back.

Polly was nowhere to be seen when dinner was served and neither was Freddie Fruitless or any of his entourage. Captain Humdinger had paid them a visit, and after a good dressing down they had been encouraged to have dinner in their cabin. Whether this offended Freddie was entirely irrelevant, for this was, after all, the captain's ship and his word was gospel.

What precise words were exchanged between them will never be known, except that Freddie's side of the argument was littered with angry and unmentionable expletives. Captain Humdinger, on the other hand, stood firm by his decision and with the greatest determination conveyed to Freddie that neither himself nor his entourage were welcome at his table on this voyage or any other where he was personally in command of the ship.

Roberta took it upon herself to make up a plate of food and go in search of Polly, for she had some idea where she would be hiding. The money was never recovered, and Captain Humdinger, when informed by the stewards of her outrageous exploits, did nothing but smile to himself as he secretly found himself thinking, "Well done, Polly. You really do have all the hallmarks of a true princess." He then called over a waiter and discreetly whispered in his ear a request for him to come back with a dustpan and brush, for some strange-looking feathers were mysteriously gathering under the table at which he was sitting.

It was in the dead of the night before Polly came out of her hiding place and stealthily crept back to her cabin. She found Langdon perched on her bed along with a large plate of food and a little note from Roberta.

Dear Polly,

What you did was extremely brave, and I am very proud of you. I have returned Langdon, and I need to tell you that the sisters have been to see Captain Humdinger, and he has no problem at all with what you did. He insisted that the sisters keep hold of the money and share it out with me, for he knows every penny of it will be spent easing the suffering of others. God bless you, little precious one. Perhaps one of your dreams should be that of a public speaker? Think about it!

Love,

Roberta

P. S. I hope you like the food I selected for you. Happy eating!

While she was munching her way through the plate of food, there was a knock on the door. Polly jumped up and went to open it. She was both very surprised and delighted to discover her late night visitor was Freddie. Freddie wasted no time in getting to the point of his visit.

"Polly, you say you can sing. Well, if you're as good as you say, would you like to come back with me to my suite and give me a note or two so I can decide whether or not to sign you up?"

Polly was surprised by her sudden hesitancy as she struggled to come up with a direct yes or no.

"Look, Polly," cried Freddie, a little irritated at her lack of enthusiasm. "Who else is going to give you this sort of opportunity? It's not as though you are pretty to look at," he commented disparagingly as he looked her up and down. "In fact, I've seen better ends on buses," he muttered under his breath. "So if I were you, I would jump at this momentous opportunity to come on tour with me."

Still Polly held back.

"Oh, come on, Polly. There isn't a young girl in the world who wouldn't throw themselves at me and accept such a wonderful offer! So don't make this hard for me. I'm running out of time."

Freddie paused as he searched her face for a hint of hope. Still Polly showed no sign of excitement at his amazing proposal.

"Polly, give me your answer. I need it now," he urged, putting on the charm as he spoke.

Polly drew a deep breath as she weighed up the pros and cons of this sudden and most unexpected invitation.

Finally she responded. "Freddie, much as I adore your music, I feel I must say no to your kind offer."

Freddie looked positively stunned. Nobody had ever refused him anything, especially a little skinny girl with crooked teeth and wobbly eyes! Who did she think she was to turn HIM, the famous Freddie Fruitless, down and without any reasonable explanation why?

"I don't understand," he angrily muttered. "Only yesterday you were falling at my feet to offer your services, and now you have the cheek to change your mind. I'm not only flabbergasted, but also really offended," he stormed. "And I think I can safely say that you will live to regret this stupid decision of yours."

"Look, I'm so sorry, Freddie, but truth is I have other plans."

"Oh, and what precisely might they be?" Freddie said frostily. "Go on; tell me."

"Well, before I tell you my plans, Freddie, I feel I need to be honest with you and say that I have found your attitude towards others, the staff in particular, really terrible and very ungracious. I am therefore fairly certain that I would find your childish tantrums pretty impossible to cope with if I were to join you on the road.

"Secondly, and more importantly, I am on my way to a place called Piadora, and I'm already terribly late getting there."

Freddie roared out loud. "Piadora? The place doesn't exist, you dim-witted fool," he said sourly.

"Oh, but it does," she answered with a gentle smile.

"Well, you're truly pathetic if you believe such nonsense," Freddie snorted. "I think *pathetic* sums you up nicely. Indeed 'Polly Pathetic,' has a nice ring about it, don't you think?"

Polly took a deep breath, and chose to refrain from hitting back with anything similarly insulting.

"Yes, Freddie, it may well sum me up, for there's no denying that I am a bit of a wimp, and at times I hate myself for it. But at least I am not trying to be something I'm not," she meekly replied.

"Well, you're the last person to speak when it comes to being something you're not, you hypocrite," exploded Freddie. "Here you are traveling around the world, acting like Mother Teresa, and stuffing your high-and-mighty moralistic values into everyone's faces, Miss Polly Perfect. And yes, I did get to hear about your touching little speech," he sniped with a mean note of sarcasm. "But allow me to state the obvious: everyone on board this ship knows you're nothing but a sad, sick moron whose parents abandoned you to an orphanage, probably because they did not want you. Personally, I don't blame them. Look at you. You're nothing but skin and bone with crooked teeth and eyes that wobble so much they make you look quite demented. In fact, I bet your mother was a woman of the streets who didn't even have a clue as to who the father was," he snarled, a small amount of spittle drooling down his chin as he continued to vent his fury. "Yes, I think I can safely say you're a real loser, if ever I saw one. And the only reason you're on this ship at all is that someone felt sorry for you. So take a hike, Polly Parasite," he yelled, slamming the cabin door in her face without warning.

Polly now felt really wobbly inside, and she could feel that her cheeks were well-and-truly burning, so she rushed to the bathroom to splash some cold water on her face. Once inside the bathroom she collapsed in a heap on the floor and sobbed. She felt overwhelmed by Freddie's vengeful accusations. Was she a fraud? Was she pathetic? Was she a real loser, and worse still, was she a parasite who manipulatively used other people's kindness to get by? Polly felt sick inside as she also questioned herself as to whether there was any truth in his terribly vicious accusations. I mean, at the end of the day, did she come over as Miss High-and-Mighty, thinking of herself as being better than others? All these thoughts screamed out from within her as she lay in a crumpled heap on the bathroom floor.

Polly lay on the bathroom floor for some time, sobbing her heart out, but then suddenly she pricked up her ears. She thought she could hear sweet music coming from the bedroom. No, it couldn't be. She had not turned the radio on. Then she thought she could hear a familiar voice.

"Hodgekiss, is that you?" she whispered, turning her head around to see out of the bathroom door.

There was nobody there, at least nobody that she could see. Was she now beginning to hallucinate? She strained her ears to see if she could hear any better.

"Hodgekiss, I can hear your voice. Come on, don't play with me," she cried.

Still nobody appeared in the room. Polly then pinched herself to see if she was dreaming. But no, she was definitely wide awake and by now feeling very alarmed, for she could still hear the whisperings. The strongest whisper of them all seemed to sound like Hodgekiss's very distinct but gentle voice. Was her imagination running riot?

"Get up from the floor, Polly," it seemed to be saying. "Wipe the tears from your eyes, brush the dust from under your feet, and hold your head up high."

Polly did not move, for although she was not frightened, she felt very safe exactly where she was down on the floor. "No, I'm not getting up," she thought to herself. "I'm tired of getting up, and I'm sick and tired of struggling through life. Losers know their place, and that's down here on the floor. In the gutter of life, where all who pass by can tread on me. No one will want to kick me again if I'm already down here, and let's face it, that's where I deserve to stay forever as the nobody that I am. Yes, anything else is just too painful."

"Oh Polly, whose report will you believe?" came the next whisper. "The choice is yours; the choice is yours."

Polly decided to stick her fingers in both ears to drown the whisperings out, but still they kept coming.

"You are fearfully and wonderfully made," whispered a chorus of voices chanting over and over as they repeated the same message. "...fearfully and wonderfully made."

"No, I'm not!" she screamed back at the whispers. "I'm ugly and nasty. Yes, I'm a monster, and I hate myself, and everybody hates me. I just want to go to sleep and never wake up, for I can't carry on," she wept.

Still the voices kept coming, "If you knew the future, you would cry for joy, not weep with despair," said the voices in perfect harmony.

Polly still could not work out where these voices where coming from, and she feared that she was finally going crazy.

Eventually, in a desperate bid to shut the voices up, she arose from the floor and washed her face in the sink. Then she climbed into her bed and held Langdon tightly to her fast-beating chest until she finally fell into a sound sleep.

Early the next morning the ship came into the docks. Polly gathered her belongings and, with Langdon under one arm, headed off in the direction of Roberta's cabin to say a final good-bye. As she made her way down the long corridor to Roberta's cabin, she bumped into the sisters, who were also on their way to say good-bye to the lovely Scottish lass. Minutes later they were swapping addresses and saying tearful good-byes.

"Is anyone meeting you off the ship, Roberta?" Sister Thomasina asked most innocently.

"Oh no, I don't think so," came Roberta's swift but gentle reply. "I think I have been gone too long for anyone to even remember me," she said wistfully. "But I do not mind. I'm just glad to be back on English soil, although I'll be going back to Africa as soon as possible, thanks to Polly and the generosity of all those men in the casino. How about you two?" she said, addressing the sisters.

"Good gracious no," came their equally speedy reply. "We come and go far too often for grand send-offs and the like. No, we just slip into one country and then out, often without as much as a whimper," said Sister Thomasina with an impish grin. "And likewise, we are very grateful for the extra funds this trip has brought our way," she said, smiling down at Polly as she spoke.

Polly decided this was a good time to leave before she got asked the same question, so she quickly gave all present a hug and a peck on the cheek and announced that she had to rush. She then turned on her heels and ran down the corridor as though she had a train to catch.

As she was disembarking from the vessel, she felt overwhelmed by the huge crowd of people gathered at the docks. They had streamers and banners with "Welcome" written in bold and bright colors. Polly at first wondered who the important person on board might be. Was it the president of the United States? Or was it the queen or the prime minister? She definitely assumed it must be royalty, and she did not have to wait long to find out.

As she stood at the top of the steps, she was ordered by two rather burly men to step aside so that the wonderful, fabulous Freddie Fruitless and the Backsliders could disembark before any other guests. The crowd was swelling and becoming more hysterical by the moment. Having stood to one side, Polly watched as young girls screamed and cried out, "Freddie, we adore you." They tried to reach the stairs so they could just touch his immortal body with their outstretched hands as he passed by them.

"I touched him! I touched him!" screamed a young female before passing out on the ground.

As the crowd moved forward, other girls appeared to faint. In minutes the police were given no choice but to cordon off an area for the well-being of the group as well as the safety of the crowd.

As Freddie passed Polly on the steps, he turned and waved. Polly reciprocated. Then, before putting his arm back down to his side, he suddenly shouted, "Bye, loser!" at the top of his voice. With a grin on his face he turned away and proceeded to swan down the steps, blowing big kisses toward the adoring crowd, sending his emotionally charged fans into a frenzy.

As press cameras clicked and flashed, taking snaps of every movement of a muscle Freddie made, the press stuffed microphones right up to his chin.

"Are you glad to be in England, Freddie? Is it true that one of your vocalists has resigned, or was she sacked?"

As Polly watched, she could not help but think that the world in which she lived was upside down. Yes, they appeared to hail bad as good and good as bad. The ill-tempered and inconsiderate Freddie Fruitless was being given a hero's welcome with all the stops pulled out. Whereas Roberta and the lovely sisters who were, to Polly's mind, the real heroes were left to discreetly slip off the boat into oblivion. So in Polly's young mind nothing in life added up. With Freddie gone and the crowd dispersing, Polly picked up her schoolbag and, with Langdon still under one arm, started to descend down the steps that led to dry land.

"One minute, miss," said a stern voice.

Polly felt a hand on her shoulder. She turned around quite startled, but then relaxed. It was Captain Humdinger.

"You weren't about to leave my ship without saying good-bye, were you, Polly?" he said with a grin as he stroked his white whiskers.

Polly smiled up at the captain.

"Oh, please forgive me. I know I should have come to find you to say good-bye and thank you, but I got so caught up watching Freddie and the Backsliders disembark. You should have seen the amazing welcome he received. It was truly awesome, with banners and streamers and…"

The captain put his finger over Polly's lips to stop her. He then looked into her eyes and touchingly spoke words of great wisdom.

"Dear, sweet Polly, there is a way that seems right to a man, but in truth it's the pathway that leads only to death," he said quietly, his deep voice betraying a deep sadness.

"I don't know what you mean Captain Humdinger," replied Polly.

"You will one day, Polly. Of that I assure you," he said, patting her on the back. "Now I must go back to the purser's office and sort out a few things before I too get to leave my lovely ship and head off to visit relatives. Can I get one of my crew to give you a lift anywhere?"

Polly declined his kind offer, for she wasn't entirely sure where she was meant to be heading, but she kept this little fact to herself. "After all, if you don't know where you're going, then you're bound to end up somewhere else," she thought to herself. As a result of that sobering little thought, she made the decision to study her little map as soon as she was able. But she was also greatly troubled by the thought that all her long trip around the world had done was take her round in circles and make her later than ever for tea in Piadora.

She gave the dear and kindly captain one final hug, and then with her schoolbag over her shoulder and Langdon at her side, she alighted from the vessel secretly feeling quite sad and melancholic.

Hector Humdinger stood on the bridge of his ship and watched her disembark, and his eyes remained firmly fixed on her until she was little more than a speck on the horizon. As he stroked his whiskery chin, he muttered, "Keep going, Polly. Don't give up now."

Chapter 27
DIAMONDS ARE A GIRL'S BEST FRIEND

*P*OLLY WALKED ON for about a mile or so before deciding it was time to have a rest and study her little map. She placed Langdon by her side and then started to rummage through her belongings until finally she produced the guide. As she sat and studied it intently, she thought she heard a rustling noise coming from the bushes nearby. Polly looked up but could see nothing, so with head down she continued to try and work out precisely where she was.

As Polly hated maps, and therefore map reading, she began to feel quite frustrated, for she had no idea where north was, or for that matter where south was supposed to be. When she was a member of the Girl Guides they had done plenty of map reading as they wandered the hills and downs looking for suitable places to pitch their tents, but right then she began to wish she had paid more attention.

Polly turned the map upside down to see if it now made more sense, and then she turned it sideways. Still she did not have a clue as to where she was. Polly folded up the map before informing Langdon that she was feeling very discouraged.

"Maybe we should just call it a day and go home, Langdon," she said mournfully, "But to tell you the truth, as I have no idea where we are, I am fairly certain I will have great difficulty even finding my way home. This adventure is beginning to turn into a nightmare," she complained bitterly. "Well, we had better just keep on walking, Langdon, and hope that sooner rather than later we find someone who can help us," she sighed.

It would be many hours later that Polly found herself looking for somewhere to sit down so that she could take another look at the map.

"Look, Langdon, there's a bench just over there in the distance. We will take a rest there while I peruse my map again in an attempt to get my bearings."

As she headed towards the bench, she saw a young lad approaching it from the other side. He had his hands stuffed in his pockets and was whistling. He seemed to be too deep in thought to notice Polly. He suddenly took an almighty leap over the bench as though it were a hurdle and came to land directly in front of Polly, almost knocking her down as he landed on both feet.

"Hi there. My name is Polly, and this little fellow is Langdon," said Polly brightly, patting Langdon on the nose as she spoke.

"Oh, hi there. I'm sorry I didn't see you," replied the boy with sandy colored hair and an impish grin on his freckle-covered face.

Polly noticed that he looked fairly scruffy, what with his very disheveled sandy brown hair standing on end and large, patched-up holes in his trousers, but none of this put her off.

"What's your name?" she politely asked.

"Well, that's for you to guess," replied the young boy most mischievously. "But I'll help you out by giving you a clue. My name starts with the letter *t*."

"Thomas? Trevor? Tony?" she asked, wrinkling up her nose as she attempted to guess correctly. The boy shook his head in a most determined manner.

"Am I getting warmer?" Polly asked.

"Nope, you're nowhere near," replied the boy. "Tell you what; I'll give you another clue. Do you like Shakespeare?" he asked throwing his head back as he continued to laugh heartily.

"Well, not really," Polly reluctantly admitted. "I do struggle with the strange language, for even though it's supposed to be English, it might as well be Swahili as far as I'm concerned. So please don't keep me guessing. Just put me out of my misery and tell me your name."

"Oh, all right," said the young boy resignedly. "My name is Toby."

"So, where in Shakespeare does the name *Toby* appear?" Polly demanded to know, for she was at a complete loss as to the link.

"To be or not 'Toby'—that is the question," he said, giving her an impish wink.

Polly just shrugged her shoulders, now feeling irritated, for she did not entirely understand his little joke.

"To-bee or not To-bee; don't you get it, Polly?" he said, laughing out loud. "Oh, never mind. Anyway, quite what brings you to this neck of the woods?"

"Well, I'm not entirely sure where I am," Polly sadly confessed. "I have tried looking at my map several times, and still I'm none the wiser. I've been hoping and praying that someone would turn up who could help me," she said rather wistfully.

"Here, let me have a look," said Toby, grabbing hold of her map and jumping back onto the bench to take a rest. "Jump up here and sit next to me, Polly," he said, holding out his hand to help her up. "Oh, and by the way, my full name is Toby Donati, but my friends call me Dodo, for I'm considered to be as nutty as a Dodo. If I'm honest, I'm really one crayon short of a full box! So please feel free to call me Dodo."

Polly laughed out loud, something she had not done for quite a while.

"How can you be as nutty as a Dodo? I do believe a Dodo is an extinct bird," Polly remarked.

"Whatever," Toby casually replied. "All I know is that's what my friends call me, and you can call me anything you like as long as it's not rude or insulting, OK?"

Dodo, as he was now to be known, concentrated his energies toward reading her map, intently furrowing his brow as his eyes oscillated forwards and backwards over it.

"Look, Polly. We're here, and this is where you are meant to get to next," he said, pointing with his finger at a specific spot on the map.

Polly looked at the map anxiously trying to take in his directions.

"You are heading for Gold Gulley, are you not? But before you get there you will come to some crossroads. Now, it would help a lot if you try and concentrate more, Polly," he brashly suggested, thrusting the map right under her nose. "Now, show me that you've understood all that I've said," he demanded. "Do you now know which road you take from the crossroads? Is it the left hand fork or the right? Or do you need to just continue on? It would be really helpful to me if you could point out precisely which one it is. Surely you must have some idea?"

"Well no, that's the problem. I don't really know which way I'm meant to take," said Polly rather mournfully.

"Well then, don't worry your pretty little head about it, for we'll sort that problem out when we come to it," stated Dodo reassuringly.

"Oh, all right. I'll try to put it out of my mind, but only if you are prepared to help me out when the time comes that I have to make a choice," Polly replied.

"Right, that's settled then," said Dodo handing Polly back her map, which she folded and put back in her backpack for safety. "I'm off to sail my boat at the nearby stream," he announced as he jumped down from the bench. "Care to join me?"

Polly accepted his kind invitation, and after being helped down, she turned to face her new friend. "Dodo, I know this probably sounds like a really stupid question, but where is your sailing boat?"

"It's in my pocket," Dodo replied with a smile.

"Oh," said Polly. "So you say that your boat is in your pocket?" she quizzed as she tried to work out which pocket could possibly hold the boat.

"Yep," replied Dodo.

Polly looked down at his pocket and felt very confused, for she could see no lump or bump that would suggest that he had any such item as a boat concealed in his trouser pocket. However, she felt it best not to pursue the matter, for she was just very glad to have some company.

Minutes later, they arrived at the brook and headed for the little bridge that went across it. Polly put Langdon on top of her bag before placing the bag to one side. She then sat down on the bridge and after taking off her socks and shoes she allowed her feet to dangle just above the water. Dodo on the other hand disappeared for a few minutes and came back to the little bridge holding a large stick. He then took a piece of folded paper and penknife from his pocket and began to make a boat from it.

"There, Polly, I told you I had a boat, didn't I?" he said, holding out his fine piece of craftsmanship.

As Dodo lay on his belly directing his boat with his long stick, they continued to talk. Eventually he got bored sailing his boat and found himself contemplating what he could do next to while away the day.

"I say, Polly, shall we play 'pooh sticks'?"

"What, might I ask, is 'pooh sticks,' Dodo?" asked Polly, showing more than a hint of curiosity. "I've never heard of that game."

"Well then, allow me to show you," he said, jumping up. "But first, we must go into the woods and cut ourselves some sticks."

Polly agreed to go with Dodo, but not before picking up Langdon, who was still lying on the top of her schoolbag. With the help of his penknife, in no time at all they had gathered quite a large supply of sticks for their game.

"Here, look after this for me, and I will carry the sticks," said Dodo as he handed Polly the penknife.

Polly placed the penknife in her pocket, and with Langdon safely tucked away under her arm they hurried back to the bridge to play pooh sticks with immense enthusiasm. Eventually she felt that enough was enough, and it was time to concentrate her thoughts toward getting back on her journey to Piadora.

"Dodo, if this doesn't sound too cheeky, would you like to come with me to Piadora?" she asked.

"Not sure," he muttered.

"Well, I think you might like it," Polly enthused.

"I'm sure I would, Polly, but I also like lazing around here on my belly, just sailing my..."

"Oh, please say you'll come," Polly interrupted.

"As I was just saying before you so rudely stopped me, I really like lying around and taking it easy, and I'm not sure if..."

"Come on, Dodo. Together we'll have a great time," urged Polly.

"Look here, Polly. Stop constantly interrupting me, and let me finish my sentence. I find your ways very irritating," he said crossly. "So take your interruptions and leave if you want to."

"I'm sorry, Dodo," said Polly meekly. "I never meant to offend you, and I promise I won't do it again."

"Yeah, well, the way I see it, life itself is a major interruption," said Dodo ruefully. "What I mean is, I like to do things my way and in my time, and I won't be ruled by any clock. So if I had it my way, I'd eat when I wanted to and go to school if and when I wanted to. And I'd lie here basking in the sunshine all day, every day. Yes, a life of leisure—that's the life for me, and I consider anything else to be a very annoying interruption," he said with a cheeky little grin.

"Well, if that's so, I'll leave right now," retorted Polly quite defensively.

"No, it's all right, you can stay and interrupt me until I've had enough of your interrupting, and then I will tell you to go. I think that's a pretty fair deal," said Dodo.

Polly sat back feeling there was no point in arguing with Dodo, for he really did do and say as he pleased. After a while she found herself feeling very restless and bored, and so she decided to show Dodo her collection of strange pebbles.

"How peculiar," was all he managed to say as he showed a complete lack of enthusiasm or interest in her small assortment of pebbles.

Polly went to put them back in her schoolbag, but as she did, one of the pebbles didn't make it. Polly tried to catch the pebble as it rolled across the wooden bridge. Dodo, being quick on the ball, managed to catch it before it went over the bridge and into the stream, where it would more than likely be lost forever. He then decided to playfully hold on to it.

"Come on, Dodo, hand it back," Polly pleaded.

Dodo responded by taking a halfpenny out of his trouser pocket.

"Toss you for it, Polly Brown. Heads, you lose, and I get to keep your pebble. Tails, you win, and I'll come with you to Piadora."

Polly was very reluctant to gamble away her pebble, but as she was keen to drag Dodo along with her, she hastily agreed, and the coin was tossed. Polly won.

"Well then, Dodo, it looks like you're coming with me after all," said Polly with a smile.

"Looks that way, doesn't it," retorted Dodo rather despondently. "But I might still change my mind."

"You can't. That wouldn't be fair. That's why we tossed the coin, remember?"

As Polly was arguing with him, she suddenly found herself distracted by a loud rustling noise coming from behind where they were still lying on the bridge.

"Shhh, Dodo," said Polly, putting her index finger up to his lips, "Did you hear that noise?"

Dodo got up from the floor and looked around.

"Yes, Polly, I did. It's coming from over there," he said, pointing towards a large clump of blackberry bushes.

Just as she was about to get up, she heard another noise, only this time it was louder and she could distinctly hear words or rather mutterings. She also thought she could hear the patter of paws and strange breathless panting. Polly and Dodo stood perfectly still, not moving a muscle as they stared in the direction of the bushes.

Suddenly they saw the tallest lady they had ever seen emerge from the bushes with two dogs on long leashes padding along at her side. Polly assumed that the lady had not seen them, for she was still loudly murmuring.

"Oh sugar, sugar, sugar," she moaned, as she stooped over to furiously brush off the leaves that had attached themselves to her long, flowing gown. She then proceeded to pick out, one-by-one, the prickly thorns that had also become embedded into material and were threatening to snag and completely ruin her outfit.

Polly momentarily considered the thought that this lady was definitely not suitably dressed for a casual stroll in the country-side with her dogs, but before she had time to ponder more on this disturbing little thought the lady looked up and caught sight of Polly and Dodo.

"Hi, I'm Polly, and my friend here is Dodo," she said in her very friendly fashion, moving a few steps forward to greet the lady.

The mysterious lady smiled back, and as she did so her whole face lit up and began to glow. Before long her whole body was also lit up like one bright light. Polly's mouth dropped open, and her eyes nearly popped out of her head as she continued to observe the illuminated lady. As she moved nearer towards her, Polly found herself totally mesmerized by her grace and beauty. Not only did she have the finest porcelain features with translucent white skin and chiseled bone structure, but she was dressed from head to toe in a gown that was the most delightfully beautiful shade of pink. Her hair was covered by a black hat, which had enormous ostrich plumes that reached toward the sky. She was indeed strikingly beautiful.

Polly could only stand in awe and marvel at her elegance and sophistication as the lady provocatively waltzed towards them. She came to a halt in front of star-struck Polly. She then put out her right hand, which Polly noticed was bedecked with sparkling jewels, for Polly to shake. Polly's hands trembled as she allowed her small hand to be clasped. The dogs held back, just sitting on their haunches with their tongues hanging out and panting.

"Nice to meet you both," said the lady with the smoothly enticing manner. "Now let me introduce myself, my dear. My name is Soogara, and I am none other than the Cotton Candy Queen. And these here are my pets Grovelock and Grubstick," she said, pointing down at them.

Polly still said nothing, preferring to stand and gaze upon her, feeling utterly spellbound by her beauty. Dodo remained distracted with one hand tucked firmly into his trouser pocket, the other playing with a stick. There could be no denying that this woman was extraordinarily beautiful, but he was experiencing strange and very uncomfortable feelings as he stood in her presence.

"A queen? You say that you are a queen?" stammered Polly, not certain as to whether this was all a dream or illusion.

"Yes, I said 'queen,' didn't I?" retorted the lady, who, upon realizing that she had raised her voice to an angry level, immediately softened it to a tone more sugar-sweet. "Well, my little precious one, what is a young girl like you doing in the middle of the countryside?" she asked, completely ignoring Polly's young friend.

Dodo used this opportunity to remove himself from her presence, for his concerns about this lady were deepening by the minute. He therefore opted to go and sit down on the same rock that Polly had left Langdon.

"Well, actually I'm pretty lost," Polly cheerfully confessed. "You see, Langdon and I..." she said, pointing behind her to where Dodo was now seated and holding tightly onto Langdon, "well, we were on our way to Piadora, and it's a long story but we became sidetracked. Now we are trying to get back on the road that will take us there. My friend Dodo, or rather Toby, has done his best to read the map, and still we are unsure as to which road I am meant to be taking," she explained. "So are you able to help us?" inquired Polly, her face visibly desperate as she made direct eye contact with the stunningly beautiful lady.

"I might be able to help you. That is, if you would allow me the pleasure of perusing your little map," replied the Cotton Candy Queen in a syrupy sweet voice.

"Of course; here it is," said Polly gratefully as she quickly handed over the map.

As the Cotton Candy Queen studied the map, her two dogs got up and came to settle by her feet.

"Oh, my dear sweet thing, you are most certainly very lost, for you are a very long way from Piadora. In fact, I am surprised that you have not yet given up and gone home. If it was me in your shoes," she said, looking down at Polly's tatty footwear and making a grimace, "I would tear up this little map and forget any of this existed."

"Oh, but I can't do that," Polly miserably sighed. "For my only hope in life is to find Piadora. Besides, Langdon and I have nothing to go home too," she said rather mournfully.

"Oh well, in that case, it's a good job I turned up, then, isn't it?" Soogara smoothly stated.

Soogara agreed to help Polly, suggesting that she walk with her, at least until they came to the crossroads that were very clearly printed on the map.

"I will then leave you to make your own way when we get to the crossroads. But please take note, it is most important that you take the turning to the left, otherwise you will find yourself more lost than ever! Yes, should you forget to take the left turning you will discover that you have just gone around in a circle."

Polly felt so relieved as well as thankful that she had bumped into Soogara when all seemed lost. She decided that Soogara must be a really lovely and kind person.

"Anyway, bring your friend, Dodo, and come with me."

Polly turned and moved towards the rock to fetch her bag.

"Come on, Dodo, it's time to leave. I don't know why you're holding back, come on."

"Go with her, you don't need me anymore," he said, acting rather surly and flicking Polly's pebble back at her. Polly picked up the pebble and placed it in her pocket.

"Come on, Dodo, don't be such a spoilsport."

Dodo didn't answer. He just lowered his head and continued to sulk.

"OK, Dodo, I'm asking you for the final time; please come. I want you to come."

Polly then picked up her schoolbag, tucked Langdon under her arm, and began walking away from Dodo. She turned around one final time and called out to her friend to join them.

Eventually, although I have to say reluctantly, he decided that he might as well go with them, as he had nothing else that he particularly wanted to do.

As they walked and talked, Soogara's pet dogs, Grovelock and Grubstick, faithfully padded alongside, their tongues hanging out and their hauntingly beady eyes firmly fixed on Polly. It was not too long before Polly took it upon herself to casually remark that Soogara was the most beautiful queen she had ever met.

"Have you always been this pretty?" Polly innocently asked. "And if so, what sort of face cream do you apply at night to keep your skin so soft?" she asked in her most outspoken manner. "I wish I was pretty like you, instead of being a plain, ugly monster," she added, giving one of her deep sighs.

"Yes, my dear, I had noticed," said Soogara, nonchalantly flicking at Polly's hair in a rather contemptuous manner. "Now tell me, dear, what self-respecting hairdresser would cut your hair in such an awful style? For it really does look quite frightful," she said, throwing up her hands to express her clear disapproval.

"Oh, I know it does," replied Polly rather sadly. "My hair used to be long. It was always braided for me, but now..." Polly's voice trailed off.

"Enough," said Soogara. "Let me get my scissors and try to shape it around your face, for I do believe you need all the help you can get."

Polly was delighted when Soogara miraculously produced a pair of pink scissors, though she was very alarmed at their size, for they looked more like gardening shears! But still, she happily allowed Soogara free reign to do as she wished with her hair.

"Oh my goodness, you do have such terribly split ends, my dear," said Soogara in a most disdainful tone of voice. "Yes, your hair, dear girl, is in atrocious condition. So, you would be well advised to change your shampoo and throw in some conditioner to the final rinse," she confided as she happily snipped away at Polly's limp hair, throwing the cut strands rather dramatically over her shoulder in utter disgust.

"There, perfect!" Soogara declared with an air of self-satisfaction. "Now I will extend my services and braid them for you."

Polly could only beam her deep appreciation, for she was so happy to have some help at last.

"Yes, I do believe there is a great improvement," said Soogara as she scanned Polly up and down with a wicked glint in her eyes.

"Does it look nice?" Polly excitedly asked Soogara.

"*Nice* isn't the word I would use, but it has done much to improve your sad and sorry features," she murmured, curling her bottom lip as she spoke.

"Thank you so much, Soogara," said Polly giving her a big smile. "I have always wanted to feel pretty."

"Oh, my little one, pretty is one thing, but perhaps this is a good time to tell you my little closely guarded secret," whispered Soogara enticingly into Polly's readily pricked-up ear.

"Secret! What secret?" Polly eagerly asked.

"Well, my little peach dumpling, you could, if you really wanted to, have looks almost as fine and flawless as mine; but only if you wanted it badly enough," Soogara cooed.

"What do you mean by that?" Polly inquired.

"Exactly what I just said," replied Soogara with a half smile. "I have the power to do anything I like, and that includes, should I wish, the ability to make you beautiful."

"Well, I think beauty is in the eye of the beholder," interrupted Dodo, who had managed to catch up with them and had caught the end of their secretive little conversation. "And anyway, Polly, I think you are perfectly lovely just the way you are, so you do not need any more help from this so-called trumped-up beauty queen."

"Excuse me, young man. Are you something of an expert on such matters?" Soogara turned and asked in distinctly icy tones.

"No, but..."

"No buts. You either are, or you're not; which is it to be?" snapped Soogara.

Dodo remained silent, just wishing he'd never bothered to voice his personal opinion on the matter.

"I see. Just as I suspected. Judging by the large amount of putrefying-looking spots dotted all over your scrawny face, it is perfectly obvious that you know nothing whatsoever about the art of true beauty! Am I correct?" she very snidely snorted.

Dodo stood, staring into her flaming eyes, and went quite red in the face.

"Just as I suspected!" she frostily snapped. "So it would pay you to keep your unwanted opinions to yourself. Do I make myself clear?" she raged.

"Perfectly," replied Dodo as he shrunk backwards, fearing the possibility of being physically attacked was more than probable if he provoked her any further. He shrugged his shoulders and decided there and then to stay well out of any further conversation between the two of them.

"Let them get on with it, for that woman is right off the wall," he sulkily muttered under his breath as he moved away, choosing to lag well behind them. For he didn't like being spoken to in such a harsh and demoralizing manner.

"Now then, where was I?" said Soogara, turning to fix her ice-cold stare on Polly. "Ah, yes, I tell you now with my hand on my heart that I have the power to transform you into a real beauty queen, fit for any pageant."

"Really!" gasped Polly. "You mean that you really could make me as beautiful as yourself?" she asked with touching innocence.

"I did not say AS beautiful!" Soogara icily snapped. "For it is quite impossible for anyone—and I repeat, anyone—to become as beautiful to behold as myself," she snarled. "However," she said, pausing for a moment to take back control of her fiery temper. "I could do much to improve your sad and sorry little features.

That is all I'm prepared to say," she replied, softening her voice once again until it became as sweet as the sweetest honeycomb.

"Oh please, please make me beautiful," Polly pleaded and begged.

"Not so fast, my little one. Not so fast. Great beauty comes with a price."

"Oh, now you tell me," said Polly, slumping her shoulders and instantly feeling downcast.

"Everything comes with a price, I'll have you know, young lady," hissed Soogara.

"Well, that's it then, isn't it?" replied Polly rather sulkily shrugging her shoulders. "I don't have any money I can give you, so I'll just have to carry on looking like Quasimodo."

"And quite who is this Quasimodo?" Soogara snorted.

"What! You haven't heard of Quasimodo?"

"No, I don't believe I have ever heard of this Quasi…So tell me now, who is he?"

"Well," said Polly, perking up a little. "He once lived in the bell tower of the Notre Dame Cathedral in Paris."

"And why a bell tower?" Soogara asked.

"Well, because he was an ugly monster that made people so afraid, so he had to be hidden away. That's why he lived in the bell-tower," replied Polly most informatively.

"Oh," said Soogara, distorting her face and momentarily shutting her eyes to show her contempt and disapproval. "Well, in that case, I'm jolly glad to have never met him, for ugly is one thing I cannot abide. Anyway, as I was saying before I was so rudely interrupted, everything, without exception, comes with a price tag."

"So, what is the price of your help, Soogara?" Polly impatiently asked.

"Well, for one thing, my little one, you would have to abandon all thoughts of going to Piadora and choose to stay with me."

"And then what?" Polly rather flippantly asked.

"Then, my dear, you will find yourself taking on my character-istics and, ultimately, a slice of my infinite beauty. That is surely not too much to ask, is it?" said Soogara most persuasively as she fanned her long eyelashes seductively in an attempt to encourage Polly to forget about Piadora and stay with her.

Polly thought long and hard, for she was not good at making decisions. She wanted to ask Dodo's advice, but as she turned to ask him for his opinion, she could clearly see he was deliberately straggling behind, making no effort whatsoever to catch up with them. Perhaps he doesn't like girl talk, Polly concluded. It was therefore left up to her to make up her own mind and, I might add, without a daisy to help her. So it was only after much thought, as well as plentiful amounts of internal agonizing, that she finally came to a decision.

"I'm really sorry, Soogara," Polly said softly, faltering as she spoke. "I'd love to stay with you, especially as I am really desperate to become beautiful, but I think I will have to say no to your kind offer. I must follow my heart, and that tells me that I must choose to make it to Piadora. Therefore," she said rather clumsily as her voice was still faltering, "I think it might be for the best if we said our good-byes here before I change my mind."

"Don't go yet!" Soogara spat back. "I would really love your company, at least for a while longer. For I am so lonely, so very lonely," she said putting on her most sickly sweet voice as she began to shed large crocodile tears in her manipulative attempt to get Polly to stay.

"Please say you'll stay a while," Soogara pleaded, "for I have only just met you. And if you were to leave me now I would be all on my own without anyone to talk to," she simpered, at the same time producing a long chiffon handkerchief to loudly blow into. "Yes, I would be so alone and so afraid, and oh, so cold all by myself," she sniffed before once again blowing louder still into her hanky.

"Now where have I seen this before?" thought Polly as she cast her mind back to dear Aunt Mildred and her famous hankies before choosing, rather unwisely, to dismiss the connection between Aunt Mildred and Soogara.

"Please, Polly, stay. Even if it's only for a while, I beg you."

Polly felt put into a corner, for she did not wish to upset Soogara, but she was also beginning to feel very concerned that her dream of reaching Piadora was beginning to vanish. However, she really empathized with Soogara, as she too knew firsthand what it was like to feel lonely and cry all night. So against her better judgment she felt she must put aside her own desires and stay with Soogara at least until morning.

And so it was, with the greatest reluctance, that she allowed Soogara's powers of persuasion to do their work and change Polly's mind, albeit temporarily.

"Soogara, I can't speak for Dodo, but I will stay with you at least until the morning. But then I will have to head off in search of Piadora. I hope that makes you feel a bit better."

"Good," replied Soogara brightly. "As a reward for your great kindness in staying, I am going to treat you to as much cotton candy as your young heart desires. I hope you like strawberry flavor, for I have never met a child who doesn't," said Soogara airily.

"I've never had it before," Polly admitted. "So it really would be something of a treat to finally try some."

"Well then, you are in for a lovely surprise, my little sugar petal," Soogara happily announced. "For sugar and spice and all things nice...yes, sugar and children go together. They are indeed a perfect match, and I love sweet-toothed children so very much," she declared, flouncing her gown as her face lit up with great delight. "And Polly dear, I will let you into another little secret. The more cotton candy you eat, well then, the more beautiful you will become. Trust me!" she triumphantly smirked.

"Really?" remarked Polly. "You mean the more I eat, then the more pretty I will get?" she asked, hardly able to contain her delight.

"Absolutely!" said Soogara with a mischievous smile. "So if I were you, I'd be anxious to get started on the cotton candy, especially as you're leaving me in the morning to continue your journey. Now call Dodo and tell him to stop his brooding and catch up with us, or he will entirely miss out on this special treat."

With that said, Soogara waved her hand like a wand and began to spin around in circles, getting faster and faster with every second that passed. Polly and Dodo watched on, totally fascinated but feeling quite dizzy as Soogara spun round like the eye of a tornado. Before long, great lengths of pink sugar strands began to wind themselves around Soogara, transforming into large, pink clouds of tantalizingly sweet cotton candy, which floated off into the air around her. Eventually, Soogara weaved her way out of the enor-

POLLY BROWN

mous cloud and suggested that they might like to start eating. Dodo hung back, feeling very unsure as to whether to eat the candy. Polly, on the other hand, needed no further encouragement, for not only was she extremely hungry but it looked so wonderful and inviting. She reminded herself that at the end of the day it was very important for her to finally be given this once-in-a-lifetime opportunity to become beautiful. She quickly began to pull off large chunks of cotton candy from the fluffy cloud, stuffing extraordinarily large amounts into her open mouth in a most unseemly and very unladylike fashion. No sooner had the cotton candy melted on her tongue than she was happily pulling off more.

"Here, Dodo, have a mouthful of this," she cried, pulling off another large piece to hand to him.

Dodo cautiously placed a large portion onto his tongue, and in just a matter of seconds he too was hooked on the stuff.

"This cotton candy is really delicious," Polly cried between mouthfuls. "I've never tasted such wonderful, gooey sweet stuff in my life. Soogara, how did you know that I had such a sweet tooth?"

Soogara didn't answer Polly; she just stood watching and waiting, her smile becoming larger as well as more sinister.

"Carry on eating, Polly," she urged.

Polly happily obliged, stopping only between mouthfuls to ask if she beginning to look pretty.

"Exquisite, Polly, but you still need to eat more if total perfection is what you're after."

Despite feeling quite full, Polly continued to digest more and more of the fluffy pink threads, for she was now feeling very excited and encouraged by the news that she was well on her way to becoming utterly gorgeous. Dodo was by now feeling very bloated but found that he too was unable to stop eating the candy. He continued to cram more of the pink stuff into his mouth. It seemed that no matter how much they tore off and ate, the pink cloud grew larger and larger in size. It was not too long before Polly began to feel she had eaten more than enough and needed to stop.

"Soogara, I must stop now, for I am beginning to feel very full."

"Don't stop now, Polly. No, not when you've come this far and are on the verge of becoming, oh, what's the word? I know—

eye-catching." She then turned to give both her dogs a sly wink. "Besides, you may never again have the opportunity of tasting such delicious cotton candy, and for free."

"Oh, all right then," said Polly, pulling off yet another large handful, "but please find me a mirror so I can see for myself just how much I have changed. Soogara watched on, a large smirk lighting up her countenance as large puss-filled boils began to sprout up all over Polly's face. Polly continued to cram in more cotton candy, blissfully unaware of the horrifying transformation that was taking place. Sadly for her, Dodo was equally unaware of Polly's worsening condition, as he struggled to fill his own mouth with more of the addictively sweet candy.

"Please find me a mirror, Soogara," Polly once again pleaded.

"Patience, my dear, patience. These things take time. I will give you a mirror later, trust me." Soogara continued to watch on, a bemused look written all over her face. "Perfect, I now have them both totally in my power, yes, under my personal control," she muttered.

Pretty soon both Polly and Dodo started to go green in the face, and both began to feel distinctly queasy and nauseated.

"Go on, Polly, you're almost there. Just a bit more of my candy and you will be blown away by your amazing transformation. You really will be a stunning beauty."

"I can't eat any more. I feel sick as a dog," Polly complained as she collapsed to the ground, curling up in a ball, for she was now suffering from the severest of pains. Seconds later Dodo joined her on the ground, writhing in absolute agony.

"Soogara, please help us!" cried Polly.

Soogara smirked wickedly as she coldly stood over the children, her long arms firmly folded.

"I'm sorry, Polly, but I am quite unable to help," she said, her smile broadening as she spoke. "You see, both of you did this to yourselves," she said icily before adding, "sadly, my little sugar lumps, you can always rely on a child to be greedy. Yes, that's always their downfall."

Soogara then began to laugh louder than ever. Polly curled up into an even tighter ball, so great were her stomach pains. "Please help me, Soogara, I beg you," she cried as she clutched her stomach tightly. Dodo joined her in crying and pleading for Soogara to show mercy. "Shut up, both of you," she snapped as she examined her long, talon nails. "Take your punishment like real men."

"But I'm not a man. I'm just a young girl," Polly bitterly wailed.

"And a really stupid one at that," sniped Soogara, betraying her utter contempt towards Polly.

"Both of you should have counted the cost before you so readily stuffed your faces with my cotton candy. The price for such greed is that I now own the two of you lock, stock, and barrel, and therefore I am free to do with you as I please," she spat.

"Grovelock, Grubstick, come here now, boys," she screeched, beckoning both dogs to come to her side. "Now, my precious pups, stand and watch over them until I return."

Both dogs circled Polly and Dodo, presumably to prevent them from running away, not that Polly could have escaped even if she had wanted to, for the pain inside the pit of her stomach was worsening by the minute. She looked over in Dodo's direction and was shocked to see his limp body was no longer moving.

"Dodo, wake up," she cried, but no answer came from his lifeless body.

Polly closed her eyes and waited to die. "Someone help me, please," she whispered. Then everything went blank.

Chapter 28
BEAUTY AND THE BEAST

*W*HEN POLLY FINALLY came round she was horrified to find herself tied up with thick rope in a dark, dank, rat-filled dungeon. The only light was a narrow shaft that was coming from a small high window that had large and very rusty iron bars. As she squinted, she could see that Dodo, as well as Langdon, had also been taken prisoner. Both were tied up to another wall on the other side of the dungeon, and Langdon looked a really sorry sight, for he had a ball and chain around his neck. Polly was horrified.

"Oh Langdon, I'm so sorry. What have they done to you?" she cried. "I'm to blame for this awful mess, so I must think of a way out."

Polly felt quite terrified by what might happen to them all. She was powerless to do anything, save silently pray for a miracle.

After what seemed like a very long time, Polly heard footsteps, followed by the soft padding of many feet. It was Soogara and the dogs coming down to the dungeon to check on them.

"Well, Polly, how does it feel to be a prisoner? Not very nice, is it?" she crowed. "I see your friend here is in very bad shape; in fact, I am of the opinion that he will not make it," she said, walking over to where Dodo was slumped with his hands tied behind his back.

She pressed her foot against his chest, and then with the point of her foot, she rolled him over so his face was in the dust.

"Yes, dear Polly, I think I am correct in saying that Dodo here," she said, tapping his back with her foot, "will never fill his face again; no never again!" Soogara then broke out into hysterical laughter that echoed through the chamber.

"Soogara, please let us go," Polly pleaded. "We have done nothing to upset you."

"You don't need to have done anything wrong, my precious one, but had you agreed to stay with me when I begged you, well then, I would never have been forced into this position. Sadly, you left me with no choice, and I have to admit that I do get such a kick out of seeing others suffer. It does much to make me feel good and oh so powerful." She wickedly smirked. "Besides, Vanaspi was counting on me to trap and enslave you, so he will be most happy to hear the good news of your capture."

Polly shuddered and let out a small whimper as she suddenly had a flashback to the terrible night she had been taken hostage. "Vanaspi! Oh my goodness! Hadn't that terrifying beast been the commander of the plane in which she had almost been taken hostage? He had mentioned the name Soogara, hadn't he?" Now everything fell into place and became perfectly clear. Soogara was definitely the name he had mentioned, and for Polly to be taken captive was part of the sickening plot that had been hatched that terrible night. How could Polly have forgotten that? She could have kicked herself for being such an idiot, and she would have done so if she had not been well-and-truly tied up.

Soogara continued to ramble on.

"Polly dear, I will tell you a little secret of mine: not only does Piadora exist, my child, but Vanaspi as well as my good self have been banished from that kingdom. Yes, banished forever. We can never set foot inside it ever again," she informed Polly, pretending as she did to weep piteously. "So you see, my dear, if I can't go there, then neither, my dear, can you," she snarled. "Yes, all's fair in love and war. So enjoy your very long, or maybe rather short, stay with us," she cackled with a wicked gleam in her eye as she observed the rats congregating in a corner, ready to attack their prey. "Come, my pets, it's time to leave Polly to slowly rot and die, provided the rats don't eat her first. However, we must hurry and leave instantly, for we have other children we need to seduce with candy and then enslave, and time is of the essence," she said chillingly as she moved toward the door, anxious to leave. "For it wouldn't do to keep our good friend Count Vanaspi waiting, would it?" she said smoothly as she bent over Polly's body, placing the long, sharp fingernail of her index finger under Polly's chin to tilt it upwards.

"Say ta-ta to everyone you know, and say good-bye to ever reaching Piadora, my precious little one," she hissed, pulling down hard on Polly's braid and breaking into convulsive fits of laughter that reached the most piercing decibels. "Beautiful, indeed! Well, I believe that would take a miracle of epic proportions," she sneered. She then stood up and beckoned the hounds to her side. "Come, my little pups, it's time to leave and go on another mission."

Both dogs instantly obeyed, coming straight to her side. Their long tongues hung out as they growled fiercely. She then patted their wet noses while her other hand searched deep into her gown pocket for the extraordinarily large gold key to lock the door behind her.

"Now boys, quickly say good-bye to Polly, for the rats are getting very hungry for their lunchtime snack," she cackled, simultaneously patting both hounds on their heads. "Good-bye, Polly. Oh, and before I leave, this is to encourage them to waste no time and dig in," she sneered menacingly as she produced a large handful of bread crumbs from the deep pocket of her gown and scattered them over Polly's limp body.

Soogara then turned on her heels and left the room, locking the creaky door behind her as she continued up the winding stone steps, her raucous laughter bouncing off the walls as she headed away from the dungeon. Polly listened intently until she could no longer hear their footsteps. She then turned her attention to the rats that were scurrying across the floor in her direction.

"Get off me!" she squealed loudly. "You're not having me for breakfast, lunch, or tea," she sobbed as she furiously fought to rid her body of the many rats that were now running up and down all over her.

She then looked over to where Langdon lay tied up and attached to a ball and chain. Polly immediately began to scream, for his helpless little body was entirely covered by hundreds of the evil little rodents, who were furiously biting into him and devouring large chunks of his fur. Dodo was also covered from head to toe with the hungry vermin gnawing at his clothing.

"Someone help us please!" she cried piteously as the rats continued to invade her little body, sniffing her and tickling her with their whiskers. Within moments they were tugging at her dress. Polly screamed louder than ever, but her empty cries produced nothing but echoes in the cold, damp dungeon. It was useless. She knew for certain that nobody would be able to hear her cries, so there would be no possibility of Dodo, Langdon, or herself being rescued.

Polly closed her eyes and whispered, "Good-bye, Dodo. I am so sorry to have done this to you." She then looked over to where Langdon lay on the floor, and with tears streaming down her cheeks, she cried, "Good-bye, Langdon. I love you, and I always will." She then closed her eyes and prepared to die.

Suddenly she saw a flash and opened her eyes. The rats leapt from her body and scurried back into the darkness, for they had been frightened witless by the brightness of the mysterious light. Likewise, the rats that had been covering Langdon and Dodo followed close on their heels as they too raced back to the safety of their holes.

Polly looked down to where the bright light seemed to be coming from, and to her amazement there in the now-ripped-away pocket of her dress sat a huge, stunningly bright diamond with the word *endurance* engraved on its brilliant surface. Dodo's penknife that he had asked her to hold for safekeeping lay beside the diamond. Polly felt elated, for she had quite forgotten that her pocket held these items.

Polly could only gasp as she realized that the pebble she had placed in the pocket before her dinner with Captain Humdinger had now miraculously transformed into this magnificent diamond that was lighting up the room like a candle, aided only by the shaft of sunlight that was streaming through the poky window above her. "No wonder the rats left in such a hurry," thought Polly. "This diamond is truly awesome in its brilliance."

She looked over in Langdon's direction. He was lying on his side, still tied around the neck by the ball and chain. Half his trunk was missing, as well as large bits of his rear end. Polly felt thoroughly sickened as she observed poor Langdon's savagely-torn body. She wondered if he would ever forgive her for getting them into this terrible mess.

"Oh Langdon, I am so sorry," she wept forlornly. "You deserved none of this, and I don't know how I can forgive myself; really I don't."

Polly also observed that Dodo was still lying on the floor and not moving, and she felt in the deepest despair at her powerlessness to do anything. As she was pondering on the hopelessness of their situation a small white bird came to hover on the sill of the window, attracted, presumably, by the glistening stone. It stood hovering on the sill, flapping its wings and poking its long beak between the bars. Polly stared up at the bird and, as their eyes met, she suddenly felt she had a brainstorm. Her eyes began to scour the room in search of her schoolbag. She breathed a sigh of relief. She could see it lying over next to Langdon. Now, if only she could free herself from the ropes that bound her and then somehow lure the bird into the dungeon, she could write an SOS and tie it around the bird's neck.

Polly looked at the penknife that was lying exposed next to the large diamond on her lap, and she thought that if she could somehow pry it open, then it could be used to cut through the ropes that were binding her wrists together. But how could she do this with her hands so tightly bound?

Polly struggled to pick up the penknife with her fingers. It turned out to be much more difficult than she first thought. Eventually, after failing numerous times, she finally had the penknife firmly between her thumb and index finger, and then she slowly brought the knife up to her mouth. Then, exposing her teeth, she placed the penknife sideways into her mouth, and once she had a firm grip on the blade, she pried it out of the protective casing.

After many attempts and an equal amount of frustration, the blade was finally released from its protective casing. She then let go, allowing the penknife to fall into her lap. She breathed a deep sigh of relief that the instrument had landed safely in her lap and had not fallen to the floor. Picking it up between her fingers again, she then set about the task of slowly cutting through the ropes that bound both her wrists together.

She had, on more than one occasion, given up trying, giving in to feelings of great despair. Then she would see Dodo's limp body and Langdon lying so brutally battered and blue that she would find herself trying with renewed vigor to cut through the rope like a saw through a piece of timber. Finally the cords that bound both her wrists together fell to the ground. She was then easily able to free herself of the ropes that bound her chest. As these ropes fell to the floor, Polly took a deep breath. She was free at last, and it felt good.

Polly rubbed her sore wrists before creeping over to where Dodo still lay lifeless on the cold stone floor. Much to her relief she could see he was still breathing, albeit very shallow. She knelt down and cut through the ropes that bound him before moving on to attend to Langdon. Try as she may, Polly was unable to cut through the heavy iron chains and remove the large ball. No, she could do nothing except hold his bruised and battered body in her arms and weep.

Eventually, she tenderly placed him back on the stone floor and went over to where her schoolbag still lay on the ground. She rummaged through it until she came across her gold diary and pen. Tearing out a blank sheet from the back pages of her diary, she set about drawing a picture of a castle, not forgetting to add a dungeon.

Finally, with her red lipstick given to her by Annabel, she made a large arrow sign pointing toward the bottom of the page. Using large capital letters she wrote "WE ARE HERE!" at the place she believed the dungeon was located.

She then pulled the red ribbon from her hair, and, after making a small hole, threaded the ribbon through it.

"Now all I need is the bird," she muttered to herself as she set about picking up all the bread crumbs that where scattered all over the floor. It was only a matter of minutes before she had collected herself a whole handful.

"This had better work," she mumbled, "or we're well-and-truly doomed."

She then held up her opened hand towards the window and beckoned to the little bird to come and eat. At first the bird resisted, choosing to remain hovering on the ledge, flapping its wings excitedly as it kept its firm gaze on her pleading eyes. Polly felt very frustrated and had no idea what to do next.

Suddenly she came up with a pretty crazy idea to start singing in the hope of coaxing the bird to fly down. It worked! Moments later she saw the bird wriggle through the bars, and then it swooped down, coming to land in the palm of her outstretched hand. Polly stroked its neck with her finger as it pecked at the breadcrumbs. The bird liked the attention and happily nuzzled up to Polly. It then allowed Polly to tie the note around its neck, and then once all the breadcrumbs were gone, she raised her outstretched hand towards the shaft of light and begged her little messenger to fly away. The bird at first resisted, probably because he wanted to be stroked some more, but gradually it got the message that she wanted him to fly out of the window. It fluttered its wings and flew towards the narrow bars and then finally out of the small window. Polly could only wait and pray for deliverance!

She sat and waited, then waited some more. But after many hours with no help arriving, she began to battle with intense feelings of despair. She tried really hard to remain positive, but deep inside she was beginning to give up on ever being rescued.

"If we don't get help soon, then there will be nothing left of us to find! Well, except half-eaten corpses or a large pile of bones," she sighed.

Suddenly she remembered her book on survival, given to her by dear old Corporal Beanpod. She went back to her schoolbag for another rummage.

"There, I've found it," she said, feeling rather pleased.

Polly then randomly opened it and her eyes fell on a fresh chapter entitled "Facing Danger." As this fit in rather well with her present predicament, she decided to read on.

> It is no use giving up. Only positive action can save you. People can survive seemingly impossible situations if they have the determination.

"Oh, that's just great," thought Polly rather glumly. "I think I have the will and determination, but somehow I don't think that this will be enough," she inwardly groaned as she continued to flick through the pages and read on.

> The situation will no doubt put you under immense phys-
> ical and mental pressure. ["Quite right!" thought Polly] You

will have to overcome fear and anxiety, thirst, hunger and fatigue, as well as sleep deprivation, boredom, loneliness, and isolation.

"So what's new?" Polly remarked with tongue in cheek as she thought back to her days at the orphanage.

As her eyes scanned down the long list of conditions to expect, Polly shook her head from side to side. "Yes, I think I can say without any fear of being contradicted that I, Polly Brown, am suffering from each and every one of these ailments," she tearfully concluded as she browsed up and down the list, mentally ticking off each disorder.

Wiping away the fresh tears that were now forming, she continued to pay close attention to all the advice on hand, for she desperately needed all the encouragement she could get to help lift her out of the deep depression she was now feeling.

> Confidence will help you to overcome these stresses, and physical fitness will also give you the resources to cope. Yes, the fitter you are the better you will survive, so start training now!

"Oh, yuk," groaned Polly out loud. "I hate exercise at the best of times."

It was at this point that she decided to move on to the food section. This lengthy section offered much useful advice concerning which animals were best to eat and which berries would provide sustenance in times of trouble. The book suggested various animals ranging from hares and rabbits to guinea pigs, lizards, snakes, boars, and numerous rodents, including rats. Polly shuddered as she read the list of suggestions.

"I've already been there with the hare," she loudly exclaimed, at the same time thinking back to that terrible day at the orphanage. "And there is absolutely no way that I'm ever going to eat a rat! I would much rather die, thank you very much," she snorted, feeling most disgruntled at her very limited options.

Her mood only worsened when she later read down the same page that rats carry diseases. She continued to read out loud:

So, when gutting, you must take the greatest of care not to rupture the innards. Cook thoroughly.

Polly shook her head and sputtered before deciding she was in well over her head.

"Oh, that's really great," she wailed. "One minute the rats are eating me, and now I'm expected to return the favor and eat them," she sadly groaned.

She despondently continued to flip through the pages, hoping to find further advice on food that would be more appealing and therefore more palatable. She despaired when she discovered that none of the other suggestions were the least bit helpful either. No, there was no hope of her catching a camel or a crocodile or a raccoon for that matter, at least not while she was held captive in this dingy dungeon! So at the end of the day, it was either eat rats or starve! She therefore made the wise decision to hastily move on to the section that dealt with thirst.

In the water section, she read that, "Plants and cactus, as well as the eyes of animals, are a good source of water."

Again this information only served to make her feel thoroughly queasy as she pictured herself sucking on the eyeballs of dead rats.

"I think not," she said out loud while feeling pretty disgusted. "Corporal Beanpod can have his book back." She closed her eyes tight, feeling utterly doomed.

As she sat on the stone floor alone and in the deepest depression she had experienced for some time, she decided there was only one thing left that she hadn't already tried, and this was to send up a small and rather urgent prayer for help. She felt more than a little stupid, but reasoned that as she was clean out of fresh ideas, anything was worth a try!

"After all, desperate people do desperate things," she whispered, once more closing her eyes to help her to concentrate. "So here goes."

Dear God, remember me? Now I know there have been many times in the past when I have been really angry with You. I don't want to minimize the effect all this must have

had on You, but I am in one of the worst crises that I've
ever had to face. Yes, we both know full well that I've had
many of those to date, and that sad fact makes me feel
awfully embarrassed. But I assure You, hand on heart,
that this one beats them all. It is with this in mind that
I am going to ask, or at least try and persuade, You to give
us a break and intervene on our behalf. For I am fairly
sure that if you could see us now, you would readily agree
that we are well-and-truly up a gum tree AND might
I add, without a paddle!

Polly momentarily paused to consider if there was anything
she had missed and therefore needed to add. Oh dear, I think
I meant to say, "Up the creek without a paddle." Will I ever get
anything right?

Oh, and by the way, if You do decide to send help, then
I promise I will try much harder to be nicer toward You.
Thank You for listening. Amen. Yours faithfully,

Miss Ever-So-Desperate.

She then buried her face in her hands and thought of Thomas,
"Oh, dear Thomas, how I miss you so terribly, and Eton, I miss you,
too." She then remembered her little brother, James, and felt really
guilty that she had forgotten to keep in contact with him. She determined there and then to write him a nice and very upbeat letter,
promising that when she returned she would take him with her to
Piadora, but until then she needed him to remain perfectly quiet
about her adventure.

She was in the process of neatly folding up her letter to James,
having just put the final kisses on the bottom, when she unexpectedly heard a noise. Polly immediately stopped what she was doing
and listened intently. Yes, she could definitely hear the sound of
hooves followed by snorting. The noise got louder and louder as
the sound of hooves approaching the window got nearer before
coming to an abrupt halt right outside. Although the window was
too high up for her to see out of, she knew that the horse was now

right under it, for she could hear the snorts from his flared nostrils. Polly jumped up from where she was sitting and raced over to stand directly under the window.

"Hello! Hello! Can you hear me?" cried Polly.

"Yes I can 'ear you!" shouted back a voice in broken English.

"Please, can you help us, for we are prisoners, innocent of any crimes!" Polly yelled.

"Of course, thees is why I am 'ere," replied the voice that Polly now recognized as a French accent. "Don't worree, I weel get you out of there in no time at all," called the most reassuring voice from outside the walls of the dungeon.

Polly listened and heard the man jump down from his horse. She then heard him give his horse a hearty pat on the back as he ordered him to stay put. Seconds later she heard the crunch of his heavy boots over gravel as he made his way into the castle, then everything went as silent as the grave. Polly used this opportunity to safely tuck her letter to James in her backpack along with all her other worldly possessions before going to stand back under the window.

It was only a matter of minutes before she heard the noise of feet hurriedly dashing down the stone steps towards the locked door. Eventually, the footsteps came to a halt on the other side of the thick door. He twisted the doorknob. It would not open.

"The door is well-and-truly locked!" Polly shouted from the other side.

"That ees no problem for me!" shouted the highly optimistic voice from the other side.

After much banging and just as much crashing the heavy dungeon door finally burst open, and in strode a man wearing knee-length boots, a scarlet red waistcoat, and cream breeches. He also sported the most peculiar hat on his head. Polly thought he looked as though he had come out of another century, so strange was his costume. Once in the room, the gentleman removed his hat and made a sweeping bow.

"Bonsieur, mademoiselle. Boniparti at your service."

"Thank you so very much," cried a very delighted Polly as she rushed over to give him a hug.

The strangely dressed gentleman winced as she flung her arms around his neck and hugged him much too tightly.

"I did not know that the Engleesh were so eemotional," he said in his delightfully broken accent. "In my countree it is customaree to give a kiss on both sides of the cheek, mon cherie," he said, most amused at Polly's excessively tight hug. "Allow me to introduce myself. My name is Napoli Bonaparti, and I am a French commander of the Republican army and a soldier from Paris."

"Nice to meet you, Napoli. I'm Polly," she said as she covered her mouth in her serious but futile attempt to stifle her giggles.

Napoli took no notice and carried on. "Thees is of course my third attempt to come to Engerland. My first attempt failed miserablee when my fleet of galleons was veree sadly sunk in the river Nile in Egypt by one of your admirals. I theenk 'is name was Lord Nellie—or was it Smellie? I cannot remember. All I remember ees it was the most trageec of days for us French."

"Oh, I'm sorry to hear that," Polly sympathetically replied as she sought to console him.

"Hmm," responded Napoli, giving Polly a steely look, for he did not find her words of comfort the least bit convincing. "Then my next attempt failed just as abysmellie when wee French under the command of Villeneuve met the Engleesh at the Battle of Truffles, for yet again wee took a most terrible beating," he said, giving the deepest of sighs. "Now zat I 've finally made it to Engerland, I fullee intend to pay a viseet to an old friend—or should I say fiend—the Duck of Welligog. Do you know him?"

"I think you mean 'Duke,'" said Polly with a giggle. "And the answer to your question is no, I don't know him, but I have heard of truffles, and I believe they are very nice chocolates that only adults get to eat," she said informatively as she reflected back to her guardians' New Year's Eve banquets.

"Weel, anyway," said Napoli, urgently wishing to get on with his story. "I intend to challenge 'eem to a priveet dual, for I 'ave taken all thees defeats veree personally and now I weesh to see 'im face-to-face and sort theengs out once and for all," he said with the most serious note of determination.

"Oh dear," said Polly again rather sympathetically as she continued to try to show some interest, when really she was still thinking about chocolates and how much she would like some. "It's not nice having enemies, Napoli, really it isn't, and I think you'd come away feeling a lot happier if you chose to sit down with him and sort out your list of grievances over a nice cup of tea and cake. You'd be amazed how calming tea can be, and Queen Victoria's sponge is so light and fluffy. I'd go as far as to say that it's really melt-in-your-mouth stuff," she declared with a smile.

"Hmm," was once again the only decidedly vague response that came from Napoli.

"I feel I should point out that many a war has been cut short on both sides due to a nice pot of tea. You should try it, really you should," she advised as she took a diplomatic approach to his problem.

Napoli chose not to give any response or comment to her seemingly helpful suggestion, so Polly decided that the best thing she could do was what all good Englishmen do when faced with an embarrassing silence. She changed the subject, and quickly.

"You must have found my note," said Polly cheerfully.

"Your note, ah yes," replied Napoli, as he brought his thoughts back to the present crisis. "Yes, I was riding along in thee countryside, mindeeng my own business, when a leettle bird pooped on my nice hat," he said, taking off his very strange oblong-shaped hat to show her the fresh evidence that still remained splattered all over it. "It must have been an Engleesh bird. That's all I can say," he said with a half-hearted smile. "Anyway, I stopped my 'orse and pulled out my weapon, but beefore I had time to attach the bayonet and shoot the leettle beggar from the sky, your note fluttered down to the ground. So I peecked it up and read it. The rest you know."

"Well, all I can say is a big thank you," said Polly warmly and appreciatively, "for I was beginning to think that I would be left to die in this hideous dungeon, for it is so cold, damp, and smelly."

"So eet is," agreed Napoli. "In fact, thee smell ees disgustingly pungent. Talking of castles, I find it most strange how the Engleesh love their dingy, dark, and veree damp castles in preference to our lovely chateaus. It is leetle wonder thee Engleesh are so miserable and depressed," he commented as he gave the matter serious thought.

"Yes, what weeth their rising damp as well as all the gloom, then I too would become veree depressed if I 'ad to live in one of thees dreadful places."

Polly smiled and agreed with him.

"Well, as the old saying goes, an Englishman's home is his castle," she replied with a giggle.

"Yes, but why do they 'ave to build large moats around them and 'ave such high drawbridges? To my way of theenking, it makes no sense at all."

"Well, it takes all that paraphernalia to make them feel safe," said Polly, most informatively. "We British are, as you have discovered, very reserved, and we like to hole ourselves in," she said with the greatest of authority. "You know something, Napoli, I'm pretty certain that if it was allowed, the moats around our castles would come complete with killer sharks patrolling them! For at the end of the day we are very private people, not given to allowing anyone to invade our personal space. No, as my Uncle Boritz has always drummed into us, what happens in the castle stays in the castle."

"I beleeve this to bee veree true, Polly," said Napoli, nodding his head as he considered her profound words.

"Yes, sadly we can be quite a secretive and suspicious bunch really," she rather wistfully concluded.

Their conversation was suddenly and very rudely broken by the sound of scampering dogs and loud footsteps.

"Quick, Napoli, I believe Soogara has returned. Now what can we do?" asked Polly, suddenly feeling panicked and fearful.

"Don't worree, I will deal with her, Polly, for I 'ave fought manee battles and therefore I am sometheeng of an expert in the art of war," he said very reassuringly as he touched the tip of his bayonet to ensure that it was still razor sharp. Much to Polly's relief it was.

In little more than a matter of seconds, Soogara burst into the room, Grovelock and Grubstick accompanying her. Both dogs looked frighteningly menacing as they raced forward, their sharp teeth bared. Much to Polly's surprise, Napoli also bared his teeth as he advanced toward all three of them. In seconds he was prancing around, though more like a dancer than a soldier, as he moved from one foot to another weaving his way toward them, waving and swishing his bayonet to and fro in his desperate bid to ward them off.

Polly watched on from a distance, hoping with all her heart that Napoli was as good as he made out he was. "He'd certainly be welcomed by any major ballet company if he decided on a career change," Polly secretly thought to herself as she watched him twirl and swirl, dodging the sharp and deadly fangs of both extremely vicious and bloodthirsty hounds.

"Get them!" screeched Soogara as she ordered both dogs to attack.

The dogs instantaneously transformed into the most terrifyingly ferocious bears that stood on their hind legs as they rapidly moved towards Napoli, ready to tear his flesh into little shreds with their teeth and claws.

"Take thees, you big ugly grislee!" Napoli shouted at the top of his lungs as he courageously swiped his bayonet from side to side as both bears lunged further toward him.

The battle between all three seemed to go on for an eternity before Napoli finally got the upper hand, managing to systematically swipe both bears across their throats with his bayonet. Both wounded bears yelped with the pain before turning on their haunches to make a hasty retreat.

"Get back in there and fight to the death!" Soogara screamed at her injured pets before waving her hand like a wand and changing them into vicious wolves.

Both beasts then turned to face Napoli, exposing their razor sharp fangs as they prepared to pounce on him. Napoli was having none of it. With great swiftness, he moved toward his frightening opponents and swiftly lashed out at the two of them, completely missing his intended targets with his seriously sharp bayonet. Suddenly one of the wolves sprang up, his paws landing on Napoli's chest with such force that he fell over backwards onto the ground. The wolves then set upon him.

"Oh, this is bad; in fact worse than bad," groaned Polly.

She knew she had to do something and quick. Suddenly, out of the corner of her eye, she saw her diamond still lying on the stone floor. She raced to pick it up and threw it as hard as she could at the nearest wolf that had Napoli pinned down by his giant paws, hungrily preparing to devour him. As the diamond hit the wolf directly between the eyes, it went straight through his forehead and out the other side, killing it instantly. The wolf gave one final desperate breath before slumping down hard on top of Napoli's outstretched body.

Napoli wasted no time in pushing the dead beast to one side, but as he did so, the other wolf leapt straight on top of him, and in no time at all Napoli was once again fighting for his life as the wolf savagely plunged his razor sharp teeth into his leg. Polly watched on, horrified. She knew that she had to act quickly if she was going to have any hope of saving dear Napoli from being gored to death by this ferocious beast.

She raced over to where the diamond now lay, covered in the gunk and gore from the brains of the beast she had just killed. Polly squirmed as she glanced down at her once sparkling diamond, for all entrails made her feel squeamish and thoroughly sick. Then throwing all caution to one side, she quickly picked it up and took aim.

"Take that, you ugly brute!" she cried as she hurled it in the direction of the wolf, whose large jaw was wide open as he prepared to rip another chunk out of Napoli's wounded leg.

The diamond once again miraculously hit its intended target with such powerful force that it severed the beast's main artery, causing blood to spurt like a fountain from his open wound. It was then only a matter of seconds before the beast slumped to the ground beside his fellow creature.

Polly rushed over to her bag and fumbled around inside as she reached and gathered up all the other stones she had collected, for she knew she might need to use these as missiles if this terrifying battle was to continue on any longer.

Napoli, though dazed and disheveled, managed to pick himself up from the ground and, lifting his bayonet high above his head, brought it down several times in his bid to severe the heads from the beasts.

"Yuck! How gruesome!" shouted Polly, turning her head to look away.

Soogara did not share the sentiment. Upon seeing her beloved dogs lying not only dead but now headless on the floor, she went into a senseless demonic rage. In a flash, her eyes became liquid fire, and her breath turned to billowing black smoke as she transformed into the most terrifying dragon-like beast, with wings and long talons. The vile and loathsome creature—now nearly the size of a building—flapped its powerful wings before racing toward them, breathing long paths of red-hot fire as it got closer.

Polly stood frozen to the spot feeling absolutely terrified, that is, until she suddenly remembered Ralph telling her the story of David versus Goliath. This belated thought gave her renewed courage as well as the sudden inspiration she needed to quickly make a sling from which to hurl her pebbles.

She raced over to where Dodo still lay and quickly removed one of his shoes, leaving Napoli to temporarily fend for himself. "This will have to do," she thought to herself. She then placed a pebble inside the shoe before placing the shoe in a sling, made up from a piece of material that she hurriedly tore off the hem of her dress.

Seconds later, she swung it over her head and aimed.

"Take that, you slimeball!" she yelled. She watched as the stone flew out of the sling and hit the dragon in the middle of its forehead, causing it to be momentarily dazed. "Oh bother," shouted Polly, "this one worked on Goliath!"

However, all was not lost, for with the dragon now temporarily concussed, it gave Napoli the opportunity he needed to get near enough to slash it across its huge and very wobbly potbelly.

Polly stared as thick blood spurted from the wounded monster, and then trickled like oil across the ground.

"How gross!" she loudly commented. But as she continued to watch the blood weave a path in her direction across the stone floor, it suddenly transformed itself into a pink fluffy cloud.

"Oh no, we're not going down this path again," Polly declared out loud. "There's no way I'm eating any more of that stuff; not now and not ever."

But as the cloud made its way toward Polly it started to wind its way around her torso. In seconds Polly was up to her chin in thick cotton candy that was choking her and on the verge of taking the very life out of her.

"Napoli, help me before this stuff swallows me up!" she screamed.

Napoli turned, and on seeing Polly trussed up in swathes of cotton candy, he rushed over and began to cut away the thick and sticky pink strands that were engulfing and threatening to entirely consume her. Once Polly had been freed, she hurriedly placed another pebble inside the shoe. She then swung it high above her head before releasing it.

"Take this you silly, soppy, sentimental, disconnected drainpipe!" she yelled.

"You forgot to mention 'double-decker'!" Napoli shouted back in her direction.

Polly looked quizzed.

"You meant to say, 'you seelly, soppy, sentimental, double-decker, disconnected drainpipe!'" yelled Napoli.

"Oh," was all the time Polly had to reply to Napoli's rather pompous correction as she watched her pebble fly through the air in the direction of the terrifying beast.

"Bingo!" she screamed excitedly as her pebble tore straight through the dragon's chest on impact.

"Bingo!" shouted Napoli as the dragon looked down at the gaping hole where its heart normally beat before slumping to the floor.

As it collapsed it made a most terrifying noise that forced Polly to stick both fingers in her ears. Once on the floor, its flesh began to peel away, leaving nothing but its skeletal frame. Then this too shriveled up. Polly watched in horror as she witnessed its terrifying features return to the face of Soogara before becoming little more than a skull with huge, dark eye sockets and a pile of decrepit bones lying beside it.

"Well done, mon cherie," said Napoli, focusing his attention on his severely injured leg, which was now bleeding profusely.

"Here, Napoli, allow me to help you," said Polly, as she zealously opened her survival book, frantically searching for the section that dealt with near-fatal injuries.

"It says here that 'open wounds are at risk from infection,' so we must bind that wound immediately," she instructed in a most assertive and matronly manner. "It also says 'foreign bodies must immediately be extracted, preferably with sterile tweezers.' Now do you think you have any foreign bodies in there?" Polly asked as she bent down to take a closer inspection of the wound.

"Do not insult me, Polly. I have never 'ad anee foreign bodees in my being, and I never weel, for I am 100 percent pure French. Foreign bodees indeed…," he muttered, feeling very miffed.

"Whatever," sniffed Polly, refusing to be offended by what she perceived as reluctance on his part to graciously accept her help. "Now Napoli, it says here that we must clean and irrigate the wound before we bandage it up," she said sternly. "I don't suppose you have any alcohol on you, for this will do the trick. So own up, do you have any?"

"Yes, I do have some French Brandy in my breast pocket, for I like to 'ave thee occasional tipple," Napoli rather sheepishly admitted.

"Good, then we'll use that to stop any infection spreading, and then we will use my sling to bandage your wound. Is that all right with you?" she asked, not waiting to hear his reply.

Napoli reluctantly submitted himself to Polly's very basic nursing skills, for having survived fiendish wolves and demonic dragons he felt he could survive anything!

As soon as Polly had finished bandaging his leg, he stood up from the ground to test whether he could still walk. As he hobbled across the floor he announced, "I theenk you may 'ave bound it too tightly, Polly, and eef that is thee case, then my blood flow will become restricted with verree disastrous consequences."

"Oh dear," said Polly, feeling very alarmed. "You might just be right, so come back and sit down so I can loosen it for you."

As Polly fussed over him, Napoli seemed far more concerned about the large gashes to his trousers.

"My breeches are utterly ruined," he cried as he attempted to lift himself up from the stone floor only to find Polly pushing him back down.

"Hang on a minute, young man. I just need you to answer some questions," she said in a suitably stern voice.

"Look, Polly, eef I remain on thees cold, stone floor much longer, in no time at all I weel be suffering from the flu as weel as painful piles," he moaned.

"Don't worry, this won't take too long. Honest," she said looking him directly in the eye in her attempt to reassure him.

Napoli's face showed that he remained unconvinced.

"Right, question one. Are you suffering from shock?" she asked, still staring at him eyeball to eyeball.

"No, I don't theenk so," replied Napoli.

"Well, we had still better go through the list just to make sure," Polly quite rightly insisted. "Are you cold and clammy?"

Napoli shook his head most resignedly.

"Are you dizzy or faint?"

Again he shook his head, but by now he was beginning to get a little irritated. "Polly, I theenk you are being just a leettle pedantic. I'm perfectlee fine, so pleese let me get up from thees floor," he groaned.

Still Polly continued to ignore his pretty reasonable request and carried on her thorough examination. "Have you a shallow or rapid pulse?"

Yet again, he wearily shook his head. "Polly, these ees worse then thee Spaneesh Inquisition!" he bitterly complained.

"Stay perfectly still. There's a good boy," she instructed as she took hold of his wrist and checked for his pulse before moving on. "Are you vomiting or unconscious? No, I think I can safely discount that one," she said dismissively as she turned the page of her book. "Is your skin pale or has it grayish tones?" she asked, studying his face as she briskly continued on with her interrogation. "Hmm… I think we can discount the grey area around your bristly chin, Napoli, don't you think? You say you've always looked that color. Well then, let's move on. And finally, have you lost any of the color in your lips?" she asked, studying his mouth as she spoke. "No, I think we can say with much certainty that they are still a very nice deep pink. There, I think we're done. Napoli; your health check is complete," Polly declared in a very self-satisfied manner as she rather dramatically slammed her book shut.

Napoli was very relieved as it meant he could now get up from the floor, assuming that Polly found no extra information in her book that necessitated further interrogation.

"Thank you very much, Miss Polly Pedanteec," said Napoli with a wry smile as he struggled to get back on both feet.

"Pleasure's all mine," Polly replied as she helped him to his feet.

Suddenly they could hear gentle moans coming from the other side of the room. "Quick, Napoli, I think that Dodo is finally coming around," said Polly excitedly.

Both of them rushed over to where Dodo lay still tied up and crouched down beside him.

"Where am I?" Dodo asked, giving a faint smile.

"Shhh, you are in a castle, Dodo, and we've just been rescued," explained Polly.

Napoli produced some smelling salts from his breast pocket and waved them under Dodo's nose. Dodo coughed and spluttered as he inhaled the frightfully offensive smell that the salts produced. The good news was that within minutes he was able to sit up, and Napoli could cut the cords that had bound him. Dodo was very grateful to Napoli, especially when he heard all that had taken place while he had been unconscious.

"How are you feeling, Dodo?" asked Polly, at the same time laying a comforting arm around his shoulders.

"Well, I'm better than what I was, but I'm not as good as what I was before I got as bad as what I am now," said Dodo with a faint smile as he ran his fingers through his crumpled locks.

"Well, I think it might be a good idea if I run through my book and give you a full and thorough medical health check."

"Oh no, Polly!" gasped a very distraught Napoli. "Pleese do not open your book again, otherwise we weell still be 'ere well into the next centuree," he pleaded, at the same time giving Dodo a quick and very sly nudge in the ribs to get his support.

"I'm feeling fine, Polly; honest, I've never felt better," Dodo insisted.

"I theenk you must take hees word for that, Polly," said Napoli, as he proceeded to cut the ball and chain from around Langdon's neck before retrieving the missing part of his trunk, as well as fragments of his curly tail and clumps of his faded blue fur. "And you would do weel to put all Langdon's bodee parts into your schoolbag for safetee," said Napoli, as he tried to console a very unconsolable Polly. "And then perhaps wee can patch him up at a later date," he said gently handing Polly the remains of her blue friend. "And now my friends, wee reallee must hurree along and leave here before anything else unforeseeable happens," said Napoli with the authority of a general in command.

Polly and Dodo readily agreed.

"There's no way I intend to stay around and clear this mess up," she said loftily as her eyes scanned the bloodstained floor littered with the headless corpses of the dogs, "but I must retrieve my collection of pebbles and my lovely diamond."

She then walked around the dungeon picking up the pebbles and popping them back in her bag for safekeeping. As Polly went about the task of gathering up her pebbles, she noted that the pebble that had miraculously transformed itself into a diamond was once more nothing but a smooth pebble. "Oh well, never mind," was all she thought as she popped it into her bag along with all the others.

"Come along, Polly. Wee must leeve 'ere immediately," Napoli urged as he helped Dodo to his feet. Then with an arm around his shoulder, he continued to prop him up as he headed towards the door of the dungeon. Polly nodded and then smiled to herself as the sight of both of them hobbling along like old men seemed to amuse her.

Once outside the castle, Napoli helped them climb onto the back of his horse before he too climbed up. After placing his feet into the stirrups, they galloped away from the castle as fast as they could.

Finally, when they believed they were safe and well out of harm's way, Napoli helped them down from his horse and they all took a much-needed rest under an old oak tree.

"Napoli, do you have anything we can eat?" Polly rather hopefully asked. "I for one am extremely hungry."

Napoli walked over to where his faithful steed stood and produced a tin lunchbox from his saddlebag. "Yes, I do beleeve I 'ave enuff food for the three of us, for my mother always packs much more than I can ever eet," he said with a big grin. "Right, let's see, what do wee 'ave here? Ahh yes, I 'ave almost a whole tin of escargots. Would you both like to try some?"

"How nice, but tell me, Napoli, tell me in English, what exactly they are," Polly politely asked, recoiling slightly as she peered inside his large tin.

"Snails, and they are quite delicious."

"Snails!" she squealed. "Oh, how grim! No, I don't think I want any of those, thank you, Napoli," she said as politely as she was able.

Dodo declined his kind and generous offer with equal adamance.

"Weel, I also 'ave some quiche," said Napoli, opening up another brown paper bag, "although I 'ave to say that it looks pretty shriveled up and very unappetizing," he said flatly. "However, feel free to try a peece, for eet will still taste veree delicious."

"Yes, please, I don't care what it looks like, for I'm absolutely ravenous," admitted Polly, licking her lips in anticipation.

"Bon appetite, my leetle friends," said Napoli with a smile, handing them both a piece of the sorriest looking quiche. They both gratefully accepted the food and hungrily devoured it in a matter of seconds.

"Your mum makes great quiche, Napoli," said Polly with a smile, "but then the French are supposed to be excellent cooks, aren't they?"

"Yes, they are considered to be probablee thee best in thee world," replied Napoli proudly. "But they are also brilliant warriors and strategists, and so weeth thees in mind, I must bid you both farewell and go on my way to catch up weeth Old Welligog. Now Polly, please remember that thee crossroads are just over that hill, so hopefullee you won't get lost," he said pointing in a northerly direction as he mounted his faithful and trusted steed.

"Good-bye, or rather 'au revoir,' Napoli, and thank you again for all your help," she said warmly as she sidled up to where he now sat high upon his horse and raised her hand to shake his. "Oh, and do remember my suggestion of tea and Victoria's sponge cake. It's a whole lot cheaper than another long and bloody war. Trust me on this one," she whispered as she gave him a wink.

Napoli smiled back, but was prevented from giving any response to her helpful reminder, as before he had time to open his mouth and utter a word Polly had thought of something extra to add.

"Anyway, I do think it's about time we English and French buried the hatchet and settled our differences once and for all," she remarked with the cheekiest of grins.

Polly then suddenly remembered that there was one more tiny favor she required of him. So she asked him to wait and then, turning on her heels, she rushed over to where her schoolbag still lay propped up against the oak tree. She pulled out her letter and raced back to his side.

"Please, could you pop this letter into an envelope and then post it for me?" she said breathlessly as she proceeded to stuff the letter into his hand. "The address of where it needs to be sent is written at the top of the letter, so promise me that you will do this for me, Napoli, for I am very worried for my younger brother," she pleaded with him.

Napoli agreed to her request and gave his word that like all good Frenchmen he would not forget to honor his promise to her.

"All you have to do is pop it into one of many bright red boxes that you will see littered all around the countryside; you can't miss them, Napoli," said Polly squeezing his hand to show the full extent of her appreciation.

Napoli placed the letter in his breast pocket and blew Polly a kiss before shouting, "Vivre La France!" as he waved his bayonet high into the air and galloped off at great speed into the sunset.

Polly watched until he was little more than a dot on the horizon, then casually sauntered over to where Dodo lay resting under the old oak tree. She decided not to disturb him, for he looked so peaceful lying there with his eyes closed.

Polly placed her schoolbag beside him and lay down and closed her eyes, smiling to herself as she fondly remembered Napoli, the strange Frenchman who helped save her. She hoped his meeting with the Duke of Welligog would turn into a happy event for both parties concerned.

Chapter 29
TOBIAS HITS THE JACKPOT

SOON IT GREW dark as well as very cold, and Polly decided that they should gather up their belongings and set off again to find the crossroads before it became too dark to see which road to take.

"Come on, Dodo, it's time to go," she whispered, giving him a gentle shake. Dodo didn't respond. "Dodo, wake up; come on. Stop pretending to be asleep, for we urgently need to be on our way," she pleaded.

Still Dodo did not reply. Polly then shook him really hard before she suddenly realized that her young friend had slipped back into unconsciousness. Polly felt quite beside herself with fear as she wondered what on earth she should or should not do. After all, they were out in the middle of the countryside with not a house or cottage in sight, and it was now beginning to get cold as well as dark. Pure panic clutched at her heart as the full extent of her new and awful crisis fully dawned on her.

Poor Polly felt she had little or no choice but to try and carry Dodo on her shoulders until they could find help. It was no easy matter trying to carry Dodo's heavy, limp body in piggyback fashion. This was made worse by the fact that she also had Langdon and her schoolbag to carry. She knew for certain that the route to find help was going to be a long and painful one, as now she could only go at a snail's pace because she was so weighed down.

If the truth be known, she did think of abandoning him, if only for a season, while she went in search of help. After all, no one would expect a rather frail girl like Polly to physically carry the weight of a boy any real distance, would they? And she reminded herself that she had already fought dragons in the castle and saved him from being eaten alive by the vilest, gruesome rats! So she had done more than her duty required, hadn't she?

"Yes, I don't believe anyone could point the finger at me, if, at this very difficult time, I decided to abandon him to save my own life," mumbled a very faint-hearted Polly to herself as the load of her burden in carrying Dodo had tripled, if not quadrupled.

It took Polly many harrowing hours of trudging and battling through bushes and thorny briars before she made it to the top of the hill, and finally she could head down into the valley. The downhill trip was made much easier because, since no one was around to make disapproving noises, Polly lay Dodo on the ground and then gave him a quick push before standing up straight to watch and hope that he did not go off course as he rolled over and over like a beer barrel until he reached the bottom of the valley.

As she watched his bumpy descent, she did whisper, "Forgive me," closing her eyes as she considered the terrible implications of what she had just done. For as far as she knew the poor, sick boy could now be dead! However, Polly reasoned that she had been given no choice in the matter, and doing it this way had at the very least given her the breathing space to temporarily recover from her ordeal. She was, after all, aching all over and covered in gashes from all the heath and bracken she had struggled to get through as she blindly stumbled along. Her feet soon started to swell and bleed, but still she forced herself to keep on moving.

As darkness fell, the temperature dramatically nosedived to well below zero. And as if that was not enough for her to contend with, the wind too became her latest enemy as it blew up into a gale, howling ferociously as it wickedly mocked her. Soon it became so cold that her ears and nose were burning and her hands and feet felt like frozen ice blocks. Many times she had to resort to literally dragging Dodo along by his feet, otherwise roughly pulling him along from underneath his armpits.

Finally, she collapsed into an exhausted heap by the crossroads and, with Dodo cradled in her arms, she began to sob.

Time passed and no stranger journeyed past them. There came a point in the night when Polly gave up any hope of being found alive.

"Perhaps I should just leave Dodo here and go. Otherwise both of us will die," she reasoned to herself. "Maybe he will be found in time," she falsely hoped. "At the end of the day, he is not my problem. It's not as though I've known him for years and built up some special relationship. So, as far as I am aware, loyalty doesn't come into the picture. I mean, I've done all that I can for him. Nobody will be any the wiser if I abandon him now, for, at the end of the day, no one will know that it was *me*, Polly Brown, that left him. I mean, it's not like I'm doing this without a good reason."

It seemed that for the next few hours, Polly was not only left to wrestle with the cold, but also her acute sense of conscience. Every time she allowed thoughts of abandoning him to rear up, she would find herself torn between justifying her actions and then dismissing them as heartless. More than once she found herself shouting out, "I hate my life, and I hate everything in my life!" But the only response came from the wind, howling back at her as though it personally wished to add to her inner torment. And as if all this was not enough for her to cope with, the heavens then cracked opened and unleashed the heaviest of downpours that had Polly soaked to the skin in a matter of minutes.

"I wish I'd never left the orphanage!" she bitterly yelled out into the thick blanket of darkness. "At least if I was back there, I'd have shelter from this storm as well as a bed and a blanket to cover myself up and keep warm," she most piteously wept.

As she sat on the roadside lamenting her troubles, she suddenly saw two small lights coming in her direction. Polly watched as the beams of light got nearer, only slowing down as they passed her by. Suddenly the car stopped and then reversed, coming to a standstill right in front of where she sat on the curbside.

Polly could hear the whir of the passenger window being rolled down, and then she heard someone call her name.

"Why, if it isn't none other than Miss Polly Perfect herself, or maybe I should call you Polly Putrid, for that has a much nicer ring to it. Or how about Polly Pernicious? Now that sounds just as good," said a decidedly cheery but sarcastic voice. "Fancy bumping into you again, and so soon," he laughed menacingly.

Polly looked up and through her mist of tears she could just see the outline of someone she recognized. It was Freddie Fruitless, along with his entourage.

Ignoring his insulting greetings, Polly jumped to her feet and raced over to the window.

"Freddie, I'm really glad to see you," said Polly, "for I could really use your help."

"Sure, what do you want, Polly? And do be quick, for I am late for tonight's concert, of which I am the star attraction, but I'm sure you already knew that." said Freddie airily, as though he was already very bored and had only stopped out of sheer amusement.

"Well, my friend Dodo is very sick, and I need to get him to a hospital, or if that is not possible, at least to the nearest house," she earnestly said. "Please say you'll help us, Freddie."

"Hang on a minute, Polly, if I rightly remember it was only a matter of hours ago that I was begging for your help," he rather angrily reminded her. "And, if my memory serves me correct, you turned down my offer and refused to help me out. Am I right?"

"Yes, you are," Polly sighed. "But this is different, Freddie. This is not about you or me. This is about Dodo who is so sick he could well die if I don't get him medical attention and fast."

"Sorry, Polly, I don't see the difference. When I needed your help, you flatly refused to give it to me. Unless you get down on bended knee and beg my forgiveness I am unable to offer my assistance," he said, laughing out loud as he gave one of his friends a nudge, which was the signal for all in the car to start laughing. "So it's entirely up to you."

Polly instantly obeyed and got down on one knee in the mud.

"Not good enough, girl," he snorted. "Now get down on both knees if you want me to entertain any thought of helping you out."

Polly dutifully obeyed by getting down on both knees.

"Further down, Polly Parasite," he ordered, patting her on the head with some rolled up song sheets he had in his hand. "There, that's good. Now you finally know your place, for it's down in the gutter where all beggars and misfits belong."

Freddie then began to roar with laughter. His companions were also quite beside themselves with hysterical laughter as they watched the young girl with the shabby dress kneel in the mud, shivering from head to toe.

"Oh look," observed one of the girls, as she pointed down at Polly, "her teeth are chattering and her lips are positively purple from the freezing cold," she giggled as she coaxed her companions to join in the banter.

"Right, now bow lower still," Freddie commanded.

Polly was forced to bend lower until her mouth was right in the mud.

"Perfect," said a very delighted Freddie. "Right, now say after me, 'Oh great and mighty star of the West.' Go on, say it, and say it out loud so everyone present can bear witness to your pathetic groveling," he sneered.

Polly started to repeat after him, stuttering and spluttering as she tried to speak, at the same time spitting out the mud that had passed her lips and entered her mouth. She felt like weeping, for she was feeling deeply humiliated as she followed Freddie's ridiculous instructions to the letter. But what else could she do? For she knew she was prepared to do whatever it took to save poor Dodo.

"Good, now then, repeat after me, 'Oh star-spangled jewel of the East, I bow to your supreme wisdom and humbly beg your forgiveness.'"

Polly swallowed hard and continued to repeat all that he commanded her to. Suddenly, with anger in her breast, she leapt up from the ground and, holding onto the car door for extra support, she leaned through the window to face him eyeball to eyeball.

"Freddie, you've had your fun. Now please forgive me for everything I've ever done to upset you," she said, taking a deep breath. "I promise that I never intentionally meant to hurt you. Now tell me I have done enough to make things right, and help me before it becomes too late and he dies," she cried as she then moved away and went back to where Dodo lay on the ground.

Still Freddie was unmoved.

"Please help us, I beg you!" she cried one final time as she stooped down to check Dodo's pulse which was becoming fainter by the minute.

"Just listen to her," said Freddie, turning towards his fellow passengers to make sure they too were witnessing Polly's utter demise. "'Please, Freddie, don't leave us here, for we desperately need your help,'" he mockingly mimicked in a high-pitched whine.

He then threw his head backwards and roared out loud, for his day was getting better and more fun by the minute.

"God, you are pathetic, just look at you, soaked to the skin with nobody to come to your rescue. Well, I'm glad you have had the decency to make a public apology, but I'm afraid I've changed my mind," he said, throwing his head back further still as he continued to laugh like a hyena. "So you are on your own, girl. Driver, start up the car and drive on," he barked.

For some strange reason the car automatically went into reverse, going backwards a few meters. The driver realized his mistake and quickly changed the gear stick out of reverse, causing the car to cough and splutter before it then lurched forward. And as it drove off, the front tires hit a large puddle, causing the water to rise up into the air and then descend down on top of Polly and Dodo, who was once more cradled in her arms.

A thoroughly drenched Polly parted her dripping hair that was now entirely covering her face and watched on with pure disbelief as the car raced away at great speed until all she could see were its two small, red back lights in the distance.

"Thanks a bunch, Freddie," she whispered as she violently shook her head to shake off the excess rainwater.

Polly was left with little choice other than to make Dodo as warm and comfortable as she could. She still hoped that maybe by morning help would come, if by then it was not too late. As she sat cold, wet, and terribly alone, she felt nothing but numbness inside and out. Time passed and the cold, blustery wind blew and whipped up around them, and all Polly could do was hug Dodo tightly to her chest as she struggled to keep them both as warm as she possibly could.

Suddenly, she thought she heard a small noise, and as she looked up and surveyed the road ahead she thought she could see the headlights of another car coming in her direction. "I hope it's not

Freddie coming back to mock me further," she thought resignedly as she continued to caress Dodo's forehead.

The car slowed down as it approached her. Polly's heart began to race as she wondered who it might be. And then she heard the passenger window slowly being rolled down. As she very cautiously lifted her head up, she saw a head peering out of the car window, followed by a voice that she instantly recognized.

"Hi there. Do you need any help?" said the friendly voice.

"Yes, please," replied Polly as she laid Dodo gently on the ground and moved toward the window to talk further.

"Why, it's Polly," said the familiar voice.

"Justin, is that you?" cried a very delighted Polly.

"Yes, Polly, you've guessed right, and Justin Thyme is here with me as well, for you know as well as I do that we never go anywhere without each other, for we're the inseparable twins," he said as he leapt from the car and gave her a hug.

"Polly, you're soaked through to the skin and shivering," he said in a most concerned manner, beckoning Justin Thyme to grab the blanket from the boot of the car to wrap around her.

"What on earth are you doing out here all on your own?" Justine Kase asked.

"It's a long story," said Polly wearily. "But I'm not on my own. I have a friend who is in urgent need of help," she sobbed, pointing down at Dodo, who lay motionless on the roadside.

"Enough said. Quickly let's get him out of the rain and into the warmth of the car. Justin, come over here and help us. Polly you get in first," he ordered in a very authoritarian manner.

Polly found herself feeling instantly lighter as someone else stronger was at last taking over all necessary decision making, allowing her the space to relax and release all her pent-up anxiety. She allowed Justin Thyme to help her into the backseat of the car, and then both boys lifted Dodo from the curbside and gently laid him down on the backseat with his head cradled in Polly's lap. Justin Kase then placed a thick, warm blanket over Dodo in order to stabilize his body heat.

"Am I glad to see the two of you," sighed Polly as they journeyed down the long, dark lane. "Anyway, what on earth brings you two to this neck of the woods?"

"Well, funnily enough, we are on our way to a concert," replied Justin Thyme excitedly.

"Yes, Polly. Have you ever heard of a band called Freddie Fruitless and the Backsliders?" Polly remained unusually silent. "Well, they are apparently the main artists at this concert, and we think he is just the greatest musician on Earth. We just had to fork out the money for tickets to go and see them. I must be honest with you, we are running pretty late thanks to Justin here, who took all day to get ready," he said with a small hint of frustration in his voice. "But I guess I should be used to his ways by now, for he always packs just about everything but the kitchen sink!" he said with a faint laugh, as though he was trying to cheer himself up.

"That's not fair, Justin," interrupted his friend. "I've only brought everything we need. You'll be jolly glad you brought me with you if you end up requiring anything from a first-aid kit to pajamas or a sleeping bag," he snorted as he pretended to be insulted by his friend's decidedly unfavorable comments.

"Yes, that's true," Justin Thyme admitted. "But I do think that, as usual, you've overdone the preparations. I mean who in their right mind needs three different flavors of toothpaste when one will do, and I hardly think we will be needing the strawberry bubble bath either!" he said, shaking his head as he spoke.

"Well, you'll never know what you need until you need it," responded Justin Kase. "So stop complaining, or I'll leave you to go to the concert on your ownsome lonesome," he said with a slightly twisted smile.

Polly used this break in the conversation to ask Justin Kase if he happened to have a needle and thread. It came as no great surprise to Polly to hear that he had a full sewing kit in his glove compartment. He handed it over to Polly, who used the opportunity to sew up the ripped pocket in her dress.

"Wow, you're amazing, Polly, for you've mended your pocket in no time at all. I've got lots of trousers that could do with a stitch or two," he said with a grin as Polly handed him back the sewing kit.

"Now I can put my pebbles safely back into my pocket without fear of losing them," she said on a triumphant note as she reached into her bag and collected up the pebbles before dropping them into her dress pocket for safekeeping.

"Why are you collecting stones, Polly? I hope you have no intention of throwing any of them at me?" asked Justin Kase with an impish grin.

"Don't be silly, Justin. Of course I'd never throw them at you. But to answer your question, I'm not too sure what they mean," replied Polly. "All I do know is that I need to keep them pretty close at hand, as they proved very useful during my imprisonment in the castle dungeon."

"Dungeon! Oh come on, Polly, you've got to be kidding us. Did you really say dungeon?" Justin Kase asked, his eyes widening like saucers as he turned his head to make full eye contact.

"Yes, that's exactly what I said," replied Polly in a very matter-of-fact tone of voice. "How absolutely unbelievable! So tell me, Polly, how on earth did you end up in a dungeon in the first place?" he asked with a look of sheer horror written all over his face.

"Oh, it's a very long story," said Polly. "Maybe one day I will tell you, but for now I am much too tired and weary to tell you my tales of woe."

Justin Thyme, who had been keeping an eye on the road, turned to see how Dodo was doing and began to talk to Polly. "On a more serious note, Polly, how is the little chap doing?"

"Not too good," Polly sadly replied as she caressed Dodo's forehead.

"Well, I don't want to bring you further bad news, but there is no hospital in this area of the countryside, so help us out. What would you like us to do?"

"Is there any chance you could take us to the nearest house?" Polly politely asked. "And then I can get someone to ring for an ambulance."

"That's fine by us, Polly," said Justin Thyme. "Then we really must rush, for if we miss this concert we will have wasted a considerable amount of money for nothing."

Polly smiled and said she fully understood before adding that she was just really grateful they had stopped to help.

It was not too long before they saw lights in the distance and what appeared to be a large thatched cottage with farmhouse buildings. They took a left turn and drove up a long winding lane until they could go no further. There were lights on inside the house, but when they tried to open the farm-style gate to drive up to the door, it refused to open.

"Have you any tools that can break this heavy padlock and chain to open this gate, Justin?" asked his friend.

"Yes, I have, but I am more than reluctant to start breaking into someone else's property without their permission," said Justin Kase.

"I understand your concerns, but our need is of the utmost urgency, Justin," wailed Polly. "So please just do it."

"Sorry, Polly, but I am not prepared to find myself on the wrong side of the law on your behalf," he said firmly. "I am prepared to leave you my hammer, but then it's up to you to decide whether or not you want to take such a risk."

It was with the greatest reluctance that Polly found herself agreeing to his terms, for she felt she had little choice. The boys carefully and gently carried Dodo to a spot on the grass beside the gate, and then Justin Kase went to the trunk of his car. Soon he produced a hammer, which he then gave to Polly.

"Look, Polly, we'd stay and help if we had the time, but we are now well-and-truly late getting to our concert. We've done all we can, the rest is really up to you."

Both boys gave Polly a hug and then got back into the car and raced off, leaving Polly alone to do the dastardly deed.

Polly wasted no time in breaking the chain off the gate, abandoning the hammer to the roadside as she struggled to drag Dodo across the open land until she reached the porch of the house.

Finally, and with great relief, she placed Dodo on the porch floor and rang the doorbell. Seconds later an old man in a nightshirt and cap opened the front door, holding a candle directly out in front of him so that he could have a better look at the uninvited guest.

"I say, miss, do you have any idea what time it is?" he asked in a most disgruntled manner.

"Yes," replied Polly. "And for that I truly apologize."

"Well, you know then that it's awfully late at night to be waking folks up, isn't it?" he gently rebuked.

"Look, I really am sorry," said Polly, "but my friend Dodo needs urgent medical attention."

"Who needs help?" asked the man with a crooked nose, peering over Polly's right shoulder, then her left. "I can't see anybody."

"That's because he's down at your feet," replied Polly, as she pointed to the bundle that lay in a heap on the floor of his porch.

"Oh dearie me, he does seem in a bad way," acknowledged the old man.

"Well, sir, can you help us?" Polly pleaded.

"Of course, my dear, of course I will help. By the way, I haven't introduced myself," he said, switching his candle from his right hand to his left before holding out a hand to shake Polly's. "My name is Tobias Mortimus, and what might your name be?" he politely asked.

"My name is Polly Brown, and my friend who needs your assistance is called Toby, although his friends call him Dodo," said Polly with a smile as she shook hands with Tobias.

"Right then, I will go and make up a bed for him, then telephone the hospital on your behalf."

"Thank you so much. I really appreciate your help," said Polly, experiencing an overwhelming sense of relief.

True to his word, Tobias made the urgent call to the hospital and also helped Polly to get Dodo onto a bed as they waited for medical assistance to turn up.

Polly pulled up a chair by his bedside and gently held his cold, limp hand until the white ambulance with the big red cross arrived. She then watched as Dodo was gently positioned on a stretcher by two burly men and then placed in the back of their vehicle. She thanked both the men and then stood with Tobias on the porch until the ambulance had completely disappeared from view.

"Well, I'd better be on my way," said Polly, turning to the man with the flickering candle. "Thank you again for all your kind help. You've been a real gentleman."

"Just one minute, young lady," said Tobias Mortimus very sternly. "You cannot leave here until I've received payment for my services."

Polly was very surprised and taken back by his request. "I'm sorry, Tobias," she said. "But the sad truth is I have no money that I can give you."

"Well, that's really not good enough," retorted the old and very bent over man with the crooked nose. "You see, my wife and I run this house as a profit-making guesthouse. It's how we earn our living. And let me tell you, it is great value. You get bed, breakfast, and an evening meal thrown into the bargain."

"But I don't require a bed or any breakfast or evening meal for that matter," said Polly, very puzzled by Tobias's demand for money.

"I'm not referring to you, my dear," replied Tobias. "No, indeed I'm not. I'm actually referring to your friend Dodo, for he had a bed made up especially for him, and he could have eaten breakfast if he so desired."

"That's crazy," replied Polly. "How could he have eaten breakfast? He was unconscious!" she cried.

"That's not my fault, is it?" retorted Tobias. "If a guest declines the offer of breakfast, then that really is none of my concern, but they are still expected to pay the same amount as those guests that stay for breakfast. We're not well off, I'll have you know. In fact, much of the time we struggle to make ends meet…" Tobias's voice trailed off as he considered what else he could think of to encourage Polly to pay up. "And my Marg's cooked breakfasts are the best, with sausages, eggs, bacon, fried bread, and…"

"Well, I think you're being really unfair," said Polly, feeling more than a little insulted by his unreasonable demand for money. "After all, he only lay on top of the bed for a matter of minutes while we waited for the ambulance to arrive," she reminded him.

"It makes no difference whatsoever, young lady," said Tobias strongly. "The fact of the matter is that I had to make up a bed for him, and he had sole use of a room that could have been let out to another guest," he informed her. "And may I remind you there is also the cost of the call to the hospital. If I let all my guests off their phone bills, then pretty soon I would be out of pocket."

"But it was the middle of the night, so surely the room would have still remained vacant," Polly retorted, feeling very frustrated towards this most uncharitable old man. "How can you be so heartless?"

"Enough of your impudence, girl," snorted Tobias, baring his full set of rotting teeth as he spoke. "If you don't pay up immediately, then I will be forced to wake up my Marg, and you won't like what she will have to say to you," he huffily stated. "Also I will be left with no choice but to call the police! For don't think I haven't noticed that you broke the chain off my gate. This, young lady, is a very serious offense that would be viewed as a crime worthy of a hefty prison sentence," he snarled, hoping to add full weight to his side of the argument. "So empty your bag now," he harshly ordered.

Polly bent down and picked up her bag, reluctantly handing it over. Tobias hastily grabbed the bag and immediately upended it, scattering its contents onto the porch floor. He then got down on both knees to sift through her belongings.

"Right, what have we here?" he said, picking up a long, fluffy blue thing.

"That's the half of Langdon's trunk that got bitten off by rats," Polly answered tearfully.

"Well, that's no use to me," said Tobias as he contemptuously threw it over his shoulder. "And I suppose this is the rest of Langdon," he said wearily as he held the badly bitten torso of Langdon in the air for further inspection.

"Yes sir, it is," wailed Polly, watching on horrified as Tobias discarded Langdon's damaged body in a similarly offensive manner to that of his trunk.

"Hmm, a book on survival, a torch, a pen and gold diary, a penknife; indeed, did you not know, young lady, that this is classed as an offensive weapon?" he said, holding the penknife up into the air. "The police will be really interested to know that not only did you break into my property but that you were also carrying a dangerous knife! And let me tell you girl, you could possibly face charges for potential grievous bodily harm, and that, I believe, carries a mandatory life sentence," he seethed, lying through his teeth to frighten her further.

"Oh, please, Mr. Mortimus, I promise you that the penknife does not belong to me. I was just looking after it for my friend Dodo," cried Polly, by now feeling shaken up by his hideous threats.

Tobias ignored Polly's desperate pleas as he continued to rummage through all her earthly belongings in search of something potentially valuable.

"Right, what else do we have here?" he said, muttering away to himself. "No, there is nothing here of any use to me," he snorted, feeling deeply dismayed as he got up from the floor with the intention of confronting her further. He was determined to exact his rightful payment, and she wasn't leaving until he got it!

Suddenly his eye caught hold of her ring. "What is that you have on your finger?" he demanded to know with a terrifying glint in his eye.

"Oh, it's only a ring a friend gave me. It only has sentimental value, I assure you," she replied, twisting the ring around on her finger as she attempted to answer his question.

"I'll decide whether it's worth anything or not," said Tobias with a snarl. "Now hand it over!"

Polly reluctantly agreed and tried hard to remove the ring from her finger. "It's well-and-truly stuck," she cried, pulling at the ring as hard as she was able.

"You're not getting away that easy, girl," Tobias hissed. "Come over here and let me have a go."

Polly proceeded to walk the few paces towards him. He roughly grabbed hold of her shoulder and, taking a firm grip of her hand, then tried with all his might to forcibly remove the ring from her finger. No amount of force worked. The ring was most definitely stuck, just as Polly had told him.

Tobias was getting angrier and more frustrated by the minute. He even resorted to a ridiculous attempt at biting it off Polly's finger. Drawing Polly's hand up to his mouth, he fixed the ring firmly between his teeth and gave an almighty tug.

"Ouch!" he yelped as he reeled backwards in pain, clutching his mouth with both hands and spitting out one of his rotten teeth. "You little brat! Your ring has broken one of my teeth," he angrily cried out as he continued to stumble back and forth with the pain. "Now you're going to pay my dentistry bill as well."

Polly picked up one of her handkerchiefs from the ground and handed it directly to him so that he could try to stem the flow of blood from his tooth socket.

"Right, now empty out your pockets, girl," he demanded, slightly calming down as the pain began to subside.

"But I've nothing in my pockets except pebbles," exclaimed Polly.

"Just do as I say, and that's an order!" Tobias impatiently shouted.

Polly obliged and immediately began to empty her pockets of all the pebbles she had collected. Then she stretched out her arm and opened up the palm of her hand to reveal her collection of pebbles. Tobias was instantly flabbergasted and took a giant step backwards. For there among the pebbles was a rather large and splendid-looking diamond with the word *endurance* inscribed on its sparkling surface.

"This will do very nicely," he announced with a wicked glint in his eye, his face lighting up with sheer delight, for he was indeed a very shrewd man, and he knew a valuable jewel when he saw one. "Yes, God really does help them that help themselves," he said with a mean chuckle.

"Here, take it," sniffed Polly, "for it's of no use to me, and if it means that you will allow me to go on my way, then it's yours for the keeping."

Tobias readily agreed and even went as far as helping Polly to collect up her belongings, for he was so excited to have won what he considered to be the jackpot of all jackpots.

Polly mumbled a good-bye, and then feeling nothing short of the greatest relief she walked down the pathway and hurriedly opened the gate she had used to gain entry onto his land. She wasted no time getting as far away as possible from the uncharitable Mr. Mortimus and his unfriendly guesthouse.

On her way out, she bent down and picked up the abandoned hammer, choosing to hide it under a gooseberry bush for safe-keeping, for now she was more than a little reluctant to be caught carrying such a tool in her bag.

"If an innocent penknife can get me life without parole, then heaven knows what sentence carrying a hammer might bring!" she muttered as she imagined herself being placed in a gas chamber or hangman's noose or, worse still, the guillotine!

Polly shuddered as she allowed her imagination to run riot. She made a mental note to remind herself of the exact location of the bush that hid the hammer, just in case Justin wanted it back. With the hammer now safely tucked away under a bush, well out of sight, she continued to wearily trudge down the long and very winding lane, still anxious to get as far away as she could from Mr. Mortimus and his very inhospitable establishment.

Tobias Mortimus, on the other hand, placed the precious diamond under his side of the bed, tucked away in one of his shoes for safety. He could hardly wait for the new day to dawn so that he could show Marg his exciting find. Now with this treasure in their possession, they could give up their business and retire to live like kings. He found himself quite unable to sleep as thoughts of how to spend his newfound wealth flooded his mind. "A new car, a new house, a luxury holiday, a white yacht—yes, the possibilities are indeed endless," he excitedly thought as he rubbed his sweaty hands with great glee before reaching over to blow out the wick of his candle that still burned brightly on his bedside locker.

The next morning he was up and already in his thick, cozy dressing gown long before the birds even had time to open their eyelids and let out their first twitter. He then excitedly raced downstairs to make his wife a cup of tea, something he rarely did these days. After all, it was a woman's job to wait on a man's every need, wasn't it? As they quietly sipped their sweet tea in the bed with the pillows puffed up behind them, Tobias used this precious and tender moment to share with Marg all the events that had taken place during the night while she was tucked up in bed sound asleep.

"Darling, close your eyes and open your hand, for I am about to give you a wonderful surprise that will change our lives forever."

Marg quickly obeyed, and after closing her eyes she took a deep breath, for her excitement was equal to that of her husband's. Tobias then reached down and placed a hand under his side of the bed. Then with his fingers outstretched he searched for his shoes and, upon finding them, he picked them up one at a time to give them a shake, for he could not be certain which shoe contained the hidden gemstone. Yes, it was the left shoe, for he could hear something hard rattling around. Without getting out of the bed, he lifted the shoe high up into the air and loudly bellowed, "Surprise! Surprise!" as he hastily emptied the contents of his shoe into the palm of her outstretched hand.

Marg opened her eyes and instantly froze on the spot.

"Argh!" she screamed in the highest decibels, for her eyes had just made contact with a most terrifyingly hideous insect. Then before another sound could pass from between her quivering lips, the cockroach quickly made its way onto her pajama top in order to make her full acquaintance. Quaking with fear, Marg reacted by hastily throwing off the bedclothes to leap out of the bed, accidentally knocking her teacup over as she did. The remains of her tea flew high into the air before pouring down all over her dear husband's head.

Tobias sat in the bed feeling most bewildered and stunned. As tea dripped down from his seriously lined forehead, he struggled to understand all that was happening to him. He shook his head from side to side, feeling profoundly distressed that only the night before he had gone to bed a man with considerable riches well beyond his wildest dreams, only to wake up the following morning and discover he was still nothing but a pauper. He was therefore very understandably at a complete loss for words.

This was not to be the case where poor Marg was concerned, for she was now running around the room screaming and yelling endless insults in his direction. She only stopped to briefly bend down and pick up one of her shoes, which she then hurled in his direction.

"Take this, you stupid imbecile!" she cried as her shoe flew through the air.

Considering her hysterical state of being, her aim was surprisingly accurate. Her shoe not only hit the poor man, but now knocked his teacup clean out of his hand, the contents of which were quickly soaked up by his blue and white striped pajamas. She then thundered along the upstairs landing and into the bathroom, yelling all the way. Slamming the bathroom door with a vengeance,

POLLY BROWN

she then turned on the innocent laundry basket to beat it with her bare fists. She kicked it over, cursing as the contents spilled out all over the bathroom floor.

Tobias Mortimus wisely chose to remain in the bed, well out of harm's way. He nursed his head between his hands, feeling sickened to the very pit of his stomach as he tried desperately to come to terms with all that had taken place. As he continued to shake his head from side to side in utter disbelief, he had the awful sinking feeling that although his guests would be served a mighty fine breakfast, he would probably be going without. Also, the prospect that he might well have to go without both lunch and supper plunged him further into the deepest of despair, for he knew exactly what to expect if his wife was in one of her moods, so as he sat unconsolable in his soaking wet pajamas he knew without a shadow of doubt that today of all days her mood was now positively thunderous!

Chapter 30
THE GULLEY OF LOST DREAMS

*P*OLLY LIMPED HER way back to the crossroads, all the time wondering which fork in the road she was meant to take. "Am I meant to take the left, or am I meant to take the right?" she said out loud as she struggled to remember who precisely had given her advice and what that advice might have been. "Oh well, at least I am away from that dreadful guesthouse and that horrid little weasel, Tobias Mortimus," she said in an attempt to comfort herself.

Finally, she arrived at the crossroads and sat down, still feeling thoroughly confused as to which way she should go. Unable to make a decision she decided to reach into her schoolbag and find her diary, for if nothing else she needed to remind herself by writing down where she had hidden Justin's hammer so that it could be returned to him at a later date. And as she was rummaging around for the book her, eye hit on a pebble that sat just inches away from her bag. Polly picked it up and discovered the word *faithfulness* inscribed on its smooth surface. Polly smiled to herself, for she was no longer surprised when these unusual stones seemed to mysteriously appear. She felt certain its discovery would more than likely be explained as soon as she opened up her diary. She was not to be disappointed.

The princess had found the last few days immensely challenging as well as frightening, for she had been beguiled and bewitched by the dreadfully wicked Cotton Candy Queen, who had promised her great beauty in

POLLY BROWN

return for her soul, a very foolish exchange if ever there were one! Yes, the princess had almost sold her birthright by mistakenly believing that eating cotton candy would give her the beauty she so desperately wanted. Look where her foolishness landed her! She had been taken captive along with Dodo and Langdon, and left to die in a rather dank dungeon. Her only hope for survival was to eat rats or at least suck on their eyeballs, something the young princess was not in the least prepared to do! Luckily help was on hand, and she was rescued by a very kind Frenchman named Napoli. Together they battled the Queen, who revealed herself to be an old dragon named Soogara who would use any evil method at her disposal to prevent the young and desperate princess from escaping.

However, the princess had shown herself to be very courageous and innovative, using her head as well as her pebbles to slay the giant dragon, David-and-Goliath style! However, her ordeal was not over yet, for having said good-bye to Napoli, she then discovered that Dodo's health had taken a turn for the worse and there was no help in sight. The princess was left with no choice but to carry and drag poor Dodo (we'll turn a blind eye to pushing him down a hill) until she found help.

Finally the princess believed that help had arrived when Freddie Fruitless and his entourage turned up at the scene. To her horror, he had no intention of doing any charitable act of kindness whatsoever. No, this sad and sorry character would not be happy until he had thoroughly humiliated the princess, forcing her to grovel in the mud before abandoning her and her seriously ill friend to die. This extremely sickening act was something that, at a future date, he would very much live to regret.

THE GULLEY OF LOST DREAMS

489

The princess was finally helped by two young lads who took her by car (an impressive Mini car with excellent suspension and very nice alloy wheels) to the house of Tobias Mortimus. Again the princess was to find herself sickened by this most uncharitable man when he, rather rudely, demanded payment for his help in getting Dodo the care he urgently needed.

Being the opportunist that he was, he quickly discovered he could oppress and pressure the young princess into paying up. On discovering the large diamond that Polly kept in her pocket with the other engraved stones, Tobias really thought his big day had just arrived! Tobias even had the temerity to misquote an adage to the forlorn maiden, telling her that "God helps those who help themselves." The cheek of it! He failed to finish his sentence, which then goes on to remind, "but God help them that are caught!" Just like Freddie, dear Tobias would be given ample opportunity over the coming years to reflect on his miserly and extraordinarily uncharitable ways.

However, all's well that ends well. Dodo was taken to the hospital, and the princess, having paid up, was finally free to go on her way, but not before her acts of faithfulness had been recorded and awarded. For despite being a frail young maiden, she had chosen to stick with Dodo no matter what the cost, and that cost had become higher than ever when she was forced by Freddie to kneel in the mud and beg. The princess had shown herself to be a truly faithful friend, and such people are indeed a rare breed. Now she was very tired and in need of rest. The princess closed her heavy eyelids and fell asleep on the curb of the pavement. She had nothing to fear, for she was being looked after and watched over from above. She also had

POLLY BROWN

no need to worry about what tomorrow might bring, for it would indeed look after itself.

Polly's sleep was deep and sound, and before long she found herself in the middle of a dream from which there was to be no escape. She only came around when she felt someone shaking her and calling out her name.

"Polly, wake up. Wake up," insisted the voice that she instantly recognized. Polly half opened her eyes and looked up to see who was calling out her name.

"Ralph, you startled me!" she cried as she hastily struggled to sit upright.

Ralph put out his hand to steady her before giving her a smile.

"Oh Ralph, am I glad to see you," she said with a faint smile. "I came to these crossroads and then realized I had no idea as to which fork in the road to take," she sniffed. "And then I must have fallen asleep."

Ralph patted her on the shoulder and then sat down beside her. "How is your little friend?" he asked.

"Which one are you referring to—Langdon or Dodo? If it's Dodo he is recovering in the hospital. If it's Langdon, well, he has not fared very well either," she said, opening up her schoolbag and pulling out the remains of Langdon to show him the full extent of Langdon's injuries.

"Oh dear, he does look a very sorry sight," exclaimed Ralph. "How on earth did something as terrible as this happen?"

"Well, I am not too sure you'd believe me if I told you," said Polly mournfully. "We ended up being taken prisoner by this frightful lady named Soogara who locked us up in the dungeon of a castle. It was really scary," Polly confided. "And poor Langdon had the heaviest ball and chain around his neck, and then he was attacked by rats," she sobbed.

Polly rummaged in her bag and finally produced the long length of his trunk that had become separated from the rest of his trunk. "See, Ralph?" she said, waving the bitten-off piece in front of his nose. "Poor Langdon has been through such a traumatic experience that I am not certain if he will ever really recover. It was all absolutely ghastly, I promise you."

Ralph dug deep into his pocket and produced a sewing kit. "Give him to me, Polly, and let me see what I can do to fix him," he said gently.

Polly then watched as Ralph sewed Langdon's trunk back together again. He then stitched up all the bald patches on his rear end.

"There, perfect," he declared triumphantly as he pulled the needle through for the final time. "Here, Polly, now Langdon is whole again."

Polly took Langdon from him, and as she inspected his workmanship she found herself saying, "Ralph, I do declare that this stitching is invisible. In fact your workmanship is truly amazing! For Langdon looks perfect, as though nothing had ever happened to him. How can this be?"

Ralph shook his head and laughed out loud. "Oh Polly, I have had so many years on the road that my clothes regularly wear out and need attention. You could say I've become a little bit of an expert at the art of sewing and darning."

Polly didn't necessarily fully believe him, because as he was explaining his wonderful sewing abilities she could clearly see a number of his toes poking through his striped socks. She was so pleased, however, to have Langdon back in one piece that she dismissed any thoughts of challenging his explanation.

"Oh Ralph, you're a really good man," she said with a smile. "I cannot thank you enough for mending him for me, and so professionally!"

"Are you hungry, Polly?" Ralph asked.

"Absolutely famished," admitted Polly.

"Good," said Ralph. "Well, let's head off to the Toggie Oggi Shack and get ourselves some hot food for our rumbling tummies."

"Toggie Oggi Shack? What and where on earth is that?" Polly quizzed.

"Oh, you'll find out soon enough," Ralph replied as he helped her up from the ground. "Now come on, Polly, let's not waste any more time. My stomach is rumbling just thinking about getting my hands on some deliciously hot oggies."

Polly picked up her bag and placed Langdon carefully on top of her other possessions before closing it up. She then linked her arm in Ralph's and allowed him to lead her onwards to the Toggie Oggi Shack. As they walked and talked, Polly found herself feeling lighter and happier than she had been for a very long time.

"Ralph, I've heard of tiddy oggies. They are Cornish pasties and were made for Cornish tin miners. Their hands were so black and dirty that their clever wives filled pastry with meat and vegetables so that the miners could eat the filling and then throw away the pastry shell."

"You're absolutely correct, Polly, but toggie oggies are just as special, and they are my favorite dish. Just you wait and see."

It wasn't long before they were back at the crossroads, this time sitting comfortably on a bench and munching away.

"You're quite right, Ralph. These taste really good," said Polly, throwing all table manners to one side as she hungrily devoured the piping hot sausages in batter that had been wrapped up in old newspaper for them.

"These little oggies are so scrumptious that I make it my business to visit this shack whenever I pass by this way. But as soon as you've finished, Polly, I want to hear about everything that has happened to you," said Ralph as he gave his mouth a wipe with a sheet of newspaper, leaving black print all over his mouth. Polly laughed and then took out a handkerchief to clean him up.

With their stomachs now satisfyingly filled, Polly went into the greatest of detail in her play-by-play account of all that had befallen her. She told him about Jessica, the little girl she had saved, and then she went on to tell all about her misunderstanding at the airport. "I ended up on the wrong plane, Ralph," she moaned. "And I found myself on a plane surrounded by all these foul creatures that were planning to take me hostage, as well as the French president. Can you believe that?"

Ralph smiled.

"Polly, are you sure those terrifying creatures were not just your imagination or, worse still, a mirror image of the inner demons that you constantly struggle to conquer?"

"Ralph, I can't believe you just said that," cried Polly, deeply offended by his unacceptable explanation. "No, I promise you they were very real, and they had names like Craving and Despair and…"

"Well, Polly, I hate to say it, but don't you suffer from the deepest of despair at times? And doesn't it seemingly paralyze you and make you feel that life is not worth living?"

"Yes, that's perfectly true," admitted Polly. "But what about Craving? Where does he come into it?"

Ralph was cautiously slow to give an answer, but then with a twinkle in his eye, he replied. "Do you not crave love and attention, Polly?"

"Well, yes, but I believe everybody wants love and also needs to be heard," sniffed Polly.

"I agree with you there, and I think it is fair to say that life has indeed dealt you some terribly cruel blows that have created utter carnage in your life."

"Carnage! Yes, that was the name of one of the hideous monsters on the plane," she cried. "And I also remember one monster was called Binge. Oh Ralph, that little fellow was really scary," she cried.

"Yes, I'm sure he was," replied Ralph, at the same time placing his arm gently on hers. "Look, Polly, I am not here to judge or condemn you or for that matter to argue the toss as to whether those monsters did or did not exist," he said, pausing to take a breath. "All I am saying here is that it is very helpful to look within ourselves for answers. For we all have our little monsters that try to take over our lives with the clear intention of bringing us down." Ralph gave her arm another pat as he continued on. "Polly, once we have faced our own demons, then we are halfway there in dealing with them because then they can no longer run amok, ultimately ruining our lives. Can you see that?"

Polly looked decidedly forlorn as she silently nodded her agreement. She then turned and looked, very resignedly, directly into Ralph's eyes.

"So, are you saying those disgustingly yucky and hairy slime-balls like Self-Pity could really be a part of me?"

"I'm not saying anything, Polly, for the truth is only you can answer that question. But let's put it this way, have you ever thought of self-pity as a nice companion to have around? Or how about jealousy? Is that a nice characteristic? Do you like to spend time around others who are filled with anger and hate? And come to think of it, what about Deceit? Was he a lovely monster, or did he make you cringe?"

Polly remained silent as she experienced afresh the measure of heartache she had endured at the hands of Gailey.

"Yes, Polly, I too am thinking of poor, sad Gailey. For at the end of the day, ask yourself this: were her deceitful and cruel ways merciful and kind, or did they add to Thomas's suffering as well as your own?"

Polly shook her head as fresh tears sprung to her eyes.

"Look Polly, if you could begin to understand why she behaves as she does, you will find it much easier to forgive her cruelty. Then you will come away the stronger of the two, for a lack of forgiveness is such a hindrance in getting to Piadora."

Ralph kept a comforting arm around Polly as he continued to commune with her in the gentlest of manners. He knew that her fragile heart was finding these revelations pretty tough to address.

"Polly, I want you to come with me, for I have much to show you that I think will help you continue your journey." He stood up and held his hand out for Polly to take hold of. "Come, we can continue talking as we walk."

Polly placed her hand in his and allowed herself to be pulled up onto both feet. She then bent down and picked up Langdon and her schoolbag and allowed Ralph to direct her up the right-hand fork of the crossroads.

As they continued on their journey, Polly poured out her heart about all the poverty and suffering she had seen on her travels and how unbearable it all felt. She was powerless to truly help them. She then told Ralph all about her journey home on the *Queen Mary*, as well as the terrible, upsetting confrontation with Freddie Fruitless.

"Ralph, he called me some pretty despicable things," she confided with the deepest of sadness. "He accused me of being nothing but a parasite. He said that my parents abandoned me because I was an unbearable little brat, and..."

"Oh Polly," Ralph quickly cut in. "When will you learn that you were born to soar like an eagle, high above all the idle chatter and malicious gossiping of those with nothing better to do with their time? Such people remain like insignificant little sparrows, sitting on telephone poles communicating their salacious gossip. They know no better. You, on the other hand, were created for much greater things. So, rise above all such treachery, and don't stop soaring until you reach and attain your goals, my precious one," he said, stroking his beard as he gave her plight much consideration. "Anyway, where are the blinders and earmuffs that I gave you at the beginning of your journey?"

"Sadly, I think I've lost them, and I am fairly certain that happened when Mr. Mortimus emptied my schoolbag and then rummaged through my personal possessions looking for payment."

"Hmm," Ralph said while deep in thought. "Well, in the future you had better just shut your eyes and stick your fingers in your ears when you see or hear anything that you find discouraging."

Polly dutifully nodded and then rather quickly changed the conversation. "Come to think of it, Ralph, where are we now going?" she asked, with more than a hint of curiosity.

"We, my dear, are heading for Gold Gulley," Ralph warmly replied.

"Oh right," was all Polly could find to say as he led her by the hand along winding dust tracks and over many grassy plains. Finally he stopped in his tracks and, shielding his eyes from the glare of the sun, announced, "Yes, I think we are almost there."

As they headed down into the gulley, Polly noticed a large sign that read Gold Gulley, with an arrow underneath to point the traveler in the right direction.

They walked slowly through the gulley, and Polly found herself speechless, for she did not know what to make of all she saw, and Ralph seemed more than content to remain silent, just giving her hand the occasional tiny squeeze.

As Polly surveyed the horizon, she found herself unable to contain her curiosity a moment longer. "Ralph, what on earth are you showing me all this for? And why is this place full of old rusty and abandoned ships and boats?" Ralph remained silent, which only served to provoke Polly into questioning him further.

"Please tell me why this place is called Gold Gulley when all I can see is a junkyard full of twisted, rusty wrecks that are most likely full of lethal contamination that could seriously affect our health? Come on, Ralph, be honest. Can't you smell the stench from the rust?" she cried as she ran over to where the nose of one boat was all that remained above the ground, exposed to the elements. "Why have you brought me here?"

Ralph quickly came over to where she was standing, near the decrepit remains of what was once obviously a beautiful sailing vessel.

"Polly, one question at a time," he said wearily. "You asked me why it was called Gold Gulley, and I would like to address that question first," he said. "But not before we have paid a visit to a very dear and good friend of mine who lives and works in this little shack over there," he said, pointing to a little run-down house in the distance.

Polly was about to protest, but changed her mind when she observed that Ralph had a serious look of determination written all over his wearied face. She therefore decided to stop all line of questioning and meekly follow him with Langdon safely tucked under her arm.

As they entered the tumbledown hut, they were met by an old wizened man with thinning, snowy white hair. He abandoned his melting pot to come over and welcome them.

"Polly, this is Mr. Shoestring, the smelter, and his job is to melt the precious metal down until it has been thoroughly refined."

"Nice to meet you, Mr. Shoestring," said Polly, putting out her hand toward him as she broke into a warm smile. She shook his frail hand and then instantly found herself overwhelmed by the heat.

"Ralph, it's so hot in here that I can barely breathe," she cried, wiping away the beads of perspiration that were now furiously trickling down her forehead.

"Forgive me, I hadn't noticed," he answered, slightly tongue-in-cheek.

Polly then checked on poor Langdon. If she was finding the heat too much too bear, what about him? For he had a coat of thick fur to contend with! Luckily, Langdon seemed to be fine. Polly was quick to observe that neither of the men was the least bit phased by the intensity of the heat, so she was extremely puzzled and perplexed to note that she was the only one dripping with perspiration!

As if he could read her mind, Ralph smiled and answered her question, "Oh, young Polly, both of us are used to burning heat, for we have both been through the fire so many times that it can no longer harm us. Come and take a look at Mr. Shoestring's melting furnace, and you can see for yourself what is going on," he said, gently coaxing her nearer the furnace and its open white flame.

Polly reluctantly found herself moving toward the furnace. The nearer she got, the more she found herself recoiling. For the heat from the furnace was so intense that her face felt as though it was melting like wax.

Ralph stood at her side, supporting her arm as he pointed toward Mr. Shoestring, who was busily scooping out all the impurities from a humungous gold vat.

"Polly, my friend, all gold has to go through the refiner's fire under the most intense heat until it goes from a solid form to liquid. Once all the impurities have been removed, it literally becomes see-through. Here, take a look. The purer the gold, the better the carat, and the more transparent it becomes."

"Oh," was all Polly could manage to utter before she felt the fierce heat burn into the back of her throat like a branding tong, causing her to feel right on the verge of passing out.

Ralph saw that she was struggling to stay upright and quickly guided her back outside for a breath of fresh air. Once outside, Polly was instantly relieved and took a deep breath, "Thanks, Ralph. I really thought I was about to collapse back in there," she weakly stated.

Ralph gave her a supportive smile as he led her away from the hut in search of a suitable place to sit and talk.

"Polly, Gold Gulley is officially known as the 'Graveyard of Lost Dreams.' And it has, over many years, become the burial ground of plenty of inspirational ideas that never transpired because people gave up on their dreams ever being fulfilled."

"Why on earth would they give up?" Polly asked, anxious for an immediate answer.

"Well, they gave up for many reasons, and here are but a few. Some gave up because they were unable to interpret their dreams. Others became too impatient and frustrated by the amount of obstacles in their way, and others lost all belief in themselves and their ability to see their personal dream realized. I have to say that the last one really does bring many down because they feel the most terrible inner pressure to abandon ship midstream. Sadly they never get to see their dreams manifested," he explained with more than a tinge of sadness. "Polly, as you walk with me through this gulley, please take a long, hard look at some of the names painted on the various vessels. Take this one, for instance," he said, pointing in the direction of a very dilapidated boat that lay abandoned on its side nearby to where they were standing. "The vessel is called *It Should Have Been Me*."

"What a strange name to give a boat!" Polly said with some surprise.

"Yes, it is strange. But the question you should be asking is why that particular name? I tell you with the greatest sadness that, it is because its owner never confronted his problem of envy. When he saw others around him reach their goals, instead of being glad for them, he became sad and jealous and no longer focused on his own vision, so it died with him."

"Oh dear," exclaimed Polly. "Now tell me about this boat named *Yo-Yo*."

"Well again, Polly, the owner of that particular vessel was literally like a toy yo-yo. One minute believing it could happen, the next minute throwing his hands up in the air. His life was a real emotional seesaw."

"Ralph, this one here is called by the strangest of names. Come and take a look."

"Ah yes, *Hope Deferred*. I knew its owner well. She waited many years for her dreams to come true, but as the years grew in number, so did her impatience. She prematurely threw in the towel, not realizing that the fruition of her personal and very special dream was just around the corner. Yes, that was a very sad case if ever I saw one," said Ralph, rubbing his chin thoughtfully as he went back in time. "What is also so sad is that had they fulfilled their dreams, then many others would also have benefited from them."

"What do you mean by that?" Polly quizzed.

"Well, think of a skyscraper, Polly."

Polly shut her eyes tightly and began to imagine a very tall, magnificent building. In fact, she imagined the Empire State Building in New York. She had seen many pictures of the building in various magazines.

"Now then, whoever built the first skyscraper must have visualized the finished work in his or her imagination long before it was ever drawn on a piece of paper. Then others came along who could clearly see the vision of this building, and, before long, those building plans became a reality. A beautiful, majestic building was created that soared right up in the sky and gave homes or offices to thousands of people. Polly, please understand that all dreams begin in the imagination, and I have to say that all the best dreams tend to benefit us all."

Polly tentatively nodded her agreement before deciding to climb to the top of a large mound of scrap metal that was piled high with the timber frames of many vessels.

"Ralph, take Langdon for me," she rather breathlessly called out as she carefully threw him high in the air for Ralph to catch. Luckily he did. "This one's called *Ain't That a Shame!*" she shouted down in his direction. "And this one here is called *Is This for Real?* Hey, guess what! There's even one boat called *Could Try Harder*! And I have to say that it sounds very similar to what teachers happily wrote on my many school reports," said Polly with a giggle.

Ralph smiled as he watched her climb higher and higher, stopping sporadically to call out all the different names of abandoned boats trying to guess the reason behind why they had ended up on the scrap heap.

"Polly, it is interesting to note that of all the names you have read out, there are none with names such as *Victory* or *Endurance* painted on their sides," he shouted up as his eyes caught hold of

Polly rather precariously balanced on the bow of a boat. "Come to think of it, Polly, what name would you choose if you were given the opportunity of personalizing a vessel?"

"That's easy," Polly replied with a grin. "It would be called *Land of Hope and Glory*, and before you knock it, Ralph, I know it's a song. But it never fails to inspire me and bring tears to my eyes."

Ralph held out his hand to help her descend back onto safe ground.

"Polly, I feel I must point out that there is a distinct possibility that those horrific monsters you came face-to-face with on the plane were, in fact, the Dream Stealers, whose sole purpose is to discourage and prevent wonderful dreams from ever being realized."

Polly wiped her mucky hands down the front of her dress and then sat down to listen to Ralph. She was totally unaware that her jaw was gaping as though she were catching flies. Eventually she asked the question that was dominating her thoughts.

"Yes, but what does all this have to do with Mr. Shoestring or his melting pot?" she asked, showing genuine interest.

"I just knew you were going to ask me that one, Polly," said Ralph as he gave the broadest of smiles. "And the answer is really simple. Just as gold is placed in the refiner's fire and heated to such an intense temperature to remove all impurities, so there are also times and seasons when our lives too go through fiery trials that I tend to call the *furnace of affliction*. And I think it is true that few of us are left out of these testing times. Did you notice that the liquid gold had no control over where it went?"

Polly nodded.

"Well, that's a bit like us at times. For when we are facing fiery trials, we often find ourselves feeling a bit wobbly and all over the place. And if we're honest with ourselves, we have to admit that we don't like it because when things go bad we feel out of control."

"Yes, all wobbly like jelly. That's exactly how I feel at times," Polly commented, feeling pleased that maybe she was finally getting the picture.

"You are absolutely right, Polly. Like limp jelly, strawberry flavor, if you like," he said with an impish grin. "Well, I think it's true to say that the greater the dream, the greater the cost, and ultimately the fiercer the furnace. And for the majority of people who have a dream, it remains lost in its embryonic form, never being birthed, for the cost of following after it is seen as being way too high."

Ralph looked into Polly's eyes as he spoke, for he needed to know that she was seriously taking in his reflective thoughts on this matter.

"Do you remember the night I visited you in the orphanage when you were polishing shoes?"

Polly nodded and said she did.

"Well, that particular evening I told you the story of Joseph the dreamer. Do you remember that story?"

Again Polly nodded.

"Well, his brothers hated and mocked him and abandoned him to a pit. They told their father that he was dead. You must read that story one day, Polly, for he went through some terrible trials before his dreams came true. And likewise, friends betray or abandon us—or worse still, mock us—because they cannot see where our vision is going or they do not believe in it. Hmm, I do believe there are times when it will cost us everything we are and everything we have to follow it with all our heart," he rather solemnly declared.

Polly drew a deep breath as she considered the reality of following after her dream.

"Polly, promise me that you will never forget this gulley that is filled to overflowing with abandoned shipwrecks because their owners could not pay the price."

Polly touched his hand and gave her word that she would never forget all she had seen and learned that day in Gold Gulley.

"Come on, Polly, let's get out of here. I don't suppose you fancy another round of toggie oggies, do you?"

"That sounds like a great idea, Ralph," Polly beamed. "Lead the way."

Polly picked up Langdon and her bag, and after linking her spare arm into Ralph's, the two of them went in search of the Toggie Oggi Shack to fill their hungry, empty tummies with more hot and very delicious miniature Yorkshire puddings filled with sausage and onions.

Chapter 31
PACK UP ALL YOUR CARES AND WOES

*W*ITH EVERY CRUMB well-and-truly demolished, Ralph suggested they move on.

"I'm not wishing to be rude, Ralph, but where are you taking me now?" asked Polly, slightly irritated that he wanted her to follow him yet again. For couldn't he clearly see she was exhausted and therefore in much of need of some serious shut-eye?

"I would have thought by now, Polly, you'd give up challenging me every time I make a request," said Ralph with a mock smile. "But then, I guess that's what makes you Polly Brown."

Polly was quick to realize that she was causing offense and so, without further hesitation, she leaped to her feet with renewed fervor and enthusiasm and cried, "Come on, Ralph, let's go then. You lead the way, and I will follow."

"That's sweet music to my ears," said Ralph with a grin.

They made their way down into the valley before Ralph pointed to a steep hill they needed to climb. The hill was very slippery due to the recent downpour, and Polly found herself climbing a few meters only to slide back down. Before long she was covered from head to toe with mud.

"Look at me, Ralph. I look an absolute mess!" she shrieked with laughter.

"Do I look any better?" replied Ralph, who was indeed almost unrecognizable due to the amount of mud on his beard and clothes. "Anyway, Polly, it's good to see you laughing, and I'd go as far as to say it really suits you."

Polly felt stumped for words. She had not realized she was having fun, and it only took climbing a silly muddy hill to provoke laughter and happiness to well up within her breast.

"Yes, Ralph, as usual you are right. It is good to laugh," she openly confessed.

"Well, Polly, they do say that laughter is good for the soul. Of that truth there can be no denying," he replied with a grin.

After many attempts and just as much laughter, they finally made it to the top of the hill.

"Sit down right here, Polly," Ralph ordered. For once, and much to his relief, Polly obeyed without questioning. "Now look into the valley below. What do you see?"

"Oh Ralph, I can see crowds of people at a pop concert, and there is a big sign saying that everyone's welcome. So, come on you old crooner. Let's go down and join in the fun."

Polly reached the bottom of the hill long before Ralph and stood patiently waiting for him. He arrived some minutes later, albeit a bit winded.

"I'm not as young as I once was," he complained as he struggled to get back his breath. "I'm sorry, Polly, I don't wish to spoil your fun, but I think you're going to have to count me out on this one."

"Oh come on, you spoilsport. Don't back out now. Look, there is even a shack giving away free bags of candy-coated peanuts. So what are we waiting for?"

"Polly, I'm rather surprised that so soon after your encounter with the Cotton Candy Queen, you readily rush towards the next free offer without the teeniest bit of caution."

"Isn't that what life's about, Ralph? Throwing caution to the wind and having lots of fun? Or are we intended to be real misery guts for the rest of our lives?" she said with a note of sarcasm, at the same time throwing up her hands to signal her growing despair.

"Well Polly, I personally think you would be ill-advised to go to the concert, as it is yet another distraction to prevent you from getting to Piadora."

"Piadora can wait, Ralph. For once in my life I want to have some fun."

"Oh well, at the end of the day, it is for you to make your own choices and suffer the consequences if anything goes wrong," said Ralph rather ominously. "But, I would still caution you to be very careful, for if I rightly remember, was it not Soogara who told you that nothing in life is free, and there is always a price to pay?"

"Thanks, Ralph. I will, and I'll also remember to save you some candy-coated peanuts," she said perkily, wrongly believing that he had given her his full blessing to go and join in all the fun. She gave Ralph a quick hug in the forlorn hope that this would cheer him up. She then quickly disappeared into the throng of bodies that were making a procession towards the peanut shack. Finally, and much to her delight, Polly very quickly found herself at the front of the queue. As she grabbed the bag with both hands, she very politely said, "Thank you, Mr..."

"It's Mr. Forget Your Cares and Woes," replied the man with a wicked grin on his face. "Now be a good girl and move over, for I've hundreds of other people to serve."

Polly did not obey the man's request, preferring to stand and stare at him, for she was fixated by the thought that she must know him from somewhere. The man turned away to pick up more bags, and as he swung back around to face the counter, he was surprised to see Polly still standing open-mouthed and staring at him.

"Look, young lady, off you go. Yes, go and eat, drink, and be merry, for tomorrow never comes," he said, his grin widening as he spoke.

Still Polly stood holding up the increasingly impatient queue as she stared directly into his eyes. It took the person behind her to be quite abusive and insulting before she moved out of the way so that others could collect their free bag of candy-coated peanuts. Then, with the bag clutched tightly in her hands, she weaved her way through the throng in pursuit of her two friends, Justin Kase and Justin Thyme for they had earlier in the day mentioned they were heading to a concert.

Finally she clapped eyes on them, but as she held up her arm to catch their attention, her other arm was knocked into by a passerby. The bag flew into the air, scattering her candy-coated peanuts all over the muddy grass. In a matter of seconds, Polly watched, horrified, as they were quickly trampled into the ground by the excited crowd as they danced to the rhythm of the music. Polly groaned as a voice behind her said, "Sorry about that."

Polly turned and angrily shouted, "I can't believe you did that!" followed by, "Are you blind? Can't you see where you're going?"

But she was wasting her breath, for whoever had caused the accident had already disappeared into the swelling crowd, leaving onlookers to just stare at her as if to say, "What's your problem?"

"This concert is already not going to well for me," she muttered to herself as she considered making a hasty retreat back to the hill in search of Ralph. "Not only have I lost my whole bag of peanuts, but I've made a complete idiot of myself."

As she turned to exit the crowd, she came face-to-face with her friends.

"Polly, it's great to see you," cried both the Justins at the same time. "Come and join us. We have a great view of the stage from here."

"How did you manage to get a ticket?" Justin Thyme asked. "Our tickets cost us a small fortune."

"Oh, I think they've opened it up to everyone. Maybe there weren't enough tickets sold," Polly suggested.

"Oh, never mind. It's just good to see you again."

"Justin, about that hammer, I have hidden it in some bushes..."

"Look, Polly, I can hardly hear you over the music, so talk to me later, for I am here to enjoy myself. You've already missed some of the best bands, so do me a favor and just enjoy yourself," he ordered, a huge grin lighting up his face.

Polly hesitated as she momentarily deliberated as to whether she should head back to the stall and get another free bag or whether it made more sense to just stay put and be with the boys. As she looked over in the direction of the peanut stall, she saw that the queue had now grown massive in size, so the decision to pursue another bag of candy-coated peanuts was rather sadly abandoned.

Polly wasted no time in joining in the fun. She danced and sang along, and in no time at all she had forgotten Ralph. It felt good to let her hair down for once and forget all her cares and woes. The next group to come on stage and perform was aptly named Frantic Frenzy, and their job, like their name, was to work the audience up into a hysterical frenzy. The girls on stage were extremely scantily clad as they cavorted in front of their audience, at the same time singing into their microphones in the most suggestive manner.

Polly felt slightly uncomfortable singing along to some of the words, but then thought, "Hey, this is only a pop concert, so does it really matter what they sing?" She then found herself inwardly scolding herself for being, in her own words, a stuffed T-shirt. After all, it was important to her to fit in unless, of course, she wanted to go through life alone with no real friends, and she knew the answer to that one.

"Aren't they just brilliant, Polly?" said Justin Thyme.

"Yes, I think I'm going to buy their album. Remind me of their name if at some future date I forget."

Polly nodded her agreement.

Finally, the lead singer of Frantic Frenzy came to the front of the stage and, placing the microphone up to his mouth, cried out, "Well, guys, it's good-bye from us. Have a great evening, and you've been a brilliant audience. But before we go, there are still many other groups to help you dance the night away. So see you around."

The evening wore on, and at a time when things were really in full flow, Polly, for some unfathomable reason, found she no longer wished to stay at the concert. She felt extremely tired, and she also admitted that she was already missing Ralph. Finally, with the heaviest of hearts, Polly decided to abandon the rest of the concert and go in search of Ralph.

"Justin," she cried, tapping her friend on the shoulder as she attempted to get his attention over the deafeningly loud music.

Justin moved his head closer in his attempt to listen, but still had his eyes glued to the stage. "Yes, Polly, what do you want now?" he asked, slightly irritated.

"Justin, I don't mean to be a wet rag, but I'm tired, so I think it's time I left," she shouted in his ear.

"I can't believe you want to leave so early, Polly, when the fun has only just begun!"

"Yes, I know, but I'm finding the longing to get to Piadora once again overwhelming, so I think I've been a little foolish to stay as long as I already have."

"Well, suit yourself then, Polly, but I paid a king's ransom for these tickets, so I'm staying until it's over," was his only response as he continued to sing along, his eyes still firmly fixed on the stage in front of him.

Polly felt both sad and lonely as she left her two friends and headed away from the crowd. And as she made her way to the bottom of the hill where she had abandoned Ralph, a lady cornered her.

"Come this way, love. We're showing free movies, and you'll get free cotton candy thrown into the bargain," the lady shouted in Polly's ear.

Now that little piece of information not only had Polly's heart racing faster than ever, but her feet as well, for there was no way she was going to be put through such an awful ordeal ever again. As she raced as fast as her feet would allow toward the hill that she had originally slid down, she almost missed Ralph sitting by a clump of bushes, well out of view.

"Did you enjoy the candy-coated peanuts?" asked the familiar sounding voice.

"Ralph, is that you?" she cried breathlessly.

"Come and sit down beside me, Polly, until you've caught your breath," he said as he patted the ground beside him.

Polly slumped down at his side. "Are you mad at me, Ralph?" she asked as soon as she had calmed down.

"Mad at you! Why would I be mad at you?" Ralph came back at her quickly.

"Well, for one thing I abandoned you to go to this concert, didn't I?" Polly stated.

"Polly, you didn't abandon me. I chose not to go, and there's a difference," he replied.

"Well, you were right not to come," said Polly despondently. "Because although I enjoyed the concert to begin with, eventually I found myself feeling quite disgruntled and sad as the evening progressed. Oh, and before I forget, some idiot knocked my bag of candy-coated peanuts right out of my hand. I never even got to eat any," she said, sounding most disgusted.

"Polly, that idiot you are speaking of was me," Ralph rather sheepishly confessed.

"Oh Ralph, how could you be so mean?" Polly furiously cried out to show her annoyance.

"Well, I did it for the best reason. You had already got yourself tied up in knots with Soogara, and I did not wish for you to find yourself in yet another sticky mess."

"And what precisely do you mean by that?" Polly angrily cried.

"Well, have another hard look at Mr. Forget All Your Cares and Woes, and tell me if you recognize him," Ralph ordered.

"Oh my goodness! I do recognize him! It's Vanaspi!"

"Yes, and you can be certain that if he is here, so is Soogara." Ralph commented.

"Yes, she must be, for I was offered more cotton candy while I was on my way to find you," sniffed Polly. "Look, Ralph, please accept my apology. Sometimes I'm so dumb, and I don't think straight."

"Apology accepted. But in the future, it might pay you to listen to an old man's advice. Sometimes you need saving from yourself, Polly."

Polly nodded. "You're right on that one."

"I know there are times when you think that I'm just a prehistoric, out-of-touch old man, but I have some wisdom inside this old head of mine."

"Well, even if you are a prehistoric old man, you still have the heart of an angel," she said with a beaming smile.

Chapter 32
LANGDON'S EPITAPH

*R*ALPH WALKED WITH Polly until they found a comfortable bench, and, despite it being a very cold night, Polly stretched out on the bench, placing her bag under her head to act as a pillow. Then with Ralph's warm coat around her she fell sound asleep. Ralph sat on the ground beside her and stuffed scrunched-up newspaper down the top of his shirt to keep warm as he watched guard over her.

As a new dawn broke, Ralph gave Polly a gentle shake to wake her up.

"Leave me alone," she whimpered. "I'm tired, and I want to go back to sleep," she drowsily moaned as she shifted her body over and closed her eyes.

When, hours later, Polly woke up again, she discovered that Ralph and his coat were gone. She rubbed her eyes and noticed a gold cage with a note attached standing on the ground beside her. As she peered closer, she clapped eyes on a small yellow and green bird who was not sitting on the perch provided, but remained huddled in the corner of the cage, his face and beak buried deep into his breast. Polly sat up straight and then removed the string with the attached note. She opened the note and was surprised to discover that it was from Ralph.

Dear Polly,

I did try to wake you up this morning, but to no avail. Sorry I had to take my coat back, but the sun was shining and you seemed perfectly *content and warm as you lay on the bench well out for the count. I will catch up with you later at the castle ruins in Carabunga Dike. It's position is clearly marked on your little map, so you shouldn't get lost.*

Polly momentarily abandoned the note to check her map and was very relieved to find that as Ralph had stated, it was indeed marked by a big circle. She then continued to read his note.

Before you set off, I do I have a few requests I wish to make. Before you start to object, as I'm more than certain you will, I want you to think carefully about our visit to Mr. Shoestring, as well as our tour around Gold Gulley.

Hodgekiss sends his love and says he is really looking forward to your arrival in Piadora. He also tells me that the preparations for the banquet are going very nicely, and not to worry about a party dress for he also has that problem in hand. However, in the meantime he has a couple of things he needs you to do for him.

The first request is that he needs you to take care of Herbert, his pet bird, for him. Hodgekiss tells me that Herbert is suffering from a very bad case of nerves and has not been his old self since he was rescued from the old people's shelter, where he lived for many years.

Sadly, while he lived there a number of the old folks did not fully appreciate his singing voice, so they would prod him through the bars with their walking sticks and bash his cage with their upturned walkers, which not only frightened him but also hurt his feelings, for he is a highly sensitive little bird. When these terrifying acts of violence failed to shut him up, they resorted to being very mean and regularly confiscated his bird food, hence his noticeable weight loss.

Now Herbert seems to be suffering from deep depression and has seemingly lost all will to live. This is where you come into the picture. Hodgekiss thought you might be the perfect person to help him overcome his melancholy, as he badly misses Herbert's shrill tweets and will not rest until he sees him well again and full of the joys of spring.

He has left a little book for you to browse through at your leisure, and you will find this resting on the floor of the cage. Please take time to thoroughly read it. Hopefully it will be a very useful tool in helping towards Herbert's full recovery.

Now if you are finding this unusual request hard to agree to, there is worse to come. I promise you, Polly, that if it were not absolutely essential, Hodgekiss would not even think of demanding such a difficult thing of you. Even as I put pen to paper I find myself shuddering inside at the impact the following request will have on you. Here goes: before you continue on your journey to Piadora you must say good-bye to Langdon, and to cap it all, Hodgekiss is further recommending that you bury him!

Polly dropped the note to the ground. There was more to the letter, but Polly was in no fit state to finish reading it.

"Say good-bye to Langdon? I think not!" she gasped, at the same time wrenching her hands together as she felt a tidal wave of emotion threatening to erupt from within the deepest recesses of her soul.

"How could Hodgekiss do this to me?" she furiously yelled. "I thought I could trust him, and now he has betrayed me. I can't believe he's done this to me after all Langdon has been through. Hodgekiss, you're nothing but a rat!" she screamed. "And if you had any decency about you then you would never have asked such a terrible thing of me. Well, forget Piadora, for I am heading home to the castle," she shouted, at the same time giving the cage an almighty kick that sent it rolling across the path.

"You're on your own, Sherbert Dip," she yelled out loud before picking up her bag to walk away from the bench and a very dizzy Herbert who was still reeling from his sudden and very unexpected flight across the pathway.

As she marched down the path at a furious pace, she thought back to Gold Gulley and then Mr. Shoestring with his melting pot. Polly momentarily faltered as images of all the abandoned ships and boats flooded her memory and added their weight to her growing personal conflict.

"No, forget everything," she yelled angrily while shaking her head in sheer dismay. "It was all just one big crazy dream anyway. So let the dream die," she whispered most despondently. "For I no longer care about Hodgekiss or Piadora."

Polly strutted a few more paces before stupidly turning around to take one final look at Herbert in his cage, and instantly she became filled with remorse. How could she pour out her anger on a defenseless little bird? At the end of the day the little chap was after all innocent of all crimes and had never done anything to harm her. Polly made a deep groan before slowly and most miserably walking back toward the cage. As she stood towering above the cage, everything inside her screamed out, "Walk away. Walk away while you still have a chance. Herbert is not your responsibility."

"Yes, that's right. He is not my concern. After all is said and done, I never actually offered to look after him, did I?" she reasoned with herself. "Therefore, I am not the least bit responsible if anything bad were to happen to him. No, Hodgekiss would have to take all the blame."

She was about to abandon Herbert to his destiny when other more disturbing voices began interrupting her train of thought. "Leave him here, and he will surely die," they seemed to be chanting. The chants were getting louder by the second. "Yes, poor Herbert is used to being ill-treated, so he can handle a bit more, and when he does die of hunger or exposure, no one will care, for he is only a sad little bird."

"Stop it. Stop it right now!" yelled Polly, clutching her head with both hands. "I can't carry my bag and Langdon as well as Herbert's cage. No, I only have two hands. I can't do everything," she resentfully added.

Polly slumped back down on the bench and placed the dome shaped-cage containing Herbert by her side.

Herbert, who had managed to roll over and get back on both feet, remained huddled in the corner of the cage, shaking from head to foot. His tender ego was very bruised as he struggled to come to terms with what had just happened to him. Suddenly their eyes met, and in that brief moment in time, Polly knew there was no way she could leave Herbert to his fate. No, if it meant struggling for a while until she reached the castle ruins, then so be it. For deep inside, she knew she would never forgive herself for walking away and turning her back on this scrawny and sorrowful little mite who needed some mercy shown to him.

Polly opened the cage door and tried to stroke Herbert on the head with her finger, but Herbert cowered even further.

"Well, I guess you are now my sole responsibility, Sherbert. So you could say we are now joined at the hip," she said, making a wearied sigh as she stared directly into his beady little eyes. Her eyes then made contact with the little book that was lying on the cage floor. So she opened the cage door and squeezed her hand in, picking the book up between two fingers. As soon as she had taken the book out of the cage, she read its title out loud to herself, "*Champ.*"

Being the curious young lady that she was, she opened the book and began to read.

Are you struggling with all the difficult circumstances in your life?

Polly gave a nod.

Are you constantly defeated, depressed, and suffering from low self-esteem?

Polly gave her mental assent by nodding again.

Well, don't despair, for help is at hand. Here are the ten healthy steps to transforming your life. And if you follow these simple guidelines, pretty soon you will find all melancholy disappearing, and you will be singing like a bird. Step number one. Find a mirror and stand directly in front of it. Then, smiling like a Cheshire cat, say out loud: "I am a wonderful and exciting person who radiates love and warmth to all I meet." This little exercise must be done three times a day for the next thirty days.

Polly stopped there to take a quick and furtive glance at sad, hostile Herbert. Their eyes met, and they stared at each other for quite a while. Eventually Polly broke the ice by shaking her head and making very rude and derisory comments regarding Herbert and his sorry condition.

"Sorry, Sherbert, but I guess I see you as a bit of a dipstick. I can't really see any hope for you."

Herbert did not flinch at her very undermining comments, preferring to remain huddled and motionless with his beady little eyes still permanently fixed on Polly.

"Well, anything is possible, I guess," she said resignedly. "So do me a favor, Sherb. Get up from your backside and quickly totter up your ladder and onto your perch while I adjust your cage mirror," she commanded, poking her hand into the cage to change the position of the small mirror and to wipe it clean with her index finger. "There, that's better. Now you can take a good look at yourself." She sighed.

Herbert, however, was having none of it. He just continued to stare in her direction. "Now, be a good birdie and do as I've asked," she pleaded. "Go on, jump up onto the perch." Polly might as well have been talking to herself, for Herbert had not the slightest intention of budging—not even one inch.

"OK, Sherbert Dip, have it your way," she said through gritted teeth, for she was becoming thoroughly exasperated with him. "I guess we'll have another try later when you've stopped sulking," she added resignedly, feeling very frustrated with what she perceived as downright defiance on Herbert's part.

Polly placed her bag over her shoulder, and with Langdon under one arm and her hand firmly fixed on the cage handle, she got up from the bench and began to walk in the direction of the dike and the castle ruins.

"Sherbert, I am going to take you as far as the dike, but you need to know now that after that I'm calling it a day and going home," she sniffed. "So I don't want you to think I'm abandoning you, because I'm not. Ralph is meant to meet up with us there, and that is my opportunity to hand you back over to him, OK?"

Polly walked and walked, dragging her heels as she despondently made her way to the dike. After what felt like an eternity, she finally decided that she needed to rest, for she was now staggering under the weight of her load, and the heat from the sun had made her feel horribly sticky and uncomfortable. After finding a suitable place, she unburdened herself first of the cage then of her bag and Langdon.

"Right, Sherbert, I think this is as good a time as any to redress the issues that got you in this mess, so be a good boy and do me the honor of climbing up that small ladder onto your perch."

Herbert continued to ignore her.

"OK then, Dipstick. If it's war you want, then you've got it!" she shouted giving the cage an almighty wack that sent shudders down Herbert's spine.

Polly then chose to sit with her back to the cage, thinking that ignoring him might well be the answer. It did not work. Finally, it was Polly who caved in and decided to have one more final attempt to help Herbert.

"OK, Sherb, let's look at the next chapter in the book and see if the suggestions it makes are any easier for you to follow." Polly picked up her small book and turned to chapter two, again reading it loud for the benefit of Herbert.

Well done, you've passed the first step with flying colors. Now, don't you feel much lighter and better for that? Now, it's time to take the next step toward achieving your personal goal. Again this will involve a mirror.

Polly slammed the book shut and moaned, "This has absolutely no chance of working, Sherbert, if you continue to refuse to jump on to your perch and face the mirror," she said, staring straight into his beady eyes. "Yes, I think I can say I'm wasting my time, and for what? A skinny, pathetic wimp of a bird who quite clearly has no intention of helping himself onto the road of recovery," she said, throwing the book to one side, and picking up Langdon to console herself. "Here, take a look at Langdon," she ordered, thrusting poor Langdon up to the cage bars. "Why, he has been through the most terrible ordeal, risking life and limb, and yet he has come through it all shining."

Still Herbert showed no interest in any of her ranting and railing. Polly begged on her knees, rattled the cage, jumped up and down, and continued to yell at him. He remained as cool as a cucumber, quite lost in his own little world.

"Well, you're obviously either stone deaf or a very stubborn bird, if ever there was one," she said sarcastically. "At least eat some of your bird food before you utterly waste away, you little stick insect," she cried as she attempted to coax him toward his seed tray by tapping loudly on the side of the plastic container.

Herbert continued to ignore Polly, preferring to bury his head deep into his bright yellow breast.

"Well, I'm certain eating seeds, as well as berries, came up in my SAS survival book. So would you mind if I help myself to some of yours as you don't appear to want it?" sniffed a very incensed Polly.

Polly crunched on a handful of the birdseed and instantly spat it out. "Ugh, this stuff is gross. No wonder you're seriously depressed, Sherbert. I would be too if I was forced to eat nothing but birdseed all day. Poor Corporal Beanpod! To think he's expected to eat this stuff as well when he's on jungle maneuvers. Well, that makes him a real hero in my eyes—either that or a complete idiot."

Eventually the sun started to disappear behind the trees, and Polly thought it was time to make tracks toward the dike and the castle ruins, so she placed her bag over her shoulder and once more, with Langdon under one arm and holding the cage in her other free hand, she set off. Before long she found herself struggling with her cumbersome load, and very quickly she found herself forced into dragging the birdcage along the ground. Poor Herbert buried his head even further into his breast as the thick dust from the ground circled around inside the cage, causing the poor bird to cough and wheeze as the dust threatened to choke him to death.

Finally, Polly let out a deafening squeal that even managed to have Herbert standing at attention.

"Look! We've finally made it. Look over there." she said pointing her finger, "Can you two also see the castle ruins?" she cried excitedly.

Polly wasted no time and quickly made her way down the steep hill, bumping and bashing the cage as it hit rock after rock on their descent. She headed across a muddy moor to where the ancient ruins stood.

"Gosh, this place is amazing," said Polly, slightly awed by the remains of the castle that were still standing. "This place must have been really fabulous once. Look at the columns, Langdon, and what do you think of this arched window? I bet many a princess was rescued from here by a shining knight in armor, eh Langdon? What do you think?"

Polly's fresh enthusiasm became very short-lived when she realized that Ralph was nowhere to be seen, and she was once again on her own in what felt like a desolate wilderness. Placing Langdon and Herbert down beside her, she took her bag off her back and sat down on a rock to have a good grumble.

"I can't believe he's done this to me," she wailed. "He promised to meet me here, and he's let me down. Now what do I do? I want to go home, and I can't carry Herbert the Heavy a moment longer," she moaned. "Yep, I'm absolutely exhausted, not to mention fresh out of new ideas. Come on, Sherbert, it's your turn to sort out this mess. Surely you can come up with something, you skinny birdbrain!"

Herbert still remained on the floor of the cage, his ears firmly shut to her very inflammatory remarks thought he continued staring at her most intently through his small beady eyes. As darkness fell and the wind began to whip up around them they were a sorry sight to behold.

At one point Polly went off in search of somewhere they would be less exposed to the elements, but there was nowhere suitable to be found. She also considered digging a hole and hiding in some undergrowth. She remembered that her survival book had advised that. It would preserve their body heat and keep them warm. But as she considered that option, she felt panicky. If Ralph did finally turn up, then he would not be able to spot them and they would find themselves truly abandoned. She came to the sad conclusion there was nothing they could do except see the night out, cold and exposed, sitting on large boulders in the castle ruins.

Eventually it began to rain, lightly at first, but before long it had turned into a torrential downpour. As the rain soaked through to her skin and Polly began to shiver and shake, she found herself yet again in the deepest pit of despair.

"I hate my horrible life, for nothing good ever happens to me!" she screamed into the darkness, and the only reply that came in response to her anguish was the deep, mocking howl of the icy wind as it bit deeply into her skin like sharp pine needles.

Eventually she fell to her knees on the muddy ground, curling up in a ball and wishing with all her heart that this nightmare would come to an end.

The rain continued to pour down, and the wind continued to rage. And Polly? Well, she continued to beat her fists in the mud as she vented her anger and frustration at all that she had been through, as well as what she was experiencing right up to this moment in time. How could life deal her one treacherous blow after another?

Finally, after she had reached complete exhaustion, she came up with a solution that she believed was her only way of escape: surrendering to Hodgekiss's cruel and very heartless request and burying Langdon.

She would then make her way home via the police station and place Herbert in their care. She realized that this option would involve considerable paperwork that required her to explain quite how Herbert came to be in her possession. She felt slightly panicky at the thought that they would think she had stolen him from some little old lady's house. They would almost certainly find her story of Ralph, Hodgekiss, and Piadora more than a little hard to swallow. However, she felt she had no other choice.

Polly got up from the ground and went in search of a suitable burial site. She then got down on all fours, and with her bare hands she began to remove the earth to make a large enough hole for Langdon. As she scooped up the earth she found renewed strength, mainly due to the amount of anger she was unleashing as she continued to dig. Polly then went in search of a boulder to mark the spot where he would be buried.

"Elephants need tombstones just as much as people do," she muttered as she searched high and low for a suitably smooth boulder on which to write his name and something loving to remember him by.

Pretty soon she found the perfect stone, and after searching her bag for her lipstick she began to think about a suitable inscription. After thinking hard and long she began to write in large bold capitals on the smooth surface of the boulder.

> To Langdon the elephant that I love
> I trust you'll understand
> This is the hardest thing I've ever done
> And none of this was planned
>
> I'll never forget you in all of my trials
> For you gave me great comfort and joy
> Don't forget me either friend…
> …Remember you're my favorite cuddly toy.

Polly struggled to keep her composure, but to no avail, as she finally finished writing her Poem of Remembrance only to break down and sob her heart out.

She knew she had to get this awful event over as quickly as possible before she changed her mind. She drew a deep breath and walked over to where Herbert and Langdon sat most innocently and unsuspectingly by the castle ruins. She picked up Langdon and placed him under her arm, and then as an afterthought she turned to confront Herbert, "You're coming with me as well, Sherbert," she cried. "So don't think you're getting off that lightly, for you need to be witness to the amount of pain your arrival on the scene has caused me," she informed him in the harshest of tones.

She then grabbed hold of the handle and dragged his cage over every lump and bump on the ground until she was back at the hole.

"Right, stay there," she commanded as she deliberately swung the cage around in the air before dropping it to the ground in the most inconsiderate and ill-mannered of ways.

Polly then picked up Langdon and, after getting back down on her knees, gently placed him on the hole, trying hard but failing miserably not to look at him for fear that she would break down completely. But it was no use for, as she half peeped at him lying pitifully in the muddy, blackened hole, she experienced the most indescribable pain pierce through her already shattered heart.

Polly was just about to fill in the hole, albeit reluctantly, when she found herself feeling a wave of pure rebellion welling up inside her breast. In a matter of seconds it manifested itself in the most terrifying rage. As the wind howled ferociously around her, biting into her flesh mercilessly in its taunts, she leapt to her feet and yelled, "I can't do this! What you're asking of me is downright cruel, and you should be reported to some society that protects defenseless animals. I wish I'd never met you, and I'm never coming to your stupid tea party!" she screamed at the top of her lungs before reaching into the hole to pull Langdon out by his trunk as a gesture of her complete defiance.

Holding him very tightly to her chest, she planted a kiss on his forehead before slumping down beside the hole in stony silence. Fresh tears began streaming and making track marks down her muddied face as she sat on the mushy ground, feeling both very bitter and utterly defeated. Minutes later she jumped up and, placing Langdon to one side, moved towards the boulder where she had earlier written her tribute to Langdon. She then roughly turned it full circle and then with her pen in her hand she wrote some large letters on the other side.

"There. That says it all," she angrily muttered to herself. She then moved over to the birdcage and opened the cage door wide. "Right Sherbert, you've seen all there is to see, so do me a favor and clear off," she angrily ordered. She threw herself into the hole to lie down, her arms crossed in front of her in a most defiant manner.

Of course the hole was much too small, and she only managed to fit in the middle half of her torso, making her extremely uncomfortable, but she was well past caring about such things as comfort.

Herbert, who had been watching the whole performance from the safety of his protective cage, continued to remain unmoved by her emotionally charged performance. He chose to remain huddled at the bottom of his cage with his beady eyes firmly fixed on her. And if he had any thoughts on the matter, he was being a very wise old bird by keeping them to himself. As he continued to peer directly into her eyes, Polly suddenly sat up and began to shout at him in a most hysterical and ill-tempered manner.

"Go fly away, birdbrain, for this is where it all ends. Read my tombstone if you don't believe me!" she yelled, at the same time pointing to the words inscribed on the boulder.

Herbert did not move. He just kept on looking deep into her eyes as if he were trying to reach her soul.

"Well, if you can't read, then I'll read it for you, dipstick," she cried. "It says, 'HERE LIES THE BODY OF MISS EVER-SO-MISUNDERSTOOD,' and underneath, bird-brain, if you hadn't noticed, it says RIP. So jolly well do as those three little letters suggest. Buzz off and allow me to rest in peace."

Still Herbert remained huddled in the corner, totally unmoved by all her ranting, but very glad to be in his cage with its protective bars.

"If I were you, I'd get out of here quickly," she continued to yell angrily in his direction. "If you continue to stay and give me the evil eye, I swear that soon you will find yourself becoming bird pie, and that's a promise," she threatened in a most menacing manner.

Still Herbert did not twitch a muscle as he continued to stare long and hard directly into her flaming eyes. Polly gave up and slumped backwards into the partial grave. As she continued to lie in the hole, it was not long before various insects tunneled their way through the soil, anxious to make her acquaintance. So pretty soon she had hundreds of the little things crawling and scurrying all over her, some even having the temerity to scuttle down the front of her dress.

Seconds later a family of curious and very slimy worms joined the gathering and began to weave their way merrily down her ankle socks in search of warmth. Polly froze in terror as insect after insect and bug after bug joined ranks and began to congregate on her chest as they prepared to investigate further.

Finally Polly found her voice and let out the most deafening screech. She leapt to her feet as she frantically tried to shake off the unwelcome visitors that were rather cheekily burrowing into her clothes.

"Get off me, you foul creeps!" she screamed as she gave the side of her head a hard slap to dislodge a centipede that was happily setting up home in her ear. "I hate this world! I hate this world!" she repeated over and over as she stormed off back toward the castle ruins, leaving Herbert as well as Langdon abandoned by the boulder.

Polly sat on a rock by the castle ruins for what seemed an eternity. She hardly noticed that it was still raining or that she was soaked through to the skin and shivering.

Hours passed and still she sat miserable and resolute on the stone. It was still dark when she finally surrendered and accepted that the burial must go ahead, and maybe, just maybe, Hodgekiss would one day explain why he had asked such a terrible thing of her.

Slowly she made her way back to the hole and her abandoned companions. She discovered that she needed to dig a new hole as the other one had now become a pool of squelchy thick sludge, due to the incessant downpour. She walked around until she found a fresh site and then began the difficult task of scooping out the earth for her fresh grave. Her hands were so frozen that she found herself making little progress, and as a result this new hole was not only much smaller in diameter but also shallower.

"This will have to do," she muttered to herself as she stood up to brush herself down.

She gave Langdon a final lingering kiss and then gently lay him down in the new hole. She covered him up with the soil she had removed, and with every handful that covered him, there became less of Langdon to see. Many times she wanted to just pull him back out of the earth and go home, but she ignored this overwhelming desire and continued to heap more soil on top of him.

Polly thought she was doing very well until she saw part of his trunk rising from the earth. She grabbed another handful of soil and poured it over his trunk before squashing it down firmly with both hands. No sooner had she done this than a foot arose from the grave. Polly attempted to squash this back down and was aghast to observe that his trunk had yet again defiantly arisen from the earth. Poor Polly was indeed finding the whole affair of burying Langdon impossible! Eventually she gave up trying and went in search of the boulder on which she had written her ode in memory of him.

After lodging the boulder firmly in place, she then set about making a cross with a couple of twigs and a spare red ribbon from her bag. Finally, when she had done all she could, she got up from her knees and stood for the customary minute's silence.

Then with the heaviest of hearts, she turned and walked away from the scene as fast as her legs would allow her. She passed by Herbert still sitting forlornly in his cage, and although she admitted that she was still feeling deeply resentful towards him, somehow she found it in her heart to pick up the cage and walk on, only this time at an even faster pace. She didn't dare turn her head for a final look, for she knew she couldn't. She had, after all, just buried the only real friend she had ever known, her battle-scarred and trust-worthy soulmate whom she loved more than life itself. No words could even begin to touch on the depth of anguish she was now experiencing at her loss.

Chapter 33
HERBERT'S FULL RECOVERY

*A*S POLLY CONTINUED to walk away from the castle ruins she had little idea as to which direction she was going, but the truth was that she didn't care a nut or bolt about anything, anymore. No, sadly, she didn't even care to look at her map, and she cared even less to make any form of meaningful conversation with Herbert, such were the feelings of emptiness and despair she felt inside.

The new dawn broke, and she just carried on walking. She trudged down mountain passes and wandered through valleys. She made her way across shallow streams and meandered slowly through thick undergrowth and forests, oblivious to the fact that her shoes were worn out and the lower half of her legs were covered with deep scratches and painfully large bruises.

At one point on her journey she tripped over a large boulder and tumbled headfirst down a hill, Herbert's cage rolling and crashing behind her. When Polly finally picked herself up, she discovered that not only had she twisted her ankle pretty badly, but she had also lacerated her right arm. Still, she kept walking like a dead man, and in total silence. All this was very disconcerting for poor little Herbert, who quickly decided that he much preferred being shouted at to being completely ignored.

"Tweet, tweet, tweet," came the small sound from the birdcage. But Polly was far too occupied with her thoughts to even notice his sudden unexplainable chirping as she continued to stumble along, the pain in both her ankle and arm increasing by the minute. Herbert was left with little choice but to continue on chirping as loudly as he was able in the forlorn hope that she would eventually wake up and realize that this new and very joyous noise was coming from him.

"Tweet, tweet, tweet," continued the sound from the cage as Herbert carried on chirping in his attempt to get her undivided attention.

Polly stopped in her tracks and crouched down on the ground, tentatively placing the cage protectively by her side. Her eyes then hurriedly scanned the horizon to see where the noise was coming from; then placing her index finger up to her lips, she gently commanded Herbert to remain silent.

"Shhh...Sherbert, do be quiet. There's a good boy, for I thought I heard something," she whispered, her eyes still focused on the horizon.

Polly remained crouching, her ears finely tuned as she strained to listen out for any strange or unusual movement that might explain the sounds that were by now slightly panicking her.

"No, I must have been imagining it," she said, getting up from the ground and picking up the cage as she continued to walk on.

"Tweet, tweet," continued Herbert, despairingly.

Polly stopped short and then suddenly looked down at Herbert.

"Why, Sherbert, I do believe it's you making that noise!" she cried. "Come on, boy, do it again. Go on; show me what you can do."

Polly dropped to the ground and lay on her stomach, placing the cage directly in front of her face as she made a new and very positive connection with Herbert. As she lay on the ground eyeball to eyeball with Herbert, much to Polly's delight Herbert instantly obliged by opening his little beak and producing some very charming high-pitched sounds. To add to her amazement, he voluntarily hopped on to the ladder and climbed up onto his perch.

"That's fantastic, Sherbert," she said, breaking into an encouraging smile.

Herbert further responded by standing in front of his mirror, his little head held high, and with his beak wide open and his breast swelling like an opera singer, he began to heartily twitter, "Pretty Polly. Pretty Polly."

"Oh, don't try to butter me up now, Sherbert!" Polly sniffed. "It's very impressive to hear you say my name, but it's *your* self-image we're trying to address here, not mine!"

Still Herbert ignored her, and he carried on tweeting "Pretty Polly. Pretty Polly," as he continued to admire himself in front of his little mirror.

"Well, I guess I should just feel happy and content knowing you're finally beginning to cooperate with me so I do believe congratulations are in order. It's wonderful to see you so happy, and it must surely mean that you are also now well on the road to making a full recovery. Oh, just wait until Hodgekiss and Ralph get to hear about this," she cried excitedly. "Oh dear, I almost forgot, I'm not going to ever see them again," she moaned, shrugging her shoulders as she momentarily lapsed back into a defeated state. "Well, never mind, my little sweetie. You should still feel proud of yourself, and if it were physically possible, I would give you a nice big hug. Instead you'll have to settle for a little pat on the head," she said, poking her finger through the cage bars and gently stroking him. Herbert inched closer towards Polly as if to encourage her to continue caressing his head.

"By the way, Sherbert, I'm really sorry about all the awful things I've said to you recently, for you're certainly not a dipstick or a birdbrain or any of the other horrible things I called you. I know my behavior has at times been quite inexcusable, but I can only hope you understand that I've been going through a very difficult patch; you just happened to be the easiest person to take it out on. For that I'm truly sorry," she sniffed, looking into his beady eyes and feeling very remorseful. "I promise I'll never again treat you in such an awful manner. So can we now be friends?"

Herbert nuzzled up against Polly's hand in a manner that communicated that finally all was well.

Polly remained lying flat out on the ground as she carried on gently stroking his little head and breast. Herbert continued to woozily nestle up to her, enjoying every minute of this new relationship that was now finally beginning to blossom.

"Look, Sherbert, I know I said I was going to leave you at a police station, but how about coming with me in search of Ralph?" she suggested in a surprisingly upbeat manner.

As she was putting this bright idea to Herbert, she thought she heard a rustling in the bushes. This was shortly followed by the sound of someone singing. As Polly shielded her eyes from the glare of the sun and looked in the direction of the noise, her eyes hit upon a young black boy heading in their direction holding a large stick as he made his way across a muddy field.

"Hi there," said the boy brightly.

"Oh hi. Come over and join us," Polly said with a welcoming smile.

"Don't mind if I do," he replied before adding, "I think I recognize your voice. Don't I know you from somewhere?"

Before Polly could answer that she didn't think so, the boy excitedly exclaimed, "Yes, I think you were at the concert, weren't you?"

"Yes, that's right. I was there. How on earth do you remember me when the crowd was so large?"

"Ah, you were the girl who had your bag of peanuts knocked out of your hand. I was standing nearby when it happened, and I heard all the commotion."

"Yes, I have to confess I did get pretty upset," admitted Polly ruefully.

"Well, when I heard your cries, I very nearly came over to you to share my peanuts, but then you suddenly disappeared and I don't think you returned. What happened to you?"

"So are you telling me you ate the whole lot?" she gasped, unintentionally ignoring his question.

"Yep, every little morsel," he said laughing. "I'm pretty greedy, aren't I?"

"Tell me, have you suffered any serious side effects?" quizzed Polly, her face now very serious.

"Like what?"

"Well, like sickness, dizziness, anything like that."

"Nope, nothing out of the ordinary. Although, come to think of it, I did feel a little queasy later that evening and my belly kept making the most terrible gurgling noises, but that's all. Anyway, why are you asking?"

"Oh nothing. Forget I ever mentioned it," said Polly, giving a deep sigh of relief.

"Anyway, as I was trying to tell you, before I had time to offer you to share my bag I heard you tell your friend that you were leaving," said the boy, raising his eyebrows as he waited for her to give a full explanation as to why she had left the concert when it was in full swing.

"Oh, it's a long story."

"I'm all ears," he replied with a smile so big and beautiful it could light up the stars.

As he stood and talked to Polly, she had the feeling that there was something different about him, although she was at a complete loss to pinpoint quite what that difference was.

"I promise to tell you later, but first let me introduce myself. I'm Polly, and this little fellow here," she said, pointing at Herbert, "is called Sherbert. At least that's my little pet name for him."

Polly noticed that the boy did not follow her hand as she pointed towards Sherbert and the cage, but she said nothing.

"Nice to meet you both," said the boy with the beautiful smile. "My name is Aazriah Maketti, Aazi for short," he said, breaking into another huge smile that showed off his gleaming, pearly white teeth. "Now tell me, what brings you two out here into the heart of Ballunga Forest?"

"Ballunga? Is that what this place is called?"

"Yep, and I hope you realize that it's a fairly dangerous place to set up camp. So tell you what, how about I join you and make sure that you and little Sherbert get out of here safely?"

Polly readily agreed to his help, especially as she now knew this was a dark and very dangerous place in which to loiter.

"Here, let me help you," said Aazi with a grin.

Polly thanked him as she placed the cage into his outstretched hand. "Hang on a minute while I pick up my schoolbag," she cried. "I'd forget my head if it wasn't screwed on so tightly."

Polly then limped over to where her bag still lay, and after slinging it over her shoulder she joined Aazi. They headed out of the forest clearing, making their way down into a deep valley.

Polly willingly let him walk ahead because he not only seemed to know where he was going, but also because she was still struggling with her twisted ankle. As she followed on behind him, she soon became acutely aware that Aazi walked very cautiously, as though he was studying every inch of the terrain with his outstretched stick before putting a step forward. This puzzled her, for it seemed to be quite out of character for an otherwise strong, confident boy. Again she dismissed this nagging thought, for at the end of the day she was really glad to have his company.

In no time at all Polly found herself back at the same cross-roads where previously she had allowed Ralph to sew Langdon's torn trunk back on. Even thinking back to that event caused her to shudder and momentarily feel the pain of her loss.

"I've been here before," she anxiously confessed to Aazi.

"So have I. In fact, if I'm honest, I've ended up at this precise spot a number of times," he said with a grin. "And each time I seem to take the wrong fork in the road. However, the good news is having gone up all the other wrong roads I am fairly confident that this time I will get it right."

Polly was very relieved to hear this. She too was equally fed up with taking wrong turns. While Aazi stood in the middle of the crossroads, deliberating which road they should take, Polly used the opportunity to find a suitable place to sit and rest a while. With her bag and birdcage safely by her side she sat down on a primrose-covered embankment.

"Polly, don't worry your pretty little head," he shouted in her direction. "I took this road last time," he said, raising his stick into the air. "And that road there the time before. And I definitely came up this road the first time round. So here we have it. This road that I'm now standing on is the right route for us to take!" he yelled excitedly as he pointed his long stick in a southerly direction. "There, sorted," he shouted gleefully before walking back to join her on the embankment. "Well, Polly, you have not answered my question as to why you were out in Ballunga forest all on your own."

"I'm not entirely alone, for I do have Herbert with me. Anyway it's a long and very sad story," Polly replied, pain etched across her faced as she spoke. "I don't suppose you've got a hanky or something similar that I could use as a bandage to tie round my ankle, Aazi?"

"Sure thing, Polly," replied Aazi, pulling out a large handkerchief from his trouser pocket and handing it to her. "Here, take this one as well," he said pulling out another.

"Thanks," mumbled Polly as she used the other hanky to bind up the deep gash in her arm.

"Now, back to the question that I keep asking and you keep evading, Polly. And before you say anything else, I've got all the time in the world, and I'd really like to know," he said, putting a sympathetic arm around her shoulder.

Polly felt encouraged by his kind gesture and proceeded to tell Aazi all about Uncle Boritz and Aunt Mildred, as well as the terrible loss of her dear brother Thomas.

"It was dreadful watching Thomas become so sick and being powerless to help him," she told Aazi in sad, hushed tones.

Aazi squeezed Polly's shoulder and told her that he too knew all about the pain of loss. Polly felt touched by his sincerity and continued on with her story, not stopping until she had brought him up right to date on all that had happened to her since leaving the castle.

"None of this would ever have happened if that stupid door hadn't shut on me," she moaned. "I could have just sneaked back to the dormitory and nobody would have been any the wiser."

"Yes, Polly, but it sounds to me as though living in that dreadful castle was completely destroying you. And look what happened to Thomas. I mean, that was pretty terrible. So perhaps that door shutting behind you was meant to be," he commiserated.

"You're probably right, Aazi," Polly replied rather glumly. "But many things that have since happened to me have also felt awful, some of them falling into the category of being simply too ludicrous for words."

"Yes, but you have also experienced some pretty awesome things on the way," Aazi chipped in, in an effort to console her. "I mean, a trip around the world on Concorde! And then a luxury cruise on the *Queen Mary*! Wow, Polly, I think most people would give their right eye to have seen and done such amazing things."

"I guess you're right, Aazi, but I saw a lot of heart-wrenching stuff everywhere I went, and it seemed to make me feel worse then ever."

"So let me get things right, Polly. Are you saying you would prefer not to have seen them?" quizzed Aazi.

"Yes, I guess that is what I'm trying to say, because it made me feel so powerless to help."

"So really, the truth is that you would prefer to live with your head in the sand rather than feel uncomfortable and a little distressed at seeing something of the suffering that exists in this world?"

"No, I'm not saying that," Polly retorted rather defensively, for she was now feeling a little peeved with Aazi and what she perceived to be his deliberate attempt at upsetting her. "I'm just saying that it has added a heavy toll to the many burdens I already struggle with."

"Don't be mad at me, Polly," said Aazi with a grin. "I too know much about feeling powerless, and at times it leaves me feeling frightened and helpless."

"Well, Aazi, I find that very hard to believe! For you seem so cheerful and confident, prepared to face any challenge that confronts you."

"Not so, Polly. Just like you, I have had my fair share of disasters and trials. And many times I have got so mad that I've felt my blood boil," he admitted with a fresh openness and honesty Polly had rarely seen in all her years.

"Oh, please tell me, Aazi! I have spent so much time convinced that even the very elements are conspiring against me," she cried.

"Well, Polly, as you can see, the color of my skin is a different color to yours, and you probably realize that I'm not originally from this country." Polly nodded. "My birthplace is Zimbabwe in South Africa. Have you ever heard of Zimbabwe, Polly?"

Polly shook her head and told Aazi that she had been to South Africa on her recent travels, including Durban and Cape Town, and she thought that Africa was a very beautiful place.

"Yes, Africa is, as you rightly say, very beautiful. But there are many parts where strife and civil unrest are the norm, and such things bring pain and poverty to many people. Anyway, I lived with my family in a small village in the heart of Zimbabwe. We were very poor, but happy. I had two younger brothers and a baby sister."

"You used the word *had*, Aazi. Don't you mean *have*?" She chipped in.

"Polly, please let me tell the story," said Aazi, lightly scolding her for interrupting him.

Polly apologized and promised she would try very hard not to interrupt again. Aazi cleared his throat and continued with his story.

"Well, there were bands of rebels who were sent in by the authorities to uproot us and burn down our homes to make sure we left, never to return." Aazi paused as he reflected on all that had happened. "To begin with, our village was spared, and they just threw stones at us and called us horrible names. But late one night, while we were all sound asleep, they sneaked into the village and set our houses on fire. My father died trying to save us all from the flames. He managed to get me out, but first he had to remove a huge beam that had fallen on top of my head, pinning me to the floor. The fire was so fierce that I could feel it burning my skin. But as he carried me to safety, I realized that I could not see a thing. All I could feel were his strong arms holding me tightly as he carried me to safety. I can still remember his deep voice whispering in my ear. 'Son, hold on. Please try to hold on. You're going to make it. Tell yourself you're going to make it.' That was to be the last time I heard my dad's voice," he said, his voice cracking with emotion. "I was told later that he went back into the flames to try and save my mother as well as my brothers and little sister," he continued, his eyes welling up with tears and his body trembling as he relived that most terrible event.

Polly too struggled to hold back the tears as her newfound friend relived his story. "Oh, Aazi, I am so very sorry," was all she felt capable of muttering as she took hold of his hand and tightly squeezed it.

"Shall I stop there, Polly?" he asked, his voice cracking even further.

"No, no. Please carry on if you can," she cried, clutching his hand even tighter as she encouraged him to finish his story.

"Anyway, the next thing I remember was waking up to find myself lying in a hospital bed with many machines attached to my body. My face was swollen like a hot air balloon and my eyes were covered by thick, heavy bandaging. They told me I had been asleep for well over two weeks, and I was a very lucky boy to have survived. It would be many days later before the doctors summoned up the courage to tell me that all my family had perished."

Polly put a hand up to his eyes to wipe away the tears that were now tumbling uncontrollably down his cheeks.

"Thank you, Polly," was all Aazi could mumble. He then paused for a few moments as he struggled to take a firm grip on himself. "Eventually I asked them to remove the bandages swathed around my head, and it was then, at that awful moment, that I discovered I was now blind."

Polly gasped and moved her hand up to his face to catch a lone tear that was tumbling down his face. And as she did so, she realized that he did not twitch or move his eyes in recognition of what she was doing. Now she knew what it was that had been troubling her since they had first met up.

"So how come you knew I was at the concert if you cannot see?" she asked, feeling a little perplexed.

"If you cast your mind back, you will remember that I never said I could see you. No, what I actually said was, 'I heard the commotion,' and that when you greeted me back there in the woods I recognized your voice as being that of the girl who got upset at losing her bag of peanuts. I may not be able to see, Polly, but since the accident my other senses have been heightened. My hearing has become very acute."

"Oh, dear, Aazi," cried a now very distressed Polly as she moved over to further console him with a long, comforting hug. "I am so sorry this has happened to you, really I am. It is much worse than anything I have had to endure," she said, fervently embracing him at the same time.

"Polly, you've been through an awful lot too, so let's not compare our pain. I don't think it is very helpful."

"You're right, Aazi. Both of us have been in agonizingly awful situations, feeling hopeless and desperately needing to be rescued," she said quietly, her eyes brimming with tears. "We make a right pair, don't we?" she sniffed as she fumbled in her pocket to find her hanky. "I thought there was something unusual about your eyes, for they didn't flicker at all when I put my hand up to your face. Oh Aazi, whatever you say I still believe that your suffering has been more unbearable than mine," she said softly as she continued to embrace him. "I had no idea whatsoever that you were blind, for you seem so confident and happy with life."

"I am most of the time," he answered, giving a faint smile. "As I lay in complete darkness in the hospital bed, feeling nothing but the despair, the air suddenly became filled with this strange smell that I have come to believe was the smell of hope. And before you say anything, Polly, hope does have a smell. Anyway, as I lay in the bed feeling alone and afraid for my future, a most unusual stranger requested permission to visit me. I had never met him before and I have to admit, Polly, his odor wiped out the beautiful, strange smell. He smelled really awful," he admitted with a large grin. "He told me his name was Ralph, and that he would love me to meet his friend Hodgekiss. I told him that unless his friend came to the hospital, there would be no chance of this ever happening. Anyway, he left me a book which he said one of the nurses would read to me, if I asked them nicely."

"What was it called?" Polly interrupted.

"Well, it might sound crazy to you, so promise not to laugh, but it was called *Jack and the Beanstalk*." Aazi momentarily paused, seeming quite reluctant to talk on."

"*Jack and the Beanstalk*! Why on earth would he give you that particular book?"

"Precisely, Polly. Just like you, I was amazed by his choice, and I have to admit I felt more than a little peeved, as all my life I have been referred to as poor boy." Aazi coughed before continuing with his story. "I can tell you now I found it extremely upsetting to read a story about a poor boy who climbs a beanstalk and eventually becomes rich when I was lying in a hospital bed no longer able to see and having lost my whole family and all my possessions. I became very angry with him," he confessed. "And then to cap it all, when I got over that book, he visited for a second time and produced yet another book. I'll give you three guesses as to its title."

"Go on, Aazi. Spill the beans," Polly urged.

"Well, this one was called *The Prince and the Pauper*, and yes, I found myself just as upset with this book as I did the first," he confided with a small grin.

"Likewise, Aazi, I found myself pretty miffed at being given happily-ever-after books when my life was at an all-time low. Tell me what happened next," Polly said, encouraging her new soulmate to reveal more.

"Well, I'm not sure you'd believe me if I told you," Aazi said falteringly.

"Look, Aazi, after all I've seen and done, I'm more than willing to believe anything. So please go on with your story," she pleaded.

"Well, a few days later Ralph visited me again. This time he placed a ring on my finger and put a green little hard-backed book in my hand before whispering in my ear that his friend Hodgekiss was expecting me for tea at a place called Piadora. Well, I told him that giving me another book was quite pointless, because I was blind and, as I was going to be leaving the hospital over the next few days, there would be no nice nurses around to read it to me. Just like you, Polly, I also told him in quite strong words that his other books had upset me deeply."

Aazi furrowed his brow as he continued to confide his story to Polly. "I was very surprised when Ralph then told me that this book had no writing, so there would be no problem. Before I could challenge Ralph as to why the book was necessary, he surprised me further by informing me that this special book would write itself. What's more, it would be in Braille, so he could see no problem.

"As he left my bedside, he squeezed my hand and said, 'Goodbye, little prince. My friend Hodgekiss, as well as my good self, look forward to meeting up with you again in Piadora.' Before that day, Polly, no one had ever called me a prince. I was only used to being called names like 'scumbag' or 'poor boy.' No, never in my whole life had I ever been called by such a wonderful name," said Aazi, his voice becoming strained with emotion as he spoke of this wonderful happening. "As Ralph said it, I felt a warm tingling sensation down my spine and a deep glow that remained deep inside of me throughout the rest of my stay in the hospital."

Aazi paused to give another one of his beautiful smiles that Polly found so endearing. She had to restrain herself from just grabbing hold of him to give him another reassuring hug, for she was so moved by his story.

"Also, another thing that I found strange was, after he left, a nurse came over to my bedside, presumably to check my progress. She then started to tell me off, saying there were feathers everywhere—on the bed, under the bed, and all over the floor around my bed. She assumed that in a fit of anger and frustration I had deliberately ripped open the pillow and scattered its feathers. Of course, I had absolutely no idea what she was talking about, and I told her as much. Don't you think that this is absolutely weird? Now, tell me, Polly, my whole story is pretty hard to swallow, isn't it?"

"Aazi, if I told you that I believe every single word of all you have told me, would you believe me?" Polly asked, speaking in very soft tones as she reached out to touch his hand. "For Ralph, and Hodgekiss are firm friends of mine, and I too have been invited to Piadora. In fact, that's where I was going until Ralph gave me a note that said I had to bury Langdon."

"So, Polly, are you saying that you've changed your mind and you're no longer going to Piadora?"

"Yes, I had changed my mind, that is, until I met you," Polly admitted. "But now after hearing your story, I feel very different. Not only has all my anger strangely evaporated, but I feel a renewed determination to get there," she said, breaking into a warm smile. "That is, as long as you are willing to keep me company."

"Well, that's a nice compliment, Polly," Aazi replied with a wide grin. "You know something, Polly, when I started this journey I wasn't alone. A large number of my friends asked if they could come with me," he said quietly. "But then, one by one, they found excuses to leave and go home. Sadly, many of them turned on me and even mocked me, saying that if they continued to keep my company it would be a case of the blind leading the blind," he said, a tear tumbling down his cheek as he found it so painful to recall such events. "Yes, even my best friend, Stompi, turned his back on me, telling me that I had no hope of getting there, or anywhere, as I now had this awful disability. So I eventually found myself making the journey alone, at least up until this point in time."

"Well, that's all about to change, Aazi," declared Polly with a positive note of triumph, "for I feel as though I've known you for years, and I really love you. You are now officially my new best friend."

"Ditto," laughed Aazi with a smile so bright that Polly believed it could well light up the whole constellation of stars.

As they sat and compared notes on where their journey had taken them so far, both of them were surprised to discover that they had much in common. Oh, their paths had taken them in different directions, but they soon discovered they had faced similar trials and obstacles. Before long they were butting in to each other's stories as they relived their unusual adventures.

"Did you get rescued by Captain Codswallop when, like me, you tried to save those people on the beach?" Polly asked.

"No, Polly. I don't think so. If I remember rightly, his name was Captain Hogwash."

"Hogwash!" cried Polly, unable to believe her ears.

"Yes, it was Hogwash. I'm fairly certain that was his name," Aazi answered, looking very serious.

"Captain Hogwash!" cried Polly rather hysterically as she repeated his name over and over, curling up into a ball as she continued to laugh.

"Yes, Polly. Captain Hogwash—that was definitely his name, but I don't know why you're laughing like a hyena. For Captain Codswallop sounds just as iffy, if you ask me," Aazi retorted, pretending to be offended. "And, if you think that's so funny, I was rescued later down the line by a Captain Cuttlefish, commander of a paddleboat that was cruising down the Nile. This very nice gentleman saved me from the extremely sharp snappers of a most fiercesome alligator."

Polly rolled around on the ground laughing so much that she was forced to clutch her stomach. Finally she sat up, and after wiping the many tears that had come to her eyes due to too much laughter and frivolity, she changed the tone of her voice to that of a more serious nature.

"Well, what about Soogara? Did you meet her, too?" Polly sniffed, pulling her face into a long grimace as she then made ghostly sounds. "Now, she was really scary, turning herself into the most frightfully fiercesome dragon. If it had not been for my good friend Napoli who came to my rescue, I do believe I would have been eaten alive or, worse still, consumed by fire, so terrible was my time in her dungeon."

"Soogara? Napoli? No, Polly, I have never met either of them. But I have had my fair share of dragons and demons to fight on the way, and some were pretty gruesome and frightening, I promise you. But look, I've come through it all and, as far as I'm aware, I'm still in one piece!" he said, at the same time feeling different parts of his body, pretending to check that nothing was missing.

Polly laughed. "Good for you, Aazi. I have to admit, with some of the things that I've been through recently I haven't done so well, for I've ended up in little pieces."

"Well, never mind, Polly. I too have to confess that I've had my wobbly moments when everything appeared hopeless. And tell me this, have you also collected pebbles like these?" he asked, putting his hand deep into his trouser pocket and pulling out a handful of the smooth stones. "I can feel their smoothness, but I also believe they have writing on them as well. Can you read them out for me?"

"I would be honored, as well as delighted, to tell you what each stone says if you hand them over," said Polly, reaching over to take them from his cupped hand. "Aazi, this one here says *courage*, and this next one says *loyalty*. Oh, and this one, well, it says *hope*."

"What about this one?" said Aazi, handing Polly the last remaining stone that he had missed. "I only got it yesterday."

Polly smiled as she looked at it. "Aazi, this one is just as special, and has the word *endurance*," engraved on its smooth surface.

Polly laughed out loud and then pulled out her pebbles to let Aazi have a feel of them. They then took it in turns to tell of the events that led up to receiving each pebble.

"I wonder what these pebbles mean?" said Aazi.

"I've haven't the faintest idea, but we had better keep hold of them because they must mean something, as both of us have a collection of them." Polly answered, putting hers back into her pocket for safe-keeping. Aazi followed suit, placing all the pebbles as deeply into his pocket as they would go.

"Come on, Polly. All this talk of Piadora has made me more anxious than ever to get there as soon as possible," he said jumping up from the ground. "Come on, what are we waiting for? Grab your bag and let's go," he anxiously urged, holding out his hand to pull her up from the ground. "Here, Polly, hand over Sherbert to me. He's much too heavy for you to carry."

Aazi extended his right hand so that Polly could place the cage handle securely into it. She then linked her arm through his and they set off together in search of Piadora.

"Polly, I think you're really beautiful," said Aazi as they walked along together.

Polly laughed out loud. "It's a good thing you're blind, Aazi, for beautiful is one thing I'm not."

"Polly, you must stop putting yourself down," Aazi said, gently rebuking her. "You truly need to understand that beauty really is an inner thing that has nothing to do with what you look like. Because I'm blind, it forces me to listen more intently to a person's words. I have even learned to bypass their actual words, listening more closely to what their heart is really saying. This way I can conjure up my own picture of what a person truly looks like, and therefore I can say with the greatest of confidence that you, Polly Brown, are indeed very beautiful."

Polly squeezed his arm tightly, letting out a slightly embarrassed giggle.

"Oh well, Aazi. Have it your way, if you must," she said, blushing such a deep scarlet that Polly was momentarily grateful that his blindness made him unable to see the deep color of her now very crimson cheeks.

Over the next few days, the pair became inseparable as they shared their hopes and dreams, as well as all their sorrows. Polly found herself laughing more than she had ever laughed in her whole life.

"You know something, Polly? One of my dreams is to swim up a huge waterfall," Aazi seriously confided.

"Up? Don't you mean down?" Polly giggled as she rectified his mistake.

"No, Polly. I meant what I said. I know it's a crazy dream, but all the same, it's a dream I like to think about."

Polly laughed. "I guess most people don't dare share their dreams, for they're much too afraid of being laughed at," she replied as she gave great thought to her impromptu words of wisdom.

"Never a truer word has been spoken, at least from your lips, Polly," said Aazi, breaking into laughter. "So let me tell you now, I would also love to go to the edge of the end of the constellation and, all by myself, create a new star," he said with a tone of immense seriousness. "So don't you dare laugh at me, for we all need dreams," he added with a big grin.

They talked nonstop about what music they liked, what movies they loved and hated, and much, much more. So much so that poor little Herbert found himself having to chirp louder than ever in his endeavor to remind them that the cage they were holding onto was not empty, and he did not like being totally ignored.

"I think we're meant to get the train from Heartache Pass to Heckofa Heights," Aazi told Polly. "At least, according to my map, that's our next destination."

"Yes, and according to my map, the station we need is just over the next hill," said Polly, using her map to confirm their position.

In no time at all Polly and her friends were sitting very comfortably on a magnificently built steam engine that chugged and wound its way up through many steep mountain passes, stopping only to pick up extra passengers. Before long the train carriage was full to capacity, and Polly felt obliged to give up Herbert's space on the seat to a rather elderly gentleman, so she placed Herbert and his cage on the carriage floor, safely by her feet.

They were not too far into the journey when Herbert started to frantically flap around the cage. Polly, who had been dozing, opened her eyes and peered downwards into the cage to see what was causing his sudden distress.

"Aazi, help me!" she cried. "Sherbert seems to be choking. What do you think?"

"Polly, I've no idea what's happening. Try to remember that I'm blind," Aazi rather anxiously responded. Before Polly could further panic, Herbert fell backwards off his perch and lay helpless on the floor of his cage.

"Do something, Aazi!" Polly cried out.

"I'm not a doctor or a vet, Polly," Aazi reminded her, "so I'm not entirely sure at this moment what we can do to help him, other than..."

Polly didn't wait for Aazi to finish his sentence. She flung the cage door open wide and gently lifted helpless Herbert from the floor of the cage, cupping him between her hands. With Herbert lying limp in the palm of her hand Polly began to stroke his beak.

"His breathing is awfully shallow, Aazi," she observed, feeling more concerned than ever for the poor little fellow.

"You could try mouth-to-beak resuscitation," suggested Aazi. "Although, this might prove to be very difficult. He is such a tiny bird with an even tinier beak through which to blow."

Polly quickly decided she was game for anything, for she could clearly see that Herbert's condition was rapidly deteriorating.

"Oh, don't die on me, Sherbert," she moaned as she gently pried open his beak before lifting Herbert right up to her face.

She then took a deep breath and began to blow air into his beak, hoping it would make its way down his windpipe and fill up his lungs.

"Come on, little fellow," she whispered as she used her index finger to massage his heart between breaths.

"Excuse me, miss. I know you're doing your best to resuscitate the poor little fellow, but if you press down any harder on his little chest, you'll completely finish him off," said one of the passengers, deeply concerned at the amount of pressure she was using to start up Herbert's tender heart.

Polly ignored the helpful stranger's comment as she diligently continued the mouth-to-mouth and heart massage in her desperate bid to revive him. Finally, as she was about to give up, Herbert slowly opened his beady eyes and let out a little tweet.

"He's back with us!" she cried, turning to Aazi and adding, "Oh Aazi, I do believe his singing has finally become music to my ears."

Polly continued to hold Herbert in the palm of her hand, feeling very reluctant to place him back in his cage in case of a repeat performance, for she sincerely believed that she was not up to going through any further drama with her little friend.

As the train continued to slowly chug its way through deep valleys and up very steep, mountainous passes, Polly continued to keep a close eye on Herbert. Pretty soon he was bouncing around on both feet as well as happily warbling and tweeting, with no physical evidence left of the rather unfortunate episode. Then suddenly without any warning he sprung out of her palm and began to wildly flutter at immense speed around the carriage. Polly watched, horrified, as Herbert shot around the carriage, barely missing the heads of unsuspecting passengers as he showed off his talents by going into continuous nosedives with the determination of a kamikaze pilot.

"Sherbert, come back. Come back!" shouted Polly as she leaped to her feet and frantically raced through the carriage after him. Seconds later Herbert crashed into the glass of a closed window and was sent plummeting at great speed to the floor. The terrified passengers quickly moved their feet before dropping their heads to observe the little fellow lying flat out beside them on the carriage floor.

"Oops! I'm so sorry. Please let me through. Please let me get to him," begged Polly as she crawled on all fours through numerous legs to get to where Herbert lay flat out and dazed. "Come on, boy, get up and jump into my hand," she whispered.

Herbert lay motionless for a moment and then mischievously sprang to both feet as if he were playing a game.

"Here boy. Here boy," said Polly as she gently tried to coax him toward her hand.

Herbert responded by furiously pecking at her outstretched hand as he resisted all attempts to be captured by her. Using both hands, Polly moved nearer in her attempt to catch him and put him safely back into the cage. Herbert, on the other hand, was having none of it. With a sudden and spurious flap of his wings, he was back up in air, whizzing the length of the compartment like a bomber plane as he evaded all attempts to be recaptured.

Soon she was joined by many fractious passengers who were feeling most upset that their tranquil journey had been ruined by a thoughtless and somewhat psychotic bird who went by the name of Sherbert.

"Here, Sherbert," they all cried as they climbed on seats and waved rolled-up newspapers in their hands, hoping to whack his stupid little head in a bid to finally bring him to his senses. But, try as they may, all efforts to catch him proved futile, for he was turning out to be a very stubborn and equally defiant little bird, incapable of being reasoned with.

With recapture well out of all the passengers' grasp, a very irate gentleman decided to take the matter into his own hands by winding down a window and yelling, "Clear off, you wretched, skinny little monster!"

Not only did Herbert feel very insulted, but he also wasted no time in obeying the order to leave, in a matter of seconds obliged by flying out of the window to freedom.

"Thank goodness for that," said the grumpy gentleman with the bowler hat and mustache as he sat back down and rather dramatically reopened his newspaper. "Now let's have some peace and quiet."

Polly's jaw dropped as she watched on, horrified, as Herbert flew out of the carriage window. She raced over to the open window and quickly stuck her head out, turning to face the same direction as he had flown off.

"Sherbert, come back! Come back!" she cried. It was no use, for the noise of the locomotive's engine drowned her cries, and the steam from the engine clouded her view.

Polly was forced to give up any hope of retrieving Herbert and angrily shut the window, giving the bowler-hatted gentleman a most resentful stare as she made her way back down the carriage to take her seat and rejoin Aazi.

"Oh Aazi, he's gone," she wailed pitifully as she slumped back down into her seat. "I have no idea why Hodgekiss thought he could trust me to take care of him, for I am incapable of doing anything right," she said wearily.

"Come on, Polly. Stop beating yourself up. You did your best. What more could you possibly have done? Besides, birds are generally at their happiest when they are free, don't you agree?"

Polly nodded, but it still didn't change a thing, for in her mind she had yet again failed hopelessly in her mission to protect and nurture one of Hodgekiss's pets.

"Let's hope that, unlike Ollie, Herbert doesn't turn out to be one of his favorites," she said rather mournfully.

Polly remained silently deep in thought for the rest of the journey as she went over and over the events that had taken place carefully considering whether there was anything else she could possibly have done to prevent Herbert from escaping. She sat with her eyes firmly shut, wondering how she was going to put this latest catastrophe into words when, and if, she came to meet up with Hodgekiss. No, try as she may, there were indeed no nice or acceptable words that would help ease her conscience, for when it came to the crunch she knew she would have to confess the whole truth. All she imagined she could say was, "Hmm, I don't know how to put this, but remember Ollie your caterpillar who took off on holiday? Well, the same thing has happened to Herbert. He too has done the dirty on me and gone on a rather long holiday. In fact, just like Ollie, he too will be gone forever."

Polly inwardly groaned at the prospect of meeting up with Hodgekiss.

Chapter 34
"AIN'T NO MOUNTAIN HIGH ENOUGH"

*P*OLLY BEGAN TO drift off, but in what seemed like only a matter of minutes she found herself being given a sharp nudge in the ribs by a very excited Aazi.

"Polly, wake up, I think we have arrived at Heckofa Heights! Quick, come take a look for yourself," he said, beckoning her to get up from the seat. "Come and take a look out of the window and tell me what you see."

Polly wasted no time, and in only a matter of moments she had wound down the window and declared, "I think you're right, Aazi. We really have made it!"

They then both stood with their heads hanging out of the open window with the wind blowing into their faces until the train came to a final halt. Aazi opened the door, but not before reminding Polly to grab her bag. As Polly picked up her bag, her eyes fell on the now empty cage.

"Aazi, what should I do about this?" she queried as she attempted to draw his attention to the empty cage, quite forgetting that he was unable to see.

"What are you referring to, Polly?" asked Aazi in response to her question.

"The cage, Aazi," she cried as she picked it up and rattled it. "Sherbert's empty cage."

"Oh, the cage. Well, let's take it with us, Polly, for it does seem the decent thing to do. I mean it's one thing to lose his bird, but if we also fail to give back the cage I think we will be adding insult to injury, don't you?"

"I agree," said Polly resignedly. "After all, it was Sherbert's home," she added sadly.

With her bag slung sloppily over her shoulder and the empty cage in one hand, she carefully climbed off the train and, still limping, followed Aazi toward the station's exit. As they came through the exit door Polly turned to Aazi and asked, "What next?"

"We could find a bench to sit down and examine our maps," he helpfully suggested.

"Yes, I think that's what we need to do," agreed Polly.

As they settled down on a bench, Polly rummaged through her belongings until she found her map. On closer inspection she began to feel quite panicky.

"Aazi, I don't think there are any more directions on this map. It has taken us as far as it can. Now what do we do?"

"I have no idea, Polly. Give me a minute to think, will you?"

Aazi thought long and hard as he pondered over what should happen next. Suddenly he had a bright thought.

"Polly, when you last saw Ralph, you mentioned he gave you a note."

"Yes, that's true, but that note was specifically asking me to look after Sherbert and bury Langdon. I assure you there was nothing in the letter concerning travel arrangements," cried Polly grimly.

"Well, how do you know that for certain? When you relayed the story to me, you said that you threw it to the ground in disgust when you learned that you were being asked to bury Langdon."

"Yes, so I did!" responded Polly.

"Well, Polly, the least you can do is take another look at the letter and see if it says anything else that might prove useful."

Polly reluctantly agreed to empty the contents of her bag and see if she still had that letter in her possession.

"Here it is, Aazi" she said, picking it out from amongst her widely scattered belongings. "Right, now, let me see. Ah, yes, here it is: 'Dear Polly... Sherbert is suffering from... Hodgekiss recommends burying... Hugs and kisses... Ralph.'"

"Come on, Polly. Is there anything else?"

"Oh Aazi, you are quite right. There is something else!" she excitedly cried as her eyes hit the bottom of the page. "There is a P.S.

at the bottom of the letter. It says: 'P.S. I forgot to mention that in the unlikely event that Herbert becomes free from all his sickness and malady, he will be most eager to fly to freedom. It is important you allow him to do so, otherwise there is the distinct possibility he will become ill again and all your hard work will have been for nothing. I also wish to encourage you that when and if this occurs, you are almost at your journey's end. Well done, Polly. You have almost made it to Piadora. Can you smell the pizza?"

"Polly, did you hear what you just read?" Aazi shouted excitedly.

"Yes, yes, I did. Isn't it wonderful, Aazi? I do believe that we're almost there—yes, almost at Piadora!"

She joined her friend in shouting at the top of her lungs, for now she was bursting with renewed anticipation and excitement and was unable to hold herself together any longer. She turned to give Aazi a big hug and, as she did so, she heard a thundering voice behind her.

"Right, are we all present and correct?" bellowed the unfamiliar voice.

Polly turned to see where the voice was coming from and whether it was directed at her. And as she looked up, she came eyeball-to-eyeball with a very portly, ruddy-cheeked man with an extremely whiskery face and ridiculously bushy eyebrows.

"Well, is anybody listening to me? Are we all here then?" he said with a loud snort before adding, "because if we are all present and correct, we may as well set off without further ado."

Polly remained seated, her gaze firmly fixed on the solidly built man who was dressed from head to toe in thickly padded clothes with enormous hiking boots on his equally enormous feet. He had a thick red, blue, and white striped scarf wrapped tightly around his neck and a matching woolly bobble hat. He also had large, thick goggles around his forehead and very plump red cheeks. In one hand he clutched a long stick with a spike on the end, and in his other hand he held a large clipboard. The fierce-looking man could see Polly was looking both very uncomfortable and completely bewildered.

"Please forgive my mad or rather bad manners and allow me the pleasure of introducing myself," he said with a chortle, at the same time holding out a massive and hairy hand for Polly to shake.

"My name is Sir Eggmond Hoollari, and I am here to take you on a mountaineering course. Are you ready?"

"Mountaineering course!" exclaimed Polly. "I think not! Sorry, but I hate heights, so there is no way you are going to get me up a mountain, of that I'm certain. Besides which, I have injured my ankle as well as my arm. Here, look for yourself if you don't believe me," she said, holding up her arm to show the gentleman.

The man raised a bushy eyebrow before turning his clipboard, his eyes scanning up and down the list that was attached to it.

Polly used the breather to further protest, "Look, you must have made some mistake," she continued, "for I have never enrolled on any rock-climbing or mountaineering course. Besides which, Aazi here is blind, and I'm not going anywhere without him."

The man carried on ignoring Polly as he continued to scan his list.

"Well, is your name Polly Brown and are you from the orphanage?" he asked, his eyeballs bulging from his sockets as he stared her directly in the face.

"Yes sir, I am Polly Brown, and I am from the orphanage, but there must be some mistake. You must have my name mixed up with that of someone else."

"Well, according to my notes, which were also recently confirmed by a little birdie, it says here, 'Polly Brown loves *The Sound of Music* and her favorite song in the film is 'Climb Every Mountain.' It never fails to inspire her.' Now I have to ask you, is this information true or false?"

"Yes, it's true, but..."

"No buts, young lady. It either is or it isn't. Now which is it?"

"It's true, but how did you get hold of that very private piece of information?" Polly asked, decidedly wearily.

"Never you mind, young lady," he replied, giving his nose a little tap that suggested she should not pursue this line of questioning any further.

"Now your friend here is also down for the training, at least according to my list, which I assure you is absolutely bang up to date. So Aazi from Zimbabwe, I sincerely hope that you have not the slightest intention of canceling at this late hour."

"That's downright ridiculous," Polly very rudely chipped in, "for can't you see he's blind?"

"Excellent," declared Eggmond Hoollari with a wide grin.

"You are crazy! I fail to see how being blind could possibly be seen as excellent," Polly angrily retorted.

"Well, my dear, it makes his climb much easier to deal with, for as he cannot see, he will have no fear. Just you wait!"

"Well, Sir Eggbunch Hillopee or Hillagi or whatever your name is, Aazi is not prepared to risk life and limb to go with you on some wild and crazy mountaineering trip, and that's the end of the matter," she said with a ferocity that even took her by surprise.

"Polly, I do think you should allow Aazi to speak for himself, for he might be blind but presumably he's not dumb!" he retorted, at the same time directing his attention towards Aazi. "Now then, Aazi, are you game for this adventure?"

Aazi shrugged his shoulders with seeming indifference, but before he had time to give any further consideration to the matter, Sir Eggmond slapped him on the back and said, "Of course you are, for according to my notes, you, young sir, also have an inspirational song that means the world to you. Yes, according to my notes your song is called 'The Impossible Dream,' and I believe it goes something like this," he said, as he began to sing the words of the song in a deep, croaky voice. Now am I right, young sir, or are you also going to begin protesting and challenge the accuracy of my notes?"

Aazi remained speechless. Just like Polly, he was dumbfounded that this complete stranger could know something so deeply personal, and he found himself utterly incapable of doing anything more than give the briefest of nods.

"Good, well that's settled. You're coming with me. Now then, where is everybody else that I have on my list? Have they missed the train?" he muttered as his eyes went back to further scan his list. "Now then, where is Elijah Entrecote? He is down on my list as coming with us today. And where, for that matter, is Cuthbert Cannontree? I thought I saw him hanging around the station much earlier in the day." Sir Eggmond continued down his list of absentees. "Isaiah Ichabod, Michael McFowl, Malachi Mortlock, Jemima

Jumpstart, oh, and where is that delightful young Italian girl Melissa Melistragata? She is such a little peach, I feel I could eat her for breakfast. Hmm, Penelope Possum is also missing, as is Haggai Thrupton and Simon Snodgrass..."

The list of absentees was endless. For one reason or another, none of them had made it. Polly watched as each name was dutifully crossed off the list.

"Well, I guess it's just the two of you today," said Sir Eggmond dryly.

As he was adjusting the paper on his clipboard, the two Justins exited the train station and ran over to where Polly and Aazi were sitting on the bench, arguing the toss with Sir Eggmond.

"Hey wait! Wait for us! We're coming too!" cried Justin Kase.

"Phew, I think we've made it just in time," declared a most relieved Justin Thyme, dropping his bag to the ground to wipe the sweat from his forehead.

"You lads are indeed very lucky that we haven't yet left, or you'd be quite up a gum tree," said Sir Eggmond, slightly amused as he went back to mark a tick by the two boys names on the now very disappointingly shortened list.

"Well, I have to say in my defense that, as usual, it's my friend's fault that we're late," Justin Thyme stated rather breathlessly. "He kept insisting that he needed to recheck his bag, finding further things to add to it each time. Honestly he may be my best pal, but at times he drives me nuts."

Justin Kase laughed out loud before pretending to give him a playful thump for being so rude about him.

"Oh, stop complaining. I've got us out of many sticky situations by having the right gear with me. Oh, by the way Polly, when we get back from Piadora we've made plans to go and see the Beatles live. Fancy coming with us?"

Polly quickly declined, for no way did she wish to set eyes upon another insect—she'd seen enough of them to last a lifetime!

"Right, pay attention everybody," said Sir Eggmond rather abruptly. "We are going to walk down to where I have set up base camp, and I'm sure that you will be pleased to know that my Sherpas are at present brewing up a jolly nice cup of tea for us. It will also give me the opportunity to treat your injuries, Polly, for your arm and ankle appear to be in pretty bad shape. Once we've got you sorted, we will have supper before checking our equipment, and then it's into our sleeping bags for a small rest before heading up the mountain at the break of dawn. Oh, and do be encouraged— I haven't lost anyone off the side of this particular mountain face for quite a while."

Polly took a deep gulp as she considered his words of comfort anything but reassuring.

Less than an hour later Polly and her friends found themselves huddled inside a large tent, and Sir Eggmond wasted no time in attending to her injuries.

"You've got yourself a nasty cut there, Polly," said Sir Eggmond as he removed her makeshift bandage. "Hmm, I think this calls for some special ointment, don't you? And while we're at it, I think we will apply a bit to that rather swollen ankle."

Moments later, Polly found her wound being swabbed in warm antiseptic water before he went on to apply his medicinal ointment.

"There, that should do it," he stated, feeling rather pleased with himself. "Now rub it deep into the wound. There's a good girl."

"Sir Eggmond, this ointment is very strange, for I'm getting a warm tingly feeling right up my arm, and now I can feel it all around my ankle. Yes, I can feel the same warm sensation," said Polly, feeling rather delighted.

"That's excellent, Polly, for it shows that my ointment is working efficiently," he said with a smile.

"What's it called? I'd very much like to get hold of some," Polly asked unable to hide her curiosity.

"Well, that's my little secret, Polly, but I tell you hand on heart that this ointment has the most wonderful, miraculous healing properties. Yes, it will heal just about any condition on the planet. There, I think we're done, and now I think it's high time we concerned ourselves with more important things, such as filling our tummies. I don't know about you, but I'm absolutely famished," he said with a smile.

Minutes later they were all digging in to a bowl of steaming homemade soup and munching on thick slices of bread. As Polly consumed every morsel she was offered, she laid aside all suspicious thoughts concerning his miracle ointment.

"This soup is delicious. What's in it?" asked Polly.

"It's my own secret recipe. I call it Chicken Shack Soup," beamed a very proud Sir Eggmond. "Let me tell you, Polly, this soup has enough nutrients and vegetables to keep you healthy for a week up in the mountains. I lived on the stuff when I last climbed the Himalayas; I hope you've heard of them," he said with a chortle.

"Yes sir, I have. I learned all about them in my geography classes. Aren't they the highest group of mountains in the world?"

"You're absolutely correct, young lady. That is, with the exception of Piadora. Although not too many people know it, she is, I believe, the highest of them all."

"Oh, great," said Polly, experiencing a deep, sinking feeling. She was very afraid for herself. "So this mountain—which takes years of experience to climb—is the one that we will be attempting. Am I getting this right?"

"Yes, I do believe you're getting the picture, Polly. But rest assured we will be training on smaller peaks to start with, and when I'm entirely satisfied with your progress, then and only then will I allow you the privilege of climbing Piadora. So let's get on with it, shall we? Our first mountain is, I believe, none other than Kilimanjaro, and she's a real beauty. Yes, I think you'll love her."

"Kilimanjaro!" gasped Justin Thyme. "Now I know you're crazy. That 'little mountain' is known by all to be well over nineteen thousand feet high."

Polly only had time to hear "Kil..." before promptly fainting. Sir Eggmond continued giving fact after fact about Mount Kilimanjaro, blissfully unaware of what was happening all around him.

"Excuse me, Sir Eggmond, but I don't think you are fully aware that Polly is no longer with us," exclaimed Justin Kase, tapping him lightly on the shoulder as he interrupted Sir Eggmond's impromptu geography lesson.

"Well, blow my nose and rattle my toes; I do believe you are right, young Justin," replied Sir Eggmond, looking pretty flustered as he surveyed Polly lying prostrate on the floor. "I'll go and get my smelling salts straight away."

Polly came to moments later as the smell of the salts hit the back of her throat and nose, causing her to cough and splutter.

"Welcome back, Polly," said Sir Eggmond with a smile as he crouched down beside her limp body. "I thought for one minute we'd lost you. Now don't worry, young lady, I promise you that we won't be attempting Mount Everest until we have successfully conquered Kilimanjaro. You have my word on that."

"Everest?" Once again Polly only heard the first syllable before passing out a second time, and once more she had to be revived with the aid of smelling salts.

"It's high time you stopped worrying, my dear, for you are, after all, in very capable hands. Why, I won't be expecting you to climb Piadora on your own until much, much later."

"On our own!" gasped Polly. She threatened to pass out for a third time and was only prevented from doing so by the firm hand of Sir Eggmond forcing her to remain in an upright position.

"No dear, now wash your ears out, for what I actually said was on *your* own."

"By myself!" Polly shrieked. "Oh no! Someone tell me I'm dreaming," she cried, feeling utterly wretched and inconsolable.

"Yes, Polly, I do believe you're finally beginning to get the message, for on your own means precisely that—on your own. So please do give me the courtesy of paying more attention when I'm speaking, for it will go a long way in helping the entire operation run more smoothly," he said, very matter-of-fact.

"Oh, tell me I'm not hearing right," she cried pitifully, "for there's no way I can climb a mountain on my own. And tell me the truth: if Kilimanjaro is nearly twenty thousand feet, how much higher is Mount Everest?"

"Well, my dear, I have to say that it is just a teeny weenie bit higher, but I'm certain this will not pose any major problem."

"Eggmunch, you're not listening to me. Tell me right now, *how much* higher is Mount Everest?" she demanded to know, for she was now badly shaking from head to toe.

"Now don't get so worked up, Polly, for if you hadn't so rudely interrupted me I was just about to give you the answer. Mount Everest stands at just over twenty nine thousand feet high, so if my math is correct, that means it's only a mere ten thousand or so feet higher. Although I do believe it is still rising further with every year that passes," he stated most informatively.

Polly took a deep gulp, for inside she was beginning to feel quite hysterical.

"I'm really sorry, Sir Eggmond, but I think I will take a pass on this one," she declared as assertively as she felt able. "As you can see, I'm already trembling with fear, and I haven't even taken one step up the mountain."

"That's fine by me, Polly, but I do need to remind you that your personalized song says, 'Climb Every Mountain,' and I do believe the word *every* does not leave much room for you to be choosy. Would you agree?"

"Yes, but..."

"No buts, my dear, unless of course you are secretly a member of the Butter Brigade."

"The Butter Brigade? Who on earth are they?" Polly asked with some surprise.

"What? Have you never heard of them? Why, they are the group who always has some excuse for not going forward or for abandoning a specific task. Yes, when they are asked to do something, they always start with, '*But* I'm not sure,' or similarly, '*But* I don't think I can,' and so on. Yes, they are indeed the society of procrastinators who always put everything off with a *but*. So, no buts my dear, for it really doesn't suit you."

"Oh b..." was all Polly could find to say, for she seemed utterly lost for words.

"Precisely, my dear! And in the meantime, do let me know if the words to that song ever get rewritten and changed from 'climb every mountain' to 'climb the ones I fancy,' or, 'climb the ones that don't scare me.' And then ask yourself this: would I be here giving up my precious time to train and give you the necessary skills to complete this task if I did not have every confidence that you are capable of successfully completing this assignment?"

Polly remained silent, for she was no match when it came to a man such as Sir Eggmond Hoollari.

"Besides, if you take the *y* off the word *every*, you're only three letters short of the word *Everest*. Now that's rather clever, don't you think?" he said rather jovially. "Anyway, while we're at it, which one of you bright sparks would like to guess my favorite signature tune?"

"I'd rather not, but I guess you're going to tell us anyway," said Polly drily.

"Absolutely!" Sir Eggmond retorted, completely ignoring Polly's very downcast expression. "Yes, it's 'Ain't No Mountain High Enough,'" he sung out loudly, as though he were a Welsh chorister, at the same time doing a little wiggle of the hips. "Oh yes, shooby doo doo. That is, I believe, a most wonderful little number, don't you think?" he said as he continued to dance around the room in a very weird, if not old-fashioned, manner.

Polly raised her eyes up into her head, presumably to convey that she was anything but amused by all his antics. But she also conceded that there was little hope of prevailing in her quest to turn back, for she was pitting her wits against a very determined man.

"Yes, my little eager beavers," he said, turning to address them all. "While I accept that you have every reason to be concerned, you must also realize that people who insist on playing it safe rarely fulfill their dreams. Very few people make it to this point in their journey, and of those that do, many like your good selves will panic and choose to opt out, believing that to reach the summit is indeed impossible." Sir Eggmond paused to clear his throat of a little irritating tickle before going on. "But I have to add that if I, a most experienced mountain climber, say you can do it—and that includes you, Polly Brown—well then you need to put all your faith and trust in me."

Polly hung her head low as she carefully considered his words. *Faith! Trust!* These words meant nothing to her, for she had never had the privilege of having anyone in her life reliable or caring enough to put faith in, let alone to go as far as trust anyone. Indeed all her young life she had continuously been let down, and now someone who a few hours ago had been nothing more than a complete stranger was asking her to put her young life in his hands. As she sat and considered the enormity of what he was expecting from her, she felt sick to the pit of her stomach with fear and anxiety.

Sir Eggmond edged forward to give her small hand a reassuring squeeze. He knew only too well all what she was going through. He too had found himself facing great inner conflict when he scaled the highest mountains often in the most atrocious weather conditions imaginable.

"Oh Polly, don't give up now. Not when you have come this far. I know you can do it," he said. "All you need is the necessary single-mindedness, plus a healthy dose of determination. Then, trust me; *you* will conquer it," Sir Eggmond euphorically stated. "Indeed, Piadora will be the one mountain you each must climb alone, and I daresay it is not one for the faint-hearted to climb," he said, individually eyeing up each of his fear-filled students. All present in the tent chose to remain cautiously silent as they considered the full impact of what was being required of them. And all present felt their hearts were beginning to fail them as they experienced sheer terror and dread at the prospect of the climb.

"Oh, and by the way, I feel now is as good a time as any to share with you an old African proverb: 'Adversity is your best friend. It introduces you to yourself.' During this climb all of you will indeed discover an inner strength you never knew you possessed."

Then, having finished sharing this deep and thought-provoking insight with them, he rose up from where he was crouched beside Polly and strode over toward the main table that was stacked high with climbing equipment.

"Right now, listen up everybody. If anyone would like to join me in a warm mug of Rosie Lee, speak up, for now is your last chance," he announced, holding up a rather revolting-looking tin teapot that had definitely seen better days.

Polly and her friends politely declined. But Polly was still very anxious and felt she could not continue this adventure without asking about something that was really bothering her—yes, a really important issue that urgently needed to be addressed.

"Sir Eggmond, I don't wish to appear rude, but I don't think I'm suitably dressed for the occasion. You're all nicely padded up in thick, puffy clothes and thick goggles in readiness of the expedition, but look at me; my dress is made of thin cotton, and my shoes are not only worn out but have enough leaks to keep a lawn nicely watered," she said pointing downwards toward her tatty shoes.

Sir Eggmond stopped drinking his tea and followed her finger downwards until his eyes hit upon her shoes. "Hmm," was the only word that ushered forth from his extraordinarily thick lips.

"I'm a little worried that even if I manage to reach the summit without plummeting to my death, I'm just as likely to freeze and transform into a rather large ice cube, and then I may not be discovered for thousands of years," she cried as she imagined such an awful thing happening to her.

Sir Eggmond, now halfway through another mouthful of tea, crashed his tin cup down and started to splutter, "Well, rattle my toes and blow my nose; you are quite right, my dear. Of course I wouldn't expect you to go as you are. Oh no, no, no. That would never do! Did you know that well over a hundred corpses remain lost on Everest? Most of these are probably due to unsuitable or insufficient clothing." He paused and then merrily added, "Of course, I'm only joking." Polly breathed the deepest sigh of relief.

"No, the sad truth is that most of those corpses are the result of the frequent avalanches that take them unawares. And yes, I do believe that it's usually those mischievous rogues that get them," he said with much too jovial a laugh for Polly's liking.

Polly shot a glance in the direction of the two Justins who, like her, were pretending to join in and laugh at his panic button sense of humor when really they all felt sick to the very pit of their stomachs.

With his tin mug firmly back down on the table, Sir Eggmond then strolled over to a large bag. "Now then, Polly, please try this one on for size," he said, pulling out a padded outfit similar to the one he was wearing. "There, this is bound to fit, so just pop it on over your clothes and then put on your boots. I will put your shoes in my backpack for safekeeping."

Polly obeyed and struggled as she put on the puffy suit before finally managing to pull the zip right up to her chin.

"Perfect!" declared a very delighted and self-satisfied Sir Eggmond. "Now Aazi, come over here and try this one on."

Before he had time to reach deeper into the bag, Justin Kase used the breathing space as an opportunity to interrupt.

"It's all right, Sir Eggmond, we don't need anything, for we are already sorted. See, I have two outfits in my large backpack for me and my friend."

Sir Eggmond said nothing but watched with a half-amused look on his face as Justin Kase proceeded to empty out the contents of his extremely overloaded backpack onto the floor before producing the outfits.

"Look, I've got ice picks, ropes, goggles, even oxygen masks and all-weather writing paper. You name it, I've got it," said Justin very proudly. "Oh, and I've even got a Union Jack flag, so I can mark our arrival when we get to the top of the summit. Isn't that just brilliant?"

"Hmm, how peachy," was Sir Eggmond's only and very unconvincing response as he furtively rubbed his chin, remaining deep in thought. "Well, Justin, there is just one eensy weensy little problem," he muttered.

"Oh? And what's that?" asked Justin, very surprised.

"Well, you need to know now that it will be quite impossible for you to take your backpack with you when we scale the mountain."

"Why?" asked Justin with a deep note of disappointment.

"Well, I would think that the answer to your question is quite obvious," replied Sir Eggmond.

"Well, no, it isn't. Would you kindly help me out here by telling me why?" asked Justin, feeling very incensed.

"Because to climb this mountain you have to be free of any heavy load."

"Well, I'm not going anywhere without my backpack!" Justin retorted, his voice betraying his growing annoyance with Sir Eggmond. "I never go anywhere without it. Oh no, sir. I take it with me everywhere I go, just in case I run into trouble. So for just this one occasion, could you turn a blind eye and allow me to take it?" Justin pleaded.

"I'm sorry, young man, but rules are not made to be broken. And as your personal safety is of paramount importance to me, I have little choice but to ask you to leave it back here at base camp. It will be perfectly safe here, I assure you."

Polly and Aazi remained silent as Justin strenuously continued to argue his case. They were both surprised at the level of stubbornness they were witnessing from both concerned parties as Justin continued to resist and sought to get Sir Eggmond's decision overruled. Yet still Justin continued to plead his case even though his arguments were indeed falling on deaf ears.

"Justin, please just give in, for you can't win against such a determined man," said Polly wearily.

Aazi chipped in, urging Justin to rethink and just leave his backpack here at base camp, although both Aazi and Polly secretly admitted that they would feel more than relieved if the trip were called off entirely due to falling numbers.

"Look, Justin, just drop it. You're really getting nowhere," said Justin Thyme, giving his friend a sharp nudge in order to make his friend aware that he too was feeling pretty fed up with the whole conversation.

"Well, that's it then. I'm not coming with you, Sir Eggmond," Justin angrily declared before turning to his best friend. "Come on, Justin. I think it's time to leave. We don't need *his* help to get up the mountain. We've got all the necessary gear to make it on our own."

Justin Thyme shrugged his shoulders and seemed quite unsure as to whether to go or stay, for he much preferred sitting on the fence in preference to upsetting anyone. No, to do such unpleasant things, quarreling or arguing, was not in his nature. Finally, after much 'umming' and an equal amount of 'uhhing,' he braved himself to voice the decision he had come to.

"Look, guys. I'd better go with Justin. He is, after all, my best friend, and we've never done anything without each other. So I guess we'll meet up again when we get to the top of the mountain," he ruefully said, anxiously wringing his hands at the same time. "Take care, Polly. You too, Aazi, and thanks for the offer, Sir Eggmond."

He then turned on his heels and followed his stooping and heavily-laden friend out of the large tent, stopping only to turn and give a final and somewhat faint-hearted wave before disappearing into the night.

"Well, I guess we're down to just the two of you," said Sir

Eggmond with a slightly despondent note in his voice. "So let's get snuggled up in our sleeping bags for a bit of shut-eye, for we do all need to be full of the joys of spring when we start our ascent first thing tomorrow."

Chapter 35
POLLY'S LAST WILL AND TESTAMENT

*P*OLLY AND AAZI climbed into their sleeping bags and rather despondently said good night to each other, for both their hearts felt extremely weighed down. Polly was not convinced that she would be able to fall asleep for fear of what the new dawn would bring. Sir Eggmond, on the other hand, slept like a log, snoring so loudly that the tent appeared to bulge in and out with every breath he took, making it even harder for Polly to doze off. She feared the tent might well balloon off into the night if Sir Eggmond continued to snore in such a disgracefully heavy manner.

In the early hours of the next morning, Sir Eggmond arose with a spring in his step, and, after checking the equipment thoroughly, crouched down beside them to give both of them a gentle shake. "Rise and shine," he said cheerily before going over to remove the boiling kettle that was making a loud whistling noise. "Yes, and I do hope we're all feeling bright-eyed and bushy-tailed on this wonderful morning," said Sir Eggmond as he poured the tea into the pot.

Polly and Aazi very reluctantly climbed out of their sleeping bags, giving a big yawn as they stretched. Polly looked down at her arm and was surprised to see that the bandage had disappeared. She was even more surprised to discover that there was no sign of the wound ever having been there. She then looked down at her ankle, and she was just as astonished to find that all swelling had completely gone and the pain had also miraculously disappeared. Polly jumped up and down on the spot just to make sure.

POLLY BROWN

"Wow, this is great!" she cried as she felt herself becoming fitter and healthier with each jump.

After wolfing down a small but filling breakfast, Sir Eggmond loaded up his backpack, whistling to himself as he did a final check. He then directed his attention toward his young and decidedly anxious novices, who were clad from head to toe in their straight jackets and were finding it fairly difficult to walk in a straight line.

"Splendiferously stupendous," he declared as he looked them up and down. "Right then, are we ready to go? Polly, you look like a cat on a hot tin roof. Relax, there is absolutely no need for you to feel so nervous," stated Sir Eggmond. "Now will both of you please make sure you have your personal diaries with you? I find that the best place to keep it safe is in your top pocket along with your pen. This way you can write down all your thoughts and experiences along the way," he said, patting his breast pocket to indicate that his diary was securely tucked away inside.

Polly and Aazi quickly searched through their belongings for their diaries, and once found, they did as Sir Eggmond suggested and placed them in the top pocket of their puffy outfits.

"Now Polly, do you still have your earmuffs and blinkers amongst your possessions? Be a dear and go check. They too will be much needed on this expedition."

"I did have them, but then somehow I lost them," she informed him.

"Oh, dearie me," replied Sir Eggmond. "That was indeed most careless of you. For both items are considered to be very essential on this expedition." He then reached into his enormous backpack. "Here, Polly. Put these on," he said, handing her a pair of earmuffs. "And this will have to do instead of blinkers," he said, handing her a scarf. "Although at present there's no need to put either on until we start our ascent."

Polly was by now very puzzled. "What will I need this scarf for?" she asked, looking very perplexed.

"Well, that's to tie around your head in order to cover up your eyes. Yes, it will act perfectly as a blindfold," he answered in a manner that suggested he was stating the obvious.

"Blindfold? But that's crazy!" she cried. "Surely I will need both eyes to see my way safely up the mountain? For there's no way I'm playing blindman's buff!"

"Oh, my dear, this certainly is no childish game. Oh no, no," he tutted. "It's just that I prefer all my students to wear blindfolds—it's much better that way. Yes, over the years my most successful students have used them when climbing mountains, for I do believe it heightens their other senses and teaches them to implicitly trust me for their safety. It really is for the best. Trust me on this one," he said with a firm edge of confidence.

Before Polly could make any further protest, Sir Eggmond zipped up his open jacket and marched over toward the tent flap.

"Yes, I think you're now ready to climb a high mountain. So come this way," he flippantly beckoned with a gesture as he held open the flap, guiding them out into the blinding sun and snow-driven landscape of the mountainside.

Polly and Aazi dutifully obeyed his order and walked slowly and awkwardly toward the tent opening, their young and tender hearts not filled with wonder and excitement but with the greatest of fear and trepidation.

"Good luck, Aazi," whispered Polly as she reached out for one final, lingering clasp of his glove-covered hand.

"You too, Polly," responded Aazi with a half smile.

They then made their way out of the tent to follow after Sir Eggmond Hoollari, both of them privately hoping and praying that this man was not absolutely stark raving mad and that they would eventually return to the tent in one piece.

The walk to the foot of the mountain was very pleasant. As the sun came out to greet them Polly found herself feeling not only more confident, but every bit the adventurer as she followed on closely behind Sir Eggmond, who left his extraordinarily large footprints in the fresh snow.

As they walked and talked, Polly asked Aazi to sing his special song, "The Impossible Dream," to her. And as she listened to the words, she felt truly inspired and encouraged to continue on. Polly decided that she loved the song so much that she persuaded Aazi to sing it over and over again until she completely familiarized herself with all the words.

"Now that I've shared my song with you, I think it's high time that I got to hear yours," said Aazi as he tried to coax her along.

Polly agreed rather reluctantly, for she told him that she much preferred to sing along with him, especially as he had such a wonderful voice.

"You're truly gifted, Aazi," she said, giving him an encouraging tap on the shoulder. "But I guess it's only fair that as you've shared your song, then I should be willing to share mine."

Polly opened her mouth and began to sing out loud, "Climb every mountain..."

Aazi had never heard the song before, but found himself feeling equally inspired and, just like Polly, greatly encouraged to press on toward his goal. And, as he had been forced to sing his song over and over, he requested that Polly do likewise until he had learned all the words by heart. Privately, as he walked slightly ahead of them, Sir Eggmond's breast swelled with pride as he listened to the two of them singing their hearts out. He also had a permanent smile fixed on his face as he too joined in the singing, albeit quietly under his breath.

Finally, they arrived at the foot of the mountain, and he insisted they stop for a break as well as a final check of their equipment.

"Isn't she a beauty?" Sir Eggmond announced, breaking into a big smile. "Yes, doesn't she just compel you to reach for her summit? Come on, Polly. Take a proper look."

Polly shielded her eyes from the glare of the sun as she obeyed his order and looked up to the heavens. "I can't see the summit," she wailed, feeling an instant rush of panic.

"Of course you can't, my dear," responded Sir Eggmond brightly. "For, it's way up there, far beyond the clouds and quite out of view to the human eye."

Polly shuddered and closed her eyes as she seriously gave great consideration to abandoning this utterly crazy quest.

"Well, I think that this is the perfect time to tell you that although the sun is at present shining and all seems calm on the horizon, the weather report for today is not good. No, not good at all," said Sir Eggmond, shaking his head.

"Not good?" queried Polly, feeling instantly hysterical.

"Does this mean, then, that we will be heading back to camp?" she asked with a distinct note of hopefulness.

"Oh no, my dear! Certainly not! No, this is all part and parcel of the challenge," he said cheerfully as he walked toward them, holding a coil of thick rope. "Polly, be a good girl and go stand next to Aazi so I can put a rope around your waist as well."

While Sir Eggmond was dealing with Aazi, Polly found herself having a sudden and most unexpected flashback to the many times she had seen her youngest brother James tied up with ropes when they were forced to go up into the hills and valleys on walking expeditions to get them all out of Aunt Mildred's hair.

As Polly had this sudden flashback, she felt sudden pangs of remorse that she had never said good-bye to James or told him what she was doing. She could only hope he was safe and well and that she would get to see him again, and soon. Oh, how she longed to see his little face and hold him close! She found herself hoping with all her heart that her friend Napoli Bonaparti had found a red pillar box to post her letter to James before continuing his journey in search of the Duke of Welligog.

Polly brought her thoughts back to the present and to Sir Eggmond's rather rambling weather update.

"Yes, we must prepare ourselves for some pretty hostile weather conditions, such as snow blizzards and possible avalanches before we reach the summit."

By this point, Polly was going crazy inside and felt right on the verge of throwing up, and found her fear getting worse by the minute.

"Polly dear, don't look so morose. You're now safely tied up with the rope, so please do us all a favor and pop your blindfold on," Sir Eggmond asked rather nonchalantly.

Polly hesitated, and rightly so! What with all his scary talk about blizzards and avalanches, any right-thinking person would question the wisdom of putting on a blindfold if they were about to scale a high, and very dangerous, mountain, wouldn't they?

"Come on, Polly. Don't be so skeptical. Be a good dear and put it on quickly, for you are now holding us up. Here, allow me the pleasure of helping you," said Sir Eggmond as he took the scarf from her severely trembling hands and began to tie it around her eyes. "Perfectissimo!" he muttered as he knotted it tightly at the back of her head. "Now, Aazi, please allow me to check that your rope is not only tight enough but thoroughly secure," he said, giving the rope a little tug for safety's sake. "Good, now let me help you further by allowing me to position your earmuffs on your head for you. There," he said, stepping back a few paces to look Aazi up and down.

"Yes, Polly, they say that within an hour or so visibility will be quite poor."

"What's the point of telling us that?" exclaimed Polly rather hysterically. "I mean, neither of us can see a jolly thing now, let alone in a few hours' time!"

"Oh Polly, there really is no need to get quite so stroppy," he quipped. "Just be a good dear and pop your earmuffs on, and then we'll start our ascent. Now hurry along, my little peanuts. I'm looking forward to this climb almost as much as the two of you!"

Polly chose to ignore him, preferring to place her earmuffs very firmly over her ears, for she believed she'd heard more than enough from Sir "Loop the Loop" Hooligooli!"

The bad weather conditions were upon them much sooner than Polly or Sir Eggmond had anticipated. However, she was left with little choice but to continue her ascent. Both she and Aazi were securely tied up to the same thick rope as Sir Eggmond. Before long, she could no longer feel her fingers, for they had gone thoroughly numb in spite of her thick protective gloves. Her lips and nose turned purple as she battled against thick snow storms and cruel icy blizzards.

"Someone should come up with an idea for nosemuffs," she thought to herself as she pondered whether her nose might drop off due to frostbite. An hour or so later she could no longer feel her toes, for they too had come out in sympathy with her nose and were now also thoroughly numb.

Finally, they arrived on a flat plateau, and Sir Eggmond untied their ropes. Aazi and Polly slumped to the ground to take a well-earned rest. Polly used this as an excuse to pull off her blindfold and was just about to remove her earmuffs so that she could start chatting away to Aazi when she heard the deafening voice of Sir Eggmond bellowing; "HELP!"

Polly felt a strong wave of fear rush through her body as his voice had a blood-curdling tone of urgency in it. Sir Eggmond then began to wave his arms frantically in the air, shouting and hollering in her direction.

"We need to get help!" he yelled through cupped hands so that the sound of his voice would travel further.

Polly staggered to her feet and then trudged as fast as she was able over to where he stood, waving both arms in the air. She could hear the loud beat of her heart as it hammered away deafeningly in her ears. Her breathing became shorter and quicker as she felt overtaken by fear. She continued to make her way toward Sir Eggmond, afraid of what she might find.

She could see that Aazi was still sitting where she had left him, so she knew the crisis had nothing to do with him. What on earth was going on?

"Aazi, don't move, stay where you are until I get back!" she shouted back in his direction. Aazi waved a hand to show that he had heard her.

As Polly came nearer to Sir Eggmond, she noticed two bodies lying sprawled out in the snow. Her heart picked up speed as she edged nearer and nearer. "Oh, my goodness! It's the two Justins!" she screamed. "Oh, please tell me they're not dead!" she cried out in horror as she raced over to where they lay sprawled out and motionless. She fell on both knees and checked their pulses. "I can feel a faint pulse. Yes, both of them have a pulse, and they're both still breathing. Quick, Sir Eggmond," she shouted in his direction, "we urgently need your help."

As Polly attended to both boys, she noticed that the snow around them was spotted with their blood. She could also see that there were long drag marks in the snow that looked as though some ferocious animal, perhaps a bear, had unsuccessfully tried to drag their bodies along. If this was true, why had the animal or animals changed their mind and abandoned the boys?

POLLY BROWN

As Polly searched their bodies for clues, she came across deep puncture wounds in their skin. "Sir Eggmond, come here quickly and take a look," she cried.

Sir Eggmond ignored her cries and carried on talking into a most strange looking contraption that was connected by long wires to a large black box. Polly cried out for his help again as the enormity of the boys' injuries came to bear heavily upon her. Finally, he came over to where Polly knelt between the two boys and got down on both knees beside her.

As Sir Eggmond observed their atrociously severe wounds, he rubbed his chin thoughtfully and remarked, "I do believe that this has all the hallmarks of Vanaspi's ferocious dogs of darkness. Yes, those puncture wounds would suggest that those very savage, vicious brutes are more than likely behind this tragedy," he sniffed, shaking his head from side to side as he inspected their wounds more closely.

"How do you know it was them and not some big grizzly?" cried Polly.

"Because no bear would venture this far up a mountain. Also, if you look carefully at the trail they have left behind in the snow, then you will see they are the paw marks of dogs or wolves. If it were a bear, the prints would be much larger and less of them. I believe our arrival on this glacier has probably saved these two boys' lives, as those hounds have now fled," he stated as he continued to inspect their wounds. "Had we arrived much later, I do believe we would be witnessing a very different scene of utter carnage. Those vicious animals would have ripped them to pieces before delivering what was left of them back to their master."

"Oh, Sir Eggmond, this is a terrible thing to have happened to them. If only they had listened to you earlier, then this would never have happened," she tearfully cried.

"Yes, but sadly, youth always think they know best, Polly. It sometimes takes a tragedy of mammoth proportions before we will listen to those older and wiser than ourselves who love us and want the best for us."

"What can we do now? We must get them help—and soon," Polly miserably stated.

"Don't worry, Polly. I have made a call to search and rescue, and they are at present mobilizing a medical team. In fact, the air rescue helicopter should be with us very shortly."

"That is such good news, Sir Eggmond," Polly said, feeling overcome with relief.

"Yes, but until help arrives we must do all within our power to keep them both warm and comfortable."

"Yes, yes," said Polly, eager to do anything she could to help. "Just tell me what to do."

"Polly, you go and search through Justin Kase's bag, which is lying over there. I need bandages and scissors and anything we can use as pillows to prop up their legs and stop the hemorrhaging. Also, I will need some large rolls of aluminum foil to wrap around their bodies in order to prevent further heat loss. Go quickly while I stay here and concern myself with stemming the blood flow until you get back."

Polly quickly jumped up from the ground and headed in the direction of Justin's large backpack. While she was gone, Sir Eggmond reached into the pocket of his thickly-padded jacket and produced two old-fashioned medicinal bottles.

"Hmm, I do believe that both the Hoolie Koolie and the Hubber Blubber ointment will be required if these boys are to have any hope of surviving this dreadfully savage attack." He then glanced quickly over his shoulder to where Polly was kneeling as she rummaged through Justin's backpack. He discreetly removing the cork out of both bottles and applied his special miracle working balm. "Brrr, I do hope that help is quick in coming," Sir Eggmond muttered to himself as he blew into his cupped hands. "I do declare my feathers are beginning to freeze up, and I'm feeling decidedly itchy!"

"Here, I've also found Justin's first-aid box," Polly cried, waving it in the air as she raced back to where the seriously injured boys lay.

"Excellent," said Sir Eggmond as he rather expediently shuffled around in the large box, searching for bandages.

"Sshh, Sir Eggmond, I think I can hear something," said Polly.

She was indeed absolutely correct. For the noise was that of the rotary blades of a helicopter as it came into view from over a mountain peak in search of them. Polly jumped up from her knees and began to wave both hands in the air in an effort to get their attention. Minutes later the helicopter touched down safely on a wide section of the plateau.

Polly watched as both boys were connected to drips before being carried away on stretchers to be transported to the nearest hospital. Polly waved the helicopter off and then went over to where Aazi had obediently been sitting throughout the whole drama. When the helicopter had finally disappeared from view, Sir Eggmond made his way over to join them.

"Oh Aazi, I'm so glad you didn't see the boys, for they looked in a terrible state," she forlornly sobbed. "I just hope they will pull through."

Aazi simply nodded as he quietly answered her, "Yes, Polly, I hope so, too."

Sir Eggmond, on hearing their conversation, chipped in, "Look, Polly, I believe they are in good hands. Believe me when I say that Hope in Your Heart Hospital has the best nursing staff in the whole world. Yes, they couldn't be in better and more capable hands, trust me. Now, I do believe that a nice, steaming hot cup of tea is in order. So while I brew the tea, I will leave you to find the food packages from my backpack, for we need to build up our energy before we move on."

"But, Sir Eggmond, surely we are not going on! Not after what has just happened!" Polly cried out, feeling very alarmed and upset.

"And why not?" replied Sir Eggmond, acting as though he was totally taken by surprise.

"Because, if something so terrible could happen to them, there is nothing to say that we won't be next!" she mumbled.

"Oh dear, Polly. Don't make a crisis out of a drama!" Sir Eggmond snorted.

"What?" shrieked Polly, unable to believe her ears. "You think I'm overreacting? Is that what you're saying? You're really unbelievable. I can't believe I agreed to come with…"

"Polly, be a dear and calm down. There will always be casualties of war, but does an army give up and go home when a few of their men are sadly injured?"

"No," replied Polly. "But…"

"No buts. You're absolutely correct. The wounded are always given every bit of help that is on hand, and then the regiment regroup and move on with more determination than ever to take hold and capture the land. Have you not watched all the old war films?"

Polly nodded, not because she wanted to, but because she had lost the argument. He was right. In all the old war movies the remaining soldiers never gave up. They just heroically pushed on.

"Good. Then you know this to be true. I'm sure that both boys will be back on their feet in no time at all. And Justin Kase will be filling his backpack with even more 'just in case' items he believes he needs for forthcoming adventures. Just you wait and see."

Polly broke out into a smile as she pictured her friend finally unable to close his bag due to severe overspill.

"Right then, let's get our lunch organized, and then we can move on."

As they munched on their sandwiches washed down with warm, sweet tea, Polly noticed an eagle flying through the air above them.

"Oh, Aazi, I wish you could see just how beautiful and majestic this bird is as it flies through the air and swoops down. It is so powerful, yet graceful."

"Yes, and of all the birds on our planet, the eagle is the only one that soars into the sunlight rays, flying effortlessly on the wind's currents as it basks in the heavens, totally at peace with its Creator," Sir Eggmond-all knowingly chipped in. "We could learn a lot from these creatures if we took the time to study them. Right then, my little chicken dippers, drink up, for we must move on before it gets dark," Sir Eggmond said rather briskly as he took the empty mugs from out of their hands. "Go and grab your things, and let's press on."

With their thick ropes once again attached to Sir Eggmond's waist, they began to climb further toward the mountain peak. Polly deliberately chose not to put her blindfold back on and hoped that Sir Eggmond would not notice.

As they scaled the mountain, Polly could not resist the urge to look down to check on Aazi, who was at the end of her rope. Suddenly, icy fear gripped her, causing her heart to race faster. She began to feel blind panic as she could no longer see land, only ice peaks and then more ice peaks, as well as thick cotton wool clouds that were moving through the heavens at great speed. Polly shut her eyes tightly, and between the tiny whimpers that were now escaping past her purplish-blue lips she prayed that this nightmare climb would come to an end fast. The wind howled mercilessly and a ferocious ice storm blew up, but still they kept climbing higher and higher into the clouds.

"We just need to get over this precipice, and then we will call it a day," Sir Eggmond shouted down to them before pointing ahead, waving a pickax in his outstretched hand.

On hearing this, Polly felt a surge of relief run through her pushed-to-the-limit young body, for she was seriously convinced that she was on the verge of cracking up. The last bit of the climb really took its toll on Polly, and as she followed behind Sir Eggmond, placing her feet in all the little contraptions he had hammered into the mountain face, she felt all her energy ebb away.

"I can't do it. I can't go any further!" she cried out loud.

"Yes, you can, Polly. Just breathe deeply into your oxygen mask. Go on; that's it. Take a deep breath. Come on; just a few feet. You're almost there," Sir Eggmond encouragingly shouted back down in her direction.

Polly then turned again to see how Aazi was progressing, and was very relieved to see that he was faithfully following on with his head bowed low as he felt his way up the mountain. Finally, her fingers touched the jagged edge of the precipice, and Sir Eggmond firmly grabbed hold of her arms and hauled her to safety.

"Well done, Polly. You've made it!" he cried, giving her a rather hefty slap on the back.

No sooner had the words come forth from his lips when Polly felt a sharp tug on the rope, followed by an almighty cry that came from further down the mountain. Polly froze. She instantly knew that her beloved friend was in deep trouble. She turned her head slowly, too terrified to want to look. She was horrified to see Aazi dangling on the end of the rope, crashing into jagged rocks as he repeatedly swung backwards and forwards. Before she had time to think, there was another sharp tug on the rope and she found herself going headlong over the side of the precipice, held only by the rope strapped around Sir Eggmond's waist.

"Hang on, both of you!" shouted Sir Eggmond.

Polly didn't answer, for the fall had completely winded her in spite of her oxygen mask. She was also struggling with the overwhelming pain caused by hitting one rocky crag after another as she swung back and forth, consistently crashing into the mountainside and tearing her flesh.

"Polly, try to reach that large rock," Sir Eggmond yelled down as he tightly held onto the rope that they were now both swinging from.

Polly felt as though she were clinging on for all her life with each attempt to grab hold of something solid.

Finally she managed to reach the rock that Sir Eggmond had pointed toward. As she grabbed hold, she looked down at Aazi and was horrified to discover that he was still helplessly swinging to and fro, and now had one foot tangled up in the rope. Polly panicked as she observed that the rope was almost severed in one particular spot where the jagged rocks had cut into it.

"Help us! Please help us!" she screamed.

"Polly, you need to keep your head!" Sir Eggmond shouted down at her. "Pull yourself up onto the rock, and then you can help pull Aazi up. Don't worry, I've got you both."

Polly struggled to obey his last order, for she was not only out of breath, but also clean out of the energy necessary to haul herself up onto the rock. Finally, when she was on the verge of giving up, she found renewed strength and willpower to get up onto the rock and to safety. She instantly felt ecstatic. But this was to be very short lived! As she turned around to help pull Aazi to the safety of the rock, the rope gave way, making a terrifyingly loud snapping noise. Polly could only watch on in complete horror as the little bundle she knew to be her best friend hurtled down the mountain at alarming speed before disappearing completely out of sight. Polly let out a piercing scream.

"Stay where you are, Polly," ordered Sir Eggmond, "and I will come and get you."

Polly, who was shaking with fear from head to toe, obeyed his order. In truth, she couldn't have moved a muscle even if she wanted to, for she was frozen with terror.

"We must now turn back and go in search of Aazis," said Sir Eggmond with a serious and grim look on his face. How Polly made it down the mountain she will never remember. After Aazi's fall, everything was just a blur. "I've had enough! I truly can't take any more!" screamed Polly. And as she inched her way down the mountain, her whole life flashed before her. She thought about her beloved Thomas and her younger brother James, and she saw pictures of her dear teachers, Mr. Beloski and Mrs. Bailey, flash before her eyes. She longed with all her heart to be back in the classroom with Mrs. Bailey, giving her an apple, for she missed her so much. Polly found this mental picture show very disconcerting, for she had heard that this only takes place moments before you die.

They had only been on their descent a short time when they came across a bundle lying in the snow.

"There he is!" cried Polly as she raced over to where his lifeless body lay covered in thick, white snow. Polly then fell to her knees and hugged the bundle. "Oh Aazi! Oh Aazi!" were the only words she uttered as she clutched him tightly to herself.

Sir Eggmond raced over to join them. "Well, blow my nose and rattle my toes, it's a miracle!" he shouted.

"What's a miracle, Eggcrunch?" Polly asked angrily as she looked up at him in sheer disbelief, searching his face for an answer.

"Polly, can't you see that this ledge saved him from falling to his death. That, I do believe, is a miracle!"

Polly felt speechless, for how could this strange man be calling this a miracle when her dear young friend was lying unconscious in her arms, probably about to die!

"Sir Eggmond, this is going to sound really rude, but I'm going to say it anyway. *Shut up and go get help!*" she yelled at the top of her lungs, "Or it will be you who needs an ambulance."

Sir Eggmond pretended to be shocked, "Now, now, Polly. That is not the sort of language I would expect to be coming from the mouth of a princess," he remonstrated.

Polly was so furious at his gung-ho attitude, which she mistook for indifference, that she failed to even notice that he had used the term *princess* with reference to her.

"Just go away and find that weird contraption of yours, and do something useful like calling the emergency services," she snapped.

Sir Eggmond quickly moved away, secretly smiling to himself. Having moved some distance from his distraught student, he knelt down in the snow to undo his backpack and look for his contraption to make the emergency call. In no time at all, the helicopter was back with them. Having found a safe place to land, a doctor and his crew jumped out and made their way over to where Polly still knelt in the snow, cradling Aazi. Polly looked up as the team approached, and was surprised to find that she recognized the doctor.

"Dr. Loveheart! Oh boy, am I glad to see you!" she cried, at the same time releasing Aazi from her arms into his.

She then moved over to one side so that the good doctor could take over and examine him. Dr. Loveheart looked most concerned as he took his stethoscope from around his neck and placed it onto Aazi's tiny chest.

"Well, the good thing is he's still alive, but I have to warn you, Polly, he is in pretty bad shape. There is no way of telling whether the poor lad will make it." Polly could not stop the hot tears that immediately sprang to her eyes as Dr. Loveheart went on to give a more formal diagnosis. "Yes, I'm afraid the poor little chap is in a deep coma, and only heaven knows whether he will come out of this one," he said as he gently squeezed her hand. "I think we'd better pray that the good Lord shines upon him, otherwise his time is up!" Polly began to sob loudly as she tried to take in all that the doctor was saying. "Polly, I know that this is all very hard to swallow, but I'm sure you would prefer me to be truthful, wouldn't you?"

Polly nodded before attempting to wipe away the fresh tears that were springing like a fountain from her glazed-over eyes.

Sir Eggmond, who was standing over her, chipped in, "Yes, Polly, I have to say, this has been a most peculiar expedition. To lose one student is most sad, but to lose three in one day is, I believe, positively careless of me! I really must go over my safety procedures to make sure something as terrible as this never happens again."

As Polly listened to Sir Eggmond make light of not one, not two, but three terrible tragedies, she found that she could no longer restrain herself. She leapt to her feet and stood facing him eyeball to eyeball, shaking with unspeakable rage. Her eyes were filled with wild hostility toward him. Finally, Polly opened her mouth to express her absolute outrage, but no words of remonstration would come forth.

"Cat got your tongue, Polly?" Sir Eggmond asked playfully.

Polly, still unable to express her sheer disgust, could only fold her arms and then turn on her heels to storm off and get as far away as possible from this man, whom she was beginning to loathe with all her being.

"Right, we'd better get this young lad to the hospital as quickly as possible," advised Dr. Loveheart. "Nurse, go and fetch a stretcher, and be sure to be quick."

Both nurses, who were standing by, turned and raced toward the helicopter to bring back a stretcher. After taking a few deep breaths in an attempt to calm down, Polly made her way back over to where the doctor was making Aazi comfortable as he prepared to leave the precipice.

"Can I come with you to the hospital?" Polly asked Dr. Loveheart.

Before the good doctor could reply, Sir Eggmond once again chipped in, "Oh no, no, my dear. You still have a mountain to climb. You can't possibly turn back now. Remember the army and…"

"Go away and leave me alone!" Polly screamed at Sir Eggmond. "You can forget your stupid mountain Sir Hula Hoop, or Loop the Loop, whatever your real name is. There is no way I'm going anywhere with you ever again!" she thundered.

"Temper, temper, Polly. You really must try harder to control yourself. Besides, I'm not asking you to take me with you. No, remember my previous words of comfort?" he asked, furrowing his brow as he looked her directly between the eyes. "Yes, if you rightly remember, if you cast your mind back, I specifically told you that you are to climb the rest of this mountain alone."

"Forget it! You're barking mad," she retaliated, great exasperation etched all over her face. She then turned her back on him to face Dr. Loveheart. "Please take me with you, Dr. Loveheart," she pleaded. "I want to stay with Aazi, especially if these are to be his final hours."

"I would, Polly, but I have to say that there is simply no room on the helicopter for all of us. After the stretcher has been placed inside there are only four spaces left. You need to understand that it simply isn't possible."

"Well, Doctor, if there is space for four of us, surely that means there is enough room for me," she said, looking very puzzled. "For you and your two nurses make three, and that leaves one available space. Am I right?"

"Yes, you're absolutely correct, Polly," said Dr. Loveheart with a gentle smile.

"Well, then, what's the problem? For surely that means I can take up the extra space and come back with you?"

"Ahh," said the good doctor, looking slightly embarrassed. "Well, I don't know how to tell you this, Polly, but that extra seat is already booked."

"Already booked!" repeated a very stunned Polly.

"Yes, my dear, already booked," Dr. Loveheart replied, looking and feeling most awkward.

"Booked by whom?" quizzed Polly.

"By him," said the doctor, sheepishly directing his eyes in Sir Eggmond's direction.

"Yes, by me, my dear," chipped in Sir Eggmond brightly as he strode forward to own up. "Yes, by my own admission, I took the liberty of reserving myself the last space on the helicopter when you rather rudely dismissed me to go and make an emergency call 'on my weird contraption,' to use your terminology."

Polly could only stare at him in sheer disbelief. "You mean you reserved yourself a seat on the rescue helicopter as if it were some theater booking, and intended to leave me out here all alone on the mountainside to die?" she said, shaking her head to make sure she was not dreaming.

"Come now, Polly, don't be such a spoilsport," he said, giving Dr. Loveheart a sneaky and mischievous wink. "Surely you don't think I would leave you out here all alone to be eaten by hungry wolves and bears. Oh no! You have shown yourself to be a most excellent mountain climber who needs no further tuition, and therefore I can see no further reason to be here."

Polly stood with her jaw dropped in a most unladylike manner as she struggled to take in his words.

"And just to further encourage you, if you look to your left, Polly, you will see the snow-capped peak of Piadora. Come on, Polly, be a good sport and look over to where I'm pointing," he said with a mischievous glint in his eye. "Yes, you need to set off as quickly as possible. The sun has almost gone down, and I believe darkness will be upon you before you can say 'peek-a-boo.'"

Taking a deep breath, Polly then placed her hands over her ears as an act of defiance as she refused point blank to follow his outstretched arm and look in the direction he was asking her to.

Finally, she found the words she was looking for.

"I cannot believe that you could be so utterly selfish and heartless, Sir Eggmond. For you know full well that I have hardly had any practice at mountain climbing, and from what I have experienced out here with you, I would go as far as to say that you are an utter fraud who deserves to be locked up for the rest of your life! Yes, and if they had any sense, they would throw away the key and leave you to rot," she announced as she bent down to gather up some stray rolls of bandage, which Dr. Loveheart had failed to put back in his medicine case.

"My, my! We really are going for the jugular, aren't we, Polly?"

Poor Polly was by this point so seething with frustration that she promptly used the bandages to bombard the unsuspecting Sir Eggmond. "Go on; leave me, you heartless rogue! You were no friend at all, and I never want to set eyes upon you again!" she yelled at him as he tried to duck the bandages that were coming his way at great speed.

"My, we're in a right tizzy, aren't we?" said Sir Eggmond with a grin as he continued to duck and dive as he moved nearer to the open door of the helicopter to avoid the unrolling bandages that Polly was using as missiles.

He then quickly climbed in to join the medical team, who were quite understandably very anxious to leave as soon as possible.

"Well, Polly, I hope everything works out for you!" he shouted from his seat as he waved her good-bye.

Polly responded to this gesture by turning her back and ignoring him completely. As the blades of the helicopter began to turn full circle and the machine lifted off the ground, Sir Eggmond continued to wave down at Polly before turning to Dr. Loveheart to make further comment.

"I think she's feeling a trifle upset at the moment, but we must not worry ourselves. As the saying goes, 'When the going gets tough, the tough get going,' and this young lady has remarkable tenacity. Just you wait and see!"

Polly watched on until the helicopter was little more than a speck in the sky. She then collapsed to the ground, crushed to the core of her spirit and feeling utterly overwhelmed by all that had happened.

"Take my life and give Aazi's back to him!" she yelled into the wind.

She continued to vent her fury by beating her fists in the snow until she had no fight left in her. As she continued to kneel in the snow with her head bowed very low in deep despair, she found herself unable to even cry. She had gone beyond tears into the worst and most terrifying dark night of the soul, where neither words nor tears can begin to express the depth of anguish and utter desolation that her broken heart was now experiencing.

And as she knelt in the snow, Polly reached for her gold little book with the intention of writing her last thoughts down. She opened up her book at the back and tore out a clean page. Despite her hands being severely frostbitten, she struggled to pick up her pen and slowly began to write.

Whoever finds me finds my last will and testament.

I, Polly Brown, do hereby confirm that I am in sound mind at the time of writing this. And sadly, I must point out that there are no real beneficiaries to my will for the simple reason that I don't really have anything, well, not of any value anyway. But I do bequeath all my toys, which I consider to be my worldly goods, to be shared amongst the other foster children back home at the castle. All I ask is that Percy and Petunia be kept together, as they are now officially a couple. Also as Cecil, my pet giraffe, is no longer required to stand guard over my pajamas, he is therefore free to spend the rest of his days as he chooses.

Finally, even though this is meant to be my last will and testament, I need to express one last thought. If I could turn back the clock, I would gladly exchange my life in return for Aazi's. My good friend is very unlikely to make it, and when I think of all he has been through in his short life, I am amazed, by his resilience and his joyful attitude toward everything in life. Aazi showed me that it is possible to suffer without complaining, something I have been terribly guilty of in the past. I will always miss him, and I believe he deserved to be the one to live, not me.

I have only one further request. If my body should ever be found, I would very much like to be buried next to my brother Thomas. I would also love a jar filled with poppies put on both graves. I would truly appreciate this little kind-ness.

Thank you very much.

Yours,

Polly

Polly's last will and testament took up two pieces of the paper torn from her diary. Having written it as best as she could, she folded it up and tucked it safely back into the diary. This time Polly opened her diary at the front, and she found herself having one final read of all that had been said about her. She shed a few tears as, for the first time ever, she noticed that every entry in her book had always referred to her as though she were already a princess, and this little fact felt deeply touching. Though her hands were well-and-truly frozen, she determined to read everything in the book since this would, after all, be the final time that she would read or write anything. When she thought she had come to the end, her eyes suddenly fell on fresh writing that she had never seen before.

Polly took a deep gasp of breath, and even as she was reading on, from out of nowhere a stone literally plopped on her head before coming to rest in the snow right beside her.

"Ouch! That hurt," mumbled Polly as she looked up to see where it had come from. She was startled to see a golden eagle soaring above her head. Her eyes fixed on his beady eyes, and she knew in an instant that he was the guilty party. She then picked up the pebble from the ground and could clearly see the word *love* inscribed on the stone. Polly placed it to one side and carried on reading.

The princess had proven herself to be a very obedient child, for when her two friends abandoned Sir Eggmond to make the ascent on their own she had chosen to stay. And despite having dreadful concerns about Sir Eggmond's state of mind, as well as his climbing skills, the princess chose to put away all fear and implicitly trust him regarding her safety and that of Aazi, her young soul mate and new best friend.

However, things looked very bleak and hopeless. First, the two Justins appeared to have perished, and then her best friend suffered a tragic accident, leaving the princess in a terrible state of anguish. She was then to be further insulted when she was betrayed by the man she trusted with her life, who rather sneakily left the scene of the accident, leaving her to die on the summit. The princess had used this opportunity to show off her very impressive,

POLLY BROWN

regal temper. She had a rather sudden outburst of anger and rage at Sir Hula Hoop or Loop the Loop, as she so rather naughtily called him. But then who could blame her? For the princess was now totally alone and at the mercy of a mountain that had, over the years, taken many a life away.

Still, as she sought to write her last will and testament, she had shown beyond a shadow of a doubt that she was indeed worthy of the title princess: *when she confessed that she would have willingly given up her own life in return for Aazi's, she did not realize that for a man to willingly lay down his life for a friend is the greatest show of love that any person can give.*

So, now as she knelt in the snow, abandoned and betrayed, would this be the final chapter in her trouble-filled life?

———⋅♦⋅———

Polly closed her book and then closed her eyes, with darkness creeping over the mountain and falling upon her like a thick blanket. Every fear that she had ever encountered rose up from within to mercilessly taunt her, claiming that all she had ever believed and hoped for was nothing more than a vale of lies that only the craziest of lunatics would ever have believed! I mean, who in their right mind would have listened to two smelly vagabonds with all their wild talk of Piadora? And who would have agreed to climb a dangerous mountain with a complete nut named Sir Eggmond Hoollari?

"I feel like a prize idiot to have ever believed and put my life into the hands of such a fraud," she whispered. She reasoned that no sane person would have readily agreed to such a ridiculous proposal, and so she had only herself to blame for putting all natural and logical reasoning to one side to embark on such a wildly frivolous adventure. Sadly, she was now paying the full price for her stupidity. She would die a slow and agonizingly painful death, alone and isolated on the mountainside.

Once again, she found herself thinking of the few people such as Thomas, Mrs. Bailey, and Mr. Beloski—people who had meant everything to her—and she felt her heart was on the very verge of breaking into pieces.

"How could I have let this happen to me?" she whimpered, bowing her head even lower into her lap in her futile effort to stave off the cold. "Now I'm in a complete mess with no way out!"

As she lay in the snow with her head bowed as low as her heart, she was suddenly startled by a strange sound that grew louder and louder. Polly slowly lifted her head and winced as she began to look in the direction of Piadora. For suddenly, the heavens around Piadora's summit lit up the whole sky with the most vivid swirls of deep orange and blinding gold. As she stared in stupefied silence in Piadora's direction, she heard music that she recognized.

"Oh my goodness!" she exclaimed. "I recognize that sound. Why, it's Aazi's favorite song, 'The Impossible Dream!'"

Polly continued to kneel in the snow, but now she was experiencing the strangest sensations. Unbelievable joy began to flood her whole being, at the same time releasing a powerful heat that surged through every fiber of her body until she glowed from head to foot. Polly felt utterly in awe of the beauty of Piadora. As she continued to stare in its direction, it seemed to be beckoning her to come forth as the sweet music appeared to cascade in loud crescendos over the snow-capped mountain peaks before sweeping down to wash over her. The longer she knelt, the more she began to feel an immense strength begin to build up inside her breast.

Finally, feeling totally energized from head to foot, she picked herself up from the snow, brushed herself down, and defiantly shouted into the wind, "I am going to climb this mountain, and I am going to do it for Aazi as well as myself. If I die on the way, so be it. At least I will have tried. Nothing is over until it's over, so Piadora, here I come!"

With her words echoing and repeating over and over as they bounced off the rocks and snow-capped peaks, she marched like a soldier into battle toward the bright light that was flooding Mount Piadora from the heavens to its base.

She sang and sang with all her might as she scaled the mountain with renewed fervor and determination. With every step she made, she thought less and less of the danger. No, nothing whatsoever was going to get in her way and prevent her from reaching the finishing line!

She continued to ignore the deep cuts that covered her hands from contact with the jagged rocks, the deep hunger pangs that were constantly nagging her, and the numbness that crept right through her body and gnawed deep into her bones. The higher she got, the thinner the air around her became, and the more difficult it became for her to breathe. Yet still she kept climbing, heading higher and higher into the clouds. She continued to listen to the music as she pulled herself up and over every crevice and plateau.

Soon she found herself unable to continue singing aloud due to shortness of breath, so she switched to singing inside her heart and head. Before too long, every fearful and deeply tormenting thought that had ever dared to voice an opinion was temporarily muted. Yes, Polly was so consumed with determination that she even failed to notice that the music had now changed to her song, "Climb Every Mountain." She just kept going up and up, further into the clouds.

She had been going for what seemed an eternity when up ahead her eyes fell on Piadora's highest peak, and despite the severe pain racking through every bone and muscle in her body, she determined in her heart that she was going to reach its top.

As her fingers finally and weakly touched the top of the peak, she felt certain that she was going to pass out. She was now really struggling to take even the shallowest of breaths. Her lungs felt on the verge of collapse. But as she placed her cut and profusely bleeding fingers onto the final jagged rock, she found herself praying for supernatural ability to pull herself up one final time.

Suddenly and without forewarning, her tiny hands were gripped by a much larger and most powerful hand.

Chapter 36
PIADORA AT LAST

$\mathcal{P}$OLLY REMEMBERED NOTHING else after she collapsed into the soft white snow on the peak of Piadora. She instantly fell into a deep and beautiful, healing sleep.

When she finally awoke, she found herself looking directly into the eyes of Hodgekiss.

"Well done, Polly. You've made it," he said with a warm smile as he continued to cradle her in his arms.

"Hodgekiss? Is that really you?" she asked quietly, as though she were waking up from a dream.

"Yes, Polly, it's me," replied Hodgekiss.

Polly rubbed her eyes to see if she was really awake and not just imagining everything. As she continued focusing on him, she became aware of a beautiful light glowing brightly all around him that was almost blinding in its brilliance. His eyes also appeared to sparkle like diamonds, and his voice sounded as gentle as the cool ripples of a brook. Instead of his dingy overcoat and old boots he was wearing a long, gold robe, encrusted with thousands of glistening and very precious jewels.

"But you don't look or smell like you usually do," said Polly weakly as she continued to rub her eyes. "I mean, without seeming too rude, you normally smell as though you've been scavaging through restaurant trash cans," she said, faltering, for she did not really wish to be offensive, just honest. "But now your smell is...well...heavenly, simply divine," she exclaimed.

"Yes, there's a reason for that, and I will explain everything to you later."

"Where am I?" she asked, a little dazed as she sat up straight.

"Why, you're just outside the gates of Piadora," said Hodgekiss, brushing away some stray hairs from her forehead. "Come, if you're feeling better, let's go together into Piadora, for there is much I need to show you."

Polly allowed Hodgekiss to help her up on both feet, and with her fingers firmly weaved into his they walked toward a dense pine forest.

"So where is Piadora, for I can't see it?" Polly asked Hodgekiss.

"Oh, it's there all right! You just can't see it at present, for it's obscured from view by all the thick pine trees. But I promise you, Polly, it really does exist, and it lies just beyond this forest. Come, let us walk faster. It will only be a matter of time before Piadora reveals itself to you."

As Polly walked through the forest, she could see groups of people huddled by trees or playing hide and seek. "Who are these people? And what are they doing here?" Polly privately wondered. As they continued walking she noticed that many of the trees were covered in large yellow bows from top to trunk,. "How strange," was all she could find to mutter.

"Before your curiosity gets the better of you—for I know precisely what you're thinking—let me answer your question," Hodgekiss said as he gave her small hand a squeeze. "This forest is known in these parts as Forgiveness Forest, and one of my favorite pastimes is to walk through its many trails."

"Forgiveness Forest? Hodgekiss, now what sort of name is that?" said Polly, feeling slightly confused as well as uncomfortable.

"Well, it is the forest where many people, particularly families, come together to resolve all conflicts that have been passed down from one generation to another. I really love it here," he commented, giving the gentlest of smiles. "Yes, it is so sad to see and hear of families that have been divided and even destroyed by resentment and hatred and other such terrible things. Here, in this forest, they have the opportunity to forgive and then learn to love each other again. It's a truly peaceful forest where tremendous healing takes place, with families being wonderfully restored and united. And that's really vital if they are going to enter into Piadora, for sadness and pain are not welcome visitors in Piadora.

Yes, many tears are shed out here, so many that they keep this forest well watered for me.

"Hmm, Hodgekiss," Polly murmured, still feeling a trifle puzzled. "But why the yellow ribbons?"

"Well, when reconciliation finally takes place each member of the family gets to tie one around a tree with their name on, and it becomes a constant reminder that love and forgiveness walk hand in hand and that family and friends are the most precious gifts we have. Yes, they are far more precious than gold or silver, or any precious jewel for that matter, and yet sometimes we toss them away with about as much thought as a discarded ice-cream wrapper, often for the most idiotic of reasons."

Polly nodded, for she really understood what Hodgekiss was talking about.

"You know something, Polly? Some family members have been up to their eyeballs in family feuds for countless years, and therefore haven't seen or spoken to each other for years. Sometimes it takes a family member or friend to die to alert them to the problem, but for those left behind it is then too late to put things right. That is just about the saddest thing that can happen, and yet it goes on all the time. Polly, think how sad being part of a broken family must feel like."

Polly nodded for a second time. "Yes, that is truly awful," she admitted. "But if I had a family I would never allow such a terrible thing to happen, for I constantly wish with all my heart to belong," she said with a sigh.

"Precisely, Polly. Sometimes it is only when we are denied, or we have something taken away that we begin to realize its special value. Families are like precious pearls that, like the heart, should grow larger and more beautiful with time. I don't know whether you know this little fact, but pearls grow larger in size as the sand that gets inside the shell continues to irritate the pearl. Now, isn't that amazing? At the end of the day families are no different. They should allow those irritations and things that bug them to make them grow larger like a pearl, and much more generous hearted, don't you think?" Polly continued to nod her agreement. "Well, Polly, I hate to say it, especially at this time, but you too have people you need to forgive. And I think Aunt Mildred and Uncle Boritz must come top of that list, don't you?"

"Oh my goodness, are they here?" cried Polly, feeling very shocked and uncomfortable at the prospect of suddenly meeting up with them.

"Certainly not, Polly, so don't worry. I wouldn't spring that one upon you without giving you plenty of prior warning, but you do need to give it some thought," he said in a strangely quiet tone of voice. "For when you leave Piadora to return home to the orphanage, nothing much will have changed. The other children will still be battling against each other, and your guardians are not going to change their ways. Yes, everything will continue on as normal, with one exception. You will have visited Piadora, and after this, you will never be the same again. No, you will find yourself with an inner strength that will keep you through all future times of trouble and hardship, and that's a promise," he said as he gazed deep into her eyes. "And yes, hopefully this wonderful experience will enable you to be gracious and merciful toward all those who despise and mistreat you."

"I hope you're right, Hodgekiss," Polly muttered, "for I felt at the end of my rope most of the time," she said with a tinge of sadness that betrayed her heavy heart as she thought back to her sad, empty life at the orphanage.

"But, come on, Polly. For the moment, let's put this conversation to one side. Now look straight ahead and you will see the gates of Piadora on the horizon."

"Wow, amazing!" were the only words that passed her lips as she gazed in awe and wonder toward the kingdom of Piadora.

As they raced together toward the entrance, Polly noticed that the towering gates to Piadora were very heavily guarded. This observation puzzled her, for she could not imagine any troops, with all their gear, surviving the terrifying climb up the mountain, let alone taking siege to plunder Piadora! Before she could ask Hodgekiss for the answer to the puzzle, he began to answer her thoughts.

"Polly, this is the only entrance into the city, and all who enter can only do so if they wear a ring just like the one you have on your finger. I'm glad you are still wearing it."

"So am I," said Polly, breaking into a smile and feeling most relieved as she thought back to the time when the awful Tobias Mortimus had, luckily for her, been most unsuccessful in his attempt to remove the ring from her finger as part payment for Dodo's board and lodging.

"Well, Polly, you would be quite surprised by how many people try to get into Piadora illegally, often using unlawful ways. Some have even resorted to the Trojan horse method, so great was their desire to be here. For this reason it is of the utmost importance that the gates are guarded day and night against any potential invaders."

As they neared the gate, Polly saw strange-looking men with long trumpets standing on turrets on either side of the entrance. The men placed the trumpets to their mouths and blew.

"What are they doing, Hodgekiss?" asked Polly, trying hard not to giggle.

"They are letting all those who live inside the kingdom know that we have a visitor. Yes, they are playing the trumpets of celebration."

"They are awfully loud," said Polly as she cupped her ears playfully to drown the noise.

"Yes, they are loud, but then my kingdom is very large, and it is very important that everybody hears the trumpets throughout the land. We also have other trumpets that are used to warn us of impending danger."

"Oh," said Polly, "so there are even dangers in Piadora?"

"Absolutely not, Polly, so don't worry your pretty little head. No outside attack has ever been successful, and there really is no back door they can get through," he said with a comforting smile.

Polly turned to face Hodgekiss and asked, "Have you ever heard of Soogara, the Cotton Candy Queen? For I had the most terrible time with her and some dogs she was looking after for Vanaspi."

"Oh yes, I know both of them well, for they were banished from the realm many years ago, and this has tormented them ever since. As a result they have made it their top priority to make sure others don't ever get here, such is their jealousy and wickedness. But come, Polly, now is not the time to talk of such things; we are here for a celebration and a banquet, so let's enjoy this time we have together."

Polly nodded her agreement, and as they walked through the gates she found herself overwhelmed by the crowds of people that lined the gold-paved streets to welcome her. Before long, a horse-drawn carriage fit for a princess drew up beside them, and after jumping down from his seat a gentleman bowed and opened the door.

"At your service, Princess," said the gentleman as he took a low bow. "Now, please do jump in."

Polly obliged, but not before letting out a little giggle. Hodgekiss jumped in beside her and waved at the adoring crowds as the carriage then moved away at great speed.

"Where are we going, Hodgekiss?" Polly asked, feeling the deepest sense of curiosity and an infinite amount of anticipation welling up inside her.

"Well, firstly we need to get you out of your mountain clothes into more suitable attire for a royal occasion. And secondly, we must reunite you with someone very special and close to your heart," he answered with a warm smile.

Polly looked down at her clothes and laughed, for in all the excitement and drama she had clearly forgotten she was still dressed from head to toe in her very unflattering mountaineering outfit.

As the carriage sped along the streets lined with people cheering and waving as they shouted out her name, Polly had the irresistible urge to wave back at them, but felt a little too embarrassed to reciprocate. She was, after all, only Polly Brown, a young nobody from an orphanage. Only presidents and queens normally did that sort of thing.

"You are allowed to wave back, Polly," said Hodgekiss as though he could read her thoughts. "After all, these people have watched you every step of the way, and they wished with all their hearts for you to make it. It would make them very happy if you were to wave back. Go on; give it a go, for it's really very simple. All you have to do is raise your arm and then move it from left to right. There, that's good. Now you're beginning to behave and act like a real princess."

Soon they had turned off the road and headed out into the richest lush countryside Polly had ever seen.

"Wow the views here are truly magnificent, yes, breathtaking," said Polly as she held her head outside the carriage window. "And the air smells so pure and so sweet. Why, this is all absolutely magical. Oh, Hodgekiss, look over there. Am I dreaming or can I really see golden-coated lions lying down in the grass, playfully licking fluffy white lambs? Now that's absolutely incredible! Aren't they meant to eat them?"

"Not in Piadora, Polly. For all the animals here respect each other's right to live, so there is therefore no food chain in this kingdom. Now look over there," he said, directing her attention toward a river. "If you look closely, you will see that the crocodiles are playing very nicely with the hippos. See Polly, they're using their long, spoonlike noses to splash water on their backs, helping them stay cool."

Polly could only watch on in awe and wonder as she witnessed the most amazing sights she had ever seen in her life.

"You can get out of the carriage and play with them too if you like," said Hodgekiss.

Polly wasted no time at all, for the carriage automatically stopped in its tracks, and she found herself jumping out and running over the grass in the direction of the lions and lambs in order to join in the fun.

Eventually she heard Hodgekiss call to her, "Come Polly, for we have much to do. You can come back later and play to your heart's content."

Polly nuzzled up to one of the lions and whispered, "See you later." The lion responded by giving her cheek an almighty wet lick with his large pink tongue. "We'll have another romp later," she said to one lioness as she stroked her silky coat. She then got up and raced back to the carriage.

"I can see you're going to like it here," said Hodgekiss with a grin.

As the carriage continued on its journey Polly suddenly saw people doing cartwheels in the grass.

"Stop!" she shouted as she leaned further out of the window to get a better look. "Correct me if I'm wrong, but isn't that Stanley Horlicks, the school cleaner?" she cried in amazement.

"Yes, Polly, I do believe you're right. That is dear Stanley. He turned up here yesterday, and what's more, he hasn't stopped doing cartwheels since the moment he arrived."

"But how can this be, for Mr. Horlicks suffered from such a painful back condition that he could hardly walk?" she informed Hodgekiss.

"Not anymore!" said Hodgekiss with a twinkle in his eye. "In Piadora not only can you choose to become whatever age you would like to be, but also just one small sip from the sap of the Hoolie Koolie or Hubber Blubber tree and all pain is banished forever. have to say that most of the grown-ups that arrive here instantly choose to become little children and relive their childhood, free at last from all the pain and fear that has beset them over their years. It's wonderful to see people like Stanley finally enjoying themselves, their faces radiating with happiness and childlike innocence, don't you think?"

"I agree with you on that one, but it's still extraordinary to see him leaping around like a frog with ants in his pants," retorted Polly before breaking out into a little giggle.

"Well, yes, I suppose in your eyes he does look a bit silly, but I prefer to call it touching. And as everyone else around here is doing pretty much the same thing, it doesn't really seem to matter. Now, if you cast your eyes over toward that wooded area, you cannot fail to see dear Oscar Postlewaite hanging by a rope as he swings from tree to tree. I bet you didn't know that he is well into his nineties, and yet he has the energy of a nine-year-old. Isn't that a most wonderful sight to behold?"

"Oh, my word, so he is," said Polly, bursting out with laughter as she caught sight of him. Hodgekiss too joined in the laughter.

"Polly, before you say anything else rude, you need to know that his childhood dream was to become a world-class gymnast, but his parents lacked the necessary funds, for him to realize his dream. Yes, sadly he had no choice but to settle for a very hard life working up to eighteen hours a day just to pay the bills and keep food on his table. So you can imagine how happy and fulfilled he is feeling at the moment. Yes, he hasn't come out of the woods since he arrived two weeks ago. Bless him."

"I think that's a wonderful story," said Polly chirpily.

"Now cast your eyes a little over to the left and you will see a number of golden oldies playing hopscotch. I have to admit that I go all tingly inside whenever I see them playing together and having such fun, for it warms the cockles of my heart." Polly watched as they hopped from square to square on one foot after throwing a stone onto the ground, and she felt that she was indeed in the middle of an amazing dream.

"But now I want you to close your eyes and hold out your hand, for I have something very special to return to you."

Polly's eyes visibly widened as she wondered what on earth he wished to give back to her. As she held out her hands, her eyes tightly shut, she felt something soft and furry being placed in her outstretched palm.

"Now, Polly, you can open your eyes," said Hodgekiss.

Polly opened them very slowly before letting out a loud gasp, "Langdon! I can't believe it!" she cried as she hugged him closely to her chest. "And his fur is now a lovely rich blue!" she said, almost stumbling over her words.

"Royal blue, actually," said Hodgekiss with a grin.

"Thank you, Hodgekiss," were the only words Polly could manage to find as she fought back tears of joy at being reunited with Langdon. "But how come you asked me to bury him in the first place if you wanted to give him back to me?" asked Polly, by now completely overwhelmed and puzzled.

"Well, Polly, if you really want to know why, then I will happily tell you," answered Hodgekiss.

"I really do," replied Polly as she stroked Langdon's new coat of fur.

"Polly, Langdon held all your tears and therefore all your bad memories. As you well know, an elephant never forgets. So you see, Langdon could not enter Piadora with that amount of sadness locked away inside of him, could he?"

"No, Hodgekiss, I see your point," said Polly in little more than a whisper.

"Also, you would never have managed to climb the mountain if you had been carrying him for, as discovered, you needed both hands to hold on. Remember dear Justin Kase, Polly? If you think back you

will remember that he refused to let go of all his personal possessions, and then look what happened to him on the mountain."

Polly felt a tinge of sadness as she thought back to both boys
lying seriously injured on the mountain.

"Don't worry, Polly, both boys are safe and well. I promise.
Hope in Your Heart Hospital is the best hospital in the world,
with a most dedicated team of specialists who have nursed both
boys back to life."

Polly felt truly relieved to hear the good news and broke out into
a little smile.

"There will come a day when Justin Kase realizes that it is in his
best interest to leave all his baggage behind, but until then I have no
choice but to watch on at his little antics."

"Why on earth does he need all that stuff?" said Polly with
a grin.

"Well, you laugh, Polly, but his load is his security. He hangs on
to it as though his very life depended upon it, and he cannot see
that not only is it ridiculously heavy, but it holds him back, too. But
before you get on your high horse, think how hard you found it to
part with Langdon, eh?" Polly nodded sheepishly. "I mean, what on
earth was that little episode about when you lay in Langdon's grave
and started shouting at poor, innocent little Herbert?" he asked,
looking deep into her eyes as he gently challenged her. "Yes, as we
all gathered at the gates of Piadora to hope and pray you'd carry
on and not give up, we were all left wondering what on earth you'd
think up next."

Polly hung her head, feeling most embarrassed by her unfortunate episode. "Yes, I'm sorry, Hodgekiss. I know I made quite a
scene, but I found it the most unbearable thing I have ever had to
do," she quietly confessed.

"I know that, Polly. It was the test of all tests. But I have to say that,
despite the tantrums, you did finally bury him, and I cannot express
the relief that we all felt up here. Yes, it made us want to throw a
party." he said with a wide grin. "We were all very proud of you. But
come with me, for I still have much to show you." He took her by the
hand and led her on down one of many golden paths. "Now, Polly,
I want you to be ever so quiet," he said in hushed tones.

Polly whispered "OK," before suddenly taking a deep gulp and looking down the path ahead. She could not have been more surprised by what she saw. With her voice cracking, she exclaimed "Oh, my goodness, it's Thomas!" She then quickly held her hand up to her mouth to stop any further noise from exiting.

"Yes, Polly, it's your beloved Thomas, and can you see he has Eton sitting next to him?"

"Yes, yes, I can," whispered Polly excitedly.

"Well, Polly, Thomas has many friends here, but Eton has become his best friend. I think this is because Eton reminds him to remember you. Every day as soon as the sun sets, he comes out into this forest clearing, and after setting up his easel, they both sit and talk about you and life here while Thomas paints pictures. I have to say you were right, Polly, his paintings are indeed most excellent and so colorful."

As Polly stood and watched her brother painting and looking so happy and contented, tears began to spill down her cheeks.

"I'm sorry, Hodgekiss," cried Polly. "But I just can't help myself, for I am completely overwhelmed with happiness."

"Well, carry on then, my little one. Tears of healing as well as happiness abound here, and this just about sums up what Piadora is all about."

"Oh, Hodgekiss, you have no idea how much this means to me to finally see him free of all the pain and misery he suffered in his short life. I am so grateful that I really don't know how to show it."

Hodgekiss turned and with the deepest compassion looked into Polly's eyes with such intensity that it felt as though he could see into her very soul. He then lifted his hand to her face and began to brush away her tumbling tears.

"Oh Polly, I know and understand every thought and feeling you have now and ever will have, and I wept for your brother just as I weep for all who suffer at the hands of others." As he continued to speak, Polly began to feel all the pain and anguish melt away. "Now then, young Polly, Thomas has just finished his latest painting, so before he starts another I think this would be an opportune moment for you to run over and give him one of those special hugs that you so like to give. And as for me, I am going to leave you a while to give you time to catch up with him. I will come back later, for Thomas will need to get ready for the banquet. I am not sure if you are aware, but he has a really healthy appetite these days," he said grinning from ear to ear.

"He's probably making up for all he missed out on because at the orphanage we didn't really get much to eat or drink," said Polly laughingly.

"I know," replied Hodgekiss, quickly reciting Uncle Boritz's rather famous saying: "'If you're hungry, you'll eat stale bread, and if you're thirsty you'll drink water.' Hmm... well, that might explain Thomas's extraordinary liking for apple juice, for I'll have you know that he drinks it by the gallon. Luckily we have a bountiful supply of apples, as well as every other imaginable fruit here in Piadora," said Hodgekiss as he walked toward an apple tree and plucked a red, juicy one from a hanging branch. "Here, Polly, take a bite," he said as he handed it to her.

As Polly bit into the apple, she began to feel all sorts of new sensations as the taste exploded in her mouth. "I've never tasted anything so wonderful!" she cried.

Hodgekiss laughed, "Well, Polly, here in Piadora all your senses are heightened, so everything tastes, smells, looks, sounds, and feels truly wonderful."

As Polly took another bite of the apple, she felt her legs give way from underneath her.

"What's going on?" she cried. "I feel tingly from head to toe, and every tiny atom of my body feels so full of extraordinary and powerful love that I feel as though I could burst."

Hodgekiss said nothing; he just continued to look at her and smile. Polly then chose to lie in the grass, feeling completely overwhelmed as waves of pure love washed over her.

Eventually Hodgekiss spoke. "Polly, what you are now experiencing is just a tiny glimpse of what it's like to live in Piadora. You need to understand that a glimpse is all I am able to show you, at least for the present time."

"Why is that Hodgekiss? Don't you want me to stay?"

"Of course I do, Polly, but you need to know that you have a mission in life that must be fulfilled. If I were to show you now all there is to see, well, you would definitely refuse to go back. So I need you to trust me when I say you can visit here as much as you like, but you will never experience this place in its entirety until you have completed your mission."

Polly sat up straight and implored him to change his mind and let her stay.

"Polly, we will talk further on this matter, but now is not the time. Come on," he said, holding out his hand to pull her up from the ground. "Thomas is waiting to see you, and then there are some classes which you're expected to attend."

"Classes! What classes? Surely I'm not expected to go to school in Piadora! I was beginning to feel like I was in heaven, that is, until you just mentioned classes," she said with a little moan. "Come on, Hodgekiss, tell me the truth. Tell me you're only joking," she urged.

Hodgekiss just smiled and then changed the subject, "Oh look, Polly. Here are some of my good friends coming over to say hello."

As the group walked over in their direction, Polly's jaw dropped open, for his friends all took on the appearance of beams of sunlight and were covered in long, white robes from head to toe. Massive wings covered in white feathers grew from their shoulder blades.

"Polly, allow me to introduce you to Michael; and this here is Gabriel; and then there's Harmony, Purity, and Sapphire. And this here is Orpheus; and then Raphael—he's been dying to meet you; and then there's..."

The list of introductions seemed to go for an eternity. Polly found herself surrounded by these angelic beings. Polly stood with a stupefied look on her face as her eyes met with Raphael. She felt really strange and most peculiar, for she felt as though she knew him from somewhere else. No, that was ridiculous. She'd never been here before. Besides, when had she ever met a celestial being that glowed from head to toe and dressed in a white robe? As Polly looked him up and down, her eyes hit on his feet, and she found herself having to take a deep breath.

"Those boots look exactly like the ones Ralph used to wear. In fact, I can see the same striped socks poking through the ends," she gasped.

She covered her mouth and at the same time thought that she really was losing her marbles. As she pointed towards his feet, flowers began to spring up from between his bootlaces and then out of all the holes in his worn-out boots.

Raphael pretended to be embarrassed. "Oops, I forgot to take them off at the door," he said most apologetically as all the angelic beings gave him a playful look of disapproval.

"Well, Polly, I have no idea who this Ralph character is, but tell me please, do his boots spring flowers?" Gabriel interrupted, at the same time giving a sly wink in Raphael's direction as he tried to cover up Raphael's little indiscretion.

"Well no, they don't, but I wish they did, for poor Ralph's feet smell really bad," Polly admitted with a giggle.

"Well then, we must meet Ralph sometime, Polly, even if it's only to give him a change of socks," said Gabriel, trying to look deadly serious. All gathered around began to laugh at that prospect.

"Anyway, Polly, we are all overjoyed to see you've finally made it to Piadora," interjected Raphael. "And I do hope you stay a while, for we've all come up with some wonderful games to play, assuming you're up for it."

Polly giggled. "Yes, I'd really love to. But it will have to be later, for I'm meant to be spending some time with Thomas," she said, pointing over to where he still sat on his stool, feverishly painting away on a large canvas. "Then I'm apparently expected to go to some classes," she said, playfully pulling a long face as she spoke.

"Ah yes, dear Thomas," said Michael, giving her a warm smile before turning back to address his companions. "Shall we tell her then?"

"Tell me what?" cried Polly, at the same time screwing up her forehead to make them fully aware that she was very puzzled.

"I'm not sure if we should, or shouldn't," replied Orpheus, breaking out into a giggle.

"Oh, go on. Let's tell her," Sapphire and Harmony eagerly chipped in.

"Well, all right, if you feel we must," Raphael quickly responded. "But I think it would be best coming from you," he said pointing at Michael to take over.

"Tell me! Please tell me!" cried Polly.

"Well, young Polly, cast your mind back to the day you visited the funeral director with Eton, your teddy bear," Michael gently ordered.

"How could I forget?" replied Polly.

"Well then, you must remember the drama with all the feathers that blew out of the coffin?"

"Yes, go on," said Polly, feeling quite uncertain as to where all this was leading.

"Well, it was us! Yes, we were responsible for all the mess," cried Orpheus with an impish grin as he butted in, clearly anxious to be involved in revealing the truth behind that day.

"You lot!" cried Polly now feeling completely bewildered.

"Yes, us lot!" Raphael admitted rather sheepishly before going on to spill the beans. "Yes, Polly, we were all called to come and gather at the gates of Piadora the day that Thomas died. When the call came for volunteers to go down to collect him and then bring him back to Piadora, well, we all wanted to go. I must confess that it became a little bit of a race as to who could get there first."

"Go on," stuttered Polly, utterly amazed by all she was hearing.

"Well, when we got to the funeral parlor, we decided the only way to choose who among us was going to be given the honor was to have a little game of tag. Do you know that game, Polly?" asked Raphael.

Polly nodded.

"The idea was that whoever was not out at the end of the game got to be the one to bring Thomas back. We had such fun, Polly, but we also lost an awful amount of our feathers in the process," he said with a grin.

"Yes, and you did a pretty poor job of tidying up, didn't you?" Michael interrupted, pretending to be annoyed with them.

"That's very true," Sapphire piped up, "but we didn't know what else to do when we heard the door handle turning. We couldn't allow ourselves to be discovered, so we just quickly stuffed all our feathers into the coffin and hoped for the best," she said, grinning from ear to ear before adding, "Oh, come on Michael, you have to admit it was very funny, although, we do promise never to make the same mistake again."

Polly found herself laughing along with them as they went on to recall the crazy events that then took place at the funeral service.

"That was one of the best and funniest services we've ever attended!" said Harmony, flapping her wings as she failed to contain her excitement a moment longer.

"I don't think Mrs. Scumberry would share your sentiments, Harmony. For I don't believe she has fully recovered from that one," Gabriel further reminded them all. "Yes, I would go as far as to say her pride was indeed seriously dented. At the end of the day, though, that is not a bad thing, for it introduced her to the emotion called humiliation. And as you all witnessed, she did not care much for it," he said, his voice betraying a tone of compassion. "No, she really did not take kindly to the shoe being on the other foot."

The whole group nodded in unison, their huge, beaming smiles lighting up their already brilliantly radiant faces. "Polly, please tell us you can see the funny side of it all?" Sapphire said, giving her a little nudge.

"Yes, I can see the funny side now, although I have to admit that at the time I did feel a little sorry for them both," Polly confessed as she broke out into a gentle smile.

"Right then, everyone. Let's have another game of tag," Harmony very excitedly suggested as she turned to grab hold of Polly's hand.

"I'd love to, really I would, but I want to spend some time with Thomas and then I am supposed to be attending some classes," said Polly rather ruefully.

"Classes? Oh, how wonderfully exciting, Polly. You'll really love the classes, just you wait and see. These are no ordinary classes," said Gabriel reassuringly. "So, tell you what, Polly, we'll hang around until you've done your classes and been to the banquet, and then we'll have some fun."

"Yes, by then you'll be in need of some serious exercise to burn off the all the calories," Harmony chipped in with a giggle. "So hurry up and go see Thomas before he starts another painting."

Polly wasted no further time and immediately ran over to where Thomas sat painting with Eton close at his side. "Thomas, Thomas!" she breathlessly cried as she flung both arms around his neck, almost knocking him off his seat.

The celestial beings stood joyfully watching the pair as they hugged and wept in each other's arms. Michael then turned to address the group of celestial beings, "Come my friends, for Polly and Thomas have much catching up to do, and although it is indeed wonderful to witness such touching moments in time I do believe they should be allowed their privacy."

Despite wanting to stay and continue witnessing this touching reunion, the group of celestial beings unanimously nodded their agreement and then vanished into thin air.

How long Polly stayed with Thomas is not recorded. But, it is enough to know that Polly had never felt happier or more content in the whole of her young life. Eventually, and with perfect timing, Hodgekiss returned and asked Polly to continue on with him.

"Thomas, it is almost time for you to put on your 'glad rags' and get yourself ready for the banquet," he reminded him.

"I can't wait," Thomas replied. "But tell me, do I have time to paint just one more picture as a special present for my sister?" he asked as he broke into a smile that conveyed his state of pure contentment.

"Of course, Thomas. Carry on painting, and I'll pop by later to check that you are ready," replied Hodgekiss.

Polly popped one final kiss on Thomas's forehead and told him she would catch up with him later.

"Carry on looking after Eton, Thomas. He seems really happy to be here with you," were her last spoken words as she turned and waved him good-bye.

Chapter 37
APPLES GALORE

*M*INUTES LATER, AFTER walking over the beautifully manicured green lawn and passing by the most enormous fountain, complete with cherubs spouting water from their mouths, they finally arrived at the most stunningly magnificent building. In Polly's mind, the place resembled Buckingham Palace, only better. It had huge marble and gold columns and the most ornate blanket of fresh flowers that carpeted the entire steps right up to the entrance.

Polly was afraid to walk on the carpet, for she did not wish to crush any of the delicate flowers underfoot. Hodgekiss felt her hesitancy and immediately placed his arm in hers as he encouraged her to continue on and climb up the steps. With each step she took, the flowers in front of her bloomed and then closed before blooming again. And as Polly glanced over her shoulder, she quickly saw that there was not one crushed flower, even though she had just stepped on their open petals. She could only marvel at the deliciously sweet aroma the flowers were emitting as she continued to make her way to top.

As she walked onwards, making her way toward the large, gold-encrusted doors, her eyes settled on the name that lit up above the doorway. "Wow, am I really going to the Royal Academy for Princesses in Training?" she exclaimed, open mouthed.

"Absolutely," replied Hodgekiss, giving her arm a light friendly squeeze.

Polly was filled with immense trepidation from head to toe as she walked with Hodgekiss down the long white marble corridors.

"I think this is our first port of call," Hodgekiss announced as he stopped halfway down a corridor and opened a side door. "Now, Polly, don't be nervous. They are all expecting you," he said as he gave her a gentle nudge to coax her through the door.

Polly followed Hodgekiss into the room, her eyes darting backwards then forwards as she scanned every inch of the room, taking in the faces of every child that sat behind the rows of desks.

As each child looked up and smiled in her direction, Polly had the strangest feeling that she intimately knew each and every one of them, even though she had never met any of them before! Then, as Polly redirected her eyes toward the blackboard at the front of the classroom, her eyes met with an extraordinarily huge mountain of rosy apples. Yes, they were piled high, almost to the ceiling.

"How peculiar!" was all Polly had the time to think before suddenly the mound of apples began to tumble down. Polly was momentarily lost for words as she watched all the apples tumble then roll across the floor, revealing the head and then shoulders of someone she had truly loved and lost.

"Grab a basket and catch them, children!" shouted the teacher as she grabbed an empty box and flung herself down onto the floor in an attempt to stop them escaping.

Finally, Polly found her tongue and let out a squeal of delight.

"Mrs. Bailey!" she cried as she raced over toward her.

"Why, if it's not Polly Brown," cried an equally delighted Mrs. Bailey as she got up from kneeling on the floor.

Mrs. Bailey put the box down and opened her arms to give Polly a hug. "Polly, it's so lovely to see you, but you really must stop wishing to give me apples. I really love crunchy apples, but as you can clearly see, we are simply overwhelmed by the amount that arrive daily on my classroom desk," she said, giving one of her infectious laughs that sent the whole class into fits of giggles.

"Yes, only last week we had to organize a truck to come and remove all the apples that were mounting up inside the classroom. It was making it very difficult, if not impossible, to teach my girls. They could no longer see me sitting behind my desk," she said cheerily. "Oh, and last week, there was also a day when we discovered that we were no longer able to push open the classroom door due to the apples that were filling the entire classroom." Polly did not know whether to laugh or cry. "I'm so glad you've made it, Polly, and I'm delighted to say that you're just in time for our award ceremony. So come and sit down right beside me, and then we can begin," Mrs. Bailey said, patting the chair beside her.

"Right then, children, we must as usual start our award ceremony with the school's most wonderful motto. Who wants to stand up and recite it for Polly's benefit? Please, one at a time, children, one at a time. All right then, we will let Ruby Turner do the honor today. So, come on, Ruby, and do remember to speak clearly. There's a good girl."

Ruby quickly stood up, her little face beaming from ear to ear. After straightening her dress, she gave a little cough and began: "Love is patient; love is kind. Love is giving to others, and choosing not to be blind. Love believes all things, hopes all things, and love never fails."

"Splendid," cried Mrs. Bailey gleefully as she enthusiastically clapped her hands together. "Now, my young princesses, I firmly believe that if you put our motto into practice, you will always come out trumps. But now I think we should move on to the awards presentation, for time is indeed marching on. Daisy Longtitude, please come out to the front of the class to receive your certificate and your gemstone for loyalty."

Daisy stood up and rather shyly made her way to the front of the class to receive her award. "Now then, Daisy, please show all the class your special pebble."

Daisy plunged her hand into her pocket and produced a pebble similar to the ones Polly had collected. On its smooth surface was inscribed the word *loyalty*. As she stood with her small hand outstretched, the pebble sitting in the palm of her hand instantly transformed into the most beautiful, sparkling pink gemstone.

"Well done, Daisy. And I have to say that it's so good to see you following in all your delightful sisters' footsteps. Now, how many of them have I taught in the past? Yes, let me see, there's Philippa, Judith, and of course darling Harriet. Sadly for me, they've all moved up to Mrs. O'Brien's class. Oh, how I already miss them all," she said, giving a deep sigh. "As for Sebastian and Oliver, your two fine brothers, if I'm correct they too have also moved up to Mr. Beloski's class."

On hearing Mr. Beloski's name mentioned, Polly made a loud gasp, covering her mouth quickly with her hand in order not to appear rude or thoughtless in the middle of such an important ceremony.

"Oh yes, the Longtitudes are indeed such a delightful family, and I really miss teaching them. And Daisy, it won't be too long before you too move up a class to join your older sisters," she said, giving another gentle sigh. "So Daisy, add this beautiful stone to your others, and remember to place it firmly into your crown next to your jewel for courage," she said, patting Daisy on the head as she reminded her. "Oh, and I mustn't forget to give you this," she added, handing over an important-looking scroll. "This is your certificate of authenticity."

"Thank you so much, Mrs. Bailey," said Daisy rather shyly before breaking out into a smile so huge that her cute golden locks appeared to give a twirl. Daisy then gave a rather awkward curtsy before heading back to her seat.

"Daisy dear, you really do need to work on your curtsy, for princesses are not required to do balancing acts! A royal curtsy must have flow and be graceful, so as you need to learn more poise, then I think you may well require extra tuition in this particular area."

"Thank you, Mrs. Bailey," Daisy answered, her cheeks going a deep, blushworthy pink.

"Right, my young princesses. Daisy here has received this reward for loyalty, and I need to remind you all that loyalty is an immensely wonderful gift. It is something we continually need to work on, especially when friends let us down and everything inside us wants to hit back. Daisy found this out this week, so well done, Daisy dear." Daisy continued to go a deep crimson as she broke into an overly generous smile that revealed large gaps in her pearly white teeth.

"Now then, who is next? Ah yes, Dulcie Collins, please step forward." Dulcie showed none of Daisy's hesitation as she leapt out of her seat and headed down to the front of the class, very eager to receive her award. "Hold out your hand, Dulcie, so that we can all bear witness to your award. Now girls, I do believe seeing all these pebbles transform into beautiful gemstones brings new meaning to the rather famous saying that 'a diamond is a girl's best friend.'" All the girls broke out into fits of giggles. "Right, Dulcie, what do we have here? Oh how lovely, an amber gemstone for honesty. Why, that's positively wonderful," said Mrs. Bailey, breaking out into another rather infectious giggle. "Now then, girls, I have to say that honesty is becoming a rare commodity these days, and this gift is becoming a thing of the past. Nowadays, very few people care to tell the truth, and even fewer care to be honest when it comes to keeping what does not belong to them. That terrible saying 'Finders, keepers; losers, weepers,' has sadly become the norm. Well, I tell you now, young ladies, if it does not belong to you, then it is important that you find and give it back to its owner. No ifs or buts. We actually take away something from ourselves when we act dishonestly. And, I might use this occasion to add that there is no such thing as a white lie. It is either the truth or it is a lie. Now, you may think me harsh, but one lie invariably leads to another. So truth and honesty are very honorable gifts to seek out. Enough said."

"Now then, where is young Lilly Rose sitting? Come on, Lilly, I know you're hiding, but it's your turn to come up and collect your award. So don't be shy; there's a good girl."

Polly watched as child after child went up to have some form of honor bestowed upon them by her beloved Mrs. Bailey. It made Polly smile as she witnessed the incredible glow on the face of each child as they, proud as punch, headed back toward their seats. Gabriel had been right all along, as these classes were something out of the ordinary. In fact, they were so extraordinary that she felt she could easily remain seated in this classroom for the rest of her days, such was the atmosphere of love she was experiencing.

Finally, the award ceremony came to an end. And as each young lady finished the job of attaching their newly collected jewels to their personal tiara, Mrs. Bailey walked around to the front of her desk before turning to address the whole class.

"All right, my precious princesses, we have so many apples to use up that I would like to suggest we all pick up a basket from the corner of the room and start collecting up all the apples. Now hurry along, girls, for then we shall take them to Mrs. O'Brien for her to use in her wonderful cookery classes." The young girls all nodded excitedly as, on hands and knees, they got back down on the floor to continue gathering up all the apples.

"Now, I wonder what Mrs. O'Brien will make today? Will it be April Crumble? Or will it be Appletude Pie?"

"April Crumble? Appletude Pie?" Polly echoed, furrowing her brow and looking very confused.

"Polly dearest, please unscrew your face immediately, for this will lead to deep lines on your forehead, and that will never do," said Mrs. Bailey merrily.

"Yes, Mrs. Bailey, but who has ever heard of Appletude Pie or April Crumble?"

"We have," chorused all the young ladies as in unison they popped up from the floor, still holding on tightly to their baskets of apples.

"Suzi, be a peach and tell Polly all about our rather heavenly Appletude Pie."

"Yes, Mrs. Bailey," responded Suzi, more than happy to oblige. "Appletude Pie is a wonderful apple pie made with the finest, juiciest apples and the lightest pastry, which is then sprinkled with sweetness and ladles of love. And, as we bind the ingredients together, we never fail to remind each other of just how important it is to have a good appletude, I mean, attitude toward everything we say and do. We all love making Appletude Pie," said Suzi most informatively, her golden locks lighting up her pretty face until she was positively glowing from head to toe.

"Go on, go on," Mrs. Bailey encouraged.

"And as for April Crumble, well, that reminds us that spring is here and with it comes the season of rebirth, when everything comes alive and the air smells deliciously sweet with fresh hope and purpose. So we all enjoy making April Pie almost as much as Appletude Pie," she said, breaking into one of her highly contagious giggles that in no time at all had all the other young ladies following suit. Polly continued to look most bewildered.

"What is troubling you now, Polly?" Mrs. Bailey asked with a note of concern.

"Well, earlier on I thought I heard you mention another class that had a teacher named Mrs. O'Brien?" Polly said rather nervously.

"I believe I may have mentioned her," Mrs. Bailey said rather mischievously. "Why do you ask?"

"Well, is that the Mrs. O'Brien who teaches at Snobbits Private School near the castle?" Polly rather cautiously asked, as she did not want to be disappointed.

"Polly, I do believe it is," Mrs. Bailey swiftly replied. "And I have to say she is a truly remarkable teacher with an endless talent for cooking, deportment classes, and a whole host of other fun subjects. Yes, she does indeed teach the older girls. And then at the Royal Academy for Princes, Mr. Beloski teaches the young princes…"

"I did hear right then? You did say Beloski?" Polly gasped as she instantly felt completely overwhelmed with emotion.

"Of course dear, but he teaches the boys…"

"You mean, there are boys here as well?"

"Yes, of course there are boys here at our school, Polly," Mrs. Bailey replied, pretending to be somewhat surprised that she was being asked such a silly question. "We cannot have a princesses' training academy without having one for princes, too. No, that would be most unfair, and unfairness is not a welcome visitor in Piadora. No, it never has been, and I can state with much authority that it never will be," she said in a very matter-of-fact fashion.

Polly found herself going quite weak at the knees at the prospect of meeting up with these teachers.

"Let's not waste another moment to catch up with them while we still have the time before our fencing lesson begins," said Mrs. Bailey brightly.

"Fencing classes? But I thought Piadora was safe and had no enemies?" said Polly, expressing great shock.

"Oh Polly, fencing classes are compulsory for all who visit Piadora. To answer your question more fully, you're absolutely correct in your thinking; Piadora is a perfect haven with no threats whatsoever! All who reside here live in perfect peace and harmony. But for those who are just paying us a short visit, it is imperative to be fully conversant with defense strategies and the art of warfare," she said informatively. "Yes, it is most essential that we all learn how to fight off the enemy effectively and win every battle and challenge," she stated in her very matter-of-fact manner. "Please don't panic, for not only are the classes great fun, but we already know that we are on the winning side. Now isn't that rather brilliant?"

"I don't wish to appear stupid Mrs. Bailey, but what's the point of fighting if we already know we're going to win?" Polly meekly asked.

"Well, Polly, now is not the time to go into the wheres and whys, for I really prefer to leave such delicate matters for dear Hodgekiss to deal with. But you have to understand that our fight is not with humans. Heavens no, it is not flesh and blood, but with dark and evil forces. Yes, principalities and powers that are most determined to take over the universe. Sadly, these terrifying forces of darkness cannot be seen with the naked eye, so at times it seems like a most unfair fight. Nonetheless, I assure you that not only are they real, but we wrestle with them much of the time."

Polly instantly squirmed as she thought back to the day on the plane with all those hideous and slimy monsters. As pictures of Vanaspi and Soogara flashed through her mind, icy shivers started to run full length down her spine and she shuddered from head to toe.

"Mark my words, the day is soon coming when there will be a final battle between good and evil, and we must all be ready and fully prepared. For now though, Polly, we need to get these apples over to Mrs. O'Brien's class straightaway. Girls, pick up your baskets and follow me."

Polly followed Mrs. Bailey and her little band of troopers down a long stretch of marble floored corridor until Mrs. Bailey came to a halt outside another side room. After opening the door, she turned to face Polly and told her to not feel afraid. She then linked her arm through Polly's and gently ushered her into the room.

"Polly, how wonderful to see you!" cried Mrs. O'Brien as she raced over and flung her arms around Polly's neck to give her a very warm and friendly embrace. "Now, come and sit down next to me while I continue on with my lesson."

Polly allowed Mr. O'Brien to quickly guide her to a vacant seat. She was beginning to feel as though her legs were about to give way completely! As she took her seat, she felt so overawed by everything that was happening to her that she didn't know whether to laugh or cry; as it turns out, she did both.

Once seated, Mrs. Bailey turned to her girls who were still standing huddled together with their baskets of apples and said, "Right then, girls, go and place your baskets on the table, and then make your way in an orderly fashion to the changing rooms, for do believe it's time for fencing classes to begin."

The girls all rushed to obey her order, placing basket after basket of large, juicy apples on Mrs. O'Brien's desk.

"Amanda Collins, I do believe your apples are as rosy as your cheeks," declared Mrs. O'Brien rather loudly.

"Mrs. O'Brien, I think you're right," said Mrs. Bailey with a giggle. Crimson-faced, Amanda reciprocated with a highly contagious giggle that immediately set all the other girls off into hoots of laughter.

"I'll catch up with you later on at the banquet, Mrs. O'Brien. And I will be looking forward to some lovely Appletude Pie topped with your delicious creamy custard," Mrs. Bailey called out as she took hold of the door handle to exit the room.

"And cream," added Mrs. O'Brien with a wink. "Why, we have such an abundance of apples that we will indeed be able to make plenty of pies for Mrs. Bailey, won't we girls?" cried a very delighted Mrs. O'Brien.

"And, I hope, April Crumble," chipped in Mrs. Bailey as she proceeded to leave the room with her girls following closely in her footsteps.

With the classroom door firmly shut, Mrs. O'Brien then turned her attention back to the girls that were seated, ready and waiting to act on her every order, "All right girls, settle down and listen. Let me introduce you to Polly, for she has just arrived at our Royal Academy. I expect all of you will want to go over and introduce yourselves, and don't forget to give her a nice big hug."

All the girls without exception jumped up from where they were seated and swiftly joined the growing queue, which in no time at all extended across the whole length of the room. One by one they eagerly lined up to greet her. As Polly embraced girl after girl, she found herself completely taken aback by the sheer warmth of every greeting, for they all treated her as though she was their long-lost best friend. Polly soon felt as though she was about to crack up on the inside, and worse still, there was nothing she could do to prevent it from happening! Her tender heart felt like a volcano on the verge of erupting. Without warning, Polly burst into tears.

"There, there, sweetheart," said Mrs. O'Brien as she placed a comforting arm around Polly's shoulder, at the same time giving her a hankie. "We are only making up for all the hugs you have missed out on over the years, hugs that would have come from your mother and father had they been around to give them."

Polly began to weep even louder.

"Carry on bawling, Polly dear. It's perfectly all right, for I don't think we've ever had a young princess attend this class for the first time who has not shed a few tears. It not only washes the face, but it's good for the soul, believe me," she insisted as she continued stroking Polly's hair in an attempt to comfort her.

Before long, there was not a dry eye in the classroom. All the young princesses began to shed a few tears, forcing Mrs. O'Brien to hand out brightly-colored handkerchiefs to every single one of them.

"I'm so sorry, Mrs. O'Brien. I am to blame for all of this, but I feel so overcome that I can't stop myself," sniffed Polly.

"Polly, it's perfectly all right. In fact, it was the best thing that could happen. Many of my young princesses need to shed a few tears every once in a while. It is, after all, an essential part of the healing process." Mrs. O'Brien patted her shoulder comfortingly before continuing to address her class.

"Now girls, it's time to pop those hankies away and be done with that most cruel and very wicked saying, 'Laugh and the world laughs with you; cry and you cry alone.'" Mrs. O'Brien then paused to take a deep breath before going on. "Yes, those cruel, contemptible words only serve to reveal the true blindness that lurks within the human condition and, therefore this utterly contemptible saying should be left to rot on the mountainside along with the abominable snowman," she angrily declared.

Every face in the room broke out into a smile as all present pictured her little analogy.

"For, in Piadora, love really does conquer all. And if we can't weep with those who weep, bearing and carrying their pain, well, then we have no right to rejoice with those who are glad," she said with the greatest authority, clasping her hands tightly at the same time.

Polly was finally able to stop the tears and once more compose herself. Mrs. O'Brien welcomed this opportune moment to invite Polly to join in the cookery class.

"Right, Abigail Collins. I will leave it to you and your dear sister, Emily, to organize the girls and make Appletude Pie. Before that happens, Polly, come and stand over here by the ovens."

Polly dutifully obeyed, following behind Mrs. O'Brien. She only stopped when Mrs. O'Brien, without warning, halted to stoop down over a saucepan and, with her nose almost in the pan, drew in its delicious aroma.

"Girls, can you smell the delightful aroma coming from this pan of homemade Horse Rubbish sauce as it delicately wafts through the air. It will taste so wonderful when it is served up with roast rib of beef."

As Polly stood next to her teacher, she found herself secretly wondering what was going to happen next, for she had begun to realize that in this special place the unexpected happened all the time!

"Right, Polly, stand up straight. For a true princess must have good posture. You will, of course, be attending my deportment classes before you leave Piadora," she authoratively stated, shaking her head wearily to show she was clearly dissatisfied with Polly's poor posture. "Polly, stand up straight and stop slumping. Right, now shoulders back and chin up. That's a good girl. Excellent!"

As Polly stood still, trying hard to follow Mrs. O'Brien's orders, a large book was then placed on her head.

"Splendid!" cried Mrs. O'Brien as she broke into a wide smile. "Right, Polly, now place your pan on the stove, and at the same time, open your mouth. You, my girl, are about to speak fluent French while cooking Crepe Suzettes, and all this with a book nicely balanced on the top of your head." Polly burst into fits of the giggles. "Wonderful, Polly, wonderful! A happy cook is indeed a good cook," exclaimed Mrs. O'Brien. "Now then, Belinda Collins, do kindly stop sucking the ends of your hair. Not only is it most unhygienic, but it is not the sort of royal etiquette that I would expect from one of my princesses. You could easily find yourself in the middle of a choking fit, and I firmly believe that this would be a truly unsightly thing to behold." Belinda instantly stopped, but not before flashing Mrs. O'Brien a gentle smile. "Right, now, where is Kayleigh? Ah, yes, Kayleigh Simmonds, come over here and help Polly. There's a dear."

As the young girl rushed over to where Polly stood, Mrs. O'Brien could not help but look down in the direction of the young girl's ankles.

"Kayleigh, be a dear and pull up your socks to the knee, for I do believe you're beginning to take on the appearance of a Welsh Rugby player!"

"Yes, miss," Kayleigh replied as she stooped down to pull both socks back up to her knees.

"Yes, that's a great improvement Kayleigh, and I'm very happy to say that there is much evidence to suggest that given time and much effort on your part, you will indeed become one of my most graceful princesses."

Kayleigh began to blush, for she was feeling very chuffed at being given such high praise.

"Girls! Girls! Girls! May I have your full attention?" shouted Mrs. O'Brien whilst clapping her hands very loudly together. "I want all of you to come up here and quickly gather around the stoves."

The girls immediately abandoned their desks and eagerly made their way to huddle around the stove as they watched Polly cook with a large book nicely balanced on her head while speaking in French. The girls used the opportunity to brush up on their French conversation. They fired one question after another her way. Polly could hardly believe that not only could she answer each and every question, but she also was able to answer with perfect fluency.

"Those Crepe Suzettes look absolutely delicious, Polly. I have to say you really do have a natural flair for cooking," Mrs. O'Brien stated very matter-of-factly as she plunged a teaspoon into the shallow pan and tried a small piece.

Suddenly Polly was startled by a rather loud knock on the classroom door, and as she turned on her heels to look in the direction of the door the book she had been carefully balancing on her head tumbled to the floor.

"Polly Brown! Why, it's true; you have made it!" cried Mr. Beloski as he quickly made his way over to where she was standing.

Polly's jaw dropped, as did the cooking utensil she was still holding in her hand. Mr. Beloski immediately bent down and picked up the book and the utensil. He gently placed them back in her hand, at the same time giving it a little squeeze.

"I told you in my letter that dreams do come true, didn't I Polly?" he said, still holding her small hand rather tightly.

Unable to find any satisfactory words and throwing all caution to the wind, Polly responded by throwing her arms around his neck to give him a big hug. "Mr. Beloski!" she cried breathlessly.

"Well, you're obviously just as delighted to see me," declared Mr. Beloski, giving a little chuckle as her demonstrative hug almost took the wind out of him. "But I think you'd better release me before you crack my ribs," he added perkily as he broke out into a big smile. "Thank you, Mrs. O'Brien, for allowing me to interrupt your class to come and see for myself that the rumor circulating in the princes' quarters is indeed true."

"The pleasure's all mine," Mrs. O'Brien merrily replied.

"Well, young Polly, I'd better get back to my royal princes, for their music lesson is nearly at an end. I will catch up with you later at the banquet, for I'm more than certain that you have much to share with me," he said, giving her a delightfully friendly wink.

Polly could only reply with a small nod of the head. She made a rather dreamy sigh as she watched him head out of the classroom, make a left turn, and disappear from view.

"Right, Polly, come with me. We urgently need to get you sorted out with a suitable gown for the banquet, for royal protocol demands that all princes and princesses dress up for the occasion."

"Ooh," was all Polly managed to squeak as Mrs. O'Brien took hold of her hand and gently coaxed her toward the open classroom door. "Abigail Collins, you're now in charge. So, girls, continue on cooking, and I will be back shortly," she ordered as she closed the door firmly behind them.

Moments later Polly found herself entering a most magnificent room, equipped with the largest gold and white bath she had ever seen.

"I thought we were going to be trying on ball gowns?" Polly asked, trying very hard to hide her disappointment but failing dismally.

"We are, my dear, but not before we have you smelling as sweet as a young princess should," replied Mrs. O'Brien as she began to turn on both gold taps.

Polly watched as the bath miraculously filled up to almost overflowing in just a matter of minutes. Mrs. O'Brien then unscrewed the top of a large jar filled with rose petals, which she began to scatter over the water.

"Now remind me, dearest, when was the last time you had a nice, hot bath?"

Polly thought long and hard before answering, "I think it might have been on the night I spent in a French hotel before boarding Concorde," replied Polly sketchily.

Poor Mrs. O'Brien recoiled, a look of sheer horror written all over her face. "Goodness gracious me! Was it really that long ago?"

"Oh no, wait a minute. I've got that wrong. I remember now. Yes, I took my last bath when I was on the *Queen Mary* sailing home from America," exclaimed Polly, feeling very pleased that she had finally remembered.

"Oh, dear me! That's still some time ago," said Mrs. O'Brien, discreetly throwing in an extra handful of rose petals. Her face conveyed an expression of deep concern as to the length of time that had passed since Polly last had a good, long soak. In a matter of seconds, the room was filled with the most delightfully heady, aromatic smells.

"Ah yes, positively exquisite," announced Mrs. O'Brien, wrinkling up her nose as she allowed herself to be overcome by the sweet smells now drifting around the steamy room. "Yes, Polly, you will come out of this bath smelling divine, just like a princess should, but do be a poppet and have a really long soak, for I am anxious that you really get rid of all the dirt and grime that has built up over time. Yes, I really do believe you need a lengthy royal soaking," she said, pouring yet more liquid into the bath from another smoky-glassed receptacle that stood on the bathroom shelf. "This special bath oil will soon have your skin feeling as soft as a baby's bottom," she announced, handing Polly a couple of the thickest and fluffiest white towels she had ever seen along with a purple-colored bottle containing shampoo. "This shampoo is truly excellent too, and will do wonders for your dull and lifeless hair, as well as those rather disgraceful split ends. Trust me," she said with a smile as she closed the bathroom door behind her.

Finally alone, Polly rather dreamily slipped into the luxurious bubble bath before slowly disappearing under the suds for a long soak. She held her breath and stayed submerged for as long as she was able to and repeated this over and over a number of times. When she emerged for the final time she was amazed to discover that all her scratches and cuts had miraculously disappeared, leaving her skin feeling, as Mrs. O'Brien had promised, as soft as a baby's bottom.

Eventually she sat up in the bath, and, after taking the top off the purple bottle, began the final task of washing her fairly knotted and tangled hair. As her hair nicely lathered up, she felt as though an extra pair of hands were massaging away all the painful memories from inside her head. Then after pulling out the plug with her toe, she wrapped one of the towels around her head in the style of a turban, using the other towel to wrap around her body. She climbed out of the bath, and as soon as she dried off there was a knock on the door.

"Come in!" Polly shouted, looking over toward the door.

"Perfect timing," declared Mrs. O'Brien, taking another sniff into the highly perfumed air. "Finally you smell like an English rose. Polly, please step this way."

"Don't I need to dry my hair first?" Polly questioned, pointing at her turban.

"No, I don't think so," replied Mrs. O'Brien, moving closer toward Polly and swiftly removing the towel from around her head.

Wonderful, followed by *absolutely stunning*, were the only words that came from her kind teacher's mouth as she moved full circle around Polly, expressing her deep admiration. "Polly, go look in the mirror if you do not believe me."

Polly obeyed, moving quickly toward the large, ornate, gold mirror that hung on the bathroom wall.

"Oh, my goodness!" she loudly exclaimed, quite forgetting to close her mouth afterwards.

"Yes, Polly, I believe your hair looks very sophisticated swept up from your face, for it shows off your fine features. Don't you think?" Polly could only nod as she moved her face from side to side to get a good look at her new and very chic hairdo.

"Now, come this way quickly," urged Mrs. O'Brien as she attempted to lead Polly, still cloaked in her towel, through another exit door into a very large dressing room.

"But what about my old clothes?" Polly asked as she pointed down toward her neatly piled but threadbare clothes.

"Oh, I think we can temporarily dispense with those," exclaimed Mrs. O'Brien as she reached down to pick them up, pinching the material between two fingers whilst raising her nose playfully into the air. She then unceremoniously dumped them on top of the laundry basket.

"Right, I think we're ready to move on. Come this way," she said, grabbing hold of Polly's hand and guiding her through the bathroom door into a very large dressing room that was filled to bursting with party frocks.

Polly tried on ball gown after ball gown as she anxiously deliberated on which one she liked the best. "I don't know which one to choose, for they are all so gorgeous," she wailed as she stood in front of another huge gold mirror. Finally, and much to Mrs. O'Brien's relief, Polly made the decision to choose a purple and cream frock.

"You've made an excellent choice," said Mrs. O'Brien, who was now standing by a pile of dresses that stood a mile high. "Now it is time for the accessories," she said as she handed Polly a pair of silky white elbow-length gloves. "Wonderful! Now you're a three in shoe size, aren't you? Be a dear, Polly, and slip these on," she ordered, handing her a pair of shiny gold slippers. "Amazing! All we need to add now is some jewelry. So here, allow me put this bracelet around your wrist, and then I'll put this delicate chain with a gold heart around your neck," said Mrs. O'Brien, suddenly producing an open box that contained the precious jewelry. "Perfect! I think we're done." she declared, standing back to admire her workmanship.

"But what about..." said Polly, tailing off and not finishing her sentence.

What she wanted to ask for was a tiara, as she believed that all the other girls would be wearing their crowns. But she felt far too embarrassed to make any further mention of this missing accessory, especially as she had already been given much more than she could possibly have dreamed of.

"Polly, I don't believe you need anything else, for you look decidedly beautiful," declared Mrs. O'Brien with an air of satisfaction. "Now be a good girl and give me a twirl." Polly obliged, twirling not once or twice, but several times. She danced delightedly around the room. "Polly, the good news is you won't change into a pumpkin at twelve, and that's a promise! I would therefore suggest that you leave all further dancing and prancing about until after the banquet. Unless, of course, you wish to miss out on all the scrumptious food," said Mrs. O'Brien, hurriedly glancing down at her watch. "Oh, my goodness, child, we must leave right now!" she anxiously declared as she grabbed hold of Polly's hand, pulling her toward the exit door. "For a princess to turn up late to a ball is, in my opinion, absolutely inexcusable," she muttered as she hurriedly led Polly down one marble corridor after another until she found herself standing in front of the most stately looking set of doors she had ever seen.

Before Polly could say a word, the doors opened up directly in front of her, and Mrs. O'Brien gave Polly a little push from behind. "You're on your own now, my dear. Walk like a princess and talk like one, and remember to have fun. Promise me," she instructed, giving Polly a light peck on the cheek. "Oh, and before I completely forget, I believe you may well require these," she said, pushing a soft drawstring purse into Polly's open hand.

"What's in here?" Polly asked, very surprised.

"You'll find out soon enough. Now hurry along before I turn into a freckly toad for bringing you here so late," said Mrs. O'Brien, breaking into a warm smile.

Polly hesitated, and through misty eyes she took hold of her teacher's hand. "Mrs. O'Brien, I don't know what to say. I have no way of properly expressing my gratitude for all you've done."

"You can thank me by getting your butt through that door and having a good time," replied Mrs. O'Brien with a wink. She gave Polly a hard push to encourage her to stop all further procrastination and enter the banqueting hall.

Chapter 38
TEA WITH HODGEKISS

*P*OLLY CAUTIOUSLY ENTERED the room and came across two rather long lines of smartly dressed, uniformed men, standing to attention on both sides of the doorway. At the top of the line guarding the doorway on both sides, were two rather portly men who looked similar to English butlers. They were dressed from head to toe in black with crisp, white shirts underneath their long penguin-looking jackets. Black bows were neatly tied around their necks. One held a long list in his hand, and the other held a bell at his side.

As Polly momentarily stood alone with one man on either side of her, she noticed that the one to the right was quickly scanning down his list of names. Her heart skipped a beat. For a second, she thought her name was not there.

Finally, the man raised his nose high into the air and began to rather loudly bellow while the other man dutifully rang his little bell.

"Ladies and gentlemen, may I present to you Princess Polly."

Suddenly there was the sound of trumpets, and the two lines of uniformed men raised their swords up high in front of them until the points of their swords met in the middle, forming an archway in front of her. Polly was very unsure of what to do next when Mr. Beloski suddenly appeared from nowhere and, having hurriedly walked through the line of raised swords, presented her with a little bouquet of delicately scented white orchids, mixed with miniature white rose buds and sweet freesias.

"Come this way, Polly," he said warmly as he took her hand and gently placed it through his looped arm.

They then walked slowly through the archway of raised swords to the sound of trumpets and loud bursts of applause that came from all those already gathered and seated at the extraordinarily long banqueting tables.

"I believe this is your seat," he said with a smile as he pulled out a chair from under the table. "You're seated next to your beloved brother, Thomas. So come, Polly, please take your seat, for the banquet is about to commence."

Polly momentarily ignored his request as she leaned over and gave Thomas a mighty hug. Once she was seated, a butler came over to her side to fill her crystal glass with some sparkling liquid that glistened like morning dew and tasted like pure nectar. He then handed her a starched, pristine white napkin with *HRH* sewn on in gold letters.

As Polly opened up the napkin and placed it on her lap, she used the opportunity to glance around the room in search of faces she could recognize. Every table was filled with young and old alike, and Polly could see that they came from every imaginable background, although she was unable to tell if they were rich or poor because all the guests were decked in the finest of clothes. As her eyes met with the various faces, each one broke into the warmest of smiles as though they had known her for years and were delighted to see her. Then out of the middle of nowhere, Polly found herself having a sad thought. She suddenly found herself thinking of Aazi and wished with all her heart that he too could be at her side at this wonderful banquet. No sooner had she reflected on her dear friend and her last moments spent with him when her thoughts were abruptly brought to a standstill.

"Your attention, everybody!" shouted the butler in a voice so loud that it almost shook all the dining tables.

The whole room went quiet as heads turned and looked towards the center of the main table to the only remaining vacant chair. It resembled a throne, for it was huge with plush maroon cushions, and its arms and legs were sumptuously encrusted with gold and bedecked with jewels that shone brighter than the sun. The throne was surrounded by a host of angelic beings of all shapes and sizes, their faces glowing and their wings flapping excitedly as they eagerly awaited their host.

Suddenly the trumpets began to blow, filling every heart with a joyous sense of anticipation as they continued to look in the direction of the unoccupied throne. Seconds later, Hodgekiss entered the room dressed from head to foot in white and surrounded by yet more angelic hosts as he made his way over to the throne.

"Ladies and gentlemen, please stand and raise your glasses to the king of Piadora," shouted the butler. Polly stood up and joined everyone else as they raised their glasses to acknowledge his presence.

With Hodgekiss now standing by his throne, he addressed the people, "May I remind all present that there is no need to hurry. Food is not only plentiful, but if what you desire is not brought to the table, then just hold out your hand and imagine it and I assure you it will appear.

"Wow, that's terrific news!" declared Polly as she gave Thomas an excited nudge.

"It only leaves me with one more thing to say, and that is a big thank you to Mrs. O'Brien and her young princesses. Thanks to their hard work we have enough Appletude Pie and April Crumble here to feed a whole army. Please kindly be seated and let the banquet begin."

Within a matter of seconds, Polly found her eyes feasting on a table laden with choice food. And as she watched, completely spellbound by all the food that was miraculously and very suddenly appearing on the table, she found herself wondering what on earth could possibly be missing.

The answer came as quickly as her curious thought when a young, dark-skinned boy stood up from his seat and waited in excited anticipation with his plate in his outstretched hands. In a matter of seconds a large round dough base fell into the palms of his upturned hands and instantly began to revolve around in circles. As he continued to stand, grinning from ear to ear, one topping after another fell onto the dough until it was piled high with every imaginable topping, requiring all his strength to balance it in his hands. Even then Polly saw he was struggling under its weight. She laughed out loud as she turned to nudge Thomas again and get his undivided attention.

"My favorite pizza!" cried the boy as he dropped back into his chair and then, picking up his knife and fork, began digging in. On seeing this happen, many of the other children present began to do likewise, and pretty soon all the other banqueting tables were filled with children standing with plates in their outstretched hands as pizza topping after pizza topping dropped onto revolving bread bases.

"I prefer hamburger and chips!" shouted a very tall boy with sandy colored hair. He excitedly jumped up from his seat and held out an empty plate. Seconds later he found it piled high with large, chunky chips as well as the most enormous hamburger.

"We have a banquet every day," Thomas informed Polly, "and no two banquets are ever the same. Every day there are new intakes who are invited to attend, and they all have different preferences when it comes to food. You would be amazed at all the different favorite dishes I have seen since coming here."

"Oh, my word," exclaimed Polly as she watched dear Stanley Horlicks stand watching as a large portion of bread-and-butter pudding landed on his plate, followed by a large dollop of creamy custard. "Well, that's obviously his favorite dish," said Polly, giving Thomas a nudge.

Then suddenly the child seated next to Stanley stood up and held out his plate. Seconds later this too was covered with a large pizza base that was spinning wildly. Seconds later it was piled high with blue bubble gum, chocolate raisins, blancmange, whipped cream, and lemon custard.

"See what I mean, Polly? You can have whatever your heart desires," said Thomas with a smile.

"Yuk, I'd never eat that. It's disgusting," she tittered, placing her hand over her mouth as she spoke so as not to offend.

"Well, Polly, why don't you think of something that takes your fancy and then see what happens," Thomas thoughtfully suggested.

"All right then, Thomas. I will," she said, moving her chair to one side and then standing up straight. "A plate of lasagna, please," she whispered, trembling with excitement as she held out her plate.

Sure enough, a large and very delicious-smelling portion of lasagna appeared from out of nowhere. Polly sat back down but struggled to eat it with any dignity, as she kept breaking into laughter.

Finally, having devoured every last morsel, she stood up again and this time ordered a knickerbocker glory. Polly gasped with delight as the tallest sundae glass she had ever seen suddenly appeared and balanced itself on the palm of her hand. It was filled with fruit and every imaginable ice cream flavor. She then watched delightedly as lashings of whipped cream piped itself on the top. Then, thinking it was now ready to eat, she sat back down and picked up a spoon. Suddenly, from nowhere a bright red cherry came to land on top of the cream with a loud plop, causing her to burst into more fits of the giggles.

The next few hours were utterly magical as Polly and Thomas communed while eating to their heart's content. With every mouthful Polly took, she felt as though she were going to explode, not from overeating, but because she felt intoxicated by the most inexpressible love that flooded and coursed through every fiber of her being. It was only when Polly felt she had no room left for anything else that she sat back contentedly on her chair, momentarily closing her eyes and hoping with all her heart that she would never wake up.

When all those gathered around the banqueting tables had eaten their fill, Polly turned to Thomas and rather poignantly asked, "Thomas, tell me now, who clears up this lot afterwards?" for she was feeling very concerned that anyone should have to clear up the staggering amount of mess left on the tables.

"Nobody, silly," replied Thomas with a smile.

"Nobody? How can that be?"

"Yes, Polly, you heard me right; nobody toils and sweats in Piadora. Well, not unless it's a really fun task that we all want to share. Otherwise everything is just magically whisked away."

Polly understandably found herself feeling very relieved to hear this, for she could not have left the banqueting hall without offering her help to clear up, even if it meant donning an apron and exchanging her silky white gloves for yellow rubber gloves to give her assistance with the cleaning chores.

Eventually, Hodgekiss rose to his feet and the room instantly fell silent.

"Polly, please come forward and receive your reward," he graciously commanded. "And please bring your little purse with you."

"Go on, Polly," whispered Thomas in her ear as he gave her arm an encouraging nudge.

Polly turned and smiled at Thomas before picking up her silky purse, and in no time at all she found herself standing in front of Hodgekiss, surrounded by angelic beings.

"Polly, open the bag," he ordered.

"Go on, Polly, open the bag," chorused the angelic hosts in unison as they excitedly gathered all around her. Polly fumbled with the purse strings as her long white gloves made it impossible for her to take a firm hold of the finely-weaved gold string.

"Here, Polly, allow me to help you," said Gabriel, taking the bag from her hand. "Now, open your palm upwards," he instructed as he emptied the contents of the purse into her open hand. Out tumbled all the pebbles she had collected on her journey.

"I do believe you are missing one," said Hodgekiss.

"Yes, sadly it was taken by a man called Tobias Mortimus when I stayed at his guesthouse," said Polly rather subdued. She wondered whether it was wise to say any more concerning that rather unfortunate episode.

"Oh, so you were his guest, were you?" Hodgekiss asked with a mischievous wink.

"Well, not exactly," replied Polly, still a little unsure as to how to explain what happened to the missing pebble. "To tell you the truth I took a friend to his house because we needed help, but sadly we weren't really welcome."

"Some guesthouse," commented Gabriel with a smile as he gave Hodgekiss a wink.

"Well, here it is," said Hodgekiss as he produced the missing pebble and placed it in her hand alongside all the others. "A man cannot keep what wasn't his in the first place," he mused. "Yes, Polly, our dear Mr. Mortimus hasn't been himself since the eve of your visit." All the angelic hosts surrounding his throne, holding on to his every utterance, smiled as they nodded their heads in agreement.

Polly was hardly listening, for she was much too busy gazing at the pebbles. One after another they transformed themselves into precious jewels of many colors. "They are truly beautiful," gasped Polly.

"Yes, beautiful gems for a beautiful princess," Gabriel chipped in as he removed them from her hand. He then turned away in a most secretive manner.

"Kneel down, Polly," Hodgekiss loudly commanded.

Polly did as she was told, getting down on both knees and bowing her head low. She was completely unaware that Gabriel had handed something to Hodgekiss. Seconds later, as Polly held up her head, gazing directly into Hodgekiss's eyes, she could see he was holding a jewel-encrusted crown in his hands.

"Is that for me?" she cried.

Hodgekiss said nothing as he moved toward her, his eyes blazing like white hot fire and filled with deep love and compassion toward her. He then gently placed the jewel-encrusted tiara on her head.

"Polly you are now officially a princess," he said out loud so all present could hear. "And here in Piadora, you are now to be known as Princess Polly. May you bear this honor with all the dignity and integrity you have shown as you journeyed here to Piadora," he said as he took her hand and helped her back onto her feet.

Tears of inexpressible joy tumbled down Polly's cheeks as her face lit up with pure radiance. She wiped a tear from her cheek before raising both arms to prevent her new crown from toppling off her head.

"Thank you so much," was all she was capable of saying. Her eyes sparkled and her countenance continued to glow.

"Now then, my princess, let us sit down together. For I believe we have one final treat in store for you."

Polly took her place beside him. She hadn't the faintest idea what to expect. Hodgekiss clapped both hands. "Master Bailey, let the grand finale begin."

Polly was completely taken by surprise as the sound of a full orchestra playing the sweetest music she had ever heard wafted across the enormously large banqueting hall. Looking across the hall, her eyes caught hold of the largest white grand piano she had ever seen. She believed it was her dear, sweet teacher's son Peter masterfully playing it. As she continued to stare in his direction she was eventually forced to close her eyes, as the sounds were so heavenly that they were playing gentle games with her heart, every single note melting it to a pulp. Polly felt exhilarated.

She found herself laughing out loud when he finally got around to playing "Climb Every Mountain." Hodgekiss also closed his eyes as he savored every note that wafted throughout the room.

"Not only is this is the most beautiful music I have ever heard in my life, but if it doesn't stop soon, I am certain to crack up completely," said Polly, her eyes well-and-truly glazing over as she openly confessed to such feelings.

"Feel free," replied Hodgekiss, giving her the tenderest of looks. "I too often feel deeply moved when I hear inspirational music and songs. With that in mind, I have one more surprise for you," he said, moving over to give her hand a little squeeze.

Before Polly could say anything further, Hodgekiss stood up and commanded all present to abandon their seats and gather around his throne.

"Master Bailey, the time has finally come for you to give us your rendition of the secret song that we have all been rehearsing for weeks. Maestro, begin!" he ordered.

Peter Bailey only managed to play a few bars before Polly almost collapsed into a heap laughing. "Goodness me! He's playing my little song, 'Give, Give Me Love.' Oh how incredible!" she cried through tears of euphoria, her heart feeling as though it would burst if perchance anything else wonderful were to happen to her.

How many times they sung her little song is, sadly, not recorded. However, suffice it to say that Polly had never felt so blissfully liberated as she did at that moment in time, surrounded by numerous angelic beings and all those who had attended the banquet. There was so much hugging and loving that she wished it would never come to an end. But there was still one more thing to come.

Hodgekiss ordered Polly to look across at the other end of the banqueting hall, and as she looked she saw two enormous curtains

POLLY BROWN

part. Polly could hardly believe her eyes, and she instantly began to crease up with laughter. Behind the curtains was a mountain of mattresses stacked so high they appeared to reach the ceiling.

"How many mattresses did she have to climb in *The Princess and the Pea*?" Hodgekiss playfully asked.

"One hundred," Polly replied.

"Well, we decided to do better than that, so we've stacked up well over a thousand, so it will be a bit of a climb," said Hodgekiss.

Polly hesitated. "Do I have to climb them all?" she asked.

"Only if you still do not believe you are a real princess," replied Hodgekiss, searching deep into her soul for an honest answer. "If you believe in your heart that you are a real princess, then there really is no need for further proof."

"I believe," replied Polly, her eyes sparkling as she broke into a gentle smile.

"Good," replied Hodgekiss, "but if you change your mind... Giles, come here, please" he said, beckoning his faithful butler to come forward.

Giles removed the domed top from the large silver dish he was holding, and announced, "Your pea, madam."

The lone green pea rolled across the dish as Giles moved closer so that Polly could take a better look. Polly burst out laughing before once again declining the offer.

"Oh Giles, not only have I seen enough peas to last a lifetime, but I no longer need a pea to convince myself that I am a princess who's worth loving. So thank you, but no thank you."

Chapter 39
POLLY IS SOMEWHAT ENLIGHTENED

ITH THE BANQUET finally over, Hodgekiss invited Polly to walk with him awhile, for he had much in his heart he wished to share with her. Without further adieu, Polly followed Hodgekiss out of the banqueting hall, down a long corridor, and out of the building into some beautiful gardens.

"Come on, let us walk on, for I still have a few surprises for you, Polly," said Hodgekiss as he took hold of her hand and led her through the gardens.

As they gently strolled along hand-in-hand, Hodgekiss shared many deep things with Polly. Their conversation was private and was therefore not recorded. It is fair to say that some of their conversation seemed to bring a smile to her face and other things caused her to look sad as they walked on and talked for many hours.

Eventually, her thoughts turned to her dear and absent friend, Aazi. She found herself once again feeling very sad that he was not here with her.

"Hodgekiss, I had a wonderful friend who had suffered so much at the hands of others. Yes, his life had been far worse than mine. We were coming here together when he had a terrible fall on the mountainside." Polly's voice began to crack as she thought back to the tragic day on the mountainside and the young boy who in no time at all had become her beloved soulmate.

"Oh dear, Polly, when will you learn there is little point in comparing suffering? For pain has no real barometer by which it can be gauged." Polly searched his face, giving one of her confused looks. "Look, Polly, answer me this: there are two men standing outside a hospital, one has a leg that has suffered such terrible frostbite that it urgently needs to be removed, and the other has a severe toothache that requires the tooth to be pulled from his jaw. Which one is suffering most?"

"The man who needs his leg amputated, of course," Polly hastily replied.

"Well, Polly, tell that to the man with the agonizing toothache, who may well be in danger of severe blood poisoning if the cause of his pain turns out to be from a burst abscess," said Hodgekiss. "The truth is, both men are in severe agony and require the help of an experienced specialist to rid them of their pain. Everybody's pain is unique to himself, and suffering is suffering."

"You're right, Hodgekiss. But I still miss Aazi, and he did suffer so badly."

Hodgekiss used this opportunity to give her hand a tight squeeze. "I know you do, Polly. I know you do."

After walking on a while, Polly turned to Hodgekiss and asked him, "Where are you taking me now?"

"Just carry on walking, Polly, for we are almost there," Hodgekiss replied as he then ushered her through a small open gate and then began to descend some steep steps.

Polly quietly followed on behind, gathering up her long dress so she wouldn't trip over it. In a matter of minutes, she found herself walking along a beach with the softest, silkiest white sand that stretched for miles.

"Hodgekiss, this tropical beach is like paradise," she gasped. Hodgekiss smiled.

"Hodgekiss, I really love the beach. Can I take my shoes off?" she asked. "I love the feel of the sand between my toes."

Hodgekiss nodded. Polly wasted no time. She removed her shoes, and then gathered up her long dress in her hands.

"Race you to the shoreline, Hodgekiss!" she shouted gleefully before running as fast as her legs would allow in the direction of the sea. "Hurry up, Hodgekiss, the water is fabulous and delightfully warm," she shouted breathlessly in his direction.

Hodgekiss continued to walk toward Polly, but she could see his mind was on other things.

"Polly, if you swim out a little you will soon discover that this sea is very special."

Polly looked puzzled. "I can't swim in this long dress, for once it is wet it will surely drag me under."

"Have a go and see for yourself," Hodgekiss replied.

Polly initially hesitated and then thought, why not?

Hodgekiss watched as Polly waded further out into the sea before disappearing between the waves.

When she finally emerged, she was shrieking rather loudly, "Hodgekiss, I can breathe underwater! It's amazing! It's wonderful. And what's more I don't need an oxygen tank to take me to the bottom. Oh, Hodgekiss, I saw beautiful sea horses and fish so big and so colorful. They really took my breath away. Come and join me, Hodgekiss," Polly shouted before disappearing under the water for a second time.

Hodgekiss remained at the water's edge, deep in thought, until Polly finally emerged from the water. As she walked back toward him, she was further amazed when she discovered that her beautiful long dress was perfectly dry. *Wow*, followed by *unbelievable*, were the only words she could manage to stutter as she headed back toward the shoreline.

Reluctant to leave the beach, Polly chose to linger just a few meters from where Hodgekiss stood. She continued to paddle in the soapy froth left by waves as they broke up and then raced ashore to wash over her feet. Suddenly her ears pricked up.

"Listen, Hodgekiss, even the very waves are singing," she cried. "Yes, I'm not imagining it. I can definitely hear the most magnificent harmonies as every small wave joins together to form a larger wave that crescendos before crashing down to race ashore. It's all too incredible to believe!" she cried as she then began to dance and splash around in the water as though she did not have a care in the world.

Suddenly she stopped her dancing. "Hodgekiss, can you hear what I can hear?" she gasped as she wrung her hands impromptu and strained her ears to listen harder. "I can hear the waves playing a song that I recognize. Yes, it's one that I actually know by heart," she excitedly cried. Hodgekiss looked at her and smiled as Polly continued to shout. "I can't believe it! The waves are singing Aazi's song, 'The Impossible Dream.' Hodgekiss, tell me that you can hear it, too!"

Before another word could pass from her lips, she heard a voice in the distance shouting out her name. And as she turned to face in the direction that the noise was coming from, her eyes instantly fell on a young black boy, running as fast as he could toward her.

Polly's eyes widened and her heart began to race.

"Aazi, is it really you?" she cried, as she leaped out of the water and rushed, arms outstretched, to greet him.

The pair of them collapsed onto the soft sand, still embracing each other as they hugged and laughed continuously, their young hearts filled to overflowing with joy at this wonderful and most unexpected reunion.

"Oh, Aazi, it's so good to see you!" she breathlessly cried as she clung to him, reluctant to let go of him lest he should once again disappear from her life.

"You too," replied Aazi with a huge beam as he too struggled and gasped for breath.

As they continued to embrace each other, Hodgekiss saw this as the perfect opportunity to discreetly disappear and allow them to continue this very special and intimate reunion.

"Oh, Aazi, never in my whole life have I seen such a fast runner," she laughed, still holding on to the poor boy for dear life.

Aazi joined in the laughter. "Put it this way, Polly. Back at home in my village, if I didn't catch the chicken, then I didn't get any supper. So that's how I learned to run like the wind!" he said with a cheerful chuckle.

He then gently removed her hands from around his tiny waist and rolled over to sit right beside her on the soft, silky sand, a small distance from the water's edge. "Polly, you really are as beautiful as I imagined you to be," he said, giving her arm a little squeeze.

"Oh, come on, Aazi. Don't start..."

Polly was about to continue on her usual course of personalized character assassination when suddenly she realized something almost too amazing for words.

"Aazi, you can see, can't you?" she squealed, waving one hand in front of his eyes.

"Yes, Polly, it's true. I really can see. I now have perfect vision, which is really fantastic. For it means I can pursue my dream of one day being a long-distance runner."

"Oh, this really is all too much for me," Polly cried with tears of joy and laughter streaming down her face as she hugged him some more.

The pair carried on laughing and talking as they caught up with each other. Aazi told Polly every detail of his stay in Hope in Your Heart Hospital, including how he had woken up in the hospital only to discover that he was no longer blind. Dr. Love-heart and all his team had been very excited and told him that his fall had turned out to be a real blessing in disguise, fully restoring his sight.

Polly was so pleased that she found it hard to stop her flow of tears. As they enjoyed sweet communion together, many more tears on both sides were shed. Polly spoke of many of the amazing things she had seen since her arrival in Piadora. She chose to keep some of the details from Aazi, not because she was holding back, but because she wanted him to experience the pure elation that came with each surprise. Finally, she encouraged Aazi to join her for a swim in the crystal clear ocean.

As they swam deep down towards the ocean bed, they marveled at the stunningly beautiful flora and fauna that remained the ocean's secret, as no man had gone to such depths and lived to tell the tale. They also climbed on the back of Hugo, a humpback whale, and still found time to frolic in the waves with two young dolphins named Danny and Donna that swam toward them, nudging them both with their spoon-shaped noses as they insisted on joining in the fun.

Then without warning, Aazi let out a loud scream. Polly, confused by the sudden noise, quickly turned around to see what the commotion was about.

"Quick, Polly, head for the shore!" cried Aazi, full of fear as he saw the fins of two large sharks heading right in their direction.

Polly immediately broke into laughter and shouted back, "Aazi, don't worry, it's only Biscuit and Bouncer. They've come along to see what all the excitement is about. Here, Bouncer," she cried, using her hand to splash the water as a way of communicating to the shark to come over.

Bouncer obliged and swiftly moved through the water towards Polly. "There, there," said Polly, giving him a pat on the nose followed by a kiss. "Yes, these poor darlings have spent their lives being hated and feared, yet here in Piadora they are just as lovable as every other creature. They particularly love to join in anytime there's a bit of larking around." Aazi now looked really confused, so Polly swam over to him to reassure him further. "Look, Aazi, in Piadora there are no predators, so consequently the whole of nature lives in total peace and harmony. I promise." Aazi still didn't seem to understand and stared at Polly with a look of complete incredulity plastered all over his face.

"Aazi, when I first arrived here, I saw lions lying down with lambs, and I even rolled in the grass with a huge golden lion named Lucy. She didn't hurt me at all. She just licked my face with her long pink tongue and playfully prodded me with her enormous padded paws. There is nothing here in Piadora that will ever harm you, believe me." Aazi broke into a relaxed smile.

"Come on, Aazi, let's go back to the beach. Tell you what; I'll race you. Let's see if you're as fast a swimmer as you are a runner. On your mark, get set, go!"

There were to be no winners or losers that day as they raced against each other, hoping to be the first out of the water. As their feet touched the warm, silky soft sand, they both collapsed into a heap on the sand in laughter.

Finally, Hodgekiss, escorted by angelic beings, returned to the water's edge only to find them still happily talking away.

"Polly, it is time for young Aazi to get dressed for the banquet, for it is his turn to receive his crown. And then after the banquet, Aazi, I thought we might fulfill a couple of your secret dreams."

"Which ones?" Aazi delightedly cried.

"Well now, have you not always wished to swim *up* a waterfall?" Hodgekiss asked with an amused smile.

Aazi's face lit up, and he broke into a grin. If he were honest, he was a little shocked that this well-kept secret had finally been revealed, but he was also very excited at the prospect of fulfilling one of his secret dreams.

"I don't suppose there is any chance of getting to ride on the back of a tyrannosaurus rex or a brontosaurus?" Aazi rather cheekily asked.

"That can be arranged," Hodgekiss replied. "And didn't you also dream of entering another universe to create a new star?"

Aazi's eyes now widened, and upon finding himself absolutely speechless, he could only nod in answer to the question.

"Well, how about creating a whole new constellation while we're at it? What are you waiting for? You'll have plenty of time to fulfill those dreams and still have time for a few more before tonight's banquet. Raphael will accompany you, for he's a bit of a whiz kid when it comes to such things."

Hodgekiss smiled and then turned to address Polly, inviting her to attend the evening banquet if she wished. Polly was given no choice in the matter, for Aazi tugged hard on her arm and begged her to say yes.

"You must come, and you must sit next to me," he cried.

Polly happily agreed, although she did promise herself that this time around she wouldn't eat so much.

It would be many hours later before the sumptuous banquet was over. Aazi felt overwhelmed by the awesome jewel-encrusted crown he was awarded and kept taking it off his head to admire it further.

"Polly, it's just so incredible to be able to see the different colors," he cried. "I just feel completely overcome by having swam up a waterfall and created new stars. Never in my whole life have I felt this happy."

"I feel exactly the same," said Polly as she watched him toy with his crown.

Eventually Hodgekiss came over to speak to the pair of them. He told Polly that he needed one final moment alone with her. Aazi was then asked if he would mind going with Gabriel, for he had many things he wished to show the young men. They both agreed, but not before giving each other a lingering hug as they said their good-byes. Polly reluctantly released Aazi from her firm grip, but not before turning to face Hodgekiss.

"We will see each other again, won't we?" she anxiously asked. Hodgekiss nodded.

"Thank you," said Polly, instantly showing great relief. "For having found Aazi again it would be awful if this turned out to be our last good-bye."

Polly then allowed Hodgekiss to escort her out of the banqueting hall and back toward the gardens they had previously walked through, though on this occasion they walked in perfect silence. For some reason Polly was reluctant to chatter on, for she had a slight feeling of unease, although she didn't know why. Eventually Hodgekiss turned to look her fully in the eyes and spoke, "Polly, it is time for you to return to the castle."

"Oh, please don't send me back there!" she pleaded.

"Oh, my young maiden, it's important for you to understand that it really is necessary for you to go back," he gently said.

"But why can't I stay here? Have I done or said anything wrong?" she pitifully cried. "Oh, Hodgekiss, please let me stay. Don't send me back to the orphanage, or I will surely die!" she begged.

Hodgekiss stood firm, still gazing into her eyes. He then took hold of her hand and, without saying a word, led her through the gates of Piadora. They continued to walk through forests and valleys until they reached the summit of Piadora. Hodgekiss then stopped in his tracks and turned to look down at her, flames of love and compassion pouring from him as he fixed his gaze on her. "Polly, please look down as far as your eye can see."

Polly obeyed and was surprised to discover that she could clearly see the whole of the town in which she lived. Her eyes moved farther up until they settled on the castle, and she wept.

"Why on earth would you send me back there?" she cried, feeling utterly distraught at such a prospect. Hodgekiss remained silent. Suddenly her eyes caught hold of the two Justins standing beside their Mini with the bonnet open and smoke billowing out.

"Oh dear, they're in big trouble again," Polly ruefully commented.

"Yes, they certainly are," replied Hodgekiss. "But don't worry, Justin Kase has enough tools with him to open a car mechanic shop," he said with a warm smile. "At the end of the day, that is his problem."

"What do you mean?" Polly asked with great surprise.

"Well, Polly, he has such a hard time relying on anyone else; sadly, he lacks trust. Remember his disagreement with Sir Eggmond when he refused to leave his backpack at base camp?"

Polly remembered. How could she forget?

"Polly, consider what happened to the two of them simply because they refused to listen to the wisdom of someone older and wiser than themselves."

"Yes, but in all fairness, there were times when even I thought Sir Eggmond very unreasonable, and many more times that I actually became convinced that the man was quite off his rocker! Is it any wonder they chose to abandon ship and make their own way up the mountain?" Polly retorted, eager to defend both boys' actions.

"The point is, Polly, that both you and Aazi chose to put all natural reason and logic behind and follow your heart, even though you were both fearful and way out of your depth. Both boys, on the other hand, chose not to. They believed in themselves and in their way of doing things, and as you saw for yourself it ended in disaster."

Polly had little choice but to agree with all he said as she thought back to their tragedy on the mountain.

"So he will never make it here, until he leaves all his baggage behind and begins to trust others much more than he does. Self-reliance might look good, but when it prevents us from making the right choices, it becomes harmful. We were, after all, made with a deep need to trust and rely on others. Anyway Polly, you will have plenty of opportunities to meet those two loveable lads again. Right now, though, please cast you eyes over in this direction," he said, pointing to the west.

Polly followed his outstretched hand, stopping when she came to a whitewashed farmhouse. Through an open window she could clearly see a young girl lying on her bed, weeping and crying. Polly had no idea what her problem was. A few minutes later, and through yet another window, Polly could see a woman with her head buried in her hands as she sat at the kitchen table. Another window revealed a man standing over a fireplace holding a letter, pain and great despair etched on his face. As she moved from house to house, Polly began to realize that many of the town's residents were in trouble and suffering in silence as they struggled with their private pain. She began to feel their hurt.

"Polly, you only feel the tiniest measure of their pain, but I feel it all. I feel and care for each and every person out there, especially those wracked with pain and in immense suffering. The orphans and the widows, as well as the single mothers and desperate fathers, well, they hold a very special place in my heart. But come now, what else can you see?"

Suddenly Polly let out a shriek, "Oh my goodness, I can see James! He's obviously come in search of me. Oh good gracious, Hodgekiss, can you see what I can see? Oh my goodness! It's Soogara and Vanaspi with those two terrifying hounds. James doesn't realize it, but he's about to fall into the spider's web. Hodgekiss, do something, please do something quick!"

"No, Polly. You do something!"

"Don't be daft, Hodgekiss! What on earth can I do?" she cried.

"That's for you alone to work out, Polly, for until the day the final conflict takes place with good and evil meeting up to do battle, then and only then will I interfere in the plans of man. Until that day comes, man is left to make his own choices. I tell you with a mixture of both sadness and joy that when that day finally comes, the very earth will quake and the heavens will tremble. The battle will be greater than any other that has ever taken place before. Their noise will be as the rumbling of chariots, like the roar of a fire sweeping over a field as they move forward to do battle with evil. And though evil has long prevailed, for the first time in history the enemy will become racked with great fear. Yes, I do believe that their hearts will fail them and their faces will grow pale as they witness my forces swarming forward like locusts, equipped with the fiercest determination to win. Those that stand for truth and freedom are quietly and confidently preparing themselves for this day of reckoning. And if you draw in a little closer, Polly, you will clearly see that all over the land there are thousands of lit candles sitting on window ledges. These people are your friends, even though you have never met them.

All you need to do is show them your signet ring, and to your surprise you will discover that they too wear the same ring as yours. Yes, these people are your friends, and they will help you in any way they are able. You will find these special people in every land that your foot touches. For their commission is to help others find the secret pathway to Piadora and prepare themselves for this last mighty battle. Only after this battle has been fought and won will there finally be peace between all men. So, young Polly, you are more than free to stay here in Piadora, for the choice is entirely yours. If you do stay, you will experience nothing but happiness way beyond your wildest dreams, and Thomas will no doubt be very delighted. However, if you go back, then it will be to more pain and more uncertainty, and probably more ridicule and humiliation."

Polly remained silent, totally agonized as she reluctantly weighed up the two very limited choices. That is, if they could be called choices; after all, she was no martyr! She hated pain and despair as well as all the other loathsome, negative emotions she struggled to control. She found herself temporarily at a complete loss for words, and who could blame her? After all, what sort of choice was that? To stay and live a life of abundance with every dream in her young heart fulfilled, or go back to a life filled with shame and misery. And, I hasten to add, she would also go back to being permanently hungry! Was Hodgekiss asking the impossible? Polly's eyes welled up with tears, for in her heart she knew the answer.

"Take your time, Polly," said Hodgekiss gently as he gave her hand a reassuring and comforting squeeze.

Polly took in a deep breath. "All right, Hodgekiss, I will go back."

"Polly, that's wonderful news! For now you truly know who your people are. They are the poor and brokenhearted, the crushed in spirit, and the dispossessed. They are the lame and the weary, the orphan and the widow; whether black or white, rich or poor, they come from every walk of life." Polly quietly nodded. "Oh, and Polly, I will let you in on a little secret: these are my people, too! But before you go and change back into your everyday clothes, which, I hasten to add, Mrs. O'Brien has not only washed and ironed, but sewn up a few odd holes, I want to show you one final thing. Take a look over to your right. Now look closer. Can you see the Copper Kettle tearoom?"

"Yes, yes, I can see it," Polly anxiously replied. "But wait, what on earth is going on? I can see a man in white overalls standing at the top of a ladder. He's taken down the old sign, and with his paint pot he's painting a new sign in big gold lettering." Polly paused. "Hodgekiss, I do believe the new sign says Polly's Pantry. Oh, my goodness! How can this be? Where are the Greedols? And do they know about this?" Polly cried as she turned to Hodgekiss, looking for a suitable explanation.

"Look, Polly, there will be no problem, for they are at present cruising around the Greek Islands."

"Yes, but hang on there, Hodgekiss. Every winter they close down the tearoom to go on a long cruise. They've done it every year for as long as I've known them. So what will happen if they come back to discover that the name has been changed in their absence?"

"Well, let's just say that this time their ticket is one way," Hodgekiss replied, the sides of his lips curling into a faint smile as he spoke.

"Oh right," said Polly as she suddenly caught hold of what he was trying to get at. She smiled. "Well, Hodgekiss, if I'm honest, I don't think those two will really be missed."

Hodgekiss agreed fully with Polly's assessment. "Polly, at present you are too young to own a tearoom. Your job is to attend school and try your best to work hard and leave school with plenty of exams. But the tearoom is yours, and until you are of an age where you can take over, it will be run by guardians of my choice. Their names are Mr. and Mrs. Kindlyside."

Polly laughed at their name. "I like the name. It sounds very nice," she said.

"Yes, I'm rather partial to their name, too, for their hearts are indeed as kind as their name, and these precious friends of mine have been commissioned to give you all the help and advice you need, oh, as well as nice cups of tea," said Hodgekiss, breaking into a warm smile. "But Polly, allow me to give you one final and small word of warning! When you eventually inherit the tearoom, you must remember to use it for the benefit of others as well. You must seek to leave out food for my ragamuffin friends."

"That goes without saying," Polly responded with great enthusiasm.

"Then come, my young princess, for it is time for you to get out of your glad rags and back into your old clothes."

Chapter 40
TIME TO GO HOME

*P*OLLY SOON FOUND herself back at the Princesses' School of Training. She asked to be left alone as she parted with her ball gown, replacing it with her dress and smock top. She momentarily held on to the gold ballet shoes, caressing them with her fingers before replacing them with the cheap shoes that she hated with a passion. Finally, she dispensed with the jewelry and her precious tiara.

As Polly sat on a chair and wistfully gazed at her tiara, there was a gentle knock on the door.

"Come in," she called out loud as she stood up from her chair. Mrs. O'Brien closed the door gently behind her and then quietly walked over to where Polly was now standing and sweetly placed her arms around her to give the young girl an almighty hug. Polly could no longer control the deep sadness that leaving Piadora was causing, and she openly wept on dear Mrs. O'Brien's shoulder.

"There, there, Polly. I know. I fully understand..." she said as she comforted the young maiden. "Remember, my dear, that crying is good for the soul, and it washes the face nicely, too," she said, pulling away so that she could look Polly directly in the eye. "Polly, I know this is the hardest decision you've ever had to make. But I can tell you, hand on heart, that it is the right one, and that's what makes you the beautiful princess that you really are," she said, giving Polly a kind smile as she gently and lovingly ran her fingers through Polly's hair. "Beauty really is an inner thing, Polly, nothing to do with the clothes you are wearing or the style of your hair. Trust me when I say that real beauty comes from the heart and permeates throughout the whole body, giving you a glow and radiance that cannot be bought for any princely sum. So go back to that dark and evil castle and shine forth like a beacon, for the darkness cannot stand light, and light is definitely the more powerful of both elements."

"Yes, but the castle is the darkest place I have ever known, and I can feel nothing but despair at the thought of going back there," said Polly rather tearfully.

"Polly, close your eyes and think of a room in pitch darkness, a room so very dark that you cannot even see past the end of your nose. Now light a small candle. There, see what I mean? The flicker of a small, insignificant candle will instantaneously light up a room, and suddenly you are able to see clearly. You, my young princess, are like a candle in the darkness, and as you go back to your difficult, mundane life, know that you are being watched over and protected," she said, giving Polly's hand a tight squeeze.

Polly smiled back and then turned to look over at her abandoned tiara, making a rather wistful sigh.

This action reminded her dear teacher that she still had something else rather reassuring to say to her young student. "Polly, remember to continue looking out for those rather unusual pebbles, for there is plenty of space to add many more to your crown, which, I hasten to add, will be carefully looked after for you until you return."

"Thank you, but will I ever see you again?" Polly asked through a vale of tears.

"Now, what sort of question is that? Of course you will, my dear, as I too am leaving Piadora to return to my girls, for it is almost the start of a new term at Snobbit's Preparatory School, and if nothing else the girls' cooking lessons will surely be a most disastrous affair if I'm not there to supervise them." Polly broke into a smile as Mrs. O'Brien talked on. "It is more than certain that I will bump into you, especially when you're sitting on the bus happily eavesdropping on the girls' idle chitchat!" she said, giving Polly a mischievous little wink.

Polly's smile widened, for she had never realized that Mrs. O'Brien had even noticed her on the bus, let alone the fact that her ears were constantly pricked up as she listened in on the girls' excited chatter.

"Now then, where is Sir Eggmond? He is meant to be here by now, for he has been given the task of getting you safely back down the mountain." Polly looked a little shocked at this new piece of information.

"Don't worry, my dear. It will be much, much, easier going down, I promise." Mrs. O'Brien stated very cheerily. "In fact, I hope you like parasailing!"

Polly said her good-byes to all the wonderful people she had met during her short stay in Piadora, including young Aazi, her soulmate. And he went to great lengths to reassure her that he would stay in touch. "Polly, I too have to go back to my land for there is much to do," he said as he stuffed a piece of paper into her hand.

"What's this?" Polly asked.

"It's my address, so please write. Promise you will."

Polly smiled. "Aazi, of course I will write. You are, afterall, my best friend ever."

Finally, she asked to be left alone for a few minutes with Thomas while they said a special good-bye. What they said to each other in that precious moment in time was for their ears and hearts only, but Polly gave Thomas a long lingering hug as she shed further tears.

"I love you, Thomas," she wept, large tears glistening in her eyes.

"I've told you before that I can't bear to see you crying, Polly," he gently and lovingly rebuked.

Polly smiled and agreed to try hard to stop.

"Look, sister, go back to the castle knowing I am finally safe and gloriously happy here. That must surely take some of the burden from off your shoulders."

Polly nodded.

"Well then, dear sister, this is not good-bye or even a farewell, for I watch over you every day. I promise that I will be thinking of you constantly."

Hodgekiss walked over to where Polly and Thomas stood in a deep embrace. "Come, my young princess, for it is time for you to go."

Polly turned toward Hodgekiss, her extended hand still tightly locked in the hand of Thomas as she walked away and their woven fingers finally parted. "Good-bye, Thomas," she whispered with a smile.

Polly opened the front door of the castle and was instantly greeted by Cecil Bogswater as well as Gailey Gobbstopper, who was sporting a rather ludicrous smile on her lips.

"You're wanted in the office," she said with a wicked smirk.

Polly wearily made her way down the corridor toward the office, already wondering if her visit to Piadora had been an entirely imaginary event. It felt as though it must have been as she was now once again feeling all the fear and trepidation that she had come to loathe. She looked down at her hand and saw the ring still on her finger, and she twisted it around to reassure herself that all she had experienced had been for real.

Polly knocked on the study door.

"Come in!" boomed the familiar voice of Uncle Boritz.

Polly twisted the doorknob and tentatively poked her head around the door before summoning up the necessary courage to walk in. She could see all the children seated in a circle on the floor, poking and jabbing each other as they shuffled around on their bottoms in their endeavor to get comfortable. Her heart dropped, for she knew it could only mean one thing. Yes, a family session, and as Polly glanced across the floor she could see young James sitting between two of the other children, staring into space as usual. She breathed a deep sigh of relief that thankfully he was safe and not about to be devoured by Soogara or her hounds. Gailey and Cecil interrupted her thoughts as they pushed past her to find themselves a spare space on the floor. Gailey in particular was very anxious to get a decent space for entertainment purposes.

"Well, well, Polly. It's very good of you to finally concede to gracing us with your presence," Uncle Boritz maliciously snarled. Pitstop joined in the fun, baring his sharpened teeth as he slobbered all over the floor.

"We've already been sitting here for a whole hour while they sent out a search party to find you," Tommy Pulleyblank loudly moaned, shooting a very hostile look in her direction.

"And where on earth have you been, young lady?" interjected a very solemn Aunt Mildred. "You know full well that you are on R.O.P.E. and therefore confined to the castle and its walls."

Polly remained perfectly silent, knowing that no amount of explanation or protestation would achieve a jolly thing.

Uncle Boritz moved away from behind his desk before making his way toward her. Polly could see that he was in an extremely confrontational mood.

"Yes, and before you make up some extraordinarily disgraceful tale, you will first of all need to explain this letter! So come on, speak up! We are all very anxious to hear what plausible explanation you could possibly come up with regarding this offensive letter," Uncle Boritz angrily shouted.

"What letter?" Polly innocently asked.

"This letter, you preposterous little liar!" Uncle Boritz roared as he pushed the envelope into her face.

Polly remained puzzled and genuinely confused as she struggled to come up with the right answer, particularly since Uncle Boritz had whipped it away from under her nose before she even had a chance to take the teeniest glimpse at the "so-called" offending item.

"Well, children, allow me to show all of you the letter that Polly is pretending she knows nothing about."

The letter was passed from grubby hand to grubby hand as every child was given the privilege of holding it for a second.

"So, who is this so-called Napoli? Some boyfriend who you have been secretly, and rather sneakily, meeting up with behind our backs? Speak up, girl, for we are all anxious to hear what you have got to say for yourself."

"No, no, you've got it all wrong, I haven't been seeing..."

"Silence!" thundered Uncle Boritz. "We don't want to hear any more of your lies. This is yet another prima facie case. If you don't agree, now is the only chance you will get to say so, for on the back of this letter it says, and I quote:

"Before you start your usual tricks of denying everything, you,
girl, have quite a lot to answer for. So we're now having clandestine
meetings with French boys, are we? You are indeed becoming more
like your mother with each new day that passes," he growled.

Polly remained silent with her head hung low and her shoulders
stooped. Uncle Boritz gave her no opportunity to explain herself,
she was used to that. It had always been that way.

"I have taken the liberty of reading the letter, which you covertly
attempted to send to James. It is quite obvious from its contents
that not only are you planning to escape from the castle, but there
are also specific references that clearly suggest your intention to
come back and take James. Well, your little plan is outrageous!
Let me tell you, young lady, that hell will indeed freeze over before
I allow you to do any such wicked thing. I am, therefore, compelled
to sentence you to a further three months on R.O.P.E. until you
finally come to understand that disobedience, illicit relationships,
and downright deceitfulness will, under no circumstances, be tolerated in my castle!"

Polly stood frozen to the spot and, as usual, felt utterly bewildered and flabbergasted! Uncle Boritz momentarily faltered as he
took his thick spectacles off his nose and began feverishly wiping
them. Aunt Mildred found her much-required hanky. James's eyes
gently flickered as in his vivid imagination he was now struggling
against all odds to land his spacecraft on Venus.

The jury of young and very bored children started the usual bottom shuffling. Pitstop started growling. Gailey Gobbstopper began smirking. And as Polly continued to look around his cluttered study, her eyes falling on the old typewriter with its stack of unanswered mail rather untidily heaped by its side, she knew with much certainty that everything was indeed back to normal.

Meanwhile, back in Piadora, Hodgekiss and Raphael stood on the mountaintop, quietly observing the meeting going ahead in Uncle Boritz's dingy study. Both men stood in utter silence and Hodgekiss stroked his whiskery beard. Eventually, two strangers, a woman accompanied by a man, walked over to join them.

"Didn't she look beautiful?" the woman said to Hodgekiss.

"Yes, positively glowing; a real princess," he replied with a warm smile.

"Yes, and when she received her beautiful crown, well, I can only say I had a real lump in my throat," the woman admitted. "I truly yearned to race up to her and give her a kiss and stroke her hair, but I knew that if I did I would have to tell her who I was," said the woman as she rather tightly held on to the hand of her companion.

"I know," replied Hodgekiss, his voice filled with deep compassion. "It must have been very hard to restrain yourselves from revealing your true identities, but it was a very wise move, for it would have made her decision to return to the castle harder still if she had discovered your existence here in Piadora."

"Alas, I know that is true, and dear Thomas had an equally difficult task. He honored us all by not exposing anything about us, for I know that he was bursting to tell her," said the gentle and gracious woman as her grasp became tighter still on her companion's hand. "I can hardly wait for the day to come when I finally hold her in my arms and wipe away her tears. We don't deserve such a special daughter after all we have put her through," she said, her eyes moist with tears as she spoke. "Hodgekiss, we cannot thank you enough. Both of us truly know that we don't and never have deserved such unmerited favor. Not only did we make a mess of our own lives, but as a direct result of our folly we handed our children such a sad and terrible legacy."

"Yes, I know," Hodgekiss replied, turning to face the woman to give her one of his gentle, compassionate looks. "But the good news is that all your mistakes are in the past, now forgotten as though they have never been. What we need to concern ourselves with at present is to keep praying for Polly's continued safety until she returns here to Piadora," Hodgekiss reminded the two of them.

Both the strangers nodded their agreement. The woman then reached out a hand and gently touched Hodgekiss.

"We both want to thank you from the bottom of our hearts for everything, and we will never stop thanking you, for such is the depth of our gratitude toward you."

Hodgekiss placed his hand on top of hers and just smiled. The woman acknowledged his smile, and with her companion at her side she turned to walk back toward the gates of Piadora, leaving Hodgekiss and Raphael alone once again.

Hodgekiss stood in complete silence as he focused his attention back toward the castle and continued to closely follow the drama that was unfolding in Uncle Boritz's study. As he stood deep in thought, a stray teardrop trickled unchecked down his cheek.

"It is better to place a millstone around your neck and jump into the sea than harm just one of my little ones," he murmured, brushing away the tear from his cheek.

Finally, he turned toward Raphael. "Raphael, tell me, how are the preparations for the new courthouse going?"

"They are progressing very nicely," Raphael eagerly replied.

"That's very good news. Yes, music to my ears," Hodgekiss cheerfully commented.

"Well, I think the Scumberrys will really like it, especially when they get to see how meticulous we have been concerning the décor," said Raphael with a faint smile. "The judge's desk is very nice and wide, and we've used only the best cedar wood for the docks."

"Well, I certainly can't wait for the day that they get to see it, for they will be really overwhelmed," Hodgekiss replied.

"Yes, Hodgekiss, but won't they be a bit upset when they discover that they will not be allowed any clever-tongued defense lawyer to help them be free of the charges?"

"Yes, I'm sure they might well find that small fact a trifle disheartening. However, they have always loved courtroom dramas so much that I think overall they should be very pleased with our efforts. It truly gladdens my heart to think that in the fullness of time we will be inviting them to take part in the most stunningly spectacular case of their lives."

"Yes, Hodgekiss, but won't we all be incredibly confused by Mr. Scumberry's verbosity and fancy language?" commented Raphael.

"Oh no, I think that this will only add both color and intrigue to the trial," Hodgekiss replied with a warm but serious smile. "But, come now, Raphael, we must get into our ragamuffin clothes and go in search of Megan and her friends, for by now they will be searching the trash cans, anxiously scavenging around for food to fill their empty stomachs. We don't want to keep them waiting, do we?"

Raphael nodded his agreement.

"Raphael, do we have any Appletude Pie left over from the banquet?"

"Plenty, as well as lots of April Crumble," Raphael excitedly replied.

"Excellent, my friend," said Hodgekiss as he placed an arm around Raphael's shoulder. They then turned and walked back toward the gates of Piadora.

"Do you think we should have told Polly who I really am, especially as she was expecting me to turn up for tea?" Raphael asked Hodgekiss with great sincerity.

"No, I don't think so. I think she was so caught up with life in Piadora she simply forgot you were meant to join us. Also if she were to discover your true identity, then she might rather unwittingly lean too heavily on you for support, and I'm inclined to think that this might not be the best thing for her. She needs to discover that she, Polly Brown, has inner strengths and resources which, when fully developed, will make her the truly amazing person she was born to be. So I think, Raphael—or rather, Ralph—that it would be best if we keep this little secret to ourselves." Raphael chuckled to himself as he nodded his head to show his approval.

"Oh my goodness! Look at the time!" exclaimed the storyteller, studying his watch. "I will have to leave the rest of the story for another time." He quickly closed the book, gently placing it to one side. He then took the time to observe his audience and was surprised to find a look of disappointment written all over their faces. "Didn't you like the story?" the storyteller asked, a little confused by their expressions.

"Oh, we loved it!" they all shouted out in unison.

"Well, what then is the problem?" the storyteller asked.

"We want you to carry on reading the story," shouted a voice from the back row.

"Yes, and we all want to know how we can get to Piadora!" piped up another fresh-faced boy rather brazenly.

The storyteller smiled. "Well, I will share with you a little secret: to get to Piadora, you have to long for it with all your heart and soul. I am not talking about a momentary, fleeting wish, such as wanting a bike or desiring a new fishing rod. Oh no, I am talking about a deep longing that overwhelms you and never leaves. Then you will not have to go in search of Piadora, for it will come in search of you."

The End

TO CONTACT THE AUTHOR

*I*F ANYTHING IN the book has raised personal issues for you, whatever your age, and you would like to talk to someone, please feel free to contact us. Please also contact us to let us know how you enjoyed the book.

Or should you wish to contribute to our children's work, both here and abroad, please also contact us through our Web site, www.hopeinyourheart.com, or by mail to:

Tricia Bennett
P.O. Box 1167
Wildwood, Florida 34785